Walking with Faith

New Perspectives on the Sources and Shaping of Catholic Moral Life

Walter J. Woods

A Michael Glazier Book
THE LITURGICAL PRESS
Collegeville, Minnesota

A Michael Glazier Book published by The Liturgical Press.

Cover design by David Manahan, O.S.B. Saint Matthew, manuscript illumination, detail, Der Landgrafenpsalter, 13th century, State Library of Württemberg, Germany.

1   2   3   4   5   6   7   8   9

Library of Congress Cataloging-in-Publication Data

Woods, Walter J. (Walter Joseph), 1943–
     Walking with faith : new perspectives on the sources and shaping
of Catholic moral life / Walter J. Woods.
         p.   cm.
     "A Michael Glazier book."
     Includes bibliographical references and index.
     ISBN 0-8146-5824-5 (alk. paper)
     1. Christian ethics—History.   2. Christian ethics—Catholic
authors.   3. Catholic Church—Doctrines.   4. Catholic Church-
-Doctrines—History.   I. Title.
BJ1249.W64   1998
241'.042—dc21   97-37773
                                                                CIP

A.M.D.G.

Contents

Preface

This book addresses a problem that is at once theological and pastoral; it concerns ordinary believers as well as clergy and theologians. To appreciate the difficulty, it suffices to consider Christian life within the Church community and an important exhortation of the Second Vatican Council, and then notice the principal concerns of contemporary moral theology.

Christian life is the enterprise of people who try to manage their affairs and conduct themselves in the light of Christian faith with the help of God's grace. It is lived in the "real world" by people who realize that circumstances can be extremely capricious and that they fully share the human condition. Aware of their failures and limitations, they try each day to escape the grip of evil, overcome temptations, live with integrity, and act in an upright way. This reflects common decency but also the conviction that God has blessed them and called them to witness and serve in this world. They are sustained by the hope of inheriting a share in God's eternal life. Christian life draws from the power and promises of God in Jesus Christ; it engages the experience, strength, conscience, and freedom of each believer.

Faithful people gather frequently to pray and to celebrate the liturgy. Liturgical worship not only helps to mark the passage of time and bring out its religious meaning, it draws believers' attention to God's presence, especially at the key moments of life. Assembled as a community of faith, they confess their sins in a spirit of repentance and confidence in divine mercy. God's word is proclaimed so that God's actions and requirements may be known and accepted. Baptism confers the free gift of divine grace with its freeing, forgiving, saving power. It integrates persons into the Church and entails a lifelong commitment to repentance, faith, and service. The celebration of the Eucharist focuses on the life, death, resurrection, and return of Jesus Christ, who has reconciled the human race to God and is the source of the Church's unity and each member's gifts. Penance opens a wide road to reconciliation for those who have gravely and culpably violated their baptismal commitments. These and other liturgical celebrations reflect the love of God, the faith of the Church, and the struggles and accomplishments, joys and hopes of ordinary people. They point ahead to a time when Christ will be all in all and every tear will be wiped away (Col 3:11; Rev 7:17).

Historically, Catholic theologians considered moral issues largely from the perspective of sacramental penance. Penance restores those who have gravely sinned to grace and to full participation in the life of the Church; it strengthens the virtuous in their living of grace. Theologians therefore examined human thoughts, words, deeds, and omissions in great detail and in order to determine what might constitute a sin. This effort was meant to help confessors carry out their work and was undertaken with the expectation that the confessor would take the penitent's personal condition and state in life into account and try to make an accurate judgment concerning his or her interior guilt or innocence. The ultimate concerns were the standing of particular brothers or sisters before God and the Church and helping them to live, worship, and serve as friends of God. Everyone accepted that the entire process fell within the jurisdiction of ecclesiastical authorities, who are responsible for good order in the community and for its worship.

For reasons to be seen later, the close association of moral theology and sacramental penance entailed a certain loss of balance and confusion of priorities. Too much emphasis was given to behavior and not enough to the workings of grace and conversion to God. Certain legal and philosophical theories tended to dominate the consideration of human behavior. Their influence and the penitential focus itself encouraged people to assume that Christian life was a matter of keeping laws and avoiding sins instead of praising God for God's gracious acts and responding generously to them. These theoretical and pastoral problems have prompted certain corrective actions.

One response is this exhortation of the Second Vatican Council: "Special attention needs to be given to the development of moral theology. Its scientific exposition should be more thoroughly nourished by scriptural teaching. It should show the nobility of the Christian vocation of the faithful and their obligation to bring forth fruit in charity for the life of the world" (*OT*, 16). This mandate calls for a thorough reconsideration of the sources, methods, and priorities of moral theology. It establishes an important goal that has yet to be adequately fulfilled.

Another reaction can be seen in a major shift that has taken moral theology out of the confessional and relocated it to what are hopefully more suitable contexts. Such a move should open the way to a better consideration of the sources and substance of Christian moral life and promote a positive response to the council's mandate. However, there are at least two causes for concern.

One is related to the general turn away from the penitential forum. Although this move was to be expected, it relieves theologians of the need to address a forum in which faith, repentance, grace, worship, conscience, community, and salvation simultaneously intersect with matters of behavior. In other words, there is a risk that moral theology will become less sensitive to the ecclesial and sacramental dimensions of Christian moral life, its foundation in grace, its ongoing need of faith and repentance, and its orientation to divine salvation. To the extent that these factors pass unacknowledged or are underestimated, to that extent moral theology will fail to do justice to moral life as a dimension of Christian faith.

The second difficulty flows from contemporary moral theology's intense interest in specific actions, determining whether they are good or evil, and rendering a satisfactory account of such judgments. Moral theologians consider such questions as justice, truth in speech, sexual and marital behavior, capital punishment, war, abortion, the impact of technology on human reproduction and on the maintenance of persons who are gravely ill, and structural obstacles to a more equitable distribution of material and cultural goods. The need to account for moral judgments has led theologians to draw upon presuppositions and reasoning developed by lawyers and philosophers across the centuries as well as their own predecessors and to be attentive to the impact of perspective and personal interest. The sensitivity and importance of some questions has prompted the popes and other ecclesiastical authorities to intervene on numerous occasions. While often helpful, their statements and unique claims to deference have increased the complexity of the discussion and focused attention even more intensely on details of human behavior, the methods used to determine its moral quality, and the issue of ecclesial authority itself.

No reasonable person would deny that behavior is of immense importance to persons, the community, and one's response to God. Clergy, theologians, and all responsible adults need to clarify the moral dimensions of human behavior with competence and care. The approach used in addressing this responsibility and the involvement of ecclesial authority are integral to the process and cannot be excluded from the discussion. Therefore the problem is not to be found in the debate over behavior and its moral assessment.

However, when contemporary moral theology is considered in light of Christian life as people usually pursue it and with the council's explicit exhortation in mind, it becomes apparent that too many foundational matters are insufficiently represented in the discussion, especially the dynamics and content of Christian faith, the witness of Scripture, the impact of liturgical life, the doctrinal tradition on divine grace, and the perennial requirement of apostolic charity. That is the theological side of the problem.

The other side is more general and pertains to the Church as a whole and to everyone who takes Christian life seriously. It can be expressed in a simple question: How does faith affect moral life? This question immediately raises several others: What do the Scriptures reveal about so basic a matter? How might the community's liturgical worship illuminate it? What does the Church teach about divine grace and what is its significance for Christian life? What are the moral aspects of faith? How have saints, theologians, pastors, and untold numbers of men and women of earlier generations understood and enacted the relationship between Christian faith and moral life and what is their legacy to us? These questions speak to laypersons and clergy as well as theologians.

My awareness of these questions has been sharpened by many years of study, teaching, and pastoral care, not to mention my own effort to live with faith. Discussions in the literature have addressed the strengths and deficiencies of the traditional manuals of moral theology, the proposals of revisionist thinkers, the sharp criticisms lodged against these proposals, the contrasting approaches offered by others, and the role of ecclesiastical authorities in these often heated debates. Along with many others, I have noticed that the sharpest divisions tend to radiate out from such issues as contraception and other aspects of marital or sexual behavior, the technology of human reproduction, the "hard cases" and public policy dimensions of abortion, the treatment of some extremely sick or brain-damaged patients, and the functioning of personal conscience. There are also important conversations concerning economic life, international justice, political affairs, the ordination of women and married men, among many other topics. Whatever the subject, much of the attention falls on questions of behavior, the reasoning that stands behind any proposal, and the issue of ecclesial authority.

A wider reading of theology discloses many other matters that are essential to Christian life. The Scriptures need to be read and heard; they are the indispensable foundation and the "soul of all theology" (*OT*, 16). History remembers other seasons in the life of the Church and shows that there have been more comprehensive approaches to moral life and to human experiences. It calls attention to the evolution of thought, the declarations of Church councils and other authorities, and the writings of great theologians and saints; much of this material bears directly on moral life. Systematic theology reflects on faith so that it can be presented correctly and accessibly to new generations. It offers well-developed insights on the life of the Church and on divine grace, including its necessity for personal salvation and for Christian life as a whole. Such resources are often acknowledged and seldom denied, but they tend in any case to have too little influence on the discussion of moral issues.

Over the years, classroom experiences and ongoing pastoral work have intensified my conviction that theological reflections on moral life need to draw more generously from the resources of Scripture, history, worship, and the broader theological tradition. Students appreciate the importance of theological considerations as such but are especially interested to see how theory speaks to practice and to pursue any pastoral and spiritual implications. Each week parishioners have faithfully brought their troubles, failures, joys, and successes to the Eucharistic liturgy. They are usually unfamiliar with technical language, but they know implicitly that their faith, prayer, repentance, and moral life go together and that they depend on God's love and mercy. They are hungry for inspiration and consolation, for insight and encouragement.

The council's exhortation, theological considerations, the contemporary profile of moral theology, and such experiences have prompted me to write this book. Its primary concern is not moral theology as such but moral life in the faith community. Moral life embraces much more than the particular actions or issues that moral theology has typically considered: it encompasses all ongoing deliberations and decisions insofar as they engage personal freedom and responsibility. This calls attention to the interior drama within persons and communities; it includes whatever enters a person's life so as to call for some response, whatever significantly influences that transaction, the decision itself, and any consequences for future moral deliberations. Since faith is essential to the picture, it is necessary to consider its role in moral life and the moral dimensions of faith itself. Because faith and moral life affect persons and communities as a whole, there can be little doubt that their cumulative significance is both comprehensive and foundational. This needs to be recognized and constitutes yet another reason to study Christian moral life.

However, so extensive and complex a subject can only be considered if reasonable limits are observed. This study makes no claim to being exhaustive and generally avoids particular issues of behavior or theological method that others have covered extensively. It aims to explore certain foundations and influences that give rise to Catholic moral life or have shaped its development and expression over the centuries. These specific aspects have been chosen because of their own importance and for their ability to compose a helpful portrait of moral life for clergy and Christian believers in general as well as for persons who are interested in moral theology as an academic discipline.

This book considers four sources, or influences, that have been especially important in giving Catholic moral life its present content and contours.

The first is the Sacred Scriptures. These texts highlight the historical grounds of faith and show what is entailed in the responses of faith and disbelief. Israel and the Church come into being through their acceptance of God's Covenant, which is the basic norm of life in the community. The Scriptures record the community's historical experiences, relationship to God, ongoing reflections, and practical responses. These factors exercise a primary influence upon the moral life of its members and emphasize the decisive effects of moral life on one's standing before God and God's people. The New Testament presents Jesus as "God with us" and testifies that persons are to hear and act upon his word. The injunction "repent and believe" follows immediately and emphasizes that faith and an upright moral life are inextricably related. This portion of the study presents foundational, normative aspects of faith and explores its moral dimensions.

The second influence is history. Human life is lived in time and under the sway of events that necessarily affect people, their choices, and their actions. History is the arena in which people of faith receive the mixed legacy of their ancestors and determine how they will relate to their neighbors, the prevailing culture, and the world around them. These Church-history, Church-culture, and Church-world dynamics are important in their own right and serve as unique windows on the moral and faith life of the Church. Worship and pastoral care also carry the marks of temporality, reflecting earlier times and shaping the religious and moral life of future generations. History is important as the arena in which pastoral, doctrinal, spiritual, and liturgical traditions develop and become normative. Chronologically, this book begins with the Old Testament and concludes with the Second Vatican Council (1962–5).

The third influence is sacramental praxis, especially as it pertains to baptism and penance. As the Church community celebrates these sacraments it mediates the Gospel's call to faith and conversion to the ordinary people who are its members. That perennial call highlights sin in the community but also prompts people to respond with extraordinary generosity toward God and neighbor. Pastoral policies disclose the elevated moral standards that are expected in a Christian and the minimum that can be accepted. Baptism and penance do much to illuminate Catholic moral life and have deeply affected its development up to the present time.

Finally, the tradition has been acutely sensitive to intellectual currents. Particular interpretations of human life can undermine personal faith and morality. Resources of thought can also help believers to understand and express their faith, strengthen catechetical efforts, clarify contemporary problems, and promote a more effective response to them. Especially through the work of councils and particular persons, philosophy and theology have made decisive contributions to Church life and have shaped believers' thinking about faith, morality, and moral agency.

This study is meant to illuminate the sources of moral life in faith, show how moral life in the Church has developed over the centuries, and encourage a more integral, comprehensive view. It respects the organic nature of Christian life and acknowledges the complex dynamics that affect it at each moment, including the impact of historical and contemporary events, the requirements of faith and of moral integrity, liturgical and theological activities, and an acute awareness of God's presence. This larger picture includes many important theological and pastoral developments and calls attention to the persons, texts, and issues that are associated with them.

This study primarily aims to offer new perspectives from which to view and understand moral life in the Catholic Church, but it also illuminates developments that bear with equal force on other communities of faith. It encourages a fuller appreciation of scriptural, liturgical, and theological resources and their effects on Christian faith and moral life. This study will hopefully contribute to a needed reconsideration of moral theology's methods, substance, and priorities. It promises to enrich the reflections, preaching, and pastoral care of clergy and others who share in the ministry. Most of all, I hope that this book will help members of the Church to gain deeper insight into the impact of faith on their moral life, plumb the moral depths of their faith, and live it in a more informed and committed way.

The preparation of this book drew upon the encouragement and assistance of many people. The rector of St. John's Seminary, Timothy J. Moran, supported this project from the beginning, not only through his interest but also by allowing me to forgo some responsibilities in order to have more time for research and writing. On behalf of the seminary he arranged for the services of Robert White, who checked most of the quotations and citations. The librarian of St. John's Seminary, Laurence W. McGrath, extended many personal courtesies and the benefit of his formidable knowledge of the literature. On numerous occasions, I have drawn from the professional competence, pastoral experience, and encouragement of other faculty members of St. John's Seminary; they have been good friends. Over the years colleagues, students, and parishioners have helped me to be a better theologian and to remember that theology is directed to the life and mission of God's people. For this too I am grateful.

Many colleagues generously agreed to examine portions of the manuscript at an earlier stage of its preparation and made valuable observations, corrections, and suggestions; they are Brian E. Daley, S.J.; Frank J. Matera; John W. O'Malley, S.J.; William M. Daly; Jane Freimiller; David Hollenbach, S.J.; John P. Galvin; and Jeffrey Hause. Mark L. Noonan read virtually the entire manuscript, addressed its treatment of many issues, and sharpened my understanding of the philosophical dimensions of the Christian heritage. My debt to him is especially heavy.

I am happy to acknowledge and thank all who have contributed to this book and claim exclusive responsibility for whatever shortcomings remain.

1

"You Shall Be My People"

The story of Christian moral life begins with the faith, experience, and reflection of the Hebrew people. Many centuries before Christ, they had been brought together by a God who loved them, freed them from oppression, and offered to remain with them forever. In return, God asked Israel to observe God's commandments, which chiefly required each person to worship God alone and act with justice and righteousness toward others, actions that were to be informed by a sincere love of God and neighbor. These few elements form the basis of Israel's faith, the heart of its religion, and the essence of its moral life.

This chapter will consider these foundational convictions and imperatives as they appear in the Old Testament. It will focus on the ongoing drama of human history because it is the crucible in which Hebrew people encountered the question of faith and the setting in which they enacted their response to it. Contemporary conditions and experiences also require attention because they refracted the primordial question of faith differently for succeeding generations and shaped the moral choices that confronted each of them. This study will emphasize the moral quality of the decision between faith and unbelief and show that in a community of faith daily moral choices cannot fail to have religious meaning. The intimate relationship among history, faith, and moral life will emerge as a major theme in the life of Israel.

This examination of Israel's faith and moral life is necessary in order to expose the foundations of Christian faith and moral life and to highlight issues and dynamics that are perennial in the Judeo-Christian tradition. Moreover, because the Old Testament is God's inspired word, it is essential to Christian life and must be included in any adequate theological reflection on it. This chapter will pursue its investigation in light of the chronological and theological priorities of the Old Testament itself.

It will begin by considering the roots of religion in fundamental questions about human life and its meaning. This discussion will outline the response that was typical of pagan peoples at the time Israel came into being. It will show how Israel's faith in God not only required a very different kind of religion but caused it to assess the world and human affairs in an entirely new way.

The second section will review Israel's formation as a people; explore the principal components of its faith, worship, and law; and highlight their moral dimensions. These elements are of foundational significance, both theologically and historically.

Once those fundamental matters have been presented, it will be possible to see how Israel assessed those persons and actions that violated God or neighbor. This discussion of sin will offer further insight into the relationship between human beings and God, and bring God's mercy into higher relief.

The fourth section will review pertinent developments during the centuries in which Israel was ruled by kings. The rise of the monarchy dramatically affected the nation's relationship with God. The prophets proclaimed God's blessing on the Davidic dynasty, held the kings responsible for Israel's fidelity to the Covenant, and interpreted Israel's political troubles as God's punishment on the monarchy's sins. This phase of the story highlights the ongoing imperative of faith, which each generation confronts anew, and the decisive effects of its moral choices.

The Exile brought great anguish to the Hebrew people. Even in its aftermath, they were required to deal with new and often taxing circumstances. The events of this period led many people to wonder if God had abandoned them. The same circumstances also stimulated a deeper faith and opened new perspectives on human experience. All these developments helped to form the political and religious world of Jesus and his first disciples.

The Wisdom literature of the postexilic centuries is the concern of the sixth section. This portion of the Old Testament shows how persons of faith wrestled with suffering and injustice and sorted out its effects on their relationship with God. Wisdom literature also reflects the influence of a more cosmopolitan age, which is evident in its reflections on nature and the resources of human experience.

The final section will offer some reflections on the Old Testament and its contribution to Christian moral life.

HUMAN LIFE AND THE SACRED

As people go through life, they encounter a wide range of events and experiences. Some of these are predictable, for instance, the behavior of the earth, the sun, the moon, and the stars; the planting and harvest of crops; and the cycle of birth, reproduction, and death in animals and humans. Others are capricious or unexpected, including earthquake, famine, pestilence, and disease; personal malice or kindness; or perhaps a fortuitous escape from danger. Sometimes people see their hopes, wants, or needs fulfilled while at other times they are frustrated by tragedy, injustice, or simply an unfortunate turn of events. They often try to assert control over themselves and their environment but usually find that necessity or unforeseen occurrences have the last word. Nevertheless, people usually do not assume that life is chaotic and meaningless. Sooner or later, they gather up their experiences, ponder human life as a whole, and try to find some meaning in it. If that attempt is successful, it will allow human activities to be placed within a larger context and interpreted accordingly.

The search for meaning is driven by many questions. Where does the universe come from, and where is it going? Does experience point to the activity of divine beings or other superhuman forces? What accounts for human society and its institutions? Is it possible to account for the routine and the capricious, the upright and the unjust, the pleasant and the painful in human life? Can anything illuminate present experiences or future expectations? Is there any way to know or control what is yet to happen, especially when much is at stake? What if anything can be asked or required of human beings as they make their way through life? These questions are all-embracing. They encompass earthly realities and cosmic events as well as personal and social experiences. They speak to the meaning of time or history and determine whether a society will find any rhyme, reason, or essential characteristics in it.[1]

After wrestling with such questions, ancient peoples concluded that both the cosmos and temporal events reflect a principle of unity and vitality. They worked out explicit accounts of these hidden but decisive forces and enshrined them in stories and rituals. Their interpretations of human life coalesced into a settled world view, a coherent set

---

[1] M. C. D'Arcy, *The Meaning and Matter of History: A Christian View* (New York: Meridian Books, 1961) 66–70, 79–80; Langdon Gilkey, *Maker of Heaven and Earth: A Study of the Christian Doctrine of Creation* (Garden City, N.Y.: Doubleday Anchor Books, 1965) 19–23; see also Karl Löwith, *Meaning in History: The Theological Implications of the Philosophy of History* (Chicago: University of Chicago Press, 1949) 1–19.

of assumptions and judgments about the universe, time, and human affairs. Along with story and ritual, that world view established the framework and grounds for each people's religion, government, and other essential aspects of life. In that respect, the Hebrew people were no different from their neighbors. What distinguished Israel was its faith in one God and its convictions about what its God did and required. The uniqueness of Israel's religion comes into high relief when it is contrasted with the religion and outlook of its pagan neighbors.

The Pagan World View

Ancient Near Eastern peoples firmly believed that the world is under the influence of superhuman forces. Certain places or things seemed to overflow with an energy that defied explanation but nonetheless elicited strong feelings of awe and fear. The unique quality of these objects was attributed to the action of a divine force. The influx of divine energy made them sacred, differentiated them from other places and things, and gave them a life, reality, and meaning that other objects did not have. Other places and things were profane, chaotic, and lacking in "reality." The need to distance themselves from chaos and draw close to the divine constrained ancient peoples to live within sacred zones and to organize their life and worship around sacred places and objects.

The all-important effort to commune with the sacred required some way to gain access to the divine actions that conferred reality, order, and fruitfulness on human life. That communion was achieved by means of rituals and festivals. When it settled in a new place, for example, a premodern people ritually reengaged the original act of creation so that its energy might bring their new territory out of chaos, organize it, and make it sacred. Other rituals sought to tap divine power for the benefit of such basic activities as planting or harvesting, governing, war making, or peacemaking. They did for time what sacred objects did for space; they qualified some time as sacred and left other time merely profane.

Sacred time ultimately refers to the "time" that accompanied such primordial divine activities as creation or reproduction, which took place in eternity before human time began. Sacred rituals sought to return to that primeval "time" so that people might commune with eternity. They interrupted the temporal sequence proper to profane human time and recognized its subordination to the divine and eternal events. By contrast, profane time is proper to the contingent events of ordinary life, which, to the extent that they lack a vital link with eternal divine deeds, can be no more than illusory or inconsequential.

The conviction that things have reality and importance only insofar as they share in a divine order imposes strict limits on the what people can do in their world. Whether it is a question of sacred realities that are to be respected or profane things that are chaotic and insignificant, people do not control their world and should not expect to change their environment. Furthermore, against the background of a normative eternal domain, human history can only contain a closed and dependent drama that goes on interminably but produces nothing new. Finally, because human and superhuman forces act on the same stage, human beings have both a motive and the means to try to manipulate the gods that have so much power over them. Whether it is a matter of trying to unleash demonic forces against an enemy or to appease an angry divinity, people try to intervene in divine affairs and turn them to their own purposes.

This premodern world view has direct impact on moral life. It tends to support idolatry, human sacrifice, sacred prostitution, and other obscene practices. In addition, by offering no reason to hope that things or events can ever take a new direction, and especially by suggesting that timeless forces dominate human affairs, it circumscribes human action and depreciates moral responsibility.[2]

Israel's Faith

Israel's world view was also profoundly religious, but it drew its strength from an altogether different source and developed in conscious opposition to the polytheistic thinking and behavior of contemporary nations. In contrast with its neighbors, Israel found the most powerful signs of God's presence not in the things of nature, but in the events of history. That basic discovery realigned the principal axis of faith and practice from nature to history. It stripped sacred spaces, things, and rituals in Israel of mythic significance and gave them a primarily historical meaning. It transformed the relationships between people and their world, their history, and their God and opened up

---

[2] Mircea Eliade, *The Sacred and the Profane: The Nature of Religion,* trans. Willard R. Trask (New York: Harper & Row; Harper Torchbooks, 1959); idem, *Cosmos and History: The Myth of the Eternal Return,* trans. Willard R. Trask (New York: Harper & Row; Harper Torchbooks, 1959); Gerhard Von Rad, *Old Testament Theology,* trans. D.M.G. Stalker (New York, Evanston, San Francisco, and London: Harper & Row, 1962–5) 2:110-2; Bernhard W. Anderson, *Understanding the Old Testament,* 4th ed. (Englewood Cliffs, N.J.: Prentice-Hall, 1986) 184–93; D'Arcy, *Meaning and Matter of History,* 80–1; John L. McKenzie, "Aspects of Old Testament Thought," *NJBC,* 1288–9, 1302-3; E. Jacob, "Les bases théologiques de l'éthique de l'Ancien Testament," *Congress Volume: Oxford 1959* (Leiden: J. Brill, 1960) 40.

new vistas of understanding and responsibility. The implications are many.

Above all, Israel knew that its God is Lord of history. It mocked the gods of the nations as helpless but celebrated the ability of its God to do whatever he wishes.[3] Israel recognized that although God is powerful, God does not toy with his creatures or act maliciously toward them as neighboring peoples believed their gods did. God exercises sovereignty out of love, with justice, and for the good of human beings. The confession of God's powerful deeds also transformed the meaning of time. Because history began with God's act of creation and embraces events that are unique and decisive, it cannot be bound to mythic events that never change. Emancipated from eternally recurring cyclical patterns, human affairs are free to unfold in a more linear, open-ended way that allows room for novelty.

Israel's faith entailed a similar reevaluation of the cosmos. So powerful a God must have a special kind of existence and a properly divine "space." God lives in "heaven," not on the earth where people do. To differentiate Creator and creature and to distinguish divine from human realms as Israel did was also to reject the customary division of the universe into sacred-orderly and profane-chaotic components. For Israel, the entire universe stands under God's sovereignty and none of it is divine. The same sharp differentiation of God and creatures means that there is no necessity for God's activity to intrude into human affairs as pagans assumed. More to the point, persons have no independent access to God's domain and cannot manipulate God in any way.

Israel's faith-inspired world view is also charged with moral significance. Israel's God utterly rejected human sacrifice, cultic prostitution, obscene fertility rites, and other aberrant behavior that neighboring peoples commonly practiced (e.g., Lev 18:21; 19:29; Deut 20:18; 23:17). Its desacralizing of the cosmos gave nature a new valence and opened the world to human intelligence and energy (Gen 1:26-28; 2:15). Its acknowledgment of God's sovereignty intensified people's responsibil-

---

[3] For I know that the LORD is great,
   and that our LORD is above all gods.
Whatever the LORD pleases he does,
   in heaven and on earth,
   in the seas and all deeps. . . .
The idols of the nations are silver and gold,
   the work of men's hands.
They have mouths, but they speak not,
   they have eyes, but they see not,
they have ears, but they hear not,
   nor is there any breath in their mouths (Ps 135:5-6, 15-17).

ity for their actions toward creation. Moreover, by intervening in history God made it necessary for Israel to consider history very carefully if it wished to know its God and discern God's will. Temporal affairs assumed even more importance as the stage on which Israel enacted its response to the God who had asked for its fidelity and obedience. Israel's faith therefore endowed time, or history, with a profoundly religious and intensely moral significance. That faith and its temporal imperatives distinguished Israel from its neighbors and established the foundations of its life and worship.[4]

HISTORY AND THE FAITH OF ISRAEL

When the Hebrew people pondered their own history, they were struck by the remarkable chain of events that had made them a nation. The outline of the story is well known. Abram, later named Abraham, left his ancestral home many centuries earlier. Some of his descendants went to Egypt, where they became slaves. During years of slavery their numbers increased, and so did their grievances against their masters. Under the leadership of Moses, they escaped across the Red Sea. After being freed from slavery, they had a powerful religious experience at the foot of Mount Sinai. United by history, faith, and a leadership that enjoyed divine authorization, they conquered and populated the Promised Land of Canaan and eventually set up a monarchical form of government. That history was marked by a wide range of personalities and the unpredictable turns that usually characterize human affairs. Taken as a whole, it suggested that something more than merely human activity and a measure of good luck was at work.[5]

---

[4] See G. Ernest Wright and Reginald H. Fuller, *The Book of the Acts of God: Contemporary Scholarship Interprets the Bible* (Garden City, N.Y.: Anchor Books, 1960) 3–29; McKenzie, "Aspects of Old Testament Thought," 1302–4; Paul Neuenzeit, "Time," *EBT*, 911–5; Von Rad, *Old Testament Theology*, 2:99-112; Eliade, *The Sacred and the Profane*, 110–1; idem, *Cosmos and History*, 102–12; Alan Richardson, *History Sacred and Profane* (Philadelphia: Westminster Press, 1964) 217–27; D'Arcy, *Meaning and Matter of History*, 217–25; Gilkey, *Maker of Heaven and Earth*, especially 1–116.

The question of history and its meaning has occasioned a great deal of writing. In addition to the sources already noted, see, for example, R. G. Collingwood, *The Idea of History*, rev. ed. (Oxford and New York: Oxford University Press, 1993); C. T. McIntire, ed., *God, History, and Historians: An Anthology of Modern Christian Views of History* (New York: Oxford University Press, 1977); Jean Daniélou, *The Lord of History: Reflections on the Inner Meaning of History*, trans. Nigel Abercrombie (London: Longmans; Chicago: Henry Regnery, 1958); Reinhold Niebuhr, *Faith and History: A Comparison of Christian and Modern Views of History* (New York: Charles Scribner's Sons, 1949).

[5] For the Scriptural texts pertinent to these events see Genesis 12–50, the Book of Exodus, Deuteronomy 1–11, Joshua 1–11, and 2 Samuel 1–8.

With some reflection, Israel came to understand this entire historical sequence as a sign that God had intervened in human affairs for the benefit of this people. In that light, it affirmed that Abraham left his home not by chance, but in response to God's initiative and intervention.[6] His descendants became a great nation and he himself a source of blessing because God had promised that this would be the case. The same God had freed the Hebrew slaves from bondage and united them into one nation. Such generous and powerful deeds constituted the foundation of Hebrew faith and gave God every right to require Israel to respond with fidelity and obedience. It is necessary to explore key aspects of that faith in greater detail and underline its moral dimensions.

Election, Exodus, and Covenant

Theologically speaking, this process is an example of election. In the case just described, election took place as God chose Israel, formed it as a people, and offered to sustain an intimate relationship with it. Election involved God's sovereignty and the obligation to be holy and fulfill a mission of service.[7] Election was the source of Israel's nationhood and the essentially religious texture of its life. The conviction that Israel was God's chosen people exercised a profound and decisive influence upon its faith and morality.

Although election began with the Hebrew patriarchs, it reached its climax in the Exodus, God's freeing the Israelites from slavery in Egypt through the cooperation of Moses.[8] This event was decisive, for it gave

---

Wright and Fuller propose that five particular historical events assumed fundamental significance for Hebrew faith and life. They are the promises made to the patriarchs Abraham, Isaac, and Jacob; the release of the Israelites from slavery in Egypt (the Exodus); the experience of God's will and the making of the Covenant at the foot of Mount Sinai; the conquest of Canaan; and the securing of land and government under King David. As interpreted by faith, these events formed the basis for Israel's knowledge of its God and their grasp of his will for them (*Book of the Acts of God,* 8–9).

[6] See Gen 12:1-3. Abraham's obedient response required him to trust the promise given, even though he would not see it fulfilled. The story of Abraham, Isaac, and Jacob is ultimately the story of God's promise and forms the preamble to the history of Israel. Walther Zimmerli, *Old Testament Theology in Outline,* trans. David E. Green (Edinburgh: T. & T. Clark, 1978) 28–9. See also Anderson, *Understanding the Old Testament,* 170–6.

[7] Harold Henry Rowley, *The Biblical Doctrine of Election* (London: Lutterworth Press, 1950) 45.

[8] Zimmerli, *Old Testament Theology,* 22. This event took place during the reign of Pharaoh Ramses II (1290–1224 B.C.). For the biblical account, see Exod 1:1–15:21. See also Anderson, *Understanding the Old Testament,* 48–83.

Israel its freedom and its origin as a people. More important however was the significance of the Exodus for its faith. In the Exodus experience the Israelites came to see that their God was compassionate, loving, and able to act with power in order to save them when they were dispersed, weak, and afflicted in a foreign land.[9]

Such acts of love and grace were deeply personal and religious because they created a relationship between God and Israel. The form and requirement of that relationship soon became clear. After Israel reached the safety of the Sinai desert, God declared his intentions to Moses:

> Thus you shall say to the house of Jacob, and tell the people of Israel: You have seen what I did to the Egyptians, and how I bore you on eagles' wings and brought you to myself. Now therefore, if you will obey my voice and keep my covenant, you shall be my own possession among all peoples; for all the earth is mine, and you shall be to me a kingdom of priests and a holy nation. These are the words which you shall speak to the children of Israel (Exod 19:3-6).

In secular usage, a covenant was a device by which two parties solemnly committed themselves to each other and agreed to abide by conditions that were explicitly set forth.[10] Against this background, God intended the Covenant to consolidate and perpetuate the special relationship that he had initiated with Israel. The Covenant crystallized all the dynamics and the essential content of Israel's faith and underlined its binding qualities.

Principal Aspects of the Covenant

First of all, the very offer of a covenant was an expression of divine sovereignty and initiative. Israel did not liberate itself, nor did it earn or deserve God's favorable intervention. Rather, the Covenant reflects a special love and points solely to God's sovereign goodness (Deut 4:32-40; 7:6-11). God's gracious initiatives are the foundation of Israel's faith, religion, and moral life.

In addition, the Covenant was based upon the mighty deeds of God in its history. In declaring God's deeds, the Covenant acknowledged God's primacy, power, and goodness and reminded the people of the

---

[9] See especially Exod 3:7-12. For a helpful discussion of the significance of the Exodus for Israel's faith, see Wright, *Book of the Acts of God*, 73-83.

[10] See Exod 24:3-8. See also Anderson, *Understanding the Old Testament*, 84-103; Wright, *Book of the Acts of God*, 84–98; Zimmerli, *Old Testament Theology*, 48–58; McKenzie, "Aspects of Old Testament Thought," 1297–9.

kind of God they served. Repeated references to God's deeds called attention to temporal affairs and emphasized their significance. They suggested that Israel's acceptance of the Covenant was not arbitrary or unrelated to its experiences and that faith is the proper response to a God who is strong, good, and caring (e.g., Exod 19:3-5 and Deut 4:32-40).

The theophany, or self-revelation of God to Moses (Exod 24:15-18; see also 34:5-9), left no doubt that God had given rise to the Covenant and that communion with God was its heart and soul. These aspects of God's relationship with Israel had a long history. Indeed, the Exodus was interpreted as God's fulfillment of an earlier promise to the patriarchs (Deut 6:10-12; 7:8). Israel's reflection on these promises helped it to realize that faithfulness was one of the chief attributes of its God and to celebrate God's goodness, presence, and fidelity (Exod 20:6 and Deut 7:9).[11]

Finally, the Covenant was not thrust upon an unwilling Israel by a powerful if benevolent God. So intimate and stable a relationship could not be established without Israel's free acceptance and a sincere commitment to abide by its requirements. The sacred text attests that the relationship between Israel and God was in fact freely and formally ratified: "All the words which the LORD has spoken we will do" (Exod 24:3; see also 19:7 and 24:7-8). This makes it clear that the response of faith was deliberate and responsible. Israel's free acceptance underlines the Covenant's inherently dialogical and moral qualities. Once enacted, it embodied both God's free gift and Israel's willing response. Israel would henceforth be accountable for its adherence to the Covenant and the obligations that went with it. Besides highlighting the moral quality of a foundational religious commitment, the Covenant invested Israelite moral life with an intensely religious significance.[12]

Principal Requirements of the Covenant

Love was among the most important requirement of the Covenant. God set the example by first acting lovingly toward Israel. It was fitting that God should ask for the same kind of response: "You shall love the Lord your God with all your heart, and with all your soul, and with all your might" (Deut 6:5). Furthermore, this relationship with

---

[11] Zimmerli, *Old Testament Theology,* 22–6.

[12] Ibid., 46. The free acceptance of the Covenant was not limited to those alive at the time of Moses. All succeeding generations in Israel were understood to have accepted it as well. See Deut 5:2-3; 29:10-15; Rowley, *Biblical Doctrine of Election,* 47–9.

God had to extend to one's neighbor: "You shall love your neighbor as yourself: I am the Lord" (Lev 19:18). Communion with God and neighbor established the basic dynamics and goals of the Covenant.

Integral to communion with God is holiness: "You shall be holy; for I the LORD your God am holy" (Lev 19:2; see also Exod 19:6 and Deut 7:6). In its original meaning, to be holy is to be separate, or set apart from the ordinary.[13] Because God is totally other, uncreated, and not identified with the universe or anything in it, God is holiness itself. Therefore, to say that Israel is holy is to acknowledge its dependence on God and its unique status as God's special possession. In a secondary way, holiness suggests cleanliness or purity. In this sense, Israel could only be holy by receiving these attributes as gifts from God who is their source.[14] As a nation meant to be both separate and pure, Israel was to reflect God's holiness in all areas of its life, interior, cultic, moral, personal, and political.[15] It was not allowed to be, act, or worship like other nations (Exod 20:3-6; Lev 18:1-5; Deut 4:15-19, 12:29-31). The requirements of holiness were bound to have a pervasive and powerful impact on Israel's self-awareness and life.

Love of God and holiness necessarily entail obedience. Israel owed obedience because God had demanded it, and as the practical expression of its fidelity to the Covenant. The following passages illustrate the practical unity of love and obedience:

> And now, Israel, what does the LORD your God require of you, but to fear the LORD your God, to walk in all his ways, to love him, to serve the LORD your God with all your heart and with all your soul, and to keep the commandments and statutes of the LORD, which I command you this day for your good? (Deut 10:12-13).
>
> Your fathers went down to Egypt seventy persons; and now the LORD your God has made you as the stars of heaven for multitude. "You shall therefore love the LORD your God, and keep his charge, his ordinances, and his commandments always" (Deut 10:22–11:1).

Love and communion established the context for law and obedience in Israel and were to be their inspiration. Covenant obedience was intended to express and maintain personal solidarity between God and Israel. Obedience helped to guarantee that the holiness of

---

[13] See, for example, *DBT*, 236–8.

[14] Ibid.

[15] The normative nature of holiness is clear from Lev 19:2, quoted above. See also Bruce C. Birch, *Let Justice Roll Down: The Old Testament, Ethics, and Christian Life* (Louisville, Ky.: Westminster/John Knox Press, 1991) 150; Jacob, "Les bases théologiques," 41.

Israel would be comprehensive, real, and visible in daily life.[16] Taken together, then, law and obedience in Israel have a profoundly religious source, inspiration, and purpose. Old Testament law and obedience are therefore not to be confused with similar concepts employed in modern civil life and legal codes. In order to emphasize and clarify this point, the religious quality of life in Israel needs to be considered in greater detail.

The Torah

As is true of any society, Israel's life was governed by many specific laws. The most important of these are found in the first five books of the Old Testament, the Pentateuch, or *Torah,* where they have been gathered into several identifiable collections, notably the Decalogue (Exod 20:2-17 and Deut 5:6-21); Covenant Code (Exod 20:22–23:33); Priestly Code (Lev 1–16); Holiness Code (Lev 17–26); and the Deuteronomic Law (Deut 12–26).[17] Although these bodies of law had different origins and purposes, their ultimate function was to protect the covenant relationship with God and help Israel to abide by it.[18]

The word "law" needs to be understood in light of its meaning in the Old Testament. The Hebrew word it translates, *torah,* does not mean a legally imposed behavioral obligation as it is usually understood in modern societies. *Torah* means "instruction." It includes "instructions for life, the teaching of God about what is necessary to do in order for the community to live according to God's way and in harmony with one another."[19] The Hebrew people were to receive such instruction

---

[16] Birch, *Let Justice Roll Down,* 126, 162–3; W. Eichrodt, "Covenant and Law," *Int* 20 (1966) 310. For a fuller discussion of the place of commandment in Hebrew covenant life, see Thomas W. Ogletree, *The Use of the Bible in Christian Ethics* (Philadelphia: Fortress Press, 1983) 47–85. For more on the origin of God's requirements, see Rowley, *Biblical Doctrine of Election,* 54–9.

[17] On the extent and diversity of law in the Pentateuch, see for example, *DBT,* 302–3; W. J. Harrelson, "Law in the OT," *IDB,* 3:77-89; Anderson, *Understanding the Old Testament,* 95–101; Brevard S. Childs, *Old Testament Theology in a Canonical Context* (Philadelphia: Fortress Press, 1986) 53–6; Werner H. Schmidt, *Old Testament Introduction,* trans. Matthew J. O'Connell (New York: Crossroad, 1984) 110–9.

[18] McKenzie, "Aspects of Old Testament Thought," 1299. Schmidt sums it up as follows: "Taken as a whole, the phenomenon of 'law' takes various forms and is conceptualized in various ways in the OT. The common purpose of all the laws is not to create a communion with God, since this is based on an action of God, but to preserve it and thus to show that God's gift calls for a corresponding human task" (*Old Testament Introduction,* 119).

[19] Patrick D. Miller, Jr., "The Place of the Decalogue in the Old Testament and Its Law," *Int* 43 (1989) 232.

with joy as a precious gift. In the words of Ps 119:105, *torah* is "a lamp to my feet and a light to my path."[20]

Receiving and following this *torah*, or instruction, brought the believer deeper knowledge of God and a new insight into God's will. Obedience encouraged a reciprocity of life and goodness between God and Israel and opened a very fruitful way for its members to understand God and grasp more fully the requirements of communion with God. Because God acts in human history, people can know God by carrying out the work God asks them to do:

> Knowledge and truth in the Bible involve things to do, not simply a belief in a God of nature nor an experience of the God within. God is too busy, too active, too dynamic to wait for us to experience him in the acts of worship we devise in our schedules. He is to be known by what he has done and said, by what he is now doing and saying; and he is known when we do what he commands us to do.[21]

The spirit and function of the *Torah*, then, was far removed from merely practical considerations or legalism.[22] It was intended to serve the Covenant and the communion between God and Israel. These basic religious imperatives are the proper context in which to consider the Ten Commandments and the function of worship, or cult.

The Decalogue

Of all the statutory texts one finds in the Old Testament, none is more important than the Decalogue, also known as the Ten Commandments, or following the Hebrew text, the ten "words."[23] The Decalogue appears in two different places, Exod 20:2-17, considered the older text, and Deut 5:6-21. Both passages attribute the Decalogue directly to Yahweh and explicitly relate the Decalogue to the Covenant.

[20] Birch, *Let Justice Roll Down*, 171–2.

[21] Wright, *Book of the Acts of God*, 22–3. See also Eichrodt, "Covenant and Law," 311.

[22] On this see Birch, *Let Justice Roll Down*, 164–5; Eichrodt, "Covenant and Law," 313–4; Anderson, *Understanding the Old Testament*, 149–50, 533–5.

[23] Exod 20:1. Exodus 34:27-28 uses the expression "the words of the covenant." In Semitic usage the "word" is not only the bearer of meaning directed to the mind, it carries a power of its own that reflects the stature of the speaker and is directed to its hearers' lives. By the same token, "hearing" is not a passive listening but a personal appropriation of and response to a "word." Understanding the Ten Commandments as the "Ten Words of Yahweh" highlights their interpersonal and dynamic quality. See McKenzie, "Aspects of Old Testament Thought," 1291–2; Miller, "Place of the Decalogue," 232–3; and Von Rad, *Old Testament Theology*, 2:80-98.

The Ten Commandments were the stipulations of the Covenant and are to be understood only in that light. They established the foundational requirements of national life.[24] All spoke immediately and personally to each and every Israelite, specifying the minimum religious and moral standards for life in the community. If Israel fulfilled them, it would live in keeping with its communion with God.

The first three commandments concern the Israelites' actions toward God. They sought to guarantee an authentic monotheistic faith and protect the community from idolatry. The remaining seven specified important obligations toward one's neighbor. These aimed to establish the foundation for a sound social life in Israel. Although they are largely concerned with public behavior, they embrace such interior acts as coveting a neighbor's property, animals, or relatives (Exod 20:17). Most of them are negative and begin with the phrase, "Thou shalt not" (20:13-17). By forbidding specific acts, these prohibitions attempted to prevent things that would injure a neighbor and threaten the bonds of society.[25] This approach was conservative and left much to be determined by other norms that could be added or modified as circumstances changed or as the Hebrew conscience matured.[26]

The Decalogue was ultimately intended to uphold the requirements of the Covenant or promote communion between God and Israel. The

---

[24] McKenzie, "Aspects of Old Testament Thought," 1299. McKenzie notes that it is incorrect to speak of the Ten Commandments as laws. Rather, they are the basis for law in Israel. This is a point on which there seems to be scholarly consensus.

[25] This concern with the requirements of life in society helps to account for the similarity between the Decalogue and other ancient Near East codes. This similarity does not argue against the divine authority behind the Decalogue but does suggest that God has not imposed it willfully and without regard for important human needs. On this see Robert Koch, "Vers une morale de l'Alliance?" *StMor* 6 (1968) 43–4; Edouard Hamel, *Loi naturelle et loi du Christ* (Bruges and Paris: Desclée de Brouwer, 1964) 107–28; idem, *Les dix paroles: Perspectives bibliques* (Brussels and Paris: Desclée, 1969) 27–33; A. T. Patrick, "La formation littéraire et l'origine historique du décalogue," *ETL* 40 (1964) 242–51.

[26] Hamel, *Les dix paroles*, 24–7. See also Birch, *Let Justice Roll Down*, 168–71; Miller, "The Place of the Decalogue," 233–42.
A comparison of the texts in Exodus and Deuteronomy shows that the formulation of the Decalogue also seems to have changed somewhat as time passed. The later statement of the tenth commandment (Deut 5:21) placed the prohibition against coveting the neighbor's wife in the first position, whereas the earlier text (Exod 20:17) gave priority to the neighbor's house (Schmidt, *Old Testament Introduction*, 115; Hamel, *Les dix paroles*, 91–7). This textual variation suggests that the Decalogue did not function as a fixed legal text but was a living reality that reflected the growth of moral and religious insight and mediated the Covenant to the ever-changing Israelite community. On these issues see Childs, *Old Testament Theology*, 63–83; Hamel, *Les dix paroles*, 41–97; Miller, "The Place of the Decalogue," 237–42.

most eloquent testimony to the essentially religious qualities of the commandments is the Deuteronomic call to Israel. It is a fitting summary to this discussion.

> Hear, O Israel: The LORD our God is one LORD; and you shall love the LORD your God with all your heart, and with all your soul, and with all your might. And these words which I command you this day shall be upon your heart; and you shall teach them diligently to your children, and shall talk of them when you sit in your house, and when you walk by the way, and when you lie down, and when you rise. And you shall bind them as sign upon your hand, and they shall be as frontlets between your eyes. And you shall write them on the doorposts of your house and on your gates (Deut 6:4-9).

Worship

Worship refers to the actions by which a community encounters the divine, professes its belief, and offers praise and glory to God. The first three commandments of the Decalogue (Exod 20:2-7), the detailed regulations concerning the things required for worship (e.g., 25–31), the demand for personal purity (e.g., Lev 11–18), and other provisions of Israelite law aimed to manifest God's sovereignty, protect the integrity of public worship, and enable it to enhance Israel's communion with God. Religious festivals and cultic acts reminded the Israelite community of God's mighty deeds and gave later generations a privileged means of access to them (Exod 18:10-12; Deut 6:20-24; 16:1-15; 26:1-11). The tabernacle and the ark of the covenant had a similar purpose, for they also symbolized God's presence to the chosen people (Exod 34:1-4, 27-29; 25:10-16; 26:1-37). These aspects of Israel's life and activity reflected God's holiness, kept the essential elements of faith before the community, and stimulated it to make the necessary response of praise, thanksgiving, and repentance.[27]

Israel's worship had important moral dimensions. The continual references in worship to God's mighty deeds highlighted the grounds of Hebrew faith and kept the imperative of faith before the community. Rituals and festivals placed God's presence and activity before all generations and summoned each Israelite to make a sincere commitment to God and to the Covenant. As Israel celebrated God's supremacy

---

[27] McKenzie, "Aspects of Old Testament Thought," 1299–1300; Zimmerli, *Old Testament Theology,* 114; Anderson, *Understanding the Old Testament,* 116–8. For a fuller discussion of Israelite worship, see John J. Castelot and Aelred Cody, "Religious Institutions of Israel," *NJBC,* 1253–83; or G. Henton Davies, "Worship in the OT," *IDB,* 4:879-83.

over the community and the whole universe, it was reminded of the love, loyalty, and obedience it owed to its God. Similarly, by sustaining Israel's self-understanding as a community that God had set apart and claimed for his own, worship gave the community great moral significance. Because it was holy, Israel was never to adopt the objectionable practices of neighboring peoples. It was to treat fellow Israelites with justice and act out of a genuine love of God and neighbor. Worship was to elevate the Israelites' moral life in all of its dimensions, interior and public, personal and social.[28]

A Blessing or a Curse

The Covenant obliged Israel to be loyal to its God, obey God's commandments, and conform all aspects of its life to the requirements of communion and holiness. Whatever its response, Israel needed to remember that its God is just and able to control human affairs. Practically speaking, if the community was obedient it could expect to receive good things from the hands of God. However, if it relied on its own cleverness, ignored justice, or sought after other gods, then it left itself open to catastrophe. The stark choice between a blessing and a curse drives home these points:

> See, I have set before you this day life and good, death and evil. If you obey the commandments of the LORD your God which I command you this day, by loving the LORD your God, by walking in his ways, and by keeping his commandments and his statutes and his ordinances, then you shall live and multiply, and the LORD your God will bless you in the land which you are entering to take possession of it. But if your heart turns away, and you will not hear, but are drawn away to worship other gods and serve them, I declare to you this day, that you shall perish; you shall not live long in the land which you are going over the Jordan to enter and possess. I call heaven and earth to witness against you this day, that I have set before you life and death, blessing and curse; therefore choose life, that you and your descendants may live, loving the LORD your God, obeying his voice, and cleaving to him (Deut 30:15-20).

If the blessing and the curse emphasized God's justice and power, the choice that faced Israel underlined its moral responsibility. How the community considered its choices and exercised freedom would determine its standing before God and the course of human affairs.

---

[28] Birch, *Let Justice Roll Down,* 174–6; Jacob, "Les bases théologiques," 47. Jacob notes that this unity between cult and morality is so significant that its loss was a sure sign that something had gone wrong with cult or morality, or perhaps with both.

The warnings uttered by the prophets and the Deuteronomist's account of Israel's history reflect a similar conviction. Under God's sovereignty, the nation's destiny and its relationship with God depended upon the quality of its moral life.[29]

GRACE AND SIN

The authors of the Pentateuch were deeply interested in all important aspects of the human condition as the faith of Israel illuminated it. Although they recognized humanity's social, cultural, and personal accomplishments, they were struck by the evil, suffering, and frustration that characterize human life; and they explored these experiences in the light of God's goodness and sovereignty. The well-known stories in the Book of Genesis, especially the account of Adam and Eve's disobedience (Gen 2:4b–3:24) and the murder of Abel by his brother, Cain (4:1-16), are the fruit of their reflections. These passages, which speak to the experience of humanity as a whole, link the bitter and destructive experiences of life to a refusal to respect God's requirements.[30] This general human sinfulness is the background against which the writers pondered a more immediate reality: Israel's own disloyalty to God, vividly expressed in the worship of the golden calf (Exod 32:1-6). As they considered the sinfulness of humanity and of Israel itself, they and other sacred authors developed a language that would make it possible to speak about the sources, motives, acts, and consequences of sin. These efforts helped to deepen their appreciation of God's gracious response to sinners and God's gift of forgiveness.

Adam and Eve

The story of Adam and Eve reflects on the actions of a man and a woman in the world God had made. God places Adam in a garden and gives him the vocation to till it and keep it (Gen 2:15). God allows Adam a great deal of freedom, and lays down only one injunction: "You may freely eat of every tree of the garden; but of the tree of the knowledge of good and evil you shall not eat, for in the day that you

---

[29] See Jacob, "Les bases théologiques," 41; Childs, *Old Testament Theology,* 56–7; Eichrodt, "Covenant and Law," 315.

[30] For further discussion of Genesis 1–11 see Anderson, *Understanding the Old Testament,* 159–66; Walter Brueggemann, *Genesis* (Atlanta: John Knox Press, 1982) 11–22; Claus Westermann, *Genesis 1–11: A Commentary,* rev. ed., trans. John J. Scullion (Minneapolis: Augsburg Publishing House, 1984) 1–73; Gerhard Von Rad, *Genesis: A Commentary,* trans. John H. Marks (Philadelphia: Westminster Press, 1972) 23–4.

eat of it you shall die" (2:16-17). In this instance, death is less a threat than a limit that demarcates a generous zone of freedom. Within that zone, Adam and Eve can live, work, and enjoy one another's company in peace and safety. The serpent dismisses God's prohibition and assures Eve that eating the forbidden fruit will return many benefits (3:1-5). Persuaded that their own curiosity, covetousness, and way of thinking should prevail, the couple ignores God's command and eats (3:6). That act changes everything. Overwhelmed with shame and fear, the couple try to hide from God (3:7-8), a response that reflects the destructive effects of their deed. In the dialogue that follows, God establishes the fact of their transgression and their full responsibility for it (3:9-13). The sentence is expulsion from the garden, which means alienation from God and a life of hardship on earth for man and woman alike (3:16-24, esp. 23).

This story emphasizes the direct relationship between God and the human couple. It assesses their life and work in the Garden in light of God's goodness and the boundaries that he had every right to draw. But the deeper point is that no relationship can survive and prosper unless the persons concerned are prepared to respect the limits it entails. Because man and woman have insisted on acting autonomously, they can no longer have peace with God. They begin to experience both internal stress and social tension and notice that their relationship with the world has also been profoundly disrupted. Without ever using the word, the story of Adam and Eve sketches a vivid picture of sin, with its sources and consequences.[31]

Cain and Abel

The story of Cain and Abel considers sin as it arises out of another foundational relationship, that of brothers. Cain is angry and disappointed because God accepted Abel's sacrifice but not his own. God describes the choice and the challenge that confront Cain: "If you do well, will you not be accepted? And if you do not do well, sin is couching at the door; its desire is for you, but you must master it" (Gen 4:7). Instead of mastering the beast of sin, Cain allows it to capture him: he murders his brother (4:8). The account then picks up the key issue: the relationship between Cain and God in the wake of Abel's murder. In answer to God's question, "Where is Abel your brother?" Cain replies,

---

[31] Brueggemann, *Genesis*, 40–54; Westermann, *Genesis 1–11*, 178–278; Von Rad, *Genesis*, 86-102; Anderson, *Understanding the Old Testament*, 160–3; Schmidt, *Old Testament Introduction*, 78–81; *DBT*, 329–32, 550–1; Birch, *Let Justice Roll Down*, 92–5; G. Quell and others, "Hamartano," *TDNT*, 1:281-6.

"I do not know; am I my brother's keeper?" (4:9), which is both a lie and an attempt to shed his responsibility. But God persists: "What have you done? The voice of your brother's blood is crying to me from the ground" (4:10). Convicted of fratricide, Cain is condemned to be "a fugitive and a wanderer on the earth" (4:12, 14). His life will be marked by hardship and restlessness.

This passage presupposes the internal stresses and external conflicts that occur as people live with their siblings—in the human family as well as nuclear ones. These problems require people to make choices. In the space between conflict and its resolution, sin prowls in search of prey, a metaphor that emphasizes the power of evil. The injunction, "you must master it," upholds people's capacity to respect others despite grave temptation, and therefore also their moral responsibility for whatever they do. Echoing the case of Adam and Eve, the story of Cain and Abel asserts God's sovereignty and the limited nature of human autonomy. It declares that one's relationship with God depends upon one's treatment of brother and sister. Because Cain killed his brother, he cannot have either peace with God or a happy life on earth. The message is simple: humanity's anxiety and alienation are to be blamed on its culpable violations of neighbor, violations that gravely offend God as well.[32]

The Golden Calf

The worship of the golden calf (Exod 32:1-6) reflects a more general human sinfulness, but its full significance is to be grasped in the light of Israel's liberation from Egypt and its covenant with God. This idolatry takes place immediately after God called upon the Israelites to make a sanctuary "that I may dwell in their midst" (25:8). Instead of being satisfied with that privileged means of communion, the people seek an idol. Distressed by Moses' absence, they ask Aaron to "make us gods" (32:1), and to that end they hand over their gold jewelry. Aaron makes them a molten calf, constructs an altar for it, and proclaims its worship; and the following day the people happily sacrifice to this idol (32:4-6). Upon discovering what the people had done, Moses dissuades God from consuming the people in wrath (32:7-14). Even so, their sin cannot fail to have severe consequences, especially when they do not repent and recommit themselves to the Lord (32:26). The Levites are commanded to slay a portion of the guilty (32:27-28), and a plague punishes the rest (32:35). Worst of all, having "sinned a

---

[32] Brueggemann, *Genesis*, 54–64; Westermann, *Genesis 1–11*, 279–320; Von Rad, *Genesis*, 102–9.

great sin" (32:30, 31), the people lose the special presence of God that had been offered to them (29:45-46; 33:3).

The worship of the golden calf is emblematic of Israel's disloyalty to the God who had saved it, offered it a covenant, and promised to be present to it in an altogether special way. Idolatry violates the first commandment (Exod 20:2-6) and is a personal affront to a God who is jealous as well as good (20:5; 34:14). The many references to anger on the part of Moses and God (32:9, 11, 12, 19, 22) underline the gravity and personal quality of such a sin. Although the sacred text presents the worship of the golden calf as a singular event, it leaves little doubt that it manifests a more general problem with very deep roots in the community. A sense of chronic sinfulness accounts for the blunt assessments of Israel as a "stiff-necked people" (32:9; 33:3, 5), "a stubborn people" (Deut 9:13), and "a perverse generation, children in whom is no faithfulness" (Deut 32:20). The episode of idolatry at the foot of Mount Sinai depicts Israel's chronic infidelity to God and suggests that this is to blame for the adversities that marked its history.[33]

The Language of Sin

Besides recounting episodes of sin, the sacred authors needed a language that would allow them to express the reality of sin and elaborate its many aspects. Because they were starting at the very beginning and had no precise vocabulary to call upon, they had to formulate a language of sin and refine it as they went along. In responding to this challenge, they presupposed God's loving-kindness toward Israel and its responsibility to live in communion with God and neighbor according to the Covenant. They recognized that on too many occasions Israel failed to keep faith with its God and had sinned against God.

When they searched for words to describe sin and its consequences, the sacred authors realized that certain daily events and experiences had something in common with sin. They took up these words and used them to express the reality and meaning of sin. Although they employed many other terms, rebellion against another *(pesha)*, guilt or iniquity *(awon)*, and missing a target or taking a wrong turn on a journey *(hattah)* are especially important. With several key words to speak of sin toward God, the Hebrew language gained the ability to express aspects or nuances that the one English word, "sin," cannot easily convey. This process of development and the diversity of language also accounts for the more primitive view that finds sin in legal or ritual mistakes *(asham)*.

---

[33] Terence E. Fretheim, *Exodus* (Louisville, Ky.: John Knox Press, 1991) 279–312; Anderson, *Understanding the Old Testament*, 103–6.

By the time of the eighth-century prophets, however, the Hebrew tradition had come to see that the full force of sin can be grasped only in the light of God's *hesed,* or "loving kindness." In other words, sin finds its true meaning and malice in the violation of the Covenant that binds the Israelite to God and neighbor. For this reason, when the sacred writers wish to refer to sin in its fullest and strongest sense, they normally use the word *hattah,* "to miss the mark." In this context they are referring not to a bull's eye or destination but to the Covenant and the bonds of communion it represents. This highlights sin as a culpable violation of God's love and a personal disloyalty toward God.[34]

Grace and Forgiveness

As frequent, widespread, and serious as sin is, God's grace and mercy have the final word. Although Adam and Eve were threatened with death if they disobeyed God's prohibition (Gen 2:17, 3:3), God did not kill them in response to their sin. Rather than allow the couple to be disabled by shame, God clothed them and helped them to recover their dignity (3:21). In response to Cain's fear of being killed, God placed a protecting mark on him and threatened heavy punishment on anyone who would take vengeance on him (4:15). In the aftermath of Israel's idolatry, God proclaims willingness to be merciful, and Moses asks God to forgive the people's sin and reestablish communion with them:

> "The LORD, the LORD, a God merciful and gracious, slow to anger, and abounding in steadfast love and faithfulness, keeping steadfast love for thousands, forgiving iniquity and transgression and sin, but who will by no means clear the guilty, visiting the iniquity of the fathers upon the children and the children's children, to the third and fourth generation." And Moses made haste to bow his head toward the earth, and worshipped. And he said, "If now I have found favor in thy sight, O Lord, let the Lord, I pray thee, go in the midst of us, although it is a stiff-necked people; and pardon our iniquity and our sin, and take us for thy inheritance."
> And he said, "Behold, I make a covenant" (Exod 34:6-9).

This passage celebrates the goodness and mercy of a God who might still forgive sinful Israel, return to Israel the ultimate gift of God's

---

[34] For a discussion of the language of sin in the Old Testament, see, for example, Johannes B. Bauer, "Sin," *EBT,* 849–62; Jacques Guillet, "Themes of Sin," *Themes of the Bible,* trans. Albert J. LaMothe, Jr. (Notre Dame, Ind.: Fides, 1964) 96–136; Bruce Vawter, "Missing the Mark," *The Mystery of Sin and Forgiveness,* ed. Michael J. Taylor (Staten Island: Alba House, 1971) 23–34; Kenneth Grayston, "Sin," *A Theological Word Book of the Bible,* ed. Alan Richardson (New York: Macmillan, 1962) 226–8; Von Rad, *Old Testament Theology,* 1:262-8; Quell, "Hamartano," 267–80.

presence, and revitalize the Covenant. This was something that Israel, "a stiff-necked people," did not deserve.[35]

God's gracious treatment of sinful humanity and offer of forgiveness and reconciliation to Israel are essential to Old Testament faith. Forgiveness points to the goodness and love of a God who is ever faithful, even to an unworthy and "stiff-necked people." Although its malice and destructive force are not to be underestimated, sin was not the first word nor is it to be the final word spoken between God and the human family. The first and last words belong to God, who speaks a language of grace, love, and goodness.

Whether they concern sin or forgiveness, these Old Testament passages presuppose that human beings live in relationship with God. They emphasize that moral choices directly affect that relationship and are responsible for the bitterness and alienation that mark the human condition. Having been especially blessed by God, Israel is obliged to meet specific religious and moral standards but often fails to do so. In its reflections on this sinfulness, the biblical text highlights the urgency of these obligations and Israel's full responsibility for its actions. Above all, it focuses attention on God's goodness and on the communion that God wishes to maintain with Israel.

ISRAEL UNDER GOD'S SOVEREIGNTY

In the centuries immediately following the Exodus-Sinai experience, Israel left its nomadic ways behind and settled in the Promised Land of Canaan. Soon afterward, the nation came under the rule of kings. Although there was a brief period of success and splendor, for the most part the monarchy did not secure Israel's political interests or ward off the catastrophes that eventually overtook the nation. Those unhappy results can be attributed to political or military causes, but faithful Israelites blamed them on the consistent failure of kings and their subjects to observe the Covenant. God had declared that fidelity to the Covenant would bring rich blessings while disloyalty would earn a curse. If Israel came to an evil end, it could only mean that God had inflicted a just punishment for its sins.

The Deuteronomistic history and the prophetic books[36] interpret the life and history of Israel from this intensely religious perspective. They find the key to Israel's history in God's justice and power over human

---

[35] Brueggemann, *Genesis*, 49–50, 60–1, 63; Fretheim, *Exodus*, 283–312, especially 301–10; Birch, *Let Justice Roll Down*, 95–7.

[36] Completed around the year 560 B.C., the Deuteronomistic history is the portrayal of Israel's past recorded in the books of Deuteronomy, Joshua, Judges, Samuel, and

affairs. These texts present a starkly human portrait of kings, priests, nobles, and ordinary people but leave no doubt that Israel is over-shadowed by the curse on infidelity. Their outlook will govern this consideration of the monarchy, Israel's life under its rule, and the prophetic response to the activity of kings and people alike. This dis-cussion will offer further evidence that history shapes and mediates the question of faith for the community and establishes the context for its moral life. It will point out the impact of moral choices on the reli-gious life and practical affairs of Israel.

The Rise of the Monarchy

After conquering a portion of the Promised Land of Canaan in the latter half of the thirteenth century B.C.,[37] Israel entered a turbulent period of about two centuries. During that time the hostility of neigh-boring peoples prevented the Hebrew tribes from fully settling and consolidating a national territory. They were also handicapped by their political system, a loose confederation that responded to charis-matic figures known as judges. Toward the year 1000 B.C., however, the people began to feel the need for a more stable and unified system of government. They wanted Israel to become a kingdom like the sur-rounding nations.[38]

That change of attitude brought about Saul's accession as the first king of Israel (1 Sam 10:1). However, Saul's power was more charis-matic than institutional, and he was unable to establish his own authority or the succession of his sons. His reign was marked by dra-matic personal and military conflicts and ended with his death in battle against the Philistines.[39] Saul began the monarchy, but his suc-cessors, David and Solomon, brought it to the heights of power and glory.

Kings. For further discussion of this literature and its theological concerns, see Schmidt, *Old Testament Introduction,* 136–59; Von Rad, *Old Testament Theology,* 1:306-47; Anderson, *Understanding the Old Testament,* 183–4, 359.

Chronologically, the first of the writing prophets is Amos, who preached in the mid-eighth century B.C. The spirit of prophecy seems to have petered out during the postexilic period. For an introduction to the prophets, see Bruce Vawter, "Intro-duction to Prophetic Literature," *NJBC,* 186–200; Von Rad, *Old Testament Theology,* 2:6-98; Anderson, *Understanding the Old Testament,* 247–53.

[37] See Joshua 1–12; Anderson, *Understanding the Old Testament,* 110–50.

[38] These events are reflected in Joshua 13–24, the book of Judges, and 1 Samuel 1–12. See also Anderson, *Understanding the Old Testament,* 181–210.

[39] For more concerning Saul's reign, see Birch, *Let Justice Roll Down,* 206–12; Anderson, *Understanding the Old Testament,* 214–20.

Once he secured the throne for himself, King David overwhelmed his enemies, conquered Jerusalem, and made it the national capital. With great ceremony he brought the ark of the covenant to Jerusalem, which invested the royal city with religious significance. He also took a census of the people, which made it possible to conscript an army, collect taxes more efficiently, and draft people into work brigades. These activities allowed David's highly centralized government to obtain the money and manpower it needed to assert its authority and successfully confront foreign enemies. But they also generated resistance to David and his court within Israel (1 Sam 13–31; 2 Sam; 1 Kgs 1–2).[40]

After a struggle for succession that included many disreputable actions, Solomon succeeded to David's throne.[41] Taking advantage of a favorable international climate, Solomon exercised his kingship on a grand scale. He put up lavish buildings, including the Temple, a palace complex, and outlying fortifications, and he acquired many chariots and a fleet of ships. In order to support such endeavors, Solomon established a system of tax collection that efficiently moved large amounts of money from the people to the royal court. Ignoring objections, he conscripted men for military service and compulsory work brigades. Seeking to forge stronger bonds with neighboring kings, Solomon married foreign wives and allowed them to worship their pagan gods. He did so himself in violation of God's command. Although "King Solomon excelled all the kings of the earth in riches and in wisdom" (1 Kgs 10:23), his actions reflected contemporary pagan influences more than the word of God.[42]

Toward the end of his reign, Solomon's harsh policies provoked many of his subjects to revolt against him. After he died in 922 B.C., his son and successor, Rehoboam, threatened to inflict even sterner measures on his aggrieved subjects (1 Kgs 12:1-14). In response, the ten northern tribes threw off his rule and set up a separate monarchy. The nation divided into two kingdoms, Israel in the north and Judah in the south, and never again united.[43]

---

[40] Anderson, *Understanding the Old Testament*, 221–34.

[41] For a candid account of the succession, see 2 Samuel 9–1 Kings 2; also Von Rad, *Old Testament Theology*, 1:313-4.

[42] "It must be emphasized as strongly as possible that by the end of Solomon's regime the Jerusalem state was a thoroughly paganized Syro-Hittite regime" (George E. Mendenhall, "The Monarchy," *Int* 29 [1975] 160, as quoted in Birch, *Let Justice Roll Down*, 221).

[43] King Solomon's reign is recounted in 1 Kings 3–11; see also Anderson, *Understanding the Old Testament*, 234–46, 256–61.

The Monarchy Under God's Sovereignty

The rise of the monarchy affected Israel's religion as much as its political, economic, and military affairs. The accession of Saul required people to address a new but quite fundamental issue: Who is the king of Israel, God or a human being? This question generated a deep sense of ambivalence. On the one hand, the ancient faith recognized no sovereignty but God's, and therefore had no room for a human king. This conviction accounts for the aggrieved tone of the following passage:

> Thus says the LORD, the God of Israel, "I brought up Israel out of Egypt, and I delivered you from the hand of all the Egyptians and from the hand of all the kingdoms that were oppressing you." But you have this day rejected your God, who saves you from all your calamities and your distresses; and you have said, "No! but set a king over us" (1 Sam 10:18-19; see also Judg 8:22-23).

To the extent this view prevailed, no king would ever be acceptable in Israel.

On the other hand, by establishing the monarchy in Israel, Saul and his successors confronted the ancient tradition with a reality that it had to accommodate. One sign of acceptance is the prophet Samuel's anointing of Saul as king (1 Sam 10:1). But this legitimation came with one important qualification: God gave the kingship and God could also take it away (15:10-11, 28, 35). Israelite kings could never be more than the delegates of God, who alone held dominion over the nation. God had blessed the monarchy, but the king would be accountable to the Covenant and to God's prophets. This was the conviction that inspired much of the prophets' preaching.[44]

The Davidic Covenant

Even more decisive was Nathan's prophecy that David's dynasty would last forever. The occasion was David's proposal to build a worthy house for God in Jerusalem (2 Sam 7:2). In response, the prophet proclaimed:

> The LORD declares to you that the LORD will make you a house. When your days are fulfilled and you lie down with your fathers, I will raise up your offspring after you, who shall come forth from your body, and I will establish his kingdom. He shall build a house for my name, and I will establish the throne of his kingdom for ever. I will be his father, and

[44] Birch, *Let Justice Roll Down*, 198–210; also Von Rad, *Old Testament Theology*, 1:324-37.

he shall be my son. When he commits iniquity, I will chasten him with the rod of men, with the stripes of the sons of men; but I will not take my steadfast love from him, as I took it from Saul, whom I put away from before you. And your house and your kingdom shall be made sure for ever before me; your throne shall be established forever (2 Sam 7:11-16).

This prophecy assumed great importance because it constituted a second covenant between God and Israel (2 Sam 23:5; Ps 132:10-12). By it God not only granted full acceptance to the monarchy but promised to maintain it forever, notwithstanding the sinfulness of particular kings. Especially when circumstances were dire and well-deserved punishments fell on the people, the Davidic covenant stood as a source of hope for faithful Israelites. It encouraged them to look forward to a day when God would raise up an anointed one, a *messiah*, a son of God and son of David who would bring justice and peace to Israel.[45]

The Monarchy's Sins and History

Samuel's anointing of Saul and Nathan's prophecy to David presupposed an unshakable faith in God's ability to control human history. He had given Israel the Mosaic Law and then established the monarchy in order that the people might know their God and do what was right and good in his sight. Israel's well-being depended upon its response, as the blessing-or-curse passages continually suggest (e.g., 1 Kgs 3:14; 6:11-13; 9:4-9). Reflecting these convictions, the Deuteronomist upholds God's sovereignty, sits in judgment on the actions of kings, and interprets particular misfortunes as God's just punishment for their sins. The early history of the monarchy offers vivid examples of the close link between infidelity and catastrophe.

Although he was otherwise a good king, David had Uriah killed so he could take Uriah's wife, Bathsheba, for himself (2 Sam 11:2-27). This "displeased the Lord" (11:27). In response God said through Nathan the prophet: "Behold, I will raise up evil against you out of your own house; and I will take your wives before your eyes, and give them to your neighbor, and he shall live with your wives in the sight of this sun" (12:11). Furthermore, "because by this deed you have utterly scorned the LORD, the child that is born to you shall die" (12:14). Those prophecies pointed to the tragic events that befell David's family (2 Sam 12:15–1 Kgs 2:12).

Solomon's behavior was yet more objectionable. His system of taxation caused many Israelites to lose their land, which they considered to

---

[45] Anderson, *Understanding the Old Testament*, 230–4; Von Rad, *Old Testament Theology*, 1:308-18, 334–2.

be part of their inheritance from God. His labor camps enslaved the very people whom God had set free from slavery (1 Kgs 5:13; 9:15). His worst sin was his participation in the polytheistic rites practiced by his foreign wives. On that matter, the writer's judgment is blunt: "His heart was not wholly true to the LORD his God. . . . For Solomon went after Ashtoreth the goddess of the Sidonians, and after Milcom the abomination of the Ammonites. So Solomon did what was evil in the sight of the LORD" (11:1-6; see also 11:7-11). The sentence follows immediately: "The LORD said to Solomon, 'Since this has been your mind and you have not kept my covenant and my statutes which I have commanded you, I will surely tear the kingdom from you and will give it to your servant. Yet for the sake of David your father I will not do it in your days, but I will tear it out of the hand of your son'" (11:11-12). From that moment God raised up adversaries against Solomon (11:14, 23, 26). They began the train of events that ended with the separation of the northern tribes from the Davidic dynasty in Jerusalem (12:19-20).

Although these examples focus on the monarch's deeds, the scriptural texts recognized the decisive role of the human heart. God chose David as king not by appearances but by reading his heart (1 Sam 16:7). Solomon is enjoined to walk with integrity of heart (1 Kgs 9:4) and incurs God's anger "because his heart had turned away from the LORD, the God of Israel" (1 Kgs 11:9). Kings and ordinary people ponder and decide important matters in their hearts (1 Kgs 12:26-27; 2 Kgs 23:25). These examples highlight the deliberation, freedom, and responsibility that attend human actions and are always known to God. The mysterious ways of the human heart can prompt sinners to repent the evil they have done and turn to the Lord and ask for forgiveness (1 Kgs 8:35-40, 46-53) or to refuse to do so (2 Kgs 17:13-14).[46] The possibility of forgiveness relieves an otherwise tragic account of kings who "did what was evil in the sight of the LORD" (e.g., 1 Kgs 14:22; 2 Kgs 8:18; 13:2).[47]

In the centuries that followed the break-up of the Israelite kingdom in 922 B.C., other prophets spoke God's word[48] to kings and priests, the wealthy and the humble. They confronted the guilty, named their sins, and predicted that God's punishment would overtake them if they did not repent. On a positive note, the prophets reminded Israel that God had been faithful and loving and that it needed to live up to the

---

[46] For a fuller discussion of conversion, or turning to the Lord, see J. Giblet, "Le sens de la conversion dans l'Ancien Testament," *MD* 90 (1967) 79–92.

[47] Von Rad, *Old Testament Theology*, 1:314-8.

[48] On this important topic, see Von Rad, *Old Testament Theology*, 2:80-98; Birch, *Let Justice Roll Down*, 153–4.

Covenant. In particular, Israel was to act with justice and righteousness, especially toward the poor and helpless. It was to abhor idolatry and give wholehearted worship to God alone.[49] The prophets Amos and Hosea exemplify these two key imperatives.

Amos, Prophet of Justice

Although he came from the southern kingdom of Judah, the prophet Amos preached in the northern kingdom of Israel around the year 760 B.C. During that period Israel was at peace and enjoyed considerable prosperity. But the spirit of those times also favored injustice in the marketplace and corruption in the courts. Before long a pampered class of people arose who enjoyed a conspicuous life of privilege. The behavior of this group toward the weak and the poor was more than Amos could bear.[50] He prophesied:

> Thus says the LORD:
> "For three transgressions of Israel,
>   and for four, I will not revoke the punishment;
> because they sell the righteous for silver,
>   and the needy for a pair of shoes—
> they trample the head of the poor into the dust of the earth,
>   and turn aside the way of the afflicted;
> a man and his father go in to the same maiden,
>   so that my holy name is profaned;
> they lay themselves down beside every altar
>   upon garments taken in pledge" (Amos 2:6-8; see also 4:1-2; 6:4-8; 8:4-7).

Amos indicted the people of Israel for their refusal to live in justice and righteousness, and warned them of the consequences:

> Therefore thus says the Lord GOD:
> "An adversary shall surround the land,
>   and bring down your defenses from you,
>   and your strongholds shall be plundered" (Amos 3:11).

---

[49] For further discussion of justice and righteousness as foundational requirements, see Birch, *Let Justice Roll Down*, 153–6.

Angelo Penna has examined prophetic texts to see to what extent they were influenced by the Decalogue. He finds that the prophets probably did not have a written text of the Decalogue to guide their preaching but were well aware of its spirit and content. The prophets often deepened or extended the meaning of specific commandments or specified how they would be fulfilled. See "Il Decalogo nell'interpretazione profetica," *Fondamenti biblici della teologia morale: Atti della XXII Settimana Biblica* (Paideia: Brescia, 1973) 83–116, especially 107.

[50] For example, Isa 3:14, 5:8; Amos 4:1-3; 8:4-6.

Although the people's sins were serious, Amos urged them to repent and suggested that the Lord might still show mercy:

> Hate evil, and love good,
>   and establish justice in the gate;
> it may be that the LORD, the God of hosts,
>   will be gracious to the remnant of Joseph (Amos 5:15).

If their songs and sacrifices are to be acceptable to God, people must "let justice roll down like waters, and righteousness like an ever-flowing stream" (Amos 5:24).[51]

Hosea and Faithful Worship

The prophet Hosea preached to the people of the northern kingdom between about 750 and 725 B.C. Although he did not overlook sins of injustice against others,[52] his principal concerns were cultic. He condemned priests for doing evil and for failing to help the people to know God:

> Yet let no one contend,
>   and let none accuse,
>   for with you is my contention, O priest. . . .
> My people are destroyed for lack of knowledge;
>   because you have rejected knowledge,
>   I reject you from being a priest to me. . . .
> They feed on the sin of my people;
>   they are greedy for their iniquity.

---

[51] Anderson, *Understanding the Old Testament*, 291–301.
Isaiah continued Amos' theme of justice:

> Wash yourselves; make yourselves clean;
>   remove the evil of your doings
>   from before my eyes;
> cease to do evil,
>   learn to do good;
> seek justice,
>   correct oppression;
> defend the fatherless,
>   plead for the widow (Isa 1:16-17).

[52]   There is no faithfulness or kindness,
>   and no knowledge of God in the land;
> there is swearing, lying, killing, stealing, and committing adultery;
>   they break all bounds and murder follows murder (Hos 4:1-2; see also 12:7-8).

Hosea rejected worship that was not authenticated by the practice of justice (Hos 4:6; 6:6).

> And it shall be like people, like priest;
>   I will punish them for their ways,
>   and requite them for their deeds (Hos 4:4, 6, 8-9).

His strongest condemnation fell on the people's idolatry:

> When Ephraim spoke, men trembled;
>   he was exalted in Israel;
>   but he incurred guilt through Ba'al and died.
> And now they sin more and more,
>   and make for themselves molten images,
> idols skillfully made of their silver,
>   all of them the work of craftsmen.
> Sacrifice to these, they say.
>   Men kiss calves! (Hos 13:1-2; see also 11:1-2).

Through its infidelity Israel had broken the Covenant and lost the right to be called God's people or claim God as its own (Hos 1:9). It had earned severe punishment, which would be inflicted through the activity of a foreign power (10:6; also 11:5-7). Still, Hosea spoke a word of hope that God's promise would not be revoked nor would God's loving kindness be withdrawn. In the time to come, God would rebuild Israel out of the ashes of its destruction. Particularly moving is Hosea's marital imagery:

> And in that day, says the LORD, you will call me, "My husband," and no longer will you call me, "My Ba'al." For I will remove the names of the Ba'als from her mouth, and they shall be mentioned by name no more. And I will make for you a covenant on that day with the beasts of the field, the birds of the air, and the creeping things of the ground; and I will abolish the bow, the sword, and war from the land; and I will make you lie down in safety. And I will betroth you to me for ever; I will betroth you to me in righteousness and in justice, in steadfast love, and in mercy. I will betroth you to me in faithfulness; and you shall know the LORD (Hos 2:16-20).[53]

As it happened, neither threats of punishment nor promises of renewal persuaded Israel to turn from its sins and return to the Lord. Although Hosea probably did not live to see it, the punishment he had foretold took place in the year 722 B.C. when the Assyrians conquered the northern kingdom of Israel and extinguished its political independence. The time of chastisement had begun.[54]

---

[53] Anderson, *Understanding the Old Testament*, 301–15. For further discussion of Old Testament prophecy see, for example, Birch, *Let Justice Roll Down*, 240–79; Von Rad, *Old Testament Theology*, 2:6-300; Schmidt, *Old Testament Introduction*, 171–296.

[54] Anderson, *Understanding the Old Testament*, 315–6.

Jeremiah and the Fall of Jerusalem

Having defeated Israel, Assyria was in a strong position to assert its hegemony over the southern kingdom of Judah. Its king, Hezekiah, refused to accept this situation and plotted against Assyria. It responded by attacking Judah and besieging Hezekiah (2 Kgs 18:7–19:37). Toward the end of the seventh century, however, Assyria weakened and Judah was able to regain a measure of liberty. This allowed King Josiah to pursue the Deuteronomic Reform, an important late seventh-century B.C. effort to revive Covenant ideals, uproot idolatry, and renew Hebrew worship. The Deuteronomic Reform ended with Josiah's death in 609.[55]

One of Josiah's successors, Jehoiakim, worked to dismantle the Deuteronomic Reform. His irreligious reign forms the background to some of Jeremiah's prophecies (e.g., Jer 35–36). The prophet condemned Jehoiakim for his dishonesty, cruelty, tyranny, and open idolatry (7; also 22:13-19). Jeremiah declared that these sins would be punished severely:

> Therefore thus says the LORD of hosts: Because you have not obeyed my words, behold, I will send for all the tribes of the north, says the LORD, and for Nebuchadrezzar the king of Babylon, my servant, and I will bring them against this land and its inhabitants, and against all these nations round about; I will utterly destroy them, and make them a horror, a hissing, and an everlasting reproach. Moreover, I will banish from them the voice of mirth and the voice of gladness, the voice of the bridegroom and the voice of the bride, the grinding of the millstones and the light of the lamp. This whole land shall become a ruin and a waste, and these nations shall serve the king of Babylon seventy years (Jer 25:8-11).

Jeremiah also saw that God's plan envisioned more than sin and ruin. He added a consoling word to Israel in those desperate times:

> Behold, the days are coming, says the LORD, when I will make a new covenant with the house of Israel and the house of Judah, not like the covenant which I made with their fathers when I took them by the hand to bring them out of the land of Egypt, my covenant which they broke, though I was their husband, says the LORD. But this is the covenant which I will make with the house of Israel after those days, says the LORD: I will put my law within them, and I will write it upon their hearts; and I will be their God, and they shall be my people. And no longer shall each man teach his neighbor and each his brother, saying, "know the LORD," for they shall all know me, from the least of them to

---

[55] Ibid., 373–88.

the greatest, says the LORD; for I will forgive their iniquity, and I will remember their sin no more (Jer 31:31-34).

Even at the eleventh hour, the kingdom of Judah did not turn to the Lord. About the year 600, Jehoiakim rebelled against the now ascendant Babylonia. The Babylonians invaded in 598–597, and deported the king, his mother, the prophet Ezekiel, and many others. Although the Babylonians had installed him, King Zedekiah also revolted in the year 588. The Babylonians returned and laid siege to Jerusalem. Jeremiah prophesied that surrender offered Jerusalem its only hope for survival (Jer 21:8-9). In no mood to entertain such a proposal, the royal court had Jeremiah arrested, beaten, imprisoned, and threatened with execution. But events proved that the prophet had been correct. In the summer of 587, Jerusalem fell to the Babylonian King Nebuchadrezzar, whose army destroyed the Temple, burned the city, and pulled down its walls. King Zedekiah and most of the survivors were deported to Babylonia.[56] Thus began the Babylonian Exile.

EXILE AND ITS AFTERMATH

The Exile opened a new era in the history of Israel. The conquest of Jerusalem ended the political tenure of the Davidic dynasty, compelled the Hebrew people to do without the Temple and the usual rhythm of worship, and initiated a wholesale displacement of people from Judea.[57] Those who had been allowed to remain became a minority in their own country. Even after the Exile had ended, difficult social, political, and cultural circumstances continued to challenge the Jewish people.[58] Those trying times stimulated important changes in their life

---

[56] Jer 39:1-10 gives the details, including the cruel sentence inflicted upon King Zedekiah.

At that time the Babylonian Empire extended over the territory roughly comprised by Palestine and the modern states of Iraq, Syria, and Lebanon. Its capital city, Babylon, was located on the Euphrates River, south of the present city of Baghdad. Most of the Judean deportees would have been sent to the area around Babylon itself. Anderson, *Understanding the Old Testament*, 404.

[57] The Diaspora, or dispersal of the Jewish people, had important social, cultural, and religious effects. See Lawrence H. Schiffman, *From Text to Tradition: A History of Second Temple and Rabbinic Judaism* (Hoboken, N.J.: Ktav Publishing House, 1991) 80–97.

[58] In the present context, the term "Jewish" refers to the people of Judah, the southern kingdom. Accordingly, when they speak of the Jews, scholars generally mean those carried into exile and their descendants. "Judaism" would refer to their religion, which was based upon the ancient Israelite faith as interpreted through the Exile and postexilic experiences. See Anderson, *Understanding the Old Testament,*

and thought, society and institutions. Jewish faith, literature, and religious practice likewise underwent a notable evolution. Taken together, these developments set the foundations of modern-day Judaism. They contributed important elements of the Christian heritage and shaped the environment in which Jesus lived and carried out his ministry.

The Exile Experience and Faith

Although the Exile was a national tragedy, its deeper meaning was religious.

> The catastrophic events of 587 B.C.E. shook the Israelite (Judean) community and its faith to the core. The experience of those events looms as the overwhelming reality against which several succeeding generations (before and after the return) sought to reformulate their basic understandings of relationship to God, God's ways of working in the world, and the nature of their own life as the people of God.[59]

When the Jewish people considered all that had befallen them, they were tempted to conclude that God had abandoned them. The words of Jeremiah probably rang all too true: "I have forsaken my house, I have abandoned my heritage; I have given the beloved of my soul into the hands of her enemies" (Jer 12:7). In addition, the anguish and humiliation of an entire people raised painful questions about God's justice, especially when the virtuous suffered and sinners prospered (see 12:1).[60]

The prophets of the Exile confronted these burning issues of faith and, in the depths of their people's sorrows, found new spiritual insights. Perhaps the most important was the conviction that their God continued to be with them in and through their anguish. The figure of the Suffering Servant seems to emerge out of this very crucible. Second Isaiah[61] taught that through the deprivation and misery of his servant,

---

435. For Schiffman, "Judaism" refers to "the collective religious, cultural, and legal tradition and civilization of the Jewish people as developed and passed down from biblical times until today" (*From Text to Tradition*, 1). He traces Judaism back to the Hebrew patriarchs (17).

[59] Birch, *Let Justice Roll Down*, 281.

[60] On this point, see also Jacob, "Les bases théologiques," 47.

[61] "Second Isaiah," or "Deutero-Isaiah," refers to the author of Isaiah 40–55, which dates from the later exilic period, perhaps between 550 and 540 B.C., some 150 years after the composition of Isaiah 1–39. Originating after 538 B.C. in the early postexilic period, Isaiah 56–66 comprises a third unit within the canonical book; its author is known as "Third Isaiah," or "Trito-Isaiah." See Schmidt, *Old Testament Introduction*, 257; Carroll Stuhlmueller, "Deutero-Isaiah and Trito-Isaiah," *NJBC*, 329–30.

God would "bring forth justice to the nations" and salvation to the world (Isa 42:1-4). The Exile experience helped bring to birth yet another realization: God's presence and power are universal. God's sovereignty was not limited to the Temple, to Jerusalem, or to Israel. God could be encountered anywhere and could act through any person or event whatsoever. Psalm 139:7-8 expresses this faith: "Whither shall I go from thy Spirit? / Or whither shall I flee from thy presence? / If I ascend to heaven, thou art there! / If I make my bed in Sheol, thou art there!" (See also Isa 45:22).

Supported by such reflections, the community recovered its religious bearings and found new depths to its faith. The mighty deeds of God in the past encouraged the prophets to hope that, despite all, God's love, forgiveness, and protection to Israel would one day be restored. Jeremiah prophesied: "I will forgive their iniquity, and I will remember their sin no more" (Jer 31:34). Second Isaiah declared, "I have swept away your transgressions like a cloud, / and your sins like mist; / return to me, for I have redeemed you" (Isa 44:22). Such forgiveness reflected God's loving kindness and invited Israel to turn back to the God toward whom it had been unfaithful.

Yet another element of hope was the expectation that God would create a new and faithful Israel. On that day Israel would wholeheartedly abide by the Covenant and live in communion with God as it was meant to do. Ezekiel's prophecy is eloquent:

> For I will take you from the nations, and gather you from all the countries and bring you into your own land. I will sprinkle clean water upon you, and you shall be clean from all your uncleannesses, and from all your idols I will cleanse you. A new heart I will give you, and a new spirit I will put within you; and I will take out of your flesh the heart of stone and give you a heart of flesh. And I will put my spirit within you, and cause you to walk in my statutes and be careful to observe my ordinances. You shall dwell in the land which I gave to your fathers; and you shall be my people, and I will be your God (Ezek 36:24-28).[62]

The Postexilic Period

The Exile came to an end in the year 538 B.C., shortly after Babylonia fell to the Persians. In that year the Persian king, Cyrus, decreed that

---

[62] See also Ezekiel's vision of dry bones coming back to life (37:1-11) and especially the following passage: "Thus says the Lord GOD: Behold, I will open your graves, and raise you from your graves, O my people; and I will bring you home into the land of Israel. And you shall know that I am the LORD, when I open your graves, and raise you from your graves, O my people. And I will put my spirit within you,

the Judean exiles were free to leave Mesopotamia and return to their own country (Ezra 1:1-4). Once they had begun to do so, the Judeans discovered that it was not possible to reestablish the situation that had existed before the fall of Jerusalem. The monarchy was gone, important religious institutions had been destroyed, and the community was scattered. Those who had not been deported considered the repatriates to be intruders and resented their dominance. Neighboring peoples were often hostile and economic conditions trying. Foreign cultural influences waxed strong, and outsiders held political sovereignty. These difficult circumstances set the context for Jewish life in the postexilic period. They help to account for the nationalistic feelings and religious developments that characterize this era.[63]

The Reconstruction of Jewish Life

Once it had begun to reestablish itself, the small and struggling Jewish community began to rebuild the Temple. The Persians had encouraged this action, which was necessary if the Jews were to restore this quintessential symbol of God's presence and unique place of worship. Although this large project had been interrupted for almost twenty years, it was finally completed in the year 515. The Second Temple was not as grand as the one Solomon had built, but it was a powerful sign of God's presence to the Jewish community and a focal point for its life. But the Second Temple could not eliminate religious laxity, dilute foreign influences, or make the community's political and economic circumstances any less difficult.

Around the middle of the fifth century B.C. two strong leaders took charge of the community. The priest Ezra reestablished Jewish life upon the foundation of the Mosaic Law, which he had promulgated to the community (Neh 8:1-9). Appealing to the ancient Covenant, he suppressed religious abuses, prohibited mixed marriages, and insisted upon a higher standard of religious observance. The normative role that the Torah attained in Jewish life probably reflects Ezra's work more than any other single influence. The governor Nehemiah also acted vigorously to protect the religious identity of the Jewish people.

---

and you shall live, and I will place you in your own land; then you shall know that I, the LORD, have spoken, and I have done it, says the LORD" (37:12-14).

On the history of the Exile and contemporary prophetic activity, see Birch, *Let Justice Roll Down*, 280–302; Anderson, *Understanding the Old Testament*, 427–506; Von Rad, *Old Testament Theology*, 2:263-77.

[63] The Book of Ezra provides an account of the return from exile and subsequent events. See also Anderson, *Understanding the Old Testament*, 470–1, 510–24.

He limited membership in the Jewish community to those who were Hebrews by birth. He strictly prohibited intermarriage and required the people to observe the Torah and support the Temple. These measures defended the community against the threat of syncretism, the tendency to blend foreign cultural and religious elements into traditional faith and religious practice. They accented the uniqueness and separateness of the Jewish community and helped to guarantee the survival of its spiritual legacy.[64]

Cultural and Political Developments

Persian control of Palestine lasted for about two centuries, ending with Alexander of Macedon's invasion in the year 332. Alexander's overwhelming military successes inaugurated a lengthy period in which Greek language, learning, and culture waxed strong throughout the eastern Mediterranean world. Jews living in Palestine and elsewhere fell under the influence of these Hellenistic currents and had to deal with them somehow. Some communities adopted the Greek language and modes of thought, and this persuaded Jewish scholars in Egypt to translate the Scriptures from Hebrew into Greek. Even at home many Jews were prepared to make extensive compromises with Greek culture and religion.

The strength of Hellenistic influences on Jewish life provoked a backlash. Many began to emphasize Jewish national identity and tried to keep religious faith and practice free from dilution or syncretism. This defensive reaction remained peaceful up until the time of Antiochus IV (175–163 B.C.). This imperious ruler sold the high priesthood to Jewish Hellenizers and insisted that everyone in his realm should worship the Greek god Zeus. Even worse, he banned the Torah and desecrated the Temple, forbade Jews to practice circumcision or follow their dietary rules, and compelled them to eat pork and sacrifice to idols. This persecution provoked an armed response, and in the Maccabean Wars that followed (168–164 B.C.), Jewish fighters defeated their overlords. That victory won the Jewish people about a century of national independence, which lasted until 63 B.C., when Pompey invaded and annexed Palestine to the Roman Empire. Roman domination stimu-

---

[64] Birch, *Let Justice Roll Down*, 307; Anderson, *Understanding the Old Testament*, 470–1, 507–39. Nehemiah began his governorship in the year 445 B.C., but the date of Ezra's arrival in Jerusalem is disputed. Although there is evidence in favor of 428 or 398, Anderson believes that the year 458 is more likely (*Understanding the Old Testament*, 524–7).

lated Jewish nationalism and heightened the fear that foreign influences might corrode faith and harm religious practice.[65]

Religious Developments

These cultural and political developments created the environment
in which the postexilic Jewish community carried out its daily affairs.
In the absence of the Davidic monarchy, religious institutions became
even more important to national cohesion and identity. Leadership in
the community passed to the high priests. The Mosaic Law became the
touchstone of authentic Jewish life, especially when foreign cultural
and religious pressures were strong. This enhanced the position of the
scribes, who were particularly responsible for keeping, studying, and
interpreting the Law. The higher profile of religious faith and practice
stimulated certain differences of opinion in the community. Although
everyone agreed that the Torah was normative, scholars disagreed on
its interpretation. People also differed about whether the prevailing
culture was to be embraced, merely tolerated, or actively rejected.
These disagreements gave rise to a variety of parties or subgroups
within postexilic Judaism. The Sadducees, for example, were prepared
to tolerate outside influences as long as Temple worship was undisturbed. The Pharisees, on the other hand, held for strict observance
and separation from outsiders. They asserted that besides the written
Torah, Moses had bequeathed an oral law, "the tradition of the elders,"
which also required obedience.[66]

The postexilic period witnessed important developments concerning the Sacred Scriptures. Over the course of time Jewish scholars developed a consensus about which writings were inspired and therefore
belonged to the canon of Scripture; this agreement was completed
around the year 100 B.C. During the same era, the spirit of prophecy
seems to have disappeared from the community. Apocalyptic texts,
such as the Book of Daniel, began to fill the literary vacuum. Employing vivid imagery and poetic symbolism, apocalyptic writers judge
that evil is so strong and so deeply rooted that it will only be defeated
when God directly intervenes at the end of time. Although these writers called for believers to remain faithful, their books encouraged
people to think that God's powerful suppression of evil might occur at
any moment.[67]

---

[65] Anderson, *Understanding the Old Testament*, 610–8.
[66] Ibid., 633–6.
[67] Ibid., 636–43; also Von Rad, *Old Testament Theology*, 2:301-15.

These international and domestic developments gave birth to the national and religious currents that ran strong in the first-century Palestinian Jewish community. Above all, they offer a context in which to understand the life and times, ministry and preaching of Jesus, and the various groups he encountered.

FAITH, WISDOM, AND INJUSTICE

In the period following the Exile, the Near East was controlled first by the Persians and then by the Greeks. That political situation favored travel and commerce and made it easier for people to become better acquainted with other nations. A more cosmopolitan atmosphere called attention to the human condition and encouraged people to reflect on the experiences and challenges of ordinary life. Such concerns called attention to wisdom traditions in Israel and in neighboring countries. As they surveyed the wider horizons of the postexilic period, Jewish thinkers turned to these sources in order to understand human experiences and help people to address life's challenges more effectively. Their reflections are enshrined in the Wisdom literature, especially the books of Proverbs, Ecclesiastes, Job, Sirach, and Wisdom.[68]

At first sight, some of the Wisdom books seem to be rather secular in nature. They are not concerned with Israel's patriarchal and covenant traditions and generally bypass fundamental questions of history and its religious meaning. Yet for all that, this literature is hardly irreligious, for it presupposes that true wisdom arises from faith: "The fear of the LORD is the beginning of knowledge" (Prov 1:7). Wisdom writers understood that the God who created the universe is the same God who had fashioned Israel through the Exodus and Sinai experiences.[69] These convictions give Wisdom writings an underlying coherence with Hebrew faith and allow them to develop important moral insights from the created world and human experiences in it. At the same time, Wisdom writers wrestled with an urgent religious problem that the Exile had forced to the surface: How is it possible to remain faithful when God seems to reward injustice and permit good people to suffer?

---

[68] Understood more broadly, Wisdom literature also includes passages in other books, for example, Genesis 1–11 and some of the psalms.

[69] This perhaps explains the close parallel seen between creation and the Exodus. See, for example, Psalm 136. See also Walter Vogels, "The God Who Creates Is the God Who Saves: The Book of Wisdom's Reversal of the Biblical Pattern," *EglTh* 22 (1991) 315–35.

Wisdom and Life

Of special interest is the creation theology implicit in Wisdom literature. Enlightened by their faith and sensitive to worldly realities, Wisdom authors speak of God as Creator (Eccl 12:1; Sir 24:8). They are convinced that as God's handiwork, creation has a special meaning and value. It depends upon God's ongoing creative support and is good (Wis 11:24-26; Ps 19:1). God's activity in the world is not arbitrary or capricious but benevolent and purposeful (Eccl 3:17; Sir 15:14-20; Prov 3:19). This suggests that there is a God-given harmony inherent in the world, making it a medium by which people can arrive at a knowledge of God's will. The wise and careful observer of human life therefore can come to know God and understand how to live (Wis 13:1-9). Wisdom guides people along the path of living well (Sir 19:20; Prov 2:1-22); fools on the other hand fail to understand, do evil, and come to disaster (Prov 1:20-33). Since creation, experience, and insight aΔre not limited to any one people or nation, wisdom is eclectic in its scope and universal in its reach.[70]

Within this more open, universal perspective, humanity finds its place and shoulders its responsibility.[71] Human beings are to examine their world carefully and arrange their affairs in light of the signs God has left for them to follow. If they do so, their relationships will be organized correctly and they will be better able to make wise personal decisions.[72] Carrying out those tasks always involves a tension between human autonomy and subordination to God. The wise know how to strike this balance, for they are open to illumination by God's commandments and respect the moral order latent in God's creative activity.[73]

In taking these positions, the sacred authors trust that wisdom enables people to act moderately and morally amidst the uncertainties of life. However, their ethic is oriented more to the acquisition of desirable personal qualities than to the elaboration of a systematized code of moral conduct. It tends to be individualistic and unconcerned with

---

[70] See Zimmerli, *Old Testament Theology*, 39–40; Jacob, "Les bases théologiques," 48.

[71] Childs, *Old Testament Theology*, 30–5; Birch, *Let Justice Roll Down*, 84–5.

[72] Proverbs 14:31 reflects this: "He who oppresses a poor man insults his Maker, but he who is kind to the needy honors him." See also Birch, *Let Justice Roll Down*, 331.

[73] See Walther Zimmerli, "The Place and Limit of the Wisdom in the Framework of the Old Testament Theology," *SJT* 17 (1964) 146–58. Proverbs 3:5 warns people to respect their limits: "Trust in the LORD with all your heart, and do not rely on your own insight."

social inequities. It appeals primarily to those whose education and leisure enable them to understand and follow its prescriptions.[74]

Evil and God's Justice

Israel's faith rested primarily on the conviction that God had done mighty deeds on behalf of the chosen people. Israel praised its Lord as a powerful and sovereign God who is fully able to intervene in human history. Certitude about God's power and justice allowed the Deuteronomist to promise that those who remained faithful to the Covenant would be blessed while sinners would be cursed (Deut 28). When the prophets threatened punishment for injustice, infidelity, and idolatry or encouraged people to turn back to the Lord, they were voicing a similar conviction. Therefore, to cast doubt on this bedrock presupposition about God's justice was to threaten a central component of Jewish faith and possibly precipitate a religious crisis. This is exactly what took place in light of the Exile and the later experiences of the Jewish people. Many concluded that there is no reason to worry about God's justice and power and acted as if God did not exist or does not care what people do.

Wisdom writers were fully aware of the traditional principle of just retribution. For example, the Book of Proverbs declares:

> The fear of the LORD prolongs life,
>   but the years of the wicked will be short.
> The hope of the righteous ends in gladness,
>   but the expectation of the wicked comes to nought.
> The LORD is a stronghold to him whose way is upright,
>   but destruction to evildoers (10:27-29; see also Sir 7:1-2 and Job 4:7-9).

But they also recognize that common experience contradicts the principle.

> Has not man a hard service upon earth,
>   and are not his days like the days of a hireling:
> Like a slave who longs for the shadow,
>   and like a hireling who looks for his wages,
> so I am allotted months of emptiness,
>   and nights of misery are apportioned to me (Job 7:1-3; also Eccl 4:1).

The author of Ecclesiastes observes that people's lives are controlled more by chance and caprice than by their merits (Eccl 9:11-12). He

---

[74] Birch, *Let Justice Roll Down*, 330–8.

complains of a perverse kind of justice: "In my vain life I have seen everything; there is a righteous man who perishes in his righteousness, and there is a wicked man who prolongs his life in his evil-doing" (7:15; see also Job 24:1-17).

These observations reflect a deeply felt anguish over the evil that disrupts human life, but their ultimate import is religious. Because it seems that God does not protect the virtuous or punish the guilty, suffering and injustice can undermine the faith of believers and lead some to conclude that there is no God at all (Ps 14:1). On the other hand, painful encounters with evil can also stimulate people to purify and deepen their faith. However a particular response unfolds, it tends to shape a person's relationship with God. The persistence and candor with which the Wisdom writers grappled with suffering and injustice suggest that they fully appreciated the religious dimensions of these experiences.

Faith and Evil

To be successful, any strategy of response to evil needs to be based upon a sober acknowledgment of the facts. Accordingly, the Book of Ecclesiastes frankly admits that life is hard and toilsome and that the wise and the foolish are both destined to die (Eccl 2:14-16, 22-23; 9:1-6). This realization provokes a stark response, which the author presents with great emotional honesty: "So I hated life, because what is done under the sun was grievous to me; for all is vanity and a striving after wind" (2:17; see also 4:1-3).

On the other hand, since the human condition is so difficult, he advises people to enjoy life's simple pleasures:

> Go, eat your bread with enjoyment, and drink your wine with a merry heart; for God has already approved what you do.
>
> Let your garments be always white; let not oil be lacking on your head.
>
> Enjoy life with the wife whom you love, all the days of your vain life which he has given you under the sun, because that is your portion in life and in your toil at which you toil under the sun. Whatever your hand finds to do, do it with your might; for there is no work or thought or knowledge or wisdom in Sheol, to which you are going (Eccl 9:7-9; see also 2:24; 3:12-13, 22; 8:15).

Although he offers his observations without apology, the author knows that faith is to guide a person's response to evil. He takes God's existence for granted, accepts that all good things are God's gifts (Eccl 2:24-25), and admits that no human being can know what God thinks or how he rules the universe (3:11). He suggests that God merely delays in executing a just sentence (8:11). In any case, it is necessary to maintain a reverent attitude toward God: "I know that whatever God does endures for ever; nothing can be added to it, nor anything taken from it; God has made it so, in order that men should fear before him" (3:14; see also 8:12-13).

The deepest and most engaging reflection on faith and suffering is found in the Book of Job. This wrenching problem is considered through the prism of a single human life, Job's. Job had been a just and devout Israelite, but he also suffers grave family tragedies and painful, disfiguring diseases (Job 1:13–2:7). One of Job's friends interprets that situation in light of the ancient doctrine of just retribution (4:7-9). If Job suffers, he must have sinned; therefore he should humbly repent and all will be well (8:3-7; 11:13-20; 22:21-30). But Job has not sinned (1:22; 2:10; 9:15, 20-21; 10:7; 23:11-12; 27:5-6), and he is prepared to defend his ways to God's face (13:15). As is the case with Ecclesiastes, Job complains that God does not enforce justice on earth or hear the cry of the afflicted (24:1-25). It seems that God has abandoned him in his time of need (9:11; 13:24). Job's anguish is so great that he wishes that he had been born dead (10:18-19). Utterly frustrated, he defies God to answer his claim of innocence (31:35-37).

After Job has decried his lot, defended his innocence, and turned aside all human attempts to resolve the conflict between his experience and God's justice, God finally speaks from the whirlwind (Job 38:1–41:34). But God does not directly answer Job's questions or respond to his protestations. Instead God asks Job what he contributed to the foundation of the world, what he knows of its mysteries, and how he governs or sustains it. The point is obvious: because Job has created nothing and knows nothing of these matters, he is in no position to question the God who creates and gives life to all things. Once Job is confronted with God's majesty and his own creatureliness, he confesses:

> I have uttered what I did not understand,
>   things too wonderful for me, which I did not know.
> "Hear, and I will speak;
>   I will question you, and you declare to me."
> I had heard of thee by the hearing of the ear,
>   but now my eye sees thee;
> therefore I despise myself,
>   and repent in dust and ashes (42:3-6).

The Book of Job presupposes that life is harsh, capricious, and unfair and that it is very difficult to live with suffering and injustice. The deepest anguish is spiritual, however, for such experiences seem to contradict the traditional faith that God will certainly act to uphold justice on earth. Sharp and ongoing conflict between experience and faith can place one's relationship with God in the balance and precipitate a religious and moral crisis. The Book of Job comes to grips with this perennial dilemma but does not "solve" the problem of suffering or "explain" the mysteries of God's justice. It suggests that a new vision of God is needed, and personal conversion as well. One who has come to know God in this new and deeper way will understand that God is not to be held to human expectations. Rather, God is to be praised and worshiped in all seasons and situations. By bringing these intensely religious imperatives to the fore, the Book of Job highlights the decisive importance of a right relationship with God, no matter what one's circumstances may be.[75]

Wisdom Literature and the Hebrew Tradition

The Wisdom books offer important contributions to the personal life of believers. Wisdom writers make it clear that people need to recognize and name the circumstances that cause them deep personal distress. They demonstrate that emotional and spiritual honesty—whether in prayer, in speech, or in a cry that comes from the heart—has a rightful place in the life of a believer. These points may be basic, but they are indispensable if problems are to be grasped truthfully and addressed effectively. At the same time, this literature depicts many ways to deal with the sharp edges of human experience, including prayer, discussion, forbearance, complaining, thought and reflection, the decision to live life as fully as possible, and a determination to praise God and behave uprightly in all circumstances. Whatever the appeal or usefulness of these options in particular cases, the Wisdom books emphasize the human, down-to-earth aspects of personal faith and show that it entails greater freedom and responsibility than might otherwise be apparent.

This literature is also to be considered in light of the Hebrew tradition as a whole. The faith of Israel is based upon the conviction that God has acted in human affairs and will punish transgressors and bless those who are faithful. It requires the community to worship God alone and conduct its affairs with justice and righteousness. For traditional faith,

---

[75] This discussion is indebted to Birch, *Let Justice Roll Down*, 321–53; Joseph Blenkinsopp, *Wisdom and Law in the Old Testament: The Ordering of Life in Israel and Early Judaism* (Oxford: Oxford University Press, 1995); Von Rad, *Old Testament Theology*, 1:391-459; Anderson, *Understanding the Old Testament*, 568–601.

history is the primary medium of communication between God and human beings. The Wisdom writers, however, display little concern for these pivotal aspects of the ancient faith. They are interested in exploring the resources of creation, reason, and common sense and allowing them to yield insights into God's will and more successful strategies for living. If anything, they seem to presuppose that history is marked by evil and manifests little of God's presence, power, or justice. The Book of Job reflects this same outlook, not least when it responds to the problem of evil by appealing to God's actions in creation, not history. This suggests that the Wisdom books represent a turn from history to creation on the part of the Hebrew faith tradition.[76]

This judgment should not be overstated. The tradition may have based itself on history, celebrated God's freedom (Gen 1:16-17; 4:4b-5a; Exod 33:19), and attributed the commandments to God's personal will (Exod 20:1-2), but it also recognized the natural virtue of justice and asserted it on its own merits (Gen 18:25). When the Wisdom writers turned to creation and reason, they presupposed rather than repudiated the ancient faith. When these considerations are taken into account, it is reasonable to conclude that the primary axis of Hebrew faith is historical but that the tradition recognizes the ambivalence of history and accepts the contributions that creation and reason can offer. In other words, the Wisdom books show that the grounds of religious and moral life are richer if also more complex than the earlier tradition might suggest. This conclusion will speak to the experiences and struggles of believers and also inform theologians' efforts to reflect upon faith, its sources, and its moral aspects.[77]

REFLECTIONS

This chapter has set forth the principal sources, requirements, and dynamics of Hebrew faith and watched different generations of Israelites wrestle with its contemporary meaning and claims. Whether it concerns the foundation of Israel as a unified nation or later developments, history—the unfolding of human affairs—has been a privileged medium of God's activity toward Israel and the stage on which it has responded to God. Both Israel's interpretation of historical events and

---

[76] By shifting their expectations to the end-times, apocalyptic writers suggest that God does not normally intervene in human affairs to vindicate justice. Although it looks toward eternity rather than creation, this literature represents a similar turn away from history. See Von Rad, *Old Testament Theology,* 2:303-8.

[77] Birch, *Let Justice Roll Down,* 342–5; Blenkinsopp, *Wisdom and Law,* 57–68; Von Rad, *Old Testament Theology,* 1:408-53; Anderson, *Understanding the Old Testament,* 599–601.

its part in shaping their future course are charged with religious and moral significance. It is useful to highlight some of the principal aspects and implications of Israel's faith as the Old Testament presents them, especially where they bear on moral life.

To ask whether particular historical events reflect God's activity and disclose God's expectations is to raise the question of faith and locate that question in the domain of human affairs. It is to recognize an issue that is fundamental to personal life and the organization of society. Moreover, historical change, new personal experiences, the constant appearance of younger generations, and the mysteries of the human heart keep the question of faith ever present. Even in a community of faith, faith remains a perennial issue. Raising and resolving the question of faith, thus framed and located, requires continual deliberation, decision, and responsibility. Because of what is at stake, the decision between faith and unbelief and the attempt to understand and obey God's will are to be ranked among the most important moments in a person's moral life.

By faith persons recognize that history and the universe reflect God's activity and plans. Faith brings the realization that God requires love, fidelity, and obedience. It focuses the personal life of believers, illuminates what they are to do and avoid, and calls them to follow through consistently and courageously. For these reasons, faith exercises a decisive influence on the moral life of believers. It helps them to recognize important moral imperatives, grasp their religious significance, and summon the energy to fulfill them. By the same token, their culpable failure to honor these moral requirements is reckoned as sin, a religious offense. However important moral life may be in itself, it is an aspect of the life of faith and is to be understood and considered in that light. To study the moral aspects of a faith community's life in isolation from that faith is to overlook an essential dimension of its morality.

The faith of Israel is grounded in God's gracious deeds on its behalf. Israel did not choose God; rather God chose Israel and made it God's special possession, even though all peoples belong to God. The Sinai Covenant and the Law, the Ten Commandments, the Davidic covenant, the prophetic word, and all other aspects of Israel's life are the fruit of God's loving initiatives. Even though kings and people sinned and were punished, God remained faithful, called Israel to repentance, and offered to restore divine love and care. This too is grace. Therefore God's generosity and love are altogether foundational. The life of a faith community cannot be properly understood unless God's free initiatives are fully acknowledged. The same applies to theological investigations into Old Testament moral life. To be adequate, these studies need to attribute priority to God's gifts, loving kindness, and fidelity and remember these gracious acts whenever moral and legal requirements or personal motivation and activity are considered.

In mighty deeds and through the prophetic word, God sought to love and care for Israel. God's principal intention is clear: "I will walk among you, and will be your God, and you shall be my people" (Lev 26:12). The Covenant crystallizes this offer of communion, underlines the priority of Israel's relationship with God, and assigns the community a decisive place in Hebrew life. Israel was to worship God alone, be holy as God is holy, and honor the imperatives of justice and righteousness. The community therefore assumes fundamental religious importance and becomes a basic norm for the religious and moral life of Israel. Each Israelite was to respect the requirements of holiness, abhor idolatry, and manifest justice toward the neighbor. Even in the absence of a specific injunction, the imperatives of communion govern all aspects of the community's life.

The Old Testament places a high premium on the behavioral requirements of Israelite life, but it also demonstrates an elevated concern for the interior dimensions of human activity. The community is enjoined to honor the Covenant on account of God's goodness, fidelity, and saving deeds. People are to receive God's commandments willingly and give them wholehearted, generous obedience. The sacred authors' awareness that the human heart is the source of sin, repentance, and love reflects a similar sensitivity to interior dynamics. Therefore, when assessing the quality of a decision or action, it is not sufficient to consider only the deed or omission. To be complete, this judgment needs to consider motivation and the personal aspects of the response to God's love and expectations. This reflects the human person's depth and complexity. It also recognizes the primary imperative of Israel's faith: "You shall love the Lord your God with all your heart, and with all your soul, and with all your might" (Deut 6:5).

Any adequate examination of the Old Testament will disclose the importance of justice. Justice guides God's interventions in human affairs (e.g., Prov 29:26; Isa 30:18; 42:1; Ezek 34:16) and grounds the blessings and curses that were set before the community. Justice requires the Israelite to worship God alone and behave rightly toward others. Justice prohibits idolatry, the abuse of one's neighbors, and the theft of their goods. These considerations suggest that justice occupies a pivotal place in the moral and religious life of the Israelite community. Justice is a primary imperative because it captures something of God's nature and activity, invites the response of faith, regulates behavior toward God and neighbor, and protects the bonds of communion. Injustice constitutes a moral evil and a sin because, in addition to violating God and neighbor, it can tempt people to compromise their own moral rectitude and lose faith in God.

The sacred text is acutely conscious of the relationship between Israel and its neighbors. To protect its faith, Israel was forbidden to imitate the idolatrous and obscene practices of neighboring peoples or to depict God in any way. The kings were not to tolerate the worship of foreign gods. In the difficult period after the Exile, the community was called upon to obey the Mosaic Law, support the Temple, and reject pagan religious practices. But if the Hebrew tradition understood the practical requirements of holiness, it also knew how to accept contributions from foreign sources, including the covenant format, the monarchy, the resources of human experience and wisdom, sensitivity to the universe as a reflection of God's glory, and the Greek language and modes of thought. Foreign kings were sometimes viewed as God's servants (Jer 25:9) and Israel as the hope of Gentile nations (Isa 2:2-3). This suggests that the relationship between Israel and its neighbors was complex and ambivalent. Constant attention and deliberation were needed in order to interpret new situations rightly and judge what was to be accepted or rejected from other nations and their cultures. These judgments engaged the faith and moral resources of those who made them and strongly influenced the content and development of the Israelite religious tradition. They deserve to be recognized as key moments in the community's religious and moral history.

In the postexilic era scriptural authors displayed a strong inclination to reflect upon the created universe and human experiences in it. They judged that such sources were congruent with their faith tradition and helped people to know God and understand God's will. The resources of creation and human wisdom were especially welcome when historical events visited great evil on people and God's justice was difficult to discern. This suggests that although historical faith and the covenant community remain central, reflection on the created universe and human experience can support faith and enhance moral insight. On this point the Old Testament sets a precedent for similar approaches later. It offers helpful examples of how believers use these sources and integrate them into the religious tradition.

This examination of the Old Testament has begun the study of the substance, context, and dynamics of Christian moral life. Many aspects of Israel's faith will prove to be foundational or normative for later developments. However essential this effort has been, these beginnings cannot be considered complete until the New Testament has also been examined.

2

"Repent and Believe in the Gospel"

If Christian moral life finds its remote origins in the experiences and faith of the Hebrew people, its essential content, purpose, and energy come from the person and preaching, the death and resurrection of Jesus Christ. Jesus Christ is a historical figure, a Palestinian Jew who lived, preached, gathered disciples, and died in the early decades of first century. He is also an object of faith, revered by Christian believers as God's holy one who fulfilled ancient prophecies; manifested God's love, authority, and presence on earth; and carries on God's work until the end of time. Because it depends upon Christian faith, Christian moral life can be adequately understood only if the life and work of Jesus Christ are taken into account and their historical and transcendent dimensions duly appreciated. The principal purpose of this chapter is to respond to that requirement.

In order to develop the requisite understanding of Jesus Christ and his place in Christian faith, it will be necessary to open the pages of the New Testament. This authoritative and indispensable source describes Jesus' origins, ministry, and death. It celebrates God's mercy and love in him and shows the wide range of human responses that he occasioned. The New Testament also affords insight into the Church's origins, its theological grounds and purposes, and the place it is meant to have in the lives of its members. Although they record many instances of sin and disbelief, these sacred texts seek above all to proclaim Jesus as Lord and Messiah and to encourage everyone to place their faith in him. This faith is the heart of Christian moral life.

This chapter begins by reviewing certain aspects of Jewish faith in God. Of particular interest are the images, symbols, and terms that helped to focus that faith for Jesus and his contemporaries. Familiarity

49

with them will contribute to a better understanding of Jesus' preaching and teaching and illuminate key passages in the New Testament.

The second section considers Jesus' preaching of the kingdom of God, which formed the centerpiece of his ministry. His efforts on behalf of the kingdom set him at odds with important aspects of Jewish tradition and customs and did much to make him a source of conflict. Jesus' preaching and teaching opened a deep division between those who believed in him and those who did not.

That conflict led directly to the arrest, trial, and execution of Jesus. While his disciples were still trying to come to terms with the trauma of his crucifixion, they came to see that God brought him back to life and that he continued to be present and active among them. The death and resurrection of Jesus constitute a *sine qua non* of Christian faith and are equally important for the moral life of believers. These events will be the concern of the third section.

The Church and its mission come forth from the life, death, and resurrection of Christ, as well as from his specific mandate. The New Testament details the Church's origins in faith and the preached word, outlines its importance for salvation, and points out its contributions to those who belong to it and to others. These passages do much to illuminate the relationship between Christian faith and Christian moral life.

The following section examines key passages of the New Testament to see what they disclose concerning the sources, motivation, context, and content of Christian morality.

GOD IN THE HEBREW TRADITION

The faith of the Hebrew people rested upon the conviction that God had saved and formed Israel by deeds of power and love. Although the community's sins and its experiences of adversity led some to conclude that God had abandoned them, devout Israelites knew that God remained faithful and looked forward to the day when God would visit them and bring justice and freedom to the oppressed. This expectation was widely shared among the contemporaries of Jesus and established much of the practical context of his ministry. But even more important is the faith that stood behind popular expectations. To speak of faith is to shift the focus back to God's power, activity, and fidelity and bring into view important aspects of the Hebrew tradition concerning God and God's dealings with the human race. This tradition is taken for granted by Jesus and informs his preaching and teaching. It is presupposed by the New Testament and is integral to Christian faith. The previous chapter reviewed the Hebrew tradition in some detail; the present discussion will therefore seek only to highlight those religious images, symbols, and terms that are particularly important to an understanding of Jesus and his ministry in the New Testament.[1]

The Grace of God

The notion of grace takes its source from Israel's faith-illuminated awareness that all good things are the gift of a God who acts with freedom. This divine love and goodness are apparent above all in God's election of Israel and granting it the Covenant. Throughout the centuries God continued to bless Israel and acted with loyalty and steadfast love toward it. Even when Israel turned away in sin, God stood ready to show mercy and grant forgiveness. In all these ways God acted graciously toward the chosen people. Israel never deserved such favor, loyalty, or loving kindness but received them as free gifts. The gratuitousness and unmerited kindness of God's actions help to give the word "grace" its original meaning. Of course, God's gracious and generous love called for reciprocation. Israelites were to act with justice and righteousness toward their neighbors and offer heartfelt praise to God, especially in liturgical celebrations.[2]

The Temple

At the heart of the Sinai Covenant stood God's promise to be present to this people and active on their behalf. Although the reality of God's presence was the essential point, something so important needed to be given some visibility in the community. Yet this was not easy to do. The totally other and all-holy God is not a physical being who can be seen or heard by ordinary mortals. Moreover, to prevent idolatry, God had forbidden the people to make any graven images (Exod 20:4-5). The Hebrew tradition therefore needed to find other ways to represent God's presence. Among the most important was Moses himself (33:9, 11, 14), who had been admitted to an extraordinary friendship with God (33:11). Inanimate objects such as the pillars of cloud and fire that accompanied an Israel on the move also manifested God's presence to Israel (13:21-22; 33:9-11). The same can be said of the tabernacle, or tent

---

[1] For a discussion of Israel's awareness of God's presence, see Yves Congar, *The Mystery of the Temple*, trans. Reginald F. Trevett (Westminster, Md.: Newman Press, 1962) 3–103.

[2] See Klaus Berger, "Grace," *SM*, 2:409-12; Johannes Schildenberger, "Grace," *EBT*, 337–40; C. L. Mitton, "Grace," *IDB*, 2:463-8; and especially Edward Schillebeeckx, *Christ: The Experience of Jesus as Lord*, trans. John Bowden (New York: Crossroad, 1981) 86–101.

of meeting, which God promised to make God's dwelling place (25:8; 29:42-46).[3]

A significant development in Israel's representation of God's presence took place when Solomon built the Temple. Well aware that not even the heavens could contain God (2 Chr 6:18; 1 Kgs 8:27), Solomon did not misunderstand the nature of his building. If God accepted it, it would become the place where God heard the prayers of the people and granted them forgiveness (2 Chr 6:18-21; also 1 Kgs 8:27-30). Scripture testifies that God indeed filled the Temple with the divine presence (2 Chr 7:1-3). This divine gesture informed Israel's faith and authenticated its conviction that the Temple was the primary sign and assurance of God's presence to Israel.

> The Temple is, as it were, the holiness of God established among his people. As God's holiness is the ultimate reality behind the whole destiny of the Jewish people, so the Temple will be for them that ultimate reality. It is in relation to the Temple that the whole life of Israel *will find its bearings* from the point of view of its relations with God, of its fidelity or infidelity towards him. This fact we shall find at the basis of the preaching of the prophets as far as it deals with the Temple. It is in particular the meaning contained in the great vision which inaugurated the ministry of Isaias (ch. 6) and this vision took place in the Temple. It is from his Temple that Yahweh judges and leads his people just as he had done in the days of Moses from the tent of witness.[4]

The Spirit of God

Although it accepted that tangible realities might in some manner represent the presence of Yahweh, Hebrew faith never forgot that God is immaterial, transcendent, and sovereign in exercising power. This dimension of its faith found expression in such subtle elements as breath, wind, and spirit. Sometimes, as in the act of creation, God's breath communicates existence and life (Gen 1:2; 2:7; Ps 33:6). At other times references to God's spirit emphasize the fluid and unpredictable activity of God, which inspires charismatic leadership, ecstatic prophecy, and other extraordinary behavior (e.g., Judg 14:6, 19; 1 Sam 10:6, 10; 11:6).

The rise of the monarchy led to a new turn in Hebrew thinking about God's activity. Instead of being unrestrained and always in motion, God's spirit was now seen to rest in a stable way upon the king (1 Sam 16:13). This suggested that anointing, laying on of hands, or dynastic succession might communicate the spirit to a person. According

---

[3] See also Congar, *Mystery of the Temple*, 7–19.
[4] Ibid., 50–1.

to Isaiah, the spirit would rest upon the expected Messiah (Isa 11:2; see also 42:1). The prophets proclaimed that the gift of the spirit would characterize God's decisive intervention in human life. On that day, God would pour out his spirit upon Israel like rain on dry ground, breathe life into dry bones and make them a faithful people, and put his spirit into them that all might all know the Lord (Isa 44:3-5, Ezek 37:1-14; 36:24-28; 39:29; Joel 2:28-29). The postexilic prophets attributed their preaching to God's spirit, which also emphasizes the vital link between God's spirit and God's word (Neh 9:30; Zech 7:12).[5]

The Word of God

From the very first chapter of Genesis the Scriptures manifest an acute consciousness that God's word is powerful. By God's word the heavens were created, and the earth, and everything in them (Gen 1:3, 6, 9, 11, 14, 20, 24, 26-27). By God's word, God blessed all that had been created, giving animals their fruitfulness and the human male and female their dominion over the world and the living things in it (1:22, 28). God's ten words to Israel became the fundamental stipulations of the Covenant (Exod 20:1; 34:27-28). Throughout the history of its relationship with God, Israel attributed to God's word the power to create and govern, instruct and illuminate (e.g., Deut 8:3; 32:46-47; Pss 33:2-9; 119:105; Isa 2:3; 55:10-11).

The prophetic experience both fed and deepened this respect for God's word and its power. For the prophets, being overtaken by God's word was an intensely personal experience that brought them into immediate contact with God, changed their lives forever, and empowered them for their work (e.g., Isa 6:1-13; Jer 1:1-10). That work was to give voice to God's word, which, while it was often addressed to particular persons or groups, necessarily achieved its purpose (Isa 55:10-11). In the prophets, the word comes to represent both personal intimacy with God and an assertion of divine power over the course of human history, which cannot but succeed.[6]

---

[5] Schillebeeckx, *Christ*, 536–8. Schillebeeckx gives ample references to the scriptural texts. On spirit, breath, and wind, see also Walter Kasper, *Jesus the Christ*, trans. V. Green (New York: Paulist Press; London: Burns & Oates, 1976) 254–5; Jacques Guillet, *Themes of the Bible*, trans. Albert J. LaMothe, Jr. (Notre Dame, Ind.: Fides, 1964) 225–79; Yves Congar, *I Believe in the Holy Spirit*, trans. David Smith (New York: Seabury; London: Geoffrey Chapman, 1983) 1:3-14; Robert Koch, "Spirit," *EBT*, 869–77; Michael Schmaus, "Holy Spirit," *SM*, 3:54; G.W.H. Lampe, "Holy Spirit," *IDB*, 2:626-9.

[6] Gerald O'Collins, *Christology: A Biblical, Historical, and Systematic Study of Jesus* (New York: Oxford University Press, 1995) 40–3; Guillet, *Themes of the Bible*, 270–2;

The Kingdom of God

Besides being present and active among the chosen people, the God of Israel is also faithful. This principal affirmation of faith was grounded in the facts of Israel's origins, especially the Exodus and the Sinai Covenant, and reflected promises God had made many centuries earlier to the patriarch Abraham (Gen 12:2-3, 7; 15:1-21). From their earliest days, therefore, Israelites saw that God's love is steadfast and God's word is to be trusted. This confidence in God's fidelity accounts for the importance that later generations attached to the Davidic covenant, which assured them that God's kingdom would last forever (2 Sam 7:11-16). For many, this promise meant that sooner or later God would send a faithful king to govern Israel with justice and righteousness.[7]

After the fall of Jerusalem in 587 B.C. and the subsequent demise of the Israelite monarchy, it appeared that the fulfillment of the Davidic covenant would require God's extraordinary intervention. The prophets began to look forward to an ideal king who would bring justice to the land, protection from foreign enemies, and peace and reconciliation to Israel and other peoples (e.g., Isa 11). Because the kings of Israel had been anointed, this long-anticipated ruler was sometimes referred to as the "anointed one," that is, "Messiah" in the Hebrew or "Christ" in the Greek.

By the time of Jesus, these prophecies and Israel's hard experiences had led many Jews to think that God would soon send the Messiah to restore the kingship in Israel. Some thought that this would be done by means of political and military activity and entail a violent confrontation with the Roman occupiers. Others emphasized the signs mentioned by the prophets and assumed that the kingdom would be established among those who "know God" and manifest God's justice and righteousness in their lives. In this view the kingdom of God brings salvation to persons but would also have tangible effects in human society. Reflecting the influence of eschatological or apocalyptic writings, yet another group asserted that God's intervention would be accompanied by a cosmic upheaval that would overthrow the pres-

---

Gerhard Von Rad, *Old Testament Theology,* trans. D.M.G. Stalker (New York, Evanston, San Francisco, and London: Harper & Row, 1965) 2:80-98. The prophets often know exactly when God's word comes to them (e.g., Isa 6:1; Jer 1:2-3; Hos 1:1; Mic 1:1); this is additional evidence that they situate God's intervention within the ambit of human history.

[7] Congar, *Mystery of the Temple,* 23–32. See also *DBT,* 465–6; Michael Schmaus, *Dogma* (Kansas City and London: Sheed & Ward, 1971) 3:18-24; and the discussion of the Davidic covenant in chapter 1, above, pp. 25–6.

ent evil age and inaugurate a new and eternal phase of human existence. These people were anxious to see the signs that would suggest that this cataclysmic event was near. The Jewish tradition had given rise to different ways of understanding the kingdom of God, but on one point there was general agreement: there would come a time when a faithful God, the true king of Israel, would visit and save Israel.[8]

JESUS PROCLAIMS THE KINGDOM OF GOD

The Gospels are primarily interested in the life and ministry, the death and resurrection of Jesus Christ. They record his birth at a particular time in human history (Luke 2:1-7); show him preaching, teaching, gathering disciples, and performing acts of kindness; and detail his arrest, trial, and execution. These events are of great importance because they constitute the historical basis of the Gospel accounts.[9] In the

---

[8] John L. McKenzie, "Aspects of Old Testament Thought," *NJBC*, 1309–12. The section entitled "The Messiah" was written by R. E. Brown. See also Oscar Cullmann, *The Christology of the New Testament*, rev. ed. (Philadelphia: Westminster Press, 1959) 111–7; Wolfgang Schrage, *The Ethics of the New Testament*, trans. David E. Green (Philadelphia: Fortress Press, 1988) 18; O'Collins, *Christology*, 22–46. On the kingship of God in the Old Testament, see Frank J. Matera, *New Testament Ethics: The Legacies of Jesus and Paul* (Louisville, Ky.: Westminster John Knox Press, 1996) 15–8.

Jewish expectations also focused on such other figures as the eschatological prophet, similar to Moses, whose appearance would signify God's inauguration of the end-times. Since it had become customary to anoint prophets and priests, this awaited prophet would also be "an anointed one." This suggests that the title "Christ" has more than one source of meaning and warns against identifying it with royal, political, or dynastic messianism. On this see Edward Schillebeeckx, *Jesus: An Experiment in Christology*, trans. Hubert Hoskins (New York: Crossroad, 1981) 441–72, 491–9; Cullmann, *Christology of the New Testament*, 13–42, 117–36.

[9] On the historical grounds of Christian faith, see *DBT*, 265–8; Kasper, *Jesus the Christ*, 65; and John P. Galvin, "Jesus Christ," *Systematic Theology: Roman Catholic Perspectives*, ed. Francis Schüssler Fiorenza and John P. Galvin (Minneapolis: Fortress Press, 1991) 1:261-2.

A problem arises because information about Jesus' life comes almost exclusively from the testimony of the Gospels. However, these sources are sometimes inconsistent, serve professedly religious purposes, and do not observe the canons of modern historical scholarship. Furthermore, such events as the virgin birth and the resurrection of Jesus are beyond historical proof. These factors make it difficult to ascertain key facts concerning Jesus' life. If satisfactory historical verification is not possible, does that not weaken or destroy the historical grounds of Christian faith?

Although it can be difficult to learn the historical facts, scholars can establish many details concerning the life and death of Jesus with at least reasonable certitude, although not so as to end all disagreements. Further pursuit of this interesting issue is beyond the scope of this study, which will defer to the canonical text of the New Testament. For further discussion of the historical and theological aspects of the "quest for the historical Jesus," see Galvin, "Jesus Christ," 281–92; Kasper,

final analysis, however, these sacred texts are not biographical records but witnesses of faith. They proclaim that Jesus is Messiah and Lord so that all people might share in God's life through faith in him (e.g., John 20:30-31). This goal has guided the evangelists' presentation of Jesus' words and deeds, his death and resurrection, and his charge to the disciples he left behind.

Jesus began his public ministry at a time when Palestinian Jews were acutely conscious of the Davidic covenant, prophetic assurances, apocalyptic writings, and the unpleasant realities that underlined Israel's need for God. Their expectations that God would reestablish the kingdom during their own lifetimes formed the background of Jesus' ministry and guaranteed that people would pay attention to his message: "The time is fulfilled, and the kingdom of God is at hand; repent, and believe in the gospel" (Mark 1:15).

The announcement of the kingdom of God stands at the center of Jesus' life and ministry. However, a close examination of the Gospels shows that Jesus adopted none of the views that prevailed at this time but understood the kingdom in a new and surprising way.

"The Kingdom of God Is at Hand"

Before it does anything else, Jesus' proclamation of God's kingdom asserts a fact, namely, that God was going to end the long reign of sin and evil in human life and had already begun to do so.[10] Although this proclamation pertains to each person who hears it, Jesus addressed it primarily to Israel (e.g., Matt 10:5-7; 15:24). His concern for Israel as a

---

Jesus the Christ, 26–40; Schillebeeckx, *Jesus,* 62–100; John P. Meier, "Jesus," *NJBC,* 1316–28; ibid., "The Historical Jesus: Rethinking Some Concepts," *TS* 51 (1990) 3–24.

[10] Presupposing Israel's awareness of sin, including its nuances, imagery, and language, the Gospels recognize that sin is a complex and pervasive reality in human life. Sin is constituted by the human unwillingness to live in keeping with God's grace and goodness, shown through Moses, the Covenant, the Law, and the Prophets. Sin can also refer to the state or situation that results from personal sin, including guilt, iniquity, alienation, and other evil effects. Whether understood as an act or a condition, sin separates people from God and precludes good relations with God. Since these points were part of the Jewish religious heritage, John the Baptist, Jesus, and his disciples could speak about sin and expect to be understood by their hearers. For a review of the concepts and vocabulary of sin in the New Testament, see G. Quell and others, "Hamartano," *TDNT,* 1:302-31; S. J. De Vries, "Sin, Sinners," *IDB,* 4:370-5; Johannes B. Bauer, "Sin," *EBT,* 852–62; Piet Schoonenberg, *Man and Sin: A Theological View,* trans. Joseph Donceel (Notre Dame, Ind.: University of Notre Dame Press, 1965) 3–7.

community reflects a key element of Hebrew self-awareness and faith and anticipates the universal reach of the Christian dispensation. The corporate dimensions of God's reign give the morality of the New Testament an essentially communitarian texture.[11]

The proclamation of the kingdom is heavy with implications. To begin with, the initiative and power for such an intervention belong entirely to God, who acts with an overflowing generosity (Matt 7:11; 20:15). Therefore the kingdom cannot be brought about by human ingenuity or reason, natural processes in the universe, or the flow of history. Moreover, God's action to free the emarginated and lowly from the grip of sin and evil (Luke 4:18-21) means that the kingdom will not be deferred until the end of time but is already being inaugurated (e.g., Luke 11:20, 17:21). It is God's gift to the lowly and humble here and now, and it requires an immediate response. Finally, by preaching and manifesting God's kingdom with such power and authority, Jesus suggested that God was acting in and through him and that he was himself the bearer of divine prerogatives (Luke 4:36, 41, 43; 5:20-24). God's initiative and activity supply the necessary foundation for Jesus' ministry.[12]

"Repent and Believe in the Gospel"

When Jesus called people to "repent and believe in the gospel," he specified the personal claims that were inherent in God's intervention and stipulated how people were to meet them. In other words, God's intervention itself makes it urgent for people to "repent and believe" and likewise empowers them to make the commitment that is necessary if these actions are to be sustained. As a result, Christian life has the character of a response to God's action and is to be understood in that light.[13]

The call to repent and believe does not impose two separate requirements but specifies the essential aspects of one comprehensive response. By naming two aspects, a sincere turning from the evil in one's life toward God and a wholehearted embrace of the Good News that God's kingdom is at hand, Jesus brought out the negative and positive dimensions of his message. At the same time, by binding repentance and faith closely together, he emphasized the unity of the overall response and precluded any suggestion that it is possible to

---

[11] Schrage, *Ethics of the New Testament*, 5.

[12] Ibid., 18–24, 30–7; Allen Verhey, *The Great Reversal: Ethics and the New Testament* (Grand Rapids: Eerdmans, 1984) 11–6.

[13] Schrage, *Ethics of the New Testament*, 24–30, 37–40.

embrace God's kingdom while remaining impenitent or that one might decline the intensely religious imperatives of his preaching on grounds that a morally upright life is sufficient. Repentance is a necessary part of one's faith, and a wholehearted adherence to God is required of all who would respond fully to Jesus' preaching (e.g., Matt 5:8, 20; Mark 7:15). For these reasons, the imperatives of repentance and faith are inseparable and constitute the essence of a positive and adequate response to the proclamation of the kingdom.[14]

Practical Dimensions of Repentance and Faith

Besides underlining the urgency of repentance and faith, the Gospels depict what a fitting response to the kingdom will involve. The parables of the buried treasure and the pearl of great price (Matt 13:44-45) evoke the sense of joy that should attend the discovery of God's kingdom (Luke 17:20-21) and the life-changing impact that it is meant to have (e.g., Luke 12:32-34). Nothing else is to have priority in a person's life (Matt 6:24, 33). This is exemplified in those who accept his call to be disciples, which involved serious personal sacrifices and risks (Matt 10:37-39; Mark 10:21; Luke 9:57-62, 14:26-33). The kingdom also governs the lives of those who share Jesus' ministry (e.g., Mark 1:17).

Closely related are the passages that look toward the future fulfillment of God's kingdom. The time that is left is not to be squandered but needs to be seized and used for repentance and right living (Matt 11:20-24; 24:45–25:13; Luke 13:6-9). Those who bear the required fruit will be blessed on the day of judgment, but the impenitent will be doomed to punishment (Matt 13:49-50; Luke 12:58-59; 13:5-9). Both the promise of reward and the possibility of condemnation are integral to Jesus' preaching; they emphasize the requirements of the kingdom, the personal consequences of one's response, and the moral responsibility that it involves (e.g., Matt 24:45–25:46).

In the meanwhile, all are required to be generous and merciful (Matt 5:7; 6:14-15; 18:21-35; Luke 6:27-38), actually do God's will instead of being content with lip service (Matt 7:21-27; 21:28-32; Luke 11:28), refrain from judging others (Luke 6:37), attend to the needs of the least of Jesus' disciples (Matt 25:31-46; Mark 9:41-42), and practice the great commandment of love (Luke 10:25-28). These are the imperatives that the kingdom of God imposes.[15]

Jesus' proclamation seemed to fulfill ancient prophecies and address the expectations of his people, and one might have expected it to re-

---

[14] Ibid., 40–6.
[15] Ibid., 26–30, 37–40, see also 87–115; Verhey, *Great Reversal*, 16–21.

ceive ready acceptance. That is not what happened; instead, his ministry provoked conflict and he himself became a source of intense controversy. This divided response can in large measure be understood in light of the stance that Jesus adopted toward important elements of contemporary Jewish faith and practice. He upheld the Law, yet also challenged and reinterpreted it. He accepted Israel's heritage of Wisdom sayings, yet stood ready to overrule it. He acknowledged the authority of Jewish religious leaders, yet severely criticized them. The mixed reception that people gave to Jesus and his ministry can be more easily understood when they are considered against the background of the Hebrew tradition and contemporary teachings.

Jesus and the Mosaic Law

At the outset, it is necessary to affirm that the preaching, teaching, and actions of Jesus fall squarely within the Jewish tradition, which acknowledged God's mighty deeds in human history, called Israelites to repentance, and required them to love God above all things and act with justice and righteousness toward their neighbor. For his part, Jesus showed his respect for the requirements of Hebrew faith and worship. He upheld the Mosaic Law against the Pharisees' willingness to give precedence to their oral traditions (Matt 23:16-23), even when the written commandment was clear and much was at stake (Mark 7:10-13). He defended the religious authority of the scribes and Pharisees and urged people to follow their teachings (Matt 23:2-3). In the dialogue with the rich young man, Jesus presupposes that the commandments are binding and reflect God's will (Mark 10:19). He worshiped in accordance with Jewish customs (Luke 4:16; 22:8) and accepted even small points of cultic observance, insisting only that due priorities should be observed (Luke 11:42).

The record also includes some strongly dissonant notes, as the hostility of some of Jesus' coreligionists clearly suggests. Some of that conflict can be attributed to Jesus' criticism of the scribes and Pharisees, who held positions of leadership in the Jewish community, and to their objections to Jesus (Luke 11:42-54). Some of it is due to his refusal to allow oral traditions and other human customs to take priority over the Law (Mark 7:10-13; Luke 11:42). Accordingly, Jesus shared table fellowship with notorious sinners and other disreputable people, even though that violated purity laws and was considered scandalous (Matt 9:10-13). Disregarding rabbinical customs and public expectation, he spoke freely with women, allowed sinful women to touch him, and admitted women as his disciples (Luke 7:36-50; 10:38-42; John 4:7-42, esp. vv. 9, 27). Although it might be possible to cite the

Hebrew tradition in defense of such actions, they violated deeply held convictions and would have been enough to turn powerful people against Jesus.

The difficulty went much deeper than issues of interpretation or the personal qualities of religious leaders. Jesus presupposed that, as a new and decisive act of God, the kingdom superseded important aspects of the Law of Moses. When there was a conflict, therefore, he always gave priority to the imperatives of the kingdom. This is evident in his readiness to do work on the Sabbath, which violated a strict Mosaic prohibition. Not only did Jesus allow his disciples to pluck and open corn on the Sabbath (Mark 2:23-28), but he also cured people, even though there were six other days when such work was permitted (e.g., Matt 12:9-13; Mark 3:1-5; Luke 13:10-17; John 5:8-10; 9:14-16). When he was challenged, Jesus did not merely argue that his actions upheld the priority of mercy (Matt 12:7), exposed the hypocrisy of external compliance without interior goodness (e.g., Luke 11:37-44),[16] or observed the greatest commandment of love of God and neighbor (Mark 12:28-34; Luke 10:25-37).[17] Jesus declared that "the Son of man is lord even of the sabbath" (Mark 2:28), which asserts full authority to set aside the Law of Moses whenever it conflicted with his own judgment about what needed to be done. Jesus' injunction that the cured paralytic should pick up his pallet and carry it away, even on the Sabbath (e.g., John 5:8-10), appeals to no motive of mercy or charity. It reflects the sovereign authority over the Law that Jesus asserted.

The same tension with the Law is evident in other areas of Jesus' life and ministry. He overturned the law of reciprocity, declaring that people are to love their enemies and be generous in responding to others (Matt 5:38-48). Even more telling are Jesus' dismissal of the Mosaic allowance of divorce (Mark 10:5-9) and Jewish dietary regulations (Mark 7:15-19). These examples are further signs that Jesus set himself

---

[16] See Jerome H. Neyrey, *Christ Is Community: The Christologies of the New Testament* (Wilmington: Michael Glazier, 1986) 35–9.

[17] The literature on the law of love is extensive. See, for example, Schillebeeckx, *Jesus*, 249–56; Rudolf Schnackenburg, *The Moral Teaching of the New Testament*, trans. J. Holland-Smith and W. J. O'Hara (London: Burns & Oates, 1975) 90–109; Victor Paul Furnish, *The Love Command in the New Testament* (Nashville: Abingdon Press, 1972); idem, "Love of Neighbor in the New Testament," *JRE* 10 (1982) 327–34; Brice L. Martin, "Matthew on Christ and the Law," *TS* 44 (1983) 53–70, especially 63–4; Ceslaus Spicq, *Théologie morale du Nouveau Testament* (Paris: Gabalda, 1970) 481–512; idem, *Agape dans le Nouveau Testament: Analyse des textes* (Paris: Gabalda, 1958–9); J. Coppens, "La doctrine biblique sur l'amour de dieu et du prochain," *ETL* 40 (1964) 252–99.

above the Law of Moses. In such cases he cites no precedents, elaborates no casuistry, and invokes no other authority to justify his words and deeds. He acts in his own name and with his own word. One must conclude that the ministry and person of Jesus were sometimes consistent with and sometimes in opposition to the Mosaic Law and other key elements of Jewish religious practice.[18]

Jesus and the Wisdom Tradition

The same mixture of general acceptance and radical revision also characterizes Jesus' attitude toward the Hebrew Wisdom tradition. On the one hand, he presupposes the common-sense maxims and basic standards of justice that inform a prudent, reasonable approach to human life. The Golden Rule (Matt 7:12), the impossibility of serving two masters (Matt 6:24), the fragility and limits of material possessions (Luke 12:15-21), and the symmetry between what is given and what is demanded (Luke 12:48) exemplify Wisdom's contribution to life in the kingdom of God. Jesus also cites God's original creative intent when he overrules the Mosaic toleration of divorce (Mark 10:6). On the other hand, Jesus leaves no doubt that the requirements of the kingdom can transform or displace the accepted norms of Wisdom. Even though circumstances may be trying, a disciple is to give priority to the kingdom rather than daily necessities (Matt 6:25-34). The kingdom likewise takes precedence over one's possessions, and it does not matter that they were honestly obtained (Mark 10:17-31). Love, doing good, and lending to the needy are not to be calculated by the canons of reciprocity; instead, the disciple is take God's mercy and kindness as the standard (Luke 6:32-38). These examples show that worldly wisdom sometimes supports and sometimes is overruled by the imperatives of the kingdom. True wisdom leads people to embrace goodness from the heart, hear Christ's words, and act upon them (Luke 6:43-49). Those who are truly shrewd will use scarce time and resources in order to repent and bring forth the good works that God requires (Luke 12:57-59; 13:6-9; 16:1-9).[19]

---

[18] For further discussion of Jesus' posture toward the Mosaic Law, see Verhey, *Great Reversal*, 21–7; Schrage, *Ethics of the New Testament*, 40–68; Schillebeeckx, *Jesus*, 237–43. See also Schnackenburg, *Moral Teaching of the New Testament*, 56–81; Martin, "Matthew on Christ and the Law"; Thomas W. Ogletree, *The Use of the Bible in Christian Ethics* (Philadelphia: Fortress Press, 1983) 97–116; and the discussion of the Sermon on the Mount in this chapter, below.

[19] Verhey, *Great Reversal*, 41–3, 56–8; Schrage, *Ethics of the New Testament*, 30–7, 62–8, 87–8, 98–107.

Jesus as Source of Division

Especially when he challenged prevailing views of faith and established customs, Jesus antagonized the religious leadership and provoked controversy among the people. His habit of speaking and acting on his own authority (Luke 4:32, 36-37) only intensified the conflict and gave it a more personal quality. This is evident in the way people responded to Jesus and his preaching. Those who embraced the kingdom also accepted Jesus as its divinely accredited agent (Luke 9:18-20). Those who rejected Jesus also dismissed his preaching and took offense at his behavior (Mark 6:1-6). The ministry of Jesus was of a piece with his personal warrants and claims (e.g., Luke 4:22; 7:16-17; 20:2-8), which also influenced people's responses. Was Jesus the long-awaited Messiah and prophet of God? Or was he a demoniac and a blasphemer (Matt 9:3, 34; 11:2-6; 12:22-28)? Jesus posed this question to his disciples: "But who do you say that I am?" (Matt 16:15).

Far from glossing over the conflicts that Jesus occasioned, the Gospels use the divergent responses to push the question of faith in Jesus into high relief.[20] The evangelists portray the person and activity

[20] The theme of conflict and division is especially strong in the Gospel of John; see, for example, 1:10-13; 3:18-21; 7:43; 9:16; 10:19; also Schillebeeckx, *Christ*, 331–43.

In his treatment of people's acceptance or rejection of Jesus, John sometimes expresses hostility toward "the Jews." These references are to be interpreted in light of the fact that the Gospel of John simultaneously reflects Jesus' own situation and the different one that pertained to John's late-first-century community. Accordingly, Schillebeeckx believes that originally the term "Jews" referred to the Judeans (as opposed to the Jewish Galileans), who largely rejected Jesus in his own time, especially the Jerusalem officials and Pharisees. For John's community, the term connoted the "synagogue Jews," who excommunicated those who professed faith in Jesus (see, e.g., John 9:22; 12:42). The tension in John's Gospel between Jesus and "the Jews" has its roots in the nature of Jesus' preaching and ministry and in the resulting conflict between church and synagogue. In neither case does John mean to indict the Jewish people as such, as his favorable references suggest (e.g., 4:22; 7:31; 11:45; 12:11). See Schillebeeckx, *Christ*, 331–40, 614–21; Neyrey, *Christ Is Community*, 142–4, 165–83; Raymond E. Brown, *The Gospel According to John* (Garden City: Doubleday, 1966) lxx–lxxv; idem, *The Death of the Messiah: From Gethsemane to the Grave: A Commentary on the Passion Narratives in the Four Gospels* (New York: Doubleday, 1994) 386–97, 837–9, 1419–34; Richard B. Hays, *The Moral Vision of the New Testament: A Contemporary Introduction to New Testament Ethics* (San Francisco: HarperCollins, 1996) 409–11, 424–8.

This historical and theological clarification addresses an important issue of textual interpretation and shows that John provides no warrant to extend this conflict to all the Jews of Jesus' time or of the first century, much less to their descendants. It is helpful to remember that Jesus himself, his parents, and the first disciples were Jewish. The commandment to love one's neighbor as oneself pertains to this matter, as does the Second Vatican Council's Declaration on the Relationship of the Church to Non-Christian Religions, n. 4.

of Jesus as confronting people with an inescapable choice. Either embrace Jesus as the long-awaited prophet and Messiah and receive God's kingdom through him, or reject Jesus, lose the kingdom, and be alienated from God (see John 6:66-70).[21] For many, that decision was difficult, since to accept Jesus as God's chosen one and to subscribe to his judgments on the Mosaic Law was also to become liable to excommunication from the synagogue.[22] Acutely conscious of these conflicts, the evangelists are at pains to celebrate Jesus' authority, set forth his warrants, and proclaim their faith in him. The conflict concerning Jesus and the Gospels' own testimony help to focus attention on the person of Jesus and establish a fitting context in which to consider his passion and death.[23]

Jesus as God's Presence

Among the clearest testimonies to Jesus are those that appear at the beginning of the Gospels. Noting that Mary has won God's special grace or favor, Luke attributes Jesus' conception to the extraordinary intervention of the Holy Spirit (Luke 1:35). John proclaims that Jesus is "full of grace and truth" and the source from which humanity can receive "grace upon grace" (John 1:14, 16-17). The Synoptic Gospels report that when Jesus was baptized in the Jordan, the Spirit of God descended upon him and a divine voice affirmed him as "my beloved son" (Matt 3:16-17 and parallel texts).[24]

---

[21] The process of turning one's entire life toward the person of Jesus and away from evil is denoted by the terms "metanoia" and "conversion." Its dynamics are similar to the devout and righteous response expected of the Israelite in view of God's steadfast love, especially in the Covenant.

On conversion, see Schnackenburg, *Moral Teaching of the New Testament,* 25–53; Kasper, *Jesus the Christ,* 81–3; Charles E. Curran, "Conversion: The Central Moral Message of Jesus," *A New Look at Christian Morality* (Notre Dame, Ind.: Fides, 1968) 25–71; Marc-François Lacan, "Conversion and Kingdom in the Synoptic Gospels," *Conversion: Perspectives on Personal and Social Transformation,* ed. Walter E. Conn (New York: Alba House, 1978) 97–118; Hans Urs von Balthasar, "Conversion in the New Testament," *Communio* 1 (1974) 47–59.

[22] This was the historical experience of the Church in its infancy; see, for example, the account of the cure of the blind man in John 9, especially verses 22, 34–5. On this point see Neyrey, *Christ Is Community,* 143, 151–5.

[23] Schrage, *Ethics of the New Testament,* 46–52.

[24] Congar, *I Believe in the Holy Spirit,* 1:15-29. On the contemporary religious and social context, John the Baptist, and his baptism of Jesus, see Schillebeeckx, *Jesus,* 116–39. For further discussion of the Holy Spirit as it pertains to the conception, baptism, and life of Jesus, see Schillebeeckx, *Christ,* 534–8; also Kasper, *Jesus the Christ,* 254–5; Koch, "Spirit," 878–81; Schmaus, "Holy Spirit," 3:54-6; Lampe, "Holy Spirit," 2:630-3, 38-9.

In his account of Jesus in his own synagogue at Nazareth, Luke emphasizes the remarkable declaration that Jesus makes after reading a passage from the book of the prophet Isaiah (61:1-2):

> "The Spirit of the Lord is upon me,
> because he has anointed me to preach good news to the poor.
> He has sent me to proclaim release to the captives
> and recovering of sight to the blind,
> to set at liberty those who are oppressed,
> to proclaim the acceptable year of the Lord."
>
> And he closed the book, and gave it back to the attendant, and sat down; and the eyes of all in the synagogue were fixed on him. And he began to say to them, "Today this scripture has been fulfilled in your hearing" (Luke 4:18-21; see also Matt 12:18-21).

In its context, Jesus' actions strongly suggest that he is the fulfillment of Isaiah's messianic prophecy.

These passages identify Jesus with God's saving presence and suggest that he is the ultimate expression of that presence. They also suggest that God's Holy Spirit is in some way identified with the person of Jesus. Coming as they do at the beginning of the Gospels and at the start of Jesus' ministry, these passages introduce principal themes that recur throughout the Gospels.

Another series of texts focuses on the Temple of Jerusalem, which was the quintessential sign of God's presence to Israel, the site of the most solemn of prayers and sacrifices, and the place where people had access to God.[25] By word and symbol, the Gospels suggest that Jesus first challenged and then replaced its unique religious function. The first step in this process is associated with his devout parents' presentation of the infant Jesus in the Temple. On that occasion the prophet Simeon declared that he could now depart in peace,

> "for mine eyes have seen thy salvation
> which thou hast prepared in the presence of all peoples,
> a light for revelation to the Gentiles,
> and for glory to thy people Israel" (Luke 2:30-32).

This prophecy envisioned a universal salvation that would supersede the exclusivity of the Jerusalem Temple.

Jesus' cleansing of the Temple was a dramatic and highly symbolic action (see Matt 21:12-17; Mark 11:15-18; Luke 19:45-46; John 2:13-22). On one level, Jesus acted because he would not tolerate the contradiction between what the Temple meant and how people were using it; in

---

[25] Congar, *Mystery of the Temple*, 107–11, gives the pertinent terminology and other details.

other words, he acted to protect the holiness of God's house. But there is a deeper and more radical significance. John recounts that after Jesus took this action, he declared to his critics, "Destroy this temple, and in three days I will raise it up" (John 2:19; see also Mark 14:58 and parallel texts). These words suggest that after Jesus died and rose, he would assume the functions of the Temple. The Synoptic Gospels make a similar point when they report that at the very moment Jesus died, "the curtain of the temple was torn in two, from top to bottom" (Mark 15:38 and parallel texts), which connotes the Temple's replacement by Jesus Christ. As a result, persons now have communion with God only through him.[26]

In sum, the Gospels proclaim that Jesus is God's life-giving presence for Israel and, indeed, all peoples. Matthew calls him "Emmanuel," or God with us (1:23; 28:20). Mark declares that his is the "gospel of Jesus Christ, the Son of God" (1:1). Luke affirms that even the demons know the true identity of Jesus (4:41). John composed his account in order to serve one overriding goal: "that you may believe that Jesus is the Christ, the Son of God, and that believing you may have life in his name" (John 20:31).

THE DEATH AND RESURRECTION OF JESUS

The conflict that surrounded Jesus and his ministry eventually led to a life-and-death confrontation. Over the course of time powerful figures in the religious leadership became so alarmed that they decided

---

[26] This discussion has followed Congar, *Mystery of the Temple,* 112–50, and Schillebeeckx, *Jesus,* 243–9. See also Neyrey, *Christ Is Community,* 48–9, 153–5.

To proclaim that Jesus Christ is the privileged means of communion with God is to imply that rejection of Jesus entails alienation from God. The New Testament gives ample witness to this Christ-centered interpretation of sin. See, for example, Mark 3:28-30; Luke 10:16; John 3:18; see also Neyrey, *Christ Is Community,* 45, 122–3, 148, 156–7; Schoonenberg, *Man and Sin,* 10–6; Yves Congar, "Blasphemy Against the Holy Spirit," *Concilium* 99 (1976) 47–57; I. De la Potterie, "La péché, c'est l'iniquité," *NRT* 78 (1956) 785–97; Schillebeeckx, *Christ,* 637; Spicq, *Théologie morale,* 197.

The expression, "blasphemy against the Holy Spirit" (Matt 12:31) refers to sin in the sense just noted.

> The direct and total opposition to Jesus' mission, which ascribed the signs of the kingdom (the casting out of demons) to the power of evil, is blasphemy against the Holy Spirit itself. Hence this is the ultimate sin, the final rejection of God as manifested in his active presence in the mighty works of Jesus (Lampe, "Holy Spirit," 631).

The image of alienation or separation from God is integral to the notion of sin as Israel understood it. In the New Testament this continues to be the essential element in sin; see, for example, the parable of the prodigal son (Luke 15:11-32).

to remove him from the scene. With the help of Judas, one of the Twelve, they had Jesus arrested. He was subjected to personal abuse, brought before Jewish and Roman tribunals, and finally put to death on a cross. His crucifixion was a violent and humiliating end to a holy man's life. For the Christian tradition, however, the death of Jesus represents much more. It manifests the power of overwhelming evil and all-surpassing grace. It is at the heart of Christian faith and the lives of those who share it. For all these reasons, the Gospels attend very closely to Jesus' passion and death and carefully interpret this drama in the light of faith (Matt 26:14–27:66; Mark 14–15; Luke 22:47–23:56; John 18–19).

Christian faith understands the death of Jesus to be life-giving because, among other reasons, it also affirms that something extraordinary occurred after he died and was buried. By God's power, Jesus came forth from his grave and took up a new mode of existence with God his Father. Thus transformed and empowered, Jesus was able to unify, empower, and guide the disciples he left behind. The presence of their resurrected Lord helped them to reconsider his life and death and know their true import. What is more, they found the insight and the energy they needed to carry out the mission Jesus had confided to them.

These topics require attention because Christian faith stands or falls with them. They constitute a foundational question of personal faith that each hearer of the Gospel is to resolve with deliberate and responsible freedom. Jesus' death and resurrection also give rise to the Church and its mission, which establish the context in which later believers enact their Christian life.

The Crucifixion

By preaching the kingdom of God and proclaiming that the long-expected kingdom had already begun, Jesus left little doubt that traditional institutions had become at least partially obsolete. He was aware that his words and deeds placed him in conflict with the religious authorities and the established order of Jewish faith and worship. He knew that no prophet is accepted among his own people and that most of them die violently (Luke 4:24; 13:34; Matt 5:12; 23:31).[27] Still, the

---

[27] The execution of John the Baptist (Mark 6:14-29) must have reminded Jesus of this unpleasant fact. As to Jesus himself, this statement seems to be autobiographical: "O Jerusalem, Jerusalem, killing the prophets and stoning those who are sent to you! How often would I have gathered your children together as a hen gathers her brood under her wings, and you would not!" (Matt 23:37).

Gospels testify that Jesus made his final trip to Jerusalem freely, calmly, and fully aware of what was to take place (Matt 16:21; Luke 9:51; 17:25; 22:42).[28]

Once in Jerusalem, Jesus gathered his friends together for the last time. The accounts of the Last Supper underline Jesus' acceptance of his impending death and disclose what he asked of his friends (Matt 26:26-29; Mark 14:17-25; Luke 22:14-23). As he had done so often during his active ministry, he used a meal to express God's generosity and desire to gather the lowly and emarginated into the kingdom. To demonstrate that love and service are to be the hallmarks of his disciples, he washed their feet (John 13:1-17). The cup he offered and shared with them would be his last until he drank the new wine of the kingdom of God. This gesture emphasized the bonds that united his person, God's offer of salvation, and his coming crucifixion. He enjoined his friends to continue sharing the bread and wine of thanksgiving in his memory (1 Cor 11:23-26).[29]

Shortly after the Last Supper Jesus was arrested and brought before the Sanhedrin, or supreme council, which had the power to try cases that arose under the Law (e.g., Mark 14:43-46, 53, 55-62). After considering the charges against him, which probably included blasphemy and threats against the Temple, the council concluded that Jesus was guilty of capital crimes and deserved to be put to death (14:63-64). However, that tribunal was not able to execute its sentence without the permission of the Roman authorities, so it referred the case to the procurator, Pontius Pilate (15:1). To Pilate, Jesus represented a religious troublemaker who threatened civil peace and order and who had already been condemned by a Jewish court. In due course, Pilate granted the Sanhedrin's wishes and pronounced his own sentence of death (15:12-15). Roman soldiers then flogged Jesus, led him out of the city, and publicly crucified him (15:16-25).[30]

A Crisis of Faith

The aftermath of the crucifixion involved much more than the normal experience of grieving for a deceased friend. Jesus' death cut deeper because it precipitated a crisis of faith for his disciples. Jesus

---

[28] On Jesus' approach to his own death and the attendant circumstances, see Kasper, *Jesus the Christ*, 113–9; Schillebeeckx, *Jesus*, 294–313.

[29] Kasper, *Jesus the Christ*, 114–9; Schillebeeckx, *Jesus*, 301–12.

[30] For a recent and very thorough discussion of the passion narratives and what can be known of the actual events, see Brown, *Death of the Messiah*. The Jewish and Roman legal processes are discussed on pages 454–60, 473–80, 506–60, 849–61; see also Kasper, *Jesus the Christ*, 113–4; Schillebeeckx, *Jesus*, 312–8.

had identified God's salvation with his own person, and his demise seemed to suggest that this could not be true. To make matters worse, devout Jews were aware that God's curse rests upon those who have been hanged on a tree (Deut 21:23; see also Gal 3:13). Jesus' death by crucifixion seemed to undo his earthly achievements and show that he could not possibly be the prophet and bearer of God's salvation.[31]

The followers of Jesus reflected upon his life and death in light of the resources that were available to them. Their Hebrew faith tradition allowed them to interpret Jesus' death as that of a martyred prophet, as a necessary part of God's plan of salvation, and as a personal sacrifice that brought forgiveness of sins.[32] However, a new and unexpected development also influenced their attempts to come to terms with Jesus' crucifixion. The disciples came to see that Jesus continued to be present to them, although in a highly transformed way. That realization, and the faith that it called forth, changed everything for them.

The Resurrection and the Gift of the Holy Spirit

The resurrection of Jesus is utterly central to Christian faith, and the Scriptures proclaim it forthrightly: "He has risen, he is not here" (Mark 16:6; also Matt 28:6). Although the New Testament provides no direct account of the resurrection itself, it calls attention to Jesus' empty tomb and his appearances to some of the disciples and to other witnesses (Matt 28:6, 9-10, 18-20; Luke 24:15-43).[33] It shows that the disciples, who greeted reports of Jesus' resurrection with doubt and disbelief (Mark 16:11, 13, 14; Luke 24:11, 25, 37-38), later became a confident group who were prepared to preach Christian faith from the rooftops (Mark 16:20; Acts 2:22-36). These scriptural accounts and the personal transformation of Jesus' friends are impressive, but their deeper significance lay in their reflection of God's activity in raising Jesus from the dead. By God's special intervention, Jesus has not only assumed a new spiritual existence but is invested with a full measure of divine power and authority. As a result, he is able to be present to his disciples and help them to live and work as such.

New Testament sources agree that the most important effects of the resurrection are Jesus' return to his Father (Mark 16:19; Acts 1:9) and

---

[31] On the reactions of Jesus' disciples see Kasper, *Jesus the Christ*, 124–5; also Schillebeeckx, *Jesus*, 320–9.

[32] Schillebeeckx, *Jesus*, 274–94.

[33] See, for example, Kasper, *Jesus the Christ*, 124–43; Schillebeeckx, *Jesus*, 329–79; Xavier Léon-Dufour, *Resurrection and the Message of Easter*, trans. R. N. Wilson (New York: Holt, Rinehart, & Winston, 1975).

the outpouring of the Holy Spirit on the disciples (John 20:21-23; Acts 2:1-4).[34] The Holy Spirit represents God's presence, life, freedom, and activity. The Spirit was responsible for Jesus' conception; it was given to him at his baptism; it rested upon him throughout his life. The Spirit is the advocate that Jesus promised to send after he had returned to his Father (John 14:16-17, 26). It is God's grace and power working through a new series of mighty deeds in the disciples and in the churches they established. The Holy Spirit brings forgiveness, communion with God, and insight into Jesus' teachings, and it is the means whereby Jesus will continue to be with his own until the end of time (Matt 28:16-20; Luke 24:36-53; John 14:26; 15:26; 20:19-23; Mark 16:19-20).[35]

Having helped to bring the disciples to faith in the risen Lord, the Holy Spirit empowered and directed all that they did. Their first task was to testify that the same Jesus who died and was buried had been raised up, and in his name to preach repentance for the forgiveness of sins (e.g., Luke 24:45-49; Acts 2:22-42; 1 Cor 15:3-8). They proclaimed God's reconciliation in Christ and called everyone to respond with faith (e.g., Matt 28:18-20; John 20:21-23). The disciples enjoined those who heard their word to "Repent, and be baptized every one of you in the name of Jesus Christ for the forgiveness of your sins; and you shall receive the gift of the Holy Spirit" (Acts 2:38). The Holy Spirit and the apostles' word give rise to the Church, which is the community of those who respond to the apostles' preaching with repentance, faith, and the reception of baptism.[36]

The Death and Resurrection of Jesus and Moral Life

Common human experience enabled the disciples to know the fact of Jesus' death, experience its power, and explore its meaning. But experience made it very difficult for them to grasp his resurrection, an event that was altogether extraordinary. Even so, they could only become Christian believers if they came to grips with the resurrection of Jesus. St. Paul has given this issue its classic expression:

---

[34] John uses water to represent the Holy Spirit and links the gift of the Holy Spirit to the resurrection; see John 7:37-39; 19:34; 20:19-23. Luke, on the other hand, locates the gift of the Holy Spirit on Pentecost; see Luke 24:49; Acts 2:1-4. Koch, "Spirit," 881.

[35] See Schillebeeckx, *Jesus*, 346–90.

[36] See Congar, *I Believe in the Holy Spirit*, 1:29-62; Kasper, *Jesus the Christ*, 254–7; Koch, "Spirit," 880–6; Schmaus, "Holy Spirit," 54–6; Lampe, "Holy Spirit," 630–9; Yves Congar, *The Mystery of the Church*, trans. A. V. Littledale (Baltimore: Helicon, 1960) 1–57.

> If Christ has not been raised, then our preaching is in vain and your faith is in vain. We are even found to be misrepresenting God, because we testified of God that he raised Christ, whom he did not raise if it is true that the dead are not raised. For if the dead are not raised, then Christ has not been raised. If Christ has not been raised, your faith is futile and you are still in your sins. Then those also who have fallen asleep in Christ have perished. If for this life only we have hoped in Christ, we are of all men most to be pitied.
>
> But in fact Christ has been raised from the dead, the first fruits of those who have fallen asleep (1 Cor 15:14-20).

These considerations confront all who wrestle with the question of faith in Jesus Christ. Persons are invited to contemplate his life and death, the testimony of his witnesses, and the signs of God's activity that are to be found in the lives of his disciples throughout history. Each one is called upon to assess the evidence, appreciate what is at stake, and respond to the proclamation that God raised Jesus from the dead. This kind of deliberation engages the mind, heart, and freedom of all who take it up. For that reason it not only determines whether and how persons will walk the path of faith but also constitutes a decisive moment in their moral life.

The response of faith in the resurrection of Jesus will also inform the outlook and shape the moral life of Christian believers. The resurrection reflects God's power and grace as they intervened in favor of the same Jesus who had suffered, died, and was buried. The acute consciousness of God's power and ability to transform both the ordinary and the tragic aspects of life cannot fail to change how believers consider human experience. Moreover, the new life and lordship of Jesus means that his earthly words and deeds retain their full measure of authority for those who would govern their own lives by them. His resurrection also opens a new age, which will end in a general resurrection. That underlines the urgency of the mission given by the risen Lord to his disciples and makes it necessary for them to reinterpret time, created realities, and human efforts accordingly. The impact of resurrection faith on the moral lives of Christians will be further illuminated in the following sections.[37]

THE FOUNDATION AND LIFE OF THE CHURCH

During the decades after the death and resurrection of Jesus, the earliest Christian communities began to appear in Palestine, Asia Minor, Greece, and Rome. The New Testament shows how St. Paul and the

[37] For some general perspectives, see Schrage, *Ethics of the New Testament*, 119–22.

other writers understood the origin, life, problems, and mission of these churches. Their writings allow the modern reader to gain deeper insight into Christian faith and how it influences the moral life of believers. Of particular interest are the situation of evil, alienation, and sin that formed the backdrop of the apostles' preaching; the Church's origins in faith, repentance, and baptism; its character as the community of the new covenant in Christ; and Paul's teachings about justification through faith.

The Sinful Condition of Humanity Without Jesus Christ

Especially in his Epistle to the Romans, St. Paul propounds the view that apart from Christ people are hopelessly ensnared in sin. By this he means that evil, immorality, and alienation are so pervasive and powerful that people cannot escape them but rather are pulled down by such an environment, which encourages even more sinfulness. Although Paul does not ignore the situation of individuals, he is primarily interested in two comprehensive groups: his own people, the Jews; and everyone else, the Gentiles. This reflects his essentially corporate or social view of human life, which is one of the keys to his thought. Considering his reflections on sinful humanity will call attention to another dimension of sin; highlight the effects of salvation in Christ; and emphasize the importance of repentance, faith, baptism, and the Church.[38]

The Gentiles had the ability to know God by interpreting the signs of his activity in creation, but they failed to acknowledge God (Rom 1:19-21, 28, 32). Therefore Paul judges that they are unclean and prone to evil, which they freely increase through their many sinful activities. The results are apparent in sexual license and idolatry, which are emblematic of their rejection of God (1:18-32).[39] What is worse, even though they do not have the gift of the Law, they are responsible because their consciences allow them to know God and recognize the requirements of a morally upright life. Because their own consciences

---

[38] Schillebeeckx, *Christ*, 126–32; also Jerome Murphy-O'Connor, *Becoming Human Together* (Wilmington: Michael Glazier, 1977) 13–4. This highly corporate, social outlook is shared by other New Testament writers; see, for example, such expressions as "evil and adulterous generation" (Matt 12:39; 16:4), "evil generation," "this generation" (Luke 11:29-32; see also Acts 2:40), and "the world" or "this world" (e.g., John 8:23; 9:39). On this see Schillebeeckx, *Christ*, 555–8.

[39] This passage presents Paul's indictment, which includes his mockery of the "wisdom" that refuses to acknowledge God even though God can be known through creation. See T. J. Deidun, *New Covenant Morality in Paul* (Rome: Biblical Institute Press, 1981) 89–93.

either accuse or excuse them (1:18-21; 2:14-15),[40] they can be judged imputable for their evil actions. The sinful environment and the Gentiles' willing connivance with evil led Paul to the conclusion that sin reigned supreme over them (1:24, 26, 28-31).

For their part, the Jews had received the Mosaic Law, which gave them a privileged way to know God (Rom 2:17-21; 9:4). Despite this advantage, Israel failed to keep the Law and persisted in doing evil rather than good (3:9-18). That entitled Paul to declare that sin reigned over them as well (3:9, 23; 5:12). In their case, however, the Law made sin more conspicuous than it otherwise would have been and also brought God's mercy into higher relief (3:20; 5:20-21; 7:7, 13).[41] These observations led to a sweeping conclusion that "all men, both Jews and Greeks, are under the power of sin" (3:9).

As he asserted the sinfulness of humanity, Paul called attention to the complexity of sin and emphasized the saving work of Jesus Christ. The multifaceted reality of sin is reflected in the different ways Paul speaks of it. Sometimes he refers to sin as a quasi-personal force, which exercises dominion over the human race. This is the sense in which Paul often uses the word *hamartia*, "sin" (e.g., Rom 6:16, 20). In a similar vein, he writes that all humanity suffers under the weight of *sarx*, or "flesh," a term that often denotes the human person under the rule of sin (e.g., 7:25). Paul also recognizes sinful actions and often uses the term *parabasis*, "sins" or "transgressions" to refer to them (2:23; 4:15). Once he has appreciated humanity's sinful state and its sinful deeds, Paul proclaims God's saving intervention in Jesus. From the power of Christ's death and resurrection everyone can be freed from sin and no longer receive its wages of death (5:6-11, 15-21; 6:23). Through faith, repentance, and baptism the human race can stop living according to the flesh and embrace the spirit, which works from within to bring about a complete transformation from sin to grace. There is no need to remain a slave of sin when one can instead be a servant of God in Christ (Rom 5:1-5; 6:1-11, 22-23).[42]

---

[40] This passage is evidence that Paul acknowledged individual cases and the presence of good people among the Gentiles. See the discussion in this chapter, below.

[41] See Joseph A. Fitzmyer, "Pauline Theology," *NJBC*, 1403–6; also Victor Paul Furnish, *Theology and Ethics in Paul* (Nashville: Abingdon Press, 1968) 135–62.

[42] Concerning Paul's thought on the sinfulness of humanity without Christ, see Pietro Dacquino, "La vita morale e l'azione dello Spirito secondo S. Paolo," *Fondamenti biblici della teologia morale: Atti della XXII Settimana Biblica* (Brescia: Paideia, 1973) 358–65; Alessandro Sacchi, "La legge naturale nella Lettera ai Romani," *Fondamenti biblici*, 376–81; Fitzmyer, "Pauline Theology," 1402–7; Bauer, "Sin," 858–62; Schoonenberg, *Man and Sin*, 124–40; Schillebeeckx, *Christ*, 126–54; Schnackenburg, *Moral Teaching of the New Testament*, 261–9; Alois Stöger, "Flesh,"

The Church: Humanity Reconciled in Jesus Christ

The forgiveness of sin and reconciliation with God that humanity needs is available in the Church of Christ, which is the only alternative to a world dominated by sin. As a community of reconciliation, the Church reflects the economy of salvation as it unfolded from the very beginning. After bringing the Hebrews out of Egypt, God formed them into one people. Through Moses, God gave this people a Covenant, which both reflected and called for the communion with God and neighbor that God willed. Although Israel sinned through its failure to honor the Covenant's requirements of love, justice, and righteousness, the prophets proclaimed that God would yet form a holy people, one that would know God and walk in God's ways. Jesus and his disciples were decisively influenced by this vision of a renewed and holy people of God.

That Jesus intended to form such a community is evident from the New Testament. Early in his public ministry he gathered a small group of disciples, which is the prototype of the community united inwardly and outwardly through faith in Christ.[43] In their accounts of the Last Supper, the Gospels testify that Jesus wished to establish a new covenant in his blood, "which is poured out for many for the forgiveness of sins" (Matt 26:28; see also Heb 9:15).[44] The same concern for communion born of love and forgiveness prompted Jesus to send his remaining eleven apostles forth to continue his work. He commissioned them to make disciples of all nations and baptize them, and he promised to remain with his community of disciples until the end of time (Matt 28:19-20).

Apostolic Preaching and the Response of Faith

The sinfulness of all humanity, God's saving work in Christ, and Jesus' missionary commission supplied the content and motivation of the earliest apostolic preaching. Speaking to a Jewish audience (Acts 2:14-42), Peter reviewed important prophecies and proclaimed that they not only pointed ahead to Jesus Christ but foresaw his death, resurrection, and exaltation at God's right hand. Peter concluded: "Let all

---

EBT, 273–8; Deidun, *New Covenant Morality*, 94–6; Murphy-O'Connor, *Becoming Human Together*, 81–143. See also note 10 in this chapter, above.

[43] Pierre Grelot, "Relations Between the Old and New Testaments in Jesus Christ," *Problems and Perspectives in Fundamental Theology*, ed. Rene Latourelle and Gerald O'Collins, trans. Matthew J. O'Connell (New York and Ramsey, N.J.: Paulist Press, 1982) 196.

[44] Ibid., 190; Neyrey, *Christ Is Community*, 43–5, 91–4, 123–6, 135–7.

the house of Israel therefore know assuredly that God has made him both Lord and Christ, this Jesus whom you crucified" (2:36). Moved by Peter's words, his hearers asked what they needed to do. "And Peter said to them, 'Repent, and be baptized every one of you in the name of Jesus Christ for the forgiveness of your sins; and you shall receive the gift of the Holy Spirit.' . . . And he testified with many other words and exhorted them, saying, 'Save yourselves from this crooked generation'" (2:38-39, 40). This passage suggests that a positive response to the preached word involves faith in Jesus as Lord and Christ, sincere repentance of one's sins,[45] and acceptance of baptism.

Prompted by faith and repentance, baptism unites people to the death and resurrection of Christ. Through baptism a person dies to sin and is made "alive to God in Christ Jesus" (Rom 6:11). Drawing its strength from the living waters of Christ's death and resurrection, baptism brings Christians communion with God, and through it they receive the blessings of God's love, which "has been poured into our hearts through the Holy Spirit which has been given to us" (5:5). Such love brings the gifts of grace, holiness,[46] and the promise of eternal life with God in Christ (5:17-21). Christians are to treasure the precious gifts they have received from God and, with God's grace, keep them safe by a life lived in charity.[47]

Justification by Faith

It was by reflecting on the transformation that occurs in those who received the preached word that Paul developed his doctrine of justi-

---

[45] Schnackenburg, *Moral Teaching of the New Testament*, 25–42; Spicq, *Théologie morale*, 62–8; Kasper, *Jesus the Christ*, 81–2; Lacan, "Conversion and Kingdom," 97–118.

[46] Convinced that each Christian is holy, Paul does not hesitate to tell his readers that their bodies are temples, and hence they are to live accordingly. See 1 Cor 6:19-20; Raymond Corriveau, *The Liturgy of Life: A Study of the Ethical Thought of St. Paul in His Letters to the Early Christian Communities* (Brussels: Desclée de Brouwer, 1970) 62–8; Congar, *Mystery of the Temple*, 153–7.

[47] On baptism and its gifts of grace, see Schillebeeckx, *Christ*, 146–59; Spicq *Théologie morale*, 68–80; Kasper, *Jesus the Christ*, 156–9; Corriveau, *Liturgy of Life*, 167–9, 196–7, 215–6, 224–6; Jerome Murphy-O'Connor, "Sin and Community in the New Testament," *The Mystery of Sin and Forgiveness*, ed. Michael J. Taylor (Staten Island: Alba House, 1971) 57–62; Furnish, *Theology and Ethics in Paul*, 162–81; Rudolph Schnackenburg, *Baptism in the Thought of Saint Paul*, trans. G. R. Beasley-Murray (New York: Herder & Herder, 1964).

The New Testament also refers to the same unity between God and the person by speaking of the believer as being an adopted child of God or having a spiritual rebirth. See, for example, Gal 3:26; 4:5-7; John 3:3-8; and 1 John 2:29–3:1. Schillebeeckx, *Christ*, 468–71; Spicq, *Théologie morale*, 84–102.

fication through faith. At its core, the term "justification" refers to a judicial acquittal; it speaks of an authoritative judgment that a person is not guilty of an offense. Closely allied are such concepts as "just," "righteous," and "upright." When applied to the relationship between God and humanity, the discussion of justification proceeds from the presuppositions that God alone is innocent, just, and righteous, and that humans appear before God already guilty on account of their sins. If that is the case, then the basic question is whether guilty persons can ever be acquitted by a just God. If they can, there are further questions about how that acquittal occurs and its effects.[48]

Paul considered whether exact obedience to the Mosaic Law might justify the devout and observant Jew, as he had once assumed. He rejected that possibility because it would empty the cross of Christ of its power and license people to boast of their own accomplishments (Gal 2:16-21; 3:10-14; Rom 2:17; 3:27). Moreover, his observations concerning sinful humanity as well as Christian faith convinced Paul that no sinner can ever earn God's justification. However, God can give it as a free and undeserved gift (Rom 3:24, 5:15-17). That is possible because of the obedience of Jesus Christ, whose suffering, death, and resurrection has redeemed or expiated human sins (Rom 3:24; Gal 3:13). Therefore it is in Christ, and only in Christ, that sinful persons can be acquitted of their sins and become righteous in God's sight. They gain access to justification and its blessings through faith in Jesus Christ (Rom 3:22-26; 5:1), which is born of the preached word (10:14-17). When they are justified, persons become holy, reconciled, and at peace with God through the grace and favor of God offered through Christ (5:1-11). Justification requires a sincere and explicit confession of faith (10:9-13). It is to be the foundation of a full personal commitment and to be manifest in deeds of charity (Rom 6:1-23; 12:1-21; Gal 5:13-26).[49]

---

[48] Alister E. McGrath, *Iustitia Dei: A History of the Christian Doctrine of Justification* (Cambridge and New York: Cambridge University Press, 1986) 1:1-16; Fitzmyer, "Pauline Theology," 1397–8; Furnish, *Theology and Ethics in Paul,* 143–62.

[49] Fitzmyer, "Pauline Theology," 1397–402, 1407–10; Furnish, *Theology and Ethics in Paul,* 143–62; Henri Rondet, *The Grace of Christ: A Brief History of the Theology of Grace,* trans. Tad W. Guzie (Westminster, Md.: Newman Press, 1967) 43–7.

Since the Reformation there has been considerable controversy over whether justification through Christian faith merely confers the status of righteousness upon the sinner while leaving the sinful state unchanged or whether justification causes the sinner to become upright in fact. Contemporary scholars acknowledge the forensic or declarative texture of the language Paul uses but also affirm that his statements envision a real change in the sinner as a result of justification. See, for example, Fitzmyer, "Pauline Theology," 1398; Furnish, *Theology and Ethics in Paul,* 151–4.

Baptism and the Church

Baptism and justification are equally important for the Church community. Baptism requires the Church to be a community of grace and holiness[50] that sharply contrasts with a sinful world that does not know God and has not received God's gifts in Christ.[51] Several well-known metaphors emphasize the comprehensive holiness and unity of the Church. One is the body of Christ, an image St. Paul developed and used to illuminate relationships in the Church and its unity with Christ (1 Cor 12:12-27; Eph 4:15-16).[52] Another sees the Church as a temple, the place where God dwells and through which God is present to humanity (1 Cor 3:16-17; Eph 2:21-22). To apply this powerful image to the Church is to assert that God has made it the privileged locus of God's presence to the human family.[53] Other metaphors envision the Church as the bride of Christ (Eph 5:25-27, 32) and the household of God (2:19).

The holiness and communion of the Church require that there should be a personal equality of dignity and charity among the members that overcomes all ethnic, socioeconomic, political, or gender-based divisions. St. Paul eloquently affirmed this dimension of Church life:

> For as many of you as were baptized into Christ have put on Christ. There is neither Jew nor Greek, there is neither slave nor free, there is neither male nor female; for you are all one in Christ Jesus. And if you are Christ's, then you are Abraham's offspring, heirs according to promise (Gal 3:27-29; see also Jas 2:1-13).

Although it is not always easy to honor this requirement, it is essential to the Church's internal life and to corroborate its preaching of repentance and reconciliation in a world where such diversities have been the pretext for so much evil and alienation.

The Church and Sin

Christian life in the Church is therefore to be marked by the grace and peace that each member receives in baptism. Even so, Christians

---

[50] On holiness in the New Testament, see Spicq, *Théologie morale*, 199–209; Deidun, *New Covenant Morality*, 3–32; Schillebeeckx, *Christ*, 557–8.

[51] On this point see Spicq, *Théologie morale*, 80–4; Schillebeeckx, *Christ*, 195–217, 492–3; Jerome Murphy-O'Connor, "Sin and Community in the New Testament," *The Mystery of Sin and Forgiveness*, 57–62; especially idem, *Becoming Human Together.*

[52] See Fitzmyer, "Pauline Theology," 1409–10.

[53] See also Congar, *Mystery of the Temple*, 151–235; idem, *I Believe in the Holy Spirit*, 2:52-5; Corriveau, *Liturgy of Life*, 36–62.

continue to sin, and this creates serious difficulties for the Church as well as for sinful persons themselves. The New Testament is remarkably candid in reporting instances of sin in the early Christian community, which range from the ordinary difficulties that occur between neighbors to the extremely serious offenses that threaten the integrity of the Church itself (Matt 18:15-17, 21-22; Acts 5:1-11; 1 Cor 5:1–6:11). It shows that the Church's response reflected the nature and gravity of the particular challenges.

First of all, the Church used a variety of means to prevent sin from occurring. People were urged to avoid the occasions of sin (e.g., 1 Cor 5:9-11). They were enjoined to advise and exhort one another to walk in the path of righteousness (Heb 3:13-15; 2 Tim 4:1-2). Prayer and a life of charity toward one's neighbors would also serve as protections from sin (Matt 6:9-13; 1 Cor 13:4-13; 1 Thess 4:9-12; Jas 4:11). It was also necessary to be forbearing (Rom 15:1-3; Jas 5:7-11) and avoid whatever might disturb innocent consciences (Matt 18:6-10; Rom 14:13-23).

When such efforts did not succeed and sin appeared within the community, the Church dealt with it in a number of ways. One of the most important was to urge sinners to repent and seek forgiveness, which could be obtained through prayer (Matt 6:12), confession (1 John 1:9-10; Jas 5:16), and a readiness to forgive others (Matt 6:14-15; 18:21-35). More serious cases called for the offender to be addressed directly and privately. If that appeal did not result in repentance, witnesses were to verify the offense and the need for reconciliation. If necessary, the Church itself was to require the offender to correct the problem (Matt 18:15-17). When the sin was especially grave and the offender impenitent, he or she might be noted and then avoided by the community (Rom 16:17-18; 2 Thess 3:14). For the most serious offenses, the Church expelled the offender (Matt 18:17; 1 Cor 5:1-5, 13).[54]

Perhaps because it is so drastic, expulsion serves to highlight what was at issue in cases of grave sin. By confronting the offender with expulsion, the Church sought to jar that person into repentance, "that his spirit may be saved in the day of the Lord Jesus" (1 Cor 5:5). Acute sensitivity to the corporate nature and requirements of Church life seems also to account for this practice, which protected the holiness of the community and kept its witness free of contradiction. Ultimately, the expulsion of grave sinners from the Church emphasizes the New Testament's conviction that holy Church and sinful world are two mutually exclusively domains, each with its own ruler and expected patterns of behavior. Grave sin is a repudiation of the Christian's

---

[54] See also Adela Yarbro Collins, "The Function of 'Excommunication' in Paul," *HTR* 73 (1980) 251–63; Murphy-O'Connor, *Becoming Human Together,* 180–6.

baptismal commitment and a violation of the Church's holiness, and those who will not repent of such activity show that they are unwilling to pursue a life of charity lived in God's Holy Spirit. Their behavior demonstrates that they prefer to rejoin the world of *sarx*, humanity under the domain of sin, and to live under the influence of Satan.[55] Against that background, expulsion can be understood as an action that externalizes the alienation from God and neighbor that is already present in grave offenses, especially when no repentance has been shown. The practice of expelling serious and impenitent sinners emphasizes the urgency of faith and holiness both for the Church community and for the individual member.

The Moral Dimensions of Christian Life

The New Testament is primarily interested in Jesus Christ and depicts the earliest preaching of the gospel and the beginnings of the Church in the light of his word and work. Christ, the apostles' preaching, and the Church establish the horizon in which the New Testament assesses faith and faithlessness, communion with God and alienation from God, and critical human interactions. The overriding concern of the sacred writers with the foundation, dynamics, and essential elements of Christian faith also dominates their treatment of the moral life. The New Testament takes the moral life seriously because free and responsible persons respond to God's love and call and answer the primordial challenge of repentance and faith. Through their moral life persons also answer the requirements of membership in the Church.[56]

---

[55] The expression "deliver to Satan" is practically synonymous with expulsion from the Church. See 1 Cor 5:5; 1 Tim 1:20; 5:15.

[56] Because its purposes are professedly religious, the New Testament shows no interest in ethical theories or methods and offers neither a system of moral theology nor a comprehensive code of moral behavior. See, for example, Schrage, *Ethics of the New Testament,* 1–12; Schillebeeckx, *Christ,* 587; Raymond F. Collins, "Scripture and the Christian Ethic," *Christian Morality: Biblical Foundations* (Notre Dame, Ind.: University of Notre Dame Press, 1986) 32, 42; Kasper, *Jesus the Christ,* 67; Schnackenburg, *Moral Teaching of the New Testament,* 209.

Also useful are the brief treatments of New Testament morality, for example, William D. Davies, "The Moral Teaching of the Early Church," *The Use of the Old Testament in the New and Other Essays: Studies in Honor of William Franklin Stinespring,* ed. James M. Efird (Durham, N.C.: Duke University Press, 1972) 310–32; Francis X. Murphy, "The Background to a History of Patristic Moral Thought," *StMor* 1 (1962) 54–61; and Eric F. Osborn, *Ethical Patterns in Early Christian Thought* (Cambridge and New York: Cambridge University Press, 1976) 15–49.

These considerations invite attention to those aspects of the New Testament that can shed additional light on the context, content, and internal dynamics of the Christian moral life. This section will recognize that communion with God is its principal source, context, and motive. Communion with God and neighbor gives rise to liturgical activity, which has its own effects on the moral life of believers. Moreover, since Christians need to know the practical requirements of faith and communion, they necessarily undertake the task of discernment. Because it embodies communion with God and neighbor, the Church is the proximate source of motivation and insight for Christian living. Also significant are Jesus' own teachings and such pivotal passages as the Sermon on the Mount. Finally, this discussion will consider the place of contemporary ethical standards and the issue of "natural" morality.

Christian Life: Communion with God

Life in Christ is a reality long before it becomes an object of reflection or discussion. Christian life depends upon the gift of communion with God, which is received in faith through the outpouring of the Holy Spirit. Communion with God, the reality intended by the word "grace,"[57] is at once a gift and an imperative. Through faith and baptism the Christian believer receives communion with God, celebrates it in the Eucharist, and tries to live it ever more fully in the circumstances of daily life. However necessary theology may be in helping a person to understand and discuss the gift of God's life, it is not to be confused with that gift itself. This point is important lest theology displace the much more important reality about which it speaks. The essence of the matter is that Christians have been called to living community with God, and this communion is ever to be central in their minds, hearts, and lives.[58]

---

[57] On this point Schillebeeckx (*Christ*, 179, also 464) writes as follows:

> For Paul, grace is communion with God through the mediation of Jesus Christ in the power of the spirit; it is liberation for brotherly love and for 'whatever is honourable, whatever is just, whatever is pure, whatever is lovely, whatever is gracious, if there is any excellence, if there is anything worthy of praise' (Phil. 4.8). 'Being of the same mind, having the same love, being in full accord and of one mind' (Phil. 2.2), above all being freed for love (I Cor. 13. 1-13). The goal and the final end of this saving initiative of God's grace is the *salvation of man* as the *glorification of the Father* (Rom. 5.2; II Cor. 4.15). *Charis* (grace) requires *charis* (thanksgiving) (II Cor. 9.11): 'to the glory of God the Father' (Phil. 2.llb).

[58] Communion with God is to affect the entirety of a person's life. There is to be no compartmentalization of the human being, offering some aspects but not others

Liturgical Worship

God's grace and the communion it brings are to be received and cele-brated with gratitude. The Church does this especially in the course of liturgical worship. The liturgy makes present the grace of Christ, re-news the Church's communion with God, reminds everyone that grace and communion are God's free gifts, and calls the worshipers to live in accordance with them. Although other instances of public worship are not to be depreciated, special attention is due to the Eucharist, which finds its prototype in the Last Supper (Matt 26:26-29) and is explicitly mentioned elsewhere in the New Testament (1 Cor 11:17-34).

As it celebrates the Eucharist, the community hears the word of God, which recalls God's mighty deeds in human history and points to God's activity in the world. The eucharistic bread and cup manifest the love of Christ, who shed his blood so that all might have forgive-ness and reconciliation in the community of the new covenant (1 Cor 10:16). The Eucharist reminds the congregation of Jesus' command of love (John 15:12-17) and prompts it to carry the requirements of com-munion into daily life. If the community conducts its affairs in light of the Eucharist, its activities can themselves assume a cultic value. As they conduct their daily affairs believers can render to God the wor-ship of a self-sacrificing love (Rom 12:1-2).[59]

Because it celebrates Christian faith and seeks to support people in living it more fully, the liturgy can readily influence moral life. The liturgy seeks to evoke and deepen the personal act of faith and encour-ages worshipers to base their lives on Christ. By emphasizing the com-munity and its holiness, the liturgy reaffirms the bonds of charity toward God and neighbor that are to govern the daily lives of Chris-tians. Charity affects moral life also because it urges people to act in a self-sacrificial way and often illuminates the path they need to follow. Finally, because Christian life is intended to have the quality of wor-ship, the liturgy offers a model that can have a deep and pervasive in-fluence on the entirety of a person's moral life. In a word, the liturgy is meant to promote "faith working through love" (Gal 5:6).

---

to God. On this see Matt 22:36-39; Kasper, *Jesus the Christ*, 207; Schnackenburg, *Moral Teaching of the New Testament*, 268–77.

[59] The giving of praise and thanks to God is the final and most fitting response to God's grace and favor. On these points see Berger, "Grace," 411; Schillebeeckx, *Christ*, 60–1, 98–9, 492–3, 512; Corriveau, *Liturgy of Life*, 149–55, 204–12, 226–9; Kasper, *Jesus the Christ*, 158, 213–5; Schnackenburg, *Moral Teaching of the New Testament*, 226–34; Spicq, *Théologie morale*, 37–42, 143–5. Drawing from Pauline texts, Corriveau has emphasized that the moral life is to render fitting worship to God, the activity most fitting to the Church as temple of the Holy Spirit.

Discernment

Although the general imperative of charity is easily understood, its specific requirements can sometimes be uncertain or debatable. In such cases it is helpful to have some way to know the right and charitable course of action to follow. In this connection, the New Testament first considers the *nous*, or "mind" that belongs to each person by creation. The "mind" is the locus of a person's "basic moral attitude, sensitiveness, and perceptiveness."[60] Especially when transformed by the gift of the Holy Spirit, the mind begins to work with the understanding, insight, and wisdom of a friend of God. By the grace of communion with God and the experience of living it, the believer gains a certain capacity to distinguish what is of God from what is not. Sometimes misunderstood or caricatured, this ability to discern is recognized in the New Testament (Col 1:9; 1 Cor 2:10-16; 1 John 4:1-6) and will be understood by anyone who has lived consistently out of a deep relationship with another person or a community. Discernment, which is never to be separated from the ecclesial community, helps believers to identify the concrete steps that charity requires.[61]

The Church as Criterion for Discernment

The practical and social requirements of the Church's life help Christians to determine what actions will best serve the demands of charity. Each member of the Church is expected to accept responsibility for protecting and deepening the holiness, unity, and peace proper to the Church itself. Christians are therefore to refrain from all sexual vices.[62] They ought to forgive offenses and never scandalize vulnerable members of the community.

[60] Corriveau, *Liturgy of Life*, 182; see also Rom 7:25 and 12:2.

[61] See Gérard Therrien, *Le Discernement dans les Ecrits Pauliniens* (Paris: Gabalda, 1973); Murphy-O'Connor, *Becoming Human Together*, 229–35; Schillebeeckx, *Christ*, 473–5; Schnackenburg, *Moral Teaching of the New Testament*, 168–77, 209.

A closely related question is the New Testament's understanding of conscience. On this see Eugene J. Cooper, "Man's Basic Freedom and Freedom of Conscience in the Bible: Reflections on I Corinthians 8-10," *ITQ* 42 (1975) 272–83; Paul W. Gooch, "'Conscience' in 1 Corinthians 8 and 10," *NTS* 33 (1987) 244–54; C. A. Pierce, *Conscience in the New Testament* (London: SCM, 1955); C. Spicq, "La conscience dans le Nouveau Testament," *RB* 47 (1938) 50–80; J. Stepien, "'Syneidesis': La conscience dans l'anthropologie de Saint-Paul," *RHPR* 60 (1980) 1–20; William D. Davies, "Conscience," *IDB*, 1:671-6; Schnackenburg, *Moral Teaching of the New Testament*, 287–96.

[62] Although the New Testament mentions many vices, sexual sins receive emphasis, especially in the Pauline writings (e.g., Rom 1:18-32; 1 Cor 5:1-5; 6:13-20; 1 Thess 4:1-8). The importance of high standards of sexual behavior is clear in Paul,

Paul emphasized that the strong in the Church must care for and bear the infirmities of the weak in faith. One practical case concerned meat that had been sacrificed to pagan gods prior to being offered for sale in the public market. In itself, eating this meat created no dilemma for the Christian who understood that Jesus had made all foods clean. But it could indeed disturb the consciences of people who assumed that eating such food made them accomplices in idolatry. Paul's point is clear: "'All things are lawful for me,' but not all things are helpful" (1 Cor 6:12; 10:23). He concluded that it is wrong to act upon a sound principle when doing so would needlessly confuse and scandalize one's neighbor. It is far better to abstain from meat and protect a weaker neighbor's faith. In this case charity requires that the conscience of the weaker brother or sister and not the principle should govern one's conduct (1 Cor 8:1-13; 10:23-33; Rom 14:13–15:2).[63]

Charity also prompts Christians to extend the Church's peace and unity to those inside and outside the ecclesial community. Members of the Church need to reconcile and include everyone, beginning with the poor, rejected, and sinners. Christian love is not to be content with simply showing kindness to individuals, it needs to extend the blessings of the Church's life and forgiveness to all who are willing to accept them. This reflects the primordial task of evangelization, which the risen Lord entrusted to his disciples (Matt 28:18-20; John 20:21-23). Charity requires Christians to be hospitable to all and to teach, heal, call to repentance, and perform other services needed by the human family. These activities are to be carried out in a way that reflects the Church's communion with God and neighbor (e.g., Matt 18:5-7, 10-14; Acts 2:14–3:10; 2 Cor 8:1–9:15; Jas 2:1-26).[64]

---

whose insistence on this point reflects not only a sense of decency but a decidedly religious quality as well. For Paul "sexual immorality, as the manifestation of man's radical selfishness, is constantly opposed to the selflessness of love." Deidun, *New Covenant Morality*, 96; see 89–96.

[63] Robert C. Austgen, *Natural Motivation in the Pauline Letters* (Notre Dame, Ind.: University of Notre Dame Press, 1966) 96–101; Ogletree, *Use of the Bible*, 154–5; Furnish, *Theology and Ethics in Paul*, 227–37; Murphy-O'Connor, *Becoming Human Together*, 224–9.

[64] See Schillebeeckx, *Christ*, 593–6; Murphy-O'Connor, "Sin and Community," 75–8; Schnackenburg, *Moral Teaching of the New Testament*, 177–85, 217–25. Schnackenburg offers the helpful reminder that love does not primarily reflect human effort but the "inner transformation which comes to us from God by grace" (220). This suggests that Christian life is first of all God's gift, which leaves persons with a responsibility to live well the gift they have received. Deidun agrees, noting that "the Christian imperative derives its *vis obligandi* [obligatory quality] not from what man could or should be but from what *God* is and does" (*New Covenant Morality*, 60).

The Words of Jesus

The words of Jesus are another important source for Christian moral life. The Gospels often refer to Jesus as "teacher" (Matt 19:16; Mark 5:35; John 11:28) and indicate that he frequently taught both his disciples and the public at large (Matt 4:23; Mark 4:2; Luke 19:47; John 18:19). His teachings not only emphasized the necessity of self-sacrificing love for God and neighbor (Mark 12:28-34; Matt 5:44; John 12:25; 15:9-14) but also addressed such varied matters as taxes, food, marriage and divorce, and the nature of human life after the resurrection (Matt 19:3-12; Mark 7:14-19; 12:14-17, 24-27; Luke 11:37-41). Furthermore, one of the functions of the Holy Spirit is to remind the disciples of Jesus' teachings and help them understand the meaning of Christian faith for their lives (John 16:7-15; see also Luke 12:12). These considerations suggest that Jesus' teachings are normative for believers, who will need to interpret them in light of new situations as well as his sovereignty as Lord.

St. Paul's writings offer some insight into how Jesus' words can inform the moral and religious lives of later generations. Although Paul's personal judgment is that those who are single should not marry, he acknowledges that the Lord has given no command on the matter (1 Cor 7:25) and that one who is free to do so can marry without sin (7:36-40). But the Lord himself has established that married people should not divorce their spouses (7:10-11). Even so, Paul states on his own authority, not that of the Lord, that if a Christian's unbelieving spouse leaves the marriage, the believer is free to marry anew (7:12-15). The same concern for and deference to the word of the Lord is evident in Paul's discussion of behavior at the Eucharist, which he attributes to Jesus himself and his actions at the Last Supper (11:23-26). Finally, the fact that Pauline texts seem to echo sayings of Jesus in the Gospels likewise argues that the early Church knew his teachings and accepted them as standards for its own life and actions (cf. Luke 6:28 and Rom 12:14 or Mark 7:15, 19 and Rom 14:14).[65]

The Sermon on the Mount

Many people are inclined to view the Sermon on the Mount (Matt 5:1–7:29) as a manifesto of Christian morality. Scholars agree that this

---

[65] Schrage, *Ethics of the New Testament,* 207–11; Furnish, *Theology and Ethics in Paul,* 51–65; and Davies, "Moral Teaching of the Early Church," 324–9.

There remains a question about the degree to which Jesus' words contributed to the overall content of Christian morality. For a discussion of the issues see also Murphy-O'Connor, *Becoming Human Together,* 213–37; Deidun, *New Covenant Morality,* 171–5.

passage constitutes a major component of the Gospel according to Matthew and that its content is predominantly moral or ethical. However, they caution that if this text is important, its historical and literary background remains somewhat obscure, its interpretation sometimes difficult, and its practical claims subject to debate. These caveats are salutary, but they should not deter contemporary believers from trying to understand the moral and religious content of the Sermon on the Mount.

Before engaging particular elements of this passage, it is helpful to attend to the details that give context and form to the sermon and disclose its basic agenda. In a brief preamble, Matthew declares that Jesus "went about all Galilee, teaching in their synagogues and preaching the gospel of the kingdom and healing every disease and every infirmity among the people. So his fame spread throughout all Syria. . . . And great crowds followed him from Galilee and the Decapolis and Jerusalem and Judea and from beyond the Jordan" (4:23-25). These verses recall Jesus' commitment to preach God's kingdom and his personal authority in its regard; they likewise account for his large following among the Jewish people. Jesus then goes up on a mountain (5:1), which represents sacred space where God is encountered and God's will is made known. With the crowds gathered around and the disciples nearby, Jesus sits in the manner of a religious teacher and opens his mouth to teach them (5:1-2). At the conclusion of his sermon, Jesus insists that it is not enough for people merely to hear his words; they are also to do them, and thus bear good fruit (7:15-27). They face a momentous choice: either enter by the narrow gate that leads to life, or use the wide one that leads to destruction (7:13-14); either act with wisdom and be secure, or mimic the fool and lose everything (7:24-27).

The sermon itself opens with the nine Beatitudes (Matt 5:3-12). In these well-known verses Jesus comforts those who have patiently awaited God's kingdom, mourn the absence of God's justice, or yearn for the day when God's own righteousness will prevail; he upholds those who have shown God's mercy to others, consistently and wholeheartedly done what is good, and acted to bring God's own peace to the world. Jesus promises that God will bless and vindicate them at the Last Judgment and reward all who suffer persecution for their faith in Christ. The sayings on salt and light (5:13-16) point out that faithful disciples have a necessary service to offer to the rest of the human family. The main point of the sermon follows immediately: "Think not that I have come to abolish the law and the prophets; I have come not to abolish them but to fulfill them" (5:17); and "For I tell you, unless your righteousness exceeds that of the scribes and the Pharisees, you will never enter the kingdom of heaven" (5:20).[66]

The sermon then describes the better righteousness that Jesus requires of his disciples. It considers accepted ways of fulfilling the Mosaic Law on murder, adultery, divorce, oath-taking, retaliation, and the treatment of enemies (Matt 5:21-48). In each of these cases Jesus reinterprets the Law so as to bring out its radical meaning or its implications for personal motivation. He then turns to almsgiving, prayer, and fasting (6:1-18), which were traditional expressions of Jewish piety, and insists that such practices should be directed to God alone and remain untainted by a desire for applause. Finally, the Sermon on the Mount offers various pieces of moral instruction that have much in common with traditional Wisdom sayings (6:19–7:12); these are summed up in the Golden Rule: "So whatever you wish that men would do to you, do so to them; for this is the law and the prophets" (7:12).

The members of the Jewish-Christian community for whom Matthew originally wrote would have understood all these instructions in the light of the clues noted above. They would have grasped the allusions to God's giving the commandments on Sinai (Exod 19:18-25) and to the blessing and the curse that confronted Israel in the wake of the Covenant (Deut 28:1-68, 30:1-20). In their ears, Jesus' requirement of practical obedience would have echoed the solemn requirement that

---

[66] To speak of a "righteousness that exceeds that of the scribes and the Pharisees" is to suggest that theirs is an inferior righteousness. This adverse reference reflects Matthew's position in an ongoing dispute within the late-first-century Jewish community over the nature of authentic religious fidelity. This controversy was both shaped and forced into prominence by the Roman army's destruction of the Second Temple in A.D. 70. This traumatic event removed a primary component of Jewish life and made it necessary to reconsider its foundations. As their contribution to that effort, some rabbis and Pharisees held that the Law included oral traditions as well as written texts and that this larger whole was normative for Jewish life. Such a position multiplied obligations, opened the door to more numerous authoritative interpretations, and placed a high premium on exact obedience to all specific requirements. By contrast, Matthew insists that whoever wishes to fulfill the Mosaic Law needs only to hear and do the words of Jesus. Matthew's participation in that Jewish discussion underlines his allegiance to the Mosaic tradition and makes it easier to understand why he did not regard Christian faith as a rejection of the Law or the Jewish faith tradition. See Daniel J. Harrington, *The Gospel According to Matthew* (Collegeville: The Liturgical Press, 1983) 76, 82–4, 96–9, 104–6, 109–11; Hays, *Moral Vision of the New Testament*, 421–4; Martin, "Matthew on Christ and the Law," 58–61. For a Jewish scholar's discussion of this and related developments, see Lawrence H. Schiffman, *From Text to Tradition: A History of Second Temple and Rabbinic Judaism* (Hoboken, N.J.: Ktav Publishing House, 1991) 139–70, also 12–3.

Israel was to *do* God's commandments (e.g., Deut 28:1, 15, 58; 30:14). Taken together, such details present Jesus as an extraordinary teacher who reveals and interprets God's requirements for Israel. With God's authority, the same Jesus who proclaims the kingdom also upholds the Law and the Prophets but reinterprets them to exclude the distorting effects of later traditions and to bring out the religious and moral essence of an authentic response to God. Such a response requires fidelity even amid great evil, effective work on behalf of God's justice and peace, Christian witness in the world, and a wholehearted commitment that governs desires as well as words and deeds. Jesus promises his hearers in every age that whoever accepts his words and lives by them will enjoy God's blessing, both now and at the last judgment.[67]

Christian Moral Life and Accepted Moral Standards

Any examination of St. Paul's epistles soon uncovers passages that seem to establish standards of moral living and conduct. Obvious among them are the lists of virtues and vices (e.g., Rom 1:29-31; Gal 5:19-23; Col 3:12-14) and passages that give directions for family life and relationships in society (Col 3:18–4:1; Eph 5:21–6:9). This section will consider these interesting texts to see what they might disclose concerning the source of the moral standards they represent.

A careful comparison of Paul's lists of virtues and vices with contemporary secular sources reveals striking similarities. According to many scholars, Paul derived their content from Stoic and other first-century philosophies and used the format of contemporary Jewish catechesis. This conclusion is corroborated by the nature of the items

---

[67] This discussion is indebted to Harrington, *Gospel According to Matthew,* 75–111; Schrage, *Ethics of the New Testament,* 143–52; John P. Meier, *Matthew* (Wilmington: Michael Glazier, 1980) 35–76; Martin, "Matthew on Christ and the Law"; Benedict Viviano, "The Gospel According to Matthew," *NJBC,* 639–47. See also Raymond F. Collins, "Christian Personalism and the Sermon on the Mount," *Christian Morality,* 223–37; idem, "Christian Ethic," 24–27; Jan Lambrecht, *The Sermon on the Mount: Proclamation and Exhortation* (Wilmington: Michael Glazier, 1985); Herman Hendrickx, *The Sermon on the Mount* (London: Geoffrey Chapman, 1979) 10–36, 179–83; Schnackenburg, *Moral Teaching of the New Testament,* 73–89; Reginald D. Fuller, "The Decalogue in the New Testament," *Int* 43 (1989) 246–8.

Luke has a parallel passage, the Sermon on the Plain (6:17-49), which also includes a series of Beatitudes (6:20-23). For further examination, see Luke Timothy Johnson, *The Gospel of Luke* (Collegeville: The Liturgical Press, 1991) 105–16; Robert J. Karris, "The Gospel According to Luke," *NJBC,* 694–6; Eugene LaVerdiere, *Luke* (Wilmington: Michael Glazier, 1980) 93–8.

he includes in his lists of virtues and vices. Arrogance, deceit, drunkenness, murder, licentiousness, and greed, for example, are rejected by reasonable human beings, whether they are Christian or not. Peace, patience, kindness, and self-control are virtues for everyone. A similar picture emerges when one examines the Pauline "household codes," or directions for domestic relationships. These directives reflect the social and cultural situation that prevailed in Paul's lifetime. By proposing them to Christians, he is suggesting that they can serve the risen Lord by living well whatever relationships they happen to have. It is reasonable to conclude that Paul's moral catalogues reflect the moral standards upheld by the decent people of his day.[68]

Paul's adoption of contemporary moral norms did not exclude properly Christian ones, nor does it mean that Paul had stripped his teaching of properly Christian qualities. On the contrary, the virtues are emblematic of one living in the Spirit, and the vices characterize the sinful person who is still living according to the flesh. Moreover, Christ is the source of the love and grace that is to guide and energize Christian living in all its dimensions. In any specific society or time, the believer's entire moral life is to be the fruit of the Holy Spirit.[69]

Paul's acceptance of the relationships prevailing within the family and society of his day was conditional. A Christian was expected to conduct all relationships according to the great commandment of charity, a norm that limited the exercise of some legally or socially recognized rights. Furthermore, within the Church relationships were also to be governed according to the strict baptismal equality recognized in the Epistle to the Galatians (Gal 3:26-29). Even if Christian practices were influenced by what was then considered acceptable and proper, the demands of charity and communion in the Church constituted further and more demanding criteria of community relationships.[70]

---

[68] Furnish, *Theology and Ethics in Paul*, 25–67, 84–92; Abraham J. Malherbe, ed., *Moral Exhortation: A Greco-Roman Sourcebook* (Philadelphia: Westminster Press, 1986) 13–5; for some specific texts, see especially 91–3, 98–9, 110–1, 125–9, 132–4, 139–41, 152–7. For a discussion of the moral texture of contemporary Roman, Greek, and Jewish societies, see Wayne A. Meeks, *The Moral World of the First Christians* (Philadelphia: Westminster Press, 1986); see also Raymond Collins, "Christian Ethic," *Christian Morality*, 33–8, especially 34; Austgen, *Natural Motivation*, 109–30; Schillebeeckx, *Christ*, 586–90; Schnackenburg, *Moral Teaching of the New Testament*, 110–43; Murphy-O'Connor, *Becoming Human Together*, 135–9.

[69] Raymond Collins, "Christian Ethic," 43.

[70] Schillebeeckx, *Christ*, 561–7; see also Furnish, *Theology and Ethics in Paul*, 25–111; Austgen, *Natural Motivation*, 114–21. Paul's acceptance of prevailing familial and social customs suggests the need to distinguish between culture-specific norms and exhortations and those that have general application.

Christian Moral Life and Natural Morality

A final question to be considered is whether the Epistle to the Romans reflects a "natural" morality. In this letter Paul writes:

> When Gentiles who have not the law do by nature what the law requires, they are a law to themselves, even though they do not have the law. They show that what the law requires is written on their hearts, while their conscience also bears witness and their conflicting thoughts accuse or perhaps excuse them (Rom 2:14-15).

In this well-known passage Paul recognizes that Gentiles sometimes succeed in doing what is morally good and right. This demonstrates that they can know the imperatives of sound morality and live accordingly. It also suggests that "the nations" can know God and fulfill God's will. Paul therefore convicted all people of sin, the Jew for ignoring the requirements God set forth in the Mosaic Law and the Gentile for failing to adhere to God's will as it is reflected in creation and recognized in their minds and hearts.[71]

This conclusion is consistent with the perspective of Old Testament wisdom literature, as was noted in the previous chapter. It reflects an underlying conviction, shared by Jews and Jewish Christians generally, that the world is God's creation and that life within the created world is under God's providential care. This encouraged St. Paul to assume that through reflection on experiences in the world all peoples can arrive at a knowledge of God and develop an insight into God's will for their lives. This general outlook also supported Paul's judgments about the Gentiles, their behavior, and their moral guilt or innocence.[72]

REFLECTIONS

Jesus stood within the Jewish religious tradition that began with Moses and the patriarchs and continually developed throughout the remarkable history of the Hebrew people. He presupposed that a good

---

[71] Deidun, *New Covenant Morality*, 161–7; Austgen, *Natural Motivation*, 122; Sacchi, "Legge naturale," especially 376–81. For an older view of this topic, see Josef Fuchs, *Natural Law: A Theological Investigation*, trans. Helmut Reckter and John A. Dowling (New York: Sheed & Ward, 1965) 14–37.

[72] Schillebeeckx, *Christ*, 515–30; see also Davies, "Moral Teaching of the Early Church," 329–30. It should be clear from this discussion that the term "nature" in the Epistle to the Romans does not reflect any developed philosophical argument on Paul's part and should not be interpreted in light of modern philosophical or scientific understandings of that term.

and powerful God acts within human history to confront sinners, combat the evils that afflict devout and innocent people, and call the human race to live in justice and righteousness with God and neighbor. He interpreted his life and conducted his ministry in the light of prophecies that promised that God would act definitively to reconcile the world and thus bring God's purposes to their fulfillment. These points are integral to the life and work of Jesus; they are taken for granted in the New Testament and have been assumed into Christian faith. These considerations urge Christians to appreciate the transcendent dimensions of their faith and its roots in the experiences, reflections, and faith of the Jewish people. They also emphasize the importance of human affairs and the need to evaluate them in light of God and God's deeds.

Against the background of the Hebrew religious tradition, the New Testament focuses upon the person and ministry of Jesus of Nazareth. It highlights his proclamation of the kingdom, his life-giving words, and his saving deeds. It proclaims him as the Messiah through whom God reconciles sinful humanity, the holy one whom God raised from the dead and made Lord of all. The New Testament is especially concerned that, helped by divine grace, people should receive Jesus as God's presence on earth and respond to him with repentance and faith. This response transforms persons and communities; it entails hearing and doing his word with a generous heart, acting with compassion toward one's neighbors, and contributing to the peace and unity of the Church. Such a response reflects the characteristic foundations, dynamics, and content of Christian moral life.

The New Testament describes the activity of Jesus' apostles, who continue his work with the power of the Holy Spirit. As the principal witnesses to his death and resurrection, theirs is the task of preaching the word and calling others to repentance, faith, and baptism into the Church, the community of Jesus' disciples and friends. Because these points are essential to Christian faith and moral life, they need to be faithfully handed on and made accessible to people of all times and nations. The life, death, and resurrection of Jesus Christ are always to be proclaimed. The word of God needs to be read, preached, heard, and lived by Christian believers in every generation. So long as evil, injustice, alienation, and disbelief continue, a faithful Church will need to bear witness to God's love and call people to share it through repentance and faith. These requirements flow from Christian faith and constitute moral imperatives for the disciples of Jesus.

Without depreciating the content of Christian faith or its importance, these considerations draw attention to faith as a foundational virtue in Christian life. Faith prompts people to recognize God's activity in human life; to know that this activity requires a personal response on their part; and to follow up with repentance, profession of faith, and a life of charity in the Church. Placing due emphasis upon the virtue of faith honors the witness of Sacred Scripture and highlights a pivotal aspect of moral life. At the same time, it makes it easier to see the close bonds that unite faith and moral life. In fact, to consider Christian moral life apart from its basis in faith is to truncate the subject and risk losing sight of its source in God's gift of communion through Jesus Christ and his word and the effects of repentance and ecclesial charity. If it remains a vital expression of Christian faith, the moral life of a believer will retain its integrity; be lived in joy, gratitude, and self-sacrifice; and constitute a fitting response to a good and gracious God.

The Church always needs to acknowledge God's gift of communion. The liturgical life of the Church is a principal means for the community to be reminded of this gift and to be summoned to repentance, thanksgiving, and praise of God. At the same time, worship offers a model for the community's moral life. The liturgy can help the congregation to see how God's actions have affected it and prompt it to respond gratefully, both at worship and in daily life. These considerations suggest that the liturgy is a significant moment in the Church's life. Efforts to assure that the liturgy fulfills its purposes are important from the perspectives of Christian faith and moral life. Practically speaking, the liturgy is intended to allow a congregation to know and celebrate God's gifts, call it to deeper faith, and help it to name and live more fully the implications of its faith. The homily can point out specific aspects of the relationship between moral life and faith and particularly underline how the moral life of the faithful might reflect the dynamics of worship.

The New Testament affirms that God intends to reconcile the human family to God through the Church, the community of the new covenant in the blood of Christ. The Church is integral to Christian faith and life. Its peace and unity are essential to it and are required by Christ's mandate, the baptismal commitment of Christians, and their eucharistic celebrations. Ecclesial charity also lends a needed credibility to the witness of evangelists and missionaries. It is no surprise that the New Testament judges serious violations of the Church's peace and unity to be scandalous, sinful, and deserving of prompt and effective remedial action. It is therefore necessary to emphasize the peace and unity of the Church. These gifts enhance efforts to prepare catechumens and children. They underline the essentially communitarian nature of Christian liturgy and illuminate its links with the economy of salvation and the Church itself. They encourage all to recognize the social dimensions of the Church, contribute to its peace and unity, and use ecclesial communion as a key criterion of discernment and action.

The writings of St. Paul manifest a respect for the standards of conduct prevailing among the good and decent people of his day. He was convinced that even without faith people can arrive at sound moral insights. He held people personally responsible for acting in accordance with their consciences. Although the brief passages on these points do not constitute a sustained or systematic treatment, they reflect Paul's assumption that the world and human experiences can be useful sources of insight when assessing the moral quality of particular actions. Although the New Testament is principally interested in the drama of God's encounter with the human family, it reflects a certain confidence that, despite their alienation and sin, people can know God and the right way to live. The New Testament follows the Old in accepting these more secular sources as congruent with faith and able to provide criteria for the behavior of the faith community. Although this approach is not developed, it serves as a scriptural precedent for later believers who would also look to the created universe and human experience when seeking insight into the moral quality of behavior.

To remain faithful to Christ in all seasons; to practice self-sacrificial charity without thought of notice or reward; to respond with wisdom and fidelity in difficult times and circumstances; and to hand on the words, witness, and realities of authentic Christian faith are daunting challenges. Although that is the Church's mandate, the historical record is mixed. Sometimes Christians have acted in a noble and edifying manner, but at other times their behavior has been indifferent or scandalous. Christian history embraces the surprising as well as the expected. At all times, it reflects the reciprocal relationship between faith and moral life and between the Church and the world in which it lives. In the process, Church faith, thought, and praxis have profoundly affected the politics, culture, and thinking of the wider society, especially in the West. It is time to explore these fascinating aspects of faith and life.

3

Faith, Repentance, and Accommodation

In the centuries immediately following the New Testament era Christian communities continued to pray, serve, and evangelize. At the same time, they had to address serious internal divisions and deal with the hostility of Graeco-Roman society. By the end of the fourth century, however, the Church had resolved important points of doctrine and practice, developed its institutional structure, and embraced major aspects of Roman culture and thought. These were momentous and far-reaching accomplishments, but they precipitated a serious problem, for as the Church became much larger and accepted its world more fully, it became increasingly difficult to maintain elevated standards of Christian faith, religious observance, and moral practice. These challenges and the underlying rapprochement between Church and society did much to set the agenda of fourth-century Christians and shape the environment in which they lived. What is even more important, these developments helped to form the thought and practice, attitudes and institutions of the Western Christianity that was already aborning.

This chapter will review the major developments of the early Christian centuries, especially as they pertain to the development of Christian life and worship or contributed to the mutual embrace of Graeco-Roman society and the Catholic Church. It will consider the relationships among Christian faith, moral life, and the wider society as they begin to emerge at this time and will note some of their implications. To accomplish these purposes, this chapter will follow a generally chronological approach to the material.

The first section will examine events that took place between the close of the New Testament period and the last decades of the second century. During this century small Christian communities recognized

93

that membership in the Church required sincere repentance and faith but were only beginning to work out the specifics. As nonconforming members of the wider society, Christians were vulnerable to persecution by the Roman state, and this both affected the course of internal developments and encouraged defensive responses.

The next period runs from the late second century up to Emperor Constantine's Decree of Toleration in A.D. 313. These decades witnessed a number of persecutions but also saw a dramatic expansion and adaptation by the Church in the Roman Empire. These developments directly influenced policies and practices that sought to maintain the quality of Christian life.

The following section considers the balance of the fourth century exclusive of St. Augustine of Hippo (354–430). Together with a general public acceptance, toleration and the subsequent legal establishment of Christianity supported a very rapid growth in the size of the Church and a more comprehensive embrace of Graeco-Roman society and culture. This has had profound and lasting effects on the Church's self-awareness, attitude toward society, norms of membership, institutional development, and pastoral agenda.

Faith and Repentance in a Hostile World

In the years immediately following the New Testament period, the Church was composed of small communities, most of which were located in the large cities of the Roman Empire. The agenda that faced these churches was a basic one: sort out organizational and authority-related questions, deal with verbal attacks and violent persecutions whenever they intruded, and meet the perennial requirements of faith, prayer, and charity. Although some of the contemporary Christian literature has disappeared, surviving documents and historical studies make it possible to understand many aspects of life in that early period.

This section will review the early Church's life and actions in order to see how it related faith and moral life and assessed the impact of grave sin on one's standing in the Church. It will show that, beneath disagreements about policies and practices, there was a firm consensus that faith requires the abandonment of one's sins, establishes a necessary basis for human life, and involves moral imperatives that are essential to one's communion with God and the Church.

Historical Background

The New Testament records the spread of Christianity from its origins in Palestine to Syria, Asia Minor, Greece, and Rome. From these points the Church was soon established in Italy, Gaul, Egypt, and along the northern coast of Africa. By the end of the second century the small Christian Church had begun to expand throughout the Roman Empire, a process that would continue in later centuries.

This expansion introduced Christianity into a society in which pagan rites were taken for granted and normally viewed as evidence of civic loyalty and patriotic devotion. From the perspective of the average Roman, Christians could easily be disparaged as religious eccentrics, people whose beliefs and practices failed to honor either Rome's gods or those of an ancient ethnic religion. Especially when Christians were accused of grossly immoral behavior, their position became extremely precarious. A nonconforming minority, they were vulnerable to condemnation as an irreligious, scandalous, and even seditious element in society.

This was the background to the persecutions that sporadically erupted in those early centuries. Their reasons varied, from the scapegoating that seems to explain Nero's persecution of A.D. 64 to Dalmatian's demand for divine honors in the last decades of the first century. Whatever their pretext, those early persecutions seem to have established the precedent that Christians could be arrested, punished, and even executed, especially when they were resolute in their faith. In practice, however, persecutions were the exception rather than the rule. Those that did take place, for example the one in the year 177 around Lyons, were generally local in nature and reflected the hostility of local authorities.[1] For the most part the Church was left undisturbed, since its members lived peaceably and no one could prove accusations of gross immorality. This is the reason persecutions did not stop Christianity from spreading throughout the Roman Empire and beyond. On the contrary, they contributed to its growth by publicizing the Church's faith and strengthening its internal cohesion. The Christian Church continued to expand throughout the second century and began to embrace members of the upper classes of Roman society.[2]

The Apologists

Once the Christian community began to stand out from its neighbors in the larger Roman society, it became more vulnerable to attack.

---

[1] Henry Chadwick, *The Early Church* (London: Penguin Books, 1967) 23–31. This discussion of historical background is indebted to Chadwick and to Stuart G. Hall, *Doctrine and Practice in the Early Church* (Grand Rapids: Eerdmans, 1991) 1–13.

[2] The motives prompting people to ask for membership in the Church are interesting to review. See Chadwick, *Early Church,* 54–60; Hall, *Doctrine and Practice,* 14–5. For a more comprehensive discussion of the topic, see Gustave Bardy, *La conversion au christianisme durant les premiers siècles* (Paris: Aubier, 1949) 117–293.

General suspicion, the need for scapegoats, and hostilities born of cultural and religious diversity made false charges and crude distortions seem believable to the public. This atmosphere and the dangerous precedent set by earlier persecutions demanded a response from Christian writers. They needed to defend the Christian Church from dangerous calumnies and publicize what its members really believed and did. Those who took up this challenge have become known as the apologists. The apologists are important also because they successfully persuaded many of their neighbors to abandon paganism and seek membership in the Church.

Justin Martyr was one of the many apologists who were active in the second century. He was a prominent figure and his writings are a good example of apologetic literature. Justin wrote two apologies, one addressed to the Roman emperor, the other to the Roman senate.[3] The *First Apology* begins by reminding the reader that it is the Roman practice to condemn a defendant only on the basis of that person's behavior. Simply bearing the name of Christian is not worthy of punishment; neither is it just to condemn all Christians for the crimes of a few. He then considers many of the substantive issues. Christians have been charged with atheism because they reject idols and act irreverently toward the local gods. In fact, Justin responds, the demons are behind such worship and Christians rightly reject it. But they do worship the true God and serve their God through a life of virtue. This is what the Christian God requires; it is far more excellent than the vices and wickedness associated with pagan life (chs. 5–16).

Justin sounds other themes that are common in apologetic writings. He reminds the emperor that Christians are good citizens, and in obedience to the Lord they willingly pay Caesar his taxes (ch. 17). Moreover, the teachings of Christ have echoes in the philosophers, and elements of Christian belief have parallels in pagan myths (chs. 20–3, 59–60). Christianity is therefore much more harmonious with Roman traditions and philosophy than they suspected. He ridicules the inconsistencies of pagan rituals and indicts the immorality often associated with them (ch. 24). In the course of his apology he provides a lengthy exposition of the economy of salvation, the fulfillment of

---

[3] Justin was born in Palestine of Greek parents, studied philosophy at Ephesus, and after becoming Christian, worked as a teacher in Rome. His two apologies date from about 151 and the early 160s respectively. In addition, around the year 160 Justin wrote another work, *Dialogue with Trypho*. This is the oldest extant example of an apology written to establish the truth of Christianity before a Jewish audience. See Cyril C. Richardson, trans. and ed., *Library of Christian Classics* (Philadelphia: Westminster Press, 1953) 1:228-31; Johannes Quasten, *Patrology* (Westminster, Md.: Newman Press, 1962) 1:196-204.

prophecies, and Christian teachings in general, including baptism, the Eucharist, and the practical aspects of Sunday worship (chs. 15, 31–40, 61, 65–7). Finally, Justin emphasizes the moral virtues of Christians: they do not abandon their infants or engage in odious sexual practices; rather they are patient, truthful, chaste, and ready to share their goods with the poor (chs. 16, 27, 29, 67).

The demands of its defense engaged the Church with society at large, especially its culture and philosophy. Positively, this required the apologists to account for the Church's faith, rituals, and morality in a way that was understandable to their Graeco-Roman audience. They showed that Christian faith was reasonable, its rituals noble, its morality admirable. At the same time, they pilloried pagan practices and exaggerations as stupid and quite unworthy of the cultured citizen of Rome. In making these statements, the apologists did more than defend the Church and uphold its faith and morality. They were building bridges between the Christian community and the Graeco-Roman philosophical and cultural world. These bridges, which later writers would widen and reinforce, proved to be of great importance in the later history of Roman society and Christian Church alike.[4]

Baptismal Preparation

This discussion has noted that the apologists tried to convince their neighbors to become Christians. That appeal shows that despite adverse circumstances, the early Church took its missionary task seriously and carried it out conscientiously. The success of such efforts required the Church to receive and prepare those who responded to the call to repentance and faith. Fortunately, the extant texts reveal what early Christian communities asked of those who sought to be baptized. The instruction given to people preparing for baptism discloses how the Church associated moral life with Christian faith.

One of the earliest documents is a Syrian text, the *Didache,* also known as the *Teaching of the Twelve Apostles.* Based upon the law of charity, the Ten Commandments, and the Golden Rule, its opening paragraphs are a baptismal instruction in the form of an either-or choice confronting the prospective Christian.

> Two Ways there are, one of Life and one of Death, and there is a great difference between the Two Ways. Now, the Way of Life is this: first, love

---

[4] On the early apologists in general and Justin Martyr in particular, see Francis X. Murphy, "The Background to a History of Patristic Moral Thought," *StMor* 1 (1962) 76–7; Hall, *Doctrine and Practice,* 48–56; Quasten, *Patrology,* 1:196-219.

the God who made you; secondly, your neighbor as yourself: do not do to another what you do not wish to be done to yourself (1:1-2).[5]

The instruction continues by specifying the actions that characterize the Way of Life, most of them drawn from the New Testament. Then the Way of Death is depicted, which names the vices that the Christian is to avoid.[6]

Another important text, *The Shepherd of Hermas,* originated in early second-century Rome. It too follows a two-way approach to moral catechesis and exhortation. In addition, *Hermas* presents the practical observance of right moral conduct as the way to achieve authentic knowledge. It sets forth an elevated ethic and indicates that while all should observe the Ten Commandments, those who exceed this basic norm will win even greater favor from God. Though *Hermas* was not explicitly concerned with prebaptismal preparation, his text presupposes that baptism requires a sincere repentance of one's sins and seals the new Christian for a life of virtue to be practiced wholeheartedly.[7]

These and other sources show that moral catechesis was very simple and usually built around certain common themes. One was the notion that in the human heart there are two opposite tendencies, or two opposing spirits. The hearer is urged to act upon the spirit that leads to life. Another was the exhortation to simplicity of heart; single-minded and wholehearted commitment was required of the true Christian. A third emphasis one finds in the early writers is an exhortation that Christians should pursue true wisdom. These themes were often

---

[5] This translation is from Johannes Quasten and Joseph C. Plumpe, eds., *Ancient Christian Writers: The Works of the Fathers in Translation,* 6 (New York: Newman Press, 1948). Unless otherwise noted, translations of patristic texts are from this series.

Although there are many exceptions, patristic writings are often divided into books, chapters, and verses or paragraphs. Since there is no standard format for citing texts, this study will use roman numerals to denote the book, and arabic numerals to indicate smaller units in a particular work. A colon will be used as needed to add a further level of specificity. Accordingly, a reference to I, 4:6 points to material in book 1, chapter or paragraph 4, verse 6 of the cited text.

[6] For further discussion, see Francis X. Murphy, *Moral Teaching in the Primitive Church* (Glen Rock, N.J.: Paulist Press, 1968) 18; idem, "Patristic Moral Thought," 62–3; Jan L. Womer, ed. and trans., *Morality and Ethics in Early Christianity* (Philadelphia: Fortress Press, 1987) 12–3.

The dating of the *Didache* is somewhat uncertain; Murphy places it around the year 90 while Womer agrees with Quasten (*Patrology,* 1:37) in dating this text sometime during the first half of the second century.

[7] For a discussion of the dating, authorship, and social background of *The Shepherd of Hermas,* see James S. Jeffers, *Conflict at Rome: Social Order and Hierarchy in Early Christianity* (Minneapolis: Fortress Press, 1992) 106–20.

sounded by non-Christian philosophers and preachers and were especially favored by the rabbis from whom the early Christian moralists
often took their cue.[8]

Church Life and the Need for Unity

The documents surviving from this period offer insight into the
human situation in early Church communities. The Christians of Rome,
for example, were mostly freeborn citizens, former slaves, members of
the urban poor, or people who were still slaves. Some of them were
well acquainted with the senatorial and equestrian classes at the top of
the social pyramid and tended to adopt their values and habits. Others
lacked the ordinary necessities of life and relied more immediately
upon the goodness and charity of their coreligionists. Besides being
socially and economically diverse, the Church community of Rome
represented a wide spectrum of moral and religious commitment. By
one account, the Roman Church in the background of *The Shepherd of
Hermas*

> is a fairly populous assembly, containing a segment of the rich, as well
> as numerous poor. Among both classes are many who have relapsed
> into pagan ways, become blasphemers, heretics, propagandists of a false
> *gnosis*. *Hermas* thus portrays hypocrites, ambitious clergymen, dishonest
> deacons, along with hospitable bishops, honest priests, martyrs and the
> innocent.[9]

This very human picture and basic Christian imperatives help to account for the emphasis on unity and charity that one finds in contemporary Church writings. Political motives also required unity and peace
among Christians. Because Christianity did not enjoy legal recognition
or protection, it was necessary that all members of the Church live in
an orderly, peaceable way and create no difficulties. That would encourage the authorities to ignore them. But if Christians caused problems or became a source of concern in the wider society, they risked
provoking a very adverse response from civic officials. Church leaders

[8] Murphy, *Moral Teaching*, 15–7, also 8–9; idem, "Patristic Moral Thought," 72–5.
The theme of the two ways can be traced back to Deut 11:26-28 and 30:19.
Simplicity of heart and wisdom are also celebrated in the Scriptures. For a discus-
sion of the background of some of these patristic themes, see Kenneth E. Kirk, *The
Vision of God: The Christian Doctrine of the Summum Bonum*, abr. ed. (Harrisburg, Pa.
and Wilton, Conn.: Morehouse Publishing, 1991) 53–61.

[9] Murphy, "Patristic Moral Thought," 71. See also Jeffers, *Conflict at Rome*, 97–105,
115–9, 166–87. Murphy dates *Hermas* in the third decade of the second century;
Jeffers holds that "part or all of the *Shepherd* dates to the late first century" (p. 112).

had practical as well as religious reasons to appeal for unity in their community.

The Letter of Clement of Rome, written at the end of the first century, addresses the church at Corinth. Under the pressure of persecution schism had divided that Christian community. Clement decries the jealousy, envy, and arrogance that seemed to be responsible for the turmoil. He emphasizes the need for unity in the Church and urges all to be submissive to those in charge and content with their proper place in the community. He reminds his readers that God offers mercy to those who humbly repent, shun all vices, and return to the way of peace. God's commandments should be their guide and the blood of Christ their inspiration.[10]

Ignatius of Antioch is another early writer who considered Church unity to be essential. Around the year 110 he wrote a series of epistles to the churches of Asia Minor; in them he responds to schism and speaks of what Christian life requires. The Church is to be united around one bishop, one Eucharist, and one Christ. All are expected to respect the bishop and through him be linked to the apostolic tradition and protected from heretical ideas. From the Eucharist, celebrated always under the bishop's authority, charity is nourished. Charity is the bond that unites the churches among themselves and prompts Christians to care for prisoners, widows and orphans, the hungry, and others in need.

Ignatius urges the imitation of Christ and self-giving as basic to Christian life. Significantly, he does not employ material from the Old Testament. His readers were not Jewish converts and would not have understood those scriptural references. His writings constitute a milestone because they mark the first attempt to express the Christian gospel in a manner calculated to allow people of the Hellenic world to understand it more readily.[11]

Gnosticism

Irenaeus of Lyons provides a very different perspective on Church life in the second century. His concerns were predominantly doctrinal and have particular relevance to the religious, ecclesial, and moral dimensions of Christian life. Writing shortly after the persecution of 177, Irenaeus responded to certain groups who claimed to be Christians but who asserted that they had received unique religious and spiritual

[10] For further discussion see Murphy, *Moral Teaching,* 18–9; idem, "Patristic Moral Thought," 65–7; Jeffers, *Conflict at Rome,* 90–7.

[11] Murphy, "Patristic Moral Thought," 67–9; Willy Rordorf and others, *The Eucharist of the Early Christians* (New York: Pueblo, 1978) 48–70.

knowledge from Christ. Although these people belonged to various sects, they are generally referred to as Gnostics, from the Greek word *gnosis,* which means "knowledge" or "understanding." In essence, they asserted that they alone possessed the spiritual knowledge that revealed the truth about the universe, set forth a norm for life, and brought God's salvation.

Non-Christian in its origins, Gnosticism was a very complex phenomenon with many different expressions and permutations. Although it affected Jews and pagans as well, Gnosticism was a recurring and sometimes serious problem for the Church during its first centuries. On the religious level, Gnosticism presumed that knowledge brings salvation; what one knows and not how one lives is ultimately decisive. Philosophically, Gnosticism was dualistic. It held that all of reality is divided into two realms: light and the spiritual as opposed to darkness and the material. The former is good and has its source in the divine, while the latter is evil and results from the work of demons. All things, or at least the elements of things, belong to one realm or the other.

When introduced into a Christian context, Gnosticism had serious consequences. Presupposing that matter is evil and illusory, Gnosticism declared that material beings must come from a material source, which has to be inferior to a purely spiritual supreme divinity. On this basis it denied that the Creator worshiped by both Jews and Christians can be truly divine. Its dualistic teachings and its negative judgment of corporeal reality likewise prove to be incompatible with fundamental points of Christian faith. Gnostic teachings imply that the Christ has to be a purely spiritual being and therefore cannot be identified with the earthly Jesus. Furthermore, because it was material, Jesus' body was evil and could not contribute to human salvation. For these reasons, Gnosticism rejected the incarnation of Jesus Christ and the unity of his person as well as his saving death and resurrection. Besides undermining basic Christian teachings, Gnosticism depreciated their scriptural and apostolic sources by declaring that they have been rendered obsolete by a special revelation that Gnostics claimed to have received. These were the serious problems that prompted Irenaeus to write his lengthy *Adversus haereses* (Against Heresies).[12]

---

[12] For an introduction to Gnosticism, see Giovanni Filoramo, *A History of Gnosticism,* trans. Anthony Alcock (Oxford; Cambridge, Mass.: Basil Blackwell, 1990); Kurt Rudolph, *Gnosis: The Nature and History of Gnosticism,* trans. and ed. R. McL. Wilson (San Francisco: Harper & Row, 1984); Pheme Perkins, *The Gnostic Dialogue: The Early Church and the Crisis of Gnosticism* (New York: Paulist Press, 1980). See also Hall, *Doctrine and Practice,* 36–45; Pelikan, 1:81-97.

In this work Irenaeus replies to various Gnostic leaders and defends Christian faith against their attacks. He affirms that God is an undivided supreme being who had indeed created the material universe (*AdvHaer*, II, 1–2; 9). Jesus Christ took on the same flesh that human beings have and later died and rose in a bodily manner (V, 14). He insisted that Christ gave his true teaching to his apostles who remained faithful to it. They passed Jesus' teaching to their successors who in turn did likewise. Writing about a century after the age of the apostles, Irenaeus could name the succession of bishops in major cities of the empire (III, 1–4; 13–4). This was the unbroken chain that bound contemporary believers to Jesus and his teachings. Therefore, if anyone sought authentic spiritual knowledge, they could obtain it from the bishops of the Catholic Church. The tradition the bishops have preserved constituted the norm of true knowledge in the Christian community, and none other was possible or necessary. As a corollary, Irenaeus held that a devout Christian should interpret the Scriptures only in harmony with the bishops of the Church, since this alone assured a correct understanding of them (IV, 26; 32; 33).[13]

In his response, Irenaeus did much more than refute Gnostic teachings. He established a standard by which right teaching could be identified in the Church, an issue whose importance went far beyond his own circumstances. In effect, Irenaeus argued that the norm of Christian belief was public, written, and institutional and not purely private, oral, or spiritual in nature. It is founded upon a fixed group common to the entire Church, the apostles commissioned by Christ. It appeals to a body of sacred writings that the universal Church recognized as normative. It is reflected in the consensus of local churches, especially those with an apostolic foundation.

Whatever might be the difficulties surrounding a specific point of belief, Irenaeus insisted that the Christian community had public and common criteria by which to resolve them. Once accepted, these criteria rendered suspect and perhaps illegitimate any voice that relied upon private sources in setting down requirements for others in the Church. The apostolic tradition as norm of faith therefore tended

---

The implications of Gnosticism for moral life are not easy to ascertain. It may be that this movement encouraged both an extreme asceticism and licentiousness, as has often been charged. However, Gnostic texts do not call for a libertine way of life; they urge followers to exercise self-control and act in accord with reason. See Filoramo, *History of Gnosticism*, 185–9.

[13] On Irenaeus, see Hall, *Doctrine and Practice*, 57–66; Rudolph, *Gnosis*, 11–2; Pheme Perkins, *Gnosticism and the New Testament* (Minneapolis: Fortress Press, 1993) 179–81.

to protect the community from the idiosyncrasies—be they doctrinal errors, moral aberrations, or devotional exaggerations—of any individual or group. Most of all, Irenaeus reminded everyone that they constituted one Christian community, with one faith, authenticated by a common tradition that came ultimately from one apostolic source.[14]

Sin and Reconciliation in the Christian Community

Since the early Church placed such a high premium upon unity and the practice of virtue, it gave special attention to those who failed to live up to the demands of Christian life. Though the references are few, the texts do show how Church leaders responded to offenses in the community. It has already been noted that Clement of Rome called upon the dissidents in Corinth to abandon their sins and turn in humility to a God who would certainly show them mercy. Clement presented repentance as the first step toward postbaptismal forgiveness. Repentance includes a sincere inner sorrow, suitable penances, and readiness to live the Christian virtues (*EpCor*, 7–9).[15]

The *Didache* has little to say about repentance but focuses instead on almsgiving, which seems to have been regarded as a privileged way for Christians to win forgiveness of their sins. Quoting the Gospel verse, "Give to anyone that asks you, and demand no return" (1:5, citing Luke 6:30), the *Didache* adds its own comment: "Happy the giver who complies with the commandment, for he goes unpunished" (1:5). The same point is repeated later in the text: "If you have means at your disposal, pay a ransom for your sins" (4:6).[16]

By far the most important early source concerning repentance is *The Shepherd of Hermas*. It addressed the fact that members of the Church sometimes sinned gravely even though grave sin is incompatible with

---

[14] The need to refute heretical doctrines on the basis of common, public, and legitimate criteria expedited the Church's identification of the documents that were inspired by God and entitled to a place in the canon of Scripture. While some texts were immediately accepted as inspired, it took the universal Church some centuries to reach consensus on the twenty-seven books that make up the New Testament. On this see Chadwick, *Early Church*, 42–4; Hall, *Doctrine and Practice*, 62; Perkins, *Gnosticism and the New Testament*, 190–3; Raymond E. Brown and Raymond F. Collins, "Canonicity," *NJBC*, 1043–51.

[15] Ignatius of Antioch also seems to hold out hope for the contentious in the community if they come to their senses, change their ways, and turn to God. See his *Epistle to the Smyrnaeans*, 9.

[16] The author was not naive about almsgiving. He instructed the Church to reject itinerant prophets as false prophets if they seemed interested only in collecting money or being well fed. See *Didache*, 11:6, 9, 12.

Christian life. The reality of sin caused people to ask how a sinful member of the Church might be forgiven. *Hermas* responds that through sincere repentance a Christian gains true knowledge and also receives God's forgiveness of any sins that had been committed. According to *Hermas*, repentance involves humbling and punishing the soul for its sins. It includes turning away from whatever wickedness had been in one's life and willingly embracing the good in compliance with God's commandments (Mand. IV:2).

The forthright declaration that repentance brings God's forgiveness led people to wonder how often a Christian could sin, repent, and be forgiven. Some answered that God forgave a person in baptism but insisted that there was no further forgiveness for a sinful Christian. In the context of that discussion, *Hermas* taught that since the devil is crafty and humans weak, God provides yet another opportunity for forgiveness. God's mercy gives a sinful Christian one more chance for repentance and forgiveness (Mand. IV:3), a position that is referred to as the "rule of one penance" after baptism. This solution to the problem of sin, penance, and forgiveness in the early Church commanded wide acceptance, especially because many considered *The Shepherd of Hermas* to be an inspired text.

Because of its importance, *Hermas'* rule of one penance has received considerable attention from modern scholars. It seems clear to many that *Hermas* sought to strike a balance. Against the rigorist view that would limit forgiveness to baptism alone, he allowed that a sinful Christian might hope for forgiveness after baptism. On the other hand, the danger of moral and religious laxity required that such forgiveness should be available to a person only once. This consensus does not extend to certain other questions of interpretation and meaning. Did the Church at the time of *Hermas* enforce the rule of one penance literally, or was it accommodated to human weakness? Was the rule based upon the conviction that God did not authorize the Church to forgive a Christian more than once, or did that restriction reflect only a practical Church policy and nothing more?

On the issue of praxis, some believe that *Hermas* is to be taken in his historical context and in light of what seems to be a readiness in the early Church to forgive and reconcile all repentant sinners. This leads to the conclusion that *Hermas'* rule of one penance did not actually impose limitations on the kind of sin or the number of times a repentant person could be forgiven.[17] Others disagree, arguing that its rule of one

---

[17] For example, Marie-François Berrouard, "La pénitence publique durant les six premiers siècles: Histoire et sociologie," *MD* 118 (1974) 94–7, 100–1; Berrouard cites many early texts to support his conclusion.

penance was applied literally and should be accepted at face value.[18] Whatever Church practice actually was at the start of the second century, later generations held *The Shepherd of Hermas* in great esteem and cited it to support their own custom of granting Christians only one postbaptismal reconciliation.

Beneath the question of Church praxis and *Hermas'* policy on postbaptismal penance, there is an extremely important theological issue. To appreciate it, it is helpful to recall that the early Church viewed Christian life from the perspective of baptism and its meaning. Given the general practice of baptizing adults and assuming the sincerity of their conversion, the early Church agreed that baptism forgives the sins of the catechumen, no matter how many or how grave they might have been. Baptism gives the new Christian the gifts of communion with God and membership in the Church of Christ. As long as Christians live in keeping with what they promised and received at baptism, they continue to enjoy communion with God and the Church. Communion is God's gift to the Church, and no further reconciliation is necessary for those who keep their baptismal commitment. On the other hand, Christians who violate their commitment and turn away from God's love and communion through grave sin also return themselves to the alienated state they occupied before being baptized. Grave sin entails alienation from God and the Church.

People are well able to sin and alienate themselves from God and the Church, but no amount of personal repentance can, by itself, restore sinners to communion once they have lost it through sin. Just as Christ's mandate and the Church's baptism confers communion on sinners in the first place, so also it requires God's action and the ministry of the Church if that communion is to be restored. In other words, the problem is not the quality of the sinner's repentance, but whether and how the Church can restore communion to gravely sinful Christians. Although he addresses the practical aspects of postbaptismal repentance, *Hermas* recognizes that the deeper and far more important issue is baptismal grace and the communion it brings, including how those gifts are first gained, their possible loss through grave sin, the Church's power to return them through a second reconciliation, and the basis on which the Church exercises such power.

This underlines the importance of the early Church's discussion of postbaptismal forgiveness. The gift, maintenance, and recovery of the grace and communion received in baptism concerns Christian life

---

[18] See, for example, Karl Rahner, *Theological Investigations* (New York: Crossroad, 1982) 15:79-83; Cyrille Vogel, *Le pécheur et la pénitence dans l'Église ancienne* (Paris: Cerf, 1966) 17.

itself and is essential both to the Church and to individual Christians. The penitential policy of *Hermas* recognizes that grave sins defile the Church community and cause the separation of the sinner from it. By the same token, they deprive a Christian of the seal received in baptism and exclude the Holy Spirit from that member's life.[19] *Hermas'* concern with baptismal grace and communion also accounts for his reluctance to grant forgiveness too freely—that approach might lead people to be careless with these divine gifts or trivialize grave sin. *The Shepherd of Hermas* is important both for its pastoral policy toward grave sinners and for its theological recognition that serious sins involve the loss of the baptismal seal and the gift of the Holy Spirit. On both scores it constitutes a milestone in the life of the Church.

The Communion of the Church

In its recognition that grave sin and ecclesial communion are mutually exclusive, and in placing sin and reconciliation in that context, *The Shepherd of Hermas* stands as a witness to the decisive importance of communion for Christians of the first centuries. Communion is the reality denoted by the Greek term *koinonia* and the Latin words *communio, communicatio, pax,* and *societas,* which are frequently encountered in early Christian texts. As God's gift to the Church, "*communio* is the bond that united the bishops and the faithful, the bishops among themselves, and the faithful among themselves, a bond that was both effected and at the same time made manifest by eucharistic communion. *Communio* very often means simply the Church itself."[20] Communion finds its source in the outpouring of the Holy Spirit on Pentecost. The Holy Spirit empowers the disciples to preach the word to all nations, reminds them of Jesus' teachings, and above all, endows them with unity, so that persons of every race and language can become one body of Christ, one Church of God (Acts 2).

Because of communion, it is necessary to profess authentic Christian faith, repent of one's sins and live in a morally upright way, protect the unity of Christian believers, practice charity especially toward the needy, defer to Church leaders, adhere to apostolic doctrine, and stay

---

[19] See Simile IX, 16, 18; also V, 6–7; IX, 32; Mandate X, 2. The term "grace" was not used by *Hermas*, but in the context the baptismal seal and the gift of the Holy Spirit received in baptism are equivalent to what later theologians would call grace. See Rahner, *Theological Investigations,* 15:38-41, for a further discussion of these issues and the anti-Gnostic direction of *Hermas'* thought. This presentation is indebted to Rahner.

[20] Ludwig Hertling, *Communio: Church and Papacy in Early Christianity,* trans. Jared Wicks (Chicago: Loyola University Press, 1972) 16.

clear of schismatic groups. An abiding concern for communion is reflected in the prayers and policies associated with public worship,
especially baptism, Eucharist, and penance. The decisive nature of communion accounts for the assumption, generally accepted among early
Christians, that peace with the Church brings peace with God, while
alienation or excommunication from the Church compromises one's
standing before God. In sum, communion pertains to the Church's divine constitution; more than anything else it distinguishes the Church
from other organizations and allows its practices and requirements to
be understood and assessed adequately.

Because it immediately affects Christian moral life, ecclesial communion gives rise to a comprehensive set of imperatives that embrace
doctrinal, liturgical, personal, and social matters. Although there are
many cases in which writers or people in positions of authority delineate moral imperatives and present them to others, the requirements of
communion cannot always be stipulated in advance. Even without
explicit directives, Christians are to protect and enhance Church unity
and be prepared to respond in justice and charity to the needs of others. Ecclesial communion calls people to be responsible for one another
and promote the good of the Church community itself, a task that
engages the commitment and wisdom of each believer. Above all, ecclesial communion represents the gift and presence of God in the
Christian community. It makes Christian moral life to be an inherently
religious enterprise and adds transcendent and social dimensions to
official deliberations and personal decision making.[21]

The Significance of This Period

The Church of the second century faced external hostility and internal
problems. It had to delineate norms for membership; settle questions of
behavior, governance, and doctrine; and respond to external attacks. The
Christian community responded to these challenges in light of its faith
and out of the conviction that it was the Church of Christ. As it did so, it
brought the relationship between faith and daily life into clearer view.

This is evident in the work of the apologists, who assumed that all
can recognize immoral behavior, declared that vice is unworthy of their
Roman audience, and insisted that the virtuous lives of Christians
reflect their faith. The apologists acknowledged that non-Christian
people and traditions have many good qualities but argued that these
positive attributes should lead them to faith in Christ. In speaking this

---

[21] On communion in the early Church, see Hertling, *Communio;* J.-M.-R. Tillard,
Eglise d'Églises: L'ecclésiologie de communion (Paris: Cerf, 1987).

way, the apologists engaged the moral sensitivities and the intelligence of their audience. As they invited their neighbors to faith, the apologists explained Christian beliefs and practices and showed that they require people to abandon immorality, offer authentic worship to God, and live a morally elevated life. This reflects their conviction that God wishes all persons to be saved through membership in the Christian Church, and that this requires them to walk the path of faith and repentance.

For their part, the norms for baptism and penance specified the requirements of repentance, faith, and morally upright living. These same standards, and the communion they reflect, obliged Christians to practice charity toward widows, orphans, and the needy. They likewise urged Church leaders to address schism in the community and Christians generally to respect the unity of the Church and never harm it. They account for the judgment that grave sins are incompatible with life in the Christian community, and they supported a strict but still-serviceable approach to the reconciliation of such sinners to God and the Church.

The theoretical concerns of early Church writers also point to the intimate connections among faith, ecclesial communion, and moral life. By denying Christ's divinity and the value of material reality, Gnosticism would have undermined the faith of the Church and dissolved its institutional coherence. Had its claim to private revelation been accepted, the grounds for effective administration, common faith, practical unity, and sustained charity in the Church would have disappeared. Moreover, by making enlightenment or knowledge rather than one's overall personal life the way to salvation, Gnosticism depreciated moral life and diminished its religious quality. The substantial, detailed, and sustained response of Christian leaders to Gnosticism suggests that they fully appreciated its threat to the faith and moral life of the Christian community.

Although much remained undeveloped in this early period, the principal contours of Christian moral life are already apparent. It is compatible with reason and common human decency but finds its foundation in the gifts of faith and repentance. Thought and practice concerning baptism, ecclesial communion, and penitential reconciliation reflect the profoundly religious texture of Christian moral life. Faith requires the Christian people to live in a way that respects the Golden Rule and other reasonable criteria of conduct but also promotes Church unity and meets the demands of charity.

HOLINESS AND RECONCILIATION IN A TIME OF GROWTH

This section examines the waning decades of the second century up to Constantine's Decree of Toleration in the year 313. This was a time of dramatic growth for the Church, but equally significant are the qualitative changes in the Church community. Along with larger numbers came a diminution of personal commitment to Christian life. In addition, there was a dramatic development in the relationship between Church and society and a much stronger tendency to find congruence between Christian faith and Graeco-Roman culture. This led to an important evolution in baptismal and penitential praxis and provoked serious disputes concerning the reconciliation of sinners. Throughout these decades intellectual, institutional, and liturgical aspects of Church life attained greater maturity.

These momentous developments did not weaken the Church's conviction that faith requires repentance and an upright moral life; there is still an expectation that Christians will manifest a comprehensive, sincere, and sustained commitment to Christ. But a larger Church that was moving closer to Graeco-Roman society provoked some difficult conflicts, especially concerning the nature of Christian life and the response that should be made to those of the baptized who had gravely sinned. How far could the Church go either in embracing its world or in reconciling sinful Christians before its integrity was compromised? To what extent was it possible to resolve the tension between the elevated demands of Christian life and the limited capacities of ordinary humans? During the third century these questions emerged with greater urgency and began to find some resolution.

Historical Background

In the century prior to toleration the Church's position in the empire was insecure and subject to sharp reversals. At the start of the third century, the Church was found mostly in the cities and its membership principally drawn from lower-middle-class people and craftsmen. Conditions in the empire as well as the appeal of the Church's life and preaching persuaded many people to embrace Christianity. During the first half of the century the Church enjoyed a considerable measure of peace even though there were also some persecutions.

Beginning around the year 240 and for some thirty years afterward the Roman Empire suffered a series of military defeats at the hands of the Persians to the east and Germanic tribes to the north. These traumatic events brought a measure of instability to the empire. One result was the increased hostility of pagan leaders toward Christian communities. In part, this was in reaction to the continuing attacks of Christian apologists against paganism, many of which had hit their mark. The keepers of classical Roman religion saw their customs and prestige in decline and resented the ascendancy of Christians. Influential pagans blamed the Christians for the military defeats suffered by the empire. The gods, they complained, were showing their anger because Christians had refused to worship them in the traditional manner.

Against a background of military defeats and mounting hostility toward Christians, Decius became emperor in 249. He ordered that everyone in the Roman Empire was to sacrifice to the gods and receive an official certificate testifying to that fact. Imprisonment and torture awaited those who failed to comply. Although it created a severe crisis in many Christian communities, this persecution passed within a year. Shortly afterward, in the year 251, Decius died while on campaign against Rome's Germanic enemies. Other persecutions took place in the following years; the worst was probably that of Valerius in 258.

The military losses on the frontier had important political effects, for they led the generals to take control of the army and then the government itself. Beginning around the year 260, there was a series of military coups that freed military leaders of senatorial control and incompetence. They were then able to defeat foreign armies and give the empire a welcome interlude of peace and stability. This was especially true in the East, where the borders were more easily secured. But it also involved repressive policies, especially when an emperor insisted upon social and ideological conformity.

From about 260 Roman society began to enjoy prosperity and stability. However, the vagaries of the tax system and the growing power of the landed aristocracy produced a deepening chasm between rich and poor. The government, now run by technocrats rather than the old nobility, gradually grew less interested in pagan and classical ideology and, under some emperors at least, tended to be tolerant of cultural and religious diversity. This favored the entry of Christians into influential positions, particularly when they had a classical Roman education.[22] Over time, their presence changed the ethos of the imperial court and helped to make it receptive to Emperor Constantine's historic Decree of Toleration.

This period was of great importance for the Church. In the year 260 Emperor Gallienus decreed toleration and an end to persecutions. This began a forty-year interval in which the emperors were generally too busy defending their frontiers to worry about the Church or cause it any trouble. As a result, the Christian community enjoyed a sustained period of tranquillity in which to organize its interior life still further, extend its inroads among the upper classes, and complete its own identification with the Roman world. By the end of the third century

[22] See Peter Brown, *The World of Late Antiquity, AD 150–750* (New York: Harcourt Brace Jovanovich, 1971) 22–36.

Christianity had become prominent in many of the great cities of the Mediterranean, especially in the more stable Eastern provinces of the empire.[23] That growth had a significance beyond numbers. As one scholar writes:

> The most decisive change of that time, however, cannot be reduced to a matter of the size of the Christian communities. It was more significant for the immediate future of Christianity that the leaders of the Christian Church, especially in the Greek world, found that they could identify themselves with the culture, outlook and needs of the average well-to-do civilian. From being a sect ranged against or to one side of Roman civilization, Christianity had become a church prepared to absorb a whole society. This is probably the most important *aggiornamento* in the history of the Church: it was certainly the most decisive single event in the culture of the third century. For the conversion of a Roman emperor to Christianity, of Constantine in 312, might not have happened—or, if it had, it would have taken on a totally different meaning—if it had not been preceded, for two generations, by the conversion of Christianity to the culture and ideals of the Roman world.[24]

In the third century the Christian Church had challenged and embraced the people and culture of its age. So protracted and fundamental an encounter was bound to generate dramatic effects. Some reverberated within the domestic life of the Church. Others appeared in the violently defensive reactions of a threatened pagan culture. The worst of these reactions took place in the early years of the fourth century.

At that point, the emperor Diocletian decided that it was necessary to impose a uniform social practice on the entire realm. That overall goal reflected military concerns, pagan resentments, and the anti-Christian hatred of powerful figures in the imperial government. What resulted was the last, longest, and probably the most violent persecution that the Roman Empire had ever undertaken against the Church. The persecution of Diocletian began in the year 303 and threatened Church members along with their books, worship, and property. Those who would not sacrifice to the gods as required by law were liable to imprisonment, torture, and execution on grounds that they were atheists who failed to demonstrate due loyalty to the state. Although this persecution was inconsistently pursued, it caused the Church great difficulty for a period of some ten years. Official Roman

---

[23] Ibid., 82. See 49–68, 86, for an informative discussion of life in the empire during the third century. This discussion follows Brown; Hall, *Doctrine and Practice*, 83–9; Chadwick, *Early Church*, 116–24.

[24] Peter Brown, *World of Late Antiquity*, 82.

persecution of the Christian Church ended once and for all in February of 313. At that time the ruler of the West, Constantine, and his Eastern counterpart, Licinius, jointly decreed that henceforth all religions in the empire were to enjoy legal toleration.

Apologetic Efforts

Despite the hostility of pagan leaders and occasional persecutions, the Church never ceased to speak directly to the leaders and people of the empire. As was the case in an earlier period, these efforts at communication aimed primarily to defend the Church and evangelize its neighbors. Both goals required the apologists to point out the law-abiding habits of the Christian faithful, highlight the Christian nature of pagan virtues, and emphasize the reasonableness of faith. Despite the obvious differences, this approach presumed that there was much congruence between the Christian Church and the pagan world. From this perspective it is easier to understand why some writers were favorable to the Graeco-Roman world and judged that its culture and accomplishments were harmonious with Christian faith.

Clement of Alexandria[25] is representative of those third-century writers who took an irenic, open posture toward the world and its people. In the *Exhortation to the Heathen,* Clement addresses a pagan readership and seeks to convince them of the superiority of Christian faith. After attacking the absurdity of pagan rituals and the immorality of pagan activities, he considers their philosophers and poets. Beneath their flawed efforts, he claims that one can detect a striving for the true God. Accordingly, Clement acknowledges that such philosophers as Plato, the Stoics, and the Pythagoreans had indeed found elements of truth. These discoveries, which depended upon God's assistance to them, prove that they can know truth. Building upon that fact, Clement proposes to show them a better and more certain way. He picks up the Scriptures and explains the Prophets. Here are the sources from whom anyone can find piety, truth, and salvation. The Prophets pointed the way to God's great love, which is shown best in Jesus Christ. Through baptism God's love can make people children of God and give them the kingdom.

---

[25] The date and place of Clement's birth are unknown. He received an education in philosophy and converted to Christianity. Thereafter it seems that he was in charge of the catechetical school at Alexandria and may have been ordained a presbyter. His death occurred between the years 215 and 221. For more on Clement, see Hall, *Doctrine and Practice,* 95–9; Eric F. Osborn, *Ethical Patterns in Early Christian Thought* (Cambridge and New York: Cambridge University Press, 1976) 50–80.

Clement was eloquent in exhorting his readers to hear the divine word, believe, and obey. Grace will abound and God will assimilate the believer to God. Clement describes God as "the lover of man." He continues: "For this, and nothing but this, is His only work—the salvation of man" (*Exhort,* 9).[26] Therefore people should take heart and not be discouraged or held back by attachment to ancestral traditions. God is ready to care and to help. "For God, of His great love to man, comes to the help of man, as the mother-bird flies to one of her young that has fallen out of the nest. . . . God the Father seeks His creature, and heals his transgression" (ch. 10). With such appeals, Clement encourages his pagan audience to move beyond their old life, accept faith in Christ, and receive forgiveness of their sins.

Stoicism in Christian Writings

The congruence that Clement found between pagan culture and the divine truth helps to account for his acceptance and use of Graeco-Roman philosophies, especially Stoicism. Stoicism began in Greece in the fourth century B.C., went through several stages of development, and eventually found adherents among such Romans as Cicero, Seneca, and Emperor Marcus Aurelius. It was also popular in some Christian circles.

Fundamental to Stoicism is the premise that a basic harmony underlies the universal law of nature and the right reason proper to each human being. This harmony is ultimately attributed to a single source in God, whose divine "mind" is present in the world, giving rational order to nature and endowing some creatures with reason. People of every race and culture share the same rational nature. One implication is that whoever wishes to live well should act strictly according to reason and nature, and this will lead them to respect the rights of others. In order to do this successfully, people need to be sure that their emotions do not lead to erroneous thinking. Therefore strong feelings are to be suppressed, or at least moderated, so that sound judgment can prevail. Overall, the Stoic ethic presumes that God, nature, and reason are essentially harmonious; it is universal rather than narrow in its reach; and it considers human emotion to be adverse to the rational control that a virtuous person exercises.[27]

[26] The translation is from *Ante-Nicene Fathers,* vol. 2.

[27] See Vernon J. Bourke, *History of Ethics* (Garden City, N.Y.: Doubleday, 1968) 33–8; Ludwig Edelstein, *The Meaning of Stoicism* (Cambridge: Harvard University Press, 1966). On Clement's dependence on Stoic thought see Michel Spanneut, "Les normes morales du stoicisme chez les Pères de l'Eglise," *StMor* 19 (1981) 167; for a

In his lengthy work *Paedagogus* (The Instructor), Clement displays his debt to Stoic thought. He links sin to the unreasonable and virtue to harmony, declaring: "Everything that is contrary to right reason is sin" (*Paed,* I, 13). On the other hand, "Virtue itself is a state of the soul rendered harmonious by reason in respect to the whole life" (I, 13). He adds that "Christian conduct is the operation of the rational soul in accordance with a correct judgment and aspiration after the truth, which attains its destined end through the body, the soul's consort and ally" (I, 13). In the rest of this work, Clement considers the many concrete details of ordinary daily life. His instructions often reflect prevailing customs of etiquette. But throughout his commentary, one basic norm seems to govern: moderation makes for virtue while too much or too little of anything is to be avoided.[28]

Baptismal Preparation

During the second century the size of Church communities increased dramatically. The larger numbers of converts to Christianity and the requirements of Christian life caused Church leaders to set up a regular structure for the preparation and instruction of catechumens. By the beginning of the third century this more institutionalized approach was in place and is reflected in the writings of that era. These sources document the developments in Church praxis and disclose their influence on Christian moral life.

One revealing document is the *Apostolic Tradition* of Hippolytus. This text, usually dated around the year 215, is generally attributed to Hippolytus, who became a bishop and antipope in early third-century Rome. The *Apostolic Tradition* provides a strikingly detailed picture of the customs and liturgical prayers typically used in Rome at that time. Part II of the document shows what is expected of those who seek to be admitted to the Christian community. First, the applicants' motives and quality of life are to be examined. Each receives the support of a Christian sponsor, who testifies to the applicant's ability to hear the

---

more thorough discussion of the matter see Spanneut's *Le Stoïcisme des pères de l'église: de Clément de Rome à Clément d'Alexandrie* (Paris: Ed. du Seuil, 1969).

[28] Two examples suffice to illustrate these points. One concerns table manners: "From all slavish habits and excess we must abstain, and touch what is set before us in a decorous way; keeping the hand and couch and chin free of stains; preserving the grace of the countenance undisturbed, and committing no indecorum in the act of swallowing; but stretching out the hand at intervals in an orderly manner" (*Paed,* II, 1). The other deals with the use of wine: "It has therefore been well said, 'A joy of the soul and heart was wine created from the beginning, when drunk in moderate sufficiency'" (II, 2).

word of God. Certain moral requirements are also set forth. Married people are expected to be faithful and the unmarried to avoid fornication. Those who engage in certain occupations or activities are disqualified unless they are willing to end their involvement in them. Specifically prohibited are keeping or visiting prostitutes, making idols, helping to put on public games, and working as a gladiator, soldier, executioner, civil magistrate, or magician. Prebaptismal instruction extends for three years, after which the catechumen is again examined to see if he or she has successfully lived up to the requirements of Christian faith and virtue.

The baptism itself is an impressive ceremony and involves exorcisms to rid the candidates of evil and a solemn profession of Christian faith. Newly baptized Christians are clothed in the white baptismal garment that signifies the holy life that they have received. The new Christians are anointed, admitted to the eucharistic assembly, and receive the Eucharist for the first time with the rest of the community.[29]

The writings of Clement of Alexandria and Tertullian show that the churches of North Africa and Egypt followed a similar approach. Three years were spent in preparing a catechumen. This time was used to wean the applicant from sinful habits and support the acquisition of Christian virtues. During the same period, the community carefully instructed the person in the Christian faith. During the third century the catechumenate came to be in general use throughout the Church.[30]

The establishment of a formal catechumenate suggests that, due to the numbers involved, the Church could no longer respond to each candidate on an individual basis. Instead it developed a standardized process to assure the kind of preparation that had traditionally been required of catechumens. Although a formalized catechumenate carried with it the risks that are associated with any shift from an individually tailored to an institutionalized approach, it manifested to all what baptism, and therefore Christian life, requires and means. Becoming

[29] For a fuller discussion of the catechumenate during this period, see Michel Dujarier, "L'évolution de la pastorale catéchuménale aux six premiers siècles de l'Église," *MD* 71 (1962) 48–50, 53–6; idem, *A History of the Catechumenate: The First Six Centuries,* trans. Edward J. Haasl (New York: Sadlier, 1979) 49–51.

[30] Victor Saxer, *Vie liturgique et quotidienne à Carthage vers le milieu du IIIe siècle: Le témoignage de saint Cyprien et de ses contemporains d'Afrique* (Città del Vaticano: Pontificio Istituto di Archeologia Cristiana, 1969) 72–80; concerning Tertullian, see Rordorf, *Eucharist of the Early Christians,* 150.

The Council of Elvira's requirement that prebaptismal preparation should span two years (Can. 42) is one evidence of the catechumenate in the early years of the fourth century. The council, which met in the year 305 or 306, stipulated some of the activities forbidden to candidates for baptism (e.g., Cann. 37, 59, 62). See Hefele, 1:131–72; Dujarier, *History of the Catechumenate,* 69.

Christian demands conversion of life and the sincere embrace of Christian faith.

The Christian tradition recognizes that moral life is rooted in faith, which is based upon God's loving deeds toward humanity. The care and time invested in a candidate's preparation presupposes that such a conversion is a holistic and gradual process that demands sustained personal effort and the ongoing support of a community. The catechumenate tried to protect and keep visible to all the holiness of life, importance of moral conversion, and priority of faith that are to characterize the Christian community.[31]

Penance in the Third Century

Even though the Church spent a great deal of time and effort to prepare catechumens for baptism, and notwithstanding the personal commitment that baptism represents, sin continued to occur in the Christian community. The slight failures and less serious faults of the Christian faithful did not constitute a major problem because they do not deprive a person of ecclesial communion. Prompted by sincere sorrow and using the spiritual resources of the Church, the Christian was urged to diminish and eliminate these "daily sins" by means of prayer, fasting and almsgiving, and acts of charity. Because they alienate a person from ecclesial communion, grave sins cannot be addressed in that way. Persons who cut themselves off from the Church's life do not have access to its resources, cannot restore themselves to communion, or cause their sin to be forgiven. That requires the gift of God and the ministry of the Church.

During the third century problems concerning sin, penance, forgiveness, and reconciliation assumed crisis proportions. In the background was the sense that the increased size of the Church had been accompanied by a weakening of personal commitment to Christian life and a diminution of unity in the larger churches. This sense of diluted standards and poorer internal cohesion persuaded local churches to adopt stricter policies toward gravely sinful members. A related question also vexed the Church at this time: What was the extent of its power to reconcile a Christian who had sinned gravely? In other words, although God has full power to forgive all sins, did God also delegate such power to the Church? In the third century some had begun to deny that God had authorized the Church to forgive certain sins. If this were the case, then some gravely sinful Christians would

---

[31] Hall, *Doctrine and Practice*, 15–7; Berrouard, "La pénitence publique," 104–5; Brown, *World of Late Antiquity*, 67–8; Dujarier, "L'évolution," 48–56.

have to live the rest of their lives unforgiven and alienated from the eucharistic life of the Church. This problem had pastoral as well as doctrinal dimensions. How the early Church resolved these penance-related conflicts established precedents that strongly influenced the penitential thinking and practice of later Christian generations.[32]

Tertullian's View of Penance

A key witness to Church doctrine and practice at the beginning of the third century is Tertullian. Sometime before the year 207, this major African theologian wrote a book entitled *De paenitentia* (On Penance).[33] In this work Tertullian notes that one can sin both by deed and by thought. In either case, repentance is required of the sinner and brings God's forgiveness (*DPaen*, 3–4). The first repentance is to occur prior to baptism; therefore the catechumen is expected to do sincere penance for past sins and resolve to avoid them in the future. Thus baptism—and the forgiveness and reconciliation it brings—follows sincere repentance and inaugurates a life that is free of further sin. Only with considerable reluctance does Tertullian mention the possibility of a second repentance after baptism. He fears that this possibility would make catechumens think that "there is still time left for sin" (7; see 5–7).

Despite his hesitation, Tertullian has no doubt that there is a second repentance available to sinful Christians. It may be shameful to sin but not shameful to be saved a second time. However, according to Tertullian, this second repentance is the last one available to a person. He views this repentance as a serious step that involves the sinner's conscience as well as exterior action (*DPaen*, 7–8). The external act Tertullian called *exomologesis*, a Greek word that means confession and includes acknowledgment of one's sins to the Lord, satisfaction, and penance. *Exomologesis* brings God's mercy to a sinner. He writes:

> Exomologesis, then, is a discipline which leads a man to prostrate and humble himself. It prescribes a way of life which, even in the matter of food and clothing, appeals to pity. It bids him to lie in sackcloth and ashes, to cover his body with filthy rags, to plunge his soul into sorrow, to exchange sin for suffering. Moreover, it demands that you know only

[32] See Berrouard, "La pénitence publique," 98–109.
[33] Quasten, *Ancient Christian Writers*, 28:12. Tertullian was born between 155 and 160 and became a Catholic in adulthood. He is regarded as the principal founder of Latin theology and a dominant figure in Carthage and Africa generally, at least until he drifted toward Montanism sometime after 207. He died around the year 220.

such food and drink as is plain; this means it is taken for the sake of your soul, not your belly. It requires that you habitually nourish prayer by fasting, that you sigh and weep and groan day and night to the Lord your God, that you prostrate yourself at the feet of the priests and kneel before the beloved of God, making all the brethren commissioned ambassadors of your prayer for pardon.

. . . In proportion as you have had no mercy on yourself, believe me, in just this same measure God will have mercy upon you (*DPaen*, 9).

Tertullian understands that through *exomologesis* the sinner reaches forth to the members of the Church and therefore is in touch with Christ. Christ, identified with the Church, joins in praying to God the Father and always receives what he requests. Through the cooperation of Christ and his Church, this second penance becomes a means of salvation for the sinner (*DPaen*, 10).

Some time after writing his *De paenitentia*, Tertullian is generally thought to have become a Montanist. Montanism takes its name from Montanus, its mid-second-century founder, who declared that he was a prophet sent to proclaim a new revelation from the Holy Spirit. He prophesied that the world would soon come to an end and that to prepare for it people needed to adhere to very strict moral and religious standards. For this reason, Montanist groups forbade second marriages, required heavy penances of everyone, considered flight from persecution to be shameful, and except for limited cases, did not extend forgiveness after baptism. A kind of charismatic movement, Montanism held that God required the Church to live up to a much higher standard than prevailed at that time. It was known for its moral rigorism and intolerance of failure.

As a Montanist, Tertullian wrote another work, *De pudicitia* (On Purity) in which these rigorist tendencies are explicit. In this book, Tertullian is harsh in tone and severe in judgment. A Catholic bishop had apparently granted reconciliation to people who had performed penance, or *exomologesis,* for fornication and adultery. Tertullian objects to that bishop's action, saying that he had undermined the integrity of the Christian life, defiled the Church, offended God, and encouraged others to sin in the future (*DPud*, 1). During the course of his lengthy diatribe, Tertullian defends Montanist doctrine and condemns Catholic praxis. He insists that the Church cannot reconcile Christians who had been guilty of adultery and fornication. He agrees that through the bishop, the Church can forgive lesser sins once the sinner has completed the necessary *exomologesis* (12, 18).

Tertullian's works confirm that by the start of the third century the Church clearly understood that the forgiveness of grave sins requires the prayerful involvement of the Church as well as sincere internal and external penance on the part of the sinner. At the conclusion of a penitent's *exomologesis* the bishop would restore that person's access to the Eucharist. A customary approach that wedded these personal and ecclesiological elements had begun to emerge. Along with this developing praxis, it had become the rule, at least in Africa, to grant this ecclesiastical penance only once in a person's lifetime.

From his Montanist perspective, Tertullian had begun to argue that in certain cases the Church could not even do that much and that some postbaptismal sins were unforgivable on earth. This assertion changed the discussion by recasting the question. It had concerned what penitential practice was helpful; now it asked what was possible. Tertullian's latter-day attack on Catholic practice showed how strong the tide of rigorism had become.[34]

The Approach of Cyprian and Cornelius

Also significant in the third-century drama was another outstanding African, Cyprian of Carthage. Cyprian was bishop in that large and important city[35] from 249 to 258, which were years of persecution for the Church. In 250, when Decius unleashed the first persecution in well over a generation, many members of the Church capitulated while others fled. Yet others tried to finesse their dilemma by such tactics as bribing an official to give them a false certificate of sacrifice. This created a crisis for the Church, including the community of Carthage. Some confessors, that is, those who had held firm under persecution and survived, interceded for people who had given in. These confessors presumed that their fidelity under persecution gave them authority to reconcile sinners to the Church. However, others asserted that apostates should receive no reconciliation at all. Cyprian took a middle course. He determined that apostates could indeed be reconciled but only after suitable and possibly lifelong penance. He also held that the power to adjudicate the cases of repentant sinners and to reconcile them belonged exclusively to the bishop.

---

[34] For further discussion about Tertullian and his penitential doctrine, see Rahner, *Theological Investigations,* 15:125-51; James Dallen, *The Reconciling Community: The Rite of Penance* (New York: Pueblo, 1986) 30–7; Hall, *Doctrine and Practice,* 67–73; Bernhard Poschmann, *Penance and the Anointing of the Sick,* trans. Francis Courtney (New York: Herder & Herder, 1964) 35–52; Vogel, *Le pécheur et la pénitence dans l'Église ancienne,* 19–24.

[35] Located near the site of the modern city of Tunis, Carthage was a major African seaport and during the early Christian era was one of the most important cities of the Roman Empire. It was the seat of a Catholic bishop, who usually commanded great respect in Africa and in the Church generally.

Soon after, in 252, it appeared that a new persecution was about to begin. In that context Cyprian decided to reconcile those who apostatized in the earlier persecution. He did so without any further delay, hoping that, by sharing fully in the Church's communion, former apostates would be strengthened against the expected attack. Although the anticipated persecution did not occur, Cyprian's actions were significant. He had upheld the principle that all sinners can be reconciled. He established a precedent for the shortening or canceling of the *exomologesis* that would normally be required of the repentant sinner. Cyprian vindicated the bishop's exclusive jurisdiction over the process of reconciliation and emphasized its episcopal and ecclesiological dimensions.[36]

The persecution of Decius precipitated a similar crisis in the Church of Rome. Against that background, Pope Cornelius also reconciled apostates even though they were not in any immediate danger of death. A Roman priest, Novatian, protested Cornelius' actions because he believed that the Church should be holy in practice and could not afford to reconcile such sinners. Strongly influenced by Montanist thinking, Novatian's convictions eventually prompted him to leave the Catholic community.

Novatian's actions testified to the strength of a more general reaction against the weakening of personal commitment within a larger Church. On one level it appeared that the problem was limited to the reconciliation of certain grave sinners and related doctrinal questions concerning penance. Beneath these objections lay a much deeper conflict about the nature of the Church. Montanists, Novatianists, and other rigorists viewed the Church as a holy community whose members are to be pure and altogether committed and in which authority belongs to its holy members rather than the official leadership. They demanded a policy that would protect the Church's holiness by excluding those who, in time of crisis, had failed to meet the test. They were not prepared to have the bishops accommodate penitential praxis to sinful Christians, claiming that to do so would constitute a betrayal of the Church and its mission.

Underlying Issues

The struggle that set Carthaginian and Roman rigorists against their bishops enacted a deeper and more general conflict between two op-

---

[36] Dallen, *Reconciling Community,* 37–42. See also Rahner, *Theological Investigations,* 15:152-222; Poschmann, *Penance and the Anointing of the Sick,* 52–62; see pages 75–80 of Poschmann's book for a discussion of the prerogatives of martyrs in granting reconciliation to others.

posing views of the Church. Cyprian, Cornelius, and many others believed that it was right to take a more generous approach to sinful Christians. They presupposed that the Church is composed of ordinary human beings with all their weaknesses. Therefore they upheld the moral and religious standards proper to Christian faith but did so in a way that was more tolerant and inclusive of frail humanity. This conflict was also of great importance from the perspective of Church governance. Latent in the confrontation over the reconciliation of grave sinners was a clash between charismatic and institutional figures and their respective claims to authority.

Cyprian and Cornelius succeeded in asserting their penitential policy and vindicating their hierarchical authority. But they did not end the conflicts over the nature of the Church, the source and use of sacred authority, or how and on what terms the Church should restore sinners to communion. In one way or another there were always people who insisted that the Church is to be pure and holy in its members and its daily life. The conviction that the Church is a visible, institutional society composed of people who are weak and struggling has likewise proved to be perennial.[37]

By the end of the third century, however, the principal contours of Catholic penitential practice and theory had been established. It was generally accepted that the Church had the power to reconcile all sinners, even if some were required to do sincere and often lengthy penance.[38] When the suitable moment arrived, the bishop granted them reconciliation, that is, readmittance to the eucharistic community and to the ecclesial communion that it embodies. It was agreed that penance brings forgiveness because of the spiritual power of personal conversion and that of the Church's intervention. In practice, the favor of postbaptismal penance was usually extended to a person only once. This resulted in a widespread but not necessarily uniform usage. By the beginning of the fourth century local Church councils began to promulgate canons that were to govern the practice of penance.

The Significance of This Period

In the century leading up to Constantine's Decree of Toleration, the Church grew in size and importance. But this rapid growth was as ambiguous as it was significant, for it appears that the increased numbers

---

[37] Poschmann, *Penance and the Anointing of the Sick,* 52–8; see also Berrouard, "La pénitence publique," 110–6.

[38] See also Canons 11-3 of the Council of Nicaea, which met in A.D. 325 (Tanner, 1:11-2).

can be attributed as much to social and cultural motives as to faith in Christ. On the one hand, the catechumenate, the rites of baptism, and penitential norms all testify that membership in the Church was to be based upon a mature conversion of life and a sustained commitment to Christian faith and its moral implications. On the other hand, mass apostasy during persecutions suggests that many Christians had failed to meet those standards. A similar ambivalence appears in the attitudes of Church leaders toward the wider community. To be sure, they acted to uphold the requirements of faith and strike a sharp contrast with the larger community. But they were also pointing out congruence between the Church and Graeco-Roman culture and helping to advance a reconciliation with it. Ironically, the Church's embrace of Roman culture and thought, which had done much to generate stress on pastoral practice in the first place, was already promoting a pastoral policy of acceptance toward the many who had responded to its outreach. If this policy diminished the stress between Church and world, it increased problems within the Church itself. In a larger community, it became much more difficult to maintain proper standards of repentance, faith, and ecclesial charity.

The tension between contrast and congruence was dramatically played out in the penitential controversies of this period. Rigorists and stricter Church practices aimed to secure a high level of Christian commitment, while many pastors took more lenient, even generous approaches to sinners, thus accommodating failure and implicitly lowering standards in the Christian community. Beneath these conflicts over praxis lay a deeper division over whether the institutional or the charismatic dimensions of the Church should prevail. Some believed that sacred authority rested ultimately in the hands of official leaders, while others held that it belonged to the holy and committed members of the Christian community. This more fundamental conflict could not be settled easily or quickly.

These developments again demonstrate that the motives and behavior proper to moral life affect the quality of one's faith and membership in the Church. This is obvious in the catechumenate, the content of Christian baptismal commitments, and penitential praxis itself. Moreover, those who defended a stricter or a more flexible approach both acted out of a shared premise, namely, that the moral life of Christians is of primary importance for the Church and for their own good standing in it, and that membership in the Christian community is to govern a person's moral life. The sharp and ongoing disagreement over penance suggests that the third-century Christian community found it difficult to decide what level of religious commitment and moral conduct was required by baptism and communion with God. Closely allied was the conflict over the locus of authority in the Church.

FAITH AND MORAL LIFE IN AN AGE OF ACCEPTANCE

Legal toleration opened a new era, for it guaranteed the rights of Christians and created an environment in which the Church was free to evangelize outsiders and conduct its domestic affairs without hindrance. Toleration led to unprecedented harmony with the state and eventually allowed the Catholic Church and the imperial government to become active in one another's affairs. The increasingly friendly relationship between the Church and the imperial government was a dominant feature of the fourth century.

This section will consider the period from the Decree of Toleration in 313 to the end of that century, excluding matters that pertain to St. Augustine of Hippo (354–430). It will open with a review of the principal historical events of that period, investigate apologetic and other patristic literature, and observe the increasing influence of humanistic thought. That will establish a suitable context in which to consider the Church's preparation and baptism of new members, the evolving discipline of ecclesiastical penance, and the appearance of the monastic movement. These developments show how faith, repentance, and moral life were understood and related in practice during the fourth century.

Historical Background

With the advent of legal toleration, the Church gained the opportunity to convoke a general council, which took place in 325 at Nicaea. Its purpose was to regulate the life of the Church as a whole and consider certain doctrinal controversies. Chief among these was the teaching of an Egyptian priest named Arius concerning the person of Jesus. Following the first chapter of the Gospel According to John, Arius agreed that Jesus was the *Logos*, or Word, but added that this implied that Jesus lacked a human soul. Arius also held that although the Word is called God in John's Gospel, it is not fully divine because it was united with the man Jesus and therefore must have been created at a certain point in time. These teachings meant that Jesus was neither fully God as the Father is God, nor fully human. If that were true, as a number of Church leaders immediately pointed out, then Jesus could not have been the Savior of the human race, a conclusion that contradicted traditional Christian faith. Against Arian teachings, the Council of Nicaea affirmed the full divinity of Jesus but did so in a declaration that was open to conflicting interpretations.[39] Forty years later another priest, Apollinarius, began to teach that although Jesus was fully divine, he lacked a human soul and should not be considered as fully human. This teaching was alike to Arianism in key respects and was rejected by a general council in 381, the First Council of Constantinople.[40]

In the fourth and fifth centuries the Church sifted and weighed different views about Jesus. Many of these were compatible with the ancient faith even though some gave greater weight to the divinity of Christ while others emphasized his humanity. Some views, however, were eventually declared to be incompatible with the Church's faith, or heretical. In the process, the Church slowly clarified what it could rightly assert about Jesus and his person. This doctrinal winnowing and refining, which lasted almost to the end of the seventh century, was extremely important, since it dealt with the very foundation of Christian faith: the person of the Savior. As is evident in the case of Arius, what one says about Jesus has repercussions on the possibility and nature of salvation, the value that can be attributed to human life, and what can be expected of people who wish to receive salvation. Christology has moral as well as religious implications.

Toleration had major political consequences. At first Constantine ruled only the Western portion of the empire. With the passage of time he was able to gain control of the much more christianized East. Under the influence of the apologists' arguments, he became convinced that it would be good for his empire if he showed favor to Christianity. As a patron of the Church he could also look forward to a close association with bishops, who by then had achieved considerable public standing. On his deathbed in 337, he completed his approach to the Church by receiving Christian baptism. His son and successor, Constantine II, extended this rapprochement between emperor and hierarchy; bishops now joined the court and became part of the governing class.

This newfound congeniality toward bishops did not hinder Constantine II from indulging his preference for Arian views, views that a number of the bishops also shared. This was another symptom of Nicaea's failure to suppress all forms of Arianism in the Church.

[39] See its profession of faith (Tanner, 1:5; DS, 125–6).

[40] See the profession of faith and Canon 1 of this council (Tanner, 1:24, 31; DS, 150-1); also John P. Galvin, "Jesus Christ," *Systematic Theology: Roman Catholic Perspectives,* ed. Francis Schüssler Fiorenza and John P. Galvin (Minneapolis: Fortress Press, 1991) 1:262-5. For a more detailed discussion of these issues see Aloys Grillmeier, *Christ in Christian Tradition,* 2nd rev. ed., trans. John Bowden and others (Atlanta: John Knox, 1975) 1:220-302, also 1:329-43.

What was worse, events subsequent to the Council of Nicaea form a complex tale of intrigue and violence that took decades to run its course. In the meantime, Arianism festered as both a doctrinal and a political problem and added to tensions between Greek and Latin Christians. This unhappy situation finally ended in 381 when the First Council of Constantinople reaffirmed Nicaea's rejection of Arian positions and did so in a way that commanded a consensus.[41]

In matters of culture and politics, toleration inaugurated a very fluid situation. One important reason was that the same Decree of Toleration that brought peace to the Church in 313 also protected pagan rituals and beliefs. Many Romans, especially those of an aristocratic background, continued to adhere to these traditions, believing that they were an essential part of their ancient culture, familial piety, and patriotic loyalty. One example suffices to show the power of pagan attachments: in mid-century Emperor Julian abandoned his Catholicism and tried to return pagan devotions and institutions to their former predominance in civil life. In an attempt to render Christianity mute and unappealing, he shrewdly forbade Christians to teach Greek literature. By denying them their most credible way to present Christianity as the pinnacle of true culture, he hoped to cripple their efforts at evangelization and advance his own agenda of turning traditional paganism into a "church" of its own, officially sanctioned and supported. Having earned the animosity of Christians, Julian died in 363 after a reign of three years.

One of his successors, Theodosius, adopted a sharply contrasting policy. In 380 he commanded that all in his empire were to follow the Catholic religion. In 391 he began to legislate against pagan temples and practices. Such laws not only promoted the establishment of Christianity in the empire but demonstrated the readiness of civil authorities to use the power of the law to suppress pagan and heretical Christian religious manifestations, just as Diocletian had used it to suppress Christian practices almost a century earlier. Theodosian legislation demonstrates the extent of the political change since the beginning of the fourth century.[42]

Whether the legal environment was tolerant or positively supportive, the Christian community continued to confront pagan ignorance

[41] This story is told in Chadwick, *Early Church,* 133–51; and Hall, *Doctrine and Practice,* 121–72. Arian evangelists had converted many of the Germanic tribes north of the Roman Empire to their form of Christianity. This had an impact on later events in Western Europe and North Africa. References to conciliar texts are given in the preceding note.

[42] Chadwick, *Early Church,* 152–73; see also Brown, *World of Late Antiquity,* 90–3; Hall, *Doctrine and Practice,* 161–2, 171–2.

and hostility and the responsibilities of daily life. As the apologists addressed these external challenges, the bishops attended to the preparation of catechumens, the ongoing support and guidance of ordinary believers, and the reconciliation of sinners. Both these tasks called forth a literary response. Besides reflecting the issues of the day, these writings show that fourth-century apologists and bishops saw a great deal of harmony between Christian faith and contemporary humanistic philosophies, and they borrowed heavily from secular culture and thought.

An Apologist Addresses Educated Romans

As the fourth century began, it became obvious that the Church needed to make a special effort if it wished to reach Roman intellectuals and make the Christian faith respectable and appealing to them. Unimpressed by simple explanations, these people could only be evangelized through a sophisticated and intellectually credible approach. This task once again fell to apologists, and among them the Latin-speaking Lactantius and the Greek author Eusebius of Caesarea stand out in importance.[43] For the purposes of this study a consideration of Lactantius can suffice.

Lactantius' major apologetic work was his *Divinae institutiones* (The Divine Institutes), written largely during the Great Persecution of Diocletian. In this lengthy and substantial book Lactantius addressed the cultured pagans, the educated men and women of the early fourth century. The Divine Institutes explains the error of polytheism and the necessity of a single God. It ridicules the exaggerations and inconsistencies of pagan mythology. It considers in detail the objectionable arguments and conclusions of all the major philosophers of Greece and Rome and provides a point-by-point rebuttal on the basis of experience and logic. Lactantius reminds his readers that although many Romans had tried to find wisdom and truth, in the end they all failed. In fact, they did not even live up to their own standards of conduct. He argues that adherence to the true religion is the only way to reach true wisdom. He proposes that people should begin with an examination of the prophets because they illuminate the way to Christ.

Lactantius provides a patient, systematic explanation of Catholic faith about God, Jesus, his death and resurrection, and related points of belief. He adds that faith involves adherence to the Catholic Church and avoidance of heretical sects. Lactantius then begins a discussion of

---

[43] Brown, *World of Late Antiquity,* 84. Lactantius wrote from about 300 until his death some time around 320. Eusebius died around the year 340.

justice and other virtues. He states that the law of nature that regulates the virtuous life is in fact the holy law of God. In support of this position, he cites a passage from the Roman philosopher Marcus Tullius Cicero, which describes the law of right reason as being congruent to nature, common to all, unchanging, and able to lead a person from vice to virtue. Lactantius declares that this insight is less the work of a philosopher than the God-given inspiration of a prophet (*DivInst*, VI, 8).

The first requirement of the natural law is the knowledge and worship of the one true God. Moral considerations immediately follow. Those who worship God must also possess the virtues of mercy, kindness, and humanity toward their neighbors. Since all people are united as children of God, they must practice love and give protection to those in need. They are always to reject hatred toward others and avoid injuring them (*DivInst*, VI, 10).[44] Lactantius adds that a sincere and conscientious practice of kindness can constitute the repentance that brings God's forgiveness of sins. The same noble activities bring one who is already just to even higher levels of virtue (VI, 13).

Lactantius is significant because he is yet another example of an early Christian writer who relied heavily on experience, reason, and intellectual discourse to promote faith among unbelievers. This approach necessarily emphasized the harmony between faith and reason, between Christianity and many aspects of pagan culture. This is evident in his abundant references to classic authors, the paucity of scriptural references, his closely reasoned arguments, and the endorsement of the natural law approaches used by pagan writers. According to Lactantius, Catholic faith is the apex of classical culture, Christian moral standards perfect natural ethics, and entry into the Church is the logical next step for the upright Roman. He implies that Christian faith is the only way for Roman citizens to win God's blessing on their country, while a lack of faith will bring God's punishment upon it.

This approach proved to be persuasive. It contributed to the increased numbers seeking admission to the catechumenate and encouraged educated people to take this step. Lactantius and other apologists reinforced the conviction that Christian moral life was reasonable and that it rested upon natural foundations common to all. Even when wedded to a supernatural perspective, this understanding of moral life remained essentially terrestrial in nature. Its Stoic, Aristotelian, and

[44] In the following two chapters Lactantius refers to the Roman virtue of liberality whereby the wealthy might be generous to others or underwrite public projects. He replies that the true liberality cares for the needy, especially destitute children and widows. In the same vein, he praises those who ransom captives, visit the sick, and bury the dead. Such deeds of mercy show a true liberality, which God will surely reward.

Platonic ancestry was explicitly acknowledged. Lactantius and other early Christian writers helped give Catholic moral life a decidedly more philosophical, rational, and human texture.[45]

A Bishop Writes for Christians

The same acceptance of natural morality and its Roman philosophical sources is also evident in those writers who spoke to their fellow Christians. One author who unquestionably demonstrates this is Ambrose, who was bishop in Milan from 374 until his death in 397. The text that best shows Ambrose's open and routine borrowing from secular sources is his *De officiis ministrorum* (On the Duties of the Clergy).

In this book Ambrose shows his understanding of Christian moral life and manifests his reliance upon a similarly titled moral work of Cicero, *De officiis*. Accordingly, Ambrose views Catholic moral life through Stoic lenses. In all things passion is to be controlled by reason. Human desires must always be subject to moderation. Actions are to be performed only at the right time and in the right order (*DOfMin*, I, 24). Moral life depends upon the virtue of prudence; under the rule of prudence the person will live according to the demands of justice, fortitude, and temperance (I, 27). The moral person lives according to nature by following his or her practical intelligence (I, 46).

Ambrose also enunciates with new and influential clarity the distinction between ordinary moral duties and practices that aim at perfection. Basing himself on the story of Jesus and the rich young man in Matthew's Gospel (19:16-30), he explains that the commandments are ordinary duties whose accomplishment, though required, still leave something undone. Perfection requires more generous actions, such as selling one's possessions and giving to the poor, loving one's enemies, and praying for one's persecutors (*DOfMin*, I, 11). The distinction between ordinary and higher standards of Christian life is a common theme in fourth-century Christian literature.

Baptism and the Catechumenate

From one perspective it seems that toleration had not affected the Church's approach to baptism and the catechumenate. The theological meaning of baptism remained the same. It still constituted the moment at which the Church accepted the religious and moral conversion of the candidate. It washed away sins and inaugurated a person into the holy

---

[45] See Brown, *World of Late Antiquity*, 84.

life of the Church. Accordingly, the Church continued to expect that those seeking baptism would undergo a lengthy period of preparation.

From another perspective, however, it is clear that legal toleration created a new situation in which major changes in the catechumenate and the practice of baptism took place. Toleration brought the Church new public respectability and advanced the process of reconciliation with Roman society. As a result, it became socially and politically advantageous to be a Christian, which prompted many more people to seek entry into the catechumenate but also made their motivation more ambiguous. What is more, in the rapprochement between Church and society, the Church became less able to function as a counter-community whose holiness shone forth in a sinful world.[46]

These developments exerted considerable stress upon the catechumenate. Aware of their mixed motives and unwilling to assume the obligations of baptism, people joined the catechumenate with no intention of receiving baptism until old age or perhaps their deathbed. Some Catholic parents refused to have their infants baptized, reasoning that an unruly youth or an immoral young adulthood could always be addressed by a later baptism. Common to both these responses was the concern that once baptism took place, the person would have to face the serious consequences that attended any betrayal of baptismal obligations.[47]

The increased numbers of catechumens and their more ambiguous motives led to significant changes in Church programs. The catechumenate began to function as a state of quasi membership in the Church rather than a means to foster and test the conversion of those who wished to join the eucharistic assembly. It became impossible to give each catechumen personal attention. Instead, the focus fell on the group, a development that made it easier for defective motivation to go unrecognized, especially when priests took a lax approach to baptismal preparation. During the fourth century the traditional and

---

[46] Dujarier, "L'évolution," 57–8, 79–81; Brown, *World of Late Antiquity*, 82.

[47] Joachim Jeremias, *Infant Baptism in the First Four Centuries*, trans. David Cairns (Philadelphia: Westminster Press, 1962) 87–97; A.H.M. Jones, *The Later Roman Empire, 284–602: A Social Economic and Administrative Survey* (Oxford: Basil Blackwell, 1964) 980–2; Dujarier, "L'évolution," 81–4. Among those who were born of Catholic parents but not baptized until adulthood were Basil the Great, Ambrose, John Chrysostom, Jerome, Paulinus of Nola, Augustine, and Gregory Nazianzen. Jeremias dates the phenomenon of delaying the baptism of children from about 330 and describes it as a symptom of a pagan and magical view of baptism that had been carried into Catholicism by the many who joined the Church after toleration. He notes that after about 365 the bishops began to react against this delay. Throughout this period many people continued to have their infants baptized in accordance with an ancient custom. See Jeremias, *Infant Baptism*, 91–5.

lengthy period of preparation may have been observed, but its internal dynamics had deteriorated. Toward the end of the century, the time dedicated to catechumenal preparation had already grown shorter and in some places was on its way to extinction.[48]

To compensate, bishops began to place great emphasis on the two-to-eight-week period immediately prior to baptism, which became a time of intense preparation of those who were to be baptized at the Easter Vigil. This brief interval reflected both the failure of the catechumenate and a good-faith attempt to honor the requirement of religious and moral conversion in those being baptized. However understandable this lenten effort was, it did not succeed in doing what a much more patient and substantial catechumenate had failed to accomplish.[49]

Faced with an unsatisfactory situation, bishops tried their best to maintain the original meaning of baptism. They worked to promote a sound understanding of faith in their candidates. Basil and Athanasius, for example, preached that faith had to be vital and inspired by a sincere love. A candidate was to reject past sins and internalize the virtues proper to Christian life. John Chrysostom declared that unless that were done it was better not to receive baptism at all. Gregory of Nyssa taught that the unworthy reception of baptism was offensive to God. That bishops had to say these things is further evidence that the customary approach to baptismal preparation was no longer satisfactory. They could not assume that their candidates for baptism had a sound grasp of faith or had undertaken a thorough reform of their lives.[50]

Penitential Practices

An ineffective catechumenate and a much wider baptismal door resulted in a Church with many members who were not prepared to live up to their Christian commitments. That anomalous situation generated stresses that radiated throughout Church life, notably affecting the practice of ecclesiastical penance.

---

[48] Dujarier, "L'évolution," 51; see also 57–9. There is some reason to conclude that by the end of the fourth century the catechumenate had disappeared altogether in Spain. See idem, *History of the Catechumenate*, 94.

[49] Dujarier, "L'évolution," 51, 59–60; idem, *History of the Catechumenate*, 97–100; Joseph Lécuyer, "Théologie de l'Initiation chrétienne d'après les Pères," *MD* 58 (1959) 16–8. The season of Lent originated with the time prior to Easter that was dedicated to the preparation of baptismal candidates. These efforts included liturgical rites and involved the entire community. In the course of time Lent came to assume other functions as well.

[50] Dujarier, "L'évolution," 50–3; this source provides textual citations.

The Church of the fourth century had inherited the faith and practice of earlier generations. Accordingly, it recognized that baptism required sincere faith and effective charity. Among the baptized, daily faults could be forgiven by daily penances performed in the course of Christian life.[51] Very different were the offenses that gravely violated the holiness of the Church as well as the member's baptismal commitments. Those sins involved the loss of baptismal grace and its gift of reconciliation, which excluded the offender from communion and called for sincere personal conversion, suitable penances,[52] and the intervention of the Church.[53] Ecclesiastical penance, already in place before toleration, combined all these elements.

After toleration, a rapidly expanding Church found that many more of its members had sinned and needed ecclesiastical penance if they were to be reconciled. In that context, Church councils began to enact canons whose purpose was to standardize and regulate the practice of penance. These canons tended to impose more severe penances for certain sins and diminished the bishop's freedom to respond to each sinner on an individual basis. In due course most aspects of ecclesiastical penance came to be regulated by the canons, and the overall process became known as "canonical penance."[54]

[51] See, for example, John Chrysostom's *Baptismal Instructions*, 6:23; 8:17-8; Ambrose's *DPaenA*, II, 10:95.

[52] St. Ambrose asserts that the external penances are to be motivated by sincere faith and charity (see *DPaenA*, II, 9:80, 83) and affirms that forgiveness is a matter of personal conversion to God:

> He who owes a debt to God has more help towards payment than he who is indebted to man. Man requires money for money, and this is not always at the debtor's command. God demands the affection of the heart, which is in our own power. No one who owes a debt to God is poor, except one who has made himself poor. And even if he have nothing to sell, yet has he herewith to pay. Prayer, fasting, and tears are the resources of an honest debtor, and much more abundant than if one from the price of his estate offered money without faith (*DPaenA*, II, 9:81; trans. from *A Select Library of Nicene and Post-Nicene Fathers of the Christian Church*, Second Series).

See also *DPaenA*, II, 11:104; John Chrysostom, Homily 20, "Concerning the Statues," especially 1–2, 24.

[53] This is explicit in many of the Fathers. Ambrose, for example, states that ecclesiastical penance was granted only once after baptism (*DPaenA*, II, 10:95; see also II, 11:104).

Earlier in this work, Ambrose emphasized that the Church can forgive the greatest sins (I, 13:59; II, 3:19) and that the repentant sinner benefits from the intercession of the many in the Church (I, 17). These liturgical and communitarian dimensions were integral to ecclesiastical penance.

[54] On canonical penance and its development see Berrouard, "La pénitence publique," 117–20; Poschmann, *Penance and the Anointing of the Sick*, 81–7; Dallen, *Reconciling Community*, 56–61.

The Emergence of Monasticism

As political changes, apologetical writings, a sharp increase in adult baptisms, and official penitential policies all drew the Catholic Church and the Roman world into an ever closer embrace, certain Christians decided that the resulting atmosphere of accommodation and compromise had become a liability to them. However, instead of challenging the bishops and apologists, those Christians addressed their difficulty by leaving for places—usually in the desert—where they would be free to live the gospel without hindrance or distraction. Toward the end of the third century this development gave rise to a new institution: monasticism.

Although the monastic movement first appeared at a time of expansion and accommodation, it reflects dynamics that are integral to Christian faith and present in the Church wherever it is found. Early monasticism carried on the honored traditions of widowhood and virginity; it reflected the influence of the ideal Christian community celebrated in the Acts of the Apostles (2:43-47; 4:32-35); the Gospel's exhortations to poverty and charity (Matt 19:21); and the command of Christ to abandon all things, deny oneself, and accept a share in his cross (Matt 16:24-26; also Rom 13:13-14). Monasticism emerged as a way to allow committed Christians to respond more fully to God's word, the commitments associated with baptism, and the Church's eucharistic life. Its goal was to foster the knowledge or vision of God, enable men and women[55] to do God's will more fully, and ultimately help them to receive God's salvation.[56]

---

[55] Although much of the writing about monasticism has traditionally concerned founders and their works, scholarly interest has recently turned to other, less noticed aspects of the monastic experience, including that of women. For more concerning early women ascetics, see Susanna Elm, *"Virgins of God": The Making of Asceticism in Late Antiquity* (Oxford: Clarendon Press, 1994); Elizabeth A. Clark, *Women in the Early Church* (Wilmington: Michael Glazier, 1983) 115–55; Jean Leclercq, "Monasticism and the Promotion of Women," *Women in Monasticism* (Petersham, Mass.: St. Bede's Publications, 1989) 3–15; Jo Ann McNamara, "Muffled Voices: The Lives of Consecrated Women in the Fourth Century," *Distant Echoes*, ed. John A. Nichols and Lillian Thomas Shank (Kalamazoo, Mich.: Cistercian Publications, 1984) 11–29; Jo Ann Kay McNamara, *Sisters in Arms: Catholic Nuns through Two Millennia* (Cambridge, Mass. and London: Harvard University Press, 1996) 34–88.

[56] Louis Bouyer, *Introduction to Spirituality*, trans. Mary Perkins Ryan (Collegeville: The Liturgical Press, 1961) 185–211; idem, *The Spirituality of the New Testament and the Fathers*, trans. Mary P. Ryan (London: Burns & Oates, 1963) 303–5, 317–21; David Knowles, *Christian Monasticism* (New York and Toronto: McGraw Hill, 1969) 10–1; Bernard McGinn, *The Foundations of Mysticism: Origins to the Fifth Century* (New York: Crossroad, 1991) 133–4, 200–2.

The beginning of institutional monasticism is usually identified with an Egyptian named Anthony. Born about 269, he took up residence in the desert in 285 and lived there until his death at an advanced age. In the desert, Anthony and those who joined him sought to live their Christian ideals without being held back by a Church that they considered to be too big and insufficiently committed to the religious and moral requirements of faith in Christ. Although at first they lived separately, the original Egyptian hermits soon gravitated into communities, which offered them the benefits of an organized social structure, a strict rule of life, and effective leadership. The monk Pachomius (c. 290–c. 346) was the principal founder of cenobitic monasticism, that is, monastic life in communities that are governed by a rule and a superior.

By the end of the fourth century monastic communities had taken root in widely separated parts of the Roman Empire and appeared both in urban settings and on country estates. Social and cultural factors certainly fueled the growth of monasticism, but its wide proliferation and acceptance in the Church was primarily due to religious motives and the decisive contributions made by bishops and monastic leaders.[57] This ascetic[58] movement protested against all that was "worldly" in the Church. It appealed to those who did not want to compromise with weakness but preferred to live out of a sustained

[57] Prominent among those whose teachings and practical support helped to establish and extend the early monastic movement are Basil the Great (329–79), Gregory of Nyssa (c. 335–c. 395), Gregory Nazianzen (c. 330–90), Athanasius of Alexandria (c. 300–73), Ambrose of Milan (334–97), Martin of Tours (c. 317–97), Jerome (c. 335–419), Augustine of Hippo (354–430), Evagrius of Pontus (c. 345–99), and John Cassian (c. 360–c. 433).

[58] The terms "ascetic," "ascetical," and "asceticism" are derived from the Greek word *askesis*, which means exercise or training.

> As is evident in its etymology, asceticism is essentially a *discipline*. . . . It is a systematic method to achieve self-control, a way to channel and counteract "passions," which range from the appetitive passions for food and sexual pleasure to emotions such as anger, jealousy, avarice, and hubris. . . . Asceticism is thus not primarily a dualistic phenomenon, which considers the body as evil in opposition to a soul which is good (and thus has far less of the masochistic or self-torturing notions often associated with it). As method or discipline, asceticism is not an end in itself, but aspires to a higher good: namely, to transform the practitioner into a pure vessel of divine will, and so to create the possibility for communication with the divine through some form of *unio mystica* (Elm, *Virgins of God*, 13–4).

John Cassian, a founder of Western monasticism, writes: "Our fastings, our vigils, meditation on Scripture, poverty and the privation of all things are not perfection, but the instruments for acquiring it" (*Conferences*, I, 7, as quoted in Bouyer, *Spirituality of the New Testament*, 318).

personal commitment to the gospel of Christ. On a wider horizon, monasticism provided society and the Church with many examples of people who broke free of their environment and confronted the demonic in human life.[59] Their witness made a deep impression on the people of that era.

As the monastic movement took hold, it flowed into a variety of channels. Although it began in the deserts of Egypt, monasticism found a strong resonance among city people. Lay Christians demonstrated that they could embrace the elevated requirements of the gospel without abandoning their occupations or their neighbors. Priests and bishops dedicated themselves to celibacy, prayer, poverty, and a common life while they continued to be responsible for the pastoral care and worship of the Christian people. Drawing strength from monastic and ascetical writings, the reports of travelers, and the staunch support of Church leaders, the monastic movement continued to develop in its various forms. In a short time it achieved great prestige and wide acceptance in the Church. Over the long run monasticism has had a profound impact on Christian thought, life, and worship; its influence, especially in the West, can hardly be exaggerated.[60]

The Issue of the Two Standards

The emergence of the monastic movement in the fourth century sharpened the contrast between ascetical and ordinary approaches to Christian life. Especially when interpreted in moral and religious

[59] Demonic beings and activities were taken for granted in the Roman world. By naming the demonic as a fearful source of evil and promising an effective attack against it, Christianity was able to command attention and make its agenda understandable to all. It is no accident that apologetic writings, evangelizing efforts, monastic activities, and the liturgical rites associated with candidacy for baptism all explicitly confront demonic elements in human life and declare that Christ has overcome them for the benefit of the human race. On this see Brown, *World of Late Antiquity*, 53–5; Bouyer, *Spirituality of the New Testament*, 311–4.

[60] On the origins of monasticism and its early development, see Knowles, *Christian Monasticism*, 9–36; Bouyer, *Spirituality of the New Testament*, 303–94; Jordan Aumann, *Christian Spirituality in the Catholic Tradition* (San Francisco: Ignatius Press; London: Sheed & Ward, 1985) 35–59; McGinn, *Foundations of Mysticism*, 131–82, 194–6, 200–2; Charles Kannengiesser, "The Spiritual Message of the Great Fathers," *Christian Spirituality: Origins to the Twelfth Century*, ed. Bernard McGinn and others (New York: Crossroad, 1985) 61–88; Jean Gribomont, "Monasticism and Asceticism: I. Eastern Christianity," *Christian Spirituality: Origins to the Twelfth Century*, 89–112; Jean Leclercq, "Monasticism and Asceticism: II. Western Christianity," *Christian Spirituality: Origins to the Twelfth Century*, 113–31; Brown, *World of Late Antiquity*, 96–103; Hall, *Doctrine and Practice*, 173–82; and the sources in note 55 above.

terms, as exemplified by Ambrose and others, that contrast can suggest that Christian life involves two standards. The many can be content with keeping the commandments and meeting other basic imperatives, while the few strive for perfection. This approach has the advantage of being humane and tolerant of human limitations while challenging those who wish to walk the path of religious and moral excellence. In effect, the two-standards approach domesticates the tension between toleration and perfection in the Church and recognizes there are many ways to live Christian life.

Whatever its benefits, the use of a two-standard approach brings certain dangers. Its "better way" can intimate that authentic Christian life is to be found only among ascetics who explicitly commit themselves to the strict requirements of the gospel. Its "ordinary way" can suggest that those who follow a merely natural morality lack commitment, are weak of faith, and are prone to compromise with the world. Where such views hold sway, ordinary people might conclude that little is expected of them or that they can never be as worthy as the ascetics. In that case there can be discouragement and a tendency to abandon the pursuit of religious and moral excellence. The two-standards notion can also be perilous to ascetics, especially if it leads them to take pride in their efforts or think that Christian perfection refers to a particular form of life rather than the quality of one's response to Christ.

Such difficulties can be avoided if it is remembered that all members of the Church walk a pilgrim's path. With God's help, all need to acknowledge their shortcomings and do their best each day to hear God's word and practice the virtues, especially humility, faith, and charity. That approach can bring everyone nearer to Christian perfection and is largely indifferent to one's occupation or place in the Church community.[61]

The Significance of This Period

The events of the fourth century demonstrate that efforts to defend the Church and evangelize the Roman Empire had succeeded. Toleration definitively ended state persecution of the Christian Church and

---

[61] The tension between inclusiveness and perfection is present in the Scriptures (cf. Matt 7:13-14 and 13:47; 19:23-25 and 9:10-13). The problem of the two standards has been all but perennial in the Church, especially given a tendency in Western Christianity to associate perfection with monastic life and a celibate priesthood. See Kirk, *Vision of God*, 104–12; Bouyer, *Spirituality of the New Testament*, 317–21; McGinn, *Foundations of Mysticism*, 131–3.

opened the way to the legal establishment of Catholicism in the empire. Christian writers had accepted secular philosophies and many aspects of Graeco-Roman culture. The Church presented itself as the salvation of the Roman state and opened its doors to the multitudes who sought admittance to the catechumenate. Those events leave no doubt that the Christian community and Roman society had indeed begun to embrace each other. A landmark in human history, that mutual rapprochement has had a deep and lasting impact on the life and landscape of the Christian community.

One of its most immediate effects was to make the Church a more ambiguous community. The widespread appeal of the Church overwhelmed the catechumentate and led to a decline in its effectiveness, increasing the number of those who had entered the Church without having repented of their sins or sincerely committed themselves to Christian faith. Apart from the stress on ecclesiastical penance, that anomalous situation meant that many people lacked the personal and theological foundations that are indispensable to Christian life properly understood. It likewise compromised the ability of the Church to present itself to others as the community of God's saints.

Integral to the Church's acceptance of Roman culture was its increasing reliance on secular modes of thought. To be sure, this use of contemporary intellectual resources was as helpful as it was probably inevitable. Stoic thought, for example, gave Christian leaders new tools with which to interpret the world, evaluate human behavior, and speak more effectively to contemporary audiences both inside and outside the Church. However, such modes of thought were not completely congruent with important aspects of Christian faith and moral life. To propose, as Stoicism does, that nature and a divine mind are normative for human activity is to generate dissonance with the Christian tradition, which considers history and God's sovereign freedom to be primary, and confesses the resurrected Jesus as its Lord. Moreover, the imperatives of reason and moderation were not drawn from the Gospel and tended to distract from its requirements of ready faith, unstinting commitment to Christ, and a life of self-sacrificing charity.[62]

---

[62] On this see Murphy, "Patristic Moral Thought," 61, 84–5; idem, *Moral Teaching,* 113–4. See also Osborn, *Ethical Patterns,* 198–200; Spanneut, "Les normes morales." Spanneut indicates that Stoic thinking encouraged the Fathers to describe morality as universal and immutable. However, the eclectic nature of many patristic borrowings, their acceptance of variation in some contexts, and the presence of cultural influences suggest that any generalizations about patristic approaches to morality should be formulated with great care.

In its various forms, the monastic response acted as a counterbalance to the weakening of Christian life and the Church's cozier relationship with society. It demonstrates that the Gospel maintained its power to speak to people's hearts and radically change their lives. Representing much more than the work of particular individuals, monasticism manifested the ability of God's word to call men and women to community, self-denial, prayer, and charity. Its successful institutionalization was also significant, for besides supporting the ascetic response among the Christian faithful, it gave the corporate dimensions of Christian life greater visibility and guaranteed that the ascetic response would continue to have a practical means of expression despite the passage of time.

These and associated developments reflected the attempt by early Christians to live their faith and address difficult problems that could not be ignored. The decisions and events of the fourth century transformed both Church and society and fashioned a very new and more ambiguous setting in which younger generations encountered the question of faith, interpreted its requirements, and responded to them. The record of their lives and actions offers a case study of faith enacted through moral deliberation and choice; it also invites consideration of the Church-world relationship and its impact on the faith and moral life of contemporary people. The developments of that century have yet further significance, for in them one can already glimpse some of the features that eventually characterized medieval Christendom: the practical identification of Church and society; a close association of secular and sacred; an acceptance in the Church of secular as well as Christian intellectual resources; problems due to poor levels of catechesis, sacramental praxis, and moral behavior among the faithful; and the ready acceptance of monasticism in the community. It would be difficult to find a century that had a greater or more extended impact on faith and moral life.

REFLECTIONS

During the first four centuries the young Christian community clarified its faith, developed its institutional structure, and worked out important points of discipline and worship. As it pursued this important but largely domestic agenda, the Church responded to external hostility and ignorance, at once confronting the errors of its neighbors and inviting them to religious and moral conversion. By the end of that period, the suspicion and hostility that once characterized the relationship between the Church and its world had yielded to sympathy, cooperation, and mutual acceptance. More than anything else, these momentous developments helped to establish the setting in which people considered and responded to the call of faith and enacted their moral life. The impact of these events on later generations can hardly be exaggerated.

To notice the dramatic developments in the Church's domestic life and in its relationship with Graeco-Roman society is to be brought face to face with the historical dimensions of human life. The early Christian community confronted serious internal and external challenges that could not responsibly be dismissed or underestimated. What is more, fidelity to the gospel demanded that these problems should be addressed and often suggested ways of doing so. Whatever the responses, they became part of the ongoing flow of human affairs. This dynamic guaranteed that any practical homeostasis would sooner or later yield to a new state of affairs and a different generation. The necessity of managing fluid human and ecclesial situations taxed the pastoral and theological judgment of Church leaders and ordinary believers throughout these centuries.

This calls attention to the social and historical matrix of the Church community and the moral life of its members. It suggests that the larger and ever-changing human picture helped to establish the setting of Church life, shape the question of faith for particular persons, and inform the moral life of the Christian community. Defending against attacks, evangelizing nonbelievers, catechizing new members of the Church, preaching the word, practicing charity, preserving ecclesial communion, and reconciling baptized sinners all required careful attention to persons and circumstances and demanded that they be considered in their particularity. Specific attention to human affairs was required by the dynamics of Christian faith as much as by the realities themselves.

Faith also exercised a decisive impact on moral life. The apologists pointed out the correlation between pagan myths and pagan immorality and highlighted the close bonds between Christian faith and upright living on the part of believers. The Scriptures, the expectations of those preparing for baptism, and the requirements of ecclesial communion unanimously testify that whoever wishes to share God's life must hear God's word, abandon all vices, and commit to a life of justice and charity in the Church. The monastic response stands as yet another witness to the ability of Christian faith to change people's lives and lead them to perfection. The discipline of ecclesiastical penance, and even the sharp debates that surrounded it, also showed that faith and an upright life were essential to good standing in the Church. This body of evidence also warns against interpreting Christian life in the light of historical facts alone, that is, without due regard for the faith that is its foundation and guide. To ignore the influence of faith is to overlook a constitutive element of the Christian experience and increase the likelihood of serious misunderstandings.

Christian faith was meant to influence the totality of a person's moral life. In light of God's word, individuals were reminded of the ecclesial nature of God's salvation and the consequent requirements of effective love of neighbor and the preservation of communion in the Church. Disreputable occupations were to be avoided, and one's public activity was to be the expression of a sincere personal response to God, born of repentance and faith, and enacted within the community. This suggests that Christian moral life is a comprehensive reality that is based upon God's gifts and the normative quality of the Christian community and includes both the internal commitment and deliberation of persons and their external plans and activities. Christian morality is therefore not to be seen as a truncated affair limited either to the interior world of intentions or the exterior realm of obedience to the community's norms. It presupposes God and the Church but also recognizes the importance of individual persons and upholds their responsibility for whatever they freely decide to do.

One of the most striking features of the early Church's life is the emergence of an intellectual component within its overall response to domestic and external challenges. In their conversation with pagan critics, both truth and the need to speak in a way that would appeal to their audience persuaded the apologists to emphasize the reasonable, human qualities of Christian faith and morality. Many of the Church Fathers adopted Stoic thought and found that it helped them to elaborate Christian faith and morality to outsiders and fellow believers alike. Furthermore, experience demonstrated that the challenge of Gnosticism, Arianism, and other christological errors could only be met on the basis of well-founded, logical thinking. Over time these precedents gave rise to the conviction that adequate intellectual resources were indispensable to the life and ministry of the Church. The emergence of an intellectual tradition is a major development in its own right. It helped to clarify the implications of Christian faith for contemporary issues, supplied important apologetical arguments, enabled Church leaders to expose and rebut doctrinal errors, and supported the ongoing work of Christian catechesis. But a system of thought entails particular content, assumptions, and presuppositions, and this was certainly true of Stoicism. The introduction of Stoic thought into the Christian tradition was arguably more significant for its content and long-term influence than it was as an example of using intellectual resources for apostolic or catechetical purposes.

The opposing claims of toleration and perfection had a pervasive impact on the life and activity of the early Church. The rigorist claims of Montanism and Novatianism posed acute problems, but they only took to an extreme the perfectionist currents that are inherent in Christianity, as the Scriptures (e.g., Matt 5:13-16, 48), baptismal requirements, penitential practices, and the monastic movement surely indicate. But as apologetic efforts began to bear fruit and the Christian Church and Graeco-Roman society embraced each other, more people entered the catechumenate without being prepared to live up to the requirements of baptism or even abide by more basic norms of behavior. Yet sinful humanity, once within the Church, had to be dealt with somehow, and this also reflects the Scriptures (e.g., Matt 13:24-30, 47-59; 18:21-35; Luke 9:53-55) as much as any social or cultural pressures. The resulting dilemma set commitment against mediocrity and brought the relationship between the Church and the world into high relief. The tensions that flowed between these dyads were strong and influential. They favored a broad acceptance of Graeco-Roman culture and thought; stimulated the rise of monasticism; encouraged the acceptance of a morality based upon the Ten Commandments, reason, nature, and moderation; and promoted the development of ecclesiastical penance. These effects reflect the importance of the perennial tension between perfection and toleration and show that it can have dramatic effects on persons, policies, and actions in the Church.

By the end of the fourth century, the overall effects of earlier events and decisions had become more clear. The Church had embraced the Roman people but tried to maintain the integrity of its faith, liturgical worship, and call to perfection. It showed increasing sympathy to non-Christian modes of thought but gave priority to the Scriptures and the apostolic tradition. It accepted the help of the Roman Empire but did not forget the differences between the temporal and the eternal. Important areas of Church thought and praxis had begun to mature and stabilize, but there was still room for development—and also for problems and conflicts.

At this critical juncture, a new and important figure appeared. As a Christian and an intellectual, a priest and a bishop, Augustine of Hippo interpreted the Scriptures, clarified and enriched the apostolic tradition, engaged in key controversies of his day, and helped others to live in faith, hope, and charity. He has influenced the thinking, worship, and life of Western Christianity as few have done. The next chapter will be dedicated to St. Augustine and his momentous contributions to the Church.

4

St. Augustine of Hippo

Of all Christians since apostolic times, Augustine of Hippo is among the most important and, apart from scriptural figures, has had a greater influence on Western Christianity than any other single individual. His extant works are voluminous and include controversial writings, sermons and homilies, scriptural commentaries, letters, spiritual and religious treatises, and such classics as the *Confessions* and *The City of God*. Augustine helped the Church to resolve a number of doctrinal and pastoral questions that could no longer be ignored. His writings strongly influenced Western thought, politics, sacramental praxis, spirituality, and moral life for at least a millennium, not least because they provided a comprehensive and coherent framework in which to consider crucial human, political, and religious issues and framed some of the principal questions that later thinkers pursued. Modern theologians and philosophers continue to study Augustine's texts, thereby testifying to his ongoing importance. A founder of Western monasticism, he remains to this day a guiding light for vowed religious life. Such influence is extraordinary and reflects the wide spectrum and fundamental nature of the issues Augustine dealt with, his outstanding skills as a writer, the quality of his spiritual and intellectual legacy, and the pivotal era in which he lived.

This chapter will therefore be dedicated to St. Augustine. It will explore key aspects of his work and identify some of his contributions to the outlook of the West as well as to the thought and praxis of the Church.

The chapter will first review certain developments that deeply affected the Mediterranean basin during Augustine's time. Among the most important was the large-scale entry of barbarian peoples into the Roman Empire. In addition to its immediate impact, this migration had a long-term influence on culture, religion, and society that can scarcely be overstated.

It will then be important to consider the personal history of this remarkable figure and highlight its influence on his development as a thinker and writer, ascetic and pastor.

The following section will review his arguments against the Manichees. To rebut the theories of this movement, Augustine asserted the inherent goodness of all that exists and attributed evil ultimately to human free will. His teachings shaped the Church's understanding of good and evil, sharpened its views on sin in human life, and taught succeeding generations to appreciate the decisive importance of the inner life of persons.

The fourth section will review Augustine's struggle against the Donatists, a North African schismatic group. It was in this context that he developed his views on the Church, including its relationship with Christ, the ambiguous quality of actual church communities, and the responsibilities of faithful members. Augustine's ecclesiological teachings endowed moral life with religious energy and direction and shaped the Western Church's self-understanding and behavior toward the world at large.

Augustine's theology of grace will then be considered. Augustine taught that original sin has so damaged human nature that without the grace of Christ, freely offered and freely accepted, it is impossible for anyone to avoid sin or reach salvation. He emphasized that an upright moral life is the product of true freedom and requires the help of grace.

The following section will highlight Augustine's view of the moral life and note its objective texture and the decisive functions of grace, love, and freedom. It will also consider his interpretation of human history and the task he assigned to the civil government.

The chapter concludes by identifying key aspects of Augustine's legacy and suggesting its significance for succeeding generations.

Historical Background

In the late fourth and early fifth centuries the Roman Empire experienced foreign invasions, mass migrations, internal disarray, and a heightened sense of insecurity. Catholic bishops assumed more civil authority and imperial rulers a greater measure of power within the Church. These and related events changed the world in which Augustine lived and set the context of his work; they demand attention also because they hastened the break up of the Roman Empire and laid the foundation of medieval Christian Europe.

Barbarian Invasions

Although the frontiers of the Roman Empire were usually peaceful, Rome could never take the security of its borders for granted. This was especially true during the last quarter of the fourth century and the early years of the fifth, when external pressures increased dramatically. Threatened by the Huns of eastern Europe, the barbarian peoples of central Europe had begun to move south and west, eventually colliding with the Roman Empire. The Romans used force to defend their territory but did not always succeed in repelling the invaders. To cite one instance, the Visigoths defeated a Roman army in 378 at Adrianople, in the European portion of modern-day Turkey. This important battle began many years of war in the Balkans. Visigothic and other invasions introduced foreign armies and peoples into the heartland of the Roman Empire.

One of the most significant incursions took place in December of 406, when tens of thousands of Germanic Vandals poured across the Rhine and entered Roman Gaul without significant opposition. The Vandals continued south, and by 409 they had crossed the Pyrenees and began their conquest of Spain. Drawn by the fertile lands of North Africa and anxious to secure themselves against attack by rival barbarian armies, the Vandals crossed the Straits of Gibraltar in 429. They advanced eastward along the coast of Roman Africa, terrorizing the population through murder, cruelty, looting, and general destruction. By 430 they had reached Augustine's city of Hippo and had it under siege as he lay dying. After seizing Carthage in 439, the Vandals set up their own kingdom in what is modern-day Tunisia. From this position they continually threatened Italy and the eastern Mediterranean. The Vandal kingdom in North Africa lasted until 533, when it was conquered by a Byzantine army.

The Vandals were not the only barbarian people to raise havoc within the Roman Empire. After its triumphs in the Balkans, Alaric's Visigothic army invaded Italy and in August of 410 sacked the city of Rome. In 455 Rome again fell to the Vandal general Genseric, whose soldiers spent two weeks plundering and pillaging the city. These events demonstrated just how defenseless the western portion of the empire had become. Together with their peaceful migrations, barbarian incursions profoundly altered the social, political, and religious fabric of the western empire.

Effects of Barbarian Migrations

If they did nothing else, barbarian incursions increased misery and insecurity in the empire. Because the army could no longer protect its own citizens against foreign invasion, large portions of the empire fell under the rule of outsiders, who were often cruel and harsh in their behavior. Britain, isolated from the rest of the empire by the Vandal advance into Gaul, was left to deal with invasions and other problems on its own. Invasion, occupation, and the disruption or lack of government added to such perennial problems as disease, famine, heavy taxation, corruption, and gross inefficiencies of transportation, making life extremely difficult for many people.

The power and proximity of the barbarian peoples had dramatic political effects. To take one example, the emperors began to use barbarian soldiers and employ foreign military leaders as officers in the army. At first this seemed to be an attractive way to domesticate them and profit from their military expertise. This tactic eventually placed a great deal of power in the hands of barbarian Roman generals. In 476 one of them, Odoacer, decided to use it in an unforeseen way—he overthrew the emperor and took that position for himself. A less dramatic but perhaps more significant effect of the barbarians' presence was an increased stress on the empire's many seams. East and West slowly drifted apart. Preoccupied by their many troubles, the provinces of the West turned inward, no longer expecting much help from the central administration or any other source.[1]

Yet another result of these dramatic political and demographic events was to foster closer association between Catholicism and civil life. As the empire appeared more weak, distant, and divided, the Catholic Church emerged as the one organization that could credibly claim to be able to unite the citizens of the empire. Especially after the sack of Rome in 410, people tended to look upon the Church as the bearer of Roman hopes and culture. Roman citizenship and Catholicism now seemed to go hand in hand, all the more so since the invaders were Arian and therefore heretical. Provincial bishops contributed to the identification of Catholicism with the state. They were often the only ones able to lead and encourage their local communities, act on their behalf, and deal effectively with barbarian rulers.

---

[1] That political and social turn inward was emblematic of a less obvious but more important turn carried out when Augustine relocated key issues to the interior domains of the human person. This chapter will return to this topic below. See Charles Taylor, *Sources of the Self: The Making of the Modern Identity* (Cambridge: Harvard University Press, 1989) 127–42.

Despite the upheavals of this difficult period, the Catholic Church in the West tried to meet its responsibility to preach the gospel. In the 430s Palladius and Patrick went as missionaries to Ireland. They advanced the conversion of the Celtic peoples and established the monasteries that quickly came to dominate the practice of faith in that land. Within the empire many pagans were asking for baptism, and this too contributed to the expansion and increased importance of the Catholic Church.[2]

AUGUSTINE'S PERSONAL HISTORY

St. Augustine's personal story has spoken to innumerable people across the centuries, both for reasons of human interest and because of its power to help others grapple with such perennial problems as self-knowledge, evil, love, a divided heart, the meaning of the world and its history, and God's place in human life. This study will review Augustine's personal development, not only for these reasons but also because it illuminates his faith, religious outlook, intellectual positions, and pastoral contributions.

Augustine's Early Life

Aurelius Augustinus was born in the North African town of Thagaste on November 13, 354. Although he was not baptized in his infancy, Augustine's devout Catholic mother, Monica, nonetheless gave him a religious upbringing. With the help of a wealthy patron, Augustine's parents sent him to Carthage, where he completed a mainly literary education. Although rather narrow, his schooling successfully taught him the rhetorical arts; Augustine learned how to use language well and acquired the ability to express himself clearly and persuasively. These skills enabled him to excel as a thinker, writer, debater, and preacher.

Augustine's years at Carthage were extremely formative. At the age of seventeen he began a fifteen-year common-law type of relationship with a woman with whom he had a son in the year 372. His relationships with this woman, whose name is unknown, and others in his

---

[2] See Peter Brown, *The World of Late Antiquity, AD 150–750* (New York: Harcourt Brace Jovanovich, 1971) 111–35; Pierre Courcelle, *Histoire littéraire des grandes invasions germaniques*, 3rd ed. (Paris: Études Augustiniennes, 1964); Lucien Musset, *The Germanic Invasions: The Making of Europe AD 400–600*, trans. Edward James and Columba James (London: Paul Elek, 1975) 6–41, 53–60, 125–34, 158–90, 219–22. This historical review is primarily indebted to Brown.

young adulthood, disclose a passionate individual, yet one who was acutely aware of forces in him that resisted his control. Philosophy and other intellectual pursuits also captivated this very sensitive young man. At Carthage he was deeply moved by his study of *Hortensius*, a lost philosophical work of the Roman writer Cicero. As a result of this experience, he committed himself to the pursuit of truth and vowed not to rest until he had successfully claimed wisdom as his own. To this enterprise Augustine brought acute intelligence and an amazing capacity to master difficult literature that others could only discuss second-hand.

In the grip of this enthusiasm, the young Augustine read the classic authors but rejected them since they ignored Jesus. The Old Testament also left him cold, in part because he found the inferior Latin text available to him to be aesthetically offensive. The Old Testament was also discredited for Augustine because his literal interpretation of the text led to absurd and unacceptable conclusions. What was worse, the Old Testament seemed to make God the origin of the evil that pervaded human life, and this left Augustine confused and in turmoil. The power and extent of evil in human life had long ago drawn his attention; now it focused his intellectual curiosity and channeled his restlessness.[3]

Augustine as a Manichee

In a crisis of faith and struggling to understand the origin and nature of evil, Augustine encountered the Manichees. They were a Gnostic-type religious group who acknowledged Jesus as a prophet of God. Especially since its beliefs included a cogent explanation of evil, Manichean teachings and way of life seemed to offer Augustine everything he wanted. He joined the Manichees as a "hearer," that is, a disciple who did not yet enjoy full membership.

The Manichees the young Augustine met in Carthage were followers of a Babylonian named Mani (216–76). Mani proclaimed that God had given him the latest and ultimate revelation of light for the world. He declared that he was the final and ultimate prophet after Buddha, Zoroaster, and Jesus, who had previously received more limited gifts of light. Mani taught that God had commissioned him to found the true and universal religion, which would bring all others to their fulfillment. Manichean teaching offered salvation to its followers and

---

[3] See Henry Chadwick, *The Early Church* (London: Penguin Books, 1967) 216–8; for a more thorough account of Augustine's early years, see Peter Brown, *Augustine of Hippo* (Berkeley: University of California Press, 1969) 19–45; for Augustine's own words, *Conf*, I–III.

spared them the burden of judgment. Its adherents were usually se-cretive and often engaged in ascetical practices.

Augustine found this religion appealing largely because it answered his needs. Its rejection of the Old Testament removed one source of vexation. Its art, poetry, rituals, and practices engaged his aesthetic sensitivities. Its highly rational quality, at least on the surface, played to the strong suit of a precocious and highly intellectual young man. Still, as time passed Augustine began to have his doubts. He was frus-trated because Manichean thought assigned a passive position to the person and hence offered no possibility of spiritual advancement. He became skeptical when he learned that the Manichean explanation of the moon and other heavenly lights was astronomically impossible. In 383 Augustine lost all confidence in Manicheism when a noted leader, Faustus of Milevis, proved to be totally incapable of answering his questions. He had been a Manichee for about nine years, and the fol-lowing year, when he left to teach in Rome, he remained a Manichee in little more than name only.[4]

Conversion to Philosophy

After a short time in Rome, Augustine was made professor of rhetoric in Milan, then the seat of the imperial government. Because he was ambitious for high office, he was delighted to receive so presti-gious an appointment. After arriving at Milan, he encountered Ambrose, the bishop of that city. Ambrose fascinated Augustine be-cause he was a superb orator who quoted a vast array of writers, both classic and Christian, and had a fine command of contemporary thought, including Manicheism. In the Milanese cathedral Augustine learned that the Old Testament was not always to be taken literally but sometimes required a spiritual interpretation. That discovery un-locked the Scriptures and led him to reject the materialistic world view of the Manichees as grossly truncated and useless. Ambrose had en-gaged Augustine's mind, heart, and spirit.[5]

Once again in a state of profound turmoil, Augustine began to read Plotinus and Porphyry, philosophers who were intellectual descen-dants of Plato, the classic Greek thinker. Because his thought was espe-cially lucid and persuasive, Plotinus (205–70) had an especially deep

[4] On Augustine's involvement with Manicheism, see Brown, *Augustine of Hippo,* 46–60; G. R. Evans, *Augustine on Evil* (Cambridge: Cambridge University Press, 1982) 11–6; *Conf,* IV–V. Manichean teachings will be discussed later in this chapter.

[5] For a discussion of this phase of Augustine's life, see Brown, *Augustine of Hippo,* 79–87; see also *Conf,* V, especially 13–4.

influence on Augustine. Plotinus held a unified concept of reality in which being emanates in stages from an ultimate source in the One, also called the Good, that is beyond all thought and all being. Emanation is a necessary process by which a higher source communicates being to the next-lower level such that the two are distinct but the source is not changed or lessened. Plotinus taught that from the One, at the center of all existence and prior to everything that exists, Intelligence, or Mind, emanates. Intelligence, also called *Logos* or the Word, contains the immaterial ideas from which specific things take their source. From Intelligence emanates the world-soul, from which individual human souls proceed. Human souls possess higher spiritual and lower material elements. Corporeal beings come about from the impression of the Mind's ideas upon matter through the activity of a soul.

This system envisions a reciprocal movement of energy in which being proceeds from higher to lower levels; and they in turn tend to stay in contact with the higher ones, from which they derive their being. As applied to human life, this means that the human soul, the lowest form of spiritual being, has a need to contemplate its source in the One. It also tends to return to the One and its Intelligence by a process of liberation from earthly life. Practically speaking, this would be accomplished best by a turning within so as to explore one's spiritual and mental activity, or by means of an ecstatic ascent, although ordinary people usually follow a more pedestrian process of discipline and purgation.

As Augustine considered this system, he found many parallels with the Prologue to the Gospel According to John. There, God, eternal and uncreated, is described as bringing all creatures into being through the *Logos*, the Word. Human beings, at once spiritual and material, are to receive the Word and ultimately return to God by means of Christ, who is their means of access to divine life. In addition, the ordered universe of Plotinus offered a way to account for love and asceticism, disorder and evil, in human life.

Although he rejected some aspects as repugnant to Christian faith, Augustine found the thought of Plotinus to be cogent and appealing. He studied it carefully until he had absorbed its inner coherence, insight, and logic. Once personalized in this way, it became the foundation of his intellectual development and the framework of his later presentations of Catholic faith. His philosophical discoveries changed Augustine's life: he abandoned all thought of pursuing a rhetorical career and accepted that philosophy would be central to his life from that moment on.[6]

---

[6] For an introduction to Plotinus, see Vernon J. Bourke, *History of Ethics* (Garden City, N.Y.: Doubleday, 1968) 40–4; Elmer O'Brien, *The Essential Plotinus: Represen-*

Conversion to Christ

Augustine continued to wrestle with fundamental philosophical questions, but he knew that his anguish was rooted in willfulness and in immoral living and could not be cured by intellectual efforts. His own words disclose the true dimensions of the problem:

> I was an unhappy young man, wretched as at the beginning of my adolescence when I prayed you for chastity and said: "Grant me chastity and continence, but not yet." I was afraid you might hear my prayer quickly, and that you might too rapidly heal me of the disease of lust which I preferred to satisfy rather than suppress. I had gone along "evil ways" (Ecclus. 2:10) with a sacrilegious superstition, not indeed because I felt sure of its truth but because I preferred it to the alternatives, which I did not investigate in a devout spirit but opposed in an attitude of hostility (*Conf*, VII, 7:17).[7]

Searching for some comfort, he turned to the epistles of St. Paul. These letters spoke personally to Augustine and reawakened the religious feelings of his youth, but they did not resolve the inner conflict that continued to tear him apart. He needed to change his life, yet continued to postpone the day of decision (*Conf*, VIII, 5:10–7:18).

A crisis soon overtook him. One day he found himself deeply moved by reports of the Egyptian monks who, although they had no education, stormed heaven with their lives of renunciation. Overwhelmed by the unbearable contrast between their selfless lives and his own sins and compromises, Augustine left the room in deep distress. His inner turmoil continued for some time while his best friend, Alypius, stood by and supported him as best he could. The turning point came when Augustine picked up the Scriptures and read these verses:

> Let us conduct ourselves becomingly as in the day, not in revelling and drunkenness, not in debauchery and licentiousness, not in quarrelling and jealousy. But put on the Lord Jesus Christ, and make no provision for the flesh, to gratify its desires (*Conf*, VIII, 12:29, quoting Rom 13:13–14).

This text went straight to his heart. Augustine knew that he could longer accept his evil behavior. He renounced all his hopes for marriage and a career in government. He would henceforth belong

---

tative Treatises from the Enneads (Indianapolis; Hackett, 1986), especially 13–32. See also *Conf*, VII, 9:13; Gerald Bonner, *St. Augustine of Hippo: Life and Controversies* (Philadelphia: Westminster Press, 1963) 80–7; Brown, *Augustine of Hippo*, 88–100.

[7] Quotations from this work are taken from Saint Augustine, *Confessions*, trans. Henry Chadwick (New York: Oxford University Press, 1991).

entirely to Christ, embrace chastity, and live according to the rule of faith.[8]

Once he had resolved his inner conflict, Augustine recovered his tranquillity and found that his life had regained a sense of purpose. The following months comprised a time of retreat in which he led an ascetical life of prayer and personal discipline, read widely, and conversed on serious topics with his friends. Along with Alypius and his son, Adeodatus, he began to prepare for baptism. The following year, after they had completed a demanding catechumenate, Bishop Ambrose baptized them during the Easter Vigil of 387. With his baptism, Augustine formally assumed the serious and lifelong responsibilities of a Catholic Christian.[9]

Augustine's time in northern Italy had changed him forever. His spiritual conversion and baptismal commitment governed the rest of his life. The study of Neoplatonic thought gave him the philosophical resources needed for a solid intellectual life. Patient work with the Scriptures and instruction in Catholic faith contributed to his Christian education and sharpened his capacity to understand and preach the sacred text. From these sources he established the profoundly religious, acutely intellectual, and thoroughly personal foundations of a lifetime of pastoral care and theological writing.

Monk, Priest, and Bishop

In the fall of the year 388 Augustine left Italy, never to return. He made his way back to Thagaste, his boyhood home, and took up residence on a portion of his family's property. There he gathered some like-minded men, all of whom wished to live in community as "servants of God," a group committed to perfection in living the Christian gospel. Their monastic way of life aimed to foster contemplation and won them the respect and support of their neighbors. It was during this period, perhaps in the year 390, that Augustine was bereaved of his son and a close friend, losses that affected him deeply. Early in 391, lonely and restless, he traveled to Hippo[10] in order to begin a monastery.

Since it already had a bishop, Augustine thought he was safe from being conscripted into that office. Instead he was set upon by the con-

---

[8] For a fuller account of Augustine's personal conversion see *Conf*, VIII, 8:19–12:30, Brown, *Augustine of Hippo*, 101–14.

[9] Brown, *Augustine of Hippo*, 115–27; *Conf*, IX, 1–6.

[10] Hippo was a major Roman port city. It stood near the modern Algerian city of Annaba, which is located a short distance from the Tunisian border.

gregation and brought forward to Bishop Valerius for ordination as a priest. Augustine's reputation as a servant of God, his intellectual abilities, and his fluid and persuasive manner of speaking all recommended his promotion. Immediately after his ordination, Augustine founded the monastery that had drawn him to Hippo. Having accepted the apostolic community (Acts 4:32-35) as their model, its members bound themselves to a life of celibacy, poverty, and charity in the service of the Church. Prayer and manual work were the principal elements of the daily routine.

Once ordained, Augustine undertook a sustained study of the Scriptures, which reflected deep personal interest as well as pastoral necessity. Aware of his extraordinary abilities, Bishop Valerius called upon the new priest to preach as well as teach, and especially to counteract the propaganda and proselytizing of local Manichees and Donatists. Augustine taught catechetical lessons, routed the Manichees who had the misfortune to meet him in debate, and expounded the Creed to an assembly of bishops. He became a bishop in 395, and the following year when Valerius died he succeeded to the see of Hippo. Although his new position required him to reside in the bishop's house, Augustine did not abandon the monastic way of life. He assembled in his own home a community of clerics who observed a common life of poverty, prayer, celibacy, and charity. Because most members were priests, their principal activity was not manual work but the pastoral care of the people.[11] Augustine spent the rest of his life as bishop of Hippo, and in that position he studied, preached, wrote, observed the affairs of his day, and participated in many of its controversies. He died on August 28, 430.[12]

[11] On the development of Augustine's monastic commitment and the communities in which he lived, see Adolar Zumkeller, *Augustine's Ideal of the Religious Life,* trans. Edmund Colledge (New York: Fordham University Press, 1986), especially 3–45; see also Henry E. Chadwick, "The Ascetic Ideal in the History of the Church," *Monks, Hermits, and the Ascetic Tradition,* ed. W. J. Sheils (Oxford: Basil Blackwell, 1985) 1–24; F. Van der Meer, *Augustine the Bishop: The Life and Work of a Father of the Church,* trans. Brian Battershaw and G. R. Lamb (London and New York: Sheed & Ward, 1961) 199–234; Peter Brown, *The Body and Society: Men, Women, and Sexual Renunciation in Early Christianity* (New York: Columbia University Press, 1988) 395.

Augustine is considered a founder of Western monasticism especially because he helped to adapt monasticism to an urban setting and accommodated it to the requirements of pastoral care and the clerics who provide it. His stature is also due to the monastic Rule that he bequeathed to the Church. See Zumkeller, *Augustine's Ideal;* George Lawless, *Augustine of Hippo and His Monastic Rule* (Oxford: Clarendon Press, 1987).

[12] Brown, *Augustine of Hippo,* 128–45, 189–202; Van der Meer, *Augustine the Bishop,* 129–98, 235–74.

GOOD AND EVIL

The problem of evil is perennial in human life. Experiences of frustration, failure, injustice, malice, sickness, suffering, and death confront everyone with evil and require them to work out some understanding of it. This was certainly true in the ancient world, in which human life was often precarious, difficult, and violent. At that time, philosophies and religious sects usually attributed evil less to human activity than to mythic activity, cosmic forces, or fate. Augustine developed a very different account of good and evil in opposition to Manicheism and in light of Catholic faith and his own philosophical views. This section will describe the context and characteristics of Augustine's account and suggest its importance for moral life and for the later tradition.

Manicheism

Manicheism was a religious movement that conceived of reality as being divided into two separate components, one good and the other evil. According to Manichean thought, God is good and is the source of light, the good element in the world. Evil comes from an evil creator and is identified with matter and the forces of darkness in general. Although they might often be in close proximity, good and evil, light and darkness, do not intermingle. In this world the evil of matter is stronger than the goodness of the light and continually wars against it.

On the religious plane, Manichean doctrine held that God had communicated some of his goodness—the light—to Mani, who in turn was to share it with others through his teachings and religion. Manicheism claimed to offer people the interior illumination that awakens them to a knowledge of the truth about themselves, God, and the world. Mani taught that within each person there is a spark of good that prompts him or her to try to behave well and even achieve unity with the Kingdom of Light in a state of unalloyed perfection. The good part of the self, the light, does not achieve its goals because the evil part of the person, notably the dead weight of the body and its many unruly passions, is stronger. Identified with the world and the body, evil continually attacks the spark of light within people and restrains it.[13]

---

[13] For a detailed account of this religion, see Kurt Rudolph, *Gnosis: The Nature and History of Gnosticism*, trans. and ed. R. McL. Wilson (San Francisco: Harper & Row, 1984) 326–42; Bonner, *St. Augustine of Hippo*, 157–92; Evans, *Augustine on Evil*, 11–6. See also Peter Brown, *Religion and Society in the Age of Saint Augustine* (London: Faber & Faber, 1972) 94–118, for a discussion of Manicheism in the Roman Empire.

Although Manicheism has important theological and metaphysical dimensions, its moral implications are especially interesting. Because evil is the stronger element within the world and good is passive, the goodness in people cannot prevail over the aggressive and impersonal forces of evil. It follows that the latter are to blame for the evils found in human life, whereas people are not responsible because they are ultimately quite helpless. Paradoxically, this understanding of the world and human activity leads both to rigorism and license in the moral life. On the one hand Manichean teaching encouraged extremely severe ascetical practices designed to subdue matter and expand the light in an adherent. On the other hand, its judgment that people are not morally responsible for the evil that they do tacitly encouraged those who engaged in immoral conduct (see *DMorMan*, 18-9).

Augustine's Teaching on Good and Evil

In the years following his conversion to philosophy and baptism, Augustine responded vigorously to the Manichees. He never forgot his experiences as a member of this group and drew upon his intimate understanding of it. He worked out a more satisfactory view of the human person and human activity, which not only informed his reply to the Manichees but also framed the issue of good and evil for Western thinkers ever since. Finally, he developed a more fruitful approach to the interpretation and preaching of the Sacred Scriptures. These steps enabled him to construct a better alternative to Manichean theories.[14]

In responding to the Manichees, Augustine usually began with what they agreed upon, namely, that God is completely good and exists in an eternal and immutable way. He then considered the nature of evil and pointed out that it has to be the opposite of the goodness found in God. However, since God is good in his very existence, evil has to be nonexistence. Therefore evil cannot be a substance, nature, or anything positive at all; it has to be a privation, or absence of a good that ought to be present. Since evil is not something but nothing, all created things are necessarily good and cannot be evil by their very nature (*DMorMan*, 1–5). In maintaining the goodness of all that is, Augustine carefully excluded any hint of pantheism. Following the Scriptures, he noted that God created the world out of nothing and not out of the

---

Manicheism involved many features of Gnosticism, including knowledge as a source of salvation, claims of a new and final revelation, diluting the moral significance of human behavior, and a dualistic understanding of reality.

[14] See Evans, *Augustine on Evil*, 29–111.

divine substance. Created things are therefore good but not divine, while evil is strictly a privation of good and not a substance of any kind (*Conf,* XII, 7:7; *DCivDei,* XI, 9; XII, 1–2).

When he considered the world known to human experience, Augustine taught that God is the highest and purest existence and has arranged for all other beings to have appropriate places in the overall order of things (*DCivDei,* XII, 2, 5). The order of nature reflects God's eternal law, which requires the observance of the natural order and prohibits its disruption (*CFaustMan,* XXII, 30). That order is eternal and can be compared to the meter that governs poetry or the proportions that make for beauty. Goodness is found when existing things adhere to the order that pertains to them. Evil occurs whenever and to the degree that a created, changeable being falls away from due order. In that case corruption begins to intrude, but as a diminution or loss of the being, measure, form, or order that ought to have been and not as a positive reality (*DMorMan,* 1–5).[15]

Augustine's position that evil is a privation of good includes a discussion of how evil actually occurs in human life. Here the issue is not the nature of evil but its origin. To that important question he gives two closely related answers. The principal source of evil is the misuse of human freedom. Human beings owe wholehearted obedience to God, but they nevertheless turn away from God, ignore his requirements, and sin. Augustine emphasizes that sin comes from a person's free will and from no other source. Sin "is the will to retain and follow after what justice forbids, and from which it is free to abstain" (*DDuaAn,* 11).[16] It also occurs when a person deserts what is better in order to secure something inferior. In acting that way, sinners cause evil in at least two senses: they violate due order, and by doing so they also inflict corruption on themselves (*DNatBon,* 7, 28, 34, 36; see also *DCivDei,* XII, 3, 6–8). The other source of evil is God's punishment of sinners, which is a just response to the sinner's free act of disobedience. Evil in human life therefore finds its source in the voluntary human turning away from God together with God's just punishment of sinners (*DNatBon,* 7; *DCivDei,* XII, 3).

[15] On eternal law and natural order see R. A. Markus, *Saeculum: History and Society in the Theology of Saint Augustine* (Cambridge: Cambridge University Press, 1970) 87–93.

[16] See Evans, *Augustine on Evil,* 91–118, especially 112–8; Eric F. Osborn, *Ethical Patterns in Early Christian Thought* (Cambridge and New York: Cambridge University Press, 1976) 149–53, 156–8.

Osborn notes that for Augustine personal sin has three components: suggestion, delight, and consent (156), which also highlight sin as an affective and free personal act.

The Significance of Augustine's Account

Augustine recognized the social, religious, and moral dimensions of evil and based his account upon a comprehensive view that began with God and the created universe. As a Christian believer, he upheld the absolute supremacy of God, maintained the radical difference between Creator and creatures, and acknowledged the goodness of the world. In affirming that evil is essentially a matter of privation, he was able to reconcile the goodness of God and all creatures with the manifest presence of evil in human life.

His view builds upon the assertion that as their Creator and highest good, God is entitled to receive the obedience of all people. God is also to be loved because only God can completely fulfill human persons and quiet their restlessness. Nothing other than communion with God fully satisfies the human heart (*Conf*, I, 1). Obedience and love are also to govern human activity toward the things found in the universe. Originally identified with God's eternal law, the order of nature is to be respected despite its having been corrupted by evil. Whether it refers to God or created things, Augustine's orderly universe provides sturdy, objective grounds on which to base human moral and religious life.

If Manicheism left little room for personal freedom or effort, Augustine not only upheld these dimensions of human life but assigned them an altogether decisive function. For Augustine, freedom is the foundation of a person's moral and religious life and a principal determinant of good and evil in the universe. Freedom emerges in the face of the primordial either-or choices that confront free persons each day: God or self, spirit or flesh, order or disorder, obedience or disobedience, humility or pride, charity or cupidity. Moreover, freedom is a necessary prerequisite if people are to be able to choose between such alternatives and be personally responsible for their choice. In an ordered universe that has God as its origin and highest good, these choices are to be made in light of objective criteria and not arbitrarily. By attributing so decisive a function to human freedom, Augustine immeasurably expanded and deepened the arena of human moral life. Although he upheld an objective order that comes from God, he relocated decisive activities to an interior forum, turned people's attention inward, and gave later generations a new way to think about pivotal human questions.

The religious implications of Augustine's response are also great. To say that God is the highest good of human persons and the end of all their striving is to suggest that God is ultimately at issue in all that people seek and in everything they freely do. In other words, all human loving and moral activity are charged with religious meaning, and this is the case whether people are aware of it or not. If they act rightly toward created beings, people not only observe due order but advance their true good and show deference to God. Free activity that fails to respect due order is not only evil but also sinful.[17] At a deeper level, however, the issue turns on love. People are to love God above all and everything else in a strictly subordinate way. When the question is framed in these terms, it becomes apparent that sin is a perverted striving or an aberration in loving. Sin occurs when persons love themselves, others, or things in a disordered way, perhaps even loving creatures with the kind of love that belongs to God alone.[18] Because they occur within God's good and ordered world, all free actions and every expression of love affect a person's relationship to God and can be assessed accordingly (e.g., *DCivDei*, XIV, 7, 11–3; XV, 22).[19]

CHRIST AND THE CHURCH

If Augustine worked out his understanding of evil largely in response to the Manichees, his ecclesiology was born of his struggle with the Donatists. In the course of many years of debate with this schismatic group he worked out his views concerning the Church, its internal life, sacramental theology, and relationship with the world. In doing so, Augustine did much more than address an urgent pastoral and intellectual problem. By identifying pivotal issues, establishing a frame of reference in which to consider them, and outlining a coherent view of Christian life, he influenced the practical course of Western Christianity and the agenda of its thinkers as few have ever done. The following section will describe the historical situation in which

[17] Hence the classic description of sin as "any deed, word, or desire that is contrary to the eternal law" (*CFaustMan*, XXII, 27).

[18] Hence another classic Augustinian formulation, which recognizes sin as the aversion from God by means of a disordered conversion to some creature (*De libero arbitrio* [On Free Will], II, 18:48–20:54, especially 19:53).

[19] For a discussion of Augustine's writings against the Manichees, see Bonner, *St. Augustine of Hippo*, 193–236. His theology of evil and sin is summarized in John Burnaby, *Amor Dei: A Study of the Religion of St. Augustine* (London: Hodder & Stoughton, 1938; rept.ed., Norwich: Canterbury Press, 1991) 184–90; see also Osborn, *Ethical Patterns*, 146–51, 156–7; Stanley R. Hopper, "The Anti-Manichean Writings," *A Companion to the Study of St. Augustine*, ed. Roy W. Battenhouse (New York: Oxford University Press, 1955) 148–74; J. Patout Burns, "Augustine on the Origin and Progress of Evil," *The Ethics of St. Augustine*, ed. William S. Babcock (Atlanta: Scholars Press, 1991) 67–85; William S. Babcock, "Augustine on Sin and Moral Agency," *Ethics of St. Augustine*, 87–108; Evans, *Augustine on Evil*, 112–8; Chadwick, "Ascetic Ideal."

Augustine developed his thinking about the Church, identify its main components, and note some implications for moral life.

The Donatists

When Augustine returned to Africa, he found a Christian community divided by conflicting views of the Church, episodes of violence, and long-nurtured grievances. The problem had begun some eighty years earlier during the Great Persecution of Diocletian. At that time some African bishops had seemed to comply with Diocletian's demand that they abandon Christianity and manifest their apostasy by surrendering sacred books for burning. Those bishops later asserted that they had not abandoned their faith and had merely handed over some heretical literature. Stricter members of the community rejected that defense. They charged that the offending bishops had indeed apostatized and thereby had excluded themselves from the Church. Beneath this conflict lay the old but still-vexing questions of personal holiness and reconciliation in the Church.

Following Cyprian of Carthage, some in North Africa held that a person in apostasy or schism could not validly celebrate a sacrament.[20] That principle seemed to apply to Caecilian, who had been chosen as the new bishop of Carthage in 312. Because he had been consecrated by one judged to be an apostate, some thought that he was invalidly consecrated and therefore should be rejected. A council of Numidian

---

[20] Cyprian had held that the Church's sacraments have their effects by virtue of the spiritual power of the Church itself. Therefore they could only be celebrated validly by one who enjoyed good standing in it, since anyone separated by schism, heresy, or apostasy has no access to the spiritual energy essential to the sacraments. That principle led Cyprian to disregard the baptisms of heretics. When they wished to join the Catholic Church, he did not merely receive them into ecclesial communion but baptized them again. That praxis and its underlying principle were formally upheld by several African councils and one in Asia Minor.

Those conciliar declarations notwithstanding, Cyprian and the African bishops found themselves in conflict with Pope Stephen of Rome, who declared that it was wrong to practice rebaptism. The Roman position was that whoever acts in accordance with Christ's command baptizes validly. That view linked the power of the sacraments more to Christ and less immediately to the Church or the minister. It allowed that the sacraments might be celebrated validly even by one not in communion with the Church. Pope Stephen asserted the right to have other bishops observe the Roman praxis and threatened Cyprian with excommunication over the issue. For reasons that are lost in the mist of history, no such breach seems to have occurred. The long-range significance of Cyprian's view is found in its use by the Donatists. On Cyprian's position and the resulting controversy, see Chadwick, *Early Church*, 221–2; Bonner, *St. Augustine of Hippo*, 26–8, 276–83; Stuart G. Hall, *Doctrine and Practice in the Early Church* (Grand Rapids: Eerdmans, 1991) 91–4.

bishops agreed with that conclusion and consecrated another bishop for that city. When he died soon afterward, the Numidians installed Donatus as his successor in Carthage. Their actions left Carthage with two competing bishops, Caecilian and Donatus, and a community divided between them and by the different views they represented.

After appeals were lodged with the emperor, a special council of bishops decided that Caecilian had been duly consecrated. The party of Donatus rejected that decision and held to its position. Donatus was primarily responsible for the consolidation of the schismatic party and its propagation far beyond Carthage. The Donatists, as they came to be called, considered themselves to be the true Church of pure and holy Christians. The rigorous standards of Donatism reflected the temper of many African Christians, and it soon became a powerful force in that area.[21]

After many decades of ascendancy, in the last years of the fourth century the tide began to turn against the Donatists. In part that was a result of Augustine's defense of his own congregation and his relentless campaign against Donatism. It was also related to a less patient attitude on the part of the imperial court, which had grown tired of the disturbances spawned by the schism in North Africa. Finally, in 405, after a bishop who had been severely beaten by a Donatist congregation had appealed for redress, the government issued its Edict of Unity. The Roman authorities declared that Donatism constituted a heretical sect and was consequently prohibited by earlier legislation issued in favor of the Catholic Church, a judgment that was reaffirmed 411. That stand by the state, and the risks entailed in defying it, convinced many Africans that joining a Catholic and not a Donatist congregation was the better course of action. In January of 412, Emperor Honorius outlawed Donatism altogether and decreed that Donatist adherents would be fined, their clergy exiled, and their property confiscated.[22]

Donatist Theology

Donatism is principally known for its ecclesiological beliefs, especially its conviction that the Church is identified with the visible com-

---

[21] Bonner, *St. Augustine of Hippo,* 26–32.

[22] Brown, *Augustine of Hippo,* 226–43, 330–9; Bonner, *St. Augustine of Hippo,* 237–75; Chadwick, *Early Church,* 223–4. For a study of the antecedents of the Donatist movement in North Africa, see W.H.C. Frend, *The Donatist Church: A Movement of Protest in Roman North Africa* (Oxford: Clarendon Press, 1971).

The imperial government's pressure against the Donatists succeeded in reducing their numbers and influence but did not eradicate them. Despite many adversities

munity of believers. The Donatists held that the Church enjoys an exclusive, privileged relationship with God. It therefore has to keep itself pure, holy, and safe from the world. Not surprisingly, Donatists were fond of comparing the Church to a vine that sometimes needs pruning, or Noah's ark, sealed tight against the chaos outside. They did not accommodate their praxis to the needs of the world or sinful Christians and considered it to be far better to remain a small but faithful remnant than to grow large at the expense of fidelity. That view resulted in a very strict pastoral policy, especially when it concerned apostasy during persecution. According to Donatist theology, failure in such an important matter entailed separation from the Church.[23]

At least in theory, that ecclesiology imposes strict moral requirements upon adherents. If they are to remain in good standing, they have to measure up to the demands of the Church's holiness. Those who fail in any significant way are to be pruned away from the vine of Christ. Thus the community's integrity and fidelity are preserved at the expense of the defective member. However, it is one thing to detail a strict theory and insist upon its validity; it is another to apply it consistently in real life. In the case of Donatism, there is ample evidence that they did not practice what they preached. Although their failure to live up to their own standards is one of the points Augustine drove home in his attack against Donatism, the essence of his argument lay elsewhere.[24]

Augustine's Understanding of the Church

Augustine had lived in Rome, found faith in northern Italy, and learned much from the widely read Ambrose. He could hardly agree that the Church could be limited to any one province or group. He was convinced that the Church was universal—it was the community of the baptized spread across the entire Mediterranean world and beyond. From that perspective the Donatists had to be the schismatics, especially since they had refused to maintain peace and communion with the rest of the Church. If, as they claimed, the sacraments could not be valid apart from the unity of the Church, then the Donatists should impugn their own sacraments and not those of the Catholic Church.

---

they survived in North Africa until overtaken by Islam around the end of the seventh century.

[23] Brown, *Augustine of Hippo,* 217–20; Bonner, *St. Augustine of Hippo,* 284–5; Markus, *Saeculum,* 105–32.

[24] See Epistle 185:16-17; Markus, *Saeculum,* 111–2.

Augustine himself did not draw that conclusion. He attributed the power of the sacraments not to a specific church community or the personal qualities of the minister but to Christ as the sinless high priest. Therefore even though the minister or recipient might be unworthy, the sacraments can be celebrated validly outside the Catholic communion. But since salvation was available only in the Catholic Church, he held that the sacraments could only be fruitful for one who shared its communion. Augustine concluded that it was unnecessary to doubt the validity of sacraments among separated Christians and wrong to repeat them after ecclesial reconciliation (*DBap*, I, esp. 5:7, 9:12, 14:22; III, 10:13-5; IV, 1:1, 2:2, 12:19).[25]

This understanding of sacramental efficacy reflected the differences between the two communities. Donatist congregations were small, defensive, largely composed of non-Roman peoples, and prone to exclude grave sinners. Augustine's Church was large, confident, well-connected with the imperial government, and prepared to embrace the world. His outlook also reflected his cosmopolitan background and mirrored the experience of a Church that was rapidly expanding on many fronts.

Pastoral experience also prompted Augustine to acknowledge that the Church includes the weak and strong, worthy and unworthy. Referring to his own congregation, he once wrote to a friend:

> You are like[ly] to see many drunkards, covetous, defrauders, gamblers, adulterers, fornicators, wearers of unholy charms, devotees of sorcerers, astrologers or diviners who are skilled in all kinds of unholy arts. Also you are like[ly] to notice that those crowds fill the churches on the feast

---

[25] For more concerning this aspect of Augustine's thought, see Frederick W. Dillistone, "The Anti-Donatist Writings," *Companion to the Study of St Augustine*, 181–97; Brown, *Augustine of Hippo*, 221–4; Bonner, *St. Augustine of Hippo*, 289–94.

Augustine compared the lasting effects of baptism and holy orders to the mark imposed upon the hands of Roman soldiers in order to identify them and deter desertion (*DBap*, I, 4). His views are the early ancestor of later theological references to the "indelible mark" left by baptism, confirmation, and holy orders. His theological response to Donatist sacramental theories also constituted an important precedent for the later distinction between the two basic ways an act of worship can gain its effects: *ex opere operato* and *ex opere operantis*. In the first case the effects follow upon the completion of act itself, assuming it is rightly performed; in the second they depend upon the personal prayer and worthiness of the one who performs it. There are important social and ecclesial advantages in holding that the sacraments work *ex opere operato*. It assures recipients that the validity of their sacraments depends upon secure public and christological grounds and is not vulnerable to the possible unworthiness of the minister. See also note 20 in this chapter, above.

days of the Christians which likewise fill the theatres on the ritual days of the pagans (*DCatRud*, 25:48).[26]

This situation was also open to a theological interpretation. Augustine considered the true Church to be the spiritual body of Christ, that is, the heavenly Christ and those united to him by grace and charity. The earthly Church participates in the heavenly Church and gains its holiness from that source. Therefore the spiritual endowments of the visible community do not ultimately depend upon the virtues of its members. This understanding of the Church allowed Augustine to acknowledge that some Christians were sinful and still maintain that the Church is holy.

The recognition that the Church was composed of all kinds of people did not empty Christian faith of its requirements, cancel its imperative to perfection, or trivialize the differences between faithful and sinful members of the Church. The mandates of Christ and holy Scripture as well as the certitude of God's judgment not only precluded equivocation on such points but also required Augustine to account for good and evil Christians. He held that those who live according to charity are the true members of the invisible but real Church, the body of Christ, while sinful members are counterfeit Christians. The mixed quality of the earthly Church reflects the scriptural parables of wheat and chaff and the net that contains bad fish as well as good (Matt 13:24-30, 47-50; see *DCivDei*, XVIII, 49). Although human beings cannot accurately discriminate between good and evil people,[27] God reads the hearts of all and will render a just judgment upon each person at the end of time (*DCivDei*, I, 35; XIV, 28; XVIII, 49).

In the meanwhile, Augustine upheld charity as the basic imperative of Christian life in a heterogeneous Church. Because it includes many sinful people, the local church community cannot be presented as a reliable source of support or a sure point of reference for daily moral life. Those functions devolve to those members who live in charity, assuming they can be identified. They are to seek one another out and benefit from their mutual help while always remaining alert to the sinful and their bad example.[28] With the resources of Christ available in the

[26] Translation from the Ancient Christian Writers series. For more on Augustine's community, see Van der Meer, *Augustine the Bishop*, 129–98.

[27] Augustine related his convictions about the ambiguity of the present situation and the fact of a mixed constituency in the Church to the difficulty of knowing oneself. If persons are obscure even to themselves, they cannot hope to judge others with any certitude. Markus, *Saeculum*, 123–4; *Conf*, X, 3:4, 5:7.

[28] Augustine explicitly instructed his friend Deacon Deogratias to advise prospective Christians that this is what they must do given the primacy of Christ and the actual situation within the Church. See *DCatRud*, 7, 11.

Church, the Christian needs to pursue spiritual maturity and perfection, a difficult and lifelong task. Faithful members of the Church are to accept the companionship of those who might be weak or sinful and try to bring them to repentance. Charity requires such an approach, which manifests loving concern for one's neighbors. Ultimately, however, Christian moral life depends upon Christ alone and not other human beings.[29]

With respect to human society in general, Augustine's ecclesiology lowered the wall between Church and world. Rather than expect the Catholic Church to isolate itself, he assumed that it was called upon to serve the world and its people. Its task was one of charity, to offer a sinful and broken society the reconciliation and healing it so evidently needed. This was an open, receptive, and evangelical posture and reflected contemporary trends as much as Augustine's intellectual convictions. His portrayal of a Church in service to the larger society also contrasts with that of the Donatists. It constitutes one of the most important contributions Augustine made to later generations.[30]

Before concluding this discussion, two other aspects of Augustine's ecclesiology need to be accounted for: his willingness to have civil officials force Donatists to rejoin the Catholic Church and the role he assigned to monasticism. The former highlights the function of coercion in Christian life, and the latter discloses the importance of freedom in the same context.

Coercion on Behalf of Faith

During his struggle with Donatists, Augustine had initially been reluctant to approve the use of pressure to secure their return to the Catholic Church because he saw little value in a merely external conformity to Christian requirements. Eventually, however, he endorsed the legal coercion of Donatists but insisted that it should be limited to fines and confiscations and not entail torture or execution. He changed his mind because he saw that his congregation was able to absorb initially reluctant Donatists and that many of them later expressed gratitude for having been brought into the Catholic communion. That experience supported Augustine's conviction that people are easily seduced by sin and sometimes need a measure of severity to bring them to the path of virtue. External discipline often succeeded in persuad-

---

[29] See, for example, Epistle 185:50; J. Patout Burns, *The Development of Augustine's Doctrine of Operative Grace* (Paris: Études Augustiniennes, 1980) 56–66. See also *DBap*, I, 13:21; IV, 9:13.

[30] See Brown, *Augustine of Hippo*, 221–5; Dillistone, "Anti-Donatist Writings," 189–94; Bonner, *St. Augustine of Hippo*, 287–9; Markus, *Saeculum*, 112–26.

ing people to commit themselves to what is good, the goal of any pastoral strategy.

Augustine's views reflect the frequent and often harsh use of coercion in the ancient world, a conviction that people are prone to sin, a comprehensive vision of order, and an overarching theory of Church and state in the world. From these perspectives Augustine was able to accept a limited form of legal coercion by a Catholic magistrate and viewed it as another part of the Church's overall pastoral care of its own. To him it was a reasonable expression of the Church's occasional need to be severe in order to do right toward those for whom it was responsible. However distasteful it might be, such coercion always aimed to bring the subject to a personal appropriation of faith and a committed practice of charity.[31]

The Monastery

Augustine's espousal of monasticism balances his acceptance of coercion and discloses the premium he placed upon freedom and sincere personal commitment. Monasticism reflected his own pilgrimage and the conviction, shared by many of his era, that anyone truly committed to Christianity would live an ascetic life. That entailed a turn away from the world's criteria of success and its disordered notion of the good; a simultaneous contemplation of God, the highest good; and a life of faith, hope, and self-sacrificing charity that reflects the Gospel.[32]

However important monasticism was for individuals, its ecclesial function was perhaps even greater. Especially when church communities were so ambiguous and individual Catholics grievously sinful, the monastery stood as a protest against sin within the Church and all

---

[31] For more on this interesting topic, see Epistle 185, a primary source of Augustine's own views. See also Markus, *Saeculum*, 133–53; Brown, *Religion and Society*, 260–78, 301–31; idem, *Augustine of Hippo*, 233–43; Bonner, *St. Augustine of Hippo*, 294–311.

Augustine's approval of legal coercion against Donatists has been cited as a precedent by later figures who employed violence in order to settle religious controversies. However, if Augustine can be criticized for creating a dangerous precedent, later generations are responsible for their own use of force. It is important to note that Augustine approved the use of strictly limited coercive measures only in the case of separated Christians and did not extend it to others. Because those who have been executed cannot repent and embrace a life of charity, he ruled out the use of capital punishment. See Epistle 185:26.

[32] See Chadwick, "Ascetic Ideal," 2–3, 20–2; Brown, *Augustine of Hippo*, 142–5; idem, *Body and Society*, 388, 395; and the discussion of monasticism in chapter 3, pp. 132–4, above.

compromises with evil. In a word, the monastery was a valuable counterpoint to Church and society, especially since both depended upon severity or coercion for the maintenance of order.

The monastery showed that people could live together and cooperate on the basis of freedom, generosity, and mutual respect. One scholar has summarized Augustine's convictions about the monastery as follows:

> It was constituted by the free decision of its members, not by social "necessities." In choosing freely to associate with others in a community based upon charity, the monk was entering a society constituted by the mutual love of its members, ruled by a father whose authority was a service of love, not domination. All duties in such a community were transformed into works of love. In this sort of community the outlines of the society of the saints, withdrawn from the "social necessities," were made dimly visible. The monastery, far from providing the model for other societies, defined the permanent challenge to all other forms of social existence.[33]

In proposing the monastery as a setting favorable to the ascetic life and outlining its witness to Church and society alike, Augustine indulged in no illusions that monks were necessarily better than others. His deeply rooted agnosticism about the quality of another person's life precluded that mistake as did his own experience of monastic life.[34] Nor did Augustine offer any solace to ascetics who were tempted to look down on those who had married and were raising families. The greatest heroism of all was martyrdom, he reminded a group of African nuns, and God sometimes calls married women and not virgins to that greatest asceticism.[35] Rather, monastic commitment was meant to help Christians prepare for the better life that God offered to all but could not be received in this world. The ascetics' freely undertaken renunciations and their common witness aimed to direct attention to that eternal communion of life with God. It tried to remind everyone that nothing else, and surely nothing earthly, can fully satisfy the longings of the human heart.[36]

GOD'S GRACE AND CHRISTIAN LIFE

The third major controversy of Augustine's life concerned an issue that is fundamental to faith and moral life, namely, how a person be-

[33] Markus, *Saeculum,* xvi.
[34] See ibid., 14–5, 20; Chadwick, "Ascetic Ideal," 14–5.
[35] Brown, *Body and Society,* 397-8.
[36] On Augustine and monasticism, see Chadwick, "Ascetic Ideal"; Van der Meer, *Augustine the Bishop,* 199–234; and the other sources noted in this discussion.

comes holy, or attains justification. Justification refers to the process by which a person is reconciled to God, that is, set free of his or her sins and made worthy in God's sight. On this issue too, Augustine hammered out his views during a controversy that occupied him for the last twenty years of his life. Initially his adversaries were two laymen, Pelagius and Caelestius; then he was attacked by another bishop, Julian of Eclanum; and finally he found it necessary to defend his views before his fellow monks.

Since grace and justification are basic to faith and praxis alike, this debate was extremely important. It produced solemn Church statements and voluminous theological writing. It holds implications for every Christian whether priest or monk, married or single. A review of that controversy will disclose Augustine's teaching on grace; show its effects on different areas of Christian life, including its moral dimensions; and account for the first declarations on grace by a Church council. These aspects of the Pelagian controversy have perennial importance and can be expected to illuminate later developments affecting Catholic moral life.

Pelagius' Understanding of Christian Life

About the same time Augustine traveled to Italy, Pelagius, a devout, well-educated young layman from Britain, came to Rome and took up residence in that city. It was a period in which ascetic currents waxed strong among many aristocratic Catholic families of Rome. They were committed believers who took a generous, sacrificial approach to Christian life. By aiming for perfection, they also wished to distinguish themselves from the majority of Catholics who seemed indifferent to their faith or mediocre in practicing it. Many of them adopted Pelagius as a mentor and sought to benefit from his example and teachings. He was happy to provide practical guidance and encouragement and in the process worked out a theological justification for his ascetical program.

By means of his theological writing, Pelagius aimed to address several serious problems. The first was the suspicion that the Romans' asceticism was a manifestation of Manicheism. Pelagius therefore tried to differentiate Catholic ascetical practices from Manicheism by emphasizing that personal freedom was essential to the former and denied in the latter. A closely related goal was theological: the vindication of God as the supremely just judge of human beings. If Christians enjoyed a full measure of personal freedom and it had a very wide scope of action, there could be no doubt that they were fully accountable for their behavior and truly deserved whatever judgment God rendered. By the same token, any significant limitation on human freedom or responsibility would cast a dark shadow over the justice of God's judgments. Finally, Pelagius wished to encourage his friends to their noble effort toward Christian perfection. This also prompted him to insist that sin was not an inevitable fact of life. Rather, virtue and salvation could be theirs if only they would commit themselves to their attainment. Underlying Pelagius' views was an expansive outlook on personal freedom and natural human capacities.[37]

Pelagius' convictions about the nature of ascetic and moral life went hand in hand with his theology of baptism. Like many in the early Church, he believed that baptism introduced a clean break between a person's old and sinful past and the new and virtuous life proper to Christian faith. According to that view baptism not only forgave sin, it also washed away the power of bad habits and allowed the new Christian to replace them with virtue and self control. That was to be done through a prudently applied program of ascetic discipline.

His theory of baptism had important implications. One was ecclesiological. Since baptism enabled Christians to reach holiness if they committed themselves to this goal and made suitable efforts to achieve it, nobody had a reasonable excuse to settle for anything less. Practically speaking, that meant that everyone in the Church was to adopt a demanding moral and ascetical agenda; it could no longer be left to the monks and others with a taste for asceticism. In a word, the Church of Pelagius was to be a holy society of ascetics and saints.

Another corollary was anthropological. According to Pelagius, the long-term consequences of Adam's sin were superficial and did not affect the nature or inherent capacities of the human race. The most that Adam bequeathed was his bad example, but the Christian can and should ignore it and choose to grow in virtue. By the same token, Christians do not need God to grant an inner empowerment or a transformation of free will in order for them to do good. Pelagius indeed recognized God's grace but limited it principally to creation and revelation.[38]

---

[37] Gerald Bonner, *Augustine and Modern Research on Pelagianism* ([n.p.]: Villanova Press, 1972) 31–5; Elizabeth A. Clark, *The Origenist Controversy: The Cultural Construction of an Early Christian Debate* (Princeton: Princeton University Press, 1992) 198–214; see also B. R. Rees, *The Letters of Pelagius and His Followers* (Woodbridge: Boydell Press, 1991) 2, 20–5; Brown, *Religion and Society*, 183–207. Bonner and Clark suggest that Pelagius got many of his theological ideas from another figure, Rufinus the Syrian. Although Pelagianism carries the name of one person, it was a much wider movement in the late fourth and early fifth centuries and enjoyed the support of important writers and other prominent figures.

[38] Brown, *Religion and Society*, 194–7; Rees, *Letters of Pelagius*, 7–9. Rees describes Pelagius' understanding of God's grace as "the grace of creation in the gift of free

The Question of Infant Baptism

The sack of Rome in August of 410 caused a general emigration of people from that city. Among the refugees were Pelagius and an associate and disciple, Caelestius. Once they heard that Rome had fallen, both of these men left Sicily, where they had gone for safety, and traveled to Africa. Pelagius stayed for a brief time and then continued on to the Holy Land. Caelestius remained in Africa, where he petitioned the bishop of Carthage for ordination to the priesthood. In the meanwhile he had attracted attention by disseminating some unsettling ideas concerning Adam's sin and its consequences for sacramental praxis.

Caelestius seemed to teach that Adam's fall principally affected only himself and therefore entailed no ultimate consequences for his descendants. If that was correct, then there would be no need to baptize newborn infants. Baptism might increase their sanctification but would not be required for their salvation. That teaching ran contrary to the consensus in Africa and would certainly provoke bishops who were already at odds with the Donatists over baptism. It is understandable, then, that Caelestius was soon charged with heresy and called to account before Bishop Aurelius of Carthage. At the trial Caelestius employed his legal and rhetorical skills to parry some of the charges and evade a direct response to others. When all was said and done, Caelestius failed to provide the required disclaimers, and Aurelius decreed his excommunication.[39]

Augustine's Response

Although he was not present at the trial of Caelestius, Augustine was soon informed of the proceedings and quickly made a systematic

---

will and of the capacity to do good works, the grace of revelation in the divine law of the Old Testament and Jesus' teaching in the New, and the grace of atonement in the death and resurrection of Jesus and the remission of sins through baptism" (7). For a sympathetic yet not uncritical summary of Pelagius' theology, see Robert F. Evans, *Pelagius: Inquiries and Reappraisals* (New York: Seabury, 1968) 90–121.

[39] For further details of this episode, see John Ferguson, *Pelagius: A Historical and Theological Study* (Cambridge: W. Heffer, 1956) 48–52. For a description of the proceedings, see Bonner, *St. Augustine of Hippo,* 320–2; for the bill of particulars against Caelestius, see Hefele, 2:446-9.

Caelestius was one of the key figures in the development of the Pelagian controversy. Although there is a similarity of views between Pelagius and Caelestius, it is difficult to know if Pelagius shared all the opinions that led to Caelestius' excommunication. In any case, it seems that Pelagius was concerned with the moral lives of adults and was not interested in the topic of infant baptism.

assessment of the entire matter. After considering the opinions of Caelestius as a whole, he concluded that they contradicted the faith and subverted the praxis of the Catholic Church. In particular, he interpreted the attempt to minimize the value of infant baptism as one symptom of a much more serious error: the depreciation of God's grace. If Adam's sin did not negatively affect others and if children are saved without God's grace given in baptism, then the grace of God cannot be considered indispensable to human salvation. That conclusion was unacceptable.

Once Augustine saw that those teachings threatened a fundamental tenet of Catholic faith, he resolved to oppose them with all the resources at his disposal. He began to study the works of Pelagius, especially his commentary on the Pauline epistles,[40] published a number of books and letters on the subject of sin and grace, and preached several homilies on the necessity of baptism. That campaign was all the more urgent because it seemed that the offensive opinions were spreading in Africa, and perhaps also in the East.[41]

Augustine understood that the underlying issue pertained to human salvation. The principal problem was to identify what human beings and God respectively contribute to that goal. That issue can be addressed by assessing the damage sin has inflicted upon human capacities and appreciating the need of God's grace to make up for that damage. Taking that approach to the issue, Augustine taught that Adam's sin caused substantial and enduring damage for himself and all his descendants. The first and most important consequence of that sin was guilt. What is decisive is not simply that Adam made himself guilty but that through his sin every human being became guilty as well.

Augustine arrived at that conclusion on the basis of the Scriptures, especially Romans 5:12. In English that verse reads: "Therefore as sin came into the world through one man and death through sin, and so death spread to all men because all men sinned" (*quia* omnes peccaverunt). However, Augustine's flawed Latin text rendered the last portion of the verse: "*in quo* omnes peccaverunt." After considering the

---

[40] A summary of the arguments Pelagius made is found in Evans, *Pelagius,* 73, see also 97–8.

[41] See Bonner, *St. Augustine of Hippo,* 324–8, for a description of this phase of the controversy. Prior to the year 415 Augustine employed a deferential tone in dealing with Pelagius and did not identify him with the objectionable teachings. Afterward he attributed errors to Pelagius personally and contested them much more vigorously. Evans argues that the turning point came when Augustine saw that Pelagius was trying to defend his views by an appeal to orthodox authorities, including Augustine himself. See also Evans, *Pelagius,* 66–89, especially 85.

matter, he determined that the text meant: "and so sin spread to all men, in whom [one man] all sinned." He concluded that all Adam's descendants were seminally present in him when he sinned and that every human being shares in his guilt.[42]

Adam's sin had a second effect: it inflicted a severe wound on human nature. That accounts for Adam's experience of shame and hardship and ultimately death as well. Because he had only his damaged human nature to bequeath to future human beings, disruption and evil have become part of the human condition. Adam's sin imposed guilt and a damaged human nature on all human beings. Everyone is liable to God's just punishment and lives in a world marked by evil and hardship. This deeply personal condition strongly inclines everyone to commit new sins of their own, thereby compounding their guilt (*DPecMerRem*, I, 8:8; 9:9–15:12; 21:16; 56; 62:33).

Augustine was firm in the conviction that no one can escape these consequences on their own; still less can anyone gain salvation by their own efforts. Not even careful obedience to God's will made known in the Law and the commandments can bring about these results. Human beings are helpless in this matter and must rely upon God, who alone can grant the forgiveness and salvation that they need. Through God's grace and its strengthening of free will, persons gain the power to avoid sin and obey God's will. That suggests that the unique source of all human righteousness is God, and particularly his free and sovereign gift of grace. Therefore, if persons are saved or do anything meritorious at all, they are to thank God; if they are condemned, they have only received the punishment that their sins justly deserve (See *DPecMerRem*, II, 5:5-6; *DSpirLit*, 14; 20–23:14; *DGestPel*, 8).[43]

In locating the source of all goodness exclusively in God, Augustine emphasized the power and activity of God's grace in people's lives.

---

[42] For a further discussion of this matter, see Piet Schoonenberg, *Man and Sin*, trans. Joseph Donceel (London: Sheed & Ward, 1965) 150–1; Ferguson, *Pelagius*, 54–5; Henri Rondet, *The Grace of Christ: A Brief History of the Theology of Grace*, trans. Tad W. Guzie (Westminster, Md.: Newman Press, 1967) 128–9; Bonner, *St. Augustine of Hippo*, 371–4.

[43] See also Bonner, *St. Augustine of Hippo*, 370–4. Augustine gives a precis of his teaching on sin and grace in *De natura et gratia* (On Nature and Grace), 3:3–4:4, excerpted in Bonner, *St. Augustine of Hippo*, 325–6.

On the background and origins of the doctrine of original sin, see Rees, *Letters of Pelagius*, 9; Gerald Bonner, "Les origines africaines de la doctrine augustinienne sur la chute et le péché originel," *Augustinus* 12 (1967) 97–116. This article is reprinted in Bonner's *God's Decree and Man's Destiny: Studies on the Thought of Augustine of Hippo* (London: Variorum Reprints, 1987); see also P. F. Beatrice, *Tradux peccati: Alle fonti della dottrina agostiniana del peccato originale* (Milan: Vita e Pensiero, 1978). On sin as bringing its own punishment to the sinner, see Burnaby, *Amor Dei*, 210–1.

He taught that God's grace, the gift of the Holy Spirit, is all-powerful and necessarily gains its intended effect. If God gives grace to a person, it empowers free will to do the good and ensures that he or she will act rightly and gain salvation. In that way God predestines those he chooses, the elect, to receive salvation. If God fails to extend this grace, people will continue to sin and cannot gain salvation. Augustine saw this position as an entirely reasonable one that was neither unjust nor contradictory. God's grace was necessary in view of original sin, the nature of salvation, and the work of Christ. He likewise affirmed personal freedom because it reflected Christian praxis, ordinary experience, and the principle that people can only be imputable if they act freely (*DSpirLit*, 5:3; 34; 52:30; 60:34; *DGestPel*, 7-8; *DGratChr*, I, 13:12).[44]

Augustine's position on grace brought together many elements of experience and traditional doctrine. He affirmed the basic religious truth that communion with God can only be received by human beings as God's free and undeserved gift. He accounted for the willfulness, weakness, and malice that he saw in people of all ages and conditions. His doctrine of original sin also seemed to be fully warranted by the Scriptures. These were the sources of his negative assessment of unaided human capacities; they prevented him from accepting the much more positive evaluations of those who agreed with Pelagius. He had no alternative but to attribute all good to God and God's grace. Grace alone forgives sin and communicates the power necessary if people are to do good and attain salvation. This in essence is Augustine's teaching. It is the basic doctrinal and human synthesis from which he responded to later events in this ongoing controversy.

Early Actions by Church Authorities

While the controversy between Augustine and Pelagius was still developing, events began to draw Church authorities into the dispute. In Palestine, where Pelagius had taken up residence, several visitors from the West brought charges that he harbored heretical opinions. In the year 415, their indictment was considered at two different synods at which Pelagius was called to respond. On both occasions the examination resulted in a formal judgment of acquittal and the declaration

---

[44] Augustine also knew that he had to distinguish his doctrine from Manichean notions of necessity that relieved persons of all moral responsibility. See Evans, *Pelagius*, 87–8; Osborn, *Ethical Patterns*, 167–70; Ferguson, *Pelagius*, 54–5.

that he remained within the Catholic communion. Pelagius welcomed these verdicts as a personal and theological vindication.[45]

The reaction in Africa was entirely different. Upon learning of what had happened, Augustine and his colleagues concluded that the Eastern synods had made a serious mistake. To them it seemed that the Palestinian bishops had failed to penetrate the evasions and deceptions by which Pelagius had masked his true convictions.[46] Alarmed at the prospect that his acquittal would make heretical doctrines appear acceptable, the Africans determined to address the matter themselves. At councils held at Carthage and Milevis in 416, they reaffirmed the judgment against Caelestius pronounced at Carthage five years earlier. They also decreed that both he and Pelagius should be excommunicated unless they formally repudiated the views that had been attributed to them.

To reinforce their position, the African bishops sent copies of their decisions, personal letters, and Pelagius' book *De natura* (On Nature) to Pope Innocent I. They asked him to ratify their judgment and impose his own excommunication unless the two accused individuals unambiguously condemned the heretical views at issue. In January of 417, Innocent, appalled at what he read in *De natura*, excommunicated Caelestius and Pelagius until they provided the required disclaimers. Two weeks later, Pope Innocent died.[47]

The rest of the drama unfolded very quickly. Innocent's successor, Pope Zosimus, received an appeal for reconsideration from Pelagius and additional correspondence from interested parties. While he was still deliberating the case, Emperor Honorius issued a decree banishing Pelagius and Caelestius from Italy. The next day the African hierarchy took new action in this deepening controversy. On May 1, 418, a council of over two hundred bishops meeting in Carthage promulgated a series of canons against Pelagianism.

These canons are important because they represent the first official declarations of the Church's doctrine on grace. The Council of Carthage affirmed that grace not only forgives past sins but helps persons

---

[45] For a fuller description of these events, see Bonner, *St. Augustine of Hippo*, 332–9; Ferguson, *Pelagius*, 72–92; Hefele, 2:449–55. A summary of the second trial is given in B. R. Rees, *Pelagius: A Reluctant Heretic* (Woodbridge, England: Boydell Press, 1988) 135–8.

In Palestine, St. Jerome was also active in opposition to Pelagius and his doctrines and exchanged correspondence on these matters with Augustine. See Clark, *Origenist Controversy*, 121–51, 221–7.

[46] Rees, *Pelagius: A Reluctant Heretic*, 138–9.

[47] Bonner, *St. Augustine of Hippo*, 339–41; Brown, *Augustine of Hippo*, 357–9; Hefele, 2:455–6. For some of the correspondence, see Epistles 175–7, 181–4.

to avoid new ones. The grace of justification does more than merely enlighten the mind, it empowers people to do what is good; it is necessary if they are to be able to do what they should. Also important was the statement that even saints commit sin in a true sense of the term and therefore apply the words "forgive us our trespasses" to themselves and not just to others. The Council of Carthage constitutes the starting point of the Church's official doctrinal tradition on grace and supplied a substantial foundation for subsequent work on that same subject.[48]

In the wake of the actions by the emperor and the African hierarchy, Pope Zosimus published his *Epistola tractoria,* now lost, in which he censured Pelagian teachings and excommunicated Pelagius and Caelestius. His document, which enjoyed the backing of imperial authority, also declared Catholic teaching on the disputed points. The eighteen Italian bishops who refused to endorse it were deposed from their sees. The decisions of 418 constitute a landmark in the Pelagian controversy and demarcate the end of its first phase.[49]

Significance of the First Phase of the Pelagian Controversy

The debate over Pelagian teachings developed out of a serious program of moral and spiritual betterment. Pelagius was anxious to maintain a theoretical frame of reference in which moral effort could be urged as necessary, fruitful, and decisive in Christian life. Otherwise, he feared that people would have an excuse to ignore or trivialize their commitment to Christian requirements. Such concerns led him to emphasize the capacities of human nature, diminish the effects of sin, and therefore minimize the role of God's grace as well. Pelagius and those who shared his outlook rejected Augustine's doctrines because they thought he had underestimated the power of human freedom and made the human person a puppet in God's hands.

As a monk and a pastor, Augustine was familiar with the dynamics of free will and the importance of human effort. But he was even more impressed by the difficulties inherent in the human condition. He was not prepared, as was Pelagius, to take human freedom for granted. Frailty, failure, and conflict seemed to be deeply rooted in human nature. Even with baptism, Augustine compared the Christian to the man rescued by the good Samaritan: saved from death but still in need of a lifelong convalescence in the Catholic Church. Above all he attrib-

---

[48] See Hefele, 2: 458-62; DS, 222–30.
[49] Bonner, *St. Augustine of Hippo,* 344–5; see also Ferguson, *Pelagius,* 100–15; Brown, *Religion and Society,* 191.

uted all good and all possibility of good to God alone. His convictions required him to emphasize the power of sin, both as a personal act and in its effects, and relate all salutary human acts to the free gift of God's grace.[50]

Notwithstanding its doctrinal grounds and experiential premises, Augustine's teaching on original sin and its physical propagation involved some doctrinal and pastoral aspects that were vulnerable to challenge. Despite the condemnations of 418, another bishop, Julian of Eclanum, picked up the Pelagian cause and engaged Augustine in a vigorous debate for the rest of his life.[51]

The Debate over Human Sexuality

From his place of exile in the East, Julian took up the Pelagian banner. He had been especially offended by Augustine's teaching that original sin had disrupted human sexuality and was passed on by means of sexual intercourse, which is always accompanied by passion and a loss of freedom. In response, Julian contradicted his African colleague, insisting that the sexual appetite was not disordered and required no renunciation. He taught that the sexual urges people commonly experience are the same as those of Adam and Eve prior to their sin. People were free to control their sexuality whenever they chose to do so.

Julian also attacked Augustine for saying that people were guilty of an inherited sin because that convicted them of something over which they had no control. Moreover, if he found fault with sexual urges and considered them to be the result of sin, then that was equivalent to attributing sexual feelings to the devil. In both cases that represented a lingering Manicheism in Augustine. For his part, Julian declared that God was the creator of the human sexual drive, and this good gift remained undamaged by original sin. God had made sexuality good and good it remained.[52]

Julian's attack was powerful. It was based upon the Pelagian notion that minimized original sin and restricted its effects upon human beings. He reinforced those views by trying to impeach Augustine's teaching as Manichean. On a more practical level, Julian moved the battleground from infant baptism and the efforts of ascetics to the

---

[50] Brown, *Augustine of Hippo*, 365–75.

[51] As a Pelagian sympathizer Julian had refused to sign the *Epistola tractoria* and was deposed from his southern Italian see in 419. He took refuge in the East, where he conducted his side of the debate. He was unable to have himself reinstated as a bishop and died in Sicily sometime prior to 455. Brown, *Augustine of Hippo*, 381–3; Evans, *Augustine on Evil*, 137.

[52] Brown, *Body and Society*, 408–16.

inner life of each person, and especially the realm of married sexuality. Augustine took up the challenge and responded in detail to all elements of Julian's assault. Of particular interest is his explanation of original sin's impact upon human sexuality.

Along with many in the early Church, Augustine taught that Adam's sin originated in a pride that led him freely to disobey God's command. That original sin represented Adam's rebellion and his willful disobedience of God. In opposition to Pelagianism, Augustine held that Adam's sin indeed affected all his descendants through a shared guilt and a damaged human nature. These effects of original sin are communicated to each person by generation and not merely by imitation.

Augustine recognized many symptoms of damaged human nature. However, along with death, sexual feelings are the most obvious among them. Sexual feelings often take their own course and do not abide by the dictates of personal decision. They have physiological effects that also escape control. To Augustine it was entirely reasonable that original sin should have these results. After all, Adam and Eve had rebelled against God and refused to abide by God's will. Therefore it is just that human beings should experience in their own bodies a similar rebellion of sexual feelings against their own control. Wayward sexual feelings, concupiscence, and lust are reminders of sin and how it occurs. Involved in the conception of each human being, sexual concupiscence constitutes the means by which original sin is passed—by generation and not merely by imitation—from one generation to the next (*DNupCon*, I, 7:6; 26; 27:24).

Augustine denied that linking sin, concupiscence, and sexual feelings in this way constituted Manicheism. He affirmed that sexual pleasure itself is good. What is evil is pleasure's resistance to a person's control. In a similar way, he held that the *concupiscentia nuptiarum*, the urge to marry, also is good. Marriage and sexual intercourse are part of God's original design for humanity and not the result of sin. What comes from sin is the *concupiscentia carnis*, the desire for the flesh, that is, the inclination to follow one's appetites instead of abiding by God's will. For Augustine, then, evil is found precisely in the resistance to rightful control, the inner tendency to rebel against the due order established by God. In that sense and for that reason concupiscence is evil; it remains in each person as the sign and occasion of sin (*DNupCon*, I, 1; 6:5; 8:7; II, 9:11; 14:5; 52:30–54:32; see also *DCivDei*, XIV, 11–24).[53]

---

[53] This discussion has followed Brown, *Body and Society*, 387–427; Bonner, *St. Augustine of Hippo*, 370–8; see also Ramsey, "Human Sexuality in the History of Redemption," *Ethics of St. Augustine*.

The Significance of Augustine's Teaching on Sexuality

Although Augustine may have succeeded in distancing his teaching from Manicheism, like most of his contemporaries he attached a negative significance to human sexual feelings. Sexual shame and the ordinary signs of arousal or its absence now carry the burden of sin. In the words of a renowned scholar, Augustine "presented impotence and frigidity, for the first time, as psychosomatic symptoms whose causes lay deep within the self. Sexuality was effectively taken from its physiological context and made to mirror an abiding, unhealed fissure in the soul."[54] Especially when Augustine's careful distinctions and nuances were forgotten, his symbolic and negative interpretation of human sexuality—and the association of sexual feelings and sin—were destined to have a profound and lasting influence on the development of Western thought and praxis.[55]

Predestination and Human Effort

Augustine's teachings on grace were completed in dialogue with his fellow ascetics. A monk of the monastery at Hadrumetum in North Africa brought home a copy of Augustine's letter to Sixtus, a Roman priest, in which he vigorously expounded his views on predestination (Epistle 194). In that letter, Augustine taught that God's grace is given with sovereign freedom and not in response to any human merit. He emphasized that persons have nothing good that has not come to them as God's gift. All good things—forgiveness, prayer, faith, and the other virtues—are the work of grace. Moreover, because grace involves God's divine power, it unfailingly achieves its intended effect: grace causes a person to do the good in true freedom and ultimately come to salvation. That same principle also implies that God's failure to extend

---

[54] Brown, *Body and Society*, 418.

Brown states that for Augustine "sexuality served only one, strictly delimited purpose: it spoke, with terrible precision, of one single, decisive event within the soul. It echoed in the body the unalterable consequence of mankind's first sin. It was down that single, narrow, and profound shaft that Augustine now looked, to the very origins of human frailty. Nocturnal emissions could not tell him anything about the silent shift of forces within the soul of a particular individual: they spoke to all men, and of one thing alone—of a fatal deposit of concupiscence left there by Adam's fall. It was a drastically limited vision of a complex phenomenon" (ibid., 422).

[55] For further discussion of Augustine's teachings on sexuality and marriage, see Brown, *Body and Society*; Ramsey, "Human Sexuality"; John T. Noonan, Jr., *Contraception: A History of Its Treatment by the Catholic Theologians and Canonists* (New York: Mentor Omega, 1967) 137–75.

his grace leaves some people in a state of sin and therefore liable to eternal condemnation. Augustine serenely accepts that aspect of God's justice and insists that no one has the right to question it (see also *DCivDei*, XIV, 26–7; XXI, 12). Such teachings as these were bound to offend monks whose very lives presupposed their own personal efforts. They protested that Augustine's letter had emptied free will of any real significance.

In response, Augustine wrote two works which he forwarded to the monastery. The first reaffirmed that God gives his grace with sovereign freedom and not according to human merit. Grace is a prerequisite for all human goodness and when given, always accomplishes its intended purpose. Even so, free will remains integral to human salvation and, far from being canceled or submerged by God's grace, is actually constituted by it (*DGratLibArb,* 7; 13:6; 31:15; 32:16; 41:20–45:23). That explanation did not satisfy the monks. They inferred that if Augustine was correct, then it was useless to rebuke a misbehaving or unfaithful brother. The only recourse would be to let him continue his errant ways and be content with praying for him. In his second book Augustine replied that it was indeed necessary to rebuke those who were doing wrong and not persevering in goodness. He added that such correction would prove helpful only if God's grace first empowered the offender to reform, and noted that God could bring someone to reform even in the absence of fraternal correction. Perseverance was God's gift, while anyone who failed to persevere is justly condemned (*DCorGrat,* 6:4–9:6, 10–9; 42; 43:14; see also *DCivDei,* XXI, 12).

Augustine's teaching on God's predestination of the elect to salvation also troubled the monks of southern Gaul, especially John Cassian (c. 365–c. 435). He believed that Augustine was wrong in limiting God's salvific will only to the elect and that he depreciated human free will and the importance of personal effort in the Christian life. Cassian based his objections on Tim 2:4, which recognizes Christ as the Savior who died for all, and also cited the tradition of the Church as it stood at that time.[56]

In contrast to Augustine's doctrine, Cassian and others proposed that the first stirrings of interest in Christ and his grace are to be credited, at least sometimes, to a person's free will. They taught that God offers saving grace to all, and God's grace is necessary for whatever good a person does, but people freely decide whether to accept it. While God has foreknowledge of people's actions and whether they

---

[56] After Augustine's friends in Gaul reported these objections, he replied to them in two letters to Prosper and Hilary: *De praedestinatione sanctorum* (On the Predestination of the Saints) and *De dono perseverantiae* (On the Gift of Perseverance).

will cooperate with grace, God does not predetermine anyone's response. The conflict between Augustine's position and that of the Gallic monks continued for some time after his death.[57]

However one judges Augustine's doctrine on predestination, it is clear that he did not intend to set it in opposition to human freedom. On theological grounds he held that it was equally necessary to uphold the priority, gratuity, and necessity of God's grace and also the basic importance of free will. He asked: "If there be no such thing as God's grace, how can He be the Savior of the world? If there be no such thing as free-will, how can He be its Judge?"[58] Augustine labored long and hard in his own life and urged his congregation and fellow ascetics to do the same in order to meet their responsibilities. By affirming that God's grace underlies and empowers all moral and religious accomplishments, he tried to place them upon the most secure of foundations. Amid the radical uncertainties of life and the ambiguities of human motivation, he could find no better way to encourage Christian fidelity and affirm its urgency.[59]

MORAL LIFE AND THE TWO CITIES

In light of what has already been set forth, this section will consider Augustine's view of the moral life and its relationship to human history, the created order, and God's providence. This discussion will also afford an opportunity to account for Augustine's assessment of the state, underline the essentially religious texture of his thought, and reiterate the decisive functions of grace, personal freedom, and love.

[57] Cassian was equally concerned to rebut the teachings of Pelagius and did so by asserting the necessity of grace if humans are to do good. A key text is Cassian's *Conlationes* (Conferences), 13. See Robert Floyd Rea, "Grace and Free Will in John Cassian," Ph.D. diss., St. Louis University, 1990 (Ann Arbor, Mich.: UMI Dissertation Information Service, n.d.), especially 152–205; M. John Farrelly, *Predestination, Grace, and Free Will* (Westminster, Md.: Newman Press, 1964) 96–8; Rondet, *Grace of Christ*, 145–8.

[58] Epistle 214:2, as quoted in Burnaby, *Amor Dei*, 227.

[59] Some have pointed out the correlation between the sociological and religious circumstances of the parties to the debate and their respective positions. Augustine's North African Christianity was more stagnant and full of ambiguities. On the other hand, the monks placed a premium on human effort, and Gaul saw large-scale conversions to Christianity and the missionary expeditions to Britain and Ireland. The former situation seemed to place God's role in high relief while the latter accented the human contribution in the drama of salvation. On this point and the controversy in general, see Burnaby, *Amor Dei*, 226–34; Brown, *Augustine of Hippo*, 398–407; Bonner, *St. Augustine of Hippo*, 347–50.

St. Augustine recognized that grace affects personal life in different ways and elaborated distinctions that have become traditional. See Peter C. Phan, *Grace and*

The City of God and the City of This World

As an unprecedented violation of the capital city and a stark reminder of Roman military decline, the sack of Rome in 410 traumatized people and shook the foundations of civic life as nothing else had
done. But the deepest and most far-reaching reverberations occurred
on the religious level. After 410 Christians could no longer credibly
argue that their God favored the Roman Empire or that their political
dominance guaranteed the prosperity of the Roman people. What is
more, prominent pagans attributed the sack of Rome to the Christians'
irreligious overthrow of the traditional gods (e.g., *DCivDei*, I). In the
years following 410 many people raised serious questions about the
religious foundations, purpose, and goal of human society. That encouraged Augustine to construct a new account of human life that
would recognize the hard facts of contemporary experience and interpret human history in light of Christian faith. What resulted was his
classic work, *De Civitate Dei*, or *The City of God*.

In this formidable volume, he shows that pagan accounts of human
affairs are unworthy of serious consideration and demolishes the claim
that the gods used to protect Rome (*DCivDei*, I–V). Although he addresses the deeper questions that the sack of Rome had raised, he is
primarily interested in the entire span of history from the creation of
the world until the Last Judgment, which he places within a divine
and eternal context. He acknowledges that human freedom accounts
for much that happens but affirms that God controls particular events
as well as the overall course of history and makes evil serve a good end
(IV, 33; V, 9–11; XI, 17–8; XIV, 26–7). Believers often encounter much
that is distressing, but they know that if God's ways are inscrutable,
they are never unjust (*Conf*, III, 9:17; *DCivDei*, V, 21; XII, 28; XX, 2).

Persons come into the world already marked by sin, perversity, and
the certitude of death. With the help of grace they are to abide by
God's will in justice and charity, worship God above all, and thereby
become citizens of the heavenly City who live in the hope of inheriting
the eternal peace of God's kingdom. Since persons have freedom, however, they can choose to disobey God, violate God's created order, and
love themselves or some other creature in a disordered way. By so
doing they become members of the earthly City, which is on a course
toward damnation. Persons determine which of these cities they belong to by means of their free will, particularly when they decide how
they will love and whether, helped by grace, they will turn toward

---

the Human Condition (Wilmington: Michael Glazier, 1988) 271–90; or Karl Rahner,
"Grace, II: Theological," *SM* 2:412-22.

God or turn toward the earth and remain closed in on themselves (*DCivDei*, XII, 1–9; XIII, 1–13; XIV, 28; XIX, 27–8).

As the City of God on earth, the Christian Church makes God's authority and grace, word and sacraments available to humanity. Although necessary to salvation, the historical Church community is not the ultimate reality. Much more important are Christ, his heavenly community, and his final judgment at the end of time. What will be decisive for Christians is not their membership in the earthly Church but the quality of their relationships with God and neighbor, and that is a matter of grace, justice, and charity. This view rendered many dimensions of Christian life more ambiguous, especially since the historical Church includes members of the earthly City as well as those who belong to the heavenly City, while some of the latter can also be found outside the Church (*DCivDei*, VIII, 24; XVIII, 47–51; XXI, 15–27).

The Roman Empire had its part in God's providence (*DCivDei*, V), but neither it nor any other political regime has transcendent importance. The principal purpose of civil government is to secure good order in human society by upholding the requirements of justice. Justice is the virtue that assures that God is properly worshiped and his just commands observed, and that all human beings receive what is rightfully due to them. Augustine was blunt in his assessment of states that fail to maintain justice: "Remove justice, and what are kingdoms but gangs of criminals on a large scale?" (IV, 4). This judgment recognizes that political governments can be dangerous and even illegitimate, but it does not impugn the modest but necessary service that they are to provide. Because religion is essential to justice, the state will actively promote the worship of God and love of neighbor. The Christian magistrate rules with justice, humility, mercy, and self-restraint (IV, 3; V, 24; XIX, 20–6).

An Ordered Morality of Grace, Obedience, and Freedom

God created everything good and assigned each being its proper place within an ordered universe. As human beings live in the world, they carry out many activities and try to attain happiness. The supreme obligation of moral life is that persons should know, worship, and love God above all creatures. Inasmuch as they exist, creatures are good and persons may make them the object of their moral action. At all times, however, humans are to respect the differences between Creator and creatures. This is a prerequisite for true and lasting happiness as well as an injunction of faith and reason (*DCivDei*, XII, 2, 5; XV, 22; XIX, 13).

These considerations prompted Augustine to enunciate a distinction and a criterion that are fundamental to his view of moral life. The distinction contrasts enjoyment and use. "We are said to enjoy something which gives us pleasure in itself, without reference to anything else, whereas we 'use' something when we seek it for some other purpose" (*DCivDei*, XI, 25; see also *DDoctChr*, I, 4). When applied to Christian life, Augustine identified God as the proper object of enjoyment or love, while everything else is to be a matter of use. Accordingly, God is the ultimate good whose eternal possession will fully satisfy the human heart, but God must not be used in order to gain or enjoy anything created. His criterion is that "we should use temporal things, rather than enjoy them, so that we may be fit to enjoy eternal blessings, unlike the wicked, who want to enjoy money, but to make use of God, not spending money for God, but worshipping God for money" (*DCivDei*, XI, 25; see also XV, 7). The same insight can be expressed in terms of an overarching "order of love," according to which a person is to love God above all and to love created things in a strictly subordinate way. When, with the help of grace, Christians love people or things in a way that shows honor to God and respect for his order, they act virtuously; if they love otherwise, they turn away from God and sin (XV, 4, 22).[60]

If they rely only on themselves, people will not succeed in knowing or doing what is good. One obstacle is the mind itself, which is weak and beclouded. For that reason it is very difficult to learn and understand the truth about God and the universe that morally upright activity presupposes. Moreover, free will is perverse, and persons often do other than what they realize they ought to do; in other words, they knowingly allow themselves to love created things in a disordered way. In his mercy God has provided special assistance to compensate for these defects of mind and will. God's authority, available in the Scriptures and the Church, illuminates the human mind, while the grace of Christ counteracts the effects of sin on human freedom (*DCivDei*, IX, 20; X, 29; XI, 2–4; XIV, 11).[61] Given their vulnerabilities, people need to shun pride and arrogance, embrace humility, and sub-

---

[60] See Burnaby, *Amor Dei*, 104–37, especially 104–10. For a summary of Augustine's moral doctrine see Osborn, *Ethical Patterns*, 143–82; Frederick S. Carney, "The Structure of Augustine's Ethic," *Ethics of St. Augustine*, 11–37.

[61] Augustine distinguished freedom (*libertas*) from free will (*liberum arbitrium*). The former is exercised in the pursuit of God as the highest good of persons and is the fruit of grace. The latter is an attribute of the human being under the influence of sin. It accounts for the free and therefore culpable decision to pursue a good in a disordered way, that is, to sin. On this point see, for example, *Conf*, VIII, 5:10; *DCivDei*, XI, 28; XIV, 11; Burnaby, *Amor Dei*, 226–9.

ordinate themselves to God in all things. In that way divine authority becomes the guiding light for moral life even as divine grace strengthens the will, redirects love, and leads a person in the ways of justice and charity.

Augustine takes human history seriously and acknowledges the goodness and importance of the universe. As the arenas in which God's grace and human freedom interact, he could not fail to do them justice. Nevertheless, he judges that the world and its history are full of evil and can never be the supreme good of persons. Moreover, unaided human beings find it difficult to arrive at knowledge of God and fail to do what God requires. For all these reasons Augustine directs his readers' attention past themselves, the world, and human affairs in general to the one God who is their eternal source, goal, helper, and judge. Having reminded them of their predicament and their hope, he calls human beings to resolve a primordial tension between two mutually exclusive attractions. In humility and love, persons can freely turn toward the God who helps and saves them, and by doing so, rise to share in divine life. Or, with pride and arrogance they can turn toward themselves and other created things, love them instead of God, and become earthly in the process. Persons become what they contemplate and love.[62]

Augustine's comprehensive and coherent portrayal of human life offered believers a new way to understand and evaluate it. He charged the entirety of human history with an intensely Christian significance and assigned the Catholic Church a strategic role within it. He reserved the widest possible scope of action for God's providence, gave divine grace a decisive role in the moral and religious activity of human beings, and stressed their need of divine authority. He highlighted as never before the ambivalence and ambiguity of free will but also recognized its pivotal impact on the course of history as well as each person's response to God and the ultimate direction of his or her life. By doing so, Augustine moved the central dynamics of human life to the interior forum of free will and endowed human freedom with transcendent importance. Elaborating this view of society and the

---

[62] The following passage makes this point explicitly:

> For if love of the world is there, love of God will not be there. Hold fast, rather, to the love of God, that, as God is eternal, so also you may abide in eternity; for each person is such as his love is. Do you love the earth? You will be earth. Do you love God? What shall I say? Will you be a god? I dare not say this on my own. Let us hear the Scripture: "I have said, 'You are gods and sons of the Most High, all of you'" (*Tractatus in Epist. Johannis ad Parthos* [Homilies on John's Epistle], II, 14:4; translated in The Fathers of the Church, 92; see also *DCivDei*, XII, 6; XIV, 13, 28).

human person before God was a momentous accomplishment. It responded to contemporary needs and enriched the theological and spiritual resources of the Church. Perhaps even more important was its influence on medieval Western Christianity, for it established the framework in which it considered the meaning and measure of human life, the respective responsibilities of Church and temporal authorities, the relationship between time and eternity, and the issue of justice and the inscrutable ways of God.[63]

REFLECTIONS

Augustine lived at a time when momentous religious, political, and demographic changes had begun to transform the Roman Empire. The Catholic Church of his day had grown large and strong and included many uncommitted or sinful members. Despite some hesitation, it had already begun to accommodate its thought and praxis to that anomalous situation. As it did so, however, it tried to honor the imperatives of conversion and perfection especially through its preaching, sacramental praxis, and support of monasticism. During Augustine's lifetime the tension between accommodation and perfection had become acute and began to seek some resolution.

In the early fifth century the Church was at an early stage of its development. Although the Scriptures, the apostolic tradition, common praxis, and ecclesial communion helped it to respond to new challenges, there had not been enough time for Christian intellectual traditions or schools of thought to come to maturity. Important issues had not yet been raised or stated clearly. The only philosophical accounts of reality, knowledge, and ethics then available were from non-Christian authors, especially the Stoics and Plotinus. As important as they were, the properly Christian resources at Augustine's disposal were insufficient to meet the challenges facing the Church in that era, and non-Christian thought could only be used if it was congruent with Christian faith or conformable to it. These considerations suggest that Augustine, a man of the early Church and the late ancient world, had little choice but to innovate. With limited resources at his disposal, he addressed new and difficult questions and worked out responses that

---

[63] Augustine wrote *De Civitate Dei* between the years 413 and 426. See Mary T. Clark, *Augustine* (Washington: Georgetown University Press, 1994) 94–107; Brown, *Augustine of Hippo*, 299–329; Markus, *Saeculum*; M. C. D'Arcy, *The Meaning and Matter of History: A Christian View* (New York: Meridian Books, 1961) 246–50; Karl Löwith, *Meaning in History: The Theological Implications of the Philosophy of History* (Chicago: University of Chicago Press, 1949) 166–73.

were intellectually coherent, theologically grounded, and pastorally fruitful. That he did so across a wide spectrum of issues that often went to the foundations of Christian life makes his accomplishments all the more impressive. The pioneering nature of his work also helps to account for those aspects of his legacy that later Christians found defective or unhelpful.

Augustine's personal background deeply affected his ministry and intellectual legacy. Although attention is sometimes drawn to his association with the Manichees or to his quasi-marital relationship, his own account emphasizes his conversion to Christ. In his *Confessions* Augustine admits that he had been proud, willful, and unhappy, and that he showed little interest in checking his sexual appetites; he sees such defects as signs of his sinfulness before God. He speaks of the prayers of his mother, the example of uneducated Egyptian monks, the impact of the Scriptures, and the restlessness of his conscience. Above all, Augustine attributes his conversion and baptism to God's love and the influence of divine providence in his life. Together with the baptism that it entailed, conversion to Christ was the central event of Augustine's life and became a foundation of his faith, ascetical life, intellectual pursuits, and pastoral ministry. It stands as another testimony to the life-changing power of personal decision and highlights the reciprocal influence of faith and moral life. Moral-religious conversion is as important to Augustine's intellectual legacy as it is to his personal history.

A principal aspect of that legacy are his teachings concerning the created universe and history. Although it came forth good from God's creative act, sin has made the universe evil, not in its substance but insofar as it departed from due order and hence became corrupt. History began with creation and has likewise been disrupted by sin, which takes its source from the evil wills of human beings. In the present era, therefore, the universe and history both carry the effects of sin. They respond to human activity but remain ever subject to the sovereign power of God, who rules every event with a freedom that may be inscrutable but is never unjust. These considerations call attention to God's creative and saving activity and suggest that the world and human history have no more than ancillary importance. The primary imperative of religious and moral life is that, with the help of grace, persons turn to God in humility, obedience, and charity. Because of God's freedom and the effects of sin, history and the created order, while often helpful, are not always reliable means to know God's will. The effects of sin on the human mind warn people against placing too much confidence in their own abilities to learn what God requires.

To place the accent on God's freedom, power, and providence as Augustine does is to raise the suspicion that God acts arbitrarily and that human moral activity lacks reasonable, objective criteria. If that is the case, then Christian morality becomes a very fluid enterprise that can only try to respond to God's whims. However, a careful review of Augustine's teachings shows that they do not lead to this conclusion. There is no doubt that he threw the majesty and sovereignty of God into high relief, assigned divine grace a decisive function, and insisted that the virtues of humility and obedience to God are basic to Christian life. But he repeatedly affirms that, despite human inability to see how this can be so in particular cases, God is reasonable and acts with justice. Together with the commandments and the economy of salvation in general, justice and reason supply an objective basis for Christian life and counterbalance Augustine's stress on God's freedom and power.

There can be little doubt, however, that by emphasizing each person's relationship with God and the activities of willing and loving, Augustine placed the interior life of human persons into very high relief. He acknowledged the importance of behavior but gave priority to the internal act of the will, which is its source (*DCivDei*, XIV, 11, 13), and held that, apart from God's giving or withholding of grace, a person's destiny depends ultimately upon his or her use of freedom. This concern for the internal life of persons is not unprecedented; the Scriptures also acknowledge the importance of the human heart (e.g. Deut 5:21; 6:5-6; Matt 15:8, 18-20). Augustine's contribution lay in the decisive functions that he assigned to a person's interior acts and especially to free will. By so doing he helped to change the axis of Western thinking about human life, directed its attention to an internal forum, and encouraged further exploration into the nature and effects of personal knowledge, freedom, and love.

Donatism and Pelagianism both addressed the problem of good and evil in human life. Opposed to evil and strict with sinners, they tried to promote the Church's holiness and make it evident to all. Although this goal was certainly acceptable, the means these groups used to achieve it were theologically flawed and pastorally dangerous. Augustine had no alternative but to reply, and in so doing he helped the Church sort out the theological and practical implications of good and evil, holiness and sin in Christian life. His theological predisposition to recognize ambiguity and human frailty supported the Church's practical choice to accept and assist rather than exclude imperfect people. At the same time, he emphasized the need for unceasing effort in Christian life, led an ascetical life himself, and helped to found the Western monastic tradition.

In response to Donatism, Augustine upheld the holiness of the Church and the responsibilities it imposes on individual Christians, but he redefined holiness to emphasize its transcendent dimensions. Holiness belongs first to Christ and the heavenly body of Christ, which he regarded as the true Church. The earthly Church, which participates in the holiness of the heavenly one, is the worldwide Catholic community rather than any of its local congregations. Holiness relates to the entirety of a person's life, including the quality of one's interior relationship with Christ. By reinterpreting holiness in that way, Augustine changed the coordinates by which a Christian's life is to be governed. Charity, conceived in terms of a graced relationship with Christ and responsiveness to his will, provides the basic norm of life. Charity is to transform a person's relationships and use of created goods. It requires the acceptance of uncommitted Christians and calls for suitable efforts toward their conversion. Once Augustine had located the source of holiness outside of history, his Church could more easily welcome those whom circumstances had brought to its door. No longer understood as a society composed solely of committed and holy people, the earthly Church was free to be the hospital in which Christ heals sin-wounded people. Augustine's therapeutic view of the Church profoundly influenced the Western Church and its relationship with the larger community.

Pelagianism also sought to promote holiness in the Church. Although Pelagius and his supporters tried to keep people engaged in their Christian life, they overestimated the capacities of the human person, depreciated their need for God's help, and underestimated the properly Christian dynamics of moral life. Augustine asserted that on account of sin, human nature is deeply flawed and persons can abide by God's will only if God freely extends the gift of grace. Although these teachings are important in their own right, of even greater significance is Augustine's presupposition that the underlying issue is religious, and therefore the discussion needed to reflect the relationship between God and the human family and do full justice to Christian faith. Christian faith highlighted the difference between God and creatures, the limited powers of human nature, the destructive effects of sin, and the absurdity of assuming that by their own efforts humans could ever obligate God to give them divine life or do anything else. Faith likewise speaks to daily life and prompts believers to walk in charity, humility, and gratitude. Besides informing Augustine's teachings on grace, these considerations help to focus the principal dynamics of Christian life and assure the integrity of its practice. They remind everyone that Christian moral life reflects God's free initiative and gifts and decisively affects one's relationship to God.

In the centuries following Augustine's death in 430 the Church received his teachings, assessed them carefully, and integrated many of them into its thinking and praxis. In the meanwhile, dramatic demographic, religious, and political developments transformed Europe and the Mediterranean basin. As these events were unfolding, the Church continued to carry out its daily activities of prayer, preaching, charity, and evangelization. Monasticism developed and assumed greater importance within the Church. The perennial tension between holiness and accommodation stimulated important changes in baptismal and penitential praxis. These events gave rise to the Middle Ages and influenced the evolution of religious institutions, worship, and moral life in the Catholic Church. These developments will be the subject of the following chapter.

5

Faith and Repentance
in a European Church

The invasions and turmoil of the fifth century set in motion a series of events that entailed the demise of the Roman Empire. Three distinct entities took its place: Western Christendom, composed of the barbarian nations that accepted the spiritual and political authority of the Roman pontiff; the Byzantine Empire in the East, which was the direct christianized successor of the Roman Empire; and the Islamic Arabs, who took control of North Africa, Spain, and much of the East. Differences in history, culture, language, government, and religion distinguished the Latins, Greeks, and Arabs from one another and generated tensions among them. The ebb and flow of their relationships directly influenced many aspects of Western European life.

The formation of Western Christendom was perhaps the principal development within Europe during the early Middle Ages.[1] In part, the emergence of this remarkable entity was stimulated by the rise of Islam and the loss of ecclesial communion between Western and

---

[1] R. W. Southern identifies the Middle Ages as that "period in western European history when the church could reasonably claim to be the one true state, and when men (however much they might differ about the nature of ecclesiastical and secular power) acted on the assumption that the church had an overriding political authority." The Middle Ages, therefore, begin when the unitary authority of the Roman Empire was replaced by the unitary authority of the papacy, a process that was completed by the seventh century. By the sixteenth century the political, cultural, intellectual, and religious synthesis of medieval Christendom had clearly dissolved; this marks the beginning of the modern era. R. W. Southern, *Western Society and the Church in the Middle Ages* (Baltimore: Pelican Books, 1970) 24, see also 16, 25.

Eastern Christians. But no less important were an increasingly assertive papacy and the mutual embrace of the barbarian nations and the Catholic Church. As this complex process unfolded, it both reflected and stimulated other events that shaped the religious and moral experience of European peoples. As societies became Catholic, baptism came to be conferred primarily in infancy, which left little room for a catechumenate and required a radically different approach to Christian catechesis. Traditional penitential practices proved to be less and less suited to people who had not committed themselves to Christian faith and morality. That situation favored the rise of a private penitential system, previously unknown, which eventually displaced the canonical system inherited from earlier centuries. Monasticism continued its vigorous growth, gained wide influence in society, and notably affected worship, spirituality, and morality in the Church. In addition to their effects on sacramental praxis and moral life, such developments recast the relationships among the Church, the people, and their societies and helped to bring forth the Christendom of the High Middle Ages.

This chapter will consider developments that occurred in the early Middle Ages and highlight their impact on the faith, worship, and moral tradition of the Church. Chronologically, this chapter extends from the end of the Roman era in the fifth century to the eve of the great European revival in the early eleventh century.

First to be considered are the effects of the wholesale incursion of barbarian peoples into Europe in the period between the death of St. Augustine in 430 and the pontificate of Pope Gregory I (590–604).[2] These two centuries saw important missionary activity and the conversion of many barbarian nations to Catholicism, events that established the early foundations of medieval Christendom. The chaos of those years and the rapid expansion of the Church generated severe stresses on the catechumenate, baptismal praxis, and penance. Significant changes in theory and practice occurred, with important effects on Christian life and morality.

The second section examines early Celtic monasticism. Besides helping to evangelize Western Europe, Celtic monks propagated a private form of penance that filled the void left by the practical failure of the ancient penitential system. Private penance helped to give form and

---

[2] Pope Gregory, also referred to as St. Gregory or Gregory the Great, is regarded by many as the last of the Latin Fathers of the Church. This two-century period is one of transition: when it opens the Roman Empire is intact although subject to stress; by the time of Pope Gregory the empire has been supplanted by a new political and religious dispensation.

content to moral life and highlighted its effects on one's communion with God and the Church.

It will then be necessary to account for Benedictine monasticism, including St. Benedict himself, particular characteristics of his monastic Rule, and the later development of the monastic tradition he began. In demonstrating the power of the Gospel to motivate men and women to pursue the highest standards of Christian commitment, prayer, and charity, monasticism affords another perspective from which to view the relationships among faith, worship, and moral life.

The fourth area of concern will be the process by which Continental peoples received and reshaped the penitential system of the Celtic monks, endowing it with many of the features found in modern-day sacramental penance. One of the most important contributions of the early Middle Ages, private penance has been a primary influence within Catholic moral life, pastoral ministry, and sacramental praxis.

In the early sixth century the Church settled a controversy concerning the contributions of God's grace and human freedom toward salvation. This topic is of perennial importance and bears directly on theology as well as the motivation, content, and religious quality of Christian moral life.

The following section will account for the fracturing of the Roman Empire and the emergence of Latin Christendom as a political, social, and religious entity. When viewed in the larger context of the Islamic advance throughout much of the Mediterranean basin and the increasing estrangement between East and West, it becomes clear that Western Christianity was becoming ever more self-enclosed. Its sharply narrowed political, human, and religious horizons did much to channel the later intellectual, social, religious, and moral development of Latin Catholicism.

BAPTISM AND PENANCE IN A NEW EUROPE

In the fifth and sixth centuries massive barbarian incursions fundamentally rearranged the social, religious, and political life of Western Europe and Roman Africa. Changes as dramatic and widespread as these did not occur quickly, easily, or without cost. They involved invasion, occupation, and war and brought wrenching human dislocations to much of the Western Empire, events that deeply affected the life and work of the Church. Foreign rulers, once established in Roman territory, gained the power to persecute the Church or disrupt its life, while the Church gained new opportunities for evangelization. The following discussion will be especially interested in the impact of such developments on the catechetical and penitential practices of the Church.

Historical Background

By the early fifth century strong political, social, demographic, and religious forces had already begun to transform the western reaches of the Roman Empire. As that century unfolded, the Angles and Saxons invaded and occupied much of Britain; the Vandals conquered Roman Africa; the Visigoths established themselves in Spain; and the Franks assumed prominence in Gaul. Although Italy suffered invasion and turmoil as well, the emperor in the East was able to retain control over a portion of that peninsula.

In the sixth century war and instability continued to be a common experience, mostly due to efforts by the Byzantine emperor Justinian I (527–65) to reclaim some of the territory that had fallen to the barbarians. In 533 he invaded and overthrew the Vandal kingdom in North Africa, restoring the region to Byzantine control and its people to the unrestricted practice of their Catholic faith. Shortly afterward he partially subdued the Visigoths of Spain. However, events in Italy soon revealed the limits of imperial power and the price of interminable conflict. The empire succeeded in conquering the Ostrogoths who had occupied part of Italy, but it could neither prevent a new invasion by the Lombards in 568 nor expel them afterward. The Gothic wars and the Lombard invasion inflicted great destruction in the Italian peninsula. By the time these events had run their course, aqueducts and other public facilities stood in ruins, many people had been forced from their homes, and those who remained often faced poverty and insecurity. Several epidemics of bubonic plague reduced the population even further and intensified the misery of the survivors.[3]

The rise of Clovis (c. 465–511) had a long-term influence that was greater than the wars, invasions, and distress of these centuries. When he became king of the Salian Franks around 481, Clovis' jurisdiction was limited to an area around Tournai in northern Gaul. Throughout his reign, however, he took every opportunity to expand his realm, which sometimes required war but usually occurred by peaceful means. By the time Clovis died his military, political, and diplomatic efforts had extended Frankish rule from his ancestral home east of the

---

[3] Lucien Musset, *The Germanic Invasions: The Making of Europe AD 400–600,* trans. Edward James and Columba James (London: Paul Elek, 1975) 22–115, 164–9; 176–83, 219–38; Michael Haren, *Medieval Thought: The Western Intellectual Tradition from Antiquity to the Thirteenth Century* (New York: St. Martin's Press, 1985) 59; Jean Daniélou and Henri Marrou, *The First Six Hundred Years,* trans. Vincent Cronin (New York: McGraw-Hill, 1964) 411–9; Henry Chadwick, *The Early Church* (London: Penguin Books, 1967) 247–57; Brian Tierney and Sidney Painter, *Western Europe in the Middle Ages: 300–1475* (New York: Knopf, 1970) 52–5.

Rhine to the Pyrenees of southern Gaul. His successors formed the Merovingian dynasty.

The religious dimensions of Clovis' reign are no less significant. About the year 503, the non-Christian Clovis decided to be baptized a Catholic, a step that local bishops both encouraged and welcomed. Within the Frankish kingdom, his conversion allowed him to assume the rights and duties of a Christian king toward the Church and enabled the bishops to seek his cooperation and support on matters of common interest. His adoption of the Catholic faith also had international implications, for it made him a coreligionist of Eastern Christians and made the Arians seem more alien.[4]

Clovis' conversion made it much easier for the Church to evangelize the Frankish people. In response to the preaching of bishops and the witness of monks, they became the first barbarian nation to accept the Catholic faith, setting a precedent that other peoples soon followed. By the end of the sixth century the neighboring Bergundians, Suevi, and Visigoths had abandoned Arianism in favor of Catholicism, with the result that the peoples of Gaul, Spain, and North Africa shared the same religion as most others in the Mediterranean basin. These national conversions began the melding of barbarian and Catholic into what would become medieval Christendom. Although no one could have known it at the time, Clovis' baptism helped to set in motion a train of events that eventually resulted in the mutual embrace of the peoples of Western Europe and the Catholic Church, a process that had incalculable effects on the development of life and history on that continent.[5]

During these centuries political upheaval, social displacement, military conflict, poverty, famine, and disease set the context for Church life and ministry. In these trying conditions, Christians were called to live their faith and carry out the ministries of word, worship, and service. These unstable and difficult conditions supported a number of developments in the life of the Church, especially an evolution in baptismal praxis, the practical failure of such institutions as the catechumenate and canonical penance, and the vigorous development of monasticism and ascetic approaches to Christian life.

[4] Musset, *Germanic Invasions*, 68–80; J. M. Wallace-Hadrill, *The Long-Haired Kings and Other Studies in Frankish History* (London: Methuen & Co., 1962) 163–85. Recent scholarship tends to present Clovis as a more informed, religious, and peaceable man than the traditional portrait allowed. See William M. Daly, "Clovis: How Barbaric, How Pagan?" *Speculum* 69 (1994) 619–64.

[5] See Tierney, *Western Europe in the Middle Ages*, 49–50; Daniélou, *First Six Hundred Years*, 418; Chadwick, *Early Church*, 248–50, 254–5; Musset, *Germanic Invasions*, 184–9.

Developments in Baptismal Praxis

This study has already noted that the larger numbers of people preparing for baptism and their ambiguous motivation entailed serious damage to the catechumenate.[6] Although this ancient institution continued to survive, it had been drastically shortened and no longer reliably performed its original functions. In the fifth and sixth centuries, an already tottering system was subjected to even more acute stresses. The turmoil spawned by the arrival of the barbarians as well as the sheer number of adults asking to be baptized made a lengthy and substantial catechumenate quite impossible. Even in tranquil conditions, a process that had failed in its application to Romans was not likely to succeed with barbarian candidates. By the time of Pope Gregory the Great the catechumenate, when it was observed at all, had become an abbreviated affair, sometimes lasting only a few days. Although it continued to exist in theory and was presupposed by baptismal rituals, the catechumenate no longer instructed and formed adults who were to be baptized.[7]

The dramatic increase in infant baptisms is a closely related development. The wholesale baptism of adults and the entry of entire peoples into the Catholic Church meant that eventually far fewer adults and many more infants were presented for baptism. This phenomenon reflects more than a normal sociological development. The practice of baptizing infants was legitimated by an ancient custom, strongly encouraged by the Church's preaching, and required by canonical legislation. Moreover, in an age of high infant mortality, St. Augustine's teachings on original sin and the necessity of baptism added a strong incentive for parents to have their newborn children baptized. Whatever the reasons, the general practice of infant baptism in Catholic areas of Western Europe doomed the catechumenate and made it necessary to reconsider the Church's catechetical and formational efforts.[8]

[6] See discussion in chapter 3, pp. 128–30, above.

[7] Michel Dujarier, "L'évolution de la pastorale catéchuménale aux six premiers siècles de l'Église," *MD* 71 (1962) 54, 58–60; idem, *A History of the Catechumenate: The First Six Centuries*, trans. Edward J. Haasl (New York: Sadlier, 1979) 94–100, 107–11. Dujarier calls attention to an important shift that often goes unnoticed. The loss of meaningful contact with the essentially religious significance of baptism made it more difficult for people to see that baptism is God's free gift to the candidate, which entails certain responsibilities. Instead of viewing their baptism in the light of God's election or call, people came to see it as something to be taken for granted or a ritual that conferred personal status in the community. See note 12 in this chapter, below.

[8] Bernard Hamilton, *Religion in the Medieval West* (London: Edward Arnold, 1986) 112–3; Pierre-Marie Gy, *La Liturgie dans l'histoire* (Paris: Ed. St.-Paul & Ed. Cerf,

Pastoral Consequences

The practical failure of the catechumenate, the ill-prepared baptism of many adults, and the predominance of infant baptism meant that most people received baptism without understanding its meaning. With respect to adult candidates, instruction soon became more a matter of form than substance and failed to communicate the moral and religious content and implications of Catholic faith. Since infants are too young to be catechized, the prayers and symbols used in the ceremony could hardly contribute toward their understanding or formation.[9]

Once the baptism of infants had become the rule rather than the exception, new approaches to instruction were required. At first the Church tried to direct its catechesis to parents and godparents. When that did not prove satisfactory, clergy, parents, and godparents were asked to instruct their baptized children as they grew up. Even though this latter initiative paid limited dividends, it signaled what was to become a general reliance on postbaptismal instruction to replace prebaptismal catechesis.

Although it was perhaps the best that could be done in the circumstances, that strategy was accompanied by a general decline of religious knowledge and understanding. Because adults were themselves poorly instructed and children limited in their capacity to learn, it was very difficult to teach people the grounds for their faith or communicate an adequate understanding of its essence and implications. Most people did well merely to learn the Lord's Prayer, the Creed, and perhaps some basic points concerning the sacraments and Christian morality.[10]

1990) 153; Joachim Jeremias, *Infant Baptism in the First Four Centuries*, trans. David Cairns (Philadelphia: Westminster Press, 1962) 97; Peter Cramer, *Baptism and Change in the Early Middle Ages, c. 200–c. 1150* (Cambridge: Cambridge University Press, 1993) 87–266; Henry G. J. Beck, *The Pastoral Care of Souls in South-East France During the Sixth Century* (Rome: Aedes Universitatis Gregorianae, 1950) 157–85.

[9] A small but interesting part of the problem was that the Church did not revise the baptismal ritual to reflect a significant change in practice. The ritual continued to presuppose adult candidates for baptism even after most people were being baptized in infancy. See Jean Daniélou and others, *Historical Theology* (Baltimore: Penguin Books, 1969) 200; Gy, *La Liturgie dans l'histoire*, 154–55; G. Bareille, "Catéchèse," *DTC*, 2/2:1889.

[10] In this connection it is well to advert to the lowering of cultural and educational standards in the West. In this age priests were sometimes ill-instructed and in no position to help educate their people. As a result the Church had little choice but to settle for very modest catechetical goals. A poor state of Christian education seems to have characterized the Church during the entirety of the Middle Ages, although as with any generalization there were exceptions. See E. Mangenot, "Catéchisme,"

The stresses that undermined baptismal catechesis also compromised the formational dimensions of baptism. The violence, war, and instability of the age as well as the wholesale baptism of non-Christian peoples virtually guaranteed that many ritual declarations of faith and conversion would be more formal than real. At the same time, Augustine's willingness to have the Church embrace the world and his tolerance of ecclesial ambiguity encouraged the Church to baptize more freely and to see itself as a mixed community. As a result, the Church came to include many who were grateful for baptism and sincerely sought to live Christian life to the full. But it also absorbed many others who retained pagan attitudes and practices, violent or murderous habits, an attachment to otherwise immoral practices, and a disposition ill-inclined to faith and conversion. The barbarian peoples greatly enlarged the Church but did not always add to the quality of its life.[11]

Taken together, the addition of the barbarian peoples to the Church and the disappearance of effective baptismal instruction and formation had serious long-term consequences for the public life and ministry of the Church. The poorly prepared entry of so many into the Church intensified the ambiguity of its corporate life. As a practical matter, the Church could not present its holiness as a telling contrast to conditions in a sinful world, thus damaging its witness to nonmembers. Another result was a further weakening of the ecclesiological foundations of faith, conversion, instruction, and baptism. Once the bulk of Church members lost an adequate grasp on their own faith and failed to give general evidence of an elevated moral life, it was no longer possible to deploy the Church community as a reliable point of reference for the instruction and formation of new members.

The splitting off of Christian instruction and formation from baptism tended to compromise subsequent efforts at catechesis and formation. A solid foundation in faith and conversion is required if people are to receive instruction with interest and walk the path of virtue with sincerity. Deprived of that foundation, efforts at catechesis and formation are easily frustrated for want of a comprehending and

---

DTC, 2/2:1895-9; Jordan Aumann, *Christian Spirituality in the Catholic Tradition* (San Francisco: Ignatius; London: Sheed & Ward, 1985) 77–8; Hamilton, *Religion in the Medieval West*, 71–2, 107–8, 112, 132–41; Gy, *La Liturgie*, 153–4; David Knowles with Dimitri Obolensky, *The Middle Ages* (London: Darton, Longman & Todd; New York: Paulist Press, 1969) 30; and Daniélou, *First Six Hundred Years*, 423–4.

[11] See Bareille, "Catéchèse," 1891; Tierney, *Western Europe in the Middle Ages*, 50, 67–75; Daniélou, *First Six Hundred Years*, 445–8. This discussion prescinds from an occasional practice that would have an obvious bearing on the issue: the forced conversion and baptism of barbarian peoples.

receptive subject. What is more, without an understanding of the history of salvation and the mystery of Christ, further instruction lacks its essential context, and the hearer lacks the key to its meaning. This context is likewise integral to Christian moral life and effective moral formation. Without it the Church cannot expect to present the moral dimensions of faith as an essential part of one's response to God's gift of divine life within a holy community. Once that basic source of meaning slips from sight, the life of the Church is bound to be adversely affected.[12]

Canonical Penance and Its Decline

At the beginning of the fifth century the principal contours of canonical penance had been well established on the basis of earlier usage. Its institutional dimensions closely reflected the inherent meaning of grave sin and the dynamics of conversion as the early Church understood them. Because grave sin separates people from God and the Church, Christians who had sinned in this way refrained from further participation in the Eucharist. Having recognized the dimensions of the problem, the sinner approached the bishop to seek his judgment. Once he was informed about the case, the bishop decided whether the person should be enrolled in the order of penitents[13] and admitted to formal canonical penance. If so, the bishop took account of the applicable canons and then assigned penances that were usually lengthy and difficult. After the penitent had performed them, the bishop again examined the penitent to see if the expected conversion had sufficiently matured. If so, the bishop granted reconciliation with the

[12] Dujarier, *History of the Catechumenate*, 107–9; Joseph Lécuyer, "Théologie de l'Initiation chrétienne d'après les Pères," *MD* 58 (1959) 5–21. It is instructive to compare this situation the one described in *DCatRud*, 3–4. St. Augustine's instruction of catechumens was primarily based upon the economy of salvation. Out of love God has done a great deal for the human race, beginning with Adam and Eve and continuing to the present day. The high point is the sending of his son, Jesus, to die for sinners. Persons are to respond to that love through lives of faith, hope, and charity. Such catechesis united the sacramental, ecclesial, instructional, and personal so that each element had its proper place within a coherent and dynamic whole. The necessity and importance of such preparation is not to be underestimated.

[13] The order of penitents was a distinct and publicly recognizable group of Christians. Members wore distinctive attire, attended the Liturgy of the Word at the beginning of the eucharistic celebration, but usually departed immediately afterward. The community was called upon to assist the penitents through prayer and encouragement. The order of penitents had much in common with the older order of catechumens, who also did not share the full communion of the Church, made up a distinct group, and attended only the Liturgy of the Word. See sources in the following note.

Church, which usually occurred just prior to the Easter Vigil. The reconciled Christian was then welcomed back into the eucharistic assembly.[14]

This system's symbolism and inner logic were clear and powerful. Grave sin alienated from God and the Church community, a catastrophe that should be truly exceptional. When such sin occurred, repentance was urgent and was the only road that led the sinner back to forgiveness and reconciliation. The penitent was expected to walk it by means of sincere inner sorrow and the practical efforts that together aimed to correct the causes of one's sin. The sinner did penance in an ecclesial and liturgical context under the supervision of the bishop. This approach had pedagogical benefits for the entire community. It depicted the effects of sin and showed that grace and forgiveness are bound to communion with God and the Church.

Despite these advantages, canonical penance included a number of elements that cumulatively weakened it, caused its practical failure, and ultimately led to its disappearance from the life of the Church. Perhaps the most serious problem was the ancient rule of one penance, which stipulated that individual Christians could avail themselves of canonical penance only once. On account of this rule, a recidivist could not enter the order of penitents but was instead excommunicated as an apostate from penance. Because this consequence was so drastic, fear of a subsequent fall into grave sin deterred many from seeking reconciliation even on the one occasion available to them.[15]

A second difficulty was that a reconciled penitent was expected to live a penitential life forever after. Normally that precluded sexual relations even with a spouse, business pursuits, eligibility for ordination, and the bearing of arms.[16] Canonical penance therefore imposed very severe and lifelong deprivations on all who embraced it, and this helps to explain why many grave sinners never sought canonical penance even though it offered them a way to be reconciled with the Church. These same deterrents caused Church councils and local bishops to

---

[14] See James Dallen, *The Reconciling Community: The Rite of Penance* (New York: Pueblo, 1986) 65–73; Cyrille Vogel, *Le pécheur et la pénitence au moyen âge* (Paris: Cerf, 1969) 17; Bernhard Poschmann, *Penance and the Anointing of the Sick,* trans. Francis Courtney (New York: Herder & Herder, 1964) 81–103. This description of canonical penance in the fifth century is a generalization that overlooks the variations over time and from place to place.

[15] Marie-François Berrouard, "La pénitence publique durant les six premiers siècles: Histoire et sociologie," *MD* 118 (1974) 126; Poschmann, *Penance and the Anointing of the Sick,* 104–7.

[16] For example, Council of Orleans (511), Can. 11; Council of Epaon (517), Can. 3; Council of Orleans (538), Can. 25; presented in Hefele, 4:90, 109, 208.

disqualify certain people from becoming penitents, no matter what they had done. The young, for example, and sometimes even the middle-aged were ineligible, as were married people who lacked the permission of their spouses.[17]

Changes Within Canonical Penance

As the severity of the canonical penitential system increasingly dissuaded sinners from using it, other developments transformed its internal dynamics. One was the decision of Pope Innocent I (402–17) to allow virtuous members of the Church to join the order of penitents to express their repentance of slight sins and their commitment to the Gospel.[18] This decision meant that canonical penance, in addition to its original task of reconciling grave sinners with the Church, gained a new but still secondary function: supporting faithful Christians who wished to lead even more devout lives. While certainly salutary, the dual use of canonical penance involved a certain loss of pedagogical and symbolical clarity. No longer reserved for the single, primordial, and urgent task of reconciling grave sinners to communion with God and the Church, penitential praxis began to blur the radical difference between grace, communion, and full participation in the Church's worship on the one hand and sin, alienation, and exclusion from the Eucharist on the other.[19]

In another development, canonical penance began to be celebrated at the end of a person's life. Aware that the Church was willing to grant reconciliation to its dying members,[20] sinners began to ask this

---

[17] See Council of Arles (443), Can. 22; Council of Agde (506), Can. 15; and Council of Orleans (538), Can. 24; see Hefele, 3:170; 4:79, 208; these canons are also quoted in Cyrille Vogel, "La *paenitentia in extremis* chez saint Césaire évêque d'Arles (503–542)," *SP* 5 (1962) 418; see also Beck, *Pastoral Care*, 191–200; Poschmann, *Penance and the Anointing of the Sick*, 104–7; Vogel, *Le pécheur et la pénitence*, 17–8; and Berrouard, "La pénitence publique," 126.

[18] Innocent I, Letter 25:7, 10; see Berrouard, "La pénitence publique," 127; Dallen, *Reconciling Community*, 84.

[19] The dual use of canonical penance is the ancestor of the modern distinction between a confession of necessity and one of devotion. The former is normally required of those who are guilty of mortal sin, while the latter is recommended to the faithful whose share of baptismal grace has continued intact despite their daily shortcomings and failings. This distinction reflects the Church's awareness that grace and sin are reckoned ultimately in terms of communion and alienation, which admit of no blurring or middle position.

[20] This rule is found in Can. 13 of the First Council of Nicaea (Tanner, 1:12; DS, 129) and subsequent local legislation; the same obligation was also imposed by a decretal of Pope Celestine I in 428. See Beck, *Pastoral Care*, 200; Poschmann, *Penance and the Anointing of the Sick*, 95, 100–1.

favor when they thought that death was near. Bishops readily granted these requests, but they did so with the understanding that deathbed penance involved the same requirements that pertained to sinners who were young and healthy. Accordingly, a gravely ill penitent who later recovered would be required to do the appropriate penances and could not expect to be reconciled again.[21] That prompted some bishops to hesitate before granting reconciliation to young persons who might well recover, especially when they were not known to have sinned grievously. These considerations also show that deathbed penance was regarded as an abbreviation of canonical penance, not a substitute for it.[22]

Despite its solid canonical and pastoral warrants, some contemporary authorities were quite ambivalent about deathbed reconciliations. Their doubts arose from the fact that dying people were generally unable to perform the penances that were integral to the process of reconciliation. They questioned the sincerity of those who had shown few signs of contrition or penance while they were healthy. Some concluded that it was unreasonable to think that the ritual of deathbed reconciliation necessarily forgave sinners or reconciled them with God. However, these doubts did not pertain to those who had shown sincere contrition for their sins and had done penance throughout their lives. These concerns notwithstanding, the practical decline of canonical penance, fear of God's judgment, and pastoral generosity to the dying cumulatively promoted the practice of deathbed reconciliation. In the sixth century it became quite general, and Church legislation eventually required everyone to receive it.[23]

Over the longer term, delaying penance until the time of death involved changes in the internal dynamics of ecclesiastical penance. Because sick and dying people could not *do* penance, penance or reconciliation was *given* to them. This changed penance from a demanding, time-consuming process of sincere personal conversion to a ritual that conveyed a spiritual status that could be received with little personal effort or commitment. In this context the priest is much more likely to be involved, not the bishop, which speeded the process by which priests displaced bishops as the usual ministers of penance and the penitent as the central human figure in the process of forgiveness. What is more, the sustained communitarian context and evocative

---

[21] See, for example, Council of Orange (441), Can. 3 (Hefele, 3:160).

[22] Beck, *Pastoral Care*, 191, 201.

[23] Ibid., 202–22; Vogel, "La *paenitentia in extremis*," 419–23; Poschmann, *Penance and the Anointing of the Sick*, 107–9; Berrouard, "La pénitence publique," 128; Dallen, *Reconciling Community*, 78–81.

liturgical celebrations, once integral to the process of reconciliation, shrank to the point of disappearance. Finally, the ritual of penance no longer envisioned the resumption of one's rightful place in the eucharistic assembly. Instead, it sought to prepare the person for death and God's judgment. These changes were significant, for they helped to disassociate forgiveness from the practical demands of moral reform and make reconciliation seem to be more a matter of ritual than of reintegration into the Christian community.[24]

Other Paths to Reconciliation

The fact that the Church reconciled people at the end of their lives demonstrates that reconciliation was not limited to those who had done penance according to the ancient canons. This makes it easier to understand how the Church could grant nonpenitential reconciliation in some other cases as well. These other paths to reconciliation were open to sinful members of the clergy, people who entered monastic communities, and those who voluntarily committed themselves to an ascetic way of life.

During the fourth century members of the clergy were considered ineligible for membership in the order of penitents.[25] Behind this ruling was the conviction that to admit clergy into the order of penitents would be to violate the dignity of the priesthood. Just as it was unthinkable to baptize a person twice, so also it was judged insulting to the sacrament of orders for the bishop to impose hands a second time upon a member of the clergy.[26] Therefore, instead of allowing a gravely sinful cleric to become a penitent, the Church dismissed him from the ranks of the clergy. That expulsion was considered an adequate way to address the offense. Once returned to the lay state, the cleric continued to enjoy uninterrupted access to the sacramental life of the Church. In some cases the degraded cleric was expected to enter a monastery and do penance privately for the rest of his life.[27]

[24] Dallen, *Reconciling Community*, 78–82; Beck, *Pastoral Care*, 213.

[25] Dallen, *Reconciling Community*, 83; Poschmann, *Penance and the Anointing of the Sick*, 110–1.

[26] This view was based upon the conviction that because it was associated with the giving of the Holy Spirit, the imposition of hands was a most sacred gesture that was not to be violated by misuse or duplication. The rituals of canonical penance involved a solemn imposition of hands, which would therefore appear to repeat the imposition of hands at ordination. Poschmann, *Penance and the Anointing of the Sick*, 111.

[27] Ibid., 110–3. The policy that degraded a cleric but did not admit him to canonical penance also reflected the legal principle that people were not to be made to answer twice for the same offense.

A similar policy applied to sinners who formally committed themselves to an ascetic form of life. Entry into a monastery, for example, required the Church's blessing and a public vow binding the person to a penitential life of prayer, asceticism, celibacy, and the use of distinctive attire. Because it was understood as a recommitment to one's baptismal promises, formal embrace of an ascetic life readmitted a sinner to the Eucharist; there was consequently no need for canonical penance. The same was true of the *conversi*, people who renounced ordinary lay life by formally pledging themselves to an ascetic life in the world.[28] However, many devout men and women also became monks or *conversi*, and this helps to explain why these groups were held in high esteem. In fact, membership among the *conversi* or in monastic communities strongly recommended a man's promotion to the presbyterate or episcopate.[29]

The awareness that sinners urgently needed to repent and that sincere repentance wins God's favor helped to open new channels for grave sinners. Bishops encouraged those who required but did not have access to canonical reconciliation to evoke sincere interior repentance and embrace a suitably penitential life. Especially if they were sustained over time, such efforts manifested faith and piety, contributed to the efficacy of deathbed penance, and helped a sinner to win God's eternal mercy. More interestingly, there is some evidence that sixth-century bishops, including Caesarius of Arles, sometimes accepted that sincere repentance might permit a grave sinner to return to the Eucharist without first having had recourse to canonical penance. However, neither this nor the other paths to reconciliation filled the pastoral void left by the practical failure of canonical penance.[30]

Pastoral Consequences

Taken together, these factors trace the development of penance in the fifth and sixth centuries. Although it continued to be the traditional

---

[28] The early Church regarded martyrdom as a substitute for baptism or a second baptism. Once the cessation of persecutions removed the opportunity for martyrdom, monastic profession came to be seen as its substitute. In this way the early Church accepted that monastic profession functioned as a second baptism. See Timothy Fry, ed., *The Rule of St. Benedict In Latin and English with Notes* (Collegeville: The Liturgical Press, 1981) 14–5; Daniélou, *First Six Hundred Years,* 269–70.

[29] Poschmann, *Penance and the Anointing of the Sick,* 113–6. See also Paul Galtier, "Pénitents et 'Convertis': De la pénitence latine à la pénitence celtique," *RHE* 33 (1937) 5–26, 277–305; Daniélou, *First Six Hundred Years,* 428; Vogel, *Le pécheur et la pénitence,* 22–3.

[30] Beck, *Pastoral Care,* 208–22; Albert Voog, "Le péché et la distinction des péchés dans l'oeuvre de Césaire d'Arles," *NRT* 84 (1962) 1065–71; Gerald C. Millenkamp,

and recognized means for the reconciliation of grave sinners, canonical penance had grown too rigid and severe to be generally useful.[31] Secondary purposes and deathbed situations came to predominate in practice, substantially changing the inner dynamics and public function of ecclesiastical penance. Its increasing failure in regard to grave sinners left the Church with limited resources in the face of a very difficult pastoral situation. As a rule, grave sinners who needed ecclesial reconciliation were not eligible to receive the Eucharist or participate fully in the other liturgical rites. As more people delayed their request for penance until the end of their lives, sacramental practice tended to decline. Baptism was still celebrated at the beginning of life, and perhaps penance, viaticum, and anointing of the sick helped to mark its end. But for many of the Catholic people, regular liturgical worship and full sacramental participation was no longer integral to their Christian lives. That phenomenon also reflected the moral problems of the community and a disassociation of moral life from the daily worship of the Church.[32]

From another perspective, this history suggests that, whatever the circumstances, a penitential life was considered appropriate for devout Christians and grave sinners alike. Although in these two centuries the demands of canonical penance discouraged most people from embracing it, devout or repentant Christians found ways to express their dependence on God's grace and pardon. Some members of the Church answered the Gospel's call to holiness by entering a monastery or committing themselves to an ascetic life; others fasted, prayed, or performed works of charity in a spirit of contrition for their sins. Although particular cases varied widely, it is clear that penance was held in high esteem and that penitents enjoyed official support and recognition. Their example points to the positive relationship that existed between moral life and Christian faith.

CELTIC MONASTICISM AND PENITENTIAL PRAXIS

As the Church on the Continent struggled to meet urgent penitential needs with an increasingly obsolete system, another approach to

---

"Penance in Transition and Caesarius of Arles" (S.T.D. diss., Rome: n.p., 1973) especially 19–27, 67–75.

[31] Poschmann, *Penance and the Anointing of the Sick,* 107–9, 123.

[32] On the history of penance in these centuries see E. Amann and A. Michel, "Pénitence - sacrement," *DTC,* 12/1:813-43; Berrouard, "La pénitence publique," 92, 120–8; Dallen, *Reconciling Community,* 61–3, 76–84; Poschmann, *Penance and the Anointing of the Sick,* 81–121; A.H.M. Jones, *The Later Roman Empire, 284–602: A Social Economic and Administrative Survey* (Oxford: Basil Blackwell, 1964) 981–2.

penance was taking shape in Ireland. Rooted in the monastic customs of Gaul and the East, Celtic penance placed greater reliance on ascetic practices, individual effort, and specific atonement. It was not limited to particular sins, persons, or seasons and could be repeated as needed. Once introduced into the European mainland, this form of penance was readily embraced by clergy and people and eventually won formal canonical approval. This private penitential system is the direct ancestor of sacramental penance in the modern-day Latin Church and has profoundly affected the theology, outlook, sacramental usage, and moral life of Western Christians since at least the end of the first millennium. This section will account for the rise of Celtic penance, note some of its salient characteristics, and suggest its religious and moral significance. A later section of this chapter will discuss the transplantation of Celtic penance to the Continent and its subsequent development.

Monasticism in Ireland

Although much remains unknown about the beginnings of Catholicism in Ireland, it is clear that during the fifth century St. Patrick and his co-workers evangelized the Celtic people of that land.[33] It is likely that he established bishoprics throughout Ireland in accordance with canonical tradition. However, by the early sixth century a decidedly monastic organization began to supplant the diocesan system Patrick had inaugurated. In an unprecedented manner Irish church life came to depend upon the monasteries and was subordinate to the authority of the abbots.[34]

The monastic character of early Irish Catholicism can be attributed to several factors. One was Patrick's own background. While living in southern Gaul, he had learned the mainly Eastern ascetic traditions prevalent in that area and undoubtedly introduced them to the Celts.[35]

---

[33] For more on St. Patrick, see John T. McNeill, *The Celtic Churches: A History* A.D. *200 to 1200* (Chicago and London: University of Chicago Press, 1974) 50–67; Charles Thomas, *Christianity in Roman Britain to* A.D. *500* (Berkeley and Los Angeles: University of California Press, 1981) 307–27.

[34] Henry Mayr-Harting, *The Coming of Christianity to Anglo-Saxon England* (London: B. T. Batsford, 1972) 78–93; Gerard Mitchell, "The Origins of Irish Penance," *ITQ* 22 (1955) 10–1.

[35] Dallen, *Reconciling Community*, 128, note 5. For further discussion of early Gallic monasticism and its principal founders, John Cassian and Martin of Tours, see Fry, *Rule of St. Benedict*, 51–9; Aumann, *Christian Spirituality*, 59–61; Louis Bouyer, *The Spirituality of the New Testament and the Fathers*, trans. Mary P. Ryan (London: Burns & Oates, 1963) 500–12.

Another factor was sociological. The absence of large cities meant that the bishops could not link their authority to the recognized dominance of urban areas over the surrounding countryside, while monasteries readily flourished in a mainly agricultural and rural society. Perhaps most important of all was a personal and cultural consideration, the affinity of the Celtic people for ascetic practices. Whatever the causes, the Irish church readily adopted many monastic customs. Among these, the system of penance used by the monks was especially significant and had a powerful impact on the development of penitential praxis in the Catholic West.[36]

Celtic Penance

One of the most remarkable features of Celtic Catholicism was its approach to the forgiveness of sins. Although Patrick may have brought the traditional system of canonical penance to Ireland, it never assumed a significant place in Irish life. Instead, the Celts employed a decidedly monastic system, which they had inherited from the East by way of Lérins and other monasteries of southern Gaul.[37] This system understood sin through the metaphor of sickness. When the need occurred, people found a confessor and described their sins through a detailed personal confession. In response, the confessor tried to act as a good physician by prescribing as a penance the practice of contrary virtues. Reconciliation, or forgiveness, occurred once the penitent had completed the penance; there was probably no prayer of absolution or other formal act of reconciliation.[38]

The Penitential Books

Because this penitential praxis was based upon the notion that sins are forgiven by the practice of contrary virtues, books began to circulate

---

[36] Mitchell, "Origins of Irish Penance," 10–1. On the origin of the Irish church and its monastic quality, see Tierney, *Western Europe in the Middle Ages,* 83–5; Daniélou, *First Six Hundred Years,* 452–5; Aumann, *Christian Spirituality,* 72–3; Jean Leclercq, François Vandenbroucke, and Louis Bouyer, *The Spirituality of the Middle Ages,* trans. The Benedictines of Holme Eden Abbey, Carlisle (London: Burns & Oates, 1968) 39–40.

[37] See Poschmann, *Penance and the Anointing of the Sick,* 99–100; Mitchell, "Origins of Irish Penance," 11–3.

[38] Cyrille Vogel, *Les "Libri paenitentiales"* (Turnhout: Brepols, 1978) 32–3; Vogel, *Le pécheur et la pénitence,* 20–1; Dallen, *Reconciling Community,* 103–8. Dallen disagrees with the opinion that early Celtic penance included a formal prayer of absolution or act of readmission to the Eucharist.

that tried to help confessors apply a suitable penance for any given sin. These *penitential books* began to circulate in the sixth century and were continually produced in various parts of Europe until at least the twelfth century.[39] They are important as evidence of medieval penitential praxis and as a source of sacramental penance in the Latin Church.[40]

The penitential books dealt exclusively with specific sins and the penances that were to be done for each and included no discussion of the underlying theological, pastoral, or catechetical issues. The sins were arranged in random order, without differentiation as to their kind or gravity. However, a close examination of the Penitentials shows that they frequently deal with sexual issues, including those proper to marriage.[41] Murder, homicide, personal violence, and slavery are also prominently treated in the penitential books; and sorcery, magical practices, offenses involving food and drink, and profanation of the Lord's Day are likewise listed with appropriate penances.[42]

The penances usually required the penitent to fast from specific foods or beverages, although some sins might call for sexual abstinence, renunciation of weapons, exile, or almsgiving. The nature of the deprivation generally depended upon the seriousness of the sin, its circumstances, and those of the sinner. The duration of the penance could range from a single day to an entire lifetime. Although the penitential books differed in how they paired sins and penances, they agreed in requiring a penitent to expiate particular sins with specific penances. This "taxation," or levying a penance on each sin, is the reason the term "tariff penance" is often used to refer to this penitential system.[43]

[39] For a list of the various penitential books and details on their respective dates and places of origin, see Vogel, Les "Libri paenitentiales," 60–94. For further discussion of this literature and the texts of specific books in translation, see Ludwig Bieler, ed., *The Irish Penitentials* (Dublin: Dublin Institute for Advanced Studies, 1963); John T. McNeill and Helena M. Gamer, trans., *Medieval Handbooks of Penance: A Translation of the Principal* Libri poenitentiales *and Selections from Related Documents* (New York: Octagon Books, 1965); Vogel, *Le pécheur et la pénitence*, 39–128.

[40] On this see John Mahoney, *The Making of Moral Theology: A Study of the Roman Catholic Tradition* (Oxford: Clarendon Press, 1987) 5–17; William Cosgrave, "How Celtic Penance Gave Us Personal Confession," *DL* 41 (1991) 412–22. For a different view see Poschmann, *Penance and the Anointing of the Sick*, 130–1.

[41] For more on the Penitentials' treatment of sexual behavior, see Vogel, Les "Libri paenitentiales," 104, 107–9; John T. Noonan, Jr., *Contraception: A History of Its Treatment by the Catholic Theologians and Canonists* (Cambridge, Mass. and London: Harvard University Press, 1986) 152–70; and Pierre J. Payer, *Sex and the Penitentials: The Development of a Sexual Code, 550–1150* (Toronto: University of Toronto Press, 1984).

[42] Vogel, Les "Libri paenitentiales," 104–11.

[43] Poschmann, *Penance and the Anointing of the Sick*, 126–7; McNeill, *Medieval Handbooks of Penance*, 30–5; Vogel, Les "Libri paenitentiales," 28–9, 34–9.

Because the penances stipulated in the penitential books could easily accumulate to the point of impossibility, this system included several mechanisms that mitigated its severity and kept it within reach of ordinary people. Because self-denial was the underlying goal, it was permissible to commute a penance, that is, exchange a lengthy penance for one that was possibly more severe but also shorter. Similarly, actions that wounded or killed someone or damaged a neighbor's property could be addressed by composition, a payment made to those who had suffered the loss. Redemption, or paying a fine by means of almsgiving, might also replace a penance that seemed too severe. It was even possible to have one's penance performed by others. Finally, the confessor was expected to use good judgment in assigning penances, and this too helped keep this system humane.[44]

An Assessment of Celtic Penance

Celtic penance is to be assessed in light of historical and cultural as well as theological factors. Although this system might appear overly harsh and impersonal today, many early medieval peoples found its reliance on specific expiation to be just and reasonable. Over time the penitential books helped to suppress homicide, personal violence, theft, and other offenses that damaged the community and made the offender a target for revenge. In diminishing societal violence, the Penitentials contributed to the civilizing of many European peoples. Moreover, the system of commutations, compositions, and redemptions reflected traditional legal principles that sought to displace private or familial vengeance with peaceful ways of settling grievances. Pastorally speaking, the nature of the penances as well their connection to specific sins helped recently christianized peoples to escape the influence of pagan cults and practices, weaken the grip of evil habits, and improve the moral tenor of their lives. Despite their focus on penitential expiation, the penitential books also recognized that prayer, contrition, and conversion were indispensable.[45]

[44] McNeill, *Medieval Handbooks of Penance*, 35–8; Poschmann, *Penance and the Anointing of the Sick*, 127–8; Vogel, *Les "Libri paenitentiales,"* 43–59. For some specific examples of commutations, redemptions, and substitutions, see McNeill, *Medieval Handbooks of Penance*, 142–7; Bieler, *Irish Penitentials*, 277–83; Vogel, *Le pécheur et la pénitence*, 119–28.

[45] McNeill, *Medieval Handbooks of Penance*, 25–6, 35–43, 46–50; Poschmann, *Penance and the Anointing of the Sick*, 128–9; Vogel, *Les "Libri paenitentiales,"* 108–10. Vogel agrees that by helping to suppress homicide and other violent crimes, the Penitentials contributed to the civilization of pagan and barbarian peoples. However, he does not share the general view that the Penitentials raised the moral consciousness

Celtic penance also included certain problematic aspects. Although the system of tariff penance originally viewed sin as a disease to be cured, it tended to treat sin as a crime to be punished. Over time, the prominence of the penal dimension lent an increasingly legal or punitive texture to sin and its forgiveness. In a similar way, the linking of forgiveness to the performance of difficult works and the acceptance of discomfort might suggest that forgiveness was more a matter of the sinner's expiation than God's gift of grace. The attention paid to the tangible profile of a penitent's sins also helped to emphasize external behavior at the expense of the interior drama of aversion from God and conversion to God. The privacy surrounding the encounter of penitent and confessor and the lack of a clear liturgical context likewise made the proceedings seem more individual and less ecclesial in nature.[46]

When considered as a whole, Celtic penance succeeded because it offered important advantages over the canonical system known on the Continent. It was available from any priest and did not require the intervention of the bishop. It accommodated all sins whether grave or slight and was available to anyone without regard to rank, station, or personal background. Because it was not synchronized with the liturgical calendar, it could be celebrated at any time and with little formality. Perhaps most important of all, the absence of a rule of one penance allowed penitents to use this penitential system as often as they wished and without infamy or lingering deprivations. In sum, Celtic penance met the spiritual and human needs of ordinary people in an imperfect world. This virtue explains why, once it was offered to them, the peoples of continental Europe so readily embraced the Celtic penitential system.[47]

BENEDICTINE MONASTICISM

If Celtic monasticism represented an early and highly ascetic form of Christian life, the Benedictine tradition was distinguished by its accent

---

of the European people. He finds that in many instances their approach fostered a debased understanding of morality and a false notion of religion. See Vogel, *Les "Libri paenitentiales,"* 111–2.

[46] Vogel, *Les "Libri paenitentiales,"* 111–2; McNeill, *Medieval Handbooks of Penance,* 46–50; Poschmann, *Penance and the Anointing of the Sick,* 124–31; Dallen, *Reconciling Community,* 105–8; Cosgrave, "Celtic Penance," 418–21; and Payer, *Sex and the Penitentials,* 7–10.

[47] Poschmann, *Penance and the Anointing of the Sick,* 125, 129–30; Vogel, *Le pécheur et la pénitence,* 18; idem., *Les "Libri paenitentiales,"* 36. Much has been written on Celtic penance. In addition to the sources noted in this discussion, see, for example,

on community, stability, and respect for the capacities of ordinary Christians. Benedictines contributed significantly to the evangelization of England and Germany. In time their practice of monasticism displaced other forms of monastic life in the West and exercised a strong and pervasive influence on the Latin Church generally. Benedictine monasticism requires attention also because it helped many monks and nuns[48] to know and serve God and stood as an important institutional witness to Christian perfection and its implications for moral life.

This section will therefore consider the development and contribution of Benedictine monasticism. The following section will discuss the impact of monasticism on the evangelization of Europe and the penitential praxis of the West.

The Foundation of Benedictine Monasticism

Arguably the most important and influential figure in Western monastic history is Benedict of Nursia, who was born in central Italy around the year 480. Although his well-to-do parents gave him a liberal Roman education, the young Benedict abandoned his schooling and all thought of an ordinary career. Fearing that too much learning would threaten his faith and repelled by the vices of his fellow students, Benedict left Rome to embrace a life of ascetic solitude. At Subiaco, about forty miles outside Rome, he took the garb of a hermit

---

Paul Galtier, "Les origines de la pénitence irlandaise," *RSR* 42 (1954); Daniélou, *First Six Hundred Years,* 452–5.

[48] Although it is customary to refer to "monks" and "monasticism," it is important to remember that women also embraced asceticism and have been conspicuous throughout monastic history. One recent study declares:

> In every period of monastic history, women as well as men fully lived the monastic life. The life of the nuns was unfortunately one of the neglected areas of monastic history until fairly recently. From its very beginnings, in the East, women played an important role in monasticism. The *Apophthegmata* mentions female solitaries in the desert; Pachomius established a monastery for virgins, and Basil legislated for them. Paula and Melania and the other associates of Jerome and Rufinus were among the most enthusiastic propagators of the monastic life in the Latin world. St. Gregory speaks of nuns in the entourage of St. Benedict and has left us an unforgettable portrait of St. Scholastica's power of prayer. A number of Latin rules were written especially for women. In the Anglo-Saxon world they were of special importance: one thinks of Hilda presiding over the double monastery of Whitby, and of Lioba and the other female collaborators who contributed so much to the work of Boniface and who appear so frequently in his letters (Fry, *Rule of St. Benedict,* 129; see also 129–30).

and lived in a cave for three years. There he attracted a number of followers, whom he organized into twelve small communities of twelve monks each. During this time Benedict began to prefer life in community to the solitude of a hermit.[49]

For reasons that remain somewhat obscure, Benedict left Subiaco for Monte Cassino with several of his companions. There, around the year 529, he began another monastery. This foundation was successful and came to have great influence in the area. It was during this period that Benedict wrote his Rule for monastic life, a document that became the most important and influential monastic text in the Latin Church. Benedict died at Monte Cassino in 547. Apart from his Rule, he bequeathed no writings of any kind to posterity.[50]

The Rule of St. Benedict

Benedict's approach to monasticism can be understood from a study of his Rule. Although it was based upon an earlier *Rule of the Master*, Benedict's Rule is unique because it reflects so much of his own experience and judgment.[51] Turning away from a violent and unstable world with its vice and distractions, Benedict intended the monastery to be a "school for the Lord's service" (*The Rule of St. Benedict*, Prologue, 45),[52] whose ultimate purpose is to help the monk achieve unity with God.

What distinguishes Benedictine monasticism is not its goal but the means used to reach it. Upholding the value of life in common, Benedict's Rule presupposes that charity toward others is essential to monastic life. Because it was so effective in confronting a monk with the demands of charity, Benedict required monastic stability. This commitment to reside in one community for life also diminished contact with the world and helped create an environment favorable to the Christian purposes of monastic life. Obedience to the abbot was enjoined on the monk not only for the sake of good order but to foster humility and self-denial in the monk and thereby help him become more generous in the service of God. Since it was so important to contemplation, the Rule placed a high premium on silence in the monastery. Its principal

[49] Gregory the Great, *Dialogues,* II. Most of what is known about Benedict's life comes from the *Dialogues* of Pope Gregory. See Fry, *Rule of St Benedict*, 73–9.

[50] Aumann, *Christian Spirituality*, 68–9; see also Gregory's *Dialogues*, II.

[51] See Southern, *Western Society and the Church*, 218–23; Fry, *Rule of St. Benedict*, 79–83, for very helpful discussions of Benedict's Rule in light of *The Rule of the Master*.

[52] Benedict's very troubled historical times seem also to have encouraged him to adopt an ascetic life. See Fry, *Rule of St. Benedict*, 65–7.

activities were common prayer, reading of the Scriptures, and manual work.

Reflecting its times, early Benedictine monasticism was a movement of ordinary lay Christians who had decided to turn away from a world judged to be evil in order to reach their salvation by a committed living of Christian life. That is the reason Benedict's communities did not pursue learning or undertake the pastoral care of people outside the monastery. His basic Christian purposes also help to explain why Benedict remained a lay person and his monasteries included few if any priests.[53]

Early Benedictine monasticism involved a demanding and disciplined way of life. But for all its requirements, Benedict nevertheless intended his Rule for beginners in living Christian life. For that reason he fashioned it to be humane and moderate, tolerant of human frailty, and able to accommodate human diversity. These features as much as its religious wisdom account for the general acceptance and wide influence the Rule eventually achieved.[54]

The Dominance of Benedictine Monasticism and Its Clericalization

Although the life and work of St. Benedict attracted little attention in his own time, his Rule circulated among the monasteries in Italy after his death and took its place among the other monastic rules in use during that period. It eventually found its way to Gaul, England, and in due time, other parts of Europe.

It was only in the early ninth century, during the Carolingian Reform, that legislation began to oblige all monasteries to adopt the Rule of St. Benedict. This helps to account for the dominance of the Rule and the success of Benedictine monasticism up to the eleventh century. In that same era Benedictine monasteries underwent an even more important internal transformation. They began to de-emphasize manual labor and concentrate instead on the study of the Scriptures and celebration of the liturgy. Since it concerned the composition and life of the community, this change affected far more than the daily routine of the monastery. Monastic communities began to include more priests than laymen. To take care of the temporal needs of the monastery, laymen were given a kind of associate membership in the monastery, which

---

[53] Aumann, *Christian Spirituality*, 71–2.
[54] On Benedictine monasticism and the Rule of Benedict, see ibid., 69–72; Daniélou, *First Six Hundred Years*, 429; Southern, *Western Society and the Church*, 218–23; Bouyer, *Spirituality of the New Testament*, 514–9; Tierney, *Western Europe in the Middle Ages*, 82–3. For the text of the Rule, see Fry, *Rule of St. Benedict*, 153–297; for a discussion of its context and content, see pages 84–96.

introduced a new stratification in the life of the community. Perhaps the most important effect was to be found on the religious and ecclesial levels: monasticism now tended to become a principally clerical institution associated with holy orders rather than a mainly lay movement that drew its direction and energy from baptism.[55]

Monasticism and the Moral Life

As was true of many early ascetics, St. Benedict conceived his monastic commitment as a safer and surer way to live the Christian life. In this he stands with all other monks and nuns who based their lives on the Scriptures, drew nourishment from the sacramental life of the Church, and followed its traditions of asceticism, holiness, and charity. These points are critical to an assessment of monasticism's religious and moral significance.[56]

Monasticism is oriented to basic Christian ends and seeks to promote union with God. Profoundly associated with faith, that goal motivates the monk to undertake ascetical practices and accept other forms of monastic discipline. These were intended to promote conversion from sin and a fuller knowledge of God; in the words of Benedict, they aimed to "amend faults and safeguard love" (*Rule*, Prologue, 47). Benedictine monasticism drew valuable support and direction from the liturgical cycle of seasons and prayers. It brought into high relief the obligation of love of God and neighbor, be they fellow monks or visitors to the monastery.[57]

This suggests that a monastic commitment involves powerful moral components that are rooted in faith. The first suggestion that God might be calling a person to commit himself or herself to perfection requires that person to decide whether to explore and then answer God's call. The history of Christian monasticism shows that when it is an-

---

[55] For more on later Benedictine history, see Southern, *Western Society and the Church*, 223–30; Aumann, *Christian Spirituality*, 80–88; Leclercq, *Spirituality of the Middle Ages*, 75–81; Fry, *Rule of St. Benedict*, 113–41, especially 128–9.

[56] On the relationship between monasticism and the basic sources and imperatives of Christian life, see Bouyer, *Spirituality of the New Testament*, 317–21, 523–30; idem, *Introduction to Spirituality*, trans. Mary Perkins Ryan (Collegeville: The Liturgical Press, 1961) 194–7.

[57] The Rule of St. Benedict emphasizes the need of charity in the monastery and the requirement of sincere and loving hospitality to visitors. See, for example, Prologue, 14–34; 2:22; 72:8; and chapters 4, 36–7, 53. See also Benedict M. Guevin, "Le Carême: Modèle de la vie morale du moine bénédictin," *ColCis* 55 (1993) 287–307; idem, "L'Opus Dei': source d'inspiration pour une éthique bénédictine," *ColCis* 56 (1994) 116–33.

swered positively, God's call to perfection changes people's lives profoundly. It mobilizes great personal energy, prompts a renewal of commitment to conversion, intensifies one's responsibility in charity for others, and helps to specify many details of intention and behavior. That much of the Church had become lukewarm and mediocre only makes the witness of the monks and nuns the more telling. It suggests that weak faith and ignorance of Christ may also have a correlative set of moral implications.

Because it arose on foundations proper to the Church itself, monasticism holds up to others in the Church an example of how authentic baptismal commitment can shape the lives of persons and communities. However, the clarity of its witness began to blur once clerics became more monastic and the monks started to dedicate themselves to the service of the altar. To be sure, many unimpeachable causes help to account for this dual process; among them are the appropriateness of a full Christian commitment for priestly service, such precedents as Augustine's clerical monastic house, and the heavy liturgical commitments of many post-ninth-century monasteries. But once monasticism and priesthood had gravitated together, the result suggested that the Church was composed of two distinct classes: those dedicated to religion, the monks, nuns, and priests, and everyone else, the ordinary laypeople living in the world. Although entirely unintentional, this differentiation tended to suggest that moral and religious excellence was the concern of the former, and mediocrity acceptable in the latter.[58]

The Evangelization of Europe and Private Penance

Throughout the fifth and sixth centuries the Church continued to embrace the peoples of Europe. In many cases their evangelization was less a matter of deliberate missionary endeavor than a felicitous by-product of monastic activity. In any case, the monks were principally responsible for the further extension of the Church in these centuries. In addition to founding monasteries they worked for moral and religious reform, established hierarchies in several areas, and catalyzed a significant change in the penitential praxis of the Church, activities

---

[58] Yves M.-J. Congar, *Lay People in the Church: A Study for a Theology of Laity,* rev. ed., trans. Donald Attwater (Westminster, Md.: Newman Press, 1965) 6–9; see also Leclercq, *Spirituality of the Middle Ages,* 72–5. According to Congar, this dual distinction was explicitly drawn by Gratian, the great twelfth-century canonist and one of the founders of the science of canon law. The issue of two standards in Christian life received attention in chapter 3, above.

that significantly affected the evolution of moral and religious life in Europe. This section will first consider the work of Irish monks on the Continent and then review the reestablishment of Catholicism in Britain and the evangelization of Germany, in which Benedictines were prominent. Against that background it will discuss the transplantation of Celtic penance to the Continent, its development and canonical acceptance, and will conclude with an assessment of private penance as it stood toward the end of the early Middle Ages.

The Celtic Monks in Europe

The Irish monks were among the first to contribute to the evangelization of Western Europe. This was an initially unintended result of their ascetical practices. Because they loved their native regions so much, the monks considered exile to be one of the most demanding forms of self-denial. For that reason many Irish monks chose to take up residence in distant locations. Believing that other parts of Ireland were still too close to home, some left for Britain or the Continent, where they founded monasteries and attracted others to join them.[59]

One of the most important of these early figures was St. Columbanus. Born around the year 543, Columbanus and some of his colleagues departed for Gaul in 591. He founded a monastery at Luxeuil, where he also wrote a monastic Rule and perhaps a pair of penitential books. Because he openly condemned the vices of the rulers and resisted episcopal control, Columbanus was expelled from the area. After failing to establish a monastery in the region of Bern in Switzerland, he traveled to Bobbio in northern Italy. There, after successfully founding a monastery, he died in the year 615.[60]

The rugged approach and rural origins of Columbanus and his associates recommended them to the country folk among whom they worked. They founded monasteries, preached the gospel, decried superstition and immorality, educated the people, and gave them an example of upright living and Christian dedication. Other monks did the same in Britain, Gaul, and Spain. These early Irish monastic pilgrims may have left home for primarily penitential reasons, but in the end they served a decidedly apostolic purpose. Their personal witness as well as the monasteries they established in remote locations were pri-

---

[59] See Mayr-Harting, *Coming of Christianity*, 94–102; Leclercq, *Spirituality of the Middle Ages*, 42–3; Aumann, *Christian Spirituality*, 73.

[60] McNeill, *Celtic Churches*, 155–69; Fry, *Rule of St. Benedict*, 115–6; Leclercq, *Spirituality of the Middle Ages*, 33–5; for Columbanus' teachings, see pages 35–9.

marily responsible for the evangelization of the European country-side.[61]

The Monastic Evangelization of England

The monks also carried out two different but simultaneous missions to the Anglo-Saxons of England. The first was undertaken by the Celts. Some of them had established monasteries among the original British Catholics in Wales and Cornwall. Others, based at the island monastery of Iona, brought their faith to Northumbria and neighboring areas. In 596 Pope Gregory I began the second mission when he dispatched a monk named Augustine and a group of forty associates to evangelize the Anglo-Saxons. After establishing his see at Canterbury, Augustine, now an archbishop, began his missionary work among the rulers of Kent and Essex.[62]

As time passed and the efforts of the Roman monks bore fruit, differences between Celtic and Roman usage became a source of friction. The Synod of Whitby in 664 resolved those conflicts when it decided in favor of Roman customs. Five years later Pope Vitalian sent a Byzantine prelate, Theodore of Tarsus, to be the new archbishop of Canterbury. Theodore extended the diocesan structure of the English church, established regular borders among the local churches, and presided over a number of Church councils. Of equal importance, he began a tradition of scholarship and culture in England, an endowment that would benefit the Church at large. The work of Archbishop Theodore completed the foundation of the Church in England.[63]

The Roman missions to England demonstrate the influence of monasticism in the early medieval Church. It reflected the personal concerns and background of Pope Gregory I, who was the first monk to occupy the see of Peter.[64] In sending Augustine and his companions to help evangelize the people of England, Gregory displayed his willingness to rely upon monks to carry out an important public apostolate in

---

[61] Tierney, *Western Europe in the Middle Ages*, 86; Leclercq, *Spirituality of the Middle Ages*, 34–5.

[62] McNeill, *Celtic Churches*, 15–47, 102–15; Mayr-Harting, *Coming of Christianity*, 51–77.

[63] Tierney, *Western Europe in the Middle Ages*, 86–9; Knowles, *Middle Ages*, 36–7.

[64] Pope Gregory exemplifies the early medieval Church's inclination to choose bishops from the ranks of the monks. Gregory had a deep influence upon the Church's spirituality and ministry throughout the Middle Ages. For an introduction to his life and work, see Leclercq, *Spirituality of the Middle Ages*, 3–30, 46–8; Tierney, *Western Europe in the Middle Ages*, 77–9; Judith Herrin, *The Formation of Christendom* (Princeton: Princeton University Press, 1987) 145–82; Aumann, *Christian Spirituality*, 74–7.

the Church. For their part, Theodore of Tarsus and his associates deserve credit for laying a strong foundation for the intellectual life in the monasteries and schools of England. Reinforcing the solid scholarly traditions of the Celts, they encouraged Western monasticism to surrender its early suspicion of learning and weave scholarship and culture into the fabric of monastic life.[65]

The Evangelization of the Germans

Another phase in the evangelization of Europe opened in the early eighth century when English monks began to make their own important contribution to the evangelization of the Continent. Among the most important of these was Winfrith, later named Boniface, who was born in Devon about the year 680. After visiting Rome in 718, Boniface accepted a papal request to work as a missionary among the Frisians. Four years later he was recalled to Rome and ordained a bishop. Taking up his new assignment among the Germans, he evangelized the people and established a number of Benedictine monasteries in their territory. Twenty years later the pope gave him the rank of archbishop and the authority to organize and govern the church north of the Alps. As papal legate he also worked to reform the church of Gaul and required all monasteries under his jurisdiction to adopt the Rule of St. Benedict. He died in 754.[66]

In reviewing Boniface's work, it is right to credit him with the christianization of the German people. In the process, Boniface extended monasticism in the West and relied upon it to help evangelize the people and strengthen their practice of the faith. His dependence upon English monks and nuns not only made his apostolate more effective, it manifested the power of a common faith and a shared monastic commitment to strengthen his new churches. The Benedictine Rule, which he imposed on all monasteries, added another and increasingly common component of Western Catholicism and displaced a more severe current within traditional monasticism. Finally, his reforming efforts in Gaul helped to knit that portion of the Church more closely to the see of Rome, and this too reinforced the bonds of unity within the Latin Church.[67]

---

[65] Tierney, *Western Europe in the Middle Ages*, 89; for a discussion of Celtic scholarship, see McNeill, *Celtic Churches*, 120–34; for the shift to the Benedictine Rule, Leclercq, *Spirituality of the Middle Ages*, 54–5.

[66] Tierney, *Western Europe in the Middle Ages*, 89–91; see also Leclercq, *Spirituality of the Middle Ages*, 58–60; Herrin, *Formation of Christendom*, 302, 346, 358; Knowles, *Middle Ages*, 9–11.

[67] Tierney, *Western Europe in the Middle Ages*, 90–1; Leclercq, *Spirituality of the Middle Ages*, 54–60; Herrin, *Formation of Christendom*, 358.

The Transplantation of Celtic Penance to the Continent

Celtic penance was introduced to the people of continental Europe by Columbanus and other Celtic and British monks. As they traveled to widely scattered destinations, they propagated the only system of penance they knew. They confronted the evil ways of many of their neighbors and called upon them to repent and do the penances by which they could be forgiven and reconciled. Although by modern standards it was quite severe, in the context of the times Celtic penance was a reasonable and workable way for people to address their sins, all the more so when the system of commutations and redemptions was taken into account. Filling the vacuum left by the failure of canonical penance, the monks' approach to forgiveness was readily accepted by the clergy and people of continental Europe.[68]

Eventually a reaction set in. Because the ninth-century Carolingian reformers wanted above all to reestablish ancient Church customs and subordinate local usage to Roman praxis, they condemned Celtic penance, now more properly called private penance, as being contrary to the canons and pastorally dangerous. However, despite a number of conciliar judgments against this system, it continued to flourish. Canonical authority had collided with pastoral need, and the latter prevailed.[69]

An attempt was made to compromise this issue. Church councils decided to distinguish those sins that were publicly known from those that had not come to the community's attention. They decreed that canonical penance was still required to reconcile public sinners, while those who had sinned in secret would be permitted to take advantage of the newer system of private penance. This compromise was significant because it endowed private penance with indisputable canonical legitimacy. It also meant that the Latin Church had two distinct, officially accepted systems for reconciling grave sinners.[70]

---

[68] Dallen, *Reconciling Community*, 102, 108–10; Poschmann, *Penance and the Anointing of the Sick*, 123, 131–4. It appears certain features of Continental practice may also have contributed to the favorable reception given to Celtic penance; these include the voluntary practice of penance by those who had repented of grave sin but did not intend to receive canonical penance until they were approaching death, and the informal, extracanonical return to the Eucharist that Caesarius and other bishops seem to have allowed. See Beck, *Pastoral Care*, 208–22; Voog, "Le péché et la distinction des péchés," 1065–71.

[69] Vogel, *Le pécheur et la pénitence*, 24–5; Dallen, *Reconciling Community*, 110–1; Poschmann, *Penance and the Anointing of the Sick*, 134–6; Ladislas Orsy, *The Evolving Church and the Sacrament of Penance* (Denville, N.J.: Dimension Books, 1978) 31–46. For excerpts from the relevant conciliar decrees, see Vogel, *Le pécheur et la pénitence*, 195–8.

[70] Dallen, *Reconciling Community*, 111–3; Poschmann, *Penance and the Anointing of the Sick*, 136; Vogel, *Le pécheur et la pénitence*, 26–7; see pages 199–200 for texts that enunciate the diverse treatment of public and private sins.

The Carolingian compromise did not last long. One reason was that public sins usually involved criminal behavior, and people did not want to expose themselves to punishment by civil magistrates. Another factor was that the official acceptance of private penance reinforced its place in Catholic life and led to legislation that promoted its use. Aware of people's sinfulness and concerned that they be properly prepared to receive Communion, conciliar legislation began to require Catholics to confess their sins to a priest at least once, twice, or even three times a year. These factors, the exhortation of preachers, and the ordinary need to deal with personal guilt all help to explain why private penance sank its roots ever more deeply into the soil of Catholic life, practice, and canonical usage.[71]

The Evolution of Private Penance

The system of penance that Columbanus and the other island monks imported to the Continent evolved with use and the passage of time. This evolution gradually changed primitive Celtic practice until it took on a form similar to the system used in the Latin Church today. At the same time, there were important shifts in the internal moral and religious dynamics of private penance.

In its early days on the Continent, the Celtic penitential system assumed that the performance of the assigned penances expiated sins and prepared for the reconciliation of the sinner. Therefore the penitent's confession was expected principally because it enabled the priest to assign the required penances. However, a formal reconciliation rite was soon joined to the process and was celebrated after the penances had been duly completed. In practice, penitents were asked to present themselves on Holy Thursday, at which time the bishop would formally reconcile them. Although the addition of this step highlighted the liturgical and ecclesial dimensions of sin and reconciliation, practical difficulties intruded. On account of distance, illness, or obtuseness, many penitents failed to appear on Holy Thursday.[72]

To deal with this problem priests began to reconcile their penitents immediately after they had finished their confessions, a change that was probably underway toward the end of the ninth century. Although immediate reconciliation was intended to address a practical

---

[71] Poschmann, *Penance and the Anointing of the Sick,* 138–40; Vogel, *Le pécheur et la pénitence,* 26–7. Vogel observes that the overlap between the jurisdiction of civil criminal laws and the scope of canonical penance means that the Church's ninth-century praxis had considerably evolved from that of the fifth and sixth centuries.

[72] Dallen, *Reconciling Community,* 113–4; Poschmann, *Penance and the Anointing of the Sick,* 143–5.

problem encountered in pastoral care, it catalyzed an interior shift of even greater significance. Since the reconciliation of penitents could be only as reliable as the power of the one who granted it, this practical change required a stronger emphasis on the priest and his spiritual authority. But to place a premium on the priest's power to reconcile is also to move the center of gravity in private penance from the expiation of the penitent to the absolution of the priest, which was a significant development indeed.[73]

Other considerations also eased the traditional emphasis on the penitent's efforts. Although the Celtic system originally depended upon severe and lengthy penances to accomplish its purposes, that primitive harshness eventually surrendered to the commutations and redemptions that had always been available. Moreover, an ever more general use of those mitigating devices and more modest assessments of human capacities led priests to assign lighter and easier penances. Their more lenient approach dovetailed with the emerging expectation that people should confess their sins more frequently.[74]

These developments led to a reassessment of the penitent's confession and its effects. As the burden of penances continued to lighten, the act of confessing took on more importance and began to be considered expiatory in itself. In other words, to confess was already to have done penance. The reluctance of many people to confess their sins and the embarrassment they sometimes felt on that occasion seemed to substantiate this conclusion. It is explicit, for example, in the widely disseminated eighth-century exhortation that people will be better off to blush before the priest today than to be shamed before God and all humanity at the Last Judgment.[75] So significant had the act of confessing become that by the eighth century the private penitential system as a whole began to be known simply as "confession."[76]

---

[73] Dallen, *Reconciling Community*, 113–6; Poschmann, *Penance and the Anointing of the Sick*, 143–5; concerning the Church's power of the keys, to which a priest's authority to bind and loose was attributed, see Poschmann, *Penance and the Anointing of the Sick*, 145–9.

[74] Dallen, *Reconciling Community*, 116; Poschmann, *Penance and the Anointing of the Sick*, 139–40; Vogel, *Le pécheur et la pénitence*, 28–31.

[75] See Poschmann, *Penance and the Anointing of the Sick*, 141.

[76] Dallen, *Reconciling Community*, 116–7; Poschmann, *Penance and the Anointing of the Sick*, 138, 140, 145–9; Vogel, *Le pécheur et la pénitence*, 31. Acknowledging a penitential value in the very act of confessing one's sins tends to make the identity of the hearer less important. This recognition encouraged the practice of confessing sins to whomever was available, a priest if possible, a layperson if necessary. This practice was supported by James 5:16 and age-old monastic customs. It was generally agreed that while confession to a layperson might forgive venial sins, mortal sins required confession to a priest in accordance with the Church's canonical

That development stands near the end of the evolutionary process that transformed the monastic texture and expiatory dynamics of ancient Celtic penance into a different system that was characterized by a strong emphasis on confession, immediate reconciliation, manageable penances, dependence on priestly authority, unambiguous canonical status, and assured spiritual effects. The next chapter will account for the final elements of that evolution: a theology of personal contrition and the Church's definitive decision that a fully developed private penitential system would be normative in the Latin Church.

The Significance of Private Penance

That the penitential system of the monks was so readily accepted suggests that the people of continental Europe were well aware of evil in their lives. It likewise shows that the example and preaching of the monks had convinced their neighbors that penance was the remedy for immoral and irreligious lives. Celtic penance offered an effective and understandable way to deal with the spiritual, personal, and ecclesial consequences of sin.

The system of private penance that the monks originated is also vulnerable to criticism. Its early reliance on expiation seems to place too much faith in the sinner's efforts and imply that they somehow cause God to forgive. When taken too far, the system of commutations suggests that ecclesial reconciliation is a suitable subject for calculation and can sometimes be obtained at a discount. The penitential books, whose norms were often inconsistent, ill-prioritized, and of unknown origin favored an attitude that viewed external actions and omissions as the essence of sin. Even the frequent access to forgiveness that so recommended this system can be harmful if it focuses attention on merely ritual or legal factors and distracts from the drama of personal conversion that is at the heart of Christian life. To the extent that private penance supported these errors, exaggerations, and aberrations, to that degree it is to be held responsible for misleading the people and damaging their religious and moral development.

Nevertheless, it is unlikely that either prelate or peasant would have accepted private penance if it had not satisfactorily addressed the respective needs of sinners and saints in a way that honored the religious and moral imperatives of Catholic faith. Despite its flaws and vulnerability to misuse or misunderstanding, private penance supported the lives of dedicated monks and nuns, tutored the ordinary European in

---

praxis. See Poschmann, *Penance and the Anointing of the Sick,* 142; Vogel, *Le pécheur et la pénitence,* 31; Dallen, *Reconciling Community,* 117–8.

the practical meaning of faith and conversion, and offered grave sinners the gifts of God's mercy and reconciliation with the Church.

Perhaps its greatest significance lies in its long-term formative effects. In the context of the Church's ordinary life of worship and charity, private penance helped to form the religious and moral conscience of Western Europe. This meant more than the simple lessons drawn from the commandments or a confessor's instruction on faith or morality. Over the course of the centuries it helped the people of the Church to emphasize the external dimensions of sin and forgiveness. But they also learned that one's personal life affects one's standing in the Church; moral failures involve one's relationship with God; and reform, always to be rooted in faith and conversion, is to accompany the reception of God's grace and forgiveness.

THE SECOND COUNCIL OF ORANGE ON GRACE AND FREE WILL

Although pastoral problems commanded most of the Church's energies in these centuries, doctrinal controversies sometimes demanded attention as well. In the late antique and early medieval eras the Church needed to address several lingering debates concerning the person of Christ and did so at the Councils of Ephesus (431), Chalcedon (451), and Constantinople (680–1).[77] Of greater importance for this study, however, is a primarily Western controversy over grace and free will that St. Augustine of Hippo's writings on that subject had provoked. In addition to being fundamental to Christian theology, the relationship between divine grace and personal freedom bears upon personal salvation and the Christian's own contribution to it, speaks to the question of moral effort, and directly affects the religious and moral lives of ordinary people. This section will consider the controversy that developed after Augustine's death, outline the decisions made by the Second Council of Orange in 529, and point out their significance.

The Controversy on God's Grace and Human Free Will

In the final years of his life, his fellow ascetics called upon Augustine to clarify and defend his teaching on predestination. Although he explicitly upheld free will, Augustine emphasized the infallible efficacy

---

[77] For more on these councils and their work, see John P. Galvin, "Jesus Christ," *Systematic Theology: Roman Catholic Perspectives,* ed. Francis Schüssler Fiorenza and John P. Galvin (Minneapolis: Fortress Press, 1991) 1:266-72; Stuart G. Hall, *Doctrine and Practice in the Early Church* (Grand Rapids: Eerdmans, 1991) 211–36; Chadwick,

of God's grace so strongly as to leave the impression that God's actions were decisive and human freedom was more nominal than real. A related problem was his teaching on predestination, particularly the idea that God's mercy brings salvation to some while his justice punishes many more with damnation. His critics complained that these teachings implicitly denied human free will and removed any reason for moral effort, compromised the doctrine that God wishes the salvation of all humanity, and were unsupported by the Christian tradition as it stood at that time. This controversy concerned the relationship between God's power and the personal freedom of human beings and the respective weight that is to be attributed to the divine and human contributions to salvation.

After Augustine's death, the debate unfolded in three stages. In the first, John Cassian, Vincent of Lérins, and other critics in southern Gaul continued to maintain that people sometimes choose their response to God's initial offer of salvation without the help of grace and thus control their own eternal destiny. If that is the case, then God's predestination is not sovereign and means no more than his foreknowledge of what people will freely do.[78] In response, Prosper of Aquitaine defended Augustine's teaching and also tried to gain the support of Pope Celestine (422–32). Celestine was not ready to take sides and offered only a general statement testifying to the holiness of Augustine's life and the soundness of his writings.[79]

Some time between 435 and 443, however, the Holy See intervened in the debate. Borrowing from earlier sources, it prepared a series of statements on grace and issued them as a single document. This text, known as the *Indiculus*,[80] is important because it reveals the thinking of the Holy See at that time. The *Indiculus* asserts that God's grace is necessary for all meritorious human desires and actions without excep-

---

Early Church, 192–212; Aloys Grillmeier, *Christ in Christian Tradition*, 2nd rev. ed., trans. John Bowden (Atlanta: John Knox, 1975) 1:443-554; W.H.C. Frend, *Saints and Sinners in the Early Church: Differing and Conflicting Traditions in the First Six Centuries* (Wilmington: Michael Glazier, 1985) 141–56; Herrin, *Formation of Christendom*, 250–9, 277–80; Tierney, *Western Europe in the Middle Ages*, 97–8.

[78] Since the seventeenth century this view has been known as "Semipelagianism." Those who consider this term to be too strongly colored by later debates tend to refer to characteristically Gallic teachings on grace and human effort as "Massilianism." See Henri Rondet, *The Grace of Christ: A Brief History of the Theology of Grace*, trans. Tad W. Guzie (Westminster, Md.: Newman Press, 1967) 145–6; Peter C. Phan, *Grace and the Human Condition* (Wilmington: Michael Glazier, 1988) 292.

[79] See Thomas A. Smith, *De Gratia: Faustus of Riez's Treatise on Grace and Its Place in the History of Theology* (Notre Dame: University of Notre Dame Press, 1990) 39–55. For Celestine's statement, sent to the bishops of Gaul in May of 431, see DS, 237.

[80] See DS, 238–9. For a translation, see Rondet, *Grace of Christ*, 388–94.

tion. Grace does not suppress human freedom but frees and empowers it to cooperate with God's grace. Although the *Indiculus* offered no judgment on the controverted matter of predestination, it shows that Augustine's theology of grace had already achieved considerable acceptance.

The second phase of this controversy took place some forty years later, again in southern Gaul. A priest of Riez had taught an extreme form of predestinationism, denying that Christ died for all. In response, Bishop Faustus of Riez (c. 405–c. 490) had his teachings condemned by the Councils of Arles (473) and Lyons (475). In the year 474 Faustus published a treatise on grace entitled *De gratia*, in which he tried to achieve a moderate and balanced statement of Catholic doctrine on the subject. Wishing to protect human freedom and the need of continuing efforts in the Christian life, he held, among other things, that people have a natural capacity for freedom, choice, and obedience that remains even after original sin, and he asserted that divine foreknowledge does not control what people freely do. Around the year 520 an African bishop, Fulgentius of Ruspe, learned of Faustus' doctrines and vigorously defended the necessity of grace. Fulgentius' strongly Augustinian approach kept the controversy alive until it was settled at the Second Council of Orange. This entire episode shows how difficult it was to find a moderate and sound position on grace and free will, and it underlined the necessity of some authoritative resolution of this important issue.[81]

The Second Council of Orange

That resolution occurred at the Second Council of Orange, which concluded its work on July 3, 529, under the presidency of Caesarius, bishop of Arles (c. 470–542). Although it was a provincial council that convoked only fourteen bishops, its canons declared Catholic teaching on the issue of God's grace, personal freedom, and human salvation.

[81] For the history of the question prior to the Council of Orange, see Smith, *De Gratia*, 2–5; Eugène Portalié, *A Guide to the Thought of St. Augustine*, trans. Ralph J. Bastian (Chicago: Regnery, 1960) 315–21; Rondet, *Grace of Christ*, 148–58; M. John Farrelly, *Predestination, Grace, and Free Will* (Westminster, Md.: Newman Press, 1964) 96–101; Phan, *Grace and the Human Condition*, 291–4.

For a thorough discussion of Faustus' *De gratia*, including its background, sources, and doctrine, see Smith, *De Gratia*. Smith characterizes Faustus' doctrine as follows: "It is not Pelagian, though it shares certain anthropological ground with Pelagius. It is not Augustinian, though it makes extensive use of Augustine. If it is semipelagian, it expresses a semipelagianism of the second or third generation, which has begun to understand and to incorporate Augustinianism" (233). Smith judges that "Faustus's attempt at synthesis is not entirely successful."

The theological competence of Caesarius enriched the council's teaching, and the approbation of Pope Boniface II strengthened its authority.[82]

In its doctrinal declarations the Council of Orange spoke to the entire range of issues involved in the controversy. However, the core of the matter concerned two specific points: the necessity of grace for all acts that contribute to human salvation and the issue of predestination. On the first, the council declared that the grace of Christ anticipates and causes each and every human act that contributes to salvation, including prayer, the wish to be cleansed of sin, the desire for faith, and even the very beginnings of faith (Cann. 3–5). Grace enables a person to seek baptism in the first place and to love God, believe in God, and do all that God requires for salvation (Cann. 6–8). Moreover, the need of grace does not suppress personal freedom but inspires it and enables persons to choose those things that accord with God's saving will (Can. 23). Addressing the vexed issue of predestination in its concluding statement, the council taught that all the baptized can and should, with the help of grace, do all that is necessary for their salvation. It firmly rejected the idea that God predestines some to do evil.[83]

An Assessment of the Council's Work

With its doctrinal affirmations, the Second Council of Orange completed the dogmatic foundations concerning God's grace and human salvation that the Council of Carthage had begun over a century earlier. It excluded the theory that attributed to human beings even a limited ability to act for their salvation without the help of God's grace but affirmed the need to act in accord with God's will. In repudiating the view that God's justice consigns many to eternal condemnation, Orange corrected that aspect of St. Augustine's theology and canonized what has become known as a moderate Augustinianism. By upholding God's prior and essential role in all salutary human activity, it emphasized the altogether religious foundation of Christian moral life. By

[82] For the council's decisions see DS, 370–95; for an English translation see Phan, *Grace and the Human Condition*, 301–8. DS, 396–7, gives Caesarius' own conclusion and DS, 398–400, the official approbation of Pope Boniface II. For a discussion of council's sources and the genesis of its text, see Farrelly, *Predestination, Grace, and Free Will*, 101, note 109; Rondet, *Grace and the Human Condition*, 158–62; Hefele, 4:155-65.

[83] See Farrelly, *Predestination, Grace, and Free Will*, 102–6; Rondet, *Grace and the Human Condition*, 159–60; on the role of Caesarius at the Council of Orange, see William M. Daly, "Caesarius of Arles, A Precursor of Medieval Christendom," *Traditio* 26 (1970) 7, 20–2.

calling for ceaseless prayer and good works (Can. 10), it warned every-one to pursue the Christian life actively and avoid fatalistic attitudes or passivity. The Council of Orange completed the principal elements of Catholic doctrine on grace, teachings that would not be significantly extended until the thirteenth century or seriously challenged until the sixteenth.[84]

THE BIRTH OF MEDIEVAL CHRISTENDOM

Beginning in the seventh century several developments took place that radically altered the course of European history and the growth of the Church in the West, namely, the rise of Islam, the mutual embrace of the Roman pontiffs and the Carolingian kings, and the increasing estrangement between Latin and Greek Christians. This section will review these events and consider how they encouraged Western Catholicism to became increasingly self-contained and identified with the peoples of Europe. This process shaped the nations of western and central Europe and supplied the context in which many religious de-velopments can be understood.

The Rise of Islam

The first historical event that demands attention took place not in Europe but on the Arabian peninsula. There, in the year 570, Mohammed was born. A merchant by trade, Mohammed believed that he was the recipient of divine revelations, which he wrote down in a book known as the *Koran*. Mohammed taught that God was a single being who had spoken through several prophets, the last and greatest being Mohammed himself. In addition to his strict monotheism, he taught that a person's eternal destiny depends upon right conduct in this world, which includes justice, mercy, care for the poor, and the ob-servance of religious and dietary duties. Adherents were also called upon to fight for their religion, Islam, and any who died while doing so were promised immediate admission to heavenly bliss.

---

[84] The history of theology includes a serious ninth-century dispute spawned by the predestinationist thinking of Gottschalk of Orbais (c. 805–c. 868) and the work of several local councils in that context. This episode offers further evidence that the relationship between grace and freedom can easily be the subject of exagger-ated statements, particularly when some of Augustine's stronger assertions are used without sufficient understanding. The result of this controversy was to strengthen the Church's moderate Augustinian position and emphasize for theolo-gians the universality of God's salvific will. See Rondet, *Grace of Christ,* 176–84; Farrelly, *Predestination Grace, and Free Will,* 109–11; Pelikan, 3:80-95.

In addition to being a religious teacher, Mohammed was also a capable organizer and a gifted military commander. Beginning at the city of Medina, he gathered many followers to this new faith. By a combination of religious appeal and the force of arms he was able to unite the peoples of central Arabia under his political and religious leadership. That is how things stood at the time of Mohammed's death in the year 632.[85]

His followers continued the propagation of Islam with remarkable success and speed. Supported by powerful and well-led armies, the Arabs conquered Syria by 640, defeating a sizable Byzantine army in the process. By 641 Egypt was in their hands and within another ten years the entire Persian Empire came under Islamic dominance. The conquest of the North African coast took longer, but by the end of the seventh century it too fell to the rule of the caliphs, Mohammed's successors. In 711 the Arabs invaded Spain and established a capital at Cordoba. From there they pressed their attack across the Pyrenees into Gaul, where in 732 Charles Martel decisively defeated them at the Battle of Tours. Some years earlier, in 718, Emperor Leo III broke the Arabs' siege of Constantinople, which halted their advance from the east. Despite the losses at Tours and Constantinople, in the hundred years following Mohammed's death, Islam had come to be practiced in an area that stretched from the Atlantic Ocean to the borders of China.[86]

The Impact on the Church

The importance of these Islamic victories can hardly be underestimated. Arab successes in the eastern Mediterranean reduced the Christian churches of that area to a small fraction of their former size. The ancient patriarchies of Jerusalem, Antioch, and Alexandria ceased to play a significant role in Church councils. The dominance of Islamic societies and the supremacy of their laws made many Byzantine Christians a small minority deprived of control over civil affairs. Hemmed in by their Muslim neighbors, they were increasingly cut off from their coreligionists in the West. That isolation contributed to an ignorance and misunderstanding on all sides, which helped to undermine good relations between Greek and Latin Christians.[87]

Arab successes also abetted a process of isolation and constriction in the West. With the rise of Islam and its strict legal prohibition against proselytizing or converting to Christianity, the Latin Church lost the op-

---

[85] Tierney, *Western Europe in the Middle Ages,* 91–2.
[86] Ibid., 92–5; see also Peter Brown, *The World of Late Antiquity, A.D. 150–750* (New York: Harcourt Brace Jovanovich, 1971) 189–203.
[87] Southern, *Western Society and the Church,* 53–6.

tion of sending missionaries to the southern or eastern portions of the Mediterranean basin.[88] With the barbarian peoples of Europe as the only available objects of evangelical activity, Western Christians found it easier to see the Church as primarily Latin, European, and Roman, and missionary successes among European peoples only reinforced that outlook.

The Islamic advance across Africa also cost the Church one of its most vigorous and theologically fruitful constituents. One respected scholar has expressed the meaning of Africa's loss for Roman Catholicism thus:

> Rome had now lost the most tenacious challenge, at any rate in the West, to its intentions. Carthage had been the one great Christian centre in the Latin world that could look Rome in the face. By its submergence, Rome gained undisputed status in the West, but the Western Church lost more than Africa. It lost the last survival of an older structure of ecclesiastical authority, and lost, with it, the vital contribution of a cast of mind, a theology, a conception of the Church and of its place in the world, which it had discarded in 313.[89]

When one considers the general contraction of horizons, the virtual disappearance of African Catholicism, the increasing isolation of East and West and their growing mutual ignorance, it becomes apparent that the rise of Islam has deeply affected the development of Christian history. So far as Latin Catholicism is concerned, its substantially narrowed and more decisively European horizons would increasingly dominate the development of its ecclesiastical customs, religious praxis, intellectual traditions, and moral outlook.

The Papacy and the Carolingian Monarchs

About two decades after Charles Martel ended the Arabs' drive into Gaul, his son Pepin the Short (714–68) achieved practical supremacy within the Merovingian kingdom. He did not, however, hold the kingship, which passed by inheritance to the descendants of Clovis. In an effort to legitimate his own claim on the throne, Pepin asked Pope Zachary (741–52) if he considered it appropriate that the Frankish kings lacked effective royal power. Zachary replied that the one who held supreme power was also entitled to hold the rank of king. By his

---

[88] Islamic law prevailed in the lands conquered by the Arabs. It prohibited public criticism of Islam or conversion to Christianity on pain of death. Hamilton, *Religion in the Medieval West*, 11–2.

[89] R. A. Markus, *Saeculum: History and Society in the Theology of Saint Augustine* (Cambridge: Cambridge University Press, 1970) 132.

action, Pope Zachary conferred on Pepin the spiritual and political license that he needed to claim the throne for himself.

Pepin soon reciprocated Pope Zachary's support. Papal lands had for some time been threatened by the Lombards of northern Italy, and the Byzantine authorities in Ravenna had proved to be unwilling or unable to defend them. Finally Pope Stephen II (752–7), perhaps citing the famous Donation of Constantine, strongly asserted his claim to Lombard territory and called upon Pepin to enforce it. At Pepin's invitation Pope Stephen traveled north for a face-to-face discussion and on that occasion anointed Pepin as king. As a result of their meeting, in 755 Pepin took his army into battle against the Lombards and forced them to capitulate. When they reneged on their promises of cooperation and even attacked the city of Rome, Pepin defeated them again and left Italy only after the pope was securely in control of his new territories.[90]

This series of events marks the beginning of the Carolingian dynasty and opens an important new chapter in the relations between Roman pontiffs and Frankish rulers. It also set the stage for Pope Leo III's coronation of Charlemagne as emperor, which took place in Rome on Christmas Day in the year 800. This dramatic event legitimated Charles' authority over a much-expanded realm and gave it a spiritual warrant; in the process Leo gained a stronger and more prestigious protector. The coronation of Charlemagne consolidated the positions of Europe's preeminent spiritual and political leaders and cemented their relationship. This new political and religious arrangement had considerable influence on the subsequent course of Europe's political and religious history.[91]

Relationships with the East

The political and religious alliance forged by the Roman pontiffs and the Frankish monarchs entailed a radically changed relationship between Latins and Greeks. Popes Zachary and Stephen were the politi-

---

[90] Robert Folz and others, *De l'antiquité au monde médiéval* (Paris: Presses Universitaires de France, 1972) 304–8; Herrin, *Formation of Christendom*, 352–3, 355–60, 370–9, 385–7; Southern, *Western Society and the Church*, 56–61; Maurice Keen, *A History of Medieval Europe* (London: Routledge & Kegan Paul, 1968) 17–9; Tierney, *Western Europe in the Middle Ages*, 97–101. For text of the Donation of Constantine, see Henry Bettenson, ed., *Documents of the Christian Church* (London and New York: Oxford, 1963) 98–101; see also Herrin, *Formation of Christendom*, 385–7; Tierney, *Western Europe in the Middle Ages*, 100; Southern, *Western Society and the Church*, 91–4.

The territory in north central Italy that Pepin won for the papacy was the beginning of the Papal States, which lasted until 1870. From the eighth century, therefore, the popes numbered among the civil rulers of Europe.

[91] See Knowles, *Middle Ages*, 62–3; Herrin *Formation of Christendom*, 454–62; Southern, *Western Society and the Church*, 60–1, 99.

cal subjects of the Byzantine emperor and had no right to establish civil rulers in the West. By formally recognizing Pepin's kingship and asserting temporal authority in Italy, the popes committed treason against the Byzantine emperor. Moreover, Pepin's refusal to hand over to the emperor the land he took from the Lombards amounted to a declaration of independence from Eastern political authority. But the decisive step was the coronation of Charlemagne, for by proclaiming him as emperor, Pope Leo assigned to Charles the prerogatives traditionally held by the Byzantine monarch, an act that definitively broke the political ties that bound Europe and the East.[92]

The popes' turn to the north had religious implications as well. That became clear in the crisis spawned by *iconoclasm*, a Greek-based term which means "destruction of sacred images." The problem began in the year 726 when, against a complex religious, political, and military background, Emperor Leo III (717–41) prohibited the use of sacred images in Christian worship and commanded that they should be destroyed. Since devotion to icons, or religious images, had sometimes bordered on idolatry, Leo intended to protect the Church from this threat to the integrity of its worship. But he was also prompted by political and economic motives. Leo calculated that the prohibition of images would damage the monasteries' popular appeal and hinder them from adding to their tax-exempt land holdings. His action also retaliated against a papacy that had refused to cooperate with efforts designed to raise the taxes on papal possessions.

Whatever the emperor's motives, Pope Gregory II (715–31) refused to exclude sacred images from the worship of Latin Catholics. Taking deep offense at these demands, he pointedly noted that if pressed he would call upon the barbarian nations to defend Rome against Constantinople on this point. The iconoclast crisis severely disrupted Church life in the East and alienated West and East for more than a century. The doctrinal side of the controversy was resolved in 787 when the Second Council of Nicaea reaffirmed that the devotional use of images was legitimate. The political source of the problem was finally removed in 843 when the Byzantine empress Theodora decreed that images were to be permitted in Christian worship.[93]

---

[92] Southern, *Western Society and the Church*, 60–1; Tierney, *Western Europe in the Middle Ages*, 106–8; Herrin, *Formation of Christendom*, 379–81.

[93] Herrin, *Formation of Christendom*, 307–53, 411–2, 417–24, 466–75; Tierney, *Western Europe in the Middle Ages*, 98–9; Southern, *Western Society and the Church*, 58–61; Knowles, *Middle Ages*, 86–91. For the decrees promulgated by the Second Council of Nicaea, see DS, 600–3, 605–9 (Tanner, 1:135-8).

On the theology of icons and their religious use, see Leonide Ouspensky and Vladimir Lossky, *The Meaning of Icons*, rev. ed., trans. G.E.H. Palmer and E.

An atmosphere of general suspicion and a series of doctrinal and political conflicts with the East framed the process by which the popes cast their lot with their Frankish neighbors to the north. To a degree, this only made manifest the increasingly important bonds that cultural and geographical affinity, evangelization, and ecclesiastical usage had been forging for some time. It represented another dimension of the Western response to the Arabs' religious and political successes and, more locally, the Roman response to Lombard pressures in Italy. It also reflects the demands of necessity, for when pressed to violate their religious principles and outlaw religious images, the popes had little alternative but to turn to their Catholic neighbors to the north. However understandable the papal embrace of the Frankish rulers may have been, it had profound political and religious consequences, for it helped to sever the remaining bonds of political unity between East and West and encouraged the Latin churches to go their own way without the companionship and support of their sister churches in the East.[94]

Although communion between the churches of Rome and Constantinople survived the iconoclast episode, subsequent events demonstrated just how weak those bonds had become. In 858 a new breach occurred when Rome refused to accept the election of Photius as the new patriarch of Constantinople. While that dispute was still outstanding, Latin jurisdictional encroachment in Bulgaria further offended the Byzantine Church. Roman missionaries in that country compounded the problem when they insisted upon adding the word *filioque* to the text of the Nicene Creed.[95] By about the year 880, changes

---

Kadloubovsky (Crestwood, N.Y.: St. Vladimir's Seminary Press, 1982); Paul Evdokimov, *The Art of the Icon: A Theology of Beauty* (Redondo Beach, Calif.: Oakwood Publications, 1990).

[94] Southern, *Western Society and the Church*, 58–61; Herrin, *Formation of Christendom*, 387–9; Knowles, *Middle Ages*, 97–8; Tierney, *Western Europe in the Middle Ages*, 100–1.

[95] The Latin word *filioque* means "and the son." When added to the Creed it specifies that the Holy Spirit proceeds from the Son as well as the Father. This teaching seems to have originated in sixth-century Spain as a way to affirm the divinity of Jesus as the Son of God, in opposition to the Arian doctrine that Jesus was not divine. Although they believed it was orthodox, out of deference to the ancient text the popes did not add the word *filioque* to the Creed until the eleventh century.

Byzantine theologians agreed that this addition violated a conciliar prohibition against amending the Creed. However, contrary to many Latins, they also held that the word *filioque* represented a doctrinal error. Obolensky summarizes their position: "In the Greek view the doctrine of the *Filioque*, by stating that the Holy Spirit proceeds from the Son as well as from the Father, was an unjustified inference from the dogma of the consubstantiality of the Father and the Son, weakened the monar-

in the circumstances and a more moderate approach on all sides helped to resolve these problems. But that settlement did not eliminate the underlying sources of conflict between Greek and Latin Christianity. East and West still harbored different views of papal primacy and disagreed about the doctrine to be held concerning the Holy Trinity. Especially when seen in the context of increasing cultural and political estrangement, these conflicts contributed to an environment in which the mutual excommunications of 1054 could more easily occur, actions that have symbolized the final loss of communion between Byzantine and Latin churches.[96]

REFLECTIONS

When one compares the Church of the mid-eleventh century to the Christian community as it stood six centuries earlier, it is readily apparent that momentous changes had occurred in the intervening period. Centrifugal forces and foreign invasions broke apart the Roman Empire and deprived the Church of the political structure that had supported its unity. Islam exploded into the Mediterranean world, sweeping African Catholicism off the map, depleting the ranks of Eastern Christians, and establishing new political and religious boundaries. Throughout this period Christians of East and West remained aware of their common apostolic origin and tried to honor the imperative of unity. Even so, they continued to misunderstand and offend each other until the bonds of ecclesial communion gave way under the strain. Meanwhile, with Augustine's encouragement fresh in its ears, the Latin Church embraced the peoples of Europe. Their evangelization enlarged the Church and opened the way to the remarkable political and religious condominium worked out between the Holy See and the Frankish kings. These political, social, cultural, and religious forces helped to divide Greek and Latin Christians and

---

chy of the Father, tended to sacrifice the distinction between the *hypostases* [persons of the Trinity] to the divine simplicity of the common essence, and implied a theology in which the mystical reality of the Triune God is to some extent obscured by a philosophy of essence." Knowles, *Middle Ages*, 103; see also 102.

[96] Ibid., 98–104. For further discussion of the *Filioque* controversy, see Yves Congar, *I Believe in the Holy Spirit*, trans. David Smith (New York: Seabury; London: Geoffrey Chapman, 1983) 3:49-60; The Pontifical Council for Promoting Christian Unity, "The Greek and Latin Traditions Regarding the Processions of the Holy Spirit," The Pontifical Council for Promoting Christian Unity Information Service 89 (1995, nos. 2–3) 88–92; Herrin, *Formation of Christendom*, 439–40, 462–4. For the events that led to the breach of 1054, see Southern, *Western Society and the Church*, 53–72.

unite the Latin Church and the peoples of the West. For better or worse the history, circumstances, and perspectives of Western Europe would attain unprecedented influence on Catholic religious and moral life and on the theological developments and pastoral decisions of the Western Church.

However complex its causes, the schism that separated Eastern and Western Christians breached the communion that the universal Church, orthodox and catholic, had once shared. At a more fundamental level, the estrangement of Latins and Greeks stands in sharp contrast to the will of Christ "that they may all be one" (John 17:21). By dividing the Church, the schism between East and West has compromised efforts at evangelization and made it more difficult for Latin and Greek Christians to benefit from each other's traditions of worship, thought, piety, and ecclesiastical polity and charity. Their estrangement has changed the religious and moral context for believers of East and West alike, impoverished both churches, and heightened the religious and moral responsibilities of all who appreciate the need of reconciliation and communion among Christians.

Rapid growth confronted the Church with a number of serious challenges and occasioned some major changes in its life and praxis. That expansion had begun in earnest after the Decree of Toleration in 313 and accelerated with the wholesale entry of the barbarian peoples into the Church. The resulting stresses doomed both the catechumenate and canonical penance as they had been known in the early centuries and stimulated the development of new approaches to Christian instruction, formation, forgiveness, and reconciliation. In a vastly expanded Church arguments about the accommodation of sinners became entirely moot. Accommodation was the accepted policy and absorption of society the agenda; in that context it became urgent to salvage the basic imperative of conversion to Christ and promote holiness among the people of God.

The Church's expansion and its new pastoral policies had profound effects on its life and praxis. One of the most significant was that many Catholics had not committed themselves to faith and conversion when they were baptized. Whether baptism took place in adulthood or in infancy, it seldom functioned as the authentic source and secure grounds for Christian life. That basic void began to show its effects in a general ignorance of the Scriptures, Christ, and the implications of Catholic faith. It accounts for a poor moral tone among many members of the Church. As this chapter has suggested, once those problems had become acute, they tended to perpetuate themselves from one generation to the next and became more firmly entrenched with the passage of time. This grave situation harmed the integrity of Christian moral life.

In the absence of a real conversion from sin and to Christ, the moral life of a baptized person lacks its proper and essential foundation. To the extent that it is lacking, faith cannot contribute its energy, direction, and ultimate meaning to the life of a free, aware, and responsible person.

The poor state of instruction and an absence of Christian conversion help to account for a new pastoral agenda. The ministry now had to address an anomalous but widespread deterioration in Church life. It aimed to supply the instruction and the call to conversion of life that had not been received on the occasion of baptism. In effect, the Church took the agenda of the ancient catechumenate and used it as the pastoral plan for ministry among its members. That the results were often modest shows how serious and intractable the problem had become. That the Church nevertheless tried to promote faith and conversion among its own demonstrates that even in this adverse climate it remembered how essential these foundations are for Christian life. Its efforts also suggest that the Church at least implicitly understood that the moral requirements of Christian life presuppose faith, conversion, and adequate instruction about the mysteries of faith.

A larger but less committed Church stimulated the development of the two institutions that loom large in this era: monasticism and private penance. Monasticism arose because ordinary men and women were overtaken by God's word, responded to the meaning of their baptism, and tried to live the Eucharist they celebrated. Set off from others in the Church, monastics did for the Church what the Church was called to do for the world: contrast sin with holiness, worldly concerns with prayerful faith, lassitude with commitment, and indifference with charity. The witness of the monks and nuns also showed that a commitment born of faith and conversion contributes to the mission of the Church as well as one's own life. In an age often marred by turmoil, violence, and ambiguity, their witness demonstrates the vitality and decisive results that can flow from Christian commitment. In highlighting once again a basic correlation between faith and moral life, monasticism continues a theme that is dominant in the Scriptures and constant in the history of the Church.

Although it originated among the monks, Celtic penance soon spread to the Continent, where, once woven into the texture of Church life, it began to perform several important functions. From canonical penance it inherited the primary work of reconciling gravely sinful members of the Church. It continued to support the efforts of committed members of the Church—be they monks, nuns, clergy, or laypeople—to live their Christian lives as fully as possible. In this era it picked up yet a third task that had been traditionally linked to baptism. Attending to those who had never responded to Christ's word that they repent and live according to the Gospel, the Church began to depend on private penance to lead them not merely to amend their behavior but also to base their lives on faith in Christ. These diverse purposes meant that pastoral efforts among very distinct constituencies in the Church all relied upon the rituals of penance. This greatly increased the importance of penance and made it as never before a focal point of Catholic moral, religious, and pastoral life.

Although private penance had assumed unprecedented importance in the Church, it also raised certain pastoral and theological questions. The emphasis on sinful behavior and penitential actions lent a certain ambivalence to the rites of penance. The use of the same ritual of penance for several distinct purposes tended to diffuse its focus and increase its ambiguity. Moreover, penitential praxis developed in pastoral settings that were largely uninfluenced by the Church's teaching concerning the freedom, necessity, and priority of God's grace. These factors constituted an important agenda concerning penance. They suggested a need to bring the basic dynamic of conversion into clearer focus, distinguish ends and means more adequately, and clarify how God's grace intersects with the ritual of penance. Until these pastoral and theological desiderata could be adequately addressed, penance would continue to be the occasion of problems even as it served Christian life in the Church.

By the early eleventh century the problems and accomplishments of this era had many centuries in which to develop and become established. Although dramatic events had taken place, it would not be reasonable to characterize this period as one of rapid transformation. On this point, however, the period of the High Middle Ages stands in sharp contrast to the early Middle Ages. While it would receive its legacy with great reverence for its antiquity and authority, it did so in a time of pervasive and even revolutionary change. That environment framed its consideration of the faith and praxis it had inherited and shaped much of the High Middle Ages' contribution to the Christian tradition. Its experience and activity are the principal concerns of the next chapter.

6

High Medieval Society, the Individual, and the Holy

Around the year 1000, as the first half of the Middle Ages was drawing to a close, long-established customs and accepted religious foundations communicated a sense of stability to Western European life. The pope and bishops exercised God-given spiritual authority, while the monarch had a divine mandate to rule society as a whole, including a duty to protect the Church, defend its rights, and support its ministries. For their part, the monks served a grateful society by their long hours of prayer for the living and the dead. Scholars and teachers, who normally worked in a monastery or bishop's school, carried out their traditional task of expounding classic and Christian texts. And if ordinary people were often poor, illiterate, ill-tutored in their faith, and subordinate to various authorities, they did well to accept their place in society because none better was usually available to them.

These institutions, customs, and ways of thinking were about to change. Strong religious dynamics had already inspired a monastic reform movement in the tenth century, and they now started to prompt people outside the cloister to address various abuses in the Church. A constellation of intellectual, economic, and sociological developments began to transform European life so that by the middle of the eleventh century the Continent had begun to experience a general and sustained revival.[1]

[1] See, for example, R. W. Southern, *Western Society and the Church in the Middle Ages* (Baltimore: Pelican Books, 1970) 27–36; David Knowles with Dimitri Obolensky, *The Middle Ages* (London: Darton, Longman & Todd; New York: Paulist

That reawakening also affected the Church. The papacy asserted an unprecedented jurisdiction over secular affairs as well as those of local churches. Religious currents waxed strong, begetting lay movements, new forms of religious life, nonconforming groups, better preaching, and a new strategy of pastoral care. These developments highlighted the moral dimensions of Christian life and augmented the religious heritage of later generations.

Beneath the public and tangible developments of the age, an evolution of outlook was also taking place. People began to pay more attention to the *individual* person or thing and were especially interested in exploring the life, relationships, and experiences of the human person. That process of discovery offered new insights into the interior life of persons and increased Western peoples' appreciation of it. Integral to the "turn to the person" was a fresh desire to understand more fully the person's relationships to social groups, the community, and God.[2] Another basic shift affected society's assumptions about the holy and the profane, the sacred and the secular, the spiritual and the temporal. Under the influence of contemporary developments, people began to find less congruence and more contrast within these dyads. That raised new questions about where the sacred and the secular were to be found and how the holy and the profane were to be distinguished. Increased sensitivity to the person and an evolving relationship between the spiritual and the temporal directly affected the religious and moral life of persons and also offered them new prisms through which to view foundational realities.

This chapter will consider key developments associated with the Great European Reawakening from its beginning in the mid-eleventh century up to the early thirteenth century. It will examine key social,

---

Press, 1969) 124–8, 246–7; Brian Tierney and Sidney Painter, *Western Europe in the Middle Ages: 300–1475* (New York: Knopf, 1970) 121–54, 171–6. For a panoramic portrait of the Church in the year 1000, see Joseph H. Lynch, *The Medieval Church: A Brief History* (London and New York: Longman, 1992) 116–35.

[2] To avoid misunderstanding and anachronism, modern notions should not be read back into a medieval context. At that time there was greater interest in the specific qualities and being of "singulars" or "individuals," be they persons or things. Therefore, the "individual" had a much wider meaning and was not simply taken as an abbreviated reference to the "individual person." Moreover, the "person" was not understood and explored apart from the Church, society, and God but in relationship to them. See Caroline Walker Bynum, "Did the Twelfth Century Discover the Individual?" *JEH* 31 (1980) 1–17.

Although they are surely significant, twelfth-century developments represent but one phase of a centuries-long effort by Western thinkers to gain a greater understanding of persons and individuals, work out the implications, and find suitable ways to speak of them.

attitudinal, political, and religious transformations of this period and identify their impact on religious and moral life. The examination of contemporary intellectual developments will be deferred to the next chapter.

The first section will consider the Gregorian Reform, a sustained campaign to correct abuses in the Church. This discussion will highlight the power of religious and moral imperatives in society; show how this reform movement helped to rearrange the moral, religious, and political coordinates of European society; and suggest that it worked to sharpen the contrast between the spiritual and temporal dimensions of life.

A review of the Great European Reawakening will acknowledge the overall expansion of European life, which became the context of many contemporary advances. This discussion will identify some of the moral implications of the "turn to the person," the increased self-confidence of many people, and their growing ability to understand and control their world.

The resurgence of religious fervor in this period will be the chapter's third concern. A renewed sensitivity to God, the sacred, and the Church manifested itself in new forms of lay piety, several expressions of nonconformity, and new religious orders. These were signs that people were concerned to respond to the Gospel and meet its personal and social requirements.

The following section will account for important theological work on sin and forgiveness, including its emphasis on the interior life of persons. By helping to refine the Church's understanding of sin and penance, theologians enriched its theological heritage and provided a critical element in a new strategy of pastoral care.

It will then be necessary to consider a pivotal decision of the Fourth Lateran Council of 1215. Its canon on yearly confession and Communion established a new criterion of good standing in the Church, reaffirmed the centrality of sacramental penance for the moral and religious life of believers, and constituted a basic presupposition of pastoral care in the following centuries. The ecclesial and personal implications of this decree make it a milestone in the history of the Church.

THE GREGORIAN REFORM

Named after Pope Gregory VII (1073–85), its most vigorous and influential proponent, the Gregorian Reform was one of the most significant movements in European history. It built upon an earlier monastic renewal and sought to bring Church offices, structures, and personnel into closer alignment with their spiritual and apostolic purposes. Because it required significant changes in customary practices, the Gregorian Reform precipitated a major confrontation between lay and clerical authorities. That conflict changed public policies and contributed to a tendency in later Western thinking to distinguish more sharply the sacred from the secular in human life.

Authority in Western Christian Societies

The Gregorian Reform, the conflicts it entailed, and the results it produced are to be considered in light of the understanding and use of authority that had prevailed up to that time in the West. That understanding presupposed a world in which the sacred and the spiritual predominated. Accordingly, it was commonly believed that God directed important state decisions and that such crude devices as the ordeal, accompanied as it was by a priest's prayers, manifested God's judgment on an accused person.[3] Even so, people distinguished the spiritual and temporal dimensions of life and knew that monarchs and prelates each had their rightful functions and authority. But since there was no means by which to segregate the jurisdiction of one from the other, civil and religious authority overlapped both in principle and in practice.

Experience suggested that cooperation and not separation or hostility should characterize the relationship between civil and ecclesiastical officials. Following precedents that started with Constantine in the early fourth century, Roman emperors considered it to be their God-given responsibility to protect the Church, confront its enemies, suppress heresy, convoke councils, sometimes appoint or consent to the installation of bishops and other officers, and generally see to the well being of the Church. For their part, bishops supported civil magistrates through prayers, appeals for cooperation and obedience, condemnations of behavior that offended justice or peace in the realm, and by affirming that lawful authority reflected God's will as much as practical necessity.

This understanding and governance of society returned important benefits. It emphasized society's unity and recognized the foundational importance of its temporal and spiritual dimensions. When they acted with good faith, competence, and wisdom, temporal and spirit-

---

[3] On relics, see Southern, *Western Society and the Church*, 30–1; on the ordeal see 29–30; idem, *The Making of the Middle Ages* (London: Hutchinson University Library, 1953) 94–6; and the illuminating essay in Peter Brown, *Society and the Holy in Late Antiquity* (Berkeley: University of California Press, 1982) 302–32.

ual authorities drew strength from one another, while society as a whole reaped the benefits. The involvement of civil dignitaries in ecclesiastical councils and the foundation of churches and monasteries often proved very constructive. When it flowed from a genuine concern for the Church, the participation of laity in the choice or reception of bishops made it more likely that a new incumbent would be welcome and his ministry fruitful. This practice also reflected a long canonical tradition that premised the installation of a new bishop on the consent of the community he was to serve.[4]

This arrangement also entailed certain problems. One was the lack of a suitable mechanism to arbitrate between civil and ecclesiastical authorities in cases of conflict or to moderate excesses by one or the other. More concretely, monarchs sometimes dispensed ecclesiastical offices or disposed of Church property in order to reward friends, cement political alliances, or advance enterprises that had little to do with the Church's mission. Especially when their institutional or personal interests were at issue, churchmen sometimes acted in ways that poorly served the apostolate. Whatever their rank or station, laypersons and clerics were equally vulnerable to shortsightedness, weakness of character, willfulness, the misuse of power, or the allure of immoral behavior, and this too contributed in no small measure to the difficulties that confronted ninth- and tenth-century reformers.

This background suggests that the distribution and use of authority in medieval Christian societies was quite complex. Given the overall situation, it was not easy for reformers to prevent abuses but leave constructive uses of authority unaffected or to modify the prerogatives of particular offices or persons without encountering theoretical objections and practical resistance.[5]

The Need for Reform

By the end of the ninth century there were ample signs that the Church was in difficulty. In much of Catholic Europe kings, noble families, local lords, or simply whoever was the strongest in the area

---

[4] The election by acclamation of Ambrose as bishop of Milan is well known. For provisions of later canon law, see, for example, the legislation of synods at Paris in the year 614 (Can. 2); Reims, c. 625 (Can. 25); and Chalons, c. 650 (Can. 10). Hefele 4:438, 447, 464.

[5] Knowles, *Middle Ages*, 69–79; F. L. Ganshof, *The Carolingians and the Frankish Monarchy: Studies in Carolingian History,* trans. Janet Sondheimer (London: Longman, 1971) 205–39, 244–5; Southern, *Western Society and the Church,* 180; Maurice Keen, *A History of Medieval Europe* (London: Routledge & Kegan Paul, 1968) 50–2.

had assumed considerable power over Church affairs.[6] The papacy was vulnerable to the will of the Roman aristocracy and the German kings. Church offices were sold for money and its assets bequeathed from father to son; unworthy and sometimes scandalous candidates were installed as bishop, abbot, or pastor; Church incomes were diverted; and its properties were stolen. Some priests were unqualified, had married, or lived in open concubinage. Beyond considerations of discipline, the cumulative effect of such abuses was to make the clergy less able to confront the powerful of their age with the requirements of the Gospel, address the immoral behavior of others, and carry out their own spiritual responsibilities with integrity and dignity. The entire situation was ripe for reform.[7]

The first stirrings of renewal emerged in the early tenth century and arose from principally monastic sources. Although it was not the only sign of a revitalized monasticism, the foundation of the monastery at Cluny in the year 909 was a milestone. In that year Duke William I of Aquitaine commissioned an abbot named Berno to found a monastery in which the monks would live according to the Rule of St. Benedict. Well aware of the dangers of outside control, William stipulated that the monks would elect their abbot, the monastery would be immune from all local authorities, and its abbot accountable directly to the Roman pontiff.[8] With time, the monastery of Cluny extended its influence, principally by promoting reform in other monasteries. More broadly, the prestige and example of Cluniac monks gave them considerable standing in the Church at large. Especially when supported

---

[6] For an account of this process as it occurred in various parts of Europe, see Lynch, *Medieval Church*, 102–7; see also 118–22, 126–8; Southern, *Western Society and the Church*, 32–3; Knowles, *Middle Ages*, 69–79.

[7] See Knowles, *Middle Ages*, 167–71. Although for centuries canon law had required priests of the Latin Rite to remain celibate for life and prohibited them from marrying, it did not invalidate the marriage of a man in holy orders or make the validity of any marriage depend upon the presence of an authorized priest and two witnesses. This canonical background helps to account for the existence of illicit and perhaps scandalous but nonetheless valid clerical marriages. See Christopher Brooke, *Medieval Church and Society: Collected Essays* (London: Sidgwick & Jackson, 1971) 69–99 for a fuller treatment of this problem and its place in medieval efforts to reform the Church.

[8] For the text of William's deed of foundation, see Brian Tierney, *The Crisis of Church and State, 1050–1300* (Englewood Cliffs, N.J.: Prentice-Hall, 1964) 28–9; or Lynch, *Medieval Church*, 109–10. In this era monasteries were usually subject to local authorities and not the pope. Despite William's decision to place Cluny directly under papal authority, the popes' other concerns and the intervening distance made it unlikely that they would frequently assert their authority. Practically speaking, Cluny was an independent monastery. See the sources in the following note.

by sympathetic laity, they discouraged abuses and encouraged reform in the Church. Perhaps Cluny's greatest contribution was the number of its monks who became abbots or bishops and in those positions helped to promote reform in the Church.[9]

The Gregorian Reform

Because it was principally monastic, the tenth-century reform had but limited effects in the Church at large. A more general reform required a determined program of action on the part of the papacy, the one authority that could command the respect of the entire Latin Church. That campaign began with the pontificate of Leo IX (1049–54), a cousin and appointee of Emperor Henry III of Germany.

Upon assuming office, Pope Leo IX undertook a reform of the College of Cardinals. He appointed a number of committed reformers to that body, internationalized its membership, and transformed it from a ceremonial to an advisory group on which he could rely for help in governing the Church. After holding a number of local synods that legislated against simony and concubinage, Leo traveled to northern Italy, Germany, and France, where he held similar councils and sat in judgment on prelates who had been accused of simony or violations of celibacy. Leo IX was the first pope to deploy his office in a deliberate and sustained effort to suppress lay and clerical abuses in the Church. At the same time he vigorously asserted Roman primacy over the entire Church. On both scores his pontificate was a harbinger of future developments.[10]

Pope Leo's successors reinforced and extended the reforms he had begun. Pope Nicholas II (1058–61) legislated against clerical concubinage, simony, and lay investiture, the custom by which lay authorities exercised power over the election and installation of candidates to Church offices. But his most significant actions concerned the election of the Roman pontiff. In a series of decrees he ordered that henceforth that responsibility would belong exclusively to the College of

[9] See Lynch, *Medieval Church*, 108–13; Knowles, *Middle Ages*, 166; Southern, *Making of the Middle Ages*, 157–9; Constance B. Bouchard, "Merovingian, Carolingian, and Cluniac Monasticism: Reform and Renewal in Burgundy," *JEH* 41 (1990) 365–88. For a fuller treatment of the reform movement, see Jean Leclercq and others, *The Spirituality of the Middle Ages*, trans. The Benedictines of Holme Eden Abbey, Carlisle (London: Burns & Oates, 1968) 95–110.

[10] Tierney, *Crisis of Church and State*, 27, 31–2; idem, *Western Europe in the Middle Ages*, 175–6; Lynch, *Medieval Church*, 136–40; Knowles, *Middle Ages*, 171–2, 177–8. In another attempt to assert Roman primacy, Pope Leo IX dispatched the ill-fated mission to Constantinople that ended with the mutual excommunications of 1054.

Cardinals. By placing the election in the hands of these ecclesiastics, Nicholas intended to protect the papacy from the manipulation of powerful Roman families or others and preclude this threat to the office and ministry of Peter's successor. Those noble motives did not console the German king, who concluded that such a change threatened to diminish his imperial authority and weaken his political position at home. A confrontation was inevitable.[11]

Immediate Consequences

That confrontation took place during the papacy of Cardinal Hildebrand, a determined apostle of moral and spiritual reform. Known to history as Pope Gregory VII (1073–85), Hildebrand pursued his predecessors' agenda, concentrating his attack on lay investiture. Well aware that the success of his reform program required the elimination of troublesome lay involvement in Church elections, Pope Gregory prohibited clerics from receiving an abbey, diocese, or any other Church office from the hands of a layperson.[12] He likewise abolished the monarch's traditional right to assent to canonically valid elections.

In so legislating, Pope Gregory claimed to be acting in line with the Roman pontiff's traditional rights, privileges, and authority. He enumerated these prerogatives in the famous *Dictatus papae* of 1075. Its twenty-seven statements include the following:

1. That the Roman Church was founded by God alone.
5. That the Pope may depose the absent.
8. That he alone may use the imperial insignia.
9. That the Pope is the only one whose feet are to be kissed by all princes.
12. That he may depose Emperors.
17. That no chapter or book may be regarded as canonical without his authority.
20. That no one shall dare to condemn a person who appeals to the Apostolic See.
21. That to this See the more important cases of every church should be submitted.
22. That the Roman Church has never erred, nor ever, by the witness of Scripture, shall err to all eternity.

[11] Knowles, *Middle Ages*, 172–3; Tierney, *Western Europe in the Middle Ages*, 176–7. In order to protect himself from a military response to his radical reforms, Nicholas entered into an alliance with the Normans of southern Italy. This shows just how strained relations had become between Roman pontiff and German emperor.

For one of Nicholas' early decrees on papal elections; another against lay investiture, simony, and concubinage; and the text of his treaty with the Normans, see Tierney, *Crisis of Church and State*, 42–4.

[12] Texts of two such decrees are found in Tierney, *Crisis of Church and State*, 51–2.

23. That the Roman Pontiff, if canonically ordained, is undoubtedly sanctified by the merits of St. Peter . . .

25. That without convening a synod he can depose and reinstate bishops.

27. That the Pope may absolve subjects of unjust men from their fealty.[13]

No previous pope had asserted such rights and claims simultaneously, in so forceful a way, and with the intention of exercising them all. In its context, the *Dictatus papae* amounted to an assertion that the pope held supreme authority over civil as well as religious affairs.[14] Gregory's expansive view of papal power was destined to have a major impact on the future course of European history. It provoked the resolute opposition of kings and all others whose rights, authority, and interests depended upon lay investiture, or at least a tolerant papacy.[15]

Tensions came to a climax in 1076, as Emperor Henry IV of Germany and Pope Gregory VII confronted each other over the election of an archbishop for the city of Milan. Henry insisted upon the installation of his own candidate in order to assure that this major see—and the strategic territory it governed—remained in friendly hands. He was determined to defend imperial authority over Church appointments also as a matter of principle. For his part, Pope Gregory could not afford to compromise his own position at so critical a juncture and demanded that the office should go to the person who had been canonically elected. As the parties maneuvered for advantage, Henry convened a German council, which deposed Gregory, who in turn excommunicated the emperor and freed his subjects from their allegiance to him. This led to the famous encounter at Canossa early the following year, in which Henry sought and received absolution from Gregory. Despite its dramatic qualities, Henry's submission was only momentary and did not resolve the underlying dispute.[16]

Elsewhere in Europe attempts to abolish lay investiture were strongly resisted. This problem continued to fester until a compromise was eventually worked out. In essence it provided that ecclesiastics would have the right to fill Church offices in accordance with canon law, but the one elected would pay homage to the king out of deference to his

---

[13] Ibid., 49–50; see also Lynch, *Medieval Church*, 147–8.

[14] Keen, *History of Medieval Europe*, 60–1; Southern, *Western Society and the Church*, 101–4; idem, *Making of the Middle Ages*, 134–45; Knowles, *Middle Ages*, 175, 234.

[15] For the accession and program of Pope Gregory VII, see Knowles, *Middle Ages*, 173–5.

[16] For further discussion of the confrontation between Henry and Gregory and its aftermath see Tierney, *Western Europe in the Middle Ages*, 178–84; Knowles, *Middle Ages*, 173–7; or Keen, *History of Medieval Europe*, 58–61. For some of their letters and decrees, see Tierney, *Crisis of Church and State*, 57–73.

temporal authority. Investiture into office would then occur at the hands of Church authorities. This arrangement permitted the parties to move forward on a basis all could tolerate. However, it did not eliminate the underlying conflicts of abstract principle or practical interest; these would continue to vex later generations and fuel other crises in European political history.[17]

The Increase of Papal Authority

The Gregorian Reform provoked such strong opposition because it challenged the customary distribution and exercise of authority in medieval society. In that context, to abolish lay investiture was to deprive lay authorities of their control over key appointments and other levers of power, losses that would be revolutionary in their effects. It was therefore to be expected that kings generally viewed the Gregorian Reform with alarm. If popes could defeat kings in a contest that involved their national interests—as was certainly the case with lay investiture—then royal authority would be exposed as hollow and the monarchs themselves left vulnerable to their enemies.[18]

On the larger horizon, reform activities involved a sustained program to extend papal jurisdiction over European life as a whole. Although the reformers relied upon an acknowledged primacy of the Roman see and invoked spiritual purposes, their campaign nonetheless had a clearly political dimension. Lay magistrates had to reckon with an increasingly dominant papacy. Local Church leaders were on notice that the popes would hold them accountable for their behavior and were prepared to employ all available means to give effect to papal jurisdiction. In that connection the revival of legal studies and the emerging science of canon law reinforced papal authority. On a practical level, the popes made effective use of legates, councils, authoritative letters, the ability to appoint local officials, rights of visitation, and especially the power to hear judicial appeals. This process diminished the authority of local bishops, who until that time enjoyed considerable autonomy in governing their sees. It likewise limited the power of kings. For although they did not accept the principle that spiritual authority was superior to the temporal, they often found themselves deferring to it in practice. As a result, between the eleventh

---

[17] See Knowles, *Middle Ages*, 183; Keen, *History of Medieval Europe*, 62; Lynch, *Medieval Church*, 145; Tierney, *Western Europe in the Middle Ages*, 181–2. The Concordat of Worms, concluded in 1122, formalized this arrangement in the empire. Its text is given in Tierney, *Crisis of Church and State*, 91–2.

[18] See Brown, *Society and the Holy*, 302–32; Knowles, *Middle Ages*, 225–34; Keen, *History of Medieval Europe*, 58–64.

and thirteenth centuries a great deal of authority flowed to the Roman pontiff and his court in Rome.[19]

The Demarcation of Spiritual and Temporal in Society

In addition to redistributing power in medieval society, the Gregorian Reform helped to change people's understanding of their society and its foundations. At the beginning of this period society was based upon a world view in which spiritual and temporal, sacred and secular, were ill distinguished, as has already been noted. In that environment the attack against lay investiture and the correlative requirement that Church elections should be free of simony and interference by civil rulers implied that spiritual authority is to be independent of secular jurisdiction and might overrule it when necessary. Such an assertion could only be sustained if the inherited assumptions were replaced with others that embodied a sharper distinction between spiritual and temporal domains and assigned primacy to the spiritual. By confronting the grounds, nature, and exercise of authority as it did, the Gregorian Reform helped medieval society to think about the sacred and the secular, the spiritual and the temporal, in a new way.

In the short term that reconsideration was strongly influenced by the popes' assertion of supremacy and the power they accumulated in Western Christendom. Stronger emphasis on the importance of the spiritual gave new prominence to the clergy, focused attention on their ministerial responsibilities, and enhanced their place in society. Especially when they had the advantages of education, many clerics were able to live quite comfortably and gain considerable authority in society.[20]

The long-range implications were more significant and less favorable to papal ambitions and the position of the clergy. For latent in the greater differentiation of spiritual and temporal was the distinction between Church and state. Moreover, if a sharp contrast between spiritual and temporal could work to the advantage of the Church authori-

---

[19] Southern, *Western Society and the Church,* 104–27, 188; Lynch, *Medieval Church,* 168–82; Tierney, *Western Europe in the Middle Ages,* 184; Knowles, *Middle Ages,* 179–80, 225–34, 336–7.

This phenomenon set the context for much that took place in this era, including the Crusades, the deteriorating relationship with the East, later pontificates, and Boniface VIII's famous bull *Unam sanctam* (see Tierney, *Crisis of Church and State,* 188–9). Some of these developments will be considered in chapter 8, below.

[20] The increased power and prominence of the clergy tended to separate them from the laity and give them a distinct status. In this era the word "church" began to refer to the clergy or the hierarchy instead of the community of Christian believers. Knowles, *Middle Ages,* 260.

ties, it could also work to the advantage of civil rulers. Although it would take centuries for this to develop, the state would one day establish its autonomy, gain the ability to ignore the Church, and perhaps also subordinate it. With respect to the clergy, the more they lived as a privileged class, the more they risked being embarrassed by people who lived a simpler, poorer life. Moreover, the power and lives of some priests and bishops would lead to objections that they were corrupt and their offices devoid of scriptural foundation.[21]

Religious and Moral Implications

One of the most important developments in Western political and social history, the Gregorian Reform began as a protest against immorality in the Church and the abuse of its offices, ministries, and worship. This movement stands as another sign of the power of faith and religious commitment to motivate people and shape their consciences in ways that affected society as well as the individuals concerned. Yet if the Gregorian Reform originated in response to evident abuses, its later development was more ambiguous. Religious and moral considerations could prompt a sustained challenge to lay investiture and other problems, but they could not resolve the political instability that eventually resulted. As this reform movement entered its later stages, some popes used their stronger position to advance primarily secular interests or other disedifying goals, ironic developments indeed. Over a much longer period of time, as the spiritual and ecclesiastical dimensions of life began to contrast more sharply with temporal and civil affairs, it became more difficult for people to remember that temporal concerns have spiritual dimensions and vice versa and to acknowledge that religious and moral imperatives speak to the exercise of civil jurisdiction. The history and effects of the Gregorian Reform underscores the political, moral, and spiritual complexity of this movement.[22]

---

[21] Keen, *History of Medieval Europe*, 62–4, 112–21, 137–51, 179–91; Southern, *Western Society and the Church*, 36–41, 180–1; idem, *Making of the Middle Ages*, 126–30; Brown, *Society and the Holy*, 302–32; Knowles, *Middle Ages*, 329–37; Leclercq, *Spirituality of the Middle Ages*, 259–60; Tierney, *Crisis of Church and State*, 97–210.

[22] Keen, *History of Medieval Europe*, 55–6; Lynch, *Medieval Church*, 139–40. A classic study of the Gregorian Reform is Augustin Fliche, *La Réforme grégorienne* (Louvain: "Spicilegium sacrum lovaniense"; Paris: E. Champion, 1924–37).

On the Gregorian Reform's capacity to distract the Roman pontiff from his ministry, see Bernard of Clairvaux's famous mid-twelfth-century letter to Pope Eugenius III (Tierney, *Crisis of Church and State*, 92–4); see also Southern, *Western Society and the Church*, 110–1; idem, *Making of the Middle Ages*, 146–50.

THE GREAT MEDIEVAL REAWAKENING

In the middle of the eleventh century, about the time Pope Leo IX initiated the Gregorian Reform, Europe began to stir, as if from a long slumber. Once it began, this reawakening gathered momentum and reached all important aspects of life. A revitalized and confident Europe was the setting for momentous developments in thought and in many other areas of human activity.

The Great Medieval Reawakening

Although historians agree that the medieval European revival was a momentous event, they have not yet fully understood what brought it about. Perhaps an economic expansion supplied the catalyst. Another explanation looks to an increase in crop harvests, possibly obtained as a result of a more favorable climate and better farming methods. It is also possible that these factors worked in tandem with a rise in population, more efficient transportation, and the absence of significant external threats to support the dramatic changes that occurred. Whatever the cause, by the beginning of the twelfth century Europe had come alive on many fronts and entered a period of sustained growth, confidence, and territorial expansion.

Once it began, this reawakening became self-sustaining and affected all important areas of life. Overall population began to increase, causing new villages and towns to spring up and older ones to grow. Land that had previously been considered useless or too remote was turned to productive purposes. Trade and commerce recorded a dramatic and steady rise, increasing prosperity and stimulating the development of a money-based economy and the institutions needed to sustain it. Although this expansion was initially evident in heightened agricultural

---

The use of papal power for political ends became especially problematic beginning with the pontificate of Innocent IV (1243–54). The following comment is pertinent:

> The significance of the opinions and rule of Innocent IV, however, do not lie primarily in his expositions of theory, but in the manner of his use of his plenary powers. It was by the great expansion of the financial claims of the papacy, by the use of the right of providing Roman and other clerks to benefices all over Europe, and by his ruthless use of the spiritual weapons of excommunication and interdict in contests that were in the last resort political rather than spiritual, that Innocent IV brought about a subtle change in the function of his office (Knowles, *Middle Ages,* 333).

For more on the involvement of Roman pontiffs in European political struggles, see, for example, Tierney, *Western Europe in the Middle Ages,* 386–99; idem, *Crisis of Church and State,* 180–92; or Keen, *History of Medieval Europe,* 137–51, 179–91.

and commercial activities, it also stimulated major advances in art, architecture, music, law, government, and literature.[23]

Although these developments affected society as a whole, they especially impacted the life and activities of urban areas. Cities and towns assumed importance as centers of education, commerce, finance, and industry. Because these functions had such clear social utility, towns received the special protection of laws that restricted the bearing of arms within city limits and guaranteed the liberties of its inhabitants. But if city life boasted of vitality and privilege it also exacted its cost, as the incidence of poverty, theft, civil disorder, fire, and disease suggests. Nevertheless, urban areas continued to grow and soon achieved dominance in European life. They nurtured new groups of craftsmen, merchants, traders, and financiers, whose lives and activities presented new moral and religious challenges. Cities and towns gave birth to the earliest universities, nourished all sorts of religious movements, and constituted the principal locus of pastoral work in this new age.[24]

A New Outlook on the World and on the Self

This rapid development and broad transformation of European life induced some equally significant changes in thinking and outlook. As the reawakening gathered momentum and people accumulated experiences of success in many areas of endeavor, they realized that the outcome of any effort often depended upon the quality of the intelligence and technical expertise that had been invested in it. That insight had profound effects on people's assessment of the world and their own ability to influence it. They became more skeptical of the inherited

---

[23] See Southern, *Western Society and the Church,* 34–44; idem, *Making of the Middle Ages,* 42–9, 62–7; Lynch, *Medieval Church,* 107–8; Carlo M. Cipolla, "The Origins," *The Fontana Economic History of Europe: The Middle Ages,* ed. Carlo M. Cipolla (n.p.: Collins/Fontana Books, 1972) 11–23; Knowles, *Middle Ages,* 224–8; 266–72, 389–401; Tierney, *Western Europe in the Middle Ages,* 213–54, 305–78; Keen, *History of Medieval Europe,* 65–95.

This general expansion had important effects beyond Catholic Europe. It supplied much of the energy that spilled over in the Crusades and formed the context for the extension of Catholicism to Scandinavia, Spain and Sicily, the Baltics, Poland, Hungary, and Iceland; see Knowles, *Middle Ages,* 209–13, 300–2; Tierney, *Western Europe in the Middle Ages,* 168, 189–211; Southern, *Making of the Middle Ages,* 23–37, 49–62; Lynch, *Medieval Church,* 113–4.

[24] Jacques Le Goff, "The Town as an Agent of Civilisation," *The Fontana Economic History of Europe: The Middle Ages,* 71–106, especially 75–8, 84–6, 90; Tierney, *Western Europe in the Middle Ages,* 218–24, 330–6; Keen, *History of Medieval Europe,* 70–4.

notion that the universe was composed of chaotic, irrational elements and that natural phenomena reflected miracles or other supernatural causes. Instead they began to view the universe as a coherent, unified whole that was amenable to rational examination and control.

Once accepted, this desacralized world view opened up vast new horizons to researchers and thinkers. Scholars began to assume that human reason could account for natural events in light of cause and effect. That favored the development of the empirical sciences and a more adequate method of inquiry in them. For their part, some theologians proposed that nature and reason might lead people to the knowledge of God.[25] Others speculated that nature might yield insights that would more fully illuminate the moral requirements of upright human living. Such suggestions opened up new methods to theological reflection and offered additional resources to personal faith and devotion.

To reassess the world and the competence of reason in that way is also to bring individuality in general and the human person in particular into higher relief. One of the most significant developments of the high medieval period was its fascination with individuality and its keener interest in persons, including their interior experiences and their relationships with particular groups, the community, and God. A stronger accent on the person prompted more people to become hermits during this period. It supported deeper interest in the interior life of persons and encouraged efforts to "know thyself." At the same time, friendship, that quintessential example of interpersonal experience, received new attention and respect. There was a greater tendency to examine human affiliations and encourage people to view their relationship with God in terms of friendship. Popular piety contemplated God through the lens of human experiences, attended to the earthly life of Jesus, and identified more closely with Mary, his mother.[26]

---

[25] His argument that human beings can know God's existence without the aid of supernatural revelation makes St. Anselm an early representative of this approach. Pelikan, 3:261-2.

[26] For more on the medieval reassessment of nature, reason, the individual, and the person, as well as some of its effects, see Jean Charles Payen, "La pénitence dans le contexte culturel des XIIe et XIIIe siècles," *RSPT* 61 (1977) 402–3; Leclercq, *Spirituality of the Middle Ages,* 110–5, 156–61, 243–54, 274–7; Knowles, *Middle Ages,* 185–6, 256–7; Timothy Fry, ed., *The Rule of St. Benedict in Latin and English with Notes* (Collegeville: The Liturgical Press, 1981) 127; R. W. Southern, *Medieval Humanism and Other Studies* (Oxford: Basil Blackwell, 1970) 29–60; Marie-Dominique Chenu, *Nature, Man, and Society in the Twelfth Century: Essays on New Theological Perspectives in the Latin West,* trans. Jerome Taylor and Lester K. Little (Chicago and London: University of Chicago Press, 1968) 1–48, 232–4; Colin Morris, *The Discovery of the*

The assumption that people have a greater ability to understand and control their world gave moral concerns a new prominence. To the extent that persons were recognized as free and responsible, to that extent they could be held morally accountable for their decisions and actions. The more human beings sought to control their surroundings, the more they encountered questions about the wisdom of their actions. As greater autonomy began to be attributed to the human person, it raised new questions about moral life and changed the context in which theologians and others considered them.

Finally, it has already been noted that the Gregorian Reform released powerful forces that encouraged people to move the secular and the sacred into more distinct realms, a step that had immediate consequences for moral and religious matters. The Great Medieval Reawakening strongly reinforced that phenomenon and helped to assure that its influence would be pervasive and its effects significant.[27]

THE MEDIEVAL RELIGIOUS RENEWAL

As they raised the profile of secular and temporal dimensions of life, the Gregorian Reform and the general awakening of European society threw the spiritual and sacred into much higher relief and led people to reconsider their relationship to God, one another, and the Church. As a result, this period witnessed a remarkable resurgence of religious sensitivity and commitment. It also supported a variety of responses to the question of faith and to religious imperatives in general.[28]

New Orders of Monks and Canons

At the start of the mid-eleventh century Benedictine monasticism enjoyed a virtual monopoly on monastic observance in the West. However, by the early twelfth century many Benedictine abbeys had come under sharp criticism for maintaining useless customs and a routine that ill reflected St. Benedict's Rule. The vigor and spirit of a new

---

Individual: 1050–1200 (London: S.P.C.K., 1972); Bynum, "Did the Twelfth Century Discover the Individual?" 1–17.

[27] Southern, *Western Society and the Church*, 35–8; idem, *Making of the Middle Ages*, 90–6; idem, *Medieval Humanism*, 32–3, 51–8; Le Goff, "Town as an Agent of Civilisation," 86–9.

[28] For a treatment of the context and motives behind this religious revival, see Giles Constable, "Renewal and Reform in Religious Life: Concepts and Realities," *Renaissance and Renewal in the Twelfth Century*, ed. Robert L. Benson and Giles Constable, with Carol D. Lanham (Cambridge, Mass.: Harvard University Press, 1982) 37–67.

age had also played their part, and many began to look elsewhere for a more austere monastic observance, one that would be more attuned to the individual and less enmeshed in society and its affairs. Those concerns prompted the foundation of mainly eremitical groups such as the one at Camaldoli in the eleventh century, from whom the Carthusians originated. They also supported new religious orders that featured life in common, especially the Cistercians, with their primitive Benedictine observance; rigorous discipline; and emphasis on solitude, poverty, and simplicity of life.[29]

The Augustinian or Austin canons represent a decidedly different approach to religious dedication. The "canons" were priests who did pastoral work among their neighbors but lived in common under various rules or canons that had been enacted for their benefit. By the late eleventh century, many of these groups had begun to adopt the Augustinian Rule, from which they took their name. Primarily dedicated to ministerial service, their most important contribution was to the people of the cities and towns. Although the Augustinian Rule was less austere than that of the Cistercians, the Austin canons earned respect and affection, since they willingly looked after the religious needs of ordinary people and did so unrestrained by the demands of a large organization or the weight of inherited customs. Their lives and ministry exemplified the melding of pastoral service and monastic commitment.[30]

Religious Developments Among the Laity

The monks and canons were not the only ones to respond to religious imperatives. In the High Middle Ages a resurgence of religious fervor captured the imagination of many laypeople and set an agenda for their lives as well. Although theirs was a spontaneous movement that appeared simultaneously in many parts of Europe, it drew its energy from certain common religious and societal roots.

The Scriptures were a principal source of the religious currents that swept across Europe at this time. Readings from the Bible were an integral part of the Church's liturgy, and the Scriptures had always been honored as God's word to the Christian community. The sacred text

---

[29] Fry, *Rule of St. Benedict*, 127–8; Knowles, *Middle Ages*, 185–90; Southern, *Western Society and the Church*, 230–6, 250–72. For a fuller discussion of the foundation of the Cistercians, their spirituality, and the teaching of St. Bernard of Clairvaux, see Leclercq, *Spirituality of the Middle Ages*, 187–220. On women and religious life, see Southern, *Western Society and the Church*, 309–18; Bernard Hamilton, *Religion in the Medieval West* (London: Edward Arnold, 1986) 33–5; Knowles, *Middle Ages*, 258.

[30] Southern, *Western Society and the Church*, 240–50; Knowles, *Middle Ages*, 190–2.

offered an agenda for Church reform and a charter to those who wished to live their baptismal commitment more perfectly. In this new period of religious activity people naturally turned to the Scriptures for enlightenment and inspiration.

Sociological factors were also influential. More accustomed to a rural environment, the Church had not served the towns very well even though they had become important and framed the lives and experience of many people. One problem was that not enough priests ministered in urban areas, and those who did often lacked an understanding of city people. Many priests either preached poorly or, as was frequently the case, not at all.[31] This was especially burdensome for the many illiterate people who did not understand the Latin of the liturgy and depended upon the sermon to nourish their spiritual life. To compound the problem, there was great resentment, especially among the poor, toward the wealth of some monasteries and the power and comfortable lives of many in the secular clergy. These problems deepened the laity's spiritual hunger and fostered anticlerical animosity. Especially in the more intense atmosphere of the cities, these feelings could be quite volatile and sometimes fueled significant, broad-based religious movements.[32]

In that context, itinerant preachers emerged and attracted a considerable audience in the cities and towns of Europe. Although their messages varied, they generally appealed to the Scriptures and took their themes from that source. Preachers usually proclaimed that the scriptural word was the principal or even the exclusive source of sustenance for the Christian life. They emphasized the "apostolic life" portrayed in the Acts of the Apostles, especially its imperatives of poverty and simplicity of life. Since the Bible often describes salvation coming to specific persons, it readily supported application to individuals and their particular circumstances.[33]

---

[31] Chenu, *Nature, Man, and Society,* 244–5; see also Hamilton, *Religion in the Medieval West,* 70–1.

[32] The conditions and opportunities of the towns were crucial to the medieval religious revival. If urban poverty, alienation, and dehumanization increased popular hunger for spiritual nourishment, the cities' commercial life helped some people to address it. Business needs demanded that at least some of the laity should be able to read, and that afforded them direct access to the biblical text and the ability to cite it to others. In addition, trade routes and the encounters required in commerce offered ready channels for the propagation of religious ideas. Southern, *Western Society and the Church,* 273–7; Knowles, *Middle Ages,* 224; Jeffrey Burton Russell, *Dissent and Order in the Middle Ages: The Search for Legitimate Authority* (New York: Twayne Publishers, 1992) 27–31.

[33] Leclercq, *Spirituality of the Middle Ages,* 257–61; Chenu, *Nature, Man, and Society,* 219–20; Russell, *Dissent and Order,* 24–7.

Preachers tapped into people's grievances against the clergy and their distaste for some Church practices. Preaching apostolic poverty, for example, might be framed as an indictment of wealthy churchmen and their life-style. A scripturally based demand for personal holiness could be used to condemn unworthy clerics. However, the supreme spiritual authority of the Bible might also be enlisted in an effort to attack the structures, hierarchy, and canonical system of worship that many found oppressive or unsatisfactory.[34] Moreover, when holiness was certified as the one and only requirement for authentic ministry in the Church, it could lead to the conclusion that the ordained priesthood, hierarchical authority, and much of liturgical worship were illegitimate accretions that ought to be discarded. The failures of the clergy[35] and the weight of Church institutions enabled some preachers to focus their message on personal reform and encouraged others to teach that the Bible, a direct spiritual relationship with God, and upright living were all that mattered in the Christian life.[36]

Whether these more radical prescriptions actually took hold often depended upon the theological skill of the preacher and the approach used. Although the more charismatic figures often gained a very dramatic response in the short term, their antipathy to organization and structure usually guaranteed a quick dissipation of any initial enthusiasm. But when speakers offered a well-crafted message and linked it to appealing and coherent programs of worship and governance, they sometimes succeeded in giving birth to new groups of dissident or nonconforming believers. When they were based upon dualistic or otherwise objectionable ideas, such religious bodies were judged by the Catholic Church to be not only schismatic but also heretical in nature.[37]

---

[34] Some cited the Scriptures to impugn some of the customs and obligations that had accumulated within Catholicism and particularly in monastic communities. These were rejected as spiritually useless, offensive to Christian liberty, and incompatible with the simple requirements of faith. Such judgments convinced many members of the Church that joining a monastic community would not help them to express their religious commitment. See Chenu, *Nature, Man, and Society,* 256–9.

[35] David Knowles is blunt on this point: "The anti-clerical and anti-sacramental bias [of heretical teachings] was a practical criticism of a sordid clerical proletariate, an aristocratic episcopate and grasping and exclusive monastic and capitular bodies." Knowles, *Middle Ages,* 366; see Leclercq, *Spirituality of the Middle Ages,* 259, for similar comments.

[36] On this entire discussion see Knowles, *Middle Ages,* 224–5, 365–6; Russell, *Dissent and Order,* 26–37; Leclercq, *Spirituality of the Middle Ages,* 257–61; Southern, *Western Society and the Church,* 273–7; Chenu, *Nature, Man, and Society,* 202–69.

[37] See Pelikan, 3:229–42; Chenu, *Nature, Man, and Society,* 219–30; Leclercq, *Spirituality of the Middle Ages,* 261–74; Knowles, *Middle Ages,* 365–71; Hamilton,

On the other hand, when it was channeled by Catholic faith and praxis, this religious awakening revitalized the Church and gave many of its members a more personal contact with the Gospel. One of the most important steps in that direction was a move to have the Bible distributed more widely and also to translate it into vernacular languages. Closely related was an effort by bishops to preach well-prepared homilies on the text of the Gospel read at the Sunday Eucharist. The popes strongly supported these attempts to give the faithful better access to God's word and emphasized the need for effective preaching.[38]

The laity participated fully in this renewal of religious commitment. Especially when supported by the preaching of dedicated pastors, many laypersons came to realize that baptism had already committed them to reject the devil and the world's evils. That helped them to set aside the idea that only monks and clerics could be fully committed to Christ and encouraged them to appreciate the Christian dignity of their own lives, witness, and service. Taking the Gospel itself as their "rule," some laypeople formed themselves into groups that were publicly committed to poverty, charity, and disengagement from the world. Many others resolved to live their daily lives in conformity with the Gospel. They sought to act justly, treat others with compassion, and honor the requirements of Christian life in whatever occupation they led.[39]

Religion in the Medieval West, 172–6; Russell, *Dissent and Order*, 21–67. Prominent among medieval dissident groups that held dualistic positions, ultimately Manichean in origin, were the Cathars, some of whom were known as Albigensians. The Waldensians exemplified an approach that adhered to the Scriptures but dispensed with the ordained priesthood and much of the sacramental system. See note 40, below.

The emergence of heretical groups raised difficult issues for the established religious and civil authorities. Their responses took many forms, including tolerance, preaching and teaching, efforts to convert the dissidents, and persecution.

The disruptive effects of some preachers and their heretical views, particularly about sacramental worship, caused the Church to reassert its right to authorize people to preach, prohibit unauthorized preaching, and pass judgment on what was preached. See, for example, the decree *Ad abolendum* issued by Pope Lucius III in 1184; Edward Peters, ed., *Heresy and Authority in Medieval Europe: Documents in Translation* (Philadelphia: University of Pennsylvania Press, 1980) 170–3. On these topics, see the sources cited in the present note, above.

[38] Chenu, *Nature, Man, and Society*, 248–9; see also Hamilton, *Religion in the Medieval West*, 58–63.

[39] Chenu, *Nature, Man, and Society*, 219–30, 240–6. Chenu also notes that this renewed appreciation of the lay Christian vocation stimulated efforts to elaborate "a certain evangelical morality for each secular trade and profession." He adds that the medieval religious reawakening constitutes "one of the great turning points in

The Dominican and Franciscan Friars

The social stresses of medieval cities and the pastoral challenges spawned by a general religious awakening set the stage for another significant development: the foundation of the Dominican and Franciscan Orders. These two religious groups played a major role in late medieval society and made lasting contributions to the pastoral and theological work of the Church.

The creative spark for the Dominican Order came in 1206 when a Spanish Augustinian canon named Dominic Guzman (c. 1173–1221) heard three Cistercian abbots complain of their inability to halt the heretical Albigensian movement in Languedoc.[40] He replied that people failed to take them seriously because they were too concerned with their rank and position and lacked the credibility of poor and simple men. Once Dominic made that comment it captured his imagination. Taking the apostolic mission in Luke 10:1-12 as his charter,[41] he resolved to found a group whose life and preparation would equip them to meet the challenges of pastoral work in those new and difficult times.

Dominic decided that the principal work of his group needed to be the crucial task of preaching, and he fashioned it with that purpose in mind. The Augustinian Rule would govern his community, provide a common life and the norm of apostolic poverty, and strongly orient it to the tasks of pastoral care. To serve these basic goals the Dominicans would be an order of priests who were distinguished for their doctrinal and spiritual competence. As they grew more numerous and spread across much of Europe, the Dominican friars developed an organiza-

---

the history of western Christian spirituality," since it involved the first effort to reconsider temporal and terrestrial realities as well as human efforts in their regard in light of God's ultimate plan for them. These steps were of great importance for the future development of a more adequate theology of lay commitment and work in the world (223–4).

[40] The term "Albigensian" is derived from Albi, a town in France that was a focal point of the larger "Catharist" movement. Catharists, who first appeared in Germany in 1143, were distinguished by their ascetical approach and doctrinal convictions. They typically embraced poverty and celibacy while rejecting murder, war, oaths, and the eating of meat, austerities that won them respect and admiration. Catharism taught that there are two gods, one of whom created matter—which is inherently evil—while the other is the source of pure and immaterial souls. Catharist doctrine is dualistic and represents a medieval form of a much older Manicheism (see discussion in ch. 4, above). To address Catharism effectively, the Catholic Church needed to put forth a better account of material reality and reinforce it with the practical witness of those who live poor and simple lives in the spirit of the Gospel. Arno Borst, "Catharists" *SM*, 1:269-70.

[41] Chenu, *Nature, Man, and Society*, 245; see also 214–5.

tional system that suited their wide-ranging apostolic purposes and afforded great flexibility in responding to educational opportunities and pastoral needs alike.

Their mission and way of life attracted the Dominican friars to the cities and major towns of Europe. Their need for a solid education led them to establish residences in cities where the best scholars taught and likewise helps to account for the prominence of Dominican professors in the newly founded European universities. Their presence in urban areas was also necessary for economic reasons, since only city people would have enough money to contribute to the friars, who were committed to a dependence upon alms. In return, the Dominicans willingly applied themselves to the tasks of pastoral care, with special concern to share the life of their neighbors and feed them with the bread of God's word, generously broken open through effective preaching.

The birth of the Franciscans also dates to the year 1206, when Francis (1181/2–1226), the son of a prosperous Assisi merchant, renounced all his possessions and dedicated himself to the radical "life and poverty of Jesus Christ."[42] Together with the first of his "little brothers," Francis lived by his own labors without a fixed residence, all the while preaching the urgency of conversion. His life, example, and ideals had a deep impact and seemed to tap into some very strong currents among the townspeople of central Italy. Before long the word spread, and people in every part of Europe joined his movement in large numbers.

This unexpected and rapid expansion necessitated some organization and system of governance among the Franciscans. Because he was primarily dedicated to a radically poor life and the mission of preaching, the charismatic Francis strongly resisted these pressures. But objective requirements, the insistence of some within his community, and interventions of the Holy See eventually persuaded Francis to provide some structure for his followers. As a result of these and other early changes, the initial severity of the Franciscan way of life was mitigated and Franciscans came to accept the necessity of education. Like the Dominicans, they realized that to be effective as preachers and missionaries they had to be well educated. Before long the Franciscans joined the Dominicans in the cities and towns of Europe, where they studied, taught, and preached.

Although their respective founders had different aims in view and the Dominican and Franciscan orders sometimes competed in the schools and in the community, these two groups had much in common

[42] The words of St. Francis, quoted in Southern, *Western Society and the Church*, 282.

and helped each other in important ways. Even more significant was their contribution to the pastoral mission of the Church. One scholar has described their accomplishments as follows: "Spiritually the friars were the principal formers of the lay piety of Europe in the later middle ages. They gave what the Church had hitherto lacked, systematic preaching and administration of the sacraments of penance and Eucharist, and this essential basis of the devout life was followed up by the institution of the 'third order' for laypeople, which gave the elements of the devout life—regular prayers, simple exercises of penance, and the restraints of certain indulgences or amusements—to men and women leading a family life and conducting the business of a town."[43]

The Significance of the Medieval Religious Revival

The medieval religious revival again discloses the power of faith to bring people to conversion and set an agenda for their lives. Some enacted their commitment within the Church and in light of its tradition. This is evident in the monastic commitment of many individuals, the Christian dedication of laypersons, and the service of the canons and the friars. These examples also demonstrate the enduring ability of the Church to reform itself, meet its ministerial responsibilities, and inspire personal dedication in believers of all ranks and stations. Despite the serious problems of the age, faithful members of the Church heard God's word and responded generously even in new and difficult circumstances.

However, to the extent that people had grievances against the Church or were offended by its authority, worship, or clergy, they were more likely to question whether God was acting through these channels. They might be inclined to believe that God spoke to them only through the Scriptures or by means of interior personal experiences. These sources tended to give rise to different responses and messages. When people were convinced of God's activity in their lives and certain about what God was asking of them, they might express themselves through very assertive public preaching.

Such developments show that Christians no longer drew the line of demarcation between the sacred and the profane the traditional way, with the Church squarely in the domain of the holy. In an age when some Church structures seemed not to serve religious purposes very well and

---

[43] Knowles, *Middle Ages*, 263. This entire discussion is indebted to Southern, *Western Society and the Church*, 272–99; Knowles, *Middle Ages*, 338–46; Leclercq, *Spirituality of the Middle Ages*, 283–95, 315–21. The latter two sources can also be consulted for other aspects of the early development of the these two orders of friars.

some clerics were more concerned with worldly affairs than their ministerial responsibilities, it is understandable that people associated them with the sinful and profane. Whatever the case, such a reassessment of the sacred and the profane represented an important change of attitude and thinking. For some people, the faithful individual had displaced the Church community as the focal point of God's activity on earth.

When pushed to its limit, such a reinterpretation led to an outright denial of the Church's religious legitimacy and a rejection of its ordained ministry and traditional system of liturgical worship. That radical step had a number of consequences: it redirected one's search for God; rechanneled efforts to understand God's will; and required a new basis for worship. However important that might be for individuals, the reconfiguration of the sacred and profane implied in such a move was even more significant for Western Christianity as a whole. For the first time since the Donatist schism in the fifth century, incompatible views about the Church, the implications of personal holiness or sinfulness, and the dynamics of Christian life had begun to divide believers and produce new faith communities. These religious developments could not fail to affect the dynamics and substance of the moral life as well.[44]

SIN AND REPENTANCE AS INTERIOR ACTS

The penitential praxis of the eleventh-century Church was hardly novel, but its theological basis had nevertheless remained largely unexplored. No one, for instance, had ever offered a satisfactory rationale for the penitential system as a whole or specified how it reconciled and forgave a penitent. The respective contributions of the penitent and the Church to that end had not been sorted out. Those were some of the issues that awaited theologians of the twelfth century.[45] Their contributions to the Church's understanding of human behavior, personal conscience, sin, and forgiveness bore directly on moral life, the community, and one's relationship with God.

Old Practices and New Influences

In the twelfth century the Church's rituals of forgiveness were largely concerned with external behavior. Although sincere repentance

[44] Knowles, *Middle Ages,* 365; Pelikan, 3:231.

[45] Bernhard Poschmann, *Penance and the Anointing of the Sick,* trans. Francis Courtney (New York: Herder & Herder, 1964) 156–8. For a description of eleventh-century penitential theology, see Paul Anciaux, *La Théologie du sacrement de pénitence au XIIe siècle* (Louvain: E. Nauwelaerts; Gembloux: Duculot, 1949) 7–55.

was called for, the accent fell on the confession of sinful acts and the priest's prayer of absolution. The penitent was also expected to perform penitential actions that reflected the sins committed. People knew that grave sinners could have their penances shortened or remitted altogether if they went on a pilgrimage, attended the dedication of a church, or performed other praiseworthy deeds. These practices mitigated the severity of some penitential actions, but they also threw the external dimensions of this system into even higher relief.[46]

The twelfth century's heightened sensitivity to the person supported a radical reconsideration of these customary penitential practices. A stronger emphasis on the experience and inner life of persons focused attention on God's presence to each one and highlighted the person's internal response to God. That environment encouraged theologians to give greater deference to the interior dimensions of sin and forgiveness and attribute less significance to the external aspects of sin and penance alike.[47]

Peter Abelard and His Ethics

Although many twelfth-century theologians and canonists worked on penance-related problems,[48] Peter Abelard (1079–1142) contributed most to the discussion. A gifted teacher who attracted students from all over Europe, Abelard used his intellectual powers and logical approach to engage a range of theological questions in an arresting way. His application of rational methods clarified his use of language and allowed him to reach conclusions that better reflected the sources and experiences he cited. Although it was often controversial, his work opened the door to important pastoral and theological advances and guaranteed his place in history. In his own day, however, Abelard's combative personality, widespread influence, and provocative conclusions earned him the implacable opposition of powerful adversaries.[49]

---

[46] Pierre-Marie Gy, "Les bases de la pénitence moderne," MD, 117 (1974) 64–5. In the Middle Ages pilgrimages were important both from a social and a religious perspective. On this topic, see, for example, Knowles, Middle Ages, 264–5; Poschmann, Penance and the Anointing of the Sick, 150–2.

The reliance on commutations and remissions also reflected a need to diminish the heavy burden of penances that sometimes resulted from the use of predetermined penances; this was especially welcome in an age that had become more sensitive to the individual.

[47] Payen, "La pénitence," 402–3.

[48] For an ample review see Anciaux, Théologie du sacrement de pénitence.

[49] Most of what is known about Abelard's life comes from his own autobiography, Historia calamitatum suarum, "The History of His Troubles." For short descriptions

Among Abelard's most important contributions are his discussions of sin, forgiveness, and their implications for ecclesiastical penance. His most focused treatment of penance-related issues is in a work that carries the revealing title *Scito te ipsum* (Know Thyself).[50] In this book, which is also known as the *Ethica*, or *Ethics*, Abelard presupposes the inherited practice of penance and its emphasis on sinful actions and penitential satisfactions. Convinced that actions do not capture the essence of sin or forgiveness, he reevaluated these basic realities and accounted for them in more personal terms. The result was a new penitential theology.[51]

Abelard's Teaching on Sin

At the beginning of his *Ethics*, Abelard asserts that sin consists exclusively in a free interior consent to what the person knows is evil in God's sight. Abelard expresses his position as follows: "Now this consent we properly call sin, that is, the fault of the soul by which it earns damnation or is made guilty before God. For what is that consent unless it is contempt of God and an offence against him? . . . And so our sin is contempt of the Creator and to sin is to hold the Creator in contempt, that is, to do by no means on his account what we believe we ought to do for him, or not to forsake on his account what we believe we ought to forsake" (Luscombe, 5–7).[52] Distilled to its essence, sin is "contempt of God or consent to that which we believe should be forsaken on God's account" (17; see also 66–7 and xxxiii).

---

of the man and his thought, see Luscombe, xiii–xv; or Paul L. Williams, *The Moral Philosophy of Peter Abelard* (Lanham, Md.: University Press of America, 1980) 1–44; a more extensive treatment is found in Leif Grane, *Peter Abelard: Philosophy and Christianity in the Middle Ages,* trans. Frederick Crowley and Christine Crowley (New York: Harcourt, Brace & World, 1970).

[50] Luscombe, 1–131, provides a critical Latin edition of the *Scito te ipsum* and a facing English translation. Only a portion of this work has survived: the first book in its entirety and a small fragment of the second. All citations to Abelard's *Scito te ipsum* in this discussion will be to this volume; Arabic numbered pages contain the Latin and English texts while the Roman numerals refer to Luscombe's commentary.

[51] On this see especially G. Verbeke, "Introductory Conference: Peter Abelard and the Concept of Subjectivity," *Peter Abelard: Proceedings of the International Conference, Louvain, May 10–12, 1971,* ed. E. M. Buytaert (Leuven: University Press; The Hague: Martinus Nijhof, 1974) 1–11.

[52] Strictly speaking, "sin" is found only in the act or state of alienation from God. In Abelard's words it is "the fault of the soul by which it earns damnation or is made guilty before God." In this discussion, sin does not encompass venial sin or an evil action taken by itself. This precision is necessary in order to understand the twelfth-century discussion and its connection with the foundational issue of per-

Once sin has been strictly defined in those terms, it follows that nothing else can be considered sinful in the same sense. That means that because pleasure, evil desires, and inner inclinations to vice do not necessarily involve consent, they cannot be sinful in themselves. The same is to be said of one's actions, and for the same reason (Luscombe, 3–5). Consistent with his principle, Abelard held that the evil activities people perform as a consequence of sinful consent do not increase their guilt: "The doing of deeds has no bearing upon an increase of sin and nothing pollutes the soul except what is of the soul, that is the consent which alone we have called sin, not the will which precedes it nor the doing of the deed which follows. . . . Moreover, I think everyone knows how often things that should not be done are done without sin, when, that is, they are committed under coercion or through ignorance" (23–5).

Abelard therefore affirms the strict moral indifference of all behavior considered in itself. Behavior gains moral significance only through the agent's intention. He is explicit on this point: "Works in fact, which . . . are common to the damned and the elect alike, are all indifferent in themselves and should be called good or bad only on account of the intention of the agent, not, that is, because it is good or bad for them to be done but because they are done well or badly, that is, by that intention by which it is or is not fitting that they should be done" (Luscombe, 45–7).

At first sight, to locate sin solely in consent and to derive an action's moral quality exclusively from personal intention seems to deny that human actions can be judged by an objective standard. A careful reading of the *Ethics* does not support this impression. On the basis of common experience and the testimony of the Scriptures, Abelard presupposes that some actions are required or permitted while others are prohibited. He acknowledges that people can know the standards that govern their conduct, and he recognizes that they "say or to do in speech or in deed what is not proper" (Luscombe, 67).[53] Therefore he is to be interpreted as asserting no more than his point required, namely, that strictly speaking sin occurs only when a person consents to something that violates conscience and involves contempt of God.

---

sonal justification, or sanctification, by God in the course of Christian life. In real life, this issue arises first in connection with baptism. It also occurs when a Christian loses communion with God (hence the question of sin in the sense noted above) and then wishes to recover it (hence the issue of reconciliation, or forgiveness).

[53] Abelard discussed such admittedly evil deeds as an accidental homicide, the deliberate killing of St. Stephen, and the crucifixion of Jesus. Luscombe, 57–67.

Abelard's Theology of Forgiveness

Abelard's understanding of a sinner's reconciliation presupposed the praxis of the Church at that time, particularly its requirement that the sinner should repent, confess, and make due satisfaction for sins committed. In saying how reconciliation occurred, Abelard remained consistent with his teaching on sin. Just as he had interpreted sin as an interior rebellion or disobedience toward God, so also he taught that interior repentance brings God's forgiveness and reconciliation. In his own words: "With this sigh and contrition of heart which we call true repentance sin does not remain, that is, the contempt of God or consent to evil, because the charity of God which inspires this sigh does not put up with fault. In this sigh we are instantly reconciled to God and we gain pardon for the preceding sin." As a result sinners are no longer liable to the eternal damnation that their contempt for God would have deserved (Luscombe, 89).[54]

Abelard was careful to stipulate that in order to be authentic, repentance had to meet certain standards. Above all, repentance was to be motivated by love of God and not by fear of God's just punishment for sins. He writes: "Now, repentance is properly called the sorrow of the mind over what it has done wrong, when, namely, someone is ashamed at having gone too far in something. However, this repentance at one time happens out of love of God and is fruitful, at another time because of some penalty with which we do not want to be burdened; such is that repentance of the damned" who "hate equity rather than iniquity" (Luscombe, 77, 79; see also 77–89).[55] Abelard insisted that true repentance involves a readiness to make due restitution for the damage caused by one's sin. Quoting St. Augustine, he notes: "If something which belongs to another is not returned when it can be returned, repentance is not done but is feigned" (79–81).[56] Authentic con-

---

[54] The reference to "the charity of God," the use of the term "reconciliation," and the stipulation that pardon cancels the penalty of damnation show that Abelard is primarily concerned with mortal sin.

[55] The principle that bases fruitful repentance on love of God also supplies the reason that sinners cannot be forgiven of some mortal sins until they repent of all of them. Because contempt for God and love of God are mutually exclusive, a sinner either remains entirely sinful due to the persistence of contempt or is possessed by God's love, which excludes all contempt and hence forgives all sins. See Luscombe, 91–3.

[56] The quotation is from Augustine's Epistle 153, 6:20. The strict requirement of restitution had direct application to sins of theft but implicitly covered all misdeeds, since they violated justice toward God or neighbor. It is obvious from Abelard's text that he had in mind many instances of avarice among contemporary clerics and laypeople. He also indicted incompetent, unworthy, indiscreet, or greedy confessors. See Luscombe, 105–11; 80, n. 1.

trition also includes the resolution to make one's confession to a priest in accordance with Church praxis and perform the penance he enjoins.[57]

Once he established that forgiveness occurs at the moment of true repentance, Abelard had to address the requirements of satisfaction and confession and show how they contribute to the overall goals of reconciliation and forgiveness. Satisfaction is required in order to set aright the scales of justice, which the sinner had upset through sin. Because God's pardon cancels only the eternal punishment due for mortal sin, the remaining penalties need to be satisfied, either in this life—through such things as prayer, fasting, vigils, physical deprivations, or almsgiving—or later in purgatory (Luscombe, 89, 109).[58] With respect to confession, Abelard defended its necessity in light of the exhortation found in Jas 5:16. It brings the help of another's prayer and calls for a humility that contributes much toward a sinner's debt of satisfaction. Confession to a priest is even better, since he can impose the required satisfactions, and deference to his judgment can help to correct any residual tendency to contempt for God (Luscombe, 99–101).

Finally, Abelard considered the value of the absolution pronounced by a priest. Here Abelard was as much influenced by the incompetence, favoritism, and vindictiveness of some bishops as he was by the inner logic of his overall approach. In his mind it was impossible to suppose that God was bound to endorse the official malfeasance of human confessors and ignore what was just and equitable. Therefore he taught that the Lord gave the power to forgive and retain sins only to the apostles themselves. It was not conferred on all bishops without distinction "but only on these who imitate Peter not in the sublimity of his chair but in the dignity of his merits" and who thus give the true and just judgments that heaven can accept (Luscombe, 119; see also

---

[57] Poschmann, *Penance and the Anointing of the Sick*, 159.

[58] The reference to purgatory underlines the objectivity of the debt that must be satisfied. Abelard noted that confessors who rashly commute penances do no favor to their penitents, since the satisfactions they owe but do not settle in this life will await them after death. In referring to penalties, Abelard envisioned both the debt of justice or equity created by sinful deeds and the sinner's obligation to submit to God's just punishment for having shown contempt for God.

To distinguish them from eternal punishment, the term "temporal punishment due to sin" is used to refer to the penalties that remain even after mortal sin has been forgiven. Abelard's writing discloses the reasoning behind the concept of "temporal punishment" and shows that it was conceived in objective terms and not as an arbitrary infliction. It also accounted for the Church's requirement of satisfaction even though the penitent had already been forgiven. See Poschmann, *Penance and the Anointing of the Sick*, 158.

113–27). Because of the objective claims of divine justice, Abelard held that universal authority to forgive and retain was strictly limited to a bishop's power to inflict or remove excommunications in accordance with the Church's canons (123–5).[59]

Abelard's Influence on Later Writers

Although it faithfully reflected St. Augustine's own priorities,[60] relocating the drama of sin and conversion to an internal arena entailed major theological and pastoral repercussions. Well aware that many of Abelard's positions diverged from the prevailing consensus, Bernard of Clairveaux and other key theologians judged a number of Abelard's teachings to be heretical and his basic approach unacceptable, and they called for his condemnation.[61] In 1140 their theological objections and personal antagonism caused the Council of Sens to condemn a series of statements that had been attributed to Abelard. However, on account of problems rooted in terminology[62] and the polemical atmosphere, these adverse judgments only partially reflected the views Abelard actually held.[63]

---

[59] For other treatments of Abelard's doctrine of sin and penance, see, for example, Poschmann, *Penance and the Anointing of the Sick*, 158–60; Williams, *Moral Philosophy of Peter Abelard*, 125–50; Richard E. Weingart, "Peter Abelard's Contribution to Medieval Sacramentology," *RTAM* 34 (1967) 173–7.

[60] Note, for example, Augustine's teaching that sin "is the will to retain and follow after what justice forbids, and from which it is free to abstain." See *DDuaAn*, 11; Luscombe, xxxiii–xxxv; and 14, n. 1. Abelard also recalled Augustine's teaching that all commandments essentially require charity and all prohibitions basically forbid cupidity, which implies that interior acts and not external deeds are more important (Luscombe, 25–7).

[61] See, for example, Bernard's letter to Pope Innocent II, in Peters, *Heresy and Authority*, 87–90.

[62] Abelard used terms with a greater precision than had been customary. While he agreed that the term "sin" might be predicated of behavior, he denied that actions could be sinful in the strict sense, since that can only be true of persons (see Luscombe, 57–67, also xxxiv). He also distinguished consent from will and concupiscence. The personal guilt *(culpa)* that results from having sinned was no longer confused with the penalty *(poena)*, that is, the debt a sinner owes in light of the injustice that sin involves and that remains even after guilt has been removed through forgiveness. Such distinctions ultimately helped to clarify the substantive issues. But in the short term they left Abelard more vulnerable to misunderstanding by others, especially when they were not well disposed to begin with.

[63] Among the propositions condemned were the following: Christ's executioners had not sinned and ignorance excuses from guilt; the power to absolve is not held by all successors of the apostles; and deeds, will, concupiscence, and pleasure are not sinful. See DS, 721–39; also Grane, *Peter Abelard*, 106–49; D. E. Luscombe, *The School of Peter Abelard: The Influence of Abelard's Thought in the Early Scholastic Period*

These adverse reactions notwithstanding, Abelard had raised issues and arguments that could not be ignored. Once Abelard had made his case that sin and forgiveness depend upon the interior acts of consent, disobedience, and repentance, theologians were required to revisit the questions of good and evil and their impact on persons and actions.[64] After considering this matter, most theologians acknowledged that Abelard had been correct in giving priority to persons and their interior acts. They agreed that contrition brought God's forgiveness to a sinner. With certain reservations they likewise accepted the corollary that actions are morally indifferent.[65]

That new consensus in favor of Abelard's contritionism came at the price of new theological problems, particularly concerning the value of absolution. For if God had already forgiven a sinner at the time of contrition, what then was the purpose of absolution? Some, including Peter Lombard, tried to solve the problem by teaching that, with respect to forgiveness, absolution has no more than a declarative value; that is, it merely publishes the fact that God had already forgiven the penitent. That answer was problematic because it deprived absolution of real effects. Others, especially theologians belonging to the school of St. Victor in Paris, held that absolution exercises a real causal influence over the forgiveness of sin or at least cancels the debt of eternal punishment. These views may have attributed more power to absolution, but it was difficult to see how they were consistent with God's grant of forgiveness at the time of repentance. This difficult problem needed more time for a satisfactory resolution.[66]

Advances in Sacramental Theology

While conducting this discussion, theologians had also begun to wrestle with the issue of sacraments, and particularly the problems involved in stipulating which of the Church's rituals qualified as

---

(Cambridge: Cambridge University Press, 1969) 103–42; Poschmann, *Penance and the Anointing of the Sick*, 159. The underlying conflict of methodology will be considered in the following chapter.

[64] Grane, *Peter Abelard*, 104–5.

[65] While convinced that this was correct in principle, Peter Lombard and others also held that certain actions were always evil. In this he could also claim the support of St. Augustine, who wrote, "Sin is any deed, word, or desire that is contrary to the eternal law." See Luscombe, xxxvi, 46–7, n. 1; idem, *School of Peter Abelard*, 276–7.

[66] See Lombard's *Liber quatuor sententiarum*, IV, Dist. XXVIII, Part I; Anciaux, *Théologie du sacrement de pénitence*, 322–35; Poschmann, *Penance and the Anointing of the Sick*, 160–2; Gy, "Les bases de la pénitence moderne," 66–7; Luscombe, *School of Peter Abelard*, 195–6, 278–9; Payen, "La pénitence," 406–7.

sacramental. Because he presupposed that the virtue of charity is essential to a person's communion with God, Abelard assumed that the process of forgiveness depended upon God's gift of charity to the penitent, and therefore he did not consider it to be formally sacramental.[67] However, in the following decades theologians revisited the notion of sacrament and pursued its applications. One result was evident in the *Liber quatuor sententiarum,* or *Sentences,* which Peter Lombard published around the year 1159. In that extremely influential book Lombard recognized seven sacraments instituted by Christ and counted penance among them, views that soon commanded general acceptance in the Church.[68]

Attributing sacramental value to penance brought the issue of grace into much higher relief and helped to refocus the theological discussion. It became clear that the fundamental question was the relationship of grace to contrition and to the movement of charity in a repentant sinner. Theologians also saw a need to attribute greater importance to the Church's role in the justification of a baptized sinner. Even though it would take more time for these results to occur, recognizing the sacramental quality of penance promoted a more satisfactory discussion of the relationship between contrition and absolution and facilitated efforts to work out comprehensive theological understandings of penance.[69]

The Evolution of Pastoral Praxis

Once it was endorsed by theological consensus, Abelard's contritionism had a significant impact on pastoral praxis. To begin with, if interior

---

[67] Anciaux, *Théologie du sacrement de pénitence,* 66; D. E. Luscombe, "The *Ethics* of Abelard: Some Further Considerations," *Peter Abelard: Proceedings of the International Conference, Louvain, May 10–12, 1971,* ed. E. M. Buytaert (Leuven: University Press; The Hague: Martinus Nijhof, 1974) 79, 82; see also Payen, "La pénitence," 407–8.

[68] Lombard's work became the "sole and universal" textbook for the study of theology and maintained that status until the Reformation. Knowles, *Middle Ages,* 236–7.

For Lombard's teaching on sacraments and on penance in particular, see the *Sentences,* IV, Dist. I, Part I; Dist. II, 1; and Dists. XIV–XXII. An English translation is given in Elizabeth Frances Rogers, *Peter Lombard and the Sacramental System* (Merrick, N.Y.: Richwood Publishing Co., 1976).

For more on the process whereby theologians worked out their understanding of "sacrament" and determined which rituals would count as such, see, for example, Knowles, *Middle Ages,* 240–1; Pelikan, 3:204-14; E. Amann and A. Michel, "Pénitence - sacrement," *DTC,* 12/1:944-7.

[69] Poschmann, *Penance and the Anointing of the Sick,* 162–7; Gy, "Les bases de la pénitence moderne," 67–8.

repentance was the essential human component in the drama of forgiveness, then theologians had to ask whether the inherited system of penance had attributed too much importance to the actions associated with sin and forgiveness.[70] Furthermore, by emphasizing sin as contempt for God or a rebellion against God's known will, Abelard highlighted the personal and religious dimensions of sin and allowed its malice to be more easily grasped. Abelard's recognition of conscience's pivotal role also favored attention to the circumstances in which a sin has occurred and a more objective estimation of personal culpability. This strongly influenced the future development of penance.[71]

By accenting the personal and interior aspects of sin and forgiveness, these theological currents helped people realize that their sinful deeds, no matter how grave they might have been, were less important than their respect for God and the quality of their repentance. And because the worst of sinners can repent, ordinary members of the Church were encouraged to believe that they too could have confidence in God's mercy. Moreover, since only those who despaired were beyond help, everyone else could expect to be embraced by the Church. Similarly, once confessors accepted that sin resided more in the will than in actions, they often found reasons to assign lighter penances than might otherwise have been the case. Such thinking helped to humanize the sacrament of penance and clear the way for its routine use.[72]

The Significance of These Developments

The theological consensus that the interior life of persons is decisive for their relationship with God constituted a major development in the

---

[70] Once it was accepted that sin is a matter of interior consent, people became less receptive to a penitential system that placed so much weight on actions. In other words, Abelard's approach marks the definitive end of tariff penance in the West. Payen, "La pénitence," 405; Gy, "Les bases de la pénitence moderne," 66.

[71] The following comment exemplifies Abelard's distinction between sin through actions on the one hand and sin through fault (*culpa,* which alone makes a person liable to eternal damnation), which entails a violation of one's conscience on the other: "And so we say that those who persecuted Christ or his disciples, who they thought should be persecuted, sinned in deed [*per operationem*], yet they would have sinned more gravely in fault [*per culpam*] if they had spared them against their own conscience." Luscombe, 66–7.

For a summary of Abelard's understanding of conscience, see Louis Janssens, *Freedom of Conscience and Religious Freedom* (New York: Alba House, 1965) 25–30. For the medieval discussion on conscience, see also M.-D. Chenu, *L'Éveil de la conscience dans la civilisation médiévale* (Montreal: Inst. d'Études Médiévales; Paris: Vrin, 1969); Timothy C. Potts, "Conscience," *CHLMP,* 687–704; Eric D'Arcy, *Conscience and Its Right to Freedom* (New York: Sheed & Ward, 1961) 20–47.

[72] Payen, "La pénitence," 405–6.

interpretation of grave sin and conversion among the baptized. In the circumstances of the High Middle Ages it was not possible for the Church to present itself as a community of salvation in contrast to a larger, sinful society. The system of tariff penance had tried to address the reality of sin, but that system had already lost pastoral effectiveness by the time Abelard exposed its theoretical weaknesses. In the context of the day, it was readily understandable that in elaborating a new theory of sin and forgiveness, theologians attributed greater importance to the individual person while maintaining the Church's own involvement in the sinner's reconciliation.[73]

This emphasis on a person's interior life, a milestone in the history of theology and pastoral care, brought undeniable benefits. The rituals inherited from the age of tariff penance, radically reinterpreted, became understandable to the people of a new age and more accessible to them. Emphasizing the decisive nature of one's relationship with God endowed personal life with more significance. At the same time, the conditions required for a morally significant act were brought out more clearly. These insights helped theologians and pastors to distinguish conscience from behavior and highlight the reciprocal relationship between the moral life of persons and their standing before God. As a result, theologians were better able to clarify the drama of sin and reconciliation, while pastors found new resources in their work of forming consciences, preaching to people in different walks of life, and making delicate judgments in the course of pastoral care. These were important contributions to the Church's traditions.

These advances came at a price. As has already been noted, contritionism precipitated difficult questions about the Church's ritual of penance, particularly the relationship between a sinner's contrition and the power of the keys. Attributing more importance to the interior acts of persons made it more difficult to sort out the relationships among conscience, behavior, and one's status as holy or sinful. The defense of personal conscience could sometimes seem to undermine behavioral requirements. On the other hand, to uphold norms of behavior could eclipse conscience or suggest that it is not decisive for a person's moral or religious life. Closely related questions concerned the assessment of one's standing before God. To what extent does one's status as holy or sinful depend upon behavior, as opposed to one's motives and intentions? These are some of the problems and questions that the twelfth century left for later generations to consider.

---

[73] See Poschmann, *Penance and the Anointing of the Sick,* 159–60.

THE FOURTH LATERAN COUNCIL'S PENITENTIAL PROGRAM

In response to the many problems and developments of its age, the Fourth Lateran Council of 1215 set forth regulations that had considerable effects on the life of society as well as the Church. Among its canons, the decree *Omnis utriusque sexus* is especially significant. By requiring annual confession and Communion of all members of the Church, that canon marked the end of one era in the Church and inaugurated a new chapter in the pastoral care of the Catholic people.

The Pastoral Situation

At the time of the council the pastoral situation reflected societal developments, inherited Church customs, and certain theological convictions. The practice of infant baptism reflects all of these factors. That custom was supported by parental concerns for the salvation of their children in view of the common teaching that a person has to be baptized in order to be saved.[74] However, the prevalence of infant baptism meant that virtually all members of the Church were baptized without having been instructed in the faith or having had a personal conversion to Christ. Although it was long standing, that situation remained anomalous. The deficit of understanding and commitment in the Church required a new response.

It is clear from contemporary evidence that the Catholic people were poorly instructed in their faith. To judge from legislation on this point, it appears that the basic syllabus of instruction included the Lord's Prayer, the Creed, and perhaps some basic points of morality. Yet as minimal as these expectations were, there were ample signs that many had not learned even that much, or if so, they did not grasp its meaning.[75] Widespread illiteracy, people's inability to understand the Latin of the liturgy, and the sad state of preaching compromised most attempts to improve this situation.

Although the data do not provide a clear picture, it appears that apart from monastic communities sacramental practice among adults was also rather poor. Most people received Holy Communion only three times a year, probably at Christmas, Easter, and Pentecost.[76] That

---

[74] Pierre-Marie Gy, *La Liturgie dans l'histoire* (Paris: Ed. St.-Paul and Ed. Cerf, 1990) 159.

[75] Ibid., 154–5. Some authorities did not think that personal comprehension was necessary. According to one view, the prayer was powerful in itself. Other opinions were that piety alone sufficed or even that understanding was a liability, since it sometimes led to error (154–8).

[76] Louis Braeckmans, *Confession et communion au moyen âge et au concile de Trente* (Gembloux: Duculot, 1971) 21.

seems to reflect canonical requirements, a great reverence for the Eucharist, and a corresponding fear of receiving Holy Communion unworthily. With respect to penance, Church councils had encouraged more frequent reception of this sacrament. Some bishops urged their people to confess their sins three times a year, possibly in order to prepare for the reception of Holy Communion on the stipulated feast days. Although most people seemed initially reluctant to respond to this exhortation, by the end of the eleventh century they were willing to go to sacramental confession much more often than before.[77]

Various motives might prompt a person to make use of sacramental penance. On strictly doctrinal grounds penance was obligatory only for those members of the Church who had lost the gift of grace or charity through grave sin. Those who remained faithful did not require penitential reconciliation. That discouraged attempts to require everyone to confess their sins. Nevertheless, penance was presented as a suitable remedy for venial sins, and that gave everyone a reason to use this sacrament, especially before going to Communion. In addition, doing so demonstrated that one adhered to the faith of the Catholic Church and not to heretical groups that rejected the ordained priesthood and the Church's system of liturgical worship.[78]

The Fourth Lateran Council

Pope Innocent III convoked the Fourth Lateran Council in order to address a wide range of problems and promote a reform of Church life.[79] Enacted on November 30, 1215, the council's decrees opened with a creed that declared the faith of the Church. Although that state-

---

[77] It is hard to say whether confession was presented as a prerequisite for Holy Communion at this time, but the evidence suggests that this was not usually the case. Nevertheless, it is likely that many people did in fact prepare for Holy Communion by going to confession. See Nicole Bériou, "Autour de Latran IV (1215): La naissance de la confession moderne et sa diffusion," *Pratiques de la confession* (Paris: Cerf, 1983) 77–8; Braeckmans, *Confession et communion*, 20–2; Payen, "La pénitence," 401–2, 408–13; Gy, "Les bases de la pénitence moderne," 73–4. For a recent study of the frequency of confession before the Fourth Lateran Council, see Alexander Murray, "Confession Before 1215," *TRHS* (London: Royal Historical Society, 1993) 51–81.

[78] Gy, "Les bases de la pénitence moderne," 72–3; Bériou, "Autour de Latran IV," 80; Payen, "La pénitence," 407–8.

[79] For a description of the work of the council see Knowles, *Middle Ages*, 219–20, and especially Carola Small, "The Fourth Lateran Council of 1215: A Turning Point in the History of Medieval Europe," *RST* 11, nos. 2 and 3 (May and September 1991) 66–78; Raymonde Foreville, *Latran I, II, III, et Latran IV* (Paris: Éditions de l'Orante, 1965) 227–74.

ment was in many respects traditional, it was formulated in opposition to the major heresies of the day. It asserted that membership in the Church is absolutely necessary for salvation; the Body and Blood of Christ is truly present in the eucharistic elements, but only after they are consecrated by a duly ordained priest; the baptism of children as well as adults, duly conferred by anyone at all, leads to salvation; and true repentance restores one who has fallen into grave sin.[80]

Well aware that clerical immorality and abuses fed the flames of dissent and heresy, Pope Innocent was anxious to have the council act against these problems and promote the mission of the Church. It enacted canons against simony, clerical incontinence, drunkenness, and other misbehavior that scandalized the faithful or damaged the ministry. Equally important, the council sought to have God's word effectively preached everywhere in the Church. It mandated bishops to appoint qualified priests to the task of preaching; the same priests were to hear the confessions of the people and generally do whatever was required for the good of souls. The council likewise ordered bishops to appoint and support qualified teachers who would serve as educators of the clergy. Because the care of souls is so important, bishops were solemnly warned to assure that their candidates for ordination were well prepared. They were to ordain only those who were competent to fulfill their ministerial responsibilities, especially when it concerned the priesthood.[81]

The Decree on Annual Confession and Communion

Although its other enactments are not to be underestimated, the council's canon on annual confession and Communion is especially important. It reads as follows:

> Every Christian of either sex, after attaining years of discretion, shall faithfully confess all his sins to his own priest at least once a year, and shall endeavor according to his ability to fulfill the penance enjoined him, reverently receiving the sacrament of the Eucharist at least at Easter, unless perchance, on the advice of his own priest, for some reasonable cause, he determines to abstain for a time from receiving it. Otherwise he shall both be withheld from entrance to the church while he lives and be deprived of Christian burial when he dies. Wherefore

---

[80] DS, 800–2; see also Tanner, 1:230-1. For further discussion of the council's profession of faith, see Foreville, *Latran*, 275–86.

[81] See Cann. 10, 11, 14, 15, 27, 63, and 66 (Tanner, 1:239-65; see also Foreville, *Latran*, 293–8).

this salutary enactment shall be frequently published in the churches lest anyone assume a veil of excuse in the blindness of ignorance.

But if anyone for a right reason wishes to confess his sins to a priest who is not his own, he shall first ask and obtain permission from his own priest, since otherwise the other priest cannot loose or bind him.

The priest, moreover, shall be discreet and cautious, so that in the manner of the skillful physician he may pour wine and oil upon the wounds of the injured, diligently searching out the circumstances both of the sinner and of the sin, that from these he may prudently understand what manner of advice he ought to offer him and what sort of remedy he ought to apply, employing various measures in order to heal the sick. Further, he is to give earnest heed that he does not in any wise betray the sinner by word or sign or in any other way; but if he needs more prudent advice he shall seek this cautiously without any divulging of the person, since we decree that he who shall presume to reveal a sin made known to him in the adjudication of penance, is not only to be deposed from the priestly office but also to be thrust into a strict monastery to do perpetual penance (Can. 21).[82]

The Significance of This Decree

The primary significance of this canon does not reside in its requirement of annual confession and Communion or its demand that priests maintain the secrecy of penitents' confessions. In laying down a specific standard of sacramental practice, the Lateran Council reflected only what was becoming customary and in fact demanded less than many local councils had done. Its insistence that priests must never betray a penitent continued a canonical tradition that had been developing for some centuries.[83] The real novelty and deeper significance of this canon is to be found elsewhere.

This decree is a milestone because it established a new criterion of good standing in the Catholic Church, an innovation of fundamental

---

[82] English text is from John T. McNeill, and Helena M. Gamer, trans., *Medieval Handbooks of Penance: A Translation of the Principal* Libri poenitentiales *and Selections from Related Documents* (New York: Octagon Books, 1965) 413–4. For the Latin see DS, 812–4, or Tanner, 1:245.

[83] The priest's obligation to keep strictly secret the sins of penitents was a necessary correlative of the private penitential system. People could not be expected to make use of private penance except on condition that what they revealed to the priest would never be made known to anyone else. Therefore canonical requirements of penitential secrecy developed hand in hand with private penance. On this aspect of penitential praxis up to the time of the Fourth Lateran Council, see Bertrand Kurtscheid, *A History of the Seal of Confession*, trans. F. A. Marks, ed. Arthur Preuss (St. Louis, Mo. and London: Herder, 1927) 1–118; see also Gy, "Les bases de la pénitence moderne," 75.

importance. The Scriptures and Catholic faith both understand that baptism brings membership in the Church and with it the responsibility to live the Christian life. Only grave sin or ecclesiastical excommunication compromises a baptized person's standing in the Church. Without impugning these basic realities, the Fourth Lateran Council added the requirements of annual confession and Communion. That it intended the fulfillment of these obligations to be a condition of good standing is clear from their universal application and the fact that they bound under the penalties of excommunication and denial of Christian burial.[84]

By instituting a general requirement of annual confession, the council canonized the system of private penance as it stood at the beginning of the thirteenth century, and this was another place where it plowed new ground. The significance of this step is not merely that the council endorsed a contemporary penitential ritual. Rather, with its solemn decision this general council recognized the practical demise of the ancient system of canonical penance and endowed private penance with unqualified legitimacy as the Church's ordinary way to forgive and reconcile its gravely sinful members.

The council's canon on annual confession and Communion served basic religious imperatives. By laying down a minimum standard of penitential practice, the council aimed to reinforce penance's primordial function of restoring grave sinners to communion with God and the Church and to promote its secondary goal of helping devout believers live their Christian life more fully. Implicit in its legislation is yet a third purpose, engaging uncommitted members of the Church and leading them to conversion. When this agendum is considered along with the other two, it is clear that, as a practical matter, the council was expecting sacramental penance to support a wide spectrum of efforts and activities in the Church.[85]

The council's penitential requirements had other pastoral implications. The occasion of confession would offer an opportunity for the priest to encourage and instruct each of the faithful concerning the requirements of Christian life. Furthermore, to require penance and

---

[84] Gy, *La Liturgie*, 159–60; Small, "Fourth Lateran Council," 71; Gy, "Les bases de la pénitence moderne," 68–9, 75–6. Although this requirement was principally intended to promote the quality of Catholic life, it probably had the secondary effect of exposing those who rejected the sacraments on doctrinal grounds. Bériou, "Autour de Latran IV," 80.

[85] Although this expectation had been inherited from earlier centuries, the council's action served to consolidate this approach in the Catholic Church and give it new authority. Gy, *La Liturgie*, 160; idem, "Les bases de la pénitence moderne," 68–9.

Communion as a normal part of Catholic life was to underscore the moral, religious, and ecclesial aspects of faith. It was also to assert the jurisdiction of the Church over all its members, whatever their station in society. In effect, the decree *Omnis utriusque sexus* inaugurated a new pastoral strategy in which sacramental practice was the linchpin and priestly authority the guiding force.[86]

The Aftermath of the Council

The decree *Omnis utriusque sexus* had profound and lasting effects in the Latin Church. It guided the work of local councils, which likewise required annual confession and Communion. The process of implementation and reenactment projected the council's decree into the life of local churches and kept it current even as time passed. Besides application, this canon also required careful interpretation, and that was a task that occupied theologians and canonists for many years. Their discussions eventually reached the conclusion that the canon strictly bound only those who were guilty of mortal sin.[87]

On the pastoral level, the first objective was to encourage people to fulfill the requirements of the canon and hopefully exceed its minimal expectations. That was principally accomplished by means of preaching, which was the only practical way to reach the people. At the same time, the canon presupposed that priests would be able to hear people's confessions in a correct and fruitful way. The ministries of preaching and hearing confessions demanded that priests should have the education necessary to fulfill them properly, and hence the preparation of the clergy was another area that felt the influence of the council. Although some of the secular clergy were well prepared as preachers and confessors, as a group the friars were best suited to fulfill these offices.[88]

The story of the implementation of the Fourth Lateran Council is largely that of the friars. They were men of their age, educated, dedicated, and free to serve where the need was greatest. Before long, these qualities persuaded the popes to grant them special privileges that entitled them to preach and hear confessions anywhere in the Church without the permission of the local bishop.[89] Their effectiveness in performing those critical ministries greatly advanced the pastoral goals of

---

[86] Payen, "La pénitence," 413–5; Gy, *La Liturgie*, 159–60.

[87] On this matter see Gy, "Les bases de la pénitence moderne," 77–8. For the current requirement, which explicitly presupposes the presence of mortal sin, see *CIC*, Can. 989.

[88] Payen, "La pénitence," 413, 419–20; Knowles, *Middle Ages*, 261.

[89] Knowles, *Middle Ages*, 349–50.

the council. In a passage that can aptly conclude this section, one author described postconciliar developments as follows: "The coming of the friars and the decrees of the Lateran council opened a new epoch in the pastoral life of the Church. The Lateran council gave to the clergy a programme and to the laity certain directions, which bishops and parish priests translated into a practical code, while the friars, who were soon also trained priests—indeed, the only priests trained to exercise their office—provided doctrinal and moral instruction from the pulpit, and moral and spiritual direction from the confessional."[90]

REFLECTIONS

The people of the High Middle Ages inherited a faith and praxis that were based upon the Scriptures, the Fathers and other ancient authorities, and the conviction that God's Spirit resided in the Church. Within the Church, a believer encountered a hierarchy principally composed of bishops and priests, a system of liturgical worship that had evolved over many centuries, and the imperatives of conversion and holiness of life, which were sharply focused by a legacy of monastic dedication. Although the worship and ministry of the Church aimed to promote Christian life in the baptized, many Catholics did not understand their faith or adequately respond to its requirements.

The High Middle Ages was a time of ferment and transformation. Popes and kings confronted each other over the distribution of authority in a Christian society, with dramatic effects then and for future generations. A general reawakening in European life increased people's self-confidence and encouraged them to be more assertive toward the world and in matters of religion. There was greater appreciation of individuals and human experiences, with repercussions on theology and praxis alike. Conditions in the cities impacted many more people and precipitated religious and moral crises that demanded a response. Throughout this period, sin and offensive behavior, particularly on the part of lay or clerical authorities, proved to be an especially powerful catalyst for radical change. Taken as a whole, this age demonstrates the power of faith to inspire profound transformations in society and the Church as well as within individual persons. It offers new evidence that societal developments strongly influence where people expect to find God, how they distinguish the

---

[90] Ibid., 263. The postconciliar era also included a strong impulse to organize and classify sins, virtues, and the like. It stimulated a new kind of literature, the "summas of confessors," which were intended to help priests in their ministry as confessors. This topic will be considered in chapter 8, below.

secular and sacred, and their understanding and response to the requirements of faith. As had been the case in earlier times, this era also gives evidence of the intimate and reciprocal relationship between faith and moral life.

In this historical context a greater sensitivity to the individual and to the person was to be expected. A by-product of success in a more confident age, the sustained attention to persons was also encouraged by the knowledge that God calls each one by name. Good preaching became even more important and demanded that preachers should know the religious needs of their people and address them in a fruitful way. People were more inclined to affirm the legitimacy of their religious instincts and assert themselves within the Church community. Esteem for persons fueled significant advances in lay spirituality, theology, and pastoral care. In this period, then, the person began to assume greater importance and to function more than before as a prism through which the dynamics and requirements of faith could be interpreted. Against this background, the range and novelty of high-medieval religious responses are more readily understood. As time passed, both the individual and the person tended to assume greater prominence in the thought and praxis of Western Christianity.

Inherent in this deepened awareness of the person was the affirmation that interior events can be decisive. This was implicit in the assumption that the believer has an immediate spiritual relationship with God, especially in the presence of God's word. It was explicit in Abelard's analysis of sin, forgiveness, and the inherited rituals of reconciliation. It was presupposed in the early medieval teaching that conscience determines a person's moral integrity and standing before God. Attributing a definitive function to conscience enhanced the dignity of persons and reinforced their claim to respect. The recognition that interior acts have a pivotal role in the religious and moral life of persons transformed the pastoral task and recast the questions that confronted theologians and canonists. Especially given its religious dimensions, scholars and pastors now had to take conscience into account whenever they considered personal salvation, the dynamics of Catholic worship, the strategies used in the pastoral ministry, and the nature and requirements of Christian moral life.

This period demonstrates that historical developments can radically affect the reception of religious traditions and lead people to challenge or revise elements of thought and practice that had been taken for granted. Experiences transformed people and disposed them to interpret and respond to the call of faith in new ways. If this era discloses the power of faith in human life, it also leaves no doubt that faith can be interpreted in different ways and entail very diverse responses. By the end of this period some devout people no longer believed that God worked through the Catholic Church or that its clergy and institutions were entitled to their respect. Others enacted their fidelity and service to God in the conviction that the Catholic Church was still the Bride of Christ and the community in which God was present, notwithstanding the deficiencies found in its leaders, structures, and policies. As part of their own response to God, faithful members of the Church crafted new strategies to address the serious pastoral and ecclesiastical problems of the age. In an era framed by the offensive lives of some clerics, social vitality, and increasing respect for individuals and persons, Christian believers divided over the religious legitimacy of the Catholic Church. Taken together, these diverse faith responses opened new and serious fissures in the bedrock of Western Christianity. Incompatible convictions about the Church reverberated in other areas of Christian life, especially those that concerned worship, ministry, sin, and forgiveness. With the passage of time these basic conflicts gained even greater power to polarize Christian believers and alter the course of Western history.

In reviewing these and related developments in the High Middle Ages, one can recognize the germination of many ideas, attitudes, and practices that are taken for granted today. In particular, the many divisions in Western Christianity, the dignity of persons, the sanctity of conscience, the separation of Church and state, and the place of penance and Communion in Catholic life can all be traced back to developments in the High Middle Ages. Although they could not know it, the people of that era set the first building blocks of the modern era. However, before pursuing its development any further, it is necessary to complete this study of the High Middle Ages by considering its momentous intellectual developments.

7

Faith and Reason
Reshape Western Thought

Besides transforming personal attitudes, politics, and religious practices, the Great Medieval Revival greatly stimulated European intellectual life. In an age that overflowed with energy and confidence, scholars reconsidered traditional ways of thinking and developed new sources and approaches. Dramatic advances in the arts, sciences, and ecclesiastical fields stand as monuments to the creative energies of the High Middle Ages. Reflection on faith was enriched by the resources of analytical logic and came to be pursued in the universities as well as the monasteries. Newly translated works of Aristotle and his commentators widened the horizons of Western thinkers and enabled them to organize and develop their fields in a more systematic way. Thirteenth-century scholars explored new ways of unfolding the meaning of faith for their contemporaries, set the foundations of theology and philosophy as distinct disciplines, and produced a body of literature that has helped to shape the intellectual and moral life of the West.[1]

The same developments that stimulated these advances also generated intellectual and institutional stresses. Even before the discovery of new texts the importance of analytical logic within the Christian tradition of scholarship had increased, focusing attention on the relationship

[1] See, for example, R. R. Bolgar, *The Classical Heritage and Its Beneficiaries* (Cambridge: Cambridge University Press, 1963) 130–40; David Knowles, *Evolution of Medieval Thought*, 2nd ed., ed. D. E. Luscombe and C. N. L. Brooke (London and New York: Longman, 1988) 72–6.

277

between faith and reason and leading some thinkers to pursue new intellectual approaches and others to insist on traditional ways. An influx of non-Christian texts compounded the problem. For once Western scholars recognized the quality of these sources and accepted much of their content, they had to address the discrepancies between them and Christian faith and reconsider the basic assumptions and overall framework of the learning enterprise itself. That led some to pursue more fully the rational dimensions of Christian faith and others to wonder if the pursuit of knowledge could be detached from its traditional foundations in faith and personal conversion. These contrasting responses threw the faith-reason problematic into very high relief.

This chapter accounts for key developments within Western scholarship between the tenth and thirteenth centuries, especially the wider application of analytical logic and the response to Aristotelian thought. The relationship of faith and reason was a perennial issue throughout this period.

The first section will attend to the monastic tradition of scholarship and the largely Augustinian assumptions on which it rested. The world view and intellectual work of the monks, important in their own right, is the point of departure for later developments during this period.

The renaissance of analytical logic will then be reviewed. St. Anselm of Canterbury's forthright acknowledgment that reason can serve faith is a milestone and contributed to an important intellectual evolution in Christian thought.

The following section reviews certain twelfth-century innovations, especially those of Peter Abelard. His use of logical analysis showed scholars how to take a more systematic approach to Christian sources but also seemed to suggest that rational analysis, not faith and love, was the suitable foundation for scholarship.

The reception of Aristotelian texts by Christian scholars in the new universities of Europe also requires attention. Aristotle's radically different approach, the power of his thought, and his wide interests required Christian scholars to reconsider their assumptions and decide how to integrate Aristotle and his commentators into their intellectual tradition.

No discussion of high medieval intellectual life can ignore Thomas Aquinas' contributions, which include his *Summa theologiae* with its treatment of the moral life. Although others also made major scholarly and pastoral contributions, Thomas warrants attention because he has had an influence that few others have equaled.

Shortly after Thomas died in 1274 a crisis at the University of Paris reached its climax. Because some professors continued to maintain objectionable positions even after a formal warning, the bishop of Paris decided to issue his famous condemnation of 1277. By excluding certain ways of resolving the faith-reason problematic as well as specific doctrinal positions, his act marked the end of a remarkable period in Western intellectual history and helped to guide its future development.

MONASTIC SCHOLARSHIP

Because the monks had custody of Western intellectual life at the dawn of the High Middle Ages, a study of medieval religious thought must begin in the monastery. This section will review the general state of education at that time, including its content and methodology, note the dominance of the Augustinian world view, and describe the monks' approach to scholarship.

Medieval Education

Education in the early Middle Ages reflected the poorer intellectual environment in which it was undertaken. The disruptive effects of invasions and a general weakening of European society had taken their toll. By the tenth and eleventh centuries the West's access to ancient resources of philosophy and higher learning in general was much diminished because few scholars had a reading knowledge of Greek. Even after the Carolingian Revival education involved little more than a weakened liberal arts curriculum, perhaps some legal or medical studies, and the tradition of commenting on sacred texts. One symptom of this decline was that many people remained illiterate for their entire lives. Nevertheless, monastic life required that monks should be educated, and ministerial responsibilities placed similar demands on clerics. As a result, early medieval intellectual life came to be centered in two Church institutions: the monasteries and the cathedral schools.[2]

---

[2] Michael Haren, *Medieval Thought: The Western Intellectual Tradition from Antiquity to the Thirteenth Century* (New York: St. Martin's Press, 1985) 69–72, 84–6; Jean Leclercq, *Love of Learning and the Desire for God: A Study of Monastic Culture*, trans. Catharine Misrahi (New York: Fordham University Press, 1961) 3–4, 237–41; Yves Congar, *A History of Theology*, trans. Hunter Guthrie (Garden City, N.Y.: Doubleday, 1968) 62–3; Knowles, *Evolution of Medieval Thought*, 76–9; David Knowles with Dimitri Obolensky, *The Middle Ages* (London: Darton, Longman & Todd; New York: Paulist Press, 1969) 246–7. The urban schools in parts of Italy are also to be noted.

For a discussion of some of the practical stimuli to learning in the monastery or cathedral, see R. W. Southern, *The Making of the Middle Ages* (London: Hutchinson University Library, 1953) 177–94.

These schools inherited their curriculum from the ancient Romans.[3] It was based upon the *trivium,* a trilogy composed of grammar, rhetoric, and dialectic. Grammar began with the basics of reading and writing and then taught the more advanced skills needed to understand an author. Building on sound grammatical foundations, rhetoric examined those elements of speech that limit or enhance its persuasiveness and emotional power. Dialectic dealt with the logical dimensions of human communication. It sought to account for the arguments that compelled the assent of reasonable people and to expose the fallacies that might wrongly induce that consent.[4]

The importance of the *trivium* went far beyond the technical skills it taught: reading, writing, the composition of a text, and the correct analysis and appreciation of an author's work. By developing an ability to understand and interpret human communication, the *trivium* helped to open up the literature of the past and allowed the student to explore all the things people write or speak about. Even more importantly it supplied the tools needed for a sustained and productive study of the Bible, the Fathers of the Church, and other sacred texts. The *trivium* established the foundation of all further education in the early and high medieval periods.[5]

Authoritative Texts

Throughout the early Middle Ages and for many centuries afterward education depended upon authoritative texts. Each subject was taught on the basis of classic or standard texts that were accepted as normative for that field. Both teacher and student deferred to the content and authority of these writings. The teacher's task was to expound the standard texts in a way that best helped students to learn. This exposition was not limited to mere paraphrase but included extended discussions of content, method, and other issues that the text raised. To strengthen this effort a teacher might also rely on commentaries that recognized experts had written. Because it was based on texts and authorities, this method of education was conservative. Because it required intelligent and informed commentary, including the

[3] See Haren, *Medieval Thought,* 69–72; for a detailed treatment of education in the West up to that time, see Bolgar, *Classical Heritage,* 13–58; 91–129

[4] Leclercq, *Love of Learning,* 22–3; Knowles, *Middle Ages,* 246. Composed of geometry, arithmetic, astronomy, and music, the *quadrivium* completed the study of the seven liberal arts. The *quadrivium* was often truncated or neglected in this period. See also David L. Wagner, ed., *The Seven Liberal Arts in the Middle Ages* (Bloomington: Indiana University Press, 1983).

[5] Leclercq, *Love of Learning,* 15–28; Congar, *History of Theology,* 61.

consideration of contemporary questions, it also had the capacity to accommodate pedagogical and substantive developments.

This approach was well suited to the teaching of the Scriptures and other sacred texts. As a divinely inspired text, the Bible was upheld as the supreme authority and given the greatest respect. Closely related to the Bible were the writings of the Church Fathers, especially those that were designed to help people hear and understand God's word more fully. Illuminated by these and other traditional sources, the Scriptures were expounded for the benefit of all who wished to study them. The careful and reverential attempt to open sacred texts in this way was not called "theology" but simply *sacra scriptura* (Sacred Scripture), *sacra doctrina* (sacred doctrine), or *sacra pagina* (sacred page).[6]

Sacra Pagina

The practice of *sacra pagina* was based upon the assumption that in the biblical texts, the writings of the Fathers, and other sacred sources, God had provided all that the Church community needed for its life and work. Early medieval scholars never supposed that they could add to these august texts and did not presume to cast doubt upon or contradict them. Theirs was to conserve, understand, and explain the sacred literature they had inherited in order that Christians might advance in faith, hope, and charity and come closer to God. Their attempts to understand and explain were guided by a further assumption, namely, that because God acts consistently in speaking to the Church, all authoritative Christian texts were ultimately harmonious. The principle of textual harmony governed the interpretation of sacred literature in the early Middle Ages. As was the case with the liberal arts, a teacher commenting upon the Scriptures might also address new questions and develop new insights into the sacred texts.[7]

The Augustinian World View

If subjects, texts, and methods formed the substance of medieval education, its basic horizon and ultimate goals reflected an overarching Augustinian world view. St. Augustine had formulated standard

---

[6] Congar, *History of Theology*, 50–2; G. R. Evans, *Old Arts and New Theology: The Beginnings of Theology as an Academic Discipline* (Oxford: Clarendon Press, 1980) 29. For a discussion of the meaning of *theologia* in the early Middle Ages, see idem, *Philosophy and Theology in the Middle Ages* (London and New York: Routledge, 1993) 10.

[7] Congar, *History of Theology*, 54–7; C H. Lohr, "The Medieval Interpretation of Aristotle," *CHLMP,* 80. *DCivDei,* XVIII, 40–4, shows how the principle of harmony

positions on many important questions of Christian doctrine, but he also taught later generations to interpret reality, recognize priorities in human life, and appreciate the decisive quality of interior decisions. This was one of his most significant contributions, and for many centuries it shaped the life, work, and educational efforts of the West, especially in the monasteries.

The Augustinian world view is nothing if not theocentric. It recognizes that God is the source of all that is and has created an ordered universe in which all things are good and each has its proper place. God is the judge of all persons and the goal or end toward which they are to move by virtue of their free and responsible decisions. These realities give rise to the basic dynamics of human life. God is the supreme being whose goodness and authority are to be acknowledged above all else. All things reflect God's creative activity and can help to manifest God to those who wish to know God. Human beings have come forth from God and are to return back to God. During the course of this *exitus-reditus* ("coming forth-returning back") process,[8] persons are to love God above all else and love created things only in a subordinate way. That places a high premium on free will and the decisions made in freedom.

In fact, original sin has disrupted human history and sown disorder in God's creation. The destructive effects of sin are found also within the human person, darkening the mind and perverting the will. Sin prompts people to embrace good things in a disordered way and to prefer self to God, pride to humility, cupidity to charity. God sent Jesus Christ to be a new way back to God; his grace heals human freedom and empowers it to choose rightly; his authority helps persons to know God and God's requirements. The grace and authority of Christ are to be found in the Scriptures and in the Catholic Church, which are never to be separated.

When it was brought to bear on the educational enterprise, the Augustinian world view directed attention to an interior realm. If they were to be fully successful, students and teachers needed to recognize

---

could be applied. See also John Marenbon, *Later Medieval Philosophy, (1150–1350): An Introduction* (London and New York: Routledge & Kegan Paul, 1987) 9–10; Beryl Smalley, *The Study of the Bible in the Middle Ages* (Oxford: Clarendon Press, 1983) xiv–xvii.

[8] Because it expresses the basic dynamics of creation, salvation, and eternal destiny, the *exitus-reditus* schema had been in use for centuries. Its strategic place in the thought of St. Augustine strongly recommended it to later writers. See, for example, *Conf*, XII, 28:38; XIII, 2:2; 4:5; also Peter Brown, *Augustine of Hippo* (Berkeley: University of California Press, 1969) 97–100; M.-D. Chenu, *Toward Understanding Saint Thomas*, trans. A.-M. Landry and D. Hughes (Chicago: Regnery, 1963) 304–13.

their vulnerability to sin, idle curiosity, and pride. They were to base themselves on faith in God and in Christ, bow in humility before the authority resident in the Scriptures and other sacred texts, and align all their efforts with the requirements of charity. In other words, scholarship rises on a moral foundation; it was to be the fruit of a free interior turning to God and nourished by reverence and prayer. Once those prerequisites were in order, one could explore all things and all texts and assign each its rightful place. The Augustinian outlook offered no grounds to view some things as secular and others as sacred; all things are God's good creation and are to be assessed and used in light of an ultimate criterion: the knowledge and love of God. Whatever promoted this end, even if it came from the religious, moral, and intellectual assets of pagan nations, was acceptable; whatever did not was to be left behind.[9]

Monastic Life

Monastic life is dedicated to the search for God. To that ultimate purpose all of a monk's efforts were directed, and from that goal they drew their meaning. Accordingly, all important elements of monastic life—the guidance of the abbot; the monastic community; obedience and other ascetic practices; the rhythm of liturgical worship; silence, work, and the prayerful reading of the Scriptures—all these were designed to help the monk to advance in Christian holiness. This goal governed scholarly work within the monastery, including the subjects studied, the approach used, and the specific purposes the monks sought to achieve. It accounts for the emphasis placed on the prayerful study and exegesis of God's scriptural word. The Bible was the daily companion of the monks, who were carefully taught how to read and understand it, and was also an essential component of their prayer. Fueled by a desire for unity with God, the contemplation of the

---

[9] Congar, *History of Theology*, 52–4, 61; Alasdair MacIntyre, *Three Rival Versions of Moral Enquiry: Encyclopedia, Genealogy, and Tradition* (Notre Dame, Ind: University of Notre Dame Press, 1990) 82–104; Haren, *Medieval Thought*, 84; Southern, *Making of the Middle Ages*, 164–5. The outlook of early medieval Christian scholars was strongly influenced by Augustine's *De doctrina Christiana*, which assessed pagan learning in light of its potential contribution to the knowledge of God and a life of charity; see especially II, 40: 60–1 and *Conf* VII, 9:15. See also Bernard McGinn, *The Foundations of Mysticism* (New York: Crossroad, 1991) 232–43, especially 232–4; Meyrick H. Carré, *Realists and Nominalists* (London: Oxford University Press, 1946) 1–31; Fernand van Steenberghen, *Aristotle in the West: The Origins of Latin Aristotelianism*, 2nd ed., trans. Leonard Johnston (Louvain: E. Nauwelaerts, 1970) 28–33; Evans, *Philosophy and Theology*, 24–6, 37–8.

Scriptures was meant to be an altogether personal experience that was to sustain an ever more profound interiorization of God's saving word and contribute to a more intense love and praise of God.[10]

The Monastic Intellectual Enterprise

The monastic intellectual enterprise can be understood in light of the educational system of the day, the prevailing Augustinian world view, and the monastery's overriding spiritual purposes. Above all, the monks saw learning as an essentially religious enterprise. It focused upon God's world and God's word and was to be sustained by humility and faith, a commitment to charity and personal purification, and the help of God's grace. Although it considered many topics, the goal of learning was wisdom and ultimately the apex of all knowledge, the knowledge of God.[11]

For the monks, learning was based upon experience. This reflected their conviction that all God's creation was good and might help to make God known. The experience of praying the Scriptures was essential to their effort to reflect upon the Scriptures. Habits of prayer account for their strong inclination to accent God's transcendence and mystery and to approach God and the sacred texts with humility and reverence. The biblical text as well as their own personal experiences led monastic writers to prefer the evocative grammar of images and symbols to the technical language of concepts and definitions. Given God's grace, the monks wished to inspire a prayerful love of God, which they saw as the best way to gain a knowledge of God.[12]

Monastic education was also oriented to texts. Supported by classic authors, it began with the *trivium*, especially grammatical studies, which established the foundation for further education, perhaps the

---

[10] Leclercq, *Love of Learning*, 87–184, especially 87–109. Such monastic founders as Jerome, Augustine, John Cassian, and Pope Gregory the Great had left no doubt that the Scriptures were to have a primary place in the life and prayer of monks.

[11] See *The Rule of St. Benedict*, Prologue, 4; *DCivDei*, IX, 20; XI, 2; see also Leclercq, *Love of Learning*, 3, 14–5, 24, 28–30, 239. Leclercq provides a full discussion of the cultural and intellectual sources of intellectual life in the monastery and emphasizes its spiritual purposes (13–184).

[12] See Jean Leclercq, "The Renewal of Theology," *Renaissance and Renewal in the Twelfth Century*, ed. Robert L. Benson and Giles Constable with Carol D. Lanham (Cambridge: Harvard University Press, 1982) 68–87; Marie-Dominique Chenu, *Nature, Man, and Society in the Twelfth Century: Essays on New Theological Perspectives in the Latin West*, ed. and trans. Jerome Taylor and Lester K. Little (Chicago and London: University of Chicago Press, 1968) 283, 305–7; Smalley, *Study of the Bible*, 1–82, especially 20–46; Jean Leclercq, "St. Bernard and the Christian Experience," *Worship* 41 (1967) 222–33; idem, *Love of Learning*, 233–86.

other subjects of the liberal arts. Knowledge of languages, the meaning of human speech, and other sciences that helped to clarify a text or its subject matter were necessary in order to carry out the work of *sacra scriptura*, which focused on the most important and authoritative of texts. Monastic scholars undertook the study of the Scriptures and other sacred texts in order to give praise to God and promote a prayerful love of God among the Christian people. Theirs was a service of faith that sought to transform the heart as well as to expand the mind of committed Christians, helping them find and love God more completely. Their work was a basic component of a larger spiritual vocation in which divine grace was primary and conversion to God in Christ essential.[13]

The Monks and the Moral Life

These aspects of life and learning shaped a characteristically monastic view of the moral life. They account for the monks' tendency to depreciate all human activities, intellectual and otherwise, that did not flow from faith or that distracted a person from the love of God and neighbor. Instead, they proposed that prayer, charity, and self-denial were essential to the well-ordered human life and upheld the contemplation of God and the service of one's neighbor as its goals. Their experience and Augustinian outlook led the monks to see the will as the principal determinant of human activity, including inquiry and scholarship, and an upright will prompted by God and directed to God as the foundation of Christian life. In sum, the early medieval monastic view of moral life was inspired by the Bible and patristic writings, energized by a radical commitment to God, characterized by ascetical practices, and oriented to the requirements of charity.[14]

LOGIC SERVES FAITH

The Augustinian dynamics and spiritual goals of monastic scholarship did not insulate it from contemporary intellectual and social currents. In the tenth and eleventh centuries a new interest in logic, or dialectic, gathered strength and began to exert an influence within the monastery. This section will account for the renaissance of logical studies and its impact on monastic writing, which become evident in the

---

[13] Leclercq, *Love of Learning*, 6–8, 282.

[14] For a study of monastic moral doctrine, see François Vandenbroucke, *La morale monastique du XIe au XVIe siècle: Pour l'histoire de la théologie morale* (Louvain: Editions Nauwelaerts; Lille: Librarie Giard, 1966); also Chenu, *Nature, Man, and Society*, 305–7.

work of St. Anselm of Canterbury. Anselm took logic into the service of faith and demonstrated that it could make the truths of faith more accessible to the people of his era. His integration of logic into monastic life and learning is the first in a series of developments that would eventually bring the traditional assumptions into question and encourage some scholars to adopt a radically different basis for their work.

The Rebirth of Logic

Although logic had been part of the *trivium,* scholars and teachers usually judged it to be of secondary importance. However, in the latter half of the tenth century the analytic aspects and potential of this ancient discipline began to be seen as a source of help in resolving long-standing problems in law, theology, and other fields. That stimulated interest in logic and accounts for its increasingly prominent place in the educational system of the day.[15]

The spark was struck by a monk named Gerbert of Aurillac (c. 940–1003), who died as Pope Sylvester II. From about 972 Gerbert was master of the cathedral school at Rheims, where he taught the liberal arts and gained wide renown as a teacher. Although Gerbert considered logic to be little more than a prerequisite for rhetorical studies, his skillful presentations opened the eyes of younger scholars to its potential. His influence also reflected the higher quality of his sources. Not content with the books customarily used, Gerbert worked from texts and translations that Boethius had prepared in the early sixth century.[16] These sources offered Western scholars a direct access to Aristotelian logic. By stimulating interest in logic and restoring contact

---

[15]Bolgar, *Classical Heritage,* 149–62; Knowles, *Evolution of Medieval Thought,* 85; idem, *Middle Ages,* 246–7.

[16]Concerned that Greek thought was slipping beyond the reach of the Latin-speaking West, Boethius (c. 480–524) decided to translate all the works of Plato and Aristotle into Latin. Although his project was cut short by his death, he was able to complete the translation of certain logical studies (the *Categories* and *De interpretatione* of Aristotle and Porphyry's *Isagoge,* or Introduction to Aristotle's *Categories,* which were collectively known as the *logica vetus,* or "old logic"), as well as various commentaries and works of his own, including *The Consolation of Philosophy.*

Boethius provided the medieval West with its first sustained exposure to Aristotelian thought (sometimes called the "first entry" of Aristotle), supported significant advances in logical studies, and prompted high medieval scholars to search for the other ancient texts that he had referenced.

See Haren, *Medieval Thought,* 59–69; Southern, *Making of the Middle Ages,* 171–3; Congar, *History of Theology,* 59–60; Evans, *Philosophy and Theology,* 22–3; Bernard G. Dod, "Aristoteles Latinus," CHLMP, 46, 53–4.

with one of the greatest of ancient Greek philosophers, Gerbert helped to set European thought on a new course.[17]

The Impact of Logic

This revival of interest in logic had an immediate effect on education. Especially in the eleventh century schools began to emphasize logical studies even as scholars continued to explore the impact of logic on a wide range of subjects. Competence in logic became expected in a teacher, and expert logicians readily attracted students. This new interest in logic was pursued primarily at the cathedral schools, while most of the monasteries maintained their traditional approach to education.[18]

It is doubtful that the new logic would have enjoyed such ascendancy if it did not help people to bring greater clarity and order to a world that seemed to be chaotic and disorganized. It offered a new set of intellectual resources with which to analyze things encountered in human experience. Applying the tool of logical analysis, people began to inventory the properties of a known reality and classify it according to rational criteria. They reconsidered the arguments used to support or defeat a position and the rules by which valid and invalid conclusions could be differentiated. In short, the new logic afforded another way of approaching reality and analyzing statements about it. Equally significant was its suggestion that the human mind was capable of greater things than many had assumed. Logic waxed strong on its promise to enhance human understanding, communication, and control. It set loose a powerful current of curiosity and inquiry.[19]

When the logic of analysis was applied to faith and thought about God, it received a decidedly mixed assessment. On the one hand, logic supplied many of the Church's apologetical needs. Experience had shown that arguments based on reason were particularly useful in discussions with non-Christians or when responding to those who defended erroneous doctrinal positions. Even in the absence of controversy faith has an inner inclination to reach for a better understanding of what it believes, and this rendered it receptive to the new logic of analysis. On the other hand, the objective grounds and coherent method of analytic logic could seem to invest it with authority even in matters of faith. When taken a step further, that could lead to the assumption that human reason did not need God's help in order to

[17] Haren, *Medieval Thought*, 86; Knowles, *Evolution of Medieval Thought*, 85–6; Southern, *Making of the Middle Ages*, 168–71.

[18] Haren, *Medieval Thought*, 86–7; Knowles, *Middle Ages*, 246–7.

[19] Southern, *Making of the Middle Ages*, 172–7; idem, *Medieval Humanism and Other Studies* (Oxford: Basil Blackwell, 1970) 12; Haren, *Medieval Thought*, 83–4.

understand God's nature or activity. At worst, the logic of rational analysis might displace the logic of faith and become the criterion of what was to be held in faith.[20] Even if matters did not go that far, an immoderate reliance on logical analysis might weaken the authority of the tradition and diminish the reverence people felt toward the things of God. Logical analysis brought the blessings of reason and the threat of rationalism to the community of faith.[21]

St. Anselm of Canterbury

Anselm was born in the year 1033 at Aosta in the northwestern portion of Italy. After a turbulent adolescence, during which he unsuccessfully tried to become a monk, Anselm left home and made his way to the monastery at Bec in Normandy, where he completed his education under the scholarly Lanfranc. After spending a number of years as a lay student and teacher his interest in the monastic life reawakened, and in 1060 he became a monk of the Bec community. Three years later he became the prior, and in 1078, the abbot of that monastery. During a monastic career that spanned more than thirty years, Anselm wrote many letters and most of his theological works. His life changed dramatically in 1093 when he succeeded Lanfranc as archbishop of Canterbury. Anselm's years of episcopal service were difficult ones, largely due to conflicts over lay investiture. He died on April 21, 1109.[22]

---

[20] One troubling example was supplied by Berengar of Tours (d. 1088). He appealed to dialectical methods to justify his denial of the Lord's real presence in the Eucharist. Because Berengar rested his case on rational and logical arguments, those who wished to rebut his teachings found that they needed to employ similar methods. This episode exposed the danger of dialectics and demonstrated its utility; it likewise helped Western scholars achieve a better integration of logic into their reflections. On this entire matter see, for example, Knowles, *Middle Ages,* 237–8, 247–8; Haren, *Medieval Thought,* 94–6; Bolgar, *Classical Heritage,* 154–7; Congar, *History of Theology,* 63–5; Evans, *Philosophy and Theology,* 97–108; Pelikan, 3:184-204, 256–7.

Many centuries earlier Augustine recognized that intellectual effort was necessary but insisted upon the limitations of the human mind, the risks that attend its use, and the inability of experience and reason to bring a person reliably to truth. Faith, humility, charity, and submission to God's authority offered a much surer foundation on which to base the pursuit of knowledge (see *Conf,* IV, 16:30-1; *DCivDei,* XI, 2; XII, 16; XXI, 3-9). By contrasting the dynamic or logic of faith with that of reason, Augustine helped to clarify what was involved in the encounter between Aristotle's and traditional Christian scholarship.

[21] Knowles, *Middle Ages,* 247; Pelikan, 3:255-67; Bolgar, *Classical Heritage,* 205–6; Haren, *Medieval Thought,* 84.

[22] See G. R. Evans, *Anselm* (Wilton, Conn.: Morehouse-Barlow; London: Geoffrey Chapman, 1989) 1–26; for a fuller treatment of Anselm's life and work, see R. W.

Anselm's Approach

Among his writings, the *Monologion* (Soliloquy) and its companion piece, the *Proslogion* (Address), offer a good introduction to Anselm's theological method. In the preface to the *Monologion* Anselm explicitly describes the approach he is to follow. In keeping with the request of certain brothers, he will meditate on several issues pertaining to God but depend exclusively on rational arguments to prove the conclusions he asserts.[23] Although in prescinding from scriptural and other canonical authorities Anselm departed from the customary approach, he insisted that the substance of his work remained entirely traditional. Perhaps anticipating some objections, he reassures his readers: "After frequently reexamining this treatise, I have not been able to find that I said in it anything inconsistent with the writings of the Catholic Fathers—especially with Blessed Augustine's writings" (*Mon*, 48–51).[24]

With his new approach Anselm sought to show the necessity of God's existence. He begins with the good things found in the world and argues that they gain their goodness from a source that is supremely good. In a similar way, lesser entities point to the existence of a highest and greatest being from which they derive their being. This "highest of all existing things" is called the "Supreme Good," the "Supreme Greatness," or the "Supreme Being" (*Mon*, 4:68-9). With the existence of God thus shown to be rationally necessary, Anselm then explains that the Supreme Being created the world out of nothing and continually sustains it. The rest of the work explores what can be rationally known about the Supreme Being's nature and existence.

In the *Proslogion*, which he wrote in 1077 or 1078, Anselm offers a simpler, more economical argument for the necessity of God's existence, his famous "ontological argument." It shares the same presuppositions as the *Monologion*, namely, that the existence of anything

---

Southern, *Saint Anselm: A Portrait in a Landscape* (Cambridge: University of Cambridge Press, 1990).

[23] Jasper Hopkins, *A New, Interpretive Translation of St. Anselm's Monologion and Proslogion* (Minneapolis: The Arthur J. Banning Press, 1987) 48–9. Anselm wrote the *Monologion* in 1077. He later described this work as "an example of meditating about the rational basis of faith." (*Proslogion*, Preface; ibid., 214–5).

Hopkins has provided a new translation of the *Monologion* and *Proslogion* together with the original Latin texts.

[24] In chapter 1 Anselm reiterates the utility of relying on reason but stipulates his willingness to defer to a "greater authority" in the tradition if any discrepancies should emerge (60–1).

Textual citations of the *Monologion* and *Proslogion* reference the pages in Hopkins, *New, Interpretive Translation of St. Anselm's Monologion and Proslogion*. Chapter references, if any, will appear to the left of the colon.

finite points to the necessary existence of a supreme or absolute proto-type from which the lesser example draws its being. On that basis Anselm argues that even when the fool says in his heart that there is no God, the idea of God as "something than which nothing greater can be thought" is necessarily present in the fool's mind. But if it is, then God must also exist in reality, for otherwise God could not even have a merely mental existence. "Something than which nothing greater can be thought" has to exist and cannot be thought not to exist (*Pros*, 2-3:224-9). As was the case with his earlier work, in the rest of the *Proslogion* Anselm explores what can be known of God's nature and attributes.[25]

Anselm's Presuppositions

In the *Proslogion* Anselm emphasizes that his work is one of faith: "For I do not seek to understand in order to believe, but I believe in order to understand. For I believe even this: that unless I believe, I shall not understand" (*Pros*, 1:224-5). One further evidence of his approach is that he initially called his work *Fides quaerens intellectum* (Faith Seeking Understanding) (*Pros*, Preface: 214–5). The importance of Anselm's faith suggests that his "proof" for God's existence was not principally meant to convince atheists but to reaffirm convictions that are already accepted in faith and to highlight their truth.[26]

Anselm's traditional orientation is also seen in the Augustinian and Neoplatonic world view of the *Monologion* and *Proslogion*. The arguments found in these books presuppose that all beings, including humans, originate from one spiritual source and point back to the source from which they take their being. In that context the ontological and similar arguments cogently assume that if lesser beings exist, then a supreme spiritual principle must also exist. Even if that reasoning is not generally accepted today, it is important to recognize the underlying Augustinian outlook that made it so appealing to Anselm and to his contemporaries.[27]

---

[25] For more on the *Monologion* and the *Proslogion*, see, for example, Frederick C. Copleston, *A History of Medieval Philosophy* (Notre Dame and London: University of Notre Dame Press, 1990) 72–9; Haren, *Medieval Thought*, 96–104; Evans, *Anselm*, 37–40, 49–55; G. R. Evans, *Anselm and Talking About God* (Oxford: Clarendon Press, 1978) 15–75; Stephen Gersh, "Anselm of Canterbury," *A History of Twelfth-Century Western Philosophy*, ed. Peter Dronke (Cambridge and New York: Cambridge University Press, 1988) 255–78; Southern, *Saint Anselm*, 113–37.

[26] Southern, *Medieval Humanism*, 13–4. Later tradition has accepted Anselm's expression "faith seeking understanding" as a classic description of theology.

[27] Southern, *Saint Anselm*, 71–87, especially 132–4; Gersh, "Anselm of Canterbury," 262–70; Evans, *Anselm*, 49–55.

The Necessity of the Incarnation

Shortly after he became archbishop of Canterbury, Anselm wrote another famous work, the *Cur Deus Homo* (Why God Became Man), in which he considered the incarnation of Jesus Christ and his work of redemption. In this work Anselm places the redemption in a context dominated by the requirements of justice. He frames the issue as follows: If God is just by his very being and cannot act other than in a just manner, and if human beings are guilty of sin and deserve to be condemned, how was it possible for God to save and not condemn them? Anselm must not only answer this question but also show that the demands of justice could only be met if the incarnation and redemption took place. In other words, these actions were necessary and not simply the fortuitous result of God's kindness.

The book opens with this question: "For what reason and on the basis of what necessity did God become a man and by His death restore life to the world (as we believe and confess), seeing that He could have accomplished this restoration either by means of some other person (whether angelic or human) or else by merely willing it?" (*CDH*, I, 1).[28] Although this question seeks an answer based upon rational necessity, Anselm presupposes the virtue of faith. He declares that people raised the issue "not in order to approach faith by way of reason, but in order to delight in the comprehension and contemplation of the doctrines which they believe, as well as in order to be ready, as best they can, always to give a satisfactory answer to everyone who asks of them a reason for the hope which is in us" (*CDH*, I, 1).

Anselm's book takes the form of a dialogue between Boso, a questioner, and Anselm, the respondent. His argument develops as follows: God created the human race in order that it might enjoy eternal salvation. But through original sin it refused the obedience to God that is required for salvation and became guilty. Because humanity could not satisfy the infinite offense of its sin, it had no hope of being saved. But in that case God's plan would be entirely frustrated, which is impossible. Therefore some redemption was required and could be carried out only by one who represented the guilty parties and was capable of making the infinite satisfaction that their offense required. Since this could only be done by a person who was at once divine and human, a God-Man was needed and therefore also the incarnation. Anselm concludes with a discussion of the power of Christ's death to save all repentant sinners and the greatness of God's mercy.

---

[28] Quotations are from Jasper Hopkins and Herbert Richardson, eds. and trans., *Anselm of Canterbury* (Toronto and New York: The Edwin Mellen Press, 1976) 49. Anselm completed this book in 1098 while exiled in Capua.

The *Cur Deus Homo* is a further example of Anselm's integration of analytical reasoning into the traditional approach based on faith and the first major contribution by a medieval writer to a typically Western theology of redemption. Anselm's satisfaction theory, with its accent on justice and necessity, established the starting point for later developments and a benchmark by which they could be understood and assessed.[29]

Anselm's Contribution

Standing squarely within the Augustinian-monastic tradition, St. Anselm drew many of his themes from monastic tradition: God as the source of all good in human life, the primacy of faith, the requirement that the human person should avoid sin at all costs and respond to God ever more wholeheartedly, the imperative of prayer in a person's life, and the need of deference to the Scriptures and other traditional authorities. The prominence of these motifs and the overall balance and integrity of his approach bear witness to Anselm's personal experience in the Benedictine monastery at Bec and his immersion in the monastic tradition of scholarship.[30]

Anselm's forthright embrace of dialectical modes of thought is equally pertinent to any assessment of his work. In a pastoral context, these new intellectual currents had begun to influence the way people thought and led them gradually to ask some basic questions about life and about faith.[31] Anselm's willingness to adopt the newer, more rational methods showed that he understood their concerns and wanted to address them effectively. Those methods also helped him to fulfill that pastoral agenda and meet the specific apologetical, evangelical,

---

[29] In addition to the *Cur Deus Homo*, see the summaries and discussions provided in Alister E. McGrath, *Iustitia Dei: A History of the Christian Doctrine of Justification* (Cambridge and New York: Cambridge University Press, 1986) 1:38-9, 55–60; William J. Courtenay, "Necessity and Freedom in Anselm's Conception of God," *Covenant and Causality in Medieval Thought: Studies in Philosophy, Theology, and Economic Practice* (London: Variorum Reprints, 1984); Haren, *Medieval Thought*, 102–3; Evans, *Anselm*, 71–3; idem, *Anselm and Talking About God*, 126–71; Southern, *Saint Anselm*, 197–227.

[30] Leclercq has characterized Anselm as follows: "As a spiritual father he was profoundly traditional in outlook; he was the typical Benedictine, devoted to the Rule and ever giving the first place to contemplation, harmonizing all the values inherited from the past. At the same time the gifts of God had made of him a thinker of great power, an exception, a Benedictine of genius." Jean Leclercq and others, *The Spirituality of the Middle Ages*, trans. The Benedictines of Holme Eden Abbey, Carlisle (London: Burns & Oates, 1968) 166, also 162–6; Southern, *Saint Anselm*, 69–71; James T. Gollnick, "The Monastic-Devotional Context of Anselm of Canterbury's Theology," *MS* 12 (1976) 239–48.

[31] Southern, *Medieval Humanism*, 10–2.

and catechetical goals that directed much of his writing. On an academic plane, the resources of analytic logic endowed Anselm's work with clarity, intellectual rigor, and a highly systematic quality. As the first major theologian to employ dialectics so effectively, he inaugurated an approach that later Scholastic theologians would accept and develop even further.[32]

In employing dialectical methods Anselm presupposed that faith and reason are inherently congruent. Within a traditional vision of Christian life, he enlisted reason to support the convictions of faith and highlighted faith's ability to increase understanding. That was his accomplishment. But from a historical perspective Anselm marks a point of departure. Later scholars embraced his logical methods and extended them much further. However, in employing these new methods some of them lost sight of the traditional assumptions that gave strength, power, and coherence to the works of Anselm and other monastic writers. That added to the centrifugal forces working against the Augustinian-monastic tradition and hastened the day when its assumptions no longer served as a common foundation of thought. If Anselm's underlying approach reflected tradition, his novel use of dialectical methods pointed to future developments. In due time these gave rise to a new set of assumptions that would one day come to dominate much of Western culture and thought.[33]

LOGIC ANALYZES THE SOURCES

The early decades of the twelfth century witnessed the beginning of several developments that moved scholars away from the tradition and assumptions underlying monastic scholarship and toward a very different approach. The figure who did the most to energize this process is Peter Abelard (1079–1142). By taking the initiative in several key areas, he developed tools that allowed more productive work to be

---

[32] For this reason Anselm is often cited as "the Father of Scholasticism." See, for example, Congar, *History of Theology*, 66; Leclercq, *Spirituality of the Middle Ages*, 166; or Gollnick, "Monastic-Devotional Context," 239.

The terms "Scholastic" or "Scholasticism" are somewhat ambiguous. In some cases they refer to the intellectual life of the High Middle Ages in general; in others they distinguish the intellectual work of the "schoolmen" in the towns or universities from that of the monks. According to Knowles, "Scholasticism" specifies a method that is aimed at "discovering and illustrating philosophical truth by means of a dialectic based on Aristotelian logic." Knowles, *Evolution of Medieval Thought*, 79; see also Leclercq, *Love of Learning*, 2–3. For more on the importance of dialectics to Scholasticism, see Chenu, *Toward Understanding Saint Thomas*, 58–69.

[33] Vandenbroucke, *La morale monastique*, 58–66; Evans, *Anselm*, 27–36.

done. His reflections on the problem of universals and his application of logical analysis to Christian texts were especially important.[34]

Institutional and Intellectual Background

In the heady new world of the twelfth century, logic gripped the imagination of scholars because it offered a prism with which to pierce the ambiguity that had enveloped many areas of life. Their wide-ranging curiosity was welcome in the cathedral schools and congenial to the life of the towns in which they were located. Students eagerly sought those who had a recognized competence in dialectics. The study and teaching of dialectics began to flourish in non-monastic settings, and cathedral schools grew in importance.[35]

The appearance of the "masters" was yet another sign of the transformation that occurred in the early twelfth century. The new academic rank of "master" publicly acknowledged the personal competence of a scholar and certified a person as an authoritative interpreter of the Sacred Scriptures. This approved status required a "license to teach" from Church authorities, who had overall responsibility for education. Because this rank involved criteria of competence and achievement, it helped to advance the state of the art in the various subjects. It contributed to the gradual emergence of a new approach to *sacra doctrina*, which is characterized by a logical analysis to the Scriptures and other texts and has distinct subject matter, practitioners, and criteria of judgment.[36]

A closely related phenomenon was the recovery between 1120 and mid-century of the rest of the Aristotelian logical works that Boethius had translated. These new sources, often referred to as the *logica nova*, or "new logic," offered further insights into words and language, the attributes proper to sound reasoning, and methods of logical proof. Scholars became less satisfied with the customary practice of commenting upon authoritative texts and began to identify and discuss the theoretical problems raised by their sources. Although this fostered a more speculative trend, in the twelfth century scholars continued to defer to the Scriptures and other traditional authorities.[37]

---

[34] Abelard's work on sin, forgiveness, and the role of consent in the moral act was also very important. This aspect of his thought was considered in chapter 6.

[35] Leif Grane, *Peter Abelard: Philosophy and Christianity in the Middle Ages*, trans. Frederick Crowley and Christine Crowley (New York: Harcourt, Brace & World, 1970) 21–3; Knowles, *Evolution of Medieval Thought*, 77–9; Haren, *Medieval Thought*, 87.

[36] Chenu, *Nature, Man, and Society*, 272–9; Lohr, "Medieval Interpretation of Aristotle," 82–4.

[37] Congar, *History of Theology*, 59–60; see also Dod, "Aristoteles Latinus," 46. For more on the methodological implications of the new approach to texts, see Chenu,

Abelard and the Question of Universals

The question of universals gave Abelard an opportunity to demonstrate his logical skills and build a reputation at the same time. Universals refer to the natures, essences, and attributes that different entities share in common, for example redness, roundness, animal, desk, church, state, humanity, and the like. The question concerns the source and status of such universals: on what grounds can one and the same universal be predicated of apparently distinct and different things? More particularly, it asks if categorizing things by genus and species reflects the way things are in reality, is merely the product of mental activity, or perhaps depends on foundations that are real and mental at the same time.[38] To be successful, a response has to account for universals in a way that accords with all relevant aspects of human knowledge and is free of internal inconsistency. The question of universals had been discussed by the ancient Greeks but emerged again in a controversy between two of Abelard's teachers. Abelard attacked both their positions and in the process set forth his own judgment.

The Inherited Approach

In the tradition of the pre-Socratic philosophers, Plato and Aristotle wrestled with the question of universals some four centuries before Christ. Plato (427–347 B.C.) proposed that universals reflect the knowledge of the immaterial Ideas, or Forms, that give rise to the particular

---

Nature, Man, and Society, 281–91. The *logica nova* included Aristotle's *Prior Analytics, Topics,* and *Sophistici Elenchi;* it was completed by James of Venice's translation of the *Posterior Analytics.*

[38] This ancient problem has fundamental and wide-ranging significance if only because any response to it influences or discloses a person's view of reality and knowledge.

According to Albert Keller, solutions to the problem of universals have fallen into four main groups: (1) extreme realism, which holds that universal concepts reflect a structure of reality that does not depend upon particular instances of the universal; (2) moderate realism, which says that universals are grounded in the concrete things that particularize them; (3) conceptualism, which identifies universals with mental concepts but denies that universals have any reality independent of the mind; and (4) nominalism, which denies that universals are to be identified with concepts and asserts that they have nothing more than a merely verbal or nominal status (Albert Keller, "Universals," *SM,* 6:325).

See also Ralph McInerny, *Boethius and Aquinas* (Washington: The Catholic University of America Press, 1990) 61–93; A. D. Woozley, "Universals," *EP,* 8:194-5, 199; Knowles, *Evolution of Medieval Thought,* 98–9; and other sources noted in this discussion.

things of experience. Aristotle (384–322 B.C.) agreed that universals really exist quite apart from the human mind but located them in the singular things that are encountered in the world. Although neither of these solutions won general acceptance, Plato's approach, especially as accommodated by the Neoplatonic thinkers Plotinus (c. 205–70) and Porphyry (233–c. 304), was found more congenial by Augustine and other early Christian authors. Although he did not explicitly consider the problem of universals, St. Augustine followed Plato in locating the source of knowledge and reality beyond the limits of sense experience. That is evident, for example, in his conviction that all things draw their being from a higher and ultimately spiritual principle; that a universal, immutable, and eternal order governs all things; and that learning sometimes involves the illumination or recognition of what is already known. Augustine's great authority encouraged most early medieval monastic thinkers to adopt similar presuppositions for their own reflections about human life and Christian faith.[39]

The Medieval Discussion of Universals

As it happened, a controversy about the doctrine of the Trinity made it necessary for scholars to reconsider the status of universals. Perhaps in reaction to the dominant approach, Roscelin of Compiègne (c. 1050–1125) asserted that reality primarily resides in the individual entities found in the world. He concluded that universals have no existence at all; they are merely words. Unfortunately, when he applied that theory to God, he was obliged to say that although they share one will and one power, each of the three persons of the Trinity enjoys its own proper existence. Having insisted upon the separate reality of the three divine Persons, Roscelin left himself no grounds on which to affirm the oneness of God. That exposed him to the charge of tritheism, the doctrine that there are three gods, a crude trinitarian error.

Taking the opposite tack, William of Champeaux (1070–1121) asserted that reality primarily belongs to the universal. Therefore the individual things of experience do not exist in their own right but draw their reality from the universals in which they participate. When he applied that presupposition to people, William was required to say that the reality of two persons is not original to them but comes from the essence they share in common, humanity. Critics objected that if the

[39] Carré, *Realists and Nominalists* 1–31, 36–8; Haren, *Medieval Thought*, 90–1; Knowles, *Evolution of Medieval Thought*, 100–1; Joseph Owens, "Faith, Ideas, Illumination, and Experience," *CHLMP*, 441–4; Woozley, "Universals," 195–9. For an example of Augustine's view of knowledge, see *Conf*, X, 10:17.

reality of two persons derives from a single human essence, then they are ultimately not two beings but one. However, to declare that two are one is a contradiction. That was only the beginning of William's problems. For if both Socrates and his donkey share an animal nature, then that nature would have to be rational and irrational at the same time, which is impossible. What is even worse, if God and creation exist, as all agreed they do, then according to his theory they draw their reality from a common substance. But to say that God and creation share the same substance is to fall into pantheism, an embarrassing position for any Christian thinker.[40]

Abelard constructed his own theory of universals in light of these controversies and Aristotle's classic position. He held that reality resides in the individual things of experience. However, over the course of time people notice that different things share important features. Despite their admitted differences, for example, individual human beings are alike because they all possess vegetative, animal, rational, and other aspects in common. The sifting of similarities from different beings reflects the process of abstraction; it yields the universals that appear in human thought and speech. Abelard related universals to this process. He held that they neither exist independently nor are they devoid of real foundation and meaning. He considered them to be words, but words that truly describe aspects of different things and signify the respective concepts that the universal terms reflect.[41]

The Significance of the Discussion

Abelard sought to occupy the middle ground between the sharply contrasting views that his teachers had defended. His work pointed out some of the difficulties that confront extreme solutions to the problem of universals and helped later discussions to become more productive. Abelard's more moderate approach seems to have foreshadowed the

[40] Although both Roscelin and William were Abelard's teachers, he was prominent among those who criticized their respective theories. In fact, while he was William's student, Abelard directed such withering criticism against his teacher's position that it destroyed his credibility and prompted him to abandon his teaching post. For more on the issues as they concern Roscelin and William, see Keller, "Universals," 325–6; Haren, *Medieval Thought*, 90–2; Pelikan, 3:264-7; Martin M. Tweedale, "Logic (i): From the Late Eleventh Century to the Time of Abelard," *History of Twelfth-Century Western Philosophy*, 213–6; D. E. Luscombe, "Peter Abelard," *History of Twelfth-Century Western Philosophy*, 288–92; Carré, *Realists and Nominalists*, 44–58; Knowles, *Evolution of Medieval Thought*, 101–3.

[41] Luscombe, "Peter Abelard," 287–92; Tweedale, "Logic," 216–21; Carré, *Realists and Nominalists*, 32–65; Haren, *Medieval Thought*, 92–3; Copleston, *History of Medieval Philosophy*, 81–3.

one that Thomas Aquinas would later take in working out his own response to this perennial question.[42]

By bringing these foundational issues into high relief, twelfth-century thinkers helped to assure that their successors would be more aware of the wide-ranging implications of any position they might adopt. This encouraged later scholars to address seemingly unrelated problems in a coherent way. The move toward systematic thinking was important in its own right but also had significant moral implications. Instead of discussing the moral life in a dispersed and fragmented way, as had been customary, later scholars would tend to treat it more coherently and as a part of a larger whole.[43]

The problem of universals offers an occasion to consider the extent to which reality is primarily spiritual or material, unified or multiple, and to inquire into the source and basis of human knowledge. The history of reflection on this problem can promote more coherent thinking and afford a helpful perspective from which to consider particular theories, systems, and positions, including those that address moral life, methodological issues in moral theology or ethics, and specific questions of human behavior.

Abelard's Application of Logical Analysis to Traditional Texts

As a believer, Abelard presupposed the authority of the Scriptures and the primacy of faith. However, he also assumed that it was better to understand what one believed than to live with a superficial or uncomprehending faith. As a scholar, he had concluded that the customary practice of commenting on Christian sources had reached its limits and could not be expected to shed much more light on the content of revelation. He complained that the traditional method favored a discussion of texts that often failed to promote insight into the subject at

---

[42] Jorge J. E. Gracia, "Cutting the Gordian Knot of Ontology: Thomas's Solution to the Problem of Universals," *Thomas Aquinas and His Legacy*, ed. David M. Gallagher (Washington: The Catholic University of America Press, 1994) 16–36; McInerny, *Boethius and Aquinas*, 82–93; Haren, *Medieval Thought*, 93–4; Woozley, "Universals," 198–9; Knowles, *Evolution of Medieval Thought*, 103–5; Carré, *Realists and Nominalists*, 66–100.

[43] In the early Middle Ages moral exhortations and imperatives were drawn from different sources and contexts, including the Scriptures; the writings of respected patristic authors; penitential norms; the requirements of monastic life, priestly ministry, or (somewhat later) various lay occupations; local laws and canons; and the expectations of the community. In addition, the authors studied in the *trivium* often aimed to develop moral virtues, and this was yet another source of direction for the moral life. On this last point see, for example, Philippe Delhaye, "L'Enseignement de la philosophie morale au XIIe siècle," *MS* 11 (1949) 77–99.

hand. As a dialectician, Abelard was convinced that by employing the resources of analytical logic he could do better. He resolved to bring dialectical methods to bear on Christian texts.[44]

He therefore fashioned a new method that relied upon analogies drawn from human reason to illuminate faith. Abelard expected that this approach would answer those who "asked for a human and philosophical basis [for faith], and preferred something they could understand to mere words. Talk alone was of no use, they said, if it was not accompanied by understanding. Nothing could be believed unless it was first understood, and it was ridiculous for some to preach to others on matters neither they nor their listeners could understand. Besides, the Lord Himself criticized the blind leading the blind."[45]

The Sic et Non

Although Abelard used his dialectical method in a number of works, it is most obvious in his *Sic et non* (yes and no). In that book Abelard presents 158 questions and assembles the answers that traditional authorities had given to them. Essential to the book's agenda is the obvious fact that the authorities seem to give contradictory answers to most of the questions.[46] After providing some principles of interpretation, Abelard leaves the reader to deal with the inconsistent sources. In taking this unusual approach, Abelard did not mean to imply that the authorities' differences were irreconcilable or deprived them of credibility. He intended awkward questions to stimulate curiosity and lead a reader to the truth. His book was meant to exercise the mind and promote the skillful use of the rational principles by which inconsistencies could be resolved and the underlying harmony revealed.[47]

---

[44] Grane, *Peter Abelard,* 42–4, 74–5, 86–7; Paul L. Williams, *The Moral Philosophy of Peter Abelard* (Lanham, Md.: University Press of America, 1980) 21, 53–5.

[45] From Abelard's autobiographical work, *Historia calamitatum suarum,* quoted in Grane, *Peter Abelard,* 74; see also 74–5.

[46] It was well known that Christian sources sometimes seemed to disagree, and this stimulated important advances in the interpretation of texts. Nevertheless, scholars still found it difficult to clarify or resolve all of these discrepancies. See Bolgar, *Classical Heritage,* 150–2; Smalley, *Study of the Bible,* 38–46.

[47] See Blanche B. Boyer and Richard McKeon, *Peter Abailard Sic et Non: A Critical Edition* (Chicago and London: University of Chicago Press, 1976–7); or the discussions provided in Haren, *Medieval Thought,* 108–9; Pelikan, 3:223-9; Congar, *History of Theology,* 72–4; or Copleston, *History of Medieval Philosophy,* 83. Part of the introduction to the *Sic et non* has been translated; see Brian Tierney, ed. and trans., "Peter Abelard: Yes and No," *Sources of Medieval History* (New York: Knopf, 1970) 139–42.

Assessments of Abelard's Method

Although the approach employed in the *Sic et non* probably reflected the work of canon lawyers who had begun to deal with conflicting canons, it represented an improvement in the treatment of sacred texts in general. Abelard demonstrated that his approach was better able to disclose the meaning of human statements and dispose of problems rooted in uncritical thought or speech. Using his methods, scholars were able to identify problems in their sources, deal with issues in a logically ordered way, and resolve them on the basis of rational criteria.

Nevertheless, Abelard had introduced momentous changes of premises and method. Anselm stood within the tradition when he declared that faith was a prerequisite for understanding. By asserting that "nothing could be believed unless it was first understood," Abelard reversed the sequence. This new principle implicitly withdrew the primacy from faith and associated experiences and assigned it to human reason and its powers of analysis. In fairness, it must be acknowledged that Abelard did not abandon the traditional assumptions. But once a new principle had been enunciated, it was only a matter of time before its implications were pursued.

Over the short term, scholars began to integrate Abelard's methods into the traditional approach. This was certainly reflected in two classic texts of the mid-twelfth century, Peter Lombard's *Sentences* and Gratian's *Decretum*, both of which address conflicting sources and seek to resolve the issues they raise. By the thirteenth century scholars had developed analytical methods even further, bringing forth the famous *quaestio* method, which offered a new framework in which to consider traditional texts and perform the work of *sacra doctrina*.[48] However, the more radical implications of Abelard's method were also developed. During the thirteenth century some scholars began to adopt knowledge, reason, and analysis as the starting point of their work and became less inclined to defer to sacred texts or accept the assumptions that undergirded the Augustinian-monastic approach. Over the long term, this line of development led to the establishment of new, more analytical foundations for Western thought.[49]

In the meanwhile, some of his contemporaries condemned Abelard and his methodology, none more vehemently than St. Bernard of

---

[48] For more on this development see Smalley, *Study of the Bible*, 66–82; Marenbon, *Later Medieval Philosophy*, 10–4, 27–34. One well-known text that employs the *quaestio* method is the *Summa theologiae* of Thomas Aquinas.

[49] Haren, *Medieval Thought*, 109; Congar, *History of Theology*, 72–8. For a brief discussion of Lombard's *Liber quatuor sententiarum* and Gratian's *Concordia discordantium canonum*, see Knowles, *Middle Ages*, 236–7.

Clairveaux (1090–1153). Part of his opposition can be attributed to the errors of doctrine that had been charged against Abelard's work. Bernard's difficulties were also rooted in the cultural dissonance a monk felt when confronted with a dialectical approach to theology. Above all, he was concerned with the assumptions that guided one's approach to sacred things. Responding to the challenge of rational inquiry, Bernard declares: "Why, you ask, did God do by the Blood (that is to say through the death of Christ) what he could do by the Word alone? Ask God himself. It is permitted to me to know that it was so, but why it was so I am not permitted to know." Bernard was convinced that scholars could only arrive at sound knowledge if they proceed with love, faith, and reverence as tradition had taught them to do. By adopting reason as his starting point, therefore, Abelard had already committed a basic error, one that reflected moral deficiency on his part and compromised his effort to learn.[50]

In dismissing a piety he thought was nurtured on ignorance or obscurantism, Abelard affirmed the value of understanding what is believed through faith. In condemning what he saw as intellectual arrogance that drained reverence and mystery from religion, Bernard insisted that love, penance, and prayer are essential to any attempt to know God. Although the polemical quality of their dispute might suggest otherwise, a solidly intellectual approach and one that springs from faith and love are not mutually exclusive. Both find support in the tradition, and both are needed if reflection on faith is to be balanced and fruitful. Abelard and Bernard should therefore not be set completely at odds. Each has contributed a needed insight and a helpful warning, and for that reason the Christian tradition is indebted to them both.[51]

ARISTOTLE AND CHRISTIAN SCHOLARSHIP

In the decades following Abelard's death in 1142 a series of undramatic activities took place. Some scholars worked to assimilate Abelard's methodological advances, while others found or translated previously

---

[50] Quoted text from Letter 190, *Treatise on the Errors of Abelard*, as given in Grane, *Peter Abelard*, 134; see also 106–49; Congar, *History of Theology*, 74–5; MacIntyre, *Three Rival Versions*, 91–3, 110–1.

[51] Scholastic and monastic approaches to theology have many similarities (see Leclercq, "Renewal of Theology"; idem, *Love of Learning*, 270, 277–81). In addition, G. R. Evans has noted that Bernard accepted dialectics in principle and only opposed its immoderate or destructive use. See her *The Mind of St. Bernard of Clairvaux* (Oxford: Clarendon Press, 1983) 141–73, especially 165–6. Without a solidly intellectual component, a mystical interpretation of Scripture is theologically useless

unexamined Greek, Islamic, and Jewish works. On another front, students and masters slowly fashioned the first universities. Shortly after the turn of the thirteenth century, Dominic and Francis founded their new mendicant orders. However unremarkable these activities may have seemed at first, they brought Latin scholars into touch with new texts and another approach to scholarship, created the institutional setting in which they were examined and assessed, and shaped the responses that eventually emerged. This section will follow these remarkable events up to the point where Aristotelian texts were formally adopted by the arts faculty and the friars achieved prominence in the theology faculty of the University of Paris.

The Beginning of the Universities

The remote origins of the first universities can be traced to the emergence of the masters as officially certified scholars and teachers. Their prominence made them the focal point of advanced educational activity and accounts for the increased academic importance of those places where a number of masters taught. Given the customs of the times, it was perhaps inevitable that in the cities where they were numerous students and masters formed guilds to protect their interests. Through their guilds, students and masters were able to establish rules designed to regulate many aspects of the educational enterprise and deal more effectively with Church and civil authorities. As this process of self-definition and institutionalization continued, the *universitas,* or aggregation of guilds, formalized its procedures more fully, accumulated considerable authority over its members, and gained additional exemptions from local jurisdiction, both civil and ecclesiastical. By the early years of the thirteenth century these developments had brought forth the first universities. They and similar institutions that were soon to be founded became the new centers of European intellectual life and the setting for the momentous events that were just over the horizon.[52]

(Congar, *History of Theology,* 75). Unless it is kept in touch with real problems, Scholastic method can become a purely formalistic exercise that contributes little to the Church (Chenu, *Toward Understanding Saint Thomas,* 62–3).

[52] Because the first universities (Bologna, Paris, and Oxford) resulted from unplanned and evolutionary processes, it is not possible to cite specific dates of their "foundation." Later universities can be specifically dated because they came into being by the act of a pope or other authority. See Brian Tierney and Sidney Painter, *Western Europe in the Middle Ages: 300–1475* (New York: Knopf, 1970) 330–6; Knowles, *Evolution of Medieval Thought,* 139–55; Haren, *Medieval Thought,* 137–41.

The Discovery of Non-Christian Intellectual Resources

While the first universities were taking shape, another development had been proceeding on a parallel track: the translation of important Greek, Arab, and Jewish texts. As has already been noted, Western scholars were becoming more strongly attracted to analytical logic, especially Aristotle's logical works. By the middle of the twelfth century they had learned that Aristotle had written many other books on a wide range of subjects. Curiosity about these writings fueled a serious effort to find and translate them into Latin.[53]

The entire Aristotelian corpus had been preserved in the Byzantine libraries of the eastern Mediterranean, where the Arabs found them after conquering that area. It was from Arab sources, principally in Spain, that the Europeans obtained the manuscripts they were seeking. Beginning in the twelfth century they gradually translated most of Aristotle's books into Latin. Although there were omissions and some of the early translations were flawed, most of Aristotle had been translated by the beginning of the thirteenth century. Even after that time scholars continued to bring out better and more complete translations of Aristotle's writings.

As they searched through Arab libraries, the Europeans found something they had not expected. Islamic and Jewish scholars[54] had studied Aristotle's works and considered their implications. Their reflections resulted in a large and impressive body of literature, which included commentaries on Aristotelian books. European scholars found these writings very helpful to their own effort to understand and respond to Aristotle and translated many of them as well.[55]

Challenges Latent in Aristotle's Thought

Once these newly discovered Aristotelian texts had become available in Latin translation, Western scholars began the slow process of familiarization.[56] Almost at once it became apparent that these writings

---

[53] Lohr, "Medieval Interpretation of Aristotle," 83.

[54] Most notable among them were Alkindi (d. after 870), Alfarabi (c. 873–950), Avicenna (980–1037), Avicebron (1021–70), Averroës (1126–98), and Moses Maimonides (1135–1204). See the sources in the following note for further discussion of their thought.

[55] On the translation of Aristotelian, Islamic, and Jewish works and their reception in Europe, see Dod, "Aristoteles Latinus," 46–53; van Steenberghen, *Aristotle in the West*, 61–6, 89–94; Tierney, *Western Europe in the Middle Ages*, 336–8; Haren, *Medieval Thought*, 118–37; Copleston, *History of Medieval Philosophy*, 104–49, 153–4.

[56] This last and greatest influx of Aristotelian works has been characterized as the "third entry" of Aristotle into Europe. Congar, *History of Theology*, 85–6.

were going to occasion some serious conflicts. The most obvious problem was that this prestigious ancient philosopher had taken positions that could not be reconciled with traditional Christian teachings. He held, for example, that the human soul is not immortal, which leaves no room for God's judgment of persons after their death. Other conflicts arose from the assertions that the cosmos is eternal and does not allow for divine providence, and that happiness is an entirely human achievement.[57] Although these discrepancies were disturbing, a more serious problem lay in Aristotle's understanding of reality and knowledge and in his view of the scholarly enterprise itself.

Aristotle presupposed that reality is fully accessible to the human mind and that, by analyzing sense experiences, the human mind can give a person knowledge of things that exist. Manifesting a deep and wide-ranging interest in the universe as well as human affairs, he sought to analyze how things are what they are and to say why they are what they are.[58] For Aristotle true knowledge was obtained when one did that correctly. These convictions were very different from those of the Augustinian-monastic tradition. The latter accepted that the human mind is weak and prone to error and that knowledge depends on divine illumination; the proper orientation of the will; and the virtues of faith, humility, and charity. Aristotle did not think of inquiry as an essentially religious enterprise that was to be prayerful and lead ultimately to knowledge of God. He would not have agreed that "without charity, knowledge inflates; that is, it exalts man to an arrogance which is nothing but a kind of windy emptiness" (*DCivDei*, IX, 20).

Aristotle's writings therefore offered Catholic Europe a new and discordant paradigm of reality and knowledge. It entailed a cogent conception of nature, including its human aspects, and provided an appealing framework for inquiry and reflection on a wide variety of subjects. However, this same paradigm seemed to marginalize Christian commitment, encourage a world view that owed nothing to the Christian tradition, and threaten the consensus that had sustained the Augustinian-monastic world view and its concept of scholarship. Moreover, Augustinian and Aristotelian traditions of scholarship entailed comprehensive but mutually exclusive world views, each with its own understanding of knowledge and criteria of assessment. For that reason the adherents of each tradition tended to assume that theirs

---

[57] Georg Wieland, "Happiness: The Perfection of Man," *CHLMP*, 673–7; Marenbon, *Later Medieval Philosophy*, 67–72; Haren, *Medieval Thought*, 145–7.

[58] This was done by delineating a thing's formal, material, efficient, and final causes. See discussion in chapter 9, p. 385, below.

offered the best means to structure the scholarly endeavor and to arrive at true knowledge of reality. These convictions exacerbated institutional stresses and made compromise or arbitration very difficult.
Thirteenth-century scholars therefore needed to understand the newly
recovered sources, clarify what was at stake for the Christian tradition
and for scholarship generally, and work out their responses. It would
take many decades to accomplish those tasks.[59]

The Reception of Aristotelian Works in the Arts Faculty

The consideration of Aristotelian thought took place in the new
European universities, toward which the newly translated books naturally flowed. Especially at the University of Paris the masters in the
liberal arts faculty received them with great interest and soon began to
expound them in their classes. Theologians objected to the way their
colleagues were dealing with Aristotelian texts and demanded that
they leave all subjects that touched upon faith in their own more capable hands. In 1210 this dispute prompted a local Church council to
forbid the University of Paris arts faculty to teach publicly those portions of the Aristotelian corpus that concerned "natural philosophy."
This early conflict disclosed the arts faculty's interest in these new
sources, the judgment by theologians that Aristotelian works contain
errors concerning faith, and the concern of ecclesiastical authorities
with this dispute.[60]

As the thirteenth century unfolded, Church authorities intervened
on a number of other occasions to warn of the dangers inherent in
Aristotelian texts and to place modest limits on their use. However, by
about 1240 almost everyone was satisfied that Aristotelian writings
were too important to ignore and did not deserve to be condemned.
Theologians had come to realize that Aristotelian thought offered
valuable intellectual resources that could help them set forth Catholic
faith in a more lucid, systematic way. The arts masters found themselves powerfully attracted to the approach Aristotle had used. In that
more tolerant environment theologians and arts masters alike pressed
ahead in their effort to sort out the implications of Aristotelian thought.

The results were especially dramatic in the arts faculty. Under the
influence of Aristotle some of the masters began to see themselves less

---

[59] MacIntyre, *Three Rival Versions,* 105–13; Lohr, "Medieval Interpretation of Aristotle," 83–4, 91; van Steenberghen, *Aristotle in the West,* 10–2, 15–6; see also Haren,
Medieval Thought, 146–7.

[60] van Steenberghen, *Aristotle in the West,* 66–77; Dod, "Aristoteles Latinus," 70–1;
Evans, *Philosophy and Theology,* 18–9.

as guardians of inherited truth and more as inquirers who searched for truth. Rather than defer to sacred texts as theologians did and to assume that these sources contained hidden truths to be unveiled, they preferred to treat no text as sacrosanct and to subject all of them to rational analysis. These scholars considered that whatever could be experienced by the senses, texts, and indeed the entire world was a fit object of analysis quite apart from God or creation. Knowledge arose from sense experience and was achieved by the analytical powers of reason.

Even though most of the arts professors still accepted the traditional subordination of arts to *sacra doctrina*, they had become convinced that Aristotelian texts were authoritative sources and entitled to official recognition. Therefore on March 19, 1255, the University of Paris arts faculty formally ruled that the Aristotelian corpus would be required reading for anyone who wished to qualify as a master of arts. That landmark decision, which passed without opposition from theologians and bishops, marked the acceptance of Aristotelian texts as a basis of instruction at the University of Paris. At the same time, it represented the establishment of another framework for knowledge, reflection, and scholarship, one that did not require faith in God and creation or deference to sacred sources. That framework supported a new approach to scholarly inquiry and eventually yielded philosophy in the modern sense of the term, a discipline whose premises and methods distinguish it from theology. In the meantime, it had become clear that the Augustinian-monastic world view would never again exercise an unchallenged claim to the allegiance of Western scholars.[61]

The reception of Aristotle by the University of Paris arts faculty and early ecclesiastical responses were only part of the larger story, which also included the response of the theologians at the same university, especially the friars who came to hold some of the chairs in the theology faculty.

The Friars' Entry into the University

At the very time Western scholars were beginning to reckon with Aristotelian thought, Dominic and Francis were laying the foundations of the new mendicant orders that would carry their names. To as-

---

[61] For more on these developments, see van Steenberghen, *Aristotle in the West*, 59–130, 162–7; Lohr, "Medieval Interpretation of Aristotle," 82–4, 87–91, 95–6; Haren, *Medieval Thought*, 84; Congar, *History of Theology*, 90; John F. Wippel, *Mediaeval Reactions to the Encounter Between Faith and Reason* (Milwaukee: Marquette University Press, 1995) 2–14.

sure that they were prepared to preach and carry out pastoral work effectively, Dominic insisted that his followers be well educated. Accordingly, he sent seven of his friars to the University of Paris in 1217. Two years later their number had grown to thirty, largely because of the faculty members and students who decided to join the Dominicans. Another important event occurred in 1229, when Roland of Cremona became the first Dominican master of theology. For his part, St. Francis had emphasized poverty and conversion rather than education, so when the first Franciscan friars arrived in Paris in 1219, their mission was not to study but to preach and offer the witness of apostolic poverty. That changed in 1236, when Master Alexander of Hales, who held a chair of theology at the University of Paris, took the Franciscan habit. He began a scholarly tradition within the Franciscan Order and did much to validate learning as an integral part of Franciscan life and ministry.[62]

From these auspicious beginnings the two orders of friars extended their influence at Paris and in other universities. Their increasing numbers and outstanding intellectual endowments enabled the Preachers and Minors to make impressive contributions to the intellectual life of the universities. In the theology faculties they worked from traditional Christian sources but also did much to develop an accurate understanding of Aristotle and his commentators. The theologians were well equipped to discuss critical issues with their colleagues in the arts faculty, whether those issues emerged from the non-Christian sources or from the responses of Christian scholars themselves. As they conducted these conversations, theologians also explored the impact of Aristotelian texts on *sacra doctrina* and the Christian people of their day. In all these activities the Franciscans and Dominicans carried on the Augustinian-monastic tradition, acknowledged the importance of non-Christian sources, and brought a pastoral awareness to their scholarship. Both orders produced outstanding theologians who contributed much to the intellectual debates and pastoral life of the thirteenth century and to the later Christian tradition.[63]

---

[62] James A. Weisheipl, *Friar Thomas D'Aquino: His Life, Thought, and Work* (Garden City, N.Y.: Doubleday, 1983) 23, 54–5, 57, 64–5. Weisheipl also details the succession of Dominican and Franciscan masters in the University of Paris theology faculty (65–6).

[63] Knowles, *Evolution of Medieval Thought*, 210–1; van Steenberghen, *Aristotle in the West*, 83–4. St. Albert the Great, under whom Thomas Aquinas studied in Cologne, had carefully studied Aristotelian texts and helped to assure that Thomas would have an unparalleled grasp of Aristotle's thought. Wippel, *Mediaeval Reactions*, 13; MacIntyre, *Three Rival Versions*, 115.

The Contribution of Thomas Aquinas

In their first century of existence the Franciscan and Dominican orders produced outstanding scholars, including Thomas Aquinas, who was among the most important and influential. He took a leading role in the intellectual debates at the University of Paris, forged a remarkable synthesis of Aristotelian and Christian thought, and in the process crafted a classic account of moral life. This section will consider his theological synthesis and his principal work, the *Summa theologiae*, giving special attention to its moral teachings.

An Overview of Thomas' Life

Thomas Aquinas was born at Roccasecca, a village north of Naples, in 1224 or 1225, and joined the Order of Preachers in Naples when he was about nineteen years of age. The following year he was sent to the University of Paris for his novitiate and further education, which he continued in Cologne under St. Albert the Great. Upon returning to Paris in 1252 Thomas began to teach the *Sentences* of Peter Lombard and in 1256 became a master in theology. During that time he wrote his *Scriptum super libros Sententiarum*, or glosses on the *Sentences*. Between 1259 and 1268 he served in Italy as preacher general of the Dominican Order and was placed in charge of the theological education of younger friars. In these years he wrote his *Sententia libri Ethicorum* (a commentary on the *Nicomachean Ethics* of Aristotle), completed the *Summa contra gentiles*, and began work on the *Summa theologiae*. In 1269 he returned to Paris to resume his position in the university. Three years later he was recalled to Naples, where he continued teaching and writing. He died at Fossanova on March 7, 1274, while traveling to the Council of Lyons.[64]

Thomas' Theological Synthesis

In constructing his theological system Thomas Aquinas presupposed the virtue of faith and the supreme authority of the Scriptures. He accepted the existence of a triune God and other Christian teach-

---

[64] For a fuller review of Thomas' life and works, see Ralph McInerny, *St. Thomas Aquinas* (Notre Dame and London: University of Notre Dame Press, 1982) 13–29; Chenu, *Toward Understanding Saint Thomas*; Weisheipl, *Friar Thomas D'Aquino*. This last source (355–405) gives an annotated list of Thomas' works. As was the case with other masters in theology, Thomas preached and offered expositions of *sacra pagina* as a normal part of his responsibilities. Chenu, *Toward Understanding Saint Thomas*, 233–63.

ings, notably the incarnation of Jesus Christ, his saving death and resurrection, the necessity of grace, and eternal happiness with God as the goal of human life. But from Aristotle Thomas had learned to respect the integrity proper to the things of the world. He acknowledged that each created being has its own nature and seeks its due completion or fulfillment. He agreed that knowledge about the world comes from a process of observation and abstraction from sense experiences and not by means of an inner illumination, as Augustine had held. Thomas believed that human reason was a reliable source of knowledge concerning the world and human experiences in it.

Thomas therefore assigned reality and knowledge to two distinct levels. The first pertained to God and God's revelation of things that concern human salvation. Many of these realities cannot be known without revelation and they cannot be attained without God's special empowerment. The other concerned the order of created nature and human capacities to know and understand it. On this natural level people are able to know and act on the strength of their own abilities without the assistance of grace or revelation. While this bi-level conception is quite reasonable in light of Thomas' presuppositions, it involves a basic problem: How are the natural and "supernatural" levels to be related? This question goes to the heart of Thomas' theology.

Essentially, Thomas held that the created universe has its own integrity, which God respects. That implies that between the created order and the one that is proper to God there is both continuity and discontinuity. The continuity flows from God's creation of all things, their reflection of God's purposes, and their inherent tendency to return to God as their ultimate end. The discontinuity emerges from the radical dissimilarity of Creator and creature. Even if sin had not intervened, created nature is inherently unable to attain a divine goal that stands outside and beyond it. Only if God freely endows created beings—primarily human persons with their reason and freedom—with special or supernatural powers can they successfully reach their appointed end, which is perfect fulfillment in God.

Thomas forged a new theological synthesis. Accepting that faith discloses the foundation and principal dynamics of human life, he drew upon the resources of Aristotelian thought to organize *sacra doctrina* in a systematic way and enrich it with new substance and strength. He explained obscure aspects of doctrine in light of points that were more clear or certain. He adopted natural human insights into life and how it is to be lived. The human condition, thus illuminated, he situated in a much wider horizon, in which God is known by faith to be the origin, end, and means whereby human beings live. A key axiom of his system is "Grace does not destroy nature, but perfects it" (*STh*, I, 1, a. 8, ad 2).[65]

Along with his pastoral commitments, Thomas Aquinas' presupposition of faith and the supremacy of God's revealed word distinguishes his approach from that of the Aristotelian philosophers, with whom he shared a deep respect for the universe and the power of human reason. His emphasis on the integrity of the natural order and the importance of human knowledge and reason helps to differentiate Thomas from his distinguished Franciscan colleague St. Bonaventure, who saw truth as the servant of the good and highlighted the spiritual quality of reality, interior illumination, and the importance of the will. They agreed that faith was basic to any adequate understanding of human life and that the entire universe was best understood as having come forth from a good and loving God and destined to return to God.[66]

The structure and principal contours of Thomas' synthesis reflect his own response to the vexed question of faith and reason. He fully acknowledged the created and the human and relied on them to help disclose God and God's design for humanity. He likewise accepted that human reason can know created things and arrive at a knowledge of God. Supported by these convictions, Thomas helped to bring nature and reason to a new prominence in Western Christian thought. Nevertheless, the entire created order, including humanity and its powers of reason, he situated within a supernatural context in which grace and faith predominate. This implies that however penetrating the light of reason may be, for Thomas the light of faith is also necessary and discloses truth that reason cannot or does not reliably grasp. Moreover, because God is the ultimate source of truth, and truth cannot be self-contradictory, there can be no final or irreconcilable conflict between reason and faith, or between the results of philosophical inquiry and those of theological reflection. Any apparent conflicts will be traced to errors in knowledge or reasoning.[67]

---

[65] See the entirety of q. 1, especially a. 8. See also Pelikan, 3:284-93; Congar, *History of Theology*, 85–103. For much fuller treatments, see Weisheipl, *Friar Thomas D'Aquino*; Brian Davies, *The Thought of Thomas Aquinas* (Oxford: Clarendon Press, 1992); McInerny, *St. Thomas Aquinas*.

[66] For comparisons of the work of Bonaventure and Thomas, see Congar, *History of Theology*, 119–22; Etienne Gilson, *The Philosophy of St. Bonaventure*, trans. Illtyd Trethowan and Frank J. Sheed (Paterson, N.J.: St. Anthony Guild Press, 1965) 387–9, 447–9; van Steenberghen, *Aristotle in the West*, 188–91; Anton C. Pegis, "St. Bonaventure, St. Francis, and Philosophy," *MS* 15 (1953) 12–3. For an appreciation of Thomas' accomplishment, see MacIntyre, *Three Rival Versions*, 113–26.

[67] Wippel, *Mediaeval Reactions*, 28–33.

The Summa Theologiae

Among the works of Thomas Aquinas the *Summa theologiae* is generally regarded as his most important. Thomas' extended discussion of the moral life in the second part of the *Summa theologiae* has been acknowledged as one of the most influential treatments of morality that Western thinkers have produced. Furthermore, once it was detached from the rest of the *Summa*, his treatment of moral questions took on a life of its own, deeply affecting both theology and pastoral praxis. This too recommends attention to it.

Pastoral Background

The pastoral circumstances of the thirteenth century form the background to the *Summa theologiae*. In 1215 the Fourth Lateran Council decided to organize pastoral work largely around preaching and the hearing of sacramental confessions. It required that priests should be well educated and prepared to carry out these ministries in a competent and fruitful way. In 1217, shortly after the council had issued these mandates, Pope Honorius III (1216–27) commissioned St. Dominic's new Order of Preachers to preach the word everywhere in the Church. Four years later he wrote to the bishops and asked them also to allow the Dominican friars to hear the sacramental confessions of the people in their dioceses. Those actions gave the Dominicans a general mandate to be confessors and preachers in the Catholic Church.[68]

Those responsibilities had a deep impact on the work of the Dominican order. They prompted St. Raymond of Peñafort (1175–1275) and other early Dominican scholars to publish books designed to support the confessor's ministry. These and similar works by later writers, collectively known as the "summas for confessors," aimed to give the ordinary confessor access to the best theological insights and latest canonical provisions. It became urgent for the Dominican Order to assure the sound theological and pastoral education of its members. Its pastoral responsibilities account for the strong institutional emphasis on education among the Dominicans, their significant contributions to theology and canon law, and their presence in the new universities of Europe.[69]

---

[68] Honorius issued the mandate to preach *(Gratiarum omnium)* in January of 1217. The encyclical letter to "all archbishops, bishops and prelates" *(Cum qui recipit prophetam)* was dated February 4, 1221. See Leonard E. Boyle, "Notes on the Education of the *Fratres communes* in the Dominican Order in the Thirteenth Century," *Pastoral Care, Clerical Education, and Canon Law, 1200–1400* (London: Variorum Reprints, 1981) 249–51; see also Weisheipl, *Friar Thomas D'Aquino*, 21–3.

[69] Boyle, "Education of the *Fratres communes*," 251–9, 267; see also idem, *The Setting of the Summa Theologiae of Saint Thomas* (Toronto: Pontifical Institute of Medieval

As a Dominican Thomas Aquinas shared his order's pastoral commitments. As a master in theology he fully participated in its educational responsibilities. In fact, he probably wrote the *Summa theologiae* to support the theological education of his own confreres. If so, they would be the "beginners" for whom Thomas wrote this great work. With them in mind, he intended to produce a comprehensive treatment of "whatever belongs to the Christian Religion," omitting useless material and avoiding undue repetition (*STh*, Prologue). He organized his work in a logical and systematic fashion and thus made theology easier to understand and learn.[70]

Perhaps a more specific motive also guided Thomas' writing of the *Summa theologiae*. By the 1260s the education of Dominican friars revolved around mainly canonical and penitential treatises that focused sharply on the practical aspects of pastoral work. It is likely that Thomas found this approach too narrow and considered it to be his responsibility to give Dominican pastoral education a more adequate theological foundation. If that is correct, then the *Summa theologiae* is to be understood as an attempt to provide pastors, confessors, and preachers with a sound and comprehensive theological basis for their work among the People of God.[71]

The Theological Structure of the Summa Theologiae

Thomas describes the overall approach of his work as follows: "Because the chief aim of sacred doctrine is to teach the knowledge of God, not only as He is in Himself, but also as He is the beginning of things and their last end, and especially of rational creatures, as is clear from what has been already said, therefore in our endeavor to expound this science, we shall treat: (1) Of God; (2) Of the rational creature's advance towards God; (3) Of Christ, Who as man, is our way to God" (*STh*, I, q. 2, Prologue).[72] These subjects determine the three-part

---

Studies, 1982) 1–4; Weisheipl, *Friar Thomas D'Aquino*, 23–5. The summas of confessors (*summae confessorum*) will be considered more fully in the next chapter.

[70] This study uses the English translation found in St. Thomas Aquinas, *Summa theologica*, trans. Fathers of the English Dominican Province (New York: Benziger Brothers, 1947). The identification of "beginners" with younger Dominican students follows Boyle, *Setting of the Summa Theologiae*, 8–20. See also Weisheipl, *Friar Thomas D'Aquino*, 216–9.

[71] Boyle, *Setting of the Summa Theologiae*, 7–8, 15–23.

[72] In this statement Thomas speaks of sacred doctrine (*sacra doctrina*), which has been discussed in this chapter, above. Weisheipl describes it as follows: "Sacred doctrine is that wisdom about God by which we lead our life to eternal glory. This is the wisdom of Sacred Scripture; it is the wisdom of saints. There is no higher

structure of the *Summa theologiae*, which also reflects the conviction that all things come forth from God (Part I) and are ultimately to return to God (Parts II and III). The overall *exitus-reditus* structure of this book integrates all its elements into a larger theological whole in which God, Christ, the Holy Spirit, the economy of salvation, and especially the dynamic of grace are paramount.[73] Within this essentially religious vision, the moral and religious activity of the human person finds its proper place. Thomas elaborates his moral teachings in the large and important second part of the *Summa theologiae*. First he considers morality in general, and then he attends to the virtues, vices, and states of life in considerable detail.[74] In much of his moral teaching Thomas follows the *Nicomachean Ethics* of Aristotle, which had just become fully available in Latin translation. His willingness to adopt Aristotle's account of human moral activity also reflects the basic principle, which Thomas also owed to Aristotle, that the natural and the human have their own integrity. Besides its intellectual dependence on Aristotle, it is probable that Thomas' treatment of the virtues and vices also reflects the pastoral literature in use at that time and his wish to improve upon it.[75]

The Moral and the Human

At the very beginning of his discussion of morals, St. Thomas recognized that sometimes people act in a free and deliberate way, while at other times they do things without freedom and deliberation. Because people are the masters of their actions only in the first case, only then are they personally responsible for their acts. Therefore only acts that flow from personal freedom and deliberation, called "human acts," qualify as morally significant. They alone can be judged morally good or evil. The strict identification of the moral with the human,

---

wisdom in this life." Weisheipl, *Friar Thomas D'Aquino*, 225. See also James A. Weisheipl, "The Meaning of *Sacra Doctrina* in *Summa Theologiae* I, q. 1," *Thomist* 38 (1974) 49–80; Congar, *History of Theology*, 92–6; T. O'Meara, "Grace as a Theological Structure in the *Summa theologiae* of Thomas Aquinas," *RTAM* 55 (1988) 136–7; Davies, *Thought of Thomas Aquinas*, 10–4.

[73] O'Meara, "Grace as a Theological Structure"; Servais Pinckaers, "La théologie morale à la periode de la grande scolastique," *NV* 52 (1977) 120–6; Weisheipl, *Friar Thomas D'Aquino*, 219; see also Weisheipl's discussion and general outline of Parts I and III (219–21).

[74] For Thomas' explicit statement of the distinction between general and specific treatments of morality, see *STh*, I-II, q. 6, Prologue.

[75] For an overview of Part II see Weisheipl, *Friar Thomas D'Aquino*, 256–63; see also Haren, *Medieval Thought*, 189–92; Boyle, *Setting of the Summa Theologiae*, 20–3.

thus understood, is axiomatic for St. Thomas, and establishes the foundation for the rest of his discussion (*STh*, I-II, q. 1, a. 1).[76]

Having limited his attention to human or morally significant acts, Thomas notes that people perform such acts in order to achieve something they consider to be good. All human actions therefore have an end, or purpose, at least implicitly. This end or purpose has objective and subjective dimensions, both of which are important. Objectively, certain things fulfill people as human beings; these things are good and their possession makes people flourish and enjoy happiness. Subjectively, when people identify the things that offer them happiness, they tend to act in order to obtain them. These considerations emphasize the overriding importance of the good, the end that will satisfy human beings, and the orientation of all human actions to the good. The moral life emerges at this point; it pertains to the ensemble of all deliberately voluntary actions that a person performs (*STh*, q. 1, aa. 2-3, 6; q. 5, a. 8).[77]

[76] See also Ralph McInerny, *Ethica Thomistica: The Moral Philosophy of Thomas Aquinas* (Washington: The Catholic University of America Press, 1982) 63–77; Davies, *Thought of Thomas Aquinas*, 220–6; Alan Donagan, "Thomas Aquinas on Human Action," *CHLMP*, 642–54.

Two clarifications might help to preclude misunderstandings. The first concerns the word "moral." When the term "moral" is understood in opposition to "immoral," it is taken to mean a qualitative judgment that an act is morally good. However, in the present context the term "moral" is to be understood in a different sense, namely, in opposition to "amoral." Used in this way, it identifies acts that come forth from a person's deliberation and freedom (e.g., deciding to cancel an appointment in order to care for someone who is sick) as opposed to actions that do not (e.g., crying out in reaction to sudden intense pain). The former are morally significant, while the latter are not. When the word "moral" simply refers to acts that are born of human freedom, there is as yet no judgment as to whether these acts are good or evil.

The second term that needs clarification is "freedom." When Thomas uses this word, he does not mean the lack of all restrictions in choosing one's behavior, for example, the ability to choose arbitrarily from a wide range of options. Rather, "freedom" pertains to the will inasmuch as the will is an interior or personal source of action aiming at a known good and therefore at something that it is reasonable to seek. In Thomas' words, "[T]he act of the will is nothing else than an inclination proceeding from the interior principle of knowledge" (*STh*, I-II, q. 6, a. 4). From this perspective, one's free acts are good when they seek the good as right reason knows it, while to act arbitrarily is to act without regard for the good and therefore in an evil manner. See *STh*, q. 18, a. 1; q. 19, aa. 3, 5.

[77] See also Davies, *Thought of Thomas Aquinas*, 227; Jean Porter, "Desire for God: Ground of the Moral Life in Aquinas," *TS* 47 (1986) 56–62, especially 58.

This perspective is important, for it locates the starting point of reflection about moral activity with the reality of moral activity. Because people act in a free and purposeful way to achieve what will satisfy them, moral reflection seeks to understand how people conduct themselves in that regard and to identify what goods

Moral Actions and the Good

Once he established that happiness, or the good, is the end of human life, Thomas explored its nature. Aristotle had taught that happiness occurs when a person reaches the fullness of perfection appropriate to human beings so that there is nothing more to be sought. He held that this perfection can take different forms and is the result of purely human effort. Thomas accepted Aristotle's understanding of happiness but introduced some revisions in light of Christian faith. He admitted that such earthly goods as health, friends, and sufficient possessions bring happiness but only in a partial and imperfect way. The complete and perfect fulfillment of the human being can occur only with the vision of God, and this is not the product of human effort but a gift of grace reserved for the next life (*STh*, I-II, q. 4; q. 5, aa. 3, 5).[78]

The good that comprises the ultimate end of human beings constitutes a fitting standard by which to evaluate human actions. Some of them duly serve the goal of human perfection; for this reason they are judged to be good. Those actions that hinder one's achievement of the good are on that account evil. To qualify as morally good, an action must proceed from an upright will, that is, a will oriented to the good. The action also needs to be rightly proportioned to its end "by means of a certain commensurateness, which results from the due circumstances" (*STh*, q. 7, a. 2). In other words, the moral quality of an act principally depends on why a person acted and what that person did, and secondarily on such considerations as who the person is who acted and the time, manner, place, and other circumstances surrounding the action. In all details reason constitutes the criterion of judgment. That action is good that accords with right reason; it is an action done for a fitting purpose and in the suitable way. An action that diverges from the requirements of right reason is an evil action (*STh*, q. 4, a. 4; qq. 18-20).[79]

---

and what actions will be more or less successful in achieving the end for which people act in freedom. See McInerny, *Ethica Thomistica*, 35–8; idem, "Ethics," *The Cambridge Companion to Aquinas*, 198–202, ed. Norman Kretzmann and Eleonore Stump (Cambridge and New York: Cambridge University Press, 1993).

[78] See also McInerny, *Ethica Thomistica*, 11–33; Davies, *Thought of Thomas Aquinas*, 227–32, 250–3; Wieland, "Happiness," 673–80.

[79] McInerny, *Ethica Thomistica*, 79–89; Davies, *Thought of Thomas Aquinas*, 237–9.

These considerations mean that while all voluntary actions are performed for a good that the agent intends to secure, sometimes what is sought only seems to be good but is not truly so because it is not reasonable to pursue and will not help to satisfy the person. Subjectively all actions are motivated by a good even though some of those actions are evil. See *STh*, I-II, q. 8, a. 1.

Virtue as the Intrinsic Source of Good Acts

Thomas was unambiguous in locating the origin of good actions in "habits," or "dispositions."[80] A habit enables and inclines a person to act in a certain way with consistency and ease; it is a personal attribute that tends to perdure over time. When habits incline a person to perform good actions, they are called virtues. On the other hand, when dispositions incline one to do evil acts, they are termed vices. Habits, or dispositions, have a strategic importance in Thomas' account of human morality. Good actions are the fruit of virtue, and the possession of virtue is essential to a morally upright life (*STh*, I-II, qq. 49–50; q. 54, a. 3; qq. 55–6).[81]

Thomas distinguished different kinds of virtue. Intellectual virtues enable the mind to know what is true and good. They include understanding the principles of reasoning, the ability to use those principles well, and wisdom concerning the things of God. They embrace art and prudence, which respectively involve knowledge concerning things to be made and things to be done (I-II, q. 57). The moral virtues, which pertain to one's will and other personal energies and inclinations, incline a person actually to do what is known to be reasonable and good. They primarily include prudence, justice, fortitude, and temperance.[82] The intellectual and moral virtues are oriented to the natural but imperfect fulfillment of the human being. But since perfect happiness is attached to the vision of God, which natural human capacities cannot attain, virtues of an entirely different or supernatural order are re-

---

[80] In this discussion the term "habit" has the technical meaning described. This term is not to be given the colloquial understanding, which sees a habit as an established pattern of behavior that occurs inadvertently and tends to resist modification. See the passages cited in the following note; also Romanus Cessario, *The Moral Virtues and Theological Ethics* (Notre Dame and London: University of Notre Dame Press, 1991) 34–44; Servais Pinckaers, "Virtue Is Not a Habit," *CC* 12 (1962) 65–81.

[81] See also McInerny, *Ethica Thomistica*, 91–103; Davies, *Thought of Thomas Aquinas*, 225–6, 239–40.

[82] Because of their preeminence, these virtues are called the cardinal virtues. Although he already filed prudence among the intellectual virtues, Thomas also considers it to be a moral virtue, since it is right reason concerning things to be done. *STh*, I-II, q. 57, a. 4; q. 58; q. 61, a. 2. For further discussion of the cardinal virtues see *STh*, II-II, 47–170; Josef Pieper, *The Four Cardinal Virtues*, trans. Richard Winston and others (Notre Dame, Ind.: University of Notre Dame Press, 1966); Cessario, *Moral Virtues and Theological Ethics*, 45–93; Daniel Mark Nelson, *The Priority of Prudence: Virtue and Natural Law in Thomas Aquinas and the Implications for Modern Ethics* (Ph.D. diss., Princeton University, 1986; Ann Arbor: University Microfilms International, 1986) 150–207; Jean Porter, *The Recovery of Virtue: The Relevance of Aquinas for Christian Ethics* (Louisville, Ky.: Westminster/John Knox, 1990) 124–71.

quired. These are primarily the theological virtues of faith, hope, and charity, which are freely given or infused by God. They empower persons so that they can freely act to achieve union with God (I-II, q. 62, esp. a. 1; also II-II, q. 1, a. 1; q. 23, a. 2; q. 24, a. 3).[83]

Law and Grace as the Extrinsic Sources of Good Acts

After his consideration of virtue as the interior source of human acts, St. Thomas turned to their extrinsic source. On this point his words are direct: "The extrinsic principle moving to good is God, Who both instructs us by means of His Law, and assists us by His Grace" (*STh*, I-II, q. 90, Prologue). Proceeding from a basic understanding of law as "an ordinance of reason for the common good, made by him who has care of the community, and promulgated" (q. 90, a. 4), Thomas attributes the character of law to God's providential governance of the universe, which he calls "eternal law." The natural law, which pertains especially to human beings, is "the light of natural reason, whereby we discern what is good and what is evil" (q. 91, a. 2). Practically speaking, all can know the primary requirements of the natural law: "good is to be done and pursued, and evil is to be avoided" (q. 94, a. 2).[84] This general imperative is to be made more specific in light of particular human inclinations to the good as reason grasps them.[85] Human law, which derives its validity from the natural law, is necessary both for the peace of society and in order to help people to grow in virtue (q. 95, aa. 1-2).

When he considered the new law, or the law of the Gospel, Thomas realized that it was primarily a matter of grace. "Now that which is preponderant in the law of the New Testament, and whereon all its efficacy is based, is the grace of the Holy Ghost, which is given through faith in Christ. Consequently the New Law is chiefly the grace itself of the Holy Ghost, which is given to those who believe in Christ" (*STh*, I-II, q. 106, a. 1). Its primary effect is to justify the believer. Only secondarily does the New Law embrace teachings of faith and commandments

---

[83] Davies, *Thought of Thomas Aquinas*, 240–4, 263–4. Thomas dedicates *STh*, II-II, qq. 1–46, to a comprehensive discussion of the theological virtues.

[84] In this formulation the good refers to those things that perfect the human being inasmuch as they can be known and pursued according to reason.

[85] Accordingly, Thomas specifies the good under three different inclinations toward perfection: those that humanity shares with all substances (e.g., self preservation); those that it shares with animals (e.g., sexual intercourse and the rearing of young); and those that are specific to human beings (e.g., to know the truth about God and to live in society); see *STh*, I-II, q. 94, a. 2. See also Davies, *Thought of Thomas Aquinas*, 244–9; D. E. Luscombe, "Natural Morality and Natural Law," *CHLMP*, 709–13.

that bear on human emotions and actions. Grace is a necessary prerequisite even for those moral norms found in the Scriptures, since without "the inward presence of the healing grace of faith" even the written word of the Gospel would kill (q. 106, a. 2).[86]

Thomas' Teaching on Grace

As a theologian writing in the thirteenth century, St. Thomas had the benefit of earlier discussions concerning God's grace. He knew that the Catholic tradition had resolved a number of doctrinal questions that had once been a matter of controversy, and he fully accepted its verdicts. His own work therefore presupposed that God gives grace freely through Christ and that personal salvation depends on this grace. He affirmed that without grace no one can contribute anything whatsoever to his or her salvation. This inherited body of teachings about grace and salvation constituted a starting point for Thomas' own work.

That work was also one of revision, for Thomas gave these traditional doctrines a meaning and a function they did not have in their earlier Augustinian context. Augustine had considered humanity primarily in terms of its actual situation before God. Because he understood human nature in a historical sense, Augustine focused on its sinfulness. Due to original and personal sins, the human person had lost the ability to will and act well; sin had destroyed all capacity to please God and win salvation. For Augustine grace primarily repairs the effects of sin and forgives sin itself. It enables the person to live in charity, do God's will, and be saved.

In keeping with his Aristotelian presuppositions, Thomas emphasized the human person as a created being with a set of capacities and ends that are proper to human nature itself. In its original context this view stresses the nature, experiences, and abilities of the human being as such; but it fails to recognize God as the primary point of reference for persons, and sin as a dominant factor in everyday human life. Therefore if Thomas wished to adopt Aristotle's view of human nature, he could only do so by modifying it significantly. He did so by giving grace a function that is not primarily related to sin but to nature. For Thomas, grace elevates human nature, endowing it with the capacity to reach God and attain salvation. Given the reality of sin, grace also forgives sin and repairs the damage it has caused (*STh*, I-II, qq. 106–14). By borrowing so much from Aristotle and by reconsidering the Augustinian doctrine of grace, Thomas endowed the tradition with a new theological synthesis.

---

[86] See also Davies, *Thought of Thomas Aquinas*, 260–2.

Thomas' understanding of grace affected many other areas of his theology. Because he envisioned grace as a God-given habit or disposition, he was able to relate it to virtue and the human acts that come from it. The theological virtues of faith, hope, and charity are especially important, for they communicate a share in God's life and enable persons to act in a way that is not only naturally virtuous but also supernaturally salvific. The theological virtues bring God's life; they empower the free and deliberate acts by which people contribute to their own salvation. Thomas' theology of the sacraments is also premised on humanity's need of grace and God's wish to offer all a share in the divine life. Finally, it should be emphasized once again that the plan and grace of God are inherent in the basic *exitus-reditus* architecture of the *Summa theologiae*. In other words, even before Thomas explicitly considered grace, he had already recognized that human life possesses a deeply religious meaning that is unintelligible apart from grace (*STh*, I-II, qq. 106–14; also II-II, q. 23, a. 2; q. 24, a. 2).[87]

An Assessment of Thomas' Theological Synthesis

The *Summa theologiae* is the first theological work of its kind to be produced in the West. Concerned to advance the Gospel in his own day, Thomas Aquinas employed the new resources of Aristotelian thought to organize and explain a traditional body of Christian teachings. He relied upon Christian faith to supply a context in which Aristotle's account of the moral life would take on even deeper significance. In this monumental work Thomas Aquinas integrated many different elements into one comprehensive whole, highlighted the priorities among them, and made faith and moral life more understandable to others. It manifests his Christian commitment, knowledge and love of the Scriptures, familiarity with patristic writings, respect for

---

[87] For a fuller discussion of Thomas' theology of grace, see Stephen J. Duffy, *The Dynamics of Grace: Perspectives in Theological Anthropology* (Collegeville: The Liturgical Press, 1993) 121–70; Davies, *Thought of Thomas Aquinas*, 250–96; Henri Rondet, *The Grace of Christ: A Brief History of the Theology of Grace*, trans. Tad W. Guzie (Westminster, Md.: Newman Press, 1967) 209–48; Roger Haight, *The Experience and Language of Grace* (New York: Paulist Press, 1979) 54–78. Rondet and Haight also present some criticisms of Thomas' theory of grace.

On grace as inherent to the architecture of the *STh*, see Chenu, *Toward Understanding Saint Thomas*, 310–7, especially 312–3; O'Meara, "Grace as a Theological Structure"; Pinckaers, "La théologie morale," 120–2.

Thomas considered Christ and the sacraments in *STh*, III, which was incomplete at the time of his death. See Davies, *Thought of Thomas Aquinas*, 297–376.

The foregoing discussion is especially indebted to Haight.

the Christian tradition, knowledge of Aristotle, and sensitivity to pastoral need. It is hard to overestimate the theological and pastoral importance of this work.

Thomas' discussion of Christian moral life in the second part of the *Summa* recognizes that persons enact their moral life whenever they act in a deliberate and voluntary way. Allied to that basic insight is the assertion that morally good actions draw their energy, substance, and direction from personal virtues. For this reason Thomas centers moral life not on law, duty, or obligation but on the virtues of prudence and charity. Any consideration of the former topics is always subordinated to virtue. His account of the moral life is therefore an eminently positive one. It is not primarily a means for people to avoid evil, sin, or punishment. It is rather their effort to do the good, that which serves the true fulfillment of the human person in a characteristically human way.[88]

The alignment of moral life between its source in virtue and its goal in the good favored its insertion into a sacral context. As a theologian, priest, and believer, Thomas knew that even though human beings seek happiness in this world, their origin and ultimate end is the love of the triune God. The reality of sacred history and the economy of salvation endow all aspects of human life with new dynamics and deeper meaning. In those contexts the moral life is to be the graced means for persons to enact their free response to God as their creator, savior, sanctifier, and perfect fulfillment.

THE CONDEMNATION OF RADICAL ARISTOTELIANISM

A few years after the formal adoption of Aristotelian texts by the University of Paris arts faculty in 1255, some professors began to develop the philosophical aspects of Aristotelian thought. Although that enterprise was not objectionable, some of the arts professors arrived at conclusions that contradicted Catholic faith, but they nonetheless defended their assertions on grounds afforded by Aristotle and some of his commentators. That precipitated a crisis and caused theologians and ecclesiastical authorities to respond. The ensuing events ended an important chapter in Western intellectual history and helped to frame key issues for later thinkers.

The Crisis at the University of Paris

For reasons that are not fully understood, during the mid-1260s some of the arts professors began to expound views that have been de-

[88] See, for example, Thomas S. Hibbs, "A Rhetoric of Motives: Thomas on Obligation as Rational Persuasion," *Thomist* 54 (1990) 307–9.

scribed as a "radical Aristotelianism." Although it is not always possible to reconstruct their actual opinions or even to identify all of the proponents, certain professors seem to have taught that human beings share one and the same intellect, which would compromise human freedom and responsibility and leave no room for an immortal soul. They were also charged with holding that historical events are governed by a chain of causes and effects that neither God nor human beings can influence. If that were the case, God could not act in the world, and divine providence would be meaningless. Human beings would also lack freedom, either because natural forces utterly control their affairs or because their intellects overwhelm personal freedom.[89]

The Condemnation of Radical Aristotelianism

The arts professors' influence among their students and the willingness of some to stake out positions contrary to faith did not go unchallenged. Thomas Aquinas, Bonaventure, and other theologians rebutted the objectionable positions of their colleagues.[90] In December of 1270 Stephen Tempier, the bishop of Paris, officially condemned thirteen propositions attributed to the arts faculty.[91] Despite these interventions and academic rulings that prohibited the arts professors from making any pronouncements that contradicted Christian faith, some continued to maintain their objectionable views, notably Siger of Brabant and Boethius of Dacia.[92] Since the battle over Aristotelianism continued unabated at the University of Paris, Pope John XXI (1276–7), himself a distinguished scholar, asked Bishop Tempier to investigate the matter and report his findings. Tempier commissioned sixteen theologians to prepare a bill of particulars specifying the errors being charged to the arts faculty. Instead of forwarding this list to Pope John, however, Tempier took action himself. On March 7, 1277, he publicly condemned 219 propositions as erroneous and imposed excommunication on anyone who taught, defended, or upheld any one of them.[93]

[89] Wippel, *Mediaeval Reactions*, 14–7. There is considerable evidence that Siger of Brabant, a principal figure in the arts faculty, held at least some of the objectionable positions.

[90] Bonaventure published his *Collationes de Decem Preceptis* in 1267, *De donis Spiritus Sancti* in 1268, and *Collationes in Hexaemeron* in 1273. Thomas Aquinas wrote *De unitate intellectus* (1270) in opposition to Siger of Brabant. See van Steenberghen, *Aristotle in the West*, 233–5; Weisheipl, *Friar Thomas D'Aquino*, 272–85.

[91] For the text of this condemnation, see Haren, *Medieval Thought*, 198–9.

[92] For a discussion of their positions on faith and reason, see Wippel, *Mediaeval Reactions*, 33–72.

[93] A complete translation is given in Ralph Lerner and Muhsin Mahdi, eds., *Medieval Political Philosophy: A Sourcebook* (New York: The Free Press of Glencoe,

The Meaning and Effects of the Condemnation

The significance of Tempier's act is not to be discerned only in the specific propositions he stigmatized, which were assembled in haste, unedited, and at times contradictory. Rather, his condemnation is principally to be understood in light of certain assumptions and insinuations that were latent in the prohibited statements. Original to Aristotle or his commentators, those statements presented the world as a closed and autonomous system. They left no room for God's providence and made it impossible to sustain human freedom and responsibility. Moreover, to insist that Aristotelian thought constituted valid grounds for statements that contradicted faith was to confront the Christian community with two incompatible standards of truth and an irreconcilable conflict between reason and faith. That was the problem that faced the Paris Aristotelians, their theological adversaries, and the bishop of Paris.[94]

Tempier's condemnation prohibited believers from citing the grounds of Aristotle's philosophy as a valid basis for statements that contradicted Christian faith. His judgment did not preclude scholars from studying any of Aristotle's works or pursuing his thought on its own terms. As long as philosophical discourse respected the limits of its own grounds and methods and did not draw conclusions about matters beyond its own realm, there would be no conflict with faith. The effects of the condemnation on theological reflection were more subtle. After considering the doctrines that had been condemned, theologians became less interested in maintaining that anything created, or that could be created, predisposed God's freedom in any way. They were more inclined to stress God's sovereign freedom and the inability of creation to limit or channel that freedom. They tended to locate the ultimate source of divine activity more in God's will than in God's mind. The same considerations prompted theologians to emphasize human freedom and will and depreciate the influence of the mind on human decision and action, thereby reversing the priority Thomas Aquinas had enshrined in his *Summa theologiae.*

As theologians backed away from positions that hinted too strongly of Aristotelian determinism, many of them showed a deeper sympathy

---

1963) 337–54; for an edited version, see Edward Peters, ed., *Heresy and Authority in Medieval Europe: Documents in Translation* (Philadelphia: University of Pennsylvania Press, 1980) 225–30. For the events that led up to this famous condemnation and a similar one issued by the archbishop of Canterbury, including the teachings of principal figures in the University of Paris arts faculty, see Haren, *Medieval Thought,* 194–206; Leff, *Dissolution,* 24–9; van Steenberghen, *Aristotle in the West,* 198–238; Copleston, *History of Medieval Philosophy,* 199–209.

[94] See Haren, *Medieval Thought,* 208; Leff, *Dissolution,* 24–5, 30–1.

for traditional Augustinian ways of thinking. The return to Augustine was highly congenial to Franciscan sensitivities and helped to make Franciscan scholars prominent in the fourteenth century. The rejection of radical Aristotelianism placed Thomas Aquinas under a cloud, especially since he seemed to have taught some of the condemned propositions. The Dominican Order mounted a vigorous defense of him, his works, and his orthodoxy. Although Thomas' canonization in 1324 ended all reasonable doubt about the orthodoxy of his doctrine, the decades following 1277 were less hospitable to his approach, and his influence declined.[95]

By the 1270s, then, European scholars had become acquainted with all of Aristotle's writings and understood the principal issues they presented to Christian thought. The challenge was no longer to integrate Aristotle into the received tradition but to explore the problems entailed in that integration and pursue their implications.[96]

REFLECTIONS

The story of the intellectual life of the High Middle Ages is largely one of tension, development, and divergence. Much of the energy behind that complex process was internally generated. In order to serve apologetical needs as well as to respond to the questions of devout believers, Christian thinkers sought to understand and explain the content of faith and pushed back the intellectual horizon as they did so. The competing claims of faith, reason, academic life, and pastoral service stimulated progress but also took scholars in different directions. By encouraging confidence in human efforts to know the world and by giving new prominence to the individual, the culture and attitudes of this period supported many of the intellectual currents that have been observed. However significant such internal factors were, external influences deeply affected the intellectual evolution of this period. Newly translated Aristotelian works required Western scholars to rethink their traditional Augustinian approach to scholarship. The work entailed in that reconsideration enriched the Western tradition but also increased the centrifugal forces within it. Those

---

[95] The aftermath of Tempier's act is reviewed in Copleston, *History of Medieval Philosophy,* 209–12; Haren, *Medieval Thought,* 207–11; Leff, *Dissolution,* 28–31. For the medieval discussion of freedom and determinism prior to 1277, see J. B. Korolec, "Free Will and Free Choice," *CHLMP,* 629–37. On Thomistic teachings and the condemnation of 1277, see John F. Wippel, "Thomas Aquinas and the Condemnation of 1277," *Modern Schoolman* 72 (1995) 233–72; idem, *Mediaeval Reactions,* 26–8.

[96] See Haren, *Medieval Thought,* 207, 210; Congar, *History of Theology,* 61–114; see also 59–61.

forces fueled important developments within Western thought, exacerbated old tensions and created new problems, and introduced an intellectual diversity unprecedented in its nature and depth. Because these effects are so significant for Western intellectual and cultural history, it is important to advert to their principal causes and implications. This can foster a better grasp of later developments and some of the factors that also affect moral and religious life.

High medieval developments highlighted certain tensions that were inherent in the Western intellectual tradition. One was rooted in a diversity of sources and methods. Christian scholars accepted that the Bible and other authorities were valid sources of knowledge and were to be used with reverence and humility. They also agreed that scholarship required experiential knowledge, technical competence, and logical analysis. The problem was to reconcile or integrate these two approaches, especially when they seemed to ask different things of the scholar or led to different conclusions. Another point of tension concerned Platonic and Aristotelian systems of thought, which have entered the Western Christian tradition largely through Augustine and Thomas Aquinas respectively. As a result, the tradition has come to include two contrasting ways of understanding reality, knowledge, and the relationship between human experience and God. Yet another source of stress is the contrast between a strong tendency to rely upon reason and nature and the Christian conviction that sin has impaired both personal efforts to know truth and creation itself. In the same connection, it is well to recall that the terms "nature" and "creation" have different origins and connotations and are not strictly synonymous.

These considerations suggest that to understand the later Western Christian tradition one needs to appreciate the existence and impact of such problems. They make it easier to understand why no system of thought can do justice to all relevant aspects of human life or Christian faith. The tension between the spiritual and physical origins of human experience and thought remains to this day. The conflict between natural human fulfillment and the Cross of Christ is likewise perennial. Such tensions have entered the substance of the Western tradition and contributed to its problems, vitality, and diversity.

No consideration of high medieval intellectual life would be complete without reference to the universities. By providing a forum dedicated to thought, research, and education, they kept alive the intellectual legacy of the past and augmented it with new perspectives and resources. Once they were established, the universities began to assume responsibility for Western intellectual life. In those institutions professors were not necessarily bound to the ordered life of the monastery or the pastoral responsibilities that governed the bishop's school or the friars' house of studies. Academic faculties developed their own norms and standards and worked with a greater measure of freedom. These factors contributed to the development of philosophy as a distinct discipline that was free to investigate human experience as such and its emancipation from the service of theology. They likewise promoted the emergence of theology as an academic subject that could be studied, developed, and taught like any other. The university can foster outstanding achievements and offer strong support to pastoral care, as the example of the Dominican and Franciscan masters shows. But it can also allow theology to become less attuned to the Church community and its liturgy and diminish its contribution to Christian life.

Whether they worked in the monastery, bishop's school, university, or other setting, medieval scholars have left an impressive record of intellectual commitment and accomplishment. They have shown that reason and logical analysis can make important, even indispensable contributions to the apologetical, catechetical, and pastoral needs of the Christian community. They demonstrated how new methods were able to address in a constructive way some of the serious problems latent in traditional authorities, whether on account of the sheer number of sources or the discrepancies among them. They provide a case study in the reception and integration of new texts and ways of thought and of authors who stood outside the Christian tradition. Their work occasionally led to dubious or objectionable conclusions and was frequently controversial. But overall, it was necessary and bore much fruit. These considerations highlight the place of scholarship in the faith community and the important contributions it can make. They also demonstrate the benefits of understanding, patience, and criticism. The work of high medieval thinkers and writers can speak to a wide range of present-day concerns and encourage those contemporary scholars who are faithfully addressing new or perennial problems.

High medieval scholars accomplished much in a relatively short period of time. They brought new clarity and fruitfulness to Christian sources, introduced the West to the full range of Aristotle's writings, and began to work out the stresses and implications that emerged as these two traditions were brought together. Many pursued these tasks as an integral part of their Christian commitment and perhaps also the ministry of pastoral care. These momentous accomplishments also meant that West would never again know a time when its intellectual life rested on a single set of assumptions about human life that practically everyone accepted.

The people of the late Middle Ages were the first to receive this important but mixed legacy. From end of the thirteenth century scholars worked to extend the insights of their predecessors and to pursue implications that had been left unexplored. This resulted in new systems of thought and more evidence of intellectual vitality and divergence. For their part, ordinary people had to confront human and natural disasters, unstable political situations, and a series of abuses and scandals within the Catholic Church. Such developments signaled the arrival of a new and very different age.

8

Old Approaches and New Ways

By almost any standard the Catholic Church held a commanding position in thirteenth-century Europe. The Fourth Lateran Council had acted to combat abuses and establish a new charter for pastoral care. In the universities scholars demonstrated impressive intellectual vitality as they responded to Aristotelian thought. Throughout the century new communities of friars made indispensable pastoral and intellectual contributions and stood as another sign of the Church's strength and responsiveness. The popes not only exercised authority in the Church but asserted a claim of jurisdiction over civil rulers as well. Directly or indirectly the Church projected its influence into virtually all areas of life.

This portrait gives no hint of the monumental changes that would soon overtake Western Christendom. Between the late thirteenth and early sixteenth centuries war, political conflict, and budding nationalism reshaped European life. A long series of scandals and abuses damaged the Church and cost the popes much of their prestige. Theologians placed greater emphasis on God's will, elaborated new theories of grace and justification, and reinterpreted moral life accordingly. In the arena of philosophical thought, individual entities came to be seen as the basis of knowledge and reality, displacing essences and natures from their accustomed primacy. During these centuries the interior and individual dynamics of personal faith and devotion tended to flow more strongly, sometimes complementing, at other times contrasting with the ecclesial dimensions of Christian life. Printing, intercontinental voyages, and a humanistic renaissance transformed many aspects of life. In the early sixteenth century, the Protestant Reformation left no doubt that a new age had begun.

This chapter will consider the period that extends from the late thirteenth century up to 1546, the year in which Martin Luther died and the Council of Trent held its first working sessions. That time of transition gave rise to the religious crisis of the sixteenth century, shaped important aspects of the Protestant and Catholic Reformations, and redirected the course of Western intellectual life. Of special significance are late medieval developments in thought, religious devotion, and outlook on Christian life.

The first section will review relevant aspects of late medieval history. Acquaintance with the often tragic events of the fourteenth and fifteenth centuries enhances one's appreciation of contemporary theological and religious developments and the crisis that followed.

Some of the principal intellectual developments of the late Middle Ages will be examined in the following three sections. Led by such figures as John Duns Scotus and William of Ockham, scholars reinterpreted Christian life in light of divine freedom and the utter contingency of all created things. They proposed new accounts of reality, knowledge, and human salvation and in so doing profoundly influenced Christian moral and religious life.

The penitential and devotional practices of late medieval Christians will be the subject of the fifth section. Because they shape and illuminate the bond between moral and religious life, penitential practices and literature warrant continuing attention. The mystical and spiritual movements of the age and the confraternities highlighted lay religious sensitivity and practice.

All these developments stand in the background of the Reformation, which will be examined insofar as it concerns Catholic moral life, either directly or through its impact on theology or practice. Some appreciation of the Reformation is also essential if the decisions of the Council of Trent and certain aspects of the modern Western outlook are to be adequately appreciated.

HISTORICAL BACKGROUND

The late Middle Ages were marked by momentous political conflicts, human tragedy on a grand scale, and a pattern of abuses that contributed to an unprecedented crisis for the Church in its head and its members. Although such calamities as war, famine, and epidemic were immensely destructive, the Avignon papacy, the Great Schism, and the popes' financial and political dealings scandalized Christians and damaged Church institutions as few external forces could have done. Those events strengthened national rulers, increased the urgency of Church reform, and encouraged radical solutions to its problems.

An Overview of the Period

The fourteenth century was a time of war, social conflict, and natural disaster. War and civil strife occurred frequently, with the Hundred Years' War between France and England (1337–1453) probably the most destructive. In addition, the climate had turned colder, shortening the growing season and reducing the harvests. The early years of the century witnessed several crop failures and widespread famine. Along with the burdens of war, problems on the farm generated intense social stresses, including a migration to the cities, distortions in the customary economic system, and armed rebellions. Despite the problems, this period also recorded some remarkable achievements, especially during the fifteenth century. Among these were the introduction of movable type, voyages from Europe to America and the East Indies, the expansion of commerce and finance, the rise of national governments, and an important cultural renaissance.[1]

The Bubonic Plague

The worst natural disaster was undoubtedly the epidemic of bubonic plague, or Black Death, that occurred between 1347 and 1350. Because people of that era did not understand the source of this disease or how it spreads, they were defenseless against it, especially in circumstances of poor hygiene or malnutrition. The plague could have drastic effects. In only a few months half the population of a large city might be wiped out or a small town totally depopulated. Overall, it is estimated that the bubonic plague killed about a third of the people living in Europe in the mid-fourteenth century. It is impossible to calculate the impact of this catastrophe.[2]

---

[1] Brian Tierney and Sidney Painter, *Western Europe in the Middle Ages: 300–1475* (New York: Knopf, 1970) 401–19, 467–78; R. W. Southern, *Western Society and the Church in the Middle Ages* (Baltimore: Pelican Books, 1970) 45–58; Robert E. Lerner, *The Fourteenth Century* (Ithaca: Cornell University Press, 1968) 7–13, 23–9. On the development of national governments, the corresponding limitation of Church authority, and the effects on religious history, see Steven Ozment, *The Age of Reform 1250–1550: An Intellectual and Religious History of Late Medieval and Reformation Europe* (New Haven and London: Yale University Press, 1980) 182–90; Francis Oakley, *The Western Church in the Later Middle Ages* (Ithaca and London: Cornell University Press, 1979) 71–9; Owen Chadwick, *The Reformation* (Middlesex and Baltimore: Penguin Books, 1972) 24–31; Tierney, *Western Europe in the Middle Ages,* 493–508.

[2] The bacillus responsible for the plague originates in rats and is transmitted to humans by the bite of an infected rat or rat flea, or through close contact with a diseased person. The epidemic of 1347–50 was the worst but not the only outbreak of this disease, which ravaged Europe in the sixth century and recurred from time to time until the eighteenth century. Tierney, *Western Europe in the Middle Ages,* 447–50; Lerner, *Fourteenth Century,* 13–7.

These disasters had a marked effect on the Church. By severely depleting the ranks of the clergy and the religious orders, the plague disrupted pastoral care. Moreover, the need to replace personnel who succumbed to the disease often involved a lowering of standards. The seeming irrationality of the epidemic as well as its swift and deadly effects generated hysteria, outlandish explanations, and bizarre religious manifestations. An environment dominated by war, famine, social turmoil, and plague encouraged people to think of human life as violent, difficult, and precarious. These experiences and attitudes shaped people's lives and formed the background for the great political and ecclesiastical conflicts of the age.[3]

The Popes' Claim to Sovereignty

At least since the reign of Pope Gregory VII (1073–85) the popes had claimed to possess authority over kings and emperors. Often their aim was simply to protect the Church from interference, but on other occasions the popes deployed their authority to arbitrate civil disputes or otherwise intervene in affairs of state. To justify these actions they cited canon law, agreements, or precedent. Their position also found support in the generally accepted notion that the temporal order is dependent upon the spiritual. Whatever its legal or theological foundation, the popes' claim to supremacy implied that national rulers were not fully in charge of their affairs. That situation led to serious conflicts between pope and monarch. In such cases, the outcome usually depended more on power than theory.

A Royal Challenge

At the very end of the thirteenth century, Pope Boniface VIII (1294–1303) and King Philip IV of France (1285–1314) found themselves at odds over whose authority should prevail on a matter of importance to them both. Boniface objected to a war between France and England. To stop it, he promulgated the bull *Clericis laicos* in February of 1296, which forbade the clergy from paying taxes to lay rulers without permission from the Holy See. That prohibition, which was meant to damage the kings' ability to fund their war, assumed that a pope had

---

[3] Oakley, *Western Church in the Later Middle Ages*, 115–7; David Knowles with Dimitri Obolensky, *The Middle Ages* (London: Darton, Longman & Todd; New York: Paulist Press, 1969) 437; Southern, *Western Society and the Church*, 304–9. For a fascinating study of life in the 14th century, see Barbara W. Tuchman, *A Distant Mirror: The Calamitous 14th Century* (New York: Knopf, 1978).

authority to overrule a king. Well aware of these practical and juridical implications, Philip responded by outlawing the export of money or other assets to the papal Curia. Boniface felt the loss of revenue and soon capitulated.[4]

With this victory behind him, Philip sought to weaken Boniface even further. In 1301 he had a French bishop arrested, tried, and imprisoned on charges that included heresy and treason. Because this action violated a long-standing right of bishops to be judged by the pope alone, it constituted an affront to Boniface and an assault on the hierarchy's prerogatives. The pope condemned Philip's behavior and summoned the French bishops to Rome. Philip countered by forbidding them to go. This conflict reached its climax the following summer. Knowing Boniface planned to excommunicate him, Philip sent a group of mercenaries to attack the small Italian town of Anagni, where the pope was staying. Although they captured Boniface, the local population rose to his defense, saving him from deportation or death. The pope died shortly after this episode.[5]

The Bull Unam Sanctam

In November of 1302 at the height of the battle against Philip, Boniface issued the famous bull, *Unam sanctam*.[6] In that document the pope asserted that "it is altogether necessary to salvation for every human creature to be subject to the Roman Pontiff." Whatever other meaning this statement might have had, in its context it reminded bishops that they were obliged to obey the commands of the Roman pontiff, even if that meant disobedience to their king. Turning to the vexed issue of authority, Boniface used the metaphor of the two swords, one spiritual and the other material, to explain the source and use of authority in society. Spiritual authority is exercised by priests, while secular power, though in "the hand of kings and soldiers," is nevertheless to be used "at the will and sufferance of the priest." With this imagery Boniface reasserted his claim to have God-given power to constitute and judge earthly rulers, including King Philip. In *Unam Sanctam* the theory of papal sovereignty achieved its classic if also extreme expression.[7]

[4] For the text of this bull, see Brian Tierney, *Crisis of Church and State, 1050–1300* (Englewood Cliffs, N.J.: Prentice-Hall, 1964) 175–6; see 172–9 for related texts and discussion.

[5] For further background on the conflict between Boniface and Philip, see Knowles, *Middle Ages*, 329–37, 386–8; Tierney, *Western Europe in the Middle Ages*, 388–94; Oakley, *Western Church in the Later Middle Ages*, 32–7; Southern, *Western Society and the Church*, 134–5.

[6] The text is in Tierney, *Crisis of Church and State*, 188–9.

[7] See related documents and the discussion in ibid., 180–8.

Implications of the Conflict

The struggle between Boniface and Philip concerned the nature, source, and limits of authority as well as the practical advantages that came from money, power, and loyalty. Their confrontation did not settle those important issues, but it did suggest that new realities were beginning to overtake the older world view that the pope represented. It was the first in a long series of conflicts and unexpected events that shook the Church, drained authority from the papacy, and augmented the power of civil rulers. The next episode came quickly and was to prove even more significant.

The Avignon Papacy

After the short pontificate of Benedict XI (1303–4) the cardinals elected the archbishop of Bordeaux, Bertrand de Got, to the chair of Peter. The new pope, Clement V (1305–14), did not immediately travel to Rome but remained in France, where he conferred with King Philip. In 1309 he took up residence at Avignon in order to participate in the preparations for the Council of Vienne (1311–2). After these tasks were completed, rebellions against the papacy and the general turmoil in central Italy persuaded Clement to postpone his journey to Rome.

Although Pope Clement may have intended his stay at Avignon to be nothing more than a temporary expedient, several forces conspired to keep him and his immediate successors in France. Central Italy remained turbulent and hostile to papal rule. That fact and ongoing problems with the German monarch required the popes to maintain good relations with the French. In addition, they had fortified the city of Avignon and undertaken new construction to accommodate the Curia and other Church personnel. All of these factors persuaded the popes to remain in Avignon.

Impact on the Church

The record of papal activities at Avignon is mixed. On the one hand, some of the Avignon popes lived simple, exemplary lives and tried to act in the best interests of the Church. Some, especially Pope John XXII (1316–34), increased the efficiency of Church administration and improved its judicial procedures. John and others, hoping to prepare for their return to Rome, did their best to pacify the Papal States. On the other hand, the popes' need for additional revenue required a sharp increase in Church taxes, which sometimes involved harsh collection tactics. The same need for money led to a greater reliance on the income that was received from those who obtained an appointment or benefited from other official acts, including dispensations and indulgences.[8] In a related development, the popes claimed the right to make more and more appointments that had been in local hands. That gave them many more opportunities to collect the fees that an appointee would expect to pay. Finally, the administrative apparatus and curial life-style ill compared to the simple life urged by the Gospel or the grinding poverty of many people, a point effectively driven home by the popes' adversaries.[9]

While it would be unjust to condemn the Avignon popes out of hand, the record supports the conclusion that many of their policies and actions grievously harmed the Church. The excesses involved in taxation spawned resentment and even hatred toward the pope and his Curia. Politics and financial motives placed unworthy or incompetent people in Church offices and led to the practice of appointing a

[8] A "dispensation" is an official act that exempts a particular case from a law that would otherwise apply to it.

An "indulgence" is an authoritative cancellation or reduction of the debt of satisfaction that a person owes on account of sin. Indulgences developed out of two parallel strands in the Church's penitential tradition. First, it had always been expected that repentant sinners would do penance for the sins that they had committed. It was also understood that the Church had the power to commute or exercise discretion over the penances that it had imposed. Second, the Church has always prayed for penitents. Because they are offered in and through Christ, these prayers contribute to the forgiveness and conversion of a repentant sinner.

The use of indulgences reflects both these practices. They reduce the satisfaction required of a penitent on account of sin and apply the prayers of the Church and its saints for the benefit of that person. Although granting indulgences is supported by ancient precedents as well as ecclesial charity, it is vulnerable to abuse, especially when superstition or monetary considerations are present and the urgency of sincere personal repentance is not appreciated. Indulgences can also suffer when they are conceived or used in too juridical a way. See Bernhard Poschmann, *Penance and the Anointing of the Sick*, trans. Francis Courtney (New York: Herder & Herder, 1964) 210–32; Paul Anciaux, *The Sacrament of Penance* (New York: Sheed & Ward, 1962) 166–81; Karl Rahner, "Indulgences," *SM*, 3:123-9.

In 1967 Pope Paul VI set forth Catholic doctrine concerning indulgences and revised the norms that govern them. See his "Constitutio Apostolica Sacrum Indulgentiarum recognitio promulgatur" (*Indulgentiarum doctrina*), *AAS* 59 (1967) 5–24. For an English translation, see Austin Flannery, ed., *Vatican Council II: The Conciliar and Post Conciliar Documents* (Northport, N.Y.: Costello, 1975) 62–79.

[9] The need for revenue to defray expenses of administration, gifts, and charity was neither new nor objectionable. However, the Avignon papacy had to support a significantly larger administrative apparatus and underwrite the costs of the warfare required to reassert its authority over the Papal States. In the meanwhile it did not collect the taxes normally received from this source. These circumstances required the papacy to find new sources of revenue and raise extraordinary sums of money from them.

person to several offices at the same time. This system and the absenteeism it involved injured the ministry of pastoral care. The decisions required in the exercise of late medieval realpolitik and the spectacle of popes and cardinals waging war had a similar effect.[10]

The Great Schism

By 1377 the situation in Italy had become stable enough for Pope Gregory XI (1370–8) to return to Rome, where he died a year later. As the cardinals prepared to elect his successor, the Roman people made it abundantly clear that they wanted a Roman, or at least an Italian, to be the next pope. In these awkward circumstances the cardinals chose Bartolomeo Prignano, who took the name Urban VI. Immediately upon his accession, the new pope began to mistreat people and abused the cardinals themselves. Deeply offended, they left Rome and promptly repudiated their election of Urban VI on grounds that it had been coerced by the Roman crowds. The College of Cardinals held a new conclave and unanimously elected Cardinal Robert of Geneva, cousin to the French king, who laid claim to the papacy as Clement VII.[11]

Once it had begun, the Great Schism threatened to continue indefinitely. Church law provided no tribunal in which a contested papal election could be decided. The ambiguity of the facts compounded the problem. Both Urban and Clement could say that they had been canonically elected. The claim that intimidation had voided the first election was plausible but could not be proven beyond a reasonable doubt. As a result, about half the Church supported one claimant, and the rest offered allegiance to the other. Everyone agreed that this situation was intolerable, and many attempts were made to settle it. Unfortunately, neither the use of force nor solutions based on compromise succeeded in ending the schism.[12]

The Great Schism added immensely to the Church's problems. Among other things, two competing pontiffs meant two curias, the duplication of administrative structures, and intensified efforts to raise

---

[10] Knowles, *Middle Ages*, 405–13, 437–9; Southern, *Western Society and the Church*, 133–69; Lerner, *Fourteenth Century*, 67–70; Oakley, *Western Church in the Later Middle Ages*, 40–55. Oakley gives some of the legal and ecclesiastical history that left Church offices vulnerable to being used as sources of revenue (27–31).

[11] Knowles, *Middle Ages*, 415–6.

[12] Lerner, *Fourteenth Century*, 74–5; Oakley, *Western Church in the Later Middle Ages*, 55–9; Tierney, *Western Europe in the Middle Ages*, 439–41. To underline the ambiguity of the situation, historians note that St. Catherine of Siena recognized Urban while St. Vincent Ferrer gave his allegiance to Clement.

money through taxation and the sale of Church offices and favors. Some religious orders split along national lines, and in others responsibility devolved from central to local leaders. The schism led many people to conclude that supreme authority in the Church resided not in the pope but in a general council, setting the stage for an extended struggle between papal and conciliar parties in the Church.[13]

The Church's urgent need for reform and the failure of all attempts to end the schism led many people to place their hopes in a general council. The first of these met at Pisa in 1409. After several years and much maneuvering, the Council of Constance (1414–7) finally resolved the Great Schism. It managed to depose or bring about the resignation of all claimants to the papacy and then enacted rules to govern the election of a new pope. As a result of these actions, Ottone Colonna was elected and took office as Pope Martin V (1417–31).[14]

Papal Policies After the Schism

Although Pope Martin had no rivals, he faced a number of challenges to his authority. Perhaps the most important came from a conciliar movement that had grown quite strong during the schism. Citing theology, canon law, and experience, its proponents argued that the papacy did not hold supreme authority in the Church. The Council of Constance had decreed that a general council was superior to the papacy and ordered such a council to meet on a stipulated schedule. Even apart from such constitutional considerations, many conciliarists had been urging reforms that would have limited the popes' activities and prerogatives. Pope Martin and his successors sometimes accommodated contemporary demands for a council, but they never accepted the doctrine of conciliar supremacy or practical measures that

[13] Brian Tierney, *Foundations of the Conciliar Theory: The Contributions of the Medieval Canonists from Gratian to the Great Schism* (Cambridge: University Press, 1955); Oakley, *Western Church in the Later Middle Ages*, 59–61; Knowles, *Middle Ages*, 425–9.

[14] Oakley, *Western Church in the Later Middle Ages*, 61–7; Tierney, *Western Europe in the Middle Ages*, 483–5. In an earlier attempt to end the Great Schism, the Council of Pisa deposed both the Roman and the Avignon popes. It then elected a successor, Alexander V, who was succeeded a year later by the thoroughly disreputable John XXIII. Despite good intentions, Pisa created a third claimant to the see of Peter, the first two having ignored its decree of deposition. The Council of Constance tried and deposed John in 1415; accepted the resignation of the Roman claimant, Gregory XII, later the same year; and deposed the Avignon claimant, Benedict XIII, in 1417. These actions cleared all claimants from the field, ended the schism, and opened the way for the election of Martin V, whose legitimacy virtually everyone acknowledged. See Knowles, *Middle Ages*, xxv–xxvi, 420–1; Oakley, *Western Church in the Later Middle Ages*, 64–7.

circumscribed their rights. The vindication of their supremacy, both in theory and in practice, became the primary goal of the popes' activities.[15]

Papal efforts to defeat conciliarism severely compromised efforts to reform the Church. By acting against conciliarism and resisting a conciliar exercise of Church authority, the popes neutralized the one source that seriously proposed to reform the Church. They also exploited the common interest of popes and kings to defend monarchical power against those who wanted to weaken it. If it helped to defeat the conciliarists, the popes were prepared to grant national monarchs a great deal of control over Church appointments and revenues. Those arrangements, which popes and kings found mutually advantageous, reinforced a system that compromised the apostolate and harmed the faithful. The popes were not prepared to allow Church reform to interfere with their strategy to vindicate papal supremacy in the Church.[16]

Besides carrying religious responsibilities, the popes ruled a portion of Italy, and this too affected their policies. Their involvement in the international affairs of Europe often required them to practice power politics, wage war, or make decisions that compromised the good of religion. The papacy's participation in the life of the Italian peninsula

---

[15] The Council of Constance's decree on conciliar supremacy, *Haec sancta synodus* (or *Sacrosancta*), was enacted in April of 1415; see Tanner, 1:409-10. The decree *Frequens*, requiring regular meetings of a general council, was issued in October of 1417 (Tanner, 1:438-43). See Knowles, *Middle Ages,* 420–5; Tierney, *Western Europe in the Middle Ages,* 483–90; Oakley, *Western Church in the Later Middle Ages,* 65–6.

The high-water mark of the conciliar movement is usually located at the Council of Basel (1431–49), whose antipapal actions and refusal to acknowledge the pope's authority eventually led it into schism and failure. Meanwhile, the canonically recognized gathering had been transferred from Basel to Ferrara and then to Florence. Sitting at Florence in July of 1439, the council enacted the decree *Laetentur coeli,* which explicitly acknowledged papal authority over the entire Church, including a general council. See Tanner, 1:523-8; DS, 1307. For more on the tangled history of the Council of Basel and its various adjournments, see Oakley, *Western Church in the Later Middle Ages,* 67–71; Ozment, *Age of Reform,* 172–9; Knowles, *Middle Ages,* 423–4; Tierney, *Western Europe in the Middle Ages,* 487–90.

Aiming to buttress the papal position still further, in 1460 Pope Pius II issued the bull *Exsecrabilis,* which condemned the practice of appealing papal decisions to a general council. See DS, 1375.

On the underlying canonical and theological issues, including the problem of a heretical pope, see Tierney, *Foundations of the Conciliar Theory;* Gordon Leff, *The Dissolution of the Medieval Outlook: An Essay on Intellectual and Spiritual Change in the Fourteenth Century* (New York: New York University Press, 1976) 142–3; Pelikan, 4:98-110.

[16] On these matters see Tierney, *Western Europe in the Middle Ages,* 490; Knowles, *Middle Ages,* 422, 426–9; Oakley, *Western Church in the Later Middle Ages,* 70–4; Ozment, *Age of Reform,* 182–90.

had yet another dimension. By highlighting ancient accomplishments and the present splendor of the human person, the Italian Renaissance stimulated a wide-ranging literary and cultural renewal. In that environment the Holy See promoted a vigorous artistic expansion and created a priceless legacy of art and architecture.[17]

Implications and Consequences

The impact of scandalous activities and conditions on the faith of ordinary believers, though impossible to quantify, must have been great. War, natural disaster, social conflict, political strife, and ecclesiastical crisis would have made it more difficult for a person to maintain moral equilibrium, especially when the Church, society, and the local community were themselves in disarray. However the people of these centuries responded in very trying circumstances, their actions had an influence that extended well beyond their own age. By handing on a wounded Church, a changed political landscape, and a complex legacy of problems and attitudes, the people of the late Middle Ages guaranteed that their children would eventually confront a moral and religious crisis of equal or greater proportions.

That legacy included a Church whose basic structures and offices had suffered from long-standing abuse. Because the integrity and right functioning of such institutions as the episcopate, the monasteries, and the local parish or religious house are essential to the spiritual and religious health of the Christian community, their impairment was bound to have negative consequences. The notion that Church offices could be sold and their revenues treated as an incumbent's private property, for example, did more than fill those offices with absent, unqualified, and uncommitted people. The ultimate and far more pernicious effect of such abuses was to disassociate pastoral offices and institutions from their proper spiritual goals and make them serve the prevailing political system and its profane agenda.

The Holy See's disedifying activities and especially the Great Schism are to be assessed in a similar light. Over time, the popes' political

---

[17] Oakley, *Western Church in the Later Middle Ages*, 74–6; Southern, *Western Society and the Church*, 150; Knowles, *Middle Ages*, 429–34. Knowles has characterized the fifteenth-century papacy in the following terms: "Deeply involved in Italian power politics, it attained considerable success in devious statecraft and lavish patronage of the arts and luxurious living, while ceasing to give effective spiritual leadership and guidance to the Church and sinking very low indeed in moral esteem. This must be borne in mind as a background to the religious life of the century: a worldly papacy, principally interested in Italian politics, and the centre of a rich, brilliant, worldly and often vicious court" (460).

efforts and financial policies undermined their religious and moral authority and weakened the papacy's historical claim to be the arbiter of authentic Christianity. By confronting the Church with a series of popes and antipopes, the Great Schism discredited the papacy as the primary symbol and guarantor of unity in the Latin Church. A divided papacy caused new divisions and added to religious and moral confusion in the Christian West. The abuses, compromises, and crises of this period injured Church institutions at every level.

The consequences of this institutional deterioration were great. Many struggled with confusion, no longer sure what resources were necessary and which activities important, as they pursued their spiritual journey. In seeking to encounter their God, devout people sometimes found it necessary to go around an incompetent priest, absentee bishop, worldly cardinal, or offensive pope. Some began to wonder about the very legitimacy of Church offices and whether they were essential to authentic Christian life. Such cases necessarily impacted a person's moral life. Church reform, the Church itself, and even how one ought to worship God all became issues of conscience. But the confusion and rechanneling of religious faith had another consequence. By obscuring the ecclesial context and coordinates of Christian moral life, contemporary scandals and abuses encouraged people to place moral issues in a frame of reference that was more individual and less social than would have been the case in an earlier age.[18]

JOHN DUNS SCOTUS

As a theologian, philosopher, and Franciscan, John Duns Scotus (1265–1308) presupposed the truth of Christian faith and maintained a deep respect for the Aristotelian and Augustinian traditions which he had also inherited. A thinker of uncommon brilliance, he had a remarkable capacity to deal logically and comprehensively with subtle issues. His teachings on God's freedom, the contingency of all creation, and the reality and singularity of persons and things influenced the future course of Western thought and promoted a new theology of Christian life.[19]

---

[18] For a discussion of the impact of historical events on religious institutions and symbols, see, for example, Alister E. McGrath, *The Intellectual Origins of the European Reformation* (Oxford: Basil Blackwell, 1987) 14–7; Heiko A. Oberman, "The Shape of Late Medieval Thought: The Birthpangs of the Modern Era," *The Pursuit of Holiness in Late Medieval and Renaissance Religion: Papers from the University of Michigan Conference*, ed. Charles Trinkaus with Heiko A. Oberman (Leiden: E. J. Brill, 1974) 8.

[19] For a review of Scotus' background, see Allan B. Wolter, "Reflections on the Life and Works of Scotus," *ACPQ* 67 (1993) 1–13.

The Primacy of Divine Freedom

Scotus' teaching on freedom reflected his faith that God is both free and almighty and acts out of an abundant love for human persons. He shared the Augustinian conviction that the will and its affections hold priority over the mind and its knowledge, a theme that was important to the Franciscans generally. It is also likely that Scotus constructed his doctrine of freedom in opposition to the principle of natural necessity that some radical Aristotelians had asserted. If nature entailed necessity and if this applied to God as well as all other beings as they thought, then God could only act in a necessary way. The universe would be necessary and autonomous, and the intellect would strictly control the will by means of the knowledge it provides. Scotus rejected these implications as repugnant to Christian faith.[20]

If he was to vindicate God's freedom, Scotus needed to do more than merely assert it; he had to show that freedom is essential to God's nature and activity. He knew that God's intellect could not be the source of this freedom because even God's intellect is bound to recognize truth and is constrained by what it knows. But this is not the case with the will, which has the power of self-determination and is not subject to natural necessity. Scotus accepted that the intellect influences the will by means of the knowledge and rational thinking it provides. But it does not dominate the will or constrain its freedom; rather, it is the will that both directs the mind and governs moral choices. Scotus therefore determined that God's will is paramount and is the source of divine freedom. Moreover, as the most perfect being God enjoys the greatest possible freedom; God's actions are necessarily free and cannot be constrained by any external necessity.[21]

The Contingency of Created Beings

Scotus' teaching on divine freedom had immediate implications for the status of creation. Earlier theologians had also recognized God's

---

[20] Mary Elizabeth Ingham, "The Condemnation of 1277: Another Light on Scotist Ethics," *FZPT* 37 (1990) 91–103, especially 94–5; Armand Maurer, "Some Aspects of Fourteenth-Century Philosophy," *Being and Knowing: Studies in Thomas Aquinas and Later Medieval Philosophers* (Toronto: Pontifical Institute of Medieval Studies, 1990) 449–50; also useful in relating Scotus to the earlier tradition is Efrem Bettoni, "The Originality of the Scotistic Synthesis," *John Duns Scotus, 1265–1965*, ed. John K. Ryan and Bernardine M. Bonansea (Washington: The Catholic University of America Press, 1965) 28–44. Ample references to original texts will be found in the sources cited in this discussion, especially those of Wolter, Ingham, Bonansea, Bettoni, and Adams.

[21] Ingham, "Condemnation of 1277," 96–7.

freedom and acknowledged that God could have made the universe differently or refrained from creating it at all. To express these points they distinguished between what God might have done *de potentia absoluta* ("by absolute power") and what he actually has done *de potentia ordinata* ("by ordained power") in creating the universe.[22] Scotus maintained that creation reflects God's free decision to constitute it in one particular way. God did not create the universe in view of any attributes that God was bound to recognize or respect. Rather, the universe is good only because God freely created it good. Scotus readily acknowledged that the present order of things reflects God's "ordained power" but saw that power as an expression of divine freedom—which God always exercises in "a most reasonable way"[23]—rather than a response to the anticipated merits of a given universe. For the same reason Scotus tended to relate God's "absolute power" to his extraordinary or miraculous interventions in the universe rather than to his hypothetical options prior to the act of creation. The created universe must therefore be considered nonnecessary, or contingent. The strictly contingent status of all created beings is a pivotal aspect of Scotus' thought.[24]

The Reality and Knowledge of the Individual

Scotus' doctrine concerning the priority of God's freedom and the contingency of all created things affected his views about reality and knowledge, especially his discussion of the individual entity. Here too the history of the discussion highlights both the traditional nature of Scotus' contribution and its novelty.

Western thinkers prior to Scotus presupposed that reality exists and that human beings know reality. Their problem was to account for reality and knowledge in a way that reflected human experience and was internally consistent. This task was framed by certain assumptions. Among these were the convictions that the things encountered in daily

[22] Bernardino M. Bonansea, "The Divine Will in the Teaching of Duns Scotus," *Antonianum* 56 (1981) 296–335; idem, "Duns Scotus' Voluntarism," *John Duns Scotus, 1265–1965*, 83–121; Alister E. McGrath, *Iustitia Dei: A History of the Christian Doctrine of Justification* (Cambridge and New York: Cambridge University Press, 1986) 1:119-21; see especially William J. Courtenay, "The Dialectic of Divine Omnipotence," *Covenant and Causality in Medieval Thought: Studies in Philosophy, Theology, and Economic Practice* (London: Variorum Reprints, 1984). On the teaching of Thomas Aquinas, see *STh*, I, q. 25, a. 6, especially ad 3.

[23] Bonansea, "Divine Will in the Teaching of Duns Scotus," 300.

[24] John Duns Scotus, *Contingency and Freedom: Lectura I 39*, intro., trans., and commentary A. Vos Jaczn and others (Dordrecht, Boston, London: Kluwer Academic Publishers, 1994) especially 94–129.

experience are particular and material and that they are grasped by the bodily senses in the same way. They also presupposed that the mind knows universals—for example, being, natures, and essences—in an immaterial or spiritual way. Furthermore, if the mind knows universals when it knows reality, then reality must somehow include the universal as well. Finally, all things were understood to entail a kind of mind or intelligible form, which precluded any gap between mind and matter and made all things inherently intelligible. These basic assumptions framed the question of reality and knowledge for the Western tradition and account for certain broad similarities even among dissimilar theories.

Given the prevailing assumptions, most earlier thinkers held that knowledge entails a unity between the knower and the known. More particularly, they tended to identify knowledge primarily with a person's apprehension of the universals or the intelligible forms related to the singular things of experience. Such an approach affirmed the underlying unity and rational quality of reality, its non-tangible dimensions, and the mind's ability to know universals. But it did not account for the multiplicity of the singular things encountered in daily life, how they are known, and their relationship to universals. Although these questions occasioned a variety of answers, most of them interpreted the reality and knowledge of singulars in light of the primacy that was attributed to universals.

Scotus followed this tradition insofar as it concerned being and universals. He presupposed the reality of the various natures, for example, the humanity that each person shares, the equine nature of every horse, the circularity represented by every wheel. He held that the human mind is inherently qualified to know being as such, as well as the nature of the singular things encountered in experience, and taught that such knowledge occurs by a process of abstraction. But Scotus plowed new ground when he offered his account of how it was possible for the same nature to be present in many particular instances of it. He proposed that each individual entity exists by virtue of a principle of individuation, which specifies the pertinent nature as *this* individual rather than that one. Scotus spoke of it as *haecceitas*, or "thisness." "Thisness" specifies humanity as John rather than Harry, and Alice rather than Jane; to take another example, "thisness" gives a particular tennis ball its unique existence, really distinct from all other round objects. Scotus understood the full and individual existence of all created beings to be a function of "thisness," which individuates a given nature and focuses it in one unique instance or representative of that nature.

The same emphasis on the unique existence of individual entities characterizes Scotus' view of human knowledge. His predecessors found it difficult to account for knowledge of particular things. Scotus addressed this problem by invoking the ancient principle that a greater power can do whatever a lesser power can do. If the material senses can know material singulars, so much the more can the higher intellectual faculty of knowledge also know singulars. He stipulated that the mind knows singulars not by a process of abstraction from sense experience but by a process of direct cognition, or intuition, which Scotus regarded as a higher form of knowledge. With those assertions Scotus abandoned the traditional Augustinian understanding of knowledge as interior illumination and bound human knowledge to the singulars of experience more closely than had previously been done.[25]

Moral Life

Scotus taught that the source of Christian life is God's sovereign decision to structure it as it is. The overriding imperative is to love God above all things and therefore keep the commandments, especially the Decalogue and the requirement to love one's neighbor. It is also necessary to observe the natural law and its requirement of justice, which can be known by right reason or prudence. These objective requirements confront human persons, whose freedom tends toward two

[25] In addition to knowing being as being, Scotus held that human beings can know existing things as separate and particular, for example, that there are five tennis balls on the table. What is more, he affirmed that persons can also know the "thisness" of a particular thing, which would, for example, allow a person unfailingly to pick out one particular tennis ball from among others that have identical physical characteristics. Scotus stipulated that human beings cannot know the "thisness" of particular things in this life but will be able to do so in the next life.

On Scotus' doctrine of reality and knowledge, see Mary Elizabeth Ingham, "John Duns Scotus: An Integrated Vision," *The History of Franciscan Theology*, ed. Kenan B. Osborne (St. Bonaventure, N.Y.: Franciscan Institute, 1994) 188–205; William A. Frank and Allan B. Wolter, *Duns Scotus, Metaphysician* (West Lafayette, Ind.: Purdue University Press, 1995) 108–97; Leff, *Dissolution of the Medieval Outlook*, 37–50; John F. Boler, "Intuitive and Abstractive Cognition," *CHLMP*, 460–6; Frederick C. Copleston, *A History of Medieval Philosophy* (Notre Dame and London: University of Notre Dame Press, 1990) 216–7; Joseph Owens, "Faith, Ideas, Illumination, and Experience," *CHLMP*, 455–7.

In addressing questions of being and cognition, Scotus was also taking a position on the problem of universals; on this topic see Marilyn McCord Adams, "Universals in the Early Fourteenth Century," *CHLMP*, 412–7; Martin M. Tweedale, "Duns Scotus's Doctrine on Universals and the Aphrodisian Tradition," *ACPQ* 67 (1993) 77–93, especially 89–93. See also Louis Dupré, *Passage to Modernity: An Essay in the Hermeneutics of Nature and Culture* (New Haven and London: Yale University Press, 1993) 15–41.

kinds of goods. The *bonum utile* includes all goods that serve other, more important ends. The *bonum honestum* denotes those goods that are to be loved for their own sakes and not used to secure any ulterior good. God is the ultimate *bonum honestum*. The human will has a natural desire for useful goods, the *affectio commodi*, since they can serve one's "perfection and well being." But the will also tends to love goods in a way that fully respects their inherent goodness; this is the *affectio justitiae*. Moral life takes place as persons freely resolve the tension between these two goods and the two loves that naturally tend toward the one good or the other. Moral life also entails self-determination, for at each moment persons can decide whether and how they will exercise their free will, which pertains to the interior decision as well as any outward behavior. These free decisions show whether persons are acting as justice requires and whether they do so out of love for God. Scotus' view of moral life accented freedom and love, but it presupposed objectivity and reason.[26]

The Economy of Salvation

Scotus located the ultimate source of salvation in God's free will to save the elect, a decision that can have no compelling motive outside God's will. God first decides the salvation of specific persons as the end to be achieved and then predestines them to eternal life. Although this includes all the elect, Christ was the first to be predestined for glory. Christ's life on earth reflects God's original plan, and his incarnation would have occurred even if humanity had never sinned. But God foresaw the history of sin and provided a way to repair its damage. He could have employed any means at all to save humanity from sin but freely elected to do so through the death of Christ. Therefore Christ's crucifixion may have been quite fitting, but it remains a contingent and not a necessary means to effect human redemption. Its saving power derives solely from God's free acceptance, that is, God's decision to consider it salvific.[27]

---

[26] Leff, *Dissolution of the Medieval Outlook*, 24–5, 29–30; Allan B. Wolter, *John Duns Scotus on the Will and Morality* (Washington: The Catholic University of America Press, 1986) 16; Mary Elizabeth Ingham, "Scotus and the Moral Order," *ACPQ* 67 (1993) 128–43; idem, "John Duns Scotus: An Integrated Vision," 205–10; idem, *The Harmony of Goodness: Mutuality and Moral Living According to John Duns Scotus* (Quincy, Ill.: Franciscan Press, 1996).

[27] St. Anselm held that the death of Christ was necessary while remaining an act of divine grace (*CDH*, II, 4–7). Aquinas taught that while it could not be necessary, it was inherently fitting or most appropriate (*STh*, III, q. 1, a. 2); see also James A. Weisheipl, *Friar Thomas D'Aquino: His Life, Thought, and Work. With Corrigenda and*

A strong accent on divine freedom and the contingency of all created things also characterizes the economy of salvation as it concerns particular persons. Scotus assumed that humans have a natural ability to act freely, reasonably, and lovingly. He believed that if divine grace was necessary to empower good actions, then freedom, which is at the heart of moral life, would be correspondingly diminished. For these reasons Scotus taught that grace does not precede or empower good moral acts but follows and intensifies them. When persons act in charity and perform upright deeds, God adds the gift of grace and confers supernatural worth upon them. Grace leads to the reward of salvation, which is given to those who have done God's will to the best of their ability. Even so, Scotus did not consider grace to be a necessary aspect of Christian life or of salvation, for that would limit God's freedom. Grace is the means God ordinarily uses to justify and save human beings. Grace is the crowning glory of a good moral life; it manifests God's overflowing love and normally foreshadows God's ultimate acceptance of those who have done God's will.[28]

Scotus was aware that his teachings on freedom and contingency might seem to inject great uncertainty into moral and religious life and even undermine the Christian dispensation itself. Even though God retains the right and the power to act according to the divine will, Scotus was convinced that God would remain faithful to the established dispensation and does not act capriciously. The economy of salvation therefore gains stability *ex pacto divino*, "from God's promise," rather than from any natural necessity. By basing Christian life on God's promise or covenant with humanity, Scotus recognized its contingent status but also affirmed that a good God treats persons consistently and not arbitrarily. As a Christian and a Franciscan he was convinced that Christian life finds its surest foundation in God's love, which is freely offered and generously bestowed.[29]

Addenda (Washington: The Catholic University of America Press, 1983) 314. On the issue itself, see William J. Courtenay, "Necessity and Freedom in Anselm's Conception of God," *Covenant and Causality;* McGrath, *Iustitia Dei,* 1:55-60, 63-4, 134-7; Pelikan, 3:106-18; 4:22-30, 33.

[28] One axiom of this theology is that God can do anything directly, and dispense with intermediaries. It is therefore possible that God can justify and save a person without the involvement of grace. This would not reflect the ordained arrangement but could be done by God's absolute power. Leff, *Dissolution of the Medieval Outlook,* 50–4; Copleston, *History of Medieval Philosophy,* 226–9; Ingham, "Scotus and the Moral Order"; Wolter, *John Duns Scotus on the Will and Morality,* 20–9, 47–51, 54–64, 89–98; 127–237 (esp. 207–25), 262–87, 423–47; Vernon J. Bourke, *History of Ethics* (Garden City, N.Y.: Doubleday, 1968) 103–4; McGrath, *Iustitia Dei,* 1:146-9.

[29] Ingham, "John Duns Scotus," 210–26; Leff, *Dissolution of the Medieval Outlook,* 50–1; McGrath, *Iustitia Dei,* 1:119-21, 147-8; Pelikan, 4:25-6; Wolter, *John Duns Scotus*

The Importance of Scotus' Doctrine

Scotus constructed his doctrine on Christian, Aristotelian, and Augustinian foundations. In light of earlier problems, he was especially concerned to do justice to God's freedom, power, and love; to describe volition as a rational desire; and to affirm the decisive quality of a person's free interior response. These teachings emphasized important dimensions of Christian life that he believed had not always received their due.

By determining that freedom prevails over necessity, Scotus was able to protect God's freedom and show how the divine will is the source of all that God has done. Such a view emphasizes the gratuity of God's actions, reflects the Scripture's testimony to a God who acts out of love (e.g., Exod 33:19; Deut 7:7-8; Luke 12:32; John 3:16; Eph 2:4), and reiterates a major Augustinian theme. God's sovereign freedom and its corollary, the contingency of all creation, shift the focus from God's nature to God's deeds, what God has actually done in the history of salvation, and the overflowing love that prompts God's actions. Although both creation and the Christian dispensation find their basis in God's will, God's promise of consistency endows them with reliability. Taken together, these complementary teachings emphasize the theological and objective texture of human life. At the same time, the primacy of freedom and love moves the center of gravity to the interior of the human person; it throws the tension between justice and utility into high relief and underlines the decisive quality of moral choices and the motivation that is associated with them.

With the tradition, Scotus accepted that natures, essences, and being itself enjoy real existence, but he was convinced that earlier thinkers had not sufficiently accounted for individual entities. In elaborating his principle of individuation, Scotus gave the individual a stronger foundation in reality, knowledge, and language than had been done before. This helped to direct attention from abstract natures to really existing things and invited scholars to reconsider the basis of knowledge. This shift of emphasis affected religious and moral life as well. It increased the standing of each individual person, the particular things they encounter, their direct knowledge of them, what they actually do, and the motivation associated with each act. It encouraged theologians and pastors to attend to the unique qualities of each person and each particular case. Scotus' doctrine on the individual is a milestone in Western intellectual history.

---

on the Will and Morality, 9–11, 16–20, 48–51, 54–7, 219–25, 239–61; Courtenay, "Dialectic of Divine Omnipotence," 1–13. Augustine of Hippo also held that Christian life gains its stability from God's fidelity to his own promises (see McGrath, *Iustitia Dei,* 1:119-20).

Scotus' principles also required him to reconsider the relationship between moral life and salvation. By teaching that grace is not needed for good decisions and actions, he sought to do justice to human freedom, love, and moral responsibility. His interpretation of grace as God's acceptance and enhancement of human goodness placed the accent on God's freedom and loving embrace of persons. When viewed as a whole, this picture portrays the Christian dispensation in terms of divine-human mutuality, in which God's love is primary, calls forth love from human persons, and then responds to their love with even greater generosity. This sharing of love is all the more impressive because it is free and unconstrained.

Scotus' emphasis on freedom and contingency entailed certain risks. Although he intended the very opposite, his insistence on the supremacy of God's freedom could be taken to suggest that God constituted the economy of salvation arbitrarily and without regard for human reality, impressions that are reinforced by Scotus' notions of God's absolute power and the contingency of the present order. Over time, people began to think that since key elements of Christian life have no inherent value, they might easily be depreciated or bypassed. Moreover, in the absence of reliable and necessary foundations or criteria, it became more difficult to settle arguments over what God's will might be. That tended to weaken the consensus about what is essential to Christian life.[30]

WILLIAM OF OCKHAM

Shortly after the death of Duns Scotus another Franciscan began to wrestle with many of these same issues. A thinker of uncommon power, William of Ockham (c. 1285–1349) also helped to redirect Western thought on fundamental points, with considerable implications for Christian life. The following discussion will principally attend to Ockham's teachings about reality, human knowledge, and Christian life.[31]

[30] Leff, *Dissolution of the Medieval Outlook*, 54–5; Copleston, *History of Medieval Philosophy*, 260–2; Bourke, *History of Ethics*, 103–4.

[31] Little is known of Ockham's early life. For a brief biography and a description of his works, see Copleston, *History of Medieval Philosophy*, 236–7; Ernest A. Moody, "William of Ockham," *EP*, 8:306-7; or Gordon Leff, *William of Ockham: The Metamorphosis of Scholastic Discourse* (Manchester: Manchester University Press; Totowa, N.J.: Rowman & Littlefield, 1975) xv–xx. For detailed presentations of Ockham's thought, see Leff, *William of Ockham*; Marilyn McCord Adams, *William Ockham* (Notre Dame, Ind.: University of Notre Dame Press, 1987).

It should also be noted that since about 1930 scholars have substantially revised the inherited view of William of Ockham and his teachings and shown that he should not be viewed as an extreme nominalist who deploys God's arbitrary will

Ockham's Account of Reality

William of Ockham worked out his account of reality largely in opposition to Duns Scotus. To begin with, Okham denied as contradictory his predecessor's teaching that similar things really exist as separate individuals but are nonetheless one through the nature they share, a nature that is no less real than the concrete individual. His second objection addressed Scotus' claim that the ground of all reality, experience, and knowledge is being, which he understood in a highly abstract and universal way. Scotus accepted that because they are unitary and abstract, being and natures cannot be experienced directly but can only be known by abstraction, a purely mental activity. Ockham replied that if being and natures are indeed knowable only by virtue of mental activity, there is no adequate way to distinguish them from mental imaginings. In other words, Ockham rejected Scotus' theory on grounds that it offered no reliable criterion by which to differentiate fantasy and reality.[32]

To avoid these difficulties, Ockham asserted that reality encompasses those things, and only those things, that exist independently of the human mind. He therefore held that reality pertains to the concrete singulars that are encountered in human experience and not to concepts, natures, or universals as such. By taking this position, Ockham abandoned the assumption that reality is ultimately one and is to be understood in terms of the universal. Ockham began with what is known through experience and declared that reality is radically multiple.[33]

Ockham's Theory of Knowledge

Ockham's assertion that reality is composed of many singular entities turned the question of knowledge on its head. Instead of having to account for a multiplicity of objects in light of their underlying unity, as many of his predecessors tried to do, Ockham's task was to explain how the human mind knows different singular things in an

---

so as to reduce the universe and Christian life to incoherence and utter fluidity, at least in principle. See William J. Courtenay, "Nominalism and Late Medieval Religion," *Pursuit of Holiness*, 26–59; idem, "Nominalism and Late Medieval Thought: A Bibliographical Essay," *TS* 33 (1972) 721–6; Marilyn McCord Adams, "William Ockham: Voluntarist or Naturalist?" *Studies in Medieval Philosophy*, ed. John F. Wippel (Washington: The Catholic University of America Press, 1987) 219–47; idem, "The Structure of Ockham's Moral Theory," *FS* 46 (1986) 1–35.

[32] Adams, "Universals in the Early Fourteenth Century," 417–22; Copleston, *History of Medieval Philosophy*, 217–8; Leff, *Dissolution of the Medieval Outlook*, 35, 57.

[33] Copleston, *History of Medieval Philosophy*, 239, 242; Leff, *Dissolution of the Medieval Outlook*, 35–8, 57–9.

abstract, universal, and unitary way. Beginning with concrete and singular entities, Ockham asserted that knowledge is the direct intuition of the things one encounters in experience.[34] Since this principle bound knowledge to individual things, it required Ockham to reconsider the status of concepts, essences, and generalizations. He taught that the mind notices common attributes of similar things and distills from them the concepts that facilitate the identification and discussion of such things in the future. A concept, universal, or essence is the product of mental activity. These abstractions enjoy no existence apart from the mind and cannot be the source of knowledge. Their validity depends upon the range of cases on which they are based and the accuracy with which they are formed.[35]

Implications of Ockham's Turn to the Singular

The significance of Ockham's teachings can be appreciated by considering their impact on the intellectual syntheses of Thomas Aquinas, Duns Scotus, and others who assume the real basis and universal reach of essences and natures. Once reality is located solely in singular things, and universals are understood to be the product of mental activity, arguments that begin with the universal and then move to the particular lose their validity and power. Moreover, on Ockham's premises, what is known to be true of the many is not necessarily true of particular instances that have not yet been the object of direct knowledge. In short, once the reality of essences and natures is denied, they cannot be

[34] Ockham allowed that one's concepts and mental activity can also be known, but this did not weaken the force of his primary insistence that knowledge is based on intuitive cognition of singular things. For further discussion see Boler, "Intuitive and Abstractive Cognition," 466–75; Copleston, *History of Medieval Philosophy,* 239–43; Moody, "William of Ockham," 308–10; Maurer, "Aspects of Fourteenth-Century Philosophy," 454–7; Leff, *Dissolution of the Medieval Outlook,* 59–67.

[35] Moody, "William of Ockham," 308–12; Copleston, *History of Medieval Philosophy,* 243, 247.

Ockham can be characterized as conceptualist with respect to the problem of universals. While he locates reality solely in singular things, he acknowledges that the mind can form concepts that reflect aspects of real things. Universals therefore do not have real existence but only conceptual status. Because they are reflected in the common nouns or names that refer to mental concepts, universals also have nominal status. This is the origin of the term "nominalism." See Oberman, "Shape of Late Medieval Thought," 3–25; Adams, "Universals in the Early Fourteenth Century," 417–22; idem, "William Ockham: Voluntarist or Naturalist?" 223–5; McGrath, *Intellectual Origins of the European Reformation,* 70–2; idem, *Iustitia Dei,* 1:167-70; Leff, *Dissolution of the Medieval Outlook,* 74–6; Courtenay, "Nominalism and Late Medieval Thought."

trusted to yield certain knowledge. Systems that presume otherwise lose a key source of their intellectual strength and validity.[36]

Ockham's turn to the individual entity reinforced the conviction, already present in Thomas Aquinas and others, that moral judgments need to be based upon a sound knowledge of the contingent facts of the matter at hand. Ockham focused new attention on the unique contours of each case and the need to evaluate it on its own merits. In a rapidly changing world activities connected with trade, finance, insurance, and diplomacy brought forth new and difficult questions of justice. He reminded theologians, pastors, and others that specific and accurate knowledge was necessary to a correct resolution of any problem they might need to address.[37]

Moral Life and Salvation

Following Duns Scotus, Ockham attributed primacy to God's will, which is altogether free of necessity and extends in principle to any action that does not violate the law of contradiction. However, Ockham went beyond Scotus when he presented freedom as a "liberty of indifference or contingency" that cannot be constrained by right reason or internal appetites.[38] On the human level, freedom is the hallmark and source of moral action, which is to be decided in the light of objective criteria. These criteria are the natural law and God's authoritative commands concerning actions that would otherwise be neither good nor evil. The natural law is known by right reason, which also recognizes the norm of God's authority. As a rule, therefore, persons act in a fully virtuous way when they do what right reason suggests because it is reasonable and as a way to show their love for God. Ockham was convinced that right reason and divine commands normally call for the same action, but he could not rule out the possibility that God might require something that conflicted with right reason. He also held that external actions as such are morally indifferent and gain their moral quality from the agent's free will. Overall, Ockham's moral theory recognized the normative function of natural law and right reason but assigned priority to God's freedom and that of human beings. By so doing he helped to strengthen a tendency among late medieval

---

[36] Oberman, "Shape of Late Medieval Thought," 13–4; Leff, *Dissolution of the Medieval Outlook*, 37; Ozment, *Age of Reform*, 60–1.

[37] One example is the reevaluation of maritime insurance, which a thirteenth-century papal decretal had condemned. See Louis Vereecke, "L'Assurance maritime chez les theologiens des XVe et XVIe siècles," *StMor* 8 (1970) 347–85.

[38] Adams, "William Ockham: Voluntarist or Naturalist?" 233.

theologians to interpret divine and human activity in light of free will.[39]

When Ockham considered the dynamics of salvation, he denied that persons need grace if they are to act in an upright way. Because God respects the ordained order, God rewards with grace, supernatural merit, and final salvation those who have acted reasonably, loved God, and obeyed the commandments as best they can. Ockham regarded this divine response as eminently reliable *ex pacto divino*, on account of God's promise. Even so, nothing external can bind God in any way, and neither good persons nor upright activities can have any independent claim on God. In the final analysis all merit and salvation comes entirely from God's free acceptance, which need not take account of any other considerations.[40]

The Question of Pelagianism

Although Ockham's views reflect the covenantal and personal aspects of the Scriptures, they also raise certain problems. One is the place of Christ in the process of justification. Because justification comes solely from God's free determination, it does not require that Christ should have died or even that he should have been born. The dynamics of a voluntarist, or will-based, system make Christ's role in human moral life and salvation strictly contingent and therefore in-

---

[39] Ibid, 231–42; idem, "The Structure of Ockham's Moral Theory," 1–35, especially 10–8; Leff, *William of Ockham*, 477–81, 496–8. Leff insists that if the term "voluntarism" is synonymous with subjectivism, it cannot refer to persons, since they are to conform their willing and acting to God's commands and not their own arbitrary will. Voluntarism does describe God, since his will freely decides which acts will be right and which persons meritorious.

The exclusively interior quality of Ockham's morality helps to balance his equally strong emphasis on God's will as the norm for human behavior. The requirement that a person freely will to do what is right out of a motive of love of God means that God's will is not concerned only with what is done or omitted. Behavior is important, but it remains secondary to considerations of free interior motivation and decision. That priority is not always easy to maintain, especially when there is an elevated concern about right behavior. For a discussion of Ockham's moral teachings, see also Lucan Freppert, *The Basis of Morality According to William Ockham* (Chicago: Franciscan Herald Press, 1988); Moody, "William of Ockham," 315–6; Copleston, *History of Medieval Philosophy*, 252–5.

[40] Ockham's views on merit and predestination are presented in Adams, "Structure of Ockham's Moral Theory," 18–33; idem, "William Ockham: Voluntarist or Naturalist?" 243–5; Leff, *William of Ockham*, 468–70; McGrath, *Iustitia Dei*, 1:115-7, 121-4, 137-8. The notion of acceptance is analogous to a government's determination that paper money or a coin struck from a base metal will have a monetary value that far exceeds its intrinsic worth.

herently less important. Another problem concerns Pelagianism. Ockham and his followers held that a person does not need grace in order to do God's will but that those who have lived an upright moral life can expect God to reward them with justification. That teaching is problematic because it seems to concede to human beings the ability to contribute toward their salvation without the help of God's grace.

For his part, Ockham tried to exclude any hint of Pelagianism from his theology, and was convinced that it respected Catholic faith. He based creation and the economy of salvation on God's freedom and insisted that God cannot be bound by human beings in any way or for any cause. Even though persons can and must act on their own to do what God commands, their obedience does not entitle them to salvation, which is exclusively God's free gift of love.

Although it was well crafted and made a strong claim to orthodoxy, Ockham's theology of salvation involved a very fragile synthesis. Its careful integration of objective requirements, human freedom and effort, and divine activity drew its strength and balance from the primacy of love in Christian life and a deep confidence in God's generosity and reliability. With the passage of time, however, such a synthesis became more difficult to maintain. Especially when later scholars lost sight of the whole and emphasized one or another of its elements; they were more likely to suggest that human beings earn salvation, portray God's freedom as arbitrary, or detach moral life from personal salvation.[41]

LATER THEOLOGICAL DEVELOPMENTS

John Duns Scotus and William of Ockham exercised a strong cumulative influence on later developments. In their wake, some scholars extended the will-based approach of these Franciscan thinkers and took it in new directions, especially when they developed the implications of God's absolute power. Some followed Ockham's lead and identified reality with the singulars that exist apart from the human mind. Others attributed some reality to universals. Although this

---

[41] Also relevant is late medieval scholars' ignorance of the decrees on grace issued by the Second Council of Orange in 529. This ignorance is to be kept in mind as their teachings are considered. On this entire matter see Leff, *Dissolution of the Medieval Outlook,* 50–2, 54; idem, *William of Ockham,* 470–5, 494–6, 498–501; McGrath, *Intellectual Origins of the European Reformation,* 80–5; idem, *Iustitia Dei,* 1:76-8, 83-91, 115-7, 121-4; Ozment, *Age of Reform,* 40–1; Oberman, "Shape of Late Medieval Thought," 15.

diversity is significant, of even greater importance is the emergence of sharply contrasting positions on justification and the moral life.[42]

Late Medieval Schools of Thought

The *via moderna* ("modern way" or "new way") was a school of thought that began with William of Ockham and included such later figures as Robert Holcot (d. 1349), Adam of Woodham (d. 1358), Pierre d'Ailly (1350–1420), and Gabriel Biel (c. 1420–95).[43] It is characterized by an underlying voluntarism and a readiness to apply the dialectic of God's two powers to a wide variety of issues, including justification and the moral life. *Via moderna* theologians taught that the economy of salvation merely reflects God's arbitrary will to structure it in one particular way. They often spoke of God as a legislator who requires people to love God and keep the commandments. Their covenantal interpretation of Christian life affirmed that people are naturally able to keep God's law but denied that obedience gives them any claim to justification. Moral goodness and supernatural merit do not reflect the worth of persons or their activities; they depend solely on God's arbitrary will to consider them worthy. This highly positive assessment of human capacities provoked accusations that the *via moderna* involved a Pelagian view of salvation. A reaction soon developed and consolidated in an opposing school of thought.[44]

The *schola Augustiniana moderna* ("later Augustinian school") took its name primarily from the Augustinian order with which it was associated. Over time, Augustinian theologians accepted the notion of God's two powers and that justification is God's free acceptance rather than a response to a creature's goodness. But their strongly anti-Pelagian disposition caused them to reject the positive anthropology taken for granted in the *via moderna*. Theologians of the later Augustinian school held that human beings are naturally incapable of anything good and contribute nothing to their salvation. Salvation and damnation both

---

[42] Recent research has shown that late medieval thought was far more complex and diverse than had been assumed and that more recent assessments of particular scholars and their teachings sometimes fails to do them justice. See, for example, Courtenay, "Nominalism and Late Medieval Thought"; idem, "Nominalism and Late Medieval Religion," especially 34–6; Hieko A. Oberman, "Some Notes on the Theology of Nominalism with Attention to Its Relation to the Renaissance," *HTR* 53 (1960) 54–5; McGrath, *Intellectual Origins of the European Reformation*, 69–93.

[43] See Heiko A. Oberman, *The Harvest of Medieval Theology: Gabriel Biel and Late Medieval Nominalism* (Grand Rapids: Eerdmans, 1967).

[44] McGrath, *Intellectual Origins of the European Reformation*, 75–85; idem, *Iustitia Dei*, 1:65-6, 166-72; idem, "The Anti-Pelagian Structure of 'Nominalist' Doctrines of Justification," *ETL* 57 (1981) 107–19.

depend entirely on God's predestination, which does not reflect the foreseen activity of human beings. If anyone acts in a morally upright or meritorious way, that is to be attributed solely to God's grace; if anyone ends in damnation, that too reflects God's sovereign and free choice. Such teachings emptied the moral life of theological significance, severed justification from human activity, and made it possible to wonder if a sinner might remain sinful even after justification.[45]

These schools of thought demonstrate that theologians had generally accepted the supremacy of God's will and the utter contingency of the present economy of salvation. Many also agreed that a contingent world does not yield certain knowledge about the nature of God or God's plan. These positions account for the general tendency to adopt a voluntaristic view of Christian life, base moral expectations on God's commands and prohibitions, and detach justification from moral life. The same presuppositions gave rise to sharp disagreements about such fundamental matters as anthropology, the possibility and value of moral life, Pelagianism, and justification.[46] This constellation of agreements and controversies suggests how much the theological landscape had changed since the time of Aquinas and Bonaventure.

The Significance of Late Medieval Thought

Although the specific teachings of late medieval scholars were certainly important, their fuller significance resides in their cumulative effect on the intellectual and religious life of Christian society. From the earliest times the Church community had been sensitive to intellectual currents. Augustine, Anselm, Aquinas, and other Catholic thinkers had analyzed authoritative texts and subjected them to judgment on the basis of intellectual and faith-related criteria. Over the centuries Christian scholars made important contributions to the theological and spiritual content of the Christian tradition and typically exercised a strong influence on the life and pastoral care in the Church community.

[45] Among the more important representatives of this school were Thomas Bradwardine (d. 1349), Gregory of Rimini (d. 1358), and Hugolino of Orvieto (d. 1373). Leff, *Dissolution of the Medieval Outlook*, 53–4; Alister E. McGrath, *Reformation Thought: An Introduction* (New York and Oxford: Basil Blackwell, 1988) 60–1; idem, *Intellectual Origins of the European Reformation*, 75–93, 104; idem, *Iustitia Dei*, 1:128-45 (esp. 143), 170–9.

[46] That theological disagreements became so acute also reflects confusion or paralysis in the hierarchy. The Great Schism, the disarray of the Holy See and local hierarchies, and the popes' struggle against conciliarism deprived the Church of any effective or generally acknowledged means by which it might settle conflicts about fundamental aspects of faith and praxis. See McGrath, *Intellectual Origins of the European Reformation*, 12–28; Pelikan, 4:10-68, especially 59–68.

The same continued to be true in the fourteenth and fifteenth centuries, all the more so when the weakness of the contemporary hierarchy and its inability to moderate the theological discussion are taken into account.

However, when one considers the qualitative impact of late medieval Christian scholarship on Church life, it becomes apparent that its contribution did not always serve the good of the Christian community. One evidence is its readiness to reinterpret the economy of salvation as well as the faith and praxis of the Church in ways that went well beyond what earlier generations had taken for granted. Some theologians were prepared to detach moral life from grace, grace from salvation, and salvation from moral life. Scholars enunciated radically incompatible views concerning the respective contributions of God and the human person to salvation, opening a new argument over Pelagianism and stimulating drastic attempts to avoid this heresy. Once God's arbitrary will was taken as the wellspring of human life, the Covenant became a mechanism by which God established rules and conditions for humanity's relationship with the divine. That view depreciated history and the economy of salvation. No longer expressions of God's love and desire to save a chosen people, the Decalogue and the natural law assumed a more legal, authoritarian quality and made it necessary to emphasize human obedience more than God's grace. Especially when they were mediated to priests and ordinary believers alike, such teachings were bound to have disruptive consequences for Christian life. That became ever more apparent as the religious drama of the sixteenth century unfolded.

PENANCE, PIETY, AND WORKS OF CHARITY

In the late Middle Ages people continued to seek suitable ways to express their faith and love of God. In keeping with traditional Church teachings and praxis, many had recourse to God's love and forgiveness in the sacrament of penance. People also undertook penitential activities on their own initiative, usually in a context framed by God's word, public prayer, and the service of others. Some turned inward, seeking unity with God by means of self-emptying and sincere conversion of heart, and gave rise to the spiritual and mystical movements that swept across Europe during this time. The following section will examine these approaches to communion with God and neighbor. It will also consider the influence of Renaissance humanism, which focused attention on the faith and piety of Western Christians and the legitimacy of basic Church beliefs, institutions, and practices. These developments highlighted key dimensions of moral and religious life and helped to create the context in which the religious crisis of the sixteenth century took place.

Sacramental Penance in the Late Middle Ages

Sacramental penance was a principal component of the Fourth Lateran Council's pastoral agenda. Aiming to promote a better living of Christian life by members of the Church, the council called for a well-educated clergy, better preaching, and more effective instruction. It asked priests to know their people and serve them well. Within that broader vision of pastoral care, the Fourth Lateran Council required all Catholics to confess their sins and do penance at least annually. It asked pastors to hear their parishioners' confessions carefully and discreetly and seek to rid them of sin in the manner of a good physician. Throughout this period preachers and local councils reiterated the need for people to confess their sins at least once a year and urged the advantages of a more frequent use of the sacrament.[47]

Developments in the Theology of Penance

By the end of the High Middle Ages theological accounts of forgiveness had begun to move away from the contritionist explanations of Abelard and Lombard. Thomas Aquinas taught that the quality of a penitent's contrition was decisive and held that forgiveness of a grave sinner occurred when God's gift of charity perfected that contrition. He attributed that infusion of charity to the power of absolution, an explanation that notably strengthened absolution's position within the ritual of penance. Duns Scotus took the matter further, teaching that a

---

[47] See Jean Charles Payen, "La pénitence dans le contexte culturel des XIIe et XIIIe siècles," *RSPT* 61 (1977) 399–428, 419–24; see also related discussions in chapters 6 and 7, above.

On the frequency with which people confessed their sins, see Thomas N. Tentler, *Sin and Confession on the Eve of the Reformation* (Princeton, N.J.: Princeton University Press, 1977) 70–82; Payen, "La pénitence," 427. On the use of the ritual, see Tentler, *Sin and Confession*, 82–95; James Dallen, *The Reconciling Community: The Rite of Penance* (New York: Pueblo, 1986) 157–8.

The need to form and educate the Catholic people gave rise to catechetical and other literature designed to further these purposes. The discussion below on the *Summae confessorum* is to be set within this larger pastoral context. See, for example, E. Mangenot, "Catéchisme," *DTC*, 2/2:1899-1907; Tentler, *Sin and Confession*, 28–53; Leonard E. Boyle, "*Summae Confessorum*," *Les genres littéraires dans les sources théologiques et philosophiques médiévales: Définition, critique et exploitation* (Louvain-la-Neuve: L'Institut d'études Médiévales, 1982) 230–3.

sinner could be forgiven in two distinct ways, either through perfect contrition or by means of absolution given to a penitent who was at least imperfectly contrite. In practice Scotus advised sinners not to rely on perfect contrition, since it was too difficult to verify. He urged them to receive absolution because that guaranteed the forgiveness of their sins and manifested a due concern for salvation.[48]

Those teachings influenced penitential praxis. By placing such stress on the power of absolution, Aquinas and Scotus emphasized the role of the Church in the process of forgiveness. Scotus' theology emphasized the power of absolution still further, which made the penitent's contrition correspondingly less important. Although neither he nor Aquinas depreciated contrition or satisfaction, their teachings encouraged the notion that the penitent's confession and the priest's absolution were the primary elements in the process of justification. In practice, that reinforced the Church's authority, assured penitents who acted in good faith that they were truly forgiven, and fostered adherence to the Lateran Council's decree.[49]

The Summae Confessorum

As a minister of the Church, the confessor was expected to abide by the regulations that various councils as well as the local bishop had enacted. However, it was not easy for a priest to learn of those rulings, since they were numerous, came from many different authorities, and changed with the passage of time. The confessor also had to consider the interpretations of canon lawyers and theologians. In addition, the work of the priest was framed by a theological understanding of Christian life that specified the nature of sin, how the ritual acted to bring about forgiveness, and the respective contributions of confessor and penitent toward that goal. Finally, the confessor needed to work from a sound understanding of persons, circumstances, motivations, occupations, and the various sins that people committed. The *summae confessorum* ("summas of confessors") were written in order to help the

---

[48] For a fuller discussion of the penitential teaching of Aquinas, Scotus, and others between Lateran IV and the Reformation, including references to the original sources, see A. Michel, "Pénitence, Du IVe Concile du Latran à la Réforme," *DTC*, 12/1:948-1050; Dallen, *Reconciling Community*, 146–8; Poschmann, *Penance and the Anointing of the Sick*, 168–9. Also to be noted is the declaration on penance issued by the Council of Florence in 1439 (DS, 1323; or Tanner, 1:548); see Poschmann, *Penance and the Anointing of the Sick*, 195–6.

[49] Thomas N. Tentler, "The Summa for Confessors as an Instrument of Social Control," *The Pursuit of Holiness*, 110–3; Payen, "La pénitence," 418–9.

priest learn about these essential matters and carry out his ministry competently, prudently, and fruitfully.[50]

The *summae confessorum* emerged around the year 1200 as penitential praxis began to pay greater attention to the penitent's circumstances and require the priest to respond accordingly. This literature reached its classic form in the year 1234 when St. Raymond of Peñafort published his *Summula de poenitentia*, which emphasized the canonical dimensions of penance. It prevailed throughout the thirteenth century until 1298, when a new and more theologically oriented work supplanted it, John of Freiburg's *Summa confessorum*. This last text, which drew heavily on the moral teachings of Thomas Aquinas, established the pattern to be followed by all others in the fourteenth and fifteenth centuries. Taken as a group, the *summae confessorum* strongly influenced the practice of penance in the late Middle Ages. Although none was composed after 1520, they remained in demand for about a century after that.[51]

The Summae Confessorum *and Christian Life*

The *summae confessorum* reflected a number of assumptions about the nature of Christian life. Based upon baptism, Christian life required a believer's wholehearted commitment to live rightly under the influence of charity and the other virtues. Christian life was also held to be ecclesial in nature: the Church was the community of worship and charity in which a member lived and the primary means through which God communicated grace. The *summae* were acutely aware that people often failed to live up to the requirements of Christian life.

---

[50] Tentler, "Summa for Confessors," 106, 108, 113–4, 117–9; Boyle, "Summae Confessorum," 233–6.

[51] Boyle, "Summae Confessorum"; Tentler, *Sin and Confession*, 31–9; Leonard E. Boyle, "The *Summa confessorum* of John of Freiburg and the Popularization of the Moral Teaching of St. Thomas and of Some of His Contemporaries," *St. Thomas Aquinas, 1274–1974: Commemorative Studies*, ed. A. Maurer and others (Toronto, 1974) 245–68, rept. in Leonard E. Boyle, *Pastoral Care, Clerical Education, and Canon Law, 1200–1400* (London: Variorum Reprints, 1981); Tentler, "Summa for Confessors."

One index of the popularity and influence of the *summae* is their publication history after movable type came into use in Europe in the mid-fifteenth century. Tentler provides a helpful chart of the *summae* and their various printings ("Summa for Confessors," 107).

Books to support the education and work of confessors were published in the centuries following 1520, but these can be regarded as a distinct literary and theological genre. Chapter 10, below, will examine these later works, which reflect the decrees of the Council of Trent and are often referred to as *Institutiones morales*, or "manuals of moral theology."

Although they admitted that knowledge and consent were essential considerations, these books tended to view failure from the perspective of the behavior that was incompatible with good Christian life. Those failures took various forms and differed in seriousness. But the decisive issue was whether they constituted mortal as opposed to venial sin, for only the former involved the loss of sanctifying grace and the threat of eternal damnation. The *summae* presupposed that those who had sinned mortally could only win back grace and justification if they were prepared to repent, confess, and make satisfaction for their sins as traditional Catholic faith and praxis as well as the Fourth Lateran Council required. Those assumptions illuminate the specific content of the *summae confessorum*.[52]

The *summae* were especially concerned that penitents should confess all the mortal sins they had committed. In part that requirement reflected social or practical considerations: mortal sins usually involved activity that gravely harmed others and hence needed to be proscribed as incompatible with Christian life and explicitly identified as matter to be confessed. A full confession of mortal sins was also necessary in order to assure that the penitent was actually forgiven. Behind this reasoning are the theological principle that a sin cannot be forgiven unless the sinner duly repents of it and the notion that confessing a sin manifests the required contrition. The deliberate failure to confess a mortal sin was therefore considered to manifest impenitence and made it impossible to forgive such a sinner at all. Finally, completeness was needed in order for the priest to know if he had authority to forgive the penitent's sins and whether there were any other requirements to be met.[53]

The need for a complete confession of mortal sins led the *summae* to discuss various sins in considerable detail. They catalogued sins according to their outward nature and the circumstances that might aggravate or mitigate them. Gravely evil activity was distinguished from behavior that was only slightly evil. But since even the worst of behavior is not actually sinful unless the person consents to it, the *summae* also had to address the subjective factors of understanding and freedom. Concern with completeness therefore embraced circum-

---

[52] Tentler, *Sin and Confession*, 57–66.

[53] A confessor's authority might be limited because the bishop had reserved the forgiveness of certain sins to himself or if the penitent was bound by an excommunication that precluded the reception of any sacraments so long as the excommunication remained in effect. A confessor was also expected to know which sins required restitution and hold the penitent to that obligation. Tentler, *Sin and Confession*, 123–4, 301–18; idem, "Summa for Confessors," 117–22; Payen, "La pénitence," 426; Kilian McDonnell, "The *Summae Confessorum* on the Integrity of Confession as Prolegomena for Luther and Trent," *TS* 54 (1993) 421–2.

stantial, personal, and behavioral factors, which easily became quite complex. That required technical competence, good judgment, and human sensitivity in the confessor. The need for completeness also made it necessary for penitents to make a careful examination of their consciences prior to confession and for confessors to ask questions of a penitent, at least in many cases.[54]

The confessor represented the hierarchy of the Church in the penitential encounter. He placed his "key of knowledge" of the Church's requirements and his understanding of theology, canon law, and Christian life at the penitent's service. He also held the "key of power" by which he conferred the absolution that mediated God's forgiveness. Although the summists never forgot contrition, many of them interpreted that requirement in a very lenient way. As long as penitents confessed their sins in good faith and were willing to try to do better in the future, they held that the priest's absolution forgave those sins.[55]

An Assessment of the Summae Confessorum

Any judgment about the *summae confessorum* needs to begin by acknowledging the particular view of Christian life that this literature embodied. In briefest terms it understood Christian life to be a comprehensive enterprise that involved the believer's faith, moral life, relationship with the Church, and standing with God. It assumed that each and every one of these elements needed to be in good order and that a serious defect in faith, moral life, or relationship with the Church could sever one's communion with God. That conception of Christian life united the moral and religious aspects of a believer's life and made the Church integral to them both. The Church calls persons to repentance, conversion, and faith, and its bishops exercise responsibility for the Christian community and its members. The forgiveness and reconciliation of sinful members required the Church's cooperation as well as the sinner's repentance.

At their best, the *summae confessorum* did justice to all these aspects of Christian life. They did so by regulating a sacramental praxis that helped members of the Church to learn what Christian faith involved

---

[54] Payen, "La pénitence," 423–4; Tentler, *Sin and Confession*, 104–24, 130–62; idem, "Summa for Confessors," 113–7; McDonnell, "*Summae Confessorum*," 415–21.

[55] Tentler, "Summa for Confessors," 109–113; idem, *Sin and Confession*, 318–43. The summists differed among themselves about the quality of contrition a penitent was expected to bring and its part in the process of forgiveness. This inability to agree on the relative importance of contrition and absolution reflects differences among the theologians whom the summists followed. See Tentler, *Sin and Confession*, 104–6, 233–301; see also the discussion in this section, above, on developments in the theology of penance.

and to see the ecclesial and practical implications of that faith. In the hands of competent and sensitive confessors[56] these books helped sacramental penance to be "the highest pastoral art, a just and certain discipline; making essential but possible demands on Christian consciences; preserving the divine order in Christ's Church; and assuring, as well as anything in this world could, the consoling gift of eternal salvation."[57]

Certain difficulties nevertheless attended the practice of sacramental confession. Both the nature of the ritual and the later *summae* tended to accent the externals: sinful behavior, the confession and its completeness, the requirements of the Church's canons and administrative rules, the authority of the confessor and the absolution that he pronounced. Although sincere repentance was required and one's relationship with a transcendent God acknowledged to be central, the concern with external factors constantly threatened to eclipse those invisible but essential dimensions of the penitential process. When that happened, the sacramental ritual could become a superstitious, legalistic, stifling, or anxiety-provoking exercise or, conversely, one that seemed to offer easy forgiveness to those who were prepared to observe its formalities.[58]

Another set of problems arose because it had become much more difficult to see the relationship between penance and the Christian community as such. Although theology and canonical regulations presupposed the ecclesial dimensions of sacramental penance, the prevailing praxis made it easier for people to associate the penance with the rules, the priest, or one's personal needs. People were more likely to understand penance as a means to absolve guilt instead of a ritual that reconciled a gravely sinful brother or sister to a holy community. Such a situation gave a higher profile to the legal, administrative, individual, and interior dimensions of the ritual.[59]

---

[56] See the summists' descriptions of the ideal confessor in Tentler, *Sin and Confession*, 95–104.

[57] Ibid., 368.

[58] Dallen, *Reconciling Community*, 148; Payen, "La pénitence," 427; Tentler, *Sin and Confession*, 363–8. On superstitious or abusive uses of penance and other religious actions, see Oakley, *Western Church in the Later Middle Ages*, 117–30; Jean Leclercq and others, *The Spirituality of the Middle Ages*, trans. The Benedictines of Holme Eden Abbey, Carlisle (London: Burns & Oates, 1968) 491–2, 497.

[59] Dallen, *Reconciling Community*, 158–62. See also Leclercq, *Spirituality of the Middle Ages*, 497–9, 507. Related problems concern the disappearance of the notion of baptismal initiation from medieval sacramental theology and the gradual shift from a largely corporate and participatory celebration of the Eucharist to one that tended to emphasize its individual and clerical aspects. See Pierre-Marie Gy, "La notion chretiénne d'initiation: Jalons pour une enquête," *MD* 132 (1977) 43–4; Oakley, *Western Church in the Later Middle Ages*, 80–9.

Mysticism

Late medieval Christian life was also characterized by a resurgence of piety and devotion. Its strength, character, and authenticity are reflected in the many saints and mystics who lived during this period as well as the ordinary men and women who embraced a life of Christian contemplation and charity. This upwelling of religious devotion among late medieval people readily flowed in the more personal and interior channels that the Augustinians, Cistercians, and Franciscans had opened in their souls.[60]

Among the most important aspects of late medieval spirituality was a mystical movement that waxed especially strong in the German-speaking portions of Europe, the Low Countries, and England. An ancient phenomenon, mysticism refers to a particular way of seeking union with God and a "direct, intuitive, ecstatic experience" of God.[61] It requires charity and prayer and yields a certain knowledge of God. Mysticism informed the lives of many fourteenth- and fifteenth-century figures, notably Catherine of Siena (c. 1347–80), Walter Hilton (d. 1396), Julian of Norwich (1342–c. 1442), Meister Eckhart (c. 1260–1328), John Tauler (1300–61), Henry Suso (c. 1295–1366), and Jan van Ruysbroeck (1293–1381). It influenced many others who either entered religious orders or joined nontraditional communities of people who lived a simple, celibate life and supported themselves by working in the world. In Germany, the Dominicans were asked to provide pastoral care for these groups, usually convents or communities of devout women. By means of their guidance, preaching, and writing the Dominicans propagated mystical awareness to wider audiences and helped to assure the ecclesial and theological soundness of this form of religious expression.[62]

The Devotio Moderna

The religious environment of the age also gave rise to a movement known as the *Devotio moderna*, which was begun by a well-educated

---

[60] Oakley, *Western Church in the Later Middle Ages*, 86–95. For a fuller discussion of religious orders in the late Middle Ages see Leclercq, *Spirituality of the Middle Ages*, 447–80.

[61] Oakley, *Western Church in the Later Middle Ages*, 90. For more concerning mysticism, see Andrew Louth, *The Origins of the Christian Mystical Tradition: From Plato to Denys* (Oxford: Clarendon Press, 1981); David Knowles, *What Is Mysticism?* (London: Sheed & Ward, 1979); also the partially completed four-volume work by Bernard McGinn, *The Presence of God: A History of Western Christian Mysticism* (New York: Crossroad, 1991–).

[62] Oakley, *Western Church in the Later Middle Ages*, 89–100; Leclercq, *Spirituality of the Middle Ages*, 373–428, 467–74, 499–505; see also 439–46.

Dutchman, Gerard Groote (1340–84). While in his early thirties Groote experienced a religious awakening that changed his life. Scandalized by the behavior of the clergy, the compromises of the religious, and the pantheistic strain in some contemporary spiritualities, Groote resolved to take another path. He lived in a simple, austere manner; upheld a strict morality; and dedicated himself to conversion, preaching, and charity. Above all, he tried to imitate Christ's humanity, an ongoing effort that he pursued by means of spiritual detachment and the practice of the virtues.

Before long he attracted others to his way of life and gathered them into small communities, which he directed. His followers became quite numerous and were eventually organized more formally. That process first gave birth to the Sisters of the Common Life and later to the Brothers of the Common Life. After Groote's death one of his closest disciples, Florens Radewijns (1350–1400), founded a monastery at Windesheim, which offered a stricter form of life to those brothers who wished to embrace it. From its beginnings in Holland the *Devotio moderna* quickly spread into the Low Countries and western Germany. Its principal literary monument is the *Imitation of Christ* by Thomas à Kempis (1379/80–1471).[63]

The Confraternities

If the *Devotio moderna* is sometimes taken as evidence that late medieval piety had largely turned inward and emphasized the individual,

---

[63] Oakley, *Western Church in the Later Middle Ages*, 100–13; Southern, *Western Society and the Church*, 331–56; Leclercq, *Spirituality of the Middle Ages*, 428–39. For a detailed history of this movement, see R. R. Post, *The Modern Devotion: Confrontation with Reformation and Humanism* (Leiden: E. J. Brill, 1968); John Van Engen, trans., *Devotio Moderna: Basic Writings* (New York: Paulist Press, 1988). For an overview of popular piety in this period, see Oakley, *Western Church in the Later Middle Ages*, 113-30; Leclercq, *Spirituality of the Middle Ages*, 481-505; see also the relevant chapters in Jill Raitt, ed., *Christian Spirituality: High Middle Ages and Reformation* (New York: Crossroad, 1985).

Scholars have sometimes considered the spirituality of the *Devotio moderna* to be largely individualistic. For example, Vandenbroucke suggests that by so strongly accenting the interior relationship between God and the soul, late medieval spirituality prepared the way for the Protestant Reformation to dispense with the Church's system of authority and worship and to relate faith to the interior experience of a believer responding to the scriptural word (see Leclercq, *Spirituality of the Middle Ages*, 498). Although he does not directly address Vandenbroucke's judgment, Oakley stresses the Catholic instincts and behavior of people in the *Devotio moderna*. He sees it as a forerunner not of Protestantism but of the Catholic Reformation of the sixteenth century (*Western Church in the Later Middle Ages*, 105–9).

the popularity of the confraternities argues to the opposite point, namely, that the corporate dynamics of lay spirituality remained strong and influential during this period. Dating from the thirteenth century, the confraternities reflected the influence of the friars, who promoted piety, penance, simplicity, and charity among the laity. With the passage of time these formally constituted associations of lay-persons became quite numerous and, in some places at least, came to have a significant impact on civic, political, and religious life.

Recent studies of Italian confraternities have shown that the spiritual activities of these groups included important ecclesial and social dimensions. Difficult penitential practices were encouraged as a means of identifying with the passion of Christ and to express one's contrition for sin. But these same practices presupposed the theology of the Church and the need of absolution for grave sins; they also addressed offenses that might harm the community. It was also felt that God was more likely hear prayers for the good of a city if its citizens repented of their sins and forgave one another. In addition, many confraternities embraced almsgiving and the relief of the poor, the sick, and others in distress. Some had been established to sing evening prayer, and many placed a high premium on preaching by the membership and prayer for deceased confreres. The confraternities' practice of scheduling religious devotions according to the Church's liturgical year, and their keen interest in the celebrations of Holy Week, serve as a further examples of their ecclesial consciousness.[64]

Renaissance Humanism

Italian Renaissance humanism celebrated the writings of ancient Greece and Rome as models of eloquence. This movement, which quickly spread to northern Europe, encouraged scholars to undertake a sustained study of classic writers. Many found this endeavor to be

---

[64] John Henderson, "Confraternities and the Church in Late Medieval Florence," *Voluntary Religion,* ed. W. J. Sheils and Diana Wood (Oxford: Basil Blackwell, 1986) 69–83; idem, "Penitence and the Laity in Fifteenth-Century Florence," *Christianity and the Renaissance: Image and Religious Imagination in the Quattrocento,* ed. Timothy Verdon and John Henderson (Syracuse, N.Y.: Syracuse University Press, 1990) 229–49; Timothy Verdon, "Christianity, the Renaissance, and the Study of History: Environments of Experience and Imagination," *Christianity and the Renaissance,* 23–7; Ronald F. E. Weissman, "Sacred Eloquence: Humanist Preaching and Lay Piety in Renaissance Florence," *Christianity and the Renaissance,* 250–71; Brian Pullan, "The *Scuole Grandi* of Venice: Some Further Thoughts," *Christianity and the Renaissance,* 272–301; Richard Mackenney, "Devotional Confraternities in Renaissance Venice," *Voluntary Religion,* 85–96.

quite appealing, especially since ancient texts could be used to promote good morals and raise the quality of contemporary speaking and
writing. Although these goals were worthy enough, the study of ancient authors had important side effects. It instilled a greater sensitivity to history and highlighted the differences between ancient and
modern times. It advanced the study of ancient languages, stimulated
the publication of critical texts, and brought out the need to interpret
them well. Before long, humanism improved scholars' knowledge of
Hebrew and Greek, the languages of the Bible, and supported new
research into patristic sources. The introduction of printing just after
1450 magnified the impact of these advances. It became possible for
scholars to publish dictionaries and grammars and to give critical texts
a wide circulation. Printing transformed scholarship and extended its
influence far and wide.[65]

By promoting interest in original sources, changing the nature of the
discussion, and opening it to lay participation, humanism greatly increased the pressure on the established Church order. The publication
of the Greek text of the New Testament exposed the flaws in the Vulgate,
the standard Latin translation, and led to calls for its abandonment.
Pointing to discrepancies between the Greek and Latin texts, critics
claimed that important aspects of Catholic doctrine and practice had
been based on errors in the Vulgate and therefore needed to be corrected. In addition, new research provided theologians with integral
texts of Jerome, Augustine, Origen, and other early Christian writers.
That gave scholars a solid basis for their work but also underlined the
differences between the early Church and the contemporary Christian
community. People began to cite the Fathers as authentic witnesses to
early Christian teachings and to criticize some later developments as
illegitimate. Finally, when the famous Donation of Constantine was
shown to be an eighth-century forgery, it seemed to vindicate those
who had condemned the Holy See's involvement in European politics
and that particular text for having legitimated it.[66]

Erasmus of Rotterdam (c. 1466–1536) reflected many of these influences. He was well educated, theologically competent, spiritually acute,
and a man of broad cultural and historical awareness. Erasmus' study
of the Scriptures and the Fathers led him to insist upon the spiritual

---

[65] McGrath, *Intellectual Origins of the European Reformation*, 32–43, 122–43; idem,
Reformation Thought, 11–3, 27–35; Maurice Keen, *A History of Medieval Europe* (London: Routledge & Kegan Paul, 1968) 278–81; see also Bard Thompson, *Humanists
and Reformers: A History of the Renaissance and Reformation* (Grand Rapids, Mich. and
Cambridge, England: Eerdmans, 1996) 1–368.

[66] McGrath, *Reformation Thought*, 41–9; idem, *Intellectual Origins of the European Reformation*, 122–39, 148–51, 175–90.

and salvific purposes of theology and condemn much of Scholastic discourse as useless and lifeless. His teachings on the primacy of grace, the Church as the body of Christ, the need for personal conversion, and the eschatological dimensions of Christian life reflect his deep concern for sound doctrine and spirituality. These same convictions fueled the withering criticism and biting satires that he directed against moral and institutional failures in the Church, the pretensions of some of its leaders, and the formalism that compromised monasticism and personal piety.[67]

By encouraging people to know Christian sources, appreciate their normative quality, and view the apostolic community as a model for the Church of their day, humanism profoundly affected the attitudes of many leaders in society, both clerical and lay. The writings of Erasmus show that humanism lent itself to constructive efforts to highlight the spiritual goals of Christian life and to refocus Church thought, piety, and ministry. But it also supported activities that were far more ambiguous. Armed with Scripture and its picture of the early Christian community, a few demanded that the Church give up its money and power and embrace the spiritual service of others in the poor and humble manner of Christ. Some began to present the Bible as the sole source and arbiter of Christian observance. This depreciated both the Church and its tradition of faith and praxis and implied that, with Bible in hand, the faithful had all that they needed to understand and pursue Christian life.[68]

The Significance of Late Medieval Spirituality

Whether one considers the great saints and mystics or the multitude of unnamed men and women who committed themselves to the Christian life, it is clear that late medieval peoples wished to see the face of

---

[67] John W. O'Malley, ed., *Collected Works of Erasmus: Spiritualia, Enchiridion, De contemptu mundi, De vidua Christiana* (Toronto: University of Toronto Press, 1988) ix–xxiii; Chadwick, *Reformation,* 31–9; McGrath, *Reformation Thought,* 35–41; Thompson, *Humanists and Reformers,* 333–45; also R. J. Schoeck, *Erasmus of Europe: The Making of a Humanist, 1467–1500* (Savage, Md.: Barnes & Noble Books, 1990); idem, *Erasmus of Europe: The Prince of Humanists, 1501–1536* (Edinburgh: Edinburgh University Press, 1993).

[68] Leff, *Dissolution of the Medieval Outlook,* 130–44.

McGrath notes that the *sola scriptura* principle necessarily raises the issue of textual interpretation. See his *Intellectual Origins of the European Reformation,* 152–74, and *Reformation Thought,* 104–15.

For some time dissident figures had defended the need to rely on the Scriptures alone, argued for a more spiritual Church, and condemned its political entanglements and the Donation of Constantine that seemed to be its warrant. A detailed

God. Their principled self-denial, habits of prayer, concern for motivation, and effective love of neighbor demonstrate that even in chaotic
times Christian faith retained the power to move people of all stations
and shape their moral lives. But the times also left their mark. In an era
dominated by natural disaster, political turmoil, theological exaggera-
tion, and ecclesiastical disarray, it is easy to see why devout people
moved their piety inward and accented the personal and transcendent
aspects of their faith. At a time when Church and society had grown
less cohesive and the liturgy had lost some of its communitarian texture, it was entirely reasonable to emphasize one's own faith and devotion. But the same considerations also prompted people to
participate in the liturgy or in devotions celebrated in common and to
attend even more conscientiously to the preached word, personal
penance, and the service of their neighbors, activities that addressed
the human and apostolic needs of the day. It is also clear that humanistic research and writing placed the spiritual and historical dimensions of Christian life in high relief and increased the pressure for
structural and personal reform. Whether they emphasized the individual and interior, the social and public, or the spiritual and eschatological, these responses reflected different aspects of Christian faith
and helped to shape the environment in which the Protestant and
Catholic Reformations took place.[69]

THE PROTESTANT REFORMATION

One of the most important developments in the history of Western
Christianity, the Protestant Reformation presupposed that the Catholic
Church had abandoned the sound doctrine and right practices warranted by the Scriptures and Church Fathers. It aimed to purge everything that did not accord with these authorities and bring the Church
back into conformity with them. In its origins the Reformation reflected
the complex political, ecclesiastical, intellectual, and religious history of
the late Middle Ages. In its actual unfolding it took many forms, usually
in conscious opposition to particular aspects of Catholic thought and
praxis. In its impact the Protestant Reformation reached well beyond the
realms of Christian theology, polity, and ritual and exerted a strong influence on the social, political, cultural, and intellectual life of the West as
a whole. With due regard for these facts, the wide geographic and theo-

---

account of this history is given in Gordon Leff, *Heresy in the Later Middle Ages: The
Relation of Heterodoxy to Dissent c. 1250–c. 1450* (Manchester: Manchester University
Press; New York: Barnes & Noble Books, 1967).
    [69] Leclercq, *Spirituality of the Middle Ages,* 439, 481–6, 497–9, 506–7.

logical spectrum represented by the Reformation, and its later development, this section will limit itself to the early phases of the Lutheran and Swiss Reformations and attend more particularly to their teachings on justification and the implications for Church praxis and moral life. These were the issues that generated such concern at the Council of Trent and have been so significant since the sixteenth century.[70]

Martin Luther

Martin Luther (1483–1546) learned the theology of the *Via moderna* while a student at the University of Erfurt. At that time he joined the Augustinian order and began to study St. Augustine. Although Luther did not share the humanists' fascination with ancient sources or verbal eloquence, he acknowledged that they had promoted the study of the Fathers and made it possible for people to read the original languages of the Scriptures. In 1512 he became a doctor of theology and started to teach Scripture at Wittenberg.[71]

Luther took religious discipline very seriously. He received sacramental penance often and did his best to pray, fast, and observe the other requirements of the Augustinian Rule. But he was never satisfied with his performance, and what was worse, his flaws and shortcomings began to torment his conscience. The theology of the *Via moderna* fanned the feelings of guilt that arose within him. Hinting that human accomplishments were a prerequisite for God's love, it taught that God expected people to keep the commandments and other requirements and would reward with grace and salvation those who responded as well as they could. Luther felt that if God responded to him as justice and his own behavior warranted, then he had no hope. Deeply disturbed and fearing for his salvation, he intensified his study of Pauline texts, especially the Epistle to the Romans, and sought further insight into the nature of justification.[72]

---

[70] For general discussions of the Protestant Reformation, its origins, and its later development, see Chadwick, *Reformation;* McGrath, *Reformation Thought;* idem, *Intellectual Origins of the European Reformation;* Ozment, *Age of Reform;* Heiko A. Oberman, *The Dawn of the Reformation: Essays in Late Medieval and Early Reformation Thought* (Edinburgh: T & T Clark, 1986); or idem, *Masters of the Reformation: The Emergence of a New Intellectual Climate in Europe,* trans. Dennis Martin (Cambridge: University of Cambridge Press, 1981).

[71] Chadwick, *Reformation,* 44; McGrath, *Intellectual Origins of the European Reformation,* 59–68; idem, *Reformation Thought,* 44–5.

[72] Luther's experiences with the sacrament of penance were a significant catalyst for his early theological thought and protests against Catholic praxis. See Pelikan, 4:128-38.

It was probably in the year 1515 that Luther arrived at a new understanding of God's saving grace. His reflection on the verse "He who through faith is righteous shall live" (Rom 1:17; Gal 3:11) convinced him that the prevailing theology was mistaken. God does not wait for human beings to act or reward them for their goodness. Under the bondage of sin the human will is not free and can only act sinfully. Hence God gives the gift of divine goodness to human beings who cannot help but fall short. Justification is God's free and undeserved gift of grace to the unworthy. If they do not rely upon their own works, efforts, or presumed goodness, persons can receive God's gift of justice by faith and then produce the good works it makes possible. Luther believed that this teaching was fully warranted by the Scriptures and consistent with St. Augustine's theology, especially its anti-Pelagian aspects. It became the foundation of his own understanding of Christian life and a principal source of conflict with the Catholic Church.[73]

The Lutheran Reformation

Luther fundamentally revised the prevailing understanding of justification. Although Catholic theologians held widely differing theories concerning how justification took place, they agreed on what it did. In keeping with a long-standing consensus they taught that God's gift of sanctifying grace causes a real change in the sinner; justification truly purifies sinful people, makes them to be good in their personal reality, and enables them to cooperate in their salvation. For Luther, justification does nothing of the kind. Sinful Christians remain sinful while God's justifying grace envelops them with a new righteousness. Justification sanctifies without purifying; it is essentially a forensic or declaratory event.[74]

[73] See the theological theses and explanation Luther provided in the "Heidelberg Disputation" of April 26, 1518; also his "Two Kinds of Righteousness" and "The Freedom of a Christian," *Martin Luther's Basic Theological Writings*, ed. Timothy F. Lull (Minneapolis: Fortress Press, 1989) 30–49, 155–64, 585–629. See also McGrath, *Iustitia Dei*, 2:1-20; idem, *Reformation Thought*, 67–78; Pelikan, 4:138-55; Stephen J. Duffy, *The Dynamics of Grace: Perspectives in Theological Anthropology* (Collegeville: The Liturgical Press, 1993) 173–203; Robert W. Bertram, "'Faith Alone Justifies': Luther on *Iustitia Fidei*. Theses," *Justification by Faith: Lutherans and Catholics in Dialogue VI*, ed. H. George Anderson and others (Minneapolis: Augsburg Publishing House, 1985) 172–84.

[74] McGrath, *Reformation Thought*, 83–4; idem, *Iustitia Dei*, 1:40-51, 180-7, especially 183–4; Eric W. Gritsch, "The Origins of the Lutheran Teaching on Justification," *Justification by Faith*, 162–71. Luther initially called this "alien justification" ("Two Kinds of Righteousness," *Martin Luther's Basic Theological Writings*, 157), while the *Augsburg Confession* (art. 4) expresses it through the notion of imputed justification.

Luther's theology of justification prompted him to reject many aspects of Catholic faith and practice. Because he believed that the individual Christian receives forgiveness and salvation immediately from God, Luther concluded that the Church was less intimately involved in human salvation than Catholic faith presupposed. He took issue with the Catholic Church's positions on hierarchical authority, the legitimacy and efficacy of the sacraments, penitential praxis, indulgences, and anything else that seemed to subordinate God's grace to human works or claims of personal goodness. The Church was to preach God's word, celebrate the sacraments, and help Christians to know the forgiveness and consolation that faith brings. The failures of the clergy and widespread religious abuses only reinforced Luther's claim that many Church institutions were incompatible with authentic Christian faith.[75]

Although they were certainly a serious problem, the elimination of abuses would not have answered Luther's objections. His conception of justification and his vision of Christian life conflicted with those the Catholic Church defended on grounds of principle. A formal parting of the ways was inevitable and took place in 1520. In June of that year Pope Leo X published the bull *Exsurge Domine,* condemning forty-one of Luther's statements and threatening him with excommunication if he failed to repudiate them. On December 10, Luther publicly burned a copy of the bull and also consigned canon law books and the *Summa angelica* to the flames. He was excommunicated on January 3, 1521.[76]

In the turbulent years that followed, Luther's call to reformation found a strong resonance in the German people and exercised an ever-stronger influence on their political and social affairs. In 1530 his associate Philip Melanchthon (1497–1560) produced the *Augsburg Confession,* which became a classic statement of Lutheran faith. Those develop-

---

See Lief Grane's commentary in his *The Augsburg Confession: A Commentary,* trans. John H. Rasmussen (Minneapolis: Augsburg Publishing House, 1987) 61–3.

[75] Along with many of his contemporaries, Luther charged the Roman Curia with grave moral and religious lapses; see his open letter of September 6, 1520, to Pope Leo X (Lull, *Martin Luther's Basic Theological Writings,* 586–95). The merchandising of indulgences in Germany galvanized his protest against contemporary Church practices and provoked his famous ninety-five theses of October 31, 1517 (ibid., 21–9). For historical details, see Chadwick, *Reformation,* 41–3.

Luther held that the Church's title to authenticity comes from doctrinal continuity with the Scriptures and not from historical continuity with the apostolic age (McGrath, *Reformation Thought,* 132–3).

[76] For the text of *Exsurge Domine* see DS, 1451–92. The events surrounding Luther's separation from the Catholic Church are rehearsed in "Justification by Faith (Common Statement)," *Justification by Faith,* 22–8; Chadwick, *Reformation,* 47–56.

ments revealed the strength of Luther's religious program and increased the likelihood of its general acceptance.[77]

The Swiss Reformation

Huldrych Zwingli (1484–1531) was a Swiss who had drunk deeply from humanist sources. When he began to preach in Zurich in January of 1519, Zwingli wished to stimulate a moral reform in the local church in order to bring it into conformity with the apostolic community. To reach this goal, he highlighted the spiritual relationship between God and believers and sought to strip away all historical accretions that did not accord with the Scriptures.[78]

This agenda accented moral life and accounts for Zwingli's initial inclination to deemphasize doctrinal issues. Because he believed that God justified only those who had successfully corrected their lives, he took exception to Luther's teachings on justification, fearing that they would encourage people to defer the moral reform they needed to undertake. However, after he was struck down by the plague in August of 1519, his views changed. As he wondered whether the disease would take his life, Zwingli acquired a deeper appreciation of his helplessness and God's power. Perhaps it was that experience that caused him to emphasize God's sovereignty over human life and conclude that a person's destiny depends entirely on God's free and sovereign action.[79]

That doctrinal theme received further development at the hands of John Calvin (1509–64), a Frenchman who helped to consolidate the Swiss Reformation from his base at Geneva. In 1536 Calvin published the first edition of *The Institutes of the Christian Religion*, the classic statement of Swiss reformed theology, which he progressively expanded in the 1541 and 1559 editions of the work. As was the case with Luther, Calvin accepted that justification is purely forensic and causes no real change in the justified person. What is distinctive are his assertions of divine sovereignty and its corollary, the doctrine of double predestination. According to Calvin, God actively decrees salvation or damnation for each person. Although that implies that Christ died for some and

---

[77] Grane provides the text and a commentary in *The Augsburg Confession: A Commentary*; see also Gritsch, "Origins of the Lutheran Teaching on Justification," 168–9; John F. Johnson, "Justification According to the Apology of the Augsburg Confession and the Formula of Concord," *Justification by Faith*, 185–99. The further development and spread of Lutheran Christianity is discussed in Chadwick, *Reformation*, 56–75.

[78] McGrath, *Intellectual Origins of the European Reformation*, 43–59; idem, *Iustitia Dei*, 2:32-4; idem, *Reformation Thought*, 42–4, 85.

[79] Chadwick, *Reformation*, 76–80; McGrath, *Reformation Thought*, 84–90.

not for all, Calvin held that God's salvation of the elect without regard for their merits shows his great mercy. He also taught that members of his congregations could be certain that they were among the saved. These doctrines also attracted the Council of Trent's attention.[80]

The Challenge to Catholicism

The Lutheran and Swiss Reformations were based upon the theological premise that justification is exclusively God's work in a human being. Persons contribute nothing to their own justification but simply receive and live it by faith. That basic position implies that the source of the Christian life is to be found in an immediate spiritual encounter between the believer and God. It also means that the Church's ordained priesthood and its traditional penitential practices are illegitimate, tainted by Pelagianism, and therefore need to be abolished. When their particular understanding of the economy of salvation is considered, it is evident that these views constituted a direct challenge to the faith and practice of the Catholic Church.

Although that challenge was fundamentally dogmatic in nature, it had important consequences for moral life. The assertion that free will makes no contribution to justification implied that a person's moral life has nothing to do with justification. That is a corollary of the theology of alien justification, and it is especially clear in the Calvinist doctrine of double predestination. Closely related is the matter of penitential praxis. Taken at its best, traditional penitential usage presupposed that the justification and conversion of sinners and the ongoing sanctification of believers require God's grace at every point. It also assumed that justification and sanctification involve the ministry of the Church and the sincere cooperation of the individuals concerned. Their participation was intended to be morally significant, that is, they were expected to act in an informed, intentional, and free way. However, if justification necessarily excludes all human cooperation, then the Catholic Church's traditional approach is erroneous and a believer's personal contribution has to be either fictional or Pelagian in nature.

REFLECTIONS

Although it encompasses less than three centuries, the late Middle Ages was a period of profound change in which many older approaches

[80] McGrath, *Iustitia Dei*, 2:36-9; idem, *Reformation Thought*, 90–3; Chadwick, *Reformation*, 82–96; Duffy, *Dynamics of Grace*, 203–7; Pelikan, 4:217-32.

yielded to new ways. However one judges the overall results, it is obvious that some of them were the product of unprecedented conflicts over authority in European society, dubious intellectual developments, moral and religious aberrations, and a papacy humiliated by schism and distracted by political and monetary concerns. Especially when these difficulties involved grave moral failures on the part of ecclesiastics, the abuse of persons in the name of religion, or the misappropriation of Church institutions, they damaged the Church and alienated its members. This suggests once again that scandal can powerfully affect the motivation, deliberation, and actions of others, sometimes with far-reaching effects. Scandal inflicted spiritual and moral injury and helped to spawn new divisions in the Church. This fact highlights the social dimensions of life and the close, mutual relationship between faith and moral life. It discloses the heavy cost, morally and spiritually, that can be entailed in grave personal failures, official malfeasance, or the abuse of Church institutions.

Even in difficult circumstances many sought to live up to the demands of faith and holiness. On the public level this is evident in the unceasing calls for the reform of the Church in its head and members. More personally, the promotion and use of the sacrament of penance testifies to people's wish to be forgiven of their sins and, if necessary, restored to communion with God. The turn to mysticism and the strength of the confraternities likewise show the power of Christian faith and its ability to bring people to charity, prayer, and the imitation of Christ. Sensitivity to God's infinity and independence from all created things guided the work of many theologians. At its core, Martin Luther's teaching on justification aimed to vindicate God's holiness. These considerations suggest that even in a turbulent era faith, holiness, and a right relationship with God shaped the moral life of believers. They responded vigorously to conditions that were offensive to faith, charity, or piety. They tried to make Church structures and theology as well as their personal lives conform to the requirements of the Gospel.

In this period, theological and devotional literature tended to move the accent from the corporate whole to the individual. Ockham's assertion that reality resides in the individual things encountered in experience rather than in universal essences or natures gave the individual new importance in philosophy and theology. The concern for the conscience of each penitent and the confession of each mortal sin reflected the decisive quality of individual cases. The mystics' solicitude for their personal holiness and its looser connection with the Church and the liturgy testified to the importance of individual efforts in Christian life. At pains to protect God's freedom in all cases, theologians transposed the discussion of grace from an ecclesial to an individual key. Luther was anxious for his own salvation and tried to provide solid theological grounds for the justification and consolation of each person. The Protestant Reformation presupposed that in matters of faith individual judgment was more important than that of the Church.

These considerations suggest that individual persons, experiences, and things exercised a greater and sometimes decisive role in religion, moral life, and intellectual reflection. Taken together, the emergence of the individual and the corresponding decline of the universal, the group, and the Church as a corporate entity are major developments in the history of the West. Emphasis on the individual reshaped the question of the one and the many and transformed the discussion of such foundational subjects as reality, knowledge, and grace. It helped to give the individual dimensions of faith, piety, and moral life much greater prominence and depreciated their ecclesial aspects. In time, the individual would come to be seen as the arbiter of truth, the wellspring of society, and the source of its government.

Late medieval intellectual work opened new avenues of development on some altogether foundational issues. Scholars began to base the moral good less on reality and its nature than on God's will, which retained absolute power even though it was usually thought to act consistently. Some of them located reality in the contingent singulars of experience and taught that the universal exists only in the mind or as a word. They reconsidered the function and purpose of grace, the value of human efforts, and the process of justification. The Renaissance interest in ancient texts led to important advances in their knowledge and interpretation and to a reconsideration of history itself.

These considerations show that rational analysis and speculation had developed to a high degree and gained a remarkable capacity to affect religious, moral, and doctrinal affairs. Even if this was not always their intent, scholars encouraged the notion that moral life is ultimately governed by commands and prohibitions, not by the nature of the real. They realigned objectivity from the abstract and universal to the concrete and particular, which could not fail to affect judgments about the moral quality of behavior. They placed Christian life in a new intellectual context, transformed the relationship between moral decision and personal salvation, and precipitated new debates over Pelagianism among believers. Their stress on divine freedom and the contingency of created things tended to depreciate the virtues as well as human nature itself. Besides pointing to the importance of late medieval scholarship, these effects disclose the perennial significance of such issues as reality and knowledge, the ultimate source of the moral good, the function of grace, and the relationship between moral life and the economy of salvation.

If late medieval scholarship influenced the community, the community also affected the work of scholars. An ignorance of past Church teachings on grace, the hierarchy's failure to meet its pastoral and doctrinal responsibilities, and the increasing alienation of the liturgy from its ecclesial foundations all had negative effects on intellectual discussions. It became more difficult for scholars to achieve consensus or to agree on the content of Catholic faith on important points. These considerations suggest that problematic theological methods or conclusions are sometimes related to deficiencies in the wider Christian community. That is germane to any assessment of this period or theology's contribution to it. It highlights the need for the Christian community to be in good order and intimates that to the extent the Church is in disarray, theology is likely to reflect its problems and produce mixed or unhelpful results.

This period is bracketed by the Fourth Lateran Council's decree on annual penance and Martin Luther's public rejection of Catholic penitential faith and praxis. Catholic faith asserts that the ministry of the Church and the sincere efforts of the penitent reflect God's will and are integral to the process of forgiveness. Penance presupposes the operation of God's grace and the interdependence of the religious, ecclesial, and moral aspects of Christian life. During the late Middle Ages considerable emphasis fell on a complete enumeration of mortal sins and the authority and absolution of the confessor. The technical requirements of sacramental penance loomed large and carried the risks of formalism, misunderstanding, and personal anxiety. The related praxis of indulgences, while defensible in theory, was compromised in practice by simony and other aberrations. Although abuses and exaggerations deserved to be indicted, the Protestant Reformation went further and denied the validity of traditional penitential praxis and the legitimacy and authority of the Catholic Church as a religious institution. It asserted that human works—whether of the Church or the believer—could contribute nothing to justification. With a challenge that was at once dogmatic and pastoral, ecclesial and personal, the Reformation placed the basic constitution and functioning of Christian life in question. That required the Catholic Church to declare its faith on the matter of justification, vindicate its authority, and defend sacramental penance as the means normally required for gravely sinful Christians to recover baptismal grace and the forgiveness it carries. Because it involved the relationship among God's work in persons, the ecclesial community, and the free and deliberate acts of believers, that threefold task would be as significant for Catholic moral life as for faith.

The responsibility to frame an official Catholic response to the Protestant Reformation fell largely to the Council of Trent (1545–63). It enunciated relevant aspects of Catholic faith, set forth the requirements of sacramental praxis, and legislated against abuses that had so grievously harmed Christian life. Its decrees have shaped Catholic theology, worship, and moral life from that day to this. However, before turning to the Council of Trent and other developments during the sixteenth and seventeenth centuries, it is necessary to consider the outlook and culture that have achieved supremacy in the West. That is the task of the following chapter.

9

The Modern Western Outlook

The religious crisis of the sixteenth century demonstrated that Europeans took faith very seriously. Although they differed sharply about its implications, the people of that era agreed that faith in Christ is decisive for individuals and communities. That conviction was nothing new; it reflected the consensus that had shaped European life for a thousand years. But it was not to continue. The vehemence with which Christians held their opposing views made it impossible to sustain the traditional consensus. Once Europe divided by faith, faith could no longer provide a common basis for intellectual, social, and cultural life. It then became possible to place thought, attitudes, and institutions on new foundations; consign religious convictions and practice to the realm of individual choice; and eventually secularize much of Western life.

The proliferation of religious differences and the bloodshed that they often occasioned were not the only causes of revolutionary change. Europeans came into touch with many other races, religions, and cultures thanks to the opening of intercontinental sea routes. Early modern investigations into the workings of heaven and earth enabled people to understand the universe more fully and moved them to reconsider the place of human beings in it. Political and economic struggles undermined a traditional order and changed the structure of ordinary life. In that new environment people and their worldly pursuits held center stage, while God and the churches were gradually relegated to a supporting role if not dismissed altogether. Along with the sad reality of a splintered Western Christianity, these other developments did their part to transform Western attitudes, institutions, and culture.

This chapter will examine important aspects of the remarkable series of events that dissolved the traditional consensus and gave rise to the outlook that still informs much of Western life. Even though this will require attention to events that seem far removed from the domains of Church and faith, such a study is necessary in order to appreciate contemporary attitudes toward faith and morality, the often adversarial relationship between the Church and contemporary culture, and the impact of these factors on moral life.

This first part of the discussion will review key events that nudged Europeans away from their traditional, largely religious outlook and prompted them to reconsider their institutions and attitudes. It will note some of the results and provide a historical background for later developments.

It will then be necessary to review the record of early modern investigations into the activity of the earth and heavenly bodies. These efforts did more than augment knowledge; they undermined a world view that had prevailed since ancient times, took the mystery out of the then-known universe, and hinted that it could be discovered and controlled by human beings.

The following section will consider the influence of early modern philosophers, who consolidated the new outlook and reinterpreted reality, knowledge, God, and moral life in accord with it. The prestige and writings of these thinkers persuaded many people to revise their view of the universe and the human person.

Next to be examined is the series of developments that brought forth the Enlightenment, the period of time in which the new outlook was explicitly enunciated and achieved great influence in England, France, and elsewhere. Many of its assumptions have informed Western consciousness and are enshrined in society's laws, attitudes, and institutions.

It will then be helpful to note later developments that have shaped moral and religious life since the Enlightenment.

HISTORICAL BACKGROUND

Between the fifteenth and seventeenth centuries Europe underwent a deep and often wrenching transformation that affected all important areas of its life. When it had run its course, sea routes had been opened to the Americas, southern Africa, and East Asia; Europe had lost all patience with religious warfare; new social and economic realities had emerged; and a thoroughly secular basis for international relationships had been created. These developments changed the texture of society, influenced popular attitudes, emarginated the churches, and transformed the context in which people confronted the question of faith and enacted their moral life.

Intercontinental Voyages

In 1492 the voyage of Christopher Columbus opened vast new worlds to the people of Europe. His discoveries encouraged other seafarers to see what else lay over the horizon. In 1498 da Gama sailed around the Cape of Good Hope to India, and two years later Cabral voyaged to Brazil. Others explored various parts of the Americas, and in 1521 Magellan circumnavigated the globe. It is difficult to overstate the importance of these voyages.

The opening of sea routes to East Asia, Africa, and the Americas had dramatic effects on the life of Europe and distant lands alike. It became possible for Europeans to import large quantities of spices and such staple goods as rice, sugar, and tea far more cheaply than before. Although such trade certainly helped seafaring nations and their merchants, it boosted the overall economy of Europe and raised the quality of life of many of its people. The importation of American gold and silver enriched the Spanish throne and enabled it to field large armies in Europe. European powers also found it necessary to send naval and land forces overseas in order to protect their nationals and keep indigenous peoples under control. That process projected European tensions onto a worldwide arena and began the process of colonialist expansion. What is more, it suggested that technological prowess was the key to power and wealth.

Sea transportation opened a new chapter in the history of Christian evangelization. Among others, Francis Xavier and his companions went to India in 1541 and then continued on to Japan. Jesuit missionaries entered China and won acceptance in the imperial court. Dominican and Franciscan friars accompanied the Portuguese and Spanish to the Americas, with Jesuits and others to follow soon afterward. In due course Catholic missionaries arrived in North America with the French, while Anglican, Reformed, and nonconforming Protestant groups established their own communities on the same continent. Missionaries eventually brought Christianity to every part of the world.[1]

---

[1] Owen Chadwick, *The Reformation* (Middlesex and Baltimore: Penguin Books, 1972) 321–47; R. R. Palmer and Joel Colton, *A History of the Modern World* (New York: Alfred A. Knopf, 1984) 104–12; Hermann Tüchle, "Renouveau de l'Église, mission universelle et conversions, le monde baroque," *Nouvelle Histoire de l'Église,* ed. L.-J. Rogier and others (Paris: Éditions du Seuil, 1963–75) 3:321-50.

The involvement of Europeans with indigenous peoples of other continents had significant effects on religious and moral life. New experiences and a much wider cross-cultural horizon led some people to reassess traditional Christian beliefs and practices. Activities involved in warfare, international trade, slavery, and the government and evangelization of native peoples raised difficult questions about the nature of the human being as well as about what was morally right and consistent with Christian faith. Expanded possibilities for travel, heightened concern for matters of commerce and government, and greater self-confidence helped to make the outlook of Europeans more secular and less Christian than before.

New Economic and Social Conditions

Despite warfare and religious animosity, the economic life of Europe expanded during the sixteenth and early seventeenth centuries. The population increased by more than 25 percent during that time, rising to some ninety million people by the year 1600. Because more food was required, more land came under the plow, which helped many peasants. Greater demand stimulated trade and the manufacture of clothing and other necessities. Inflation did its part by making goods more valuable over time and encouraging merchants and entrepreneurs to borrow money for their business pursuits and governments for their military expenses. Inflation did not cause economic or political instability, since prices rose in a gradual and generally predictable way.

Expansion brought certain structural changes to European socioeconomic life. One was that borrowed money became much more important. It took large amounts of capital to pay for equipment, raw materials, and labor; build the inventories needed in expanding markets; and exploit the potential of overseas trade. Mining, book publishing, maintaining an army or navy, and trade in expensive commodities likewise depended on borrowed capital. Banks became much more important and financiers more powerful. Another change occurred as economic life overflowed local limits and assumed national and international dimensions. These developments encouraged closer cooperation between national governments and business corporations and the formulation of national economic and trade policies.

These developments helped to stratify society into distinct classes with unequal shares of economic security and political power. At the top stood the monarch, the court nobility, the landed aristocracy, and a few others who enjoyed great wealth and power. Beneath them were the merchants, traders, government officials, landowners, professionals, independent craftsmen, shopkeepers, and those who owned productive land or buildings. They and their families made up the middle class. Then there were those who lacked a secure and adequate income, including landowners whose fixed rental payments did not keep up with inflation and wage earners whose income fell behind the cost of food and lodging. Because they increasingly depended on contracts with dealers, many craftsmen were vulnerable to unemployment and poverty, and they too joined the destitute and emarginated at the bottom of society. This socioeconomic stratification was a very significant development; in time it generated acute social stresses, destabilized many governments, and affected people's relationship with the Church.[2]

The Wars of Religion

As the Lutheran Reformation extended across the German-speaking regions of Europe, armed conflict generally followed in its wake. Although political, economic, and social animosities certainly played their part, once the Reformation had begun, religious antagonism became the principal cause of strife. It continued to convulse German lands until 1555, when the Peace of Augsburg established terms for peaceful coexistence between Catholics and Lutherans. It provided that those localities that had become Lutheran prior to 1552 might maintain that faith. In the future, each local ruler would have the right to adopt either the Catholic or Lutheran faith, and his subjects would then be expected to adhere to the same church or leave his jurisdiction. The Peace of Augsburg prevented religion-based war in Germany for about sixty years.[3]

The French experience was similar. John Calvin had always hoped to bring his reformation to France, but the Catholic monarch of that land opposed him and persecuted Calvinists from the outset. Even so, by about 1560 the Calvinists grew numerous enough to influence political struggles in France and strong enough to demand certain religious and political rights. In an environment marked by domestic disunity and international tension, animosities between Catholics and Calvinists became more dangerous. In March of 1562 a bloody encounter between Catholics and Huguenots, as the French Calvinists

---

[2] Palmer, *History of the Modern World,* 112–23.

[3] Chadwick, *Reformation,* 141–4. For the text of the Peace of Augsburg, see Sidney Z. Ehler and John B. Marrall, eds., *Church and State Through the Centuries: A Collection of Historic Documents with Commentaries* (London: Burns & Oates; Westminster, Md.: Newman Press, 1954) 166–73.

were now called, started a vicious circle of attack and counterattack that plunged France into a war that continued off and on for several decades. Those hostilities came to an end in 1593 when the Huguenot king, Henry IV, recognizing that only a Catholic monarch could bring peace to France, decided to adopt that faith. In 1598 Henry became politically strong enough to issue the Edict of Nantes, which guaranteed toleration to the Huguenots and official status to the Catholics. Despite attempts to repeal or limit the edict afterward, it established a workable framework for religious peace in France.[4]

In the early years of the seventeenth century the religious situation in Germany began to deteriorate once again. The Calvinists, who had increased in number, had taken control of some German states. The Catholics had lost ground, largely because their states had passed into the hands of Lutheran or secular rulers. Mutual suspicions prompted Protestant and Catholic states to organize in defense of their interests. By 1610 opposing alliances had been formed, and each side engaged the support of foreign powers. That uneasy situation gave way to open conflict in 1618 when the Protestant nobles of Bohemia revolted against their Catholic king, Ferdinand, who was also the Holy Roman Emperor. They offered the crown to the Calvinist head of the Protestant alliance in Germany, who took the title King Frederick V. To solidify his position Frederick invited military support from German Calvinists and financial help from the Dutch. The emperor counterattacked with assistance from Bavarian and Spanish forces, winning a complete victory in 1620.

That triumph had important if unexpected consequences. It gave the emperor firm control over Bohemia, Austria, and much of Germany, enabling him to renew the Counter-Reformation in those areas. The emperor's Spanish allies strengthened their position in the Rhineland and in the Netherlands. Most important of all, the empire's commanding position so threatened other states that they felt compelled to intervene. Denmark entered the war on behalf of the Protestants, and in due course Sweden and France also acted to defeat a strong imperial power in Germany. What had begun as a domestic dispute about religious rights in Germany eventually became a full-scale war for political, economic, and national supremacy in Europe. It devastated Germany and entangled much of the Continent in war for some thirty years.[5]

[4] Palmer, *History of the Modern World*, 133–6; Chadwick, *Reformation*, 153–68.
[5] Palmer, *History of the Modern World*, 137–41; Chadwick, *Reformation*, 316–8.

The Peace of Westphalia

The Thirty Years War came to an end in 1648, largely because people had grown tired of war and realized that peace could only be achieved if certain facts of life were accepted and legally recognized. The settlement was enshrined in a pair of treaties that are collectively known as the Peace of Westphalia. It acknowledged the sovereignty and independence of the Netherlands and Switzerland. On the other hand, by recognizing more than three hundred German states, it sealed the demise of the Holy Roman Empire as a major international power and guaranteed that Germany would remain divided and weak for at least another two centuries. To prevent further religious conflicts in Germany, it reaffirmed the Peace of Augsburg but extended it to the Calvinists, who would henceforth have equal status with Catholics and Lutherans. By giving political security to the three Christian communions, the Peace of Westphalia definitively ended the political Counter-Reformation and guaranteed the survival of German Protestantism.[6]

The importance of the Peace of Westphalia goes well beyond its specific provisions. It marked the emergence of the nation-state as the most important political entity in the international arena. Henceforth nations would deal with one another as equals and in light of their national interests. They would settle their differences by means of treaties where possible but reserve the right to wage war when necessary. After 1648 neither the pope nor the emperor retained any acknowledged power to command, prohibit, or regulate the conduct of national rulers. Having accepted that most of northern Europe was Lutheran or Calvinist, southern Europe Catholic, and the lands in between somewhat mixed, the Peace of Westphalia relegated the public dimensions of church life to the jurisdiction of the respective states, effectively removing religion from the international arena. In the years that followed religious rivalries continued to create problems in a number of countries, but states no longer went to war to settle disputes over faith.

The new arrangement dramatically changed the position of the churches in European society. Catholic, Lutheran, Calvinist, and Anglican churches sometimes found themselves under magistrates who asserted jurisdiction over church policies, resources, and offices. Another consequence was more subtle but perhaps more important. The destructive effects of war and persecution had persuaded many

---

[6] For the religious clauses of the Peace of Westphalia, see Ehler, *Church and State Through the Centuries*, 190–3. Pope Innocent X's bull *Zelo domus dei*, which protests these arrangements, is given on pages 194–8.

people that tolerance was a better response to religious diversity than armed conflict or the attempt to force people to follow a particular faith. Although the reasons for this judgment are readily understandable, it fostered an environment in which faith could more easily be emarginated from the public arena and religion considered as the private choice of individuals. The emergence of the nation-state and the diversity of religious allegiances also helped to place public affairs in a more secular setting. These considerations suggest that the Peace of Westphalia has been as important for religious attitudes and the place of the faith in public life as it was in setting a foundation for the relationships among modern nation-states.[7]

THE IMPACT OF EARLY MODERN PHYSICS

While Europe was reaching around the globe and adjusting to a much wider religious diversity at home, a number of individuals were making a sustained effort to expand human knowledge by means of careful observation of the universe, the earth, and the human body. Very often, though, their findings and hypotheses were greeted with skepticism or outright rejection. The problem was that their conclusions did not square with the prevailing view of the universe and therefore seemed to be impossible. The incompatibility was so great that the new science could only be accepted if many older assumptions were abandoned. That process was complex and took a great deal of time and work. In the end, however, the new approach vindicated itself, and people adopted a radically new outlook on nature, reason, knowledge, education, government, religion and the Church, the human person, and human society. In its depth, extent, and consequences, that transformation was nothing short of revolutionary.[8]

---

[7] Gerald R. Cragg, *The Church and the Age of Reason 1648–1789* (Baltimore: Penguin Books, 1970) 9–11; Palmer, *History of the Modern World,* 141–6; Chadwick, *Reformation,* 318–20, 366–7; see also 365–405.

[8] The relationships between world view and ideas concerning the universe and between philosophy and science are important. For brief introductions see R. G. Collingwood, *The Idea of Nature* (Oxford: Clarendon Press, 1945) 1–3; Herbert Butterfield, *The Origins of Modern Science 1300–1800* (New York: Free Press, 1965) 7–10.

Some historians of science have questioned whether it is appropriate to speak of a "scientific revolution" as has been customary since Herbert Butterfield popularized this view shortly after World War II. See David C. Lindberg and Robert S. Westman, eds., *Reappraisals of the Scientific Revolution* (Cambridge: Cambridge University Press, 1990). However that issue is eventually settled, there is no doubt that early modern investigations stimulated a transformation of European attitudes and thinking that was indeed revolutionary in scope.

The Traditional World View

Prior to the sixteenth century European understanding of the universe had been largely informed by Aristotelian physics. According to that great philosopher and student of nature, the earth is the fixed center of the universe. It is composed of two heavy elements, earth and water, which tend to fall, and two light ones, fire and air, whose nature is to rise. The moon, the sun, the planets, and the stars are composed of ether, an extremely light substance that is easily moved. These heavenly bodies rotate around the earth because they are carried along by invisible revolving spheres. In the second century A.D. Ptolemy's detailed mathematical and astronomical studies confirmed Aristotle's geocentric view of the universe.

Aristotle presupposed that all beings are permeated with a kind of mind, or intelligence, which is always proportioned to the particular thing. Everything in the universe is therefore endowed with orderliness and vitality. Following his Greek philosophical predecessors, Aristotle sought to account for the movement of things in the world. Besides nature itself, he identified four interrelated causes of movement or change. A formal cause gives a thing its shape, pattern, or form. A material cause gives a thing its substance. An efficient cause acts upon or changes a thing, usually from the outside. A final cause is the purpose or end of a thing and can be inherent to it. Aristotle taught that a thing is adequately known when its causes are known and that it is the physicist's task to understand all four causes of any given thing.[9]

Although some aspects were open to challenge, these astronomical and physical theories accounted for observable phenomena so well that most people found them convincing. Strengthened by the endorsement of Aristotle and Ptolemy, that array of assumptions and explanations had coalesced into a coherent world view that was in firm possession when early modern explorations into the nature and activity of the universe began.[10]

---

[9] See Aristotle's *Physics*, II, 3, 7. An example might help to illustrate the four causes: silver is the material cause of a cup made of that metal; the formal cause is its cuplike shape, which enables it to hold liquids; its efficient cause is the artisan who made it; the cup's final cause is its ability to serve as a drinking vessel. The tendency of a seed to sprout, grow, and develop flowers or of a heavy object to fall to the ground reflects their natures; these are examples of activity or motion that is inherent to a thing.

[10] Collingwood, *Idea of Nature*, 3–4, 111; W.K.C. Guthrie, *The Greek Philosophers: From Thales to Aristotle* (New York: Harper & Row, 1975) 137–8; Butterfield, *Origins of Modern Science*, 29–36. For a more detailed account of the development of Greek views of nature, see Collingwood, *Idea of Nature*, 29–92.

A New View of the Universe

The first milestone in the history of modern science is the publication in 1543 of Copernicus' *De revolutionibus orbium*. In essence Copernicus (1473–1543) proposed that the planets revolve around the sun and that the earth rotates on its axis once each day. He further suggested that all substances tend to settle into a spherical shape, and this is why things hold together. In the sixteenth century such statements were both surprising and difficult to defend. If the earth was not at the center of the universe, then the centrifugal force of its rotation should throw things off into space. But that is obviously not what happens, and Copernicus was unable to say why objects remain earthbound. Although his heliocentric theory failed to gain many adherents, it did offer the first sketch of a vastly different picture of the universe. He was suggesting that the earth is one cosmic body among many others that are similar in nature. That notion contradicted Aristotle's theory of dissimilar substances and implied that the physical laws that hold true on earth also apply everywhere else in the universe. Copernicus was on the right track, but since he could not account for certain basic phenomena, he could not overcome the power of the Aristotelian world view.[11]

The problem of gravity that so vexed Copernicus also claimed the attention of William Gilbert (c. 1540–1603). In 1600 he published the theory that magnetic attraction accounts for gravity and is a property of all substances. Building on Gilbert's work, Johann Kepler (1571–1630) hypothesized that bodies tend to remain stationary unless they are attracted to another one, a thesis that might account for gravity and the action of the tides. Even more important were the intellectual dimensions of his work. He proposed that the universe can be understood through a study of the mathematical relationships that it involves. Setting the traditional doctrine of causes aside, he held that motion is to be understood in terms of power applied from without. In other words, things are inert entities that can be understood in strictly quantitative and mechanical terms.[12] That assertion contradicted the Aristotelian view of the universe because it emphasized efficient causality but dispensed with the other three causes.[13]

Armed with one of the first telescopes, Galileo Galilei (1564–1642) discovered sunspots and the moons of Jupiter, phenomena whose ex-

---

[11] Collingwood, *Idea of Nature*, 96–8; Butterfield, *Origins of Modern Science*, 36–48.

[12] Kepler proposed that "the conception of a vital energy producing qualitative changes should be replaced by that of a mechanical energy, itself quantitative, and producing quantitative changes." Collingwood, *Idea of Nature*, 102.

[13] Butterfield, *Origins of Modern Science*, 74–8, 151–9; Collingwood, *Idea of Nature*, 101–2.

istence and irregularity could not be reconciled with the older world view. However, the principal import of his work was methodological. Galileo tried to base his conclusions on careful observations of astronomical activity, which was an important step forward. He held that astronomical observations can be understood by means of geometry and mathematics. These approaches implied that the universe is intelligible only insofar as it is observed, quantified, and measured. Although Galileo accomplished a great deal, his failure to account satisfactorily for the rise and fall of the tides showed that his theories were still somewhat inadequate. That left him vulnerable to his enemies in the academy, who defended the older view of the universe, which still seemed to offer a better account of what could be observed. Nevertheless, Galileo helped to establish the modern scientific method and extended the discussion to a wider audience. His dialogues in *The Two Principal World-Systems,* published in 1632, vigorously attacked the Aristotelian-Ptolemaic world view and helped persuade the public at large that his own concept of the universe was better.[14]

Sir Isaac Newton (1642–1727) brought together many earlier discoveries and developed coherent theoretical explanations of them. In his famous *Principia,* published in 1687, Newton showed how the laws of inertia and gravity accounted for earthly phenomena and the behavior of astronomical bodies. He further demonstrated how mathematical

---

[14] Michael Sharratt, *Galileo: Decisive Innovator* (Cambridge: Cambridge University Press, 1996) especially 16–20, 98–106, 168–70; Butterfield, *Origins of Modern Science,* 78–83. By writing his dialogues in Italian rather than Latin, Galileo bypassed his academic colleagues and appealed directly to the public. This helped to popularize his work and outlook and set an example that others would follow. This type of communication played an important role in the rise to dominance of the world view that Galileo and others promoted.

In June of 1633 Galileo was condemned by the Inquisition, a doctrinal tribunal of the Catholic Church. This well-known event has sometimes been presented as a clear manifestation of the Catholic Church's supposedly blind opposition toward modern science. On this point and the difficulty of sustaining it in light of the facts, see Rivka Feldhay, *Galileo and the Church: Political Inquisition or Critical Dialogue?* (Cambridge: Cambridge University Press, 1995) 1–10. For a fuller description of Galileo's life, work, condemnation, and rehabilitation by the Church, see Sharratt, *Galileo.* For the documents and chronology pertinent to Galileo's case, which involved disciplinary aspects as well as the relationship between modern scientific findings and biblical texts, see Maurice A. Finocchiaro, ed. and trans., *The Galileo Affair: A Documentary History* (Berkeley, Los Angeles, and London: University of California Press, 1989). In 1992 Pope John Paul II reviewed the historical record, recognized the errors that were made, and discussed the relationship of faith and science. See "Lessons of the Galileo Case," *Origins* 22 (1992–3) 369, 171–4; also Cardinal [Paul] Poupard, "Galileo: Report on Papal Commission Findings," *Origins* 22 (1992–3) 374–5.

calculations successfully predict events in the heavens and on earth. Newton's synthesis was intellectually powerful and helped make him a cultural hero. He administered the coup de grace to the world view of Aristotle and Ptolemy and did much to persuade people that the universe was "a rationally ordered machine governed by simple mathematical laws."[15] That metaphor did more than crystallize a new understanding of the universe. It hinted that the laws of physics might illuminate other areas of human life, make it easier to exercise control over them, and disclose the true place of God and the human person in the universe. The importance and power of such suggestions can hardly be overestimated.[16]

Before leaving the history of early modern physics and astronomy, it is necessary to acknowledge equally significant accomplishments in biology and chemistry. In both these fields early researchers encountered many technical problems and the resistance of traditional accounts, which took a great deal of time and work to overthrow. The achievement of William Harvey (1578–1657) in giving a correct account of the circulatory system was especially important. Building on the work of his predecessors, he validated the experimental method and opened the way to a greater knowledge of human biology. Even more significantly, as the human body surrendered its secrets to early modern investigators, it became easier to think of the body as another aspect of material nature that was open to study, understanding, and control. That new perspective helped to demystify the human body and secularize attitudes toward it. With the passage of time, that new outlook would have important scientific, human, and cultural consequences.[17]

THE INFLUENCE OF EARLY MODERN PHILOSOPHERS

The success of early modern investigations is to be measured not only by their contributions to knowledge but also by their impact on society's intellectual assumptions. As methods became more productive and discoveries accumulated, they set in motion a tectonic shift that undermined established modes of thinking and produced a world view that conformed to the newer methods and the results they obtained. However important scientific findings were to the establish-

---

[15] Dudley Shapere, "Newton, Isaac," *EP*, 5–6:491.

[16] Ibid, 489–91; idem, "Newtonian Mechanics and Mechanical Explanation," *EP*, 5–6:491-6; Butterfield, *Origins of Modern Science*, 164–70; see also Collingwood, *Idea of Nature*, 106–10.

[17] For the story of biology and chemistry, see Butterfield, *Origins of Modern Science*, 49–66, 203–21.

ment of a new outlook, that outcome cannot be fully understood unless the contribution of philosophers is also considered. They conferred intellectual legitimacy on the new world view, developed its implications, and prepared it for wide dissemination among the people of Europe. Although others did their part, René Descartes and John Locke were especially effective in consolidating and extending the new outlook.

René Descartes and the Problem of Knowledge

A brilliant geometrician and mathematician, René Descartes (1596–1650) holds a dominant place in modern Western philosophy.[18] As a philosopher Descartes was primarily concerned to establish the certitude of knowledge. To do this, he adopted a strategy of methodological doubt that required him to reject any idea whose certitude could be impugned for any reason. In pursuing this path, Descartes assumed that knowledge was certain when it had the same clarity and distinctness as mathematics or geometry. Accordingly, Descartes rejected sense-related experiences and intellectual reasoning, since both can mislead, confuse, or deceive. As he continued to press his strategy, he realized that the very activity of doubting pointed to the certitude he was seeking. If he doubted, or even if he was deceived by some evil force, then he must certainly exist. This is the context in which Descartes enunciated his famous axiom: "Cogito ergo sum," I think, therefore I am. In the activity of thinking, Descartes found the clear, distinct, and indubitable idea of his own existence. He also gained a secure starting point for his quest for certitude on other matters (*Med*, I–II).[19]

Descartes then considered his knowledge of things outside himself. Turning first to the question of God, he presupposed his own existence and his concept of God as a perfect being. But since neither his personal being nor his knowledge of God could be accounted for satisfactorily unless there was such a God, he concluded that God's existence

---

[18] Descartes was a prolific writer. His principal works include the *Discourse on Method* (1637), *Meditations on First Philosophy* (1641), *Objections* (1641), *Replies to the Objections* (1641), and *Principles of Philosophy* (1644). For a brief biography, see Bernard Williams, "Descartes, René," *EP*, 1–2:344-5.

[19] Descartes declares that his purpose is not destructive or skeptical. He employs a method of doubt only to convince nonbelievers that God truly exists and that the human soul is distinct from the body (*Med*, Prologue). See also Williams, "Descartes, René," 345–8; A. Robert Caponigri, *Renaissance to the Romantic Age* (Chicago: Henry Regnery, 1963) 161–74.

Descartes' "Cogito ergo sum" was foreshadowed many centuries earlier by a discussion in St. Augustine's *The City of God*, XI, 26.

was certain (*Med*, III).[20] The next step was to consider the many ideas he had concerning the external world and his strong tendency, shared by people in general, to assume that such ideas reflect things that actually exist. He assumed that God could not allow people to be deceived on so basic a matter because that would make God a deceiver, which is impossible. Descartes concluded that human ideas about the external world must have a counterpart in reality and a firm basis in God's goodness, and that the universe certainly exists (*Med*, III–VI).[21]

Principal Characteristics of Cartesian Thought

Descartes is known first of all for his rationalism,[22] which is most evident in his highly abstract and deductive method of knowledge. Like mathematics, true knowledge does not emerge from a person's observation of things and events. Truth and certitude are discovered within the mind itself by means of careful reflection on its activity. One starts with intuition, proceeds by means of deduction, and obtains results in the form of propositions that follow with logical necessity. Descartes judged knowledge to be certain when it is untainted by sensory input and qualified by the formal attributes of clarity, distinctness, and absence of doubt. Truth can therefore be expressed in an orderly series of abstract propositions that are certain. Cartesian rationalism takes the nature, resources, and operation of the mind as the norm for truth; it contrasts with all approaches that locate truth in the conformity of the mind to external reality.[23]

Cartesian thought is also characterized by the dualism that is entailed when mind and matter are understood as two different things that share nothing in common. The mind is a thinking thing whose ideas might reflect physical entities but are not caused by them. Physi-

---

[20] Descartes assumes that causes must have at least as much perfection and reality as the effects they bring about. His own existence and his idea of a perfect God, taken to be innate, are effects that cannot be accounted for unless such a God truly exists. This approach has much in common with the ontological argument of St. Anselm (see ch. 7, above).

[21] See also Williams, "Descartes, René," 348–51; Caponigri, *Renaissance to the Romantic Age*, 176–86.

[22] The meaning of the term "rationalism" depends upon its context. As applied to Descartes, "rationalism" refers to his highly abstract and deductive theory of knowledge; it stands in opposition to "empiricism," which bases knowledge on one's experience of the world. See, for example, Williams, "Rationalism," *EP*, 7–8:69.

[23] Caponigri, *Renaissance to the Romantic Age*, 174–6; Williams, "Descartes, René," 345–7, 350–1; also Charles Taylor, *Sources of the Self: The Making of the Modern Identity* (Cambridge, Mass.: Harvard University Press, 1989) 144–7, 155–8.

cal reality has quantity or extension but no qualitative features or inherent meaning that can speak to the mind. Dividing reality into separate "rational" and "physical" components requires a fundamental reinterpretation of the human being. If its mental and physical components are radically dissimilar, the human person can no longer be understood as a coherent unity with bodily, spiritual, and rational dimensions. What is commonly referred to as the "self" or the "person" must be identified with the mind and its thinking. That makes the person a radically immaterial and privatized being. It depersonalizes the body, making it a physical possession or material accompaniment of the immaterial self.[24]

Although he was a devout Catholic believer who intended no offense, his philosophical claims upon God were heavy with implications. Descartes invoked God's power and goodness in order to account for his own existence and to guarantee the certitude of human ideas about the universe. Accordingly, God is no longer the God of Jesus Christ who acts in human history, offers salvation to humans, and claims their worship and service; God is only a necessary element in the rationalistic project of Descartes. In other words, Descartes truncated God's divinity and relocated the question of God from a religious, historical, and personal frame of reference to one that is abstract and intellectual. God becomes a philosophical question that has little to do with human life or the experiences, decisions, and destiny of ordinary people.[25]

Cartesian thought has important moral implications as well. Although Descartes took it for granted that his fellow Catholics should adhere to their faith and obey civil laws, his intellectual system took a very different perspective. For Descartes, moral life does not respond

---

[24] Descartes is quite explicit in teaching the identity of the self with its rational faculty and distinguishing it from the body. He speaks of the thinking thing that he *is*, while referring to the body he *has*:

> Thus, simply by knowing that I exist and seeing at the same time that absolutely nothing else belongs to my nature or essence except that I am a thinking thing, I can infer correctly that my essence consists solely in the fact that I am a thinking thing. It is true that I may have (or, to anticipate, that I certainly have) a body that is very closely joined to me. But nevertheless, on the one hand I have a clear and distinct idea of myself, in so far as I am simply a thinking, non-extended thing; and on the other hand I have a distinct idea of body, in so far as this is simply an extended, non-thinking thing. And accordingly, it is certain that I am really distinct from my body, and can exist without it (*Med*, VI; p. 54).

See also Williams, "Descartes, René," 348, 353–4; Caponigri, *Renaissance to the Romantic Age*, 187–93; Taylor, *Sources of the Self*, 144–7.

[25] Williams, "Descartes, René," 348–50; Taylor, *Sources of the Self*, 156–8.

to dilemmas that arise from life in the world or among one's neighbors. Instead, it pertains to an internal drama: the ongoing conflict between one's will and bodily emotions. The best way for a person to gain relief from this conflict is to assert the will so that it prevails over contrary feelings. In that task neither the external world nor the human body can offer any help. Only the clear and distinct ideas provided by the mind are able to supply the truth that suitably guides the decisions of the will. In taking this tack, Descartes assumed that knowing truth is sufficient to prompt a person to assent to it and will accordingly. He emphasizes rational thinking and maintaining control by means of the will. He turned the focus of moral judgment away from the external world of people and things and reoriented it to the mind, will, and feelings, which are arrayed in a strictly intrapersonal forum. For these reasons, Descartes marks a turning point in the history of Western moral thought.[26]

John Locke

The English philosopher and physician John Locke (1632–1704) also considered human knowledge.[27] He disagreed that human beings are endowed with innate ideas or that knowledge can be derived simply from an analysis of the mind's activity. He rejected that approach as theoretically unsound and, because it was so amenable to abuse by academic and religious authorities, apt to lead people away from truth. Taking the opposite approach, Locke assumed that there is a real world of things apart from the mind and its ideas. He taught that the mind begins as a blank slate and that all knowledge comes from one's experiences of the world, either directly from external sensation or indirectly through reflection on the ideas that come from sensation. Because it based knowledge on experience and credited everyone with the ability to learn and understand, his approach democratized the activity of knowing. Locke emphasized that it was still necessary to observe the requirements of reason when accumulating experiences and analyzing ideas.[28]

[26] Taylor, *Sources of the Self*, 143–58; Vernon J. Bourke, *History of Ethics* (Garden City, NY: Doubleday, 1968) 154–6; Caponigri, *Renaissance to the Romantic Age*, 187–93.

[27] For a review of his life, see James Gordon Clapp, "Locke, John," *EP*, 3–4:487-89. Locke's principal works are the *Essay Concerning Human Understanding* (1689) and *Two Treatises of Government* (1690).

[28] A corollary of this approach denies that essences or natures are known. Because experiences of things or events give rise to the ideas that constitute knowledge, knowledge relates to experience and not to essences. That suggests that ideas merely represent the external world and raises the question of the relationship be-

Locke is also famous for helping to inaugurate a new theory of social life. In his view human beings are created free, rational, and equal. God and nature endow them with certain inalienable rights, primarily to life, liberty, and property. Free persons are to behave according to the natural law, which requires them to live peaceably and respect the rights of others. Because some individuals will not conform to this minimal expectation, it is necessary for people to establish a civil government to deter and punish transgressions against others. The state therefore does not emerge from a monarch's authority but is the product of a free agreement among sovereign and co-equal individuals.[29] Its principal task is to protect their lives, liberty, and property rights and to enforce contractual agreements. Even so, civil government remains little more than a necessary expedient that is always accountable to its constituents. Locke's political philosophy has been extremely influential on later thinking about human rights, the functions of government, and constitutional theory.[30]

---

tween knowledge and external realities. On these issues see, for example, Clapp, "Locke, John," 489–98; Hans Aarsleff, "Locke's Influence," *The Cambridge Companion to Locke*, ed. Vere Chappell (Cambridge: Cambridge University Press, 1994) 255–60, 262.

[29] It is important to relate Locke's political theories to contemporary events and his own interests. His assertion that political authority comes from constituents and not the monarch legitimated the Revolution of 1688, which overthrew King James II and vindicated the merchants, landowners, aristocrats, and others who led the revolution. Locke provided a theoretical foundation for the Bill of Rights of 1689, which prohibited any monarch from ignoring Parliament's laws and required parliamentary consent before taxes were imposed or armies raised. It protected people from unlawful arrest or prosecution. That act changed English constitutional arrangements in a way that restricted royal power and assigned to Parliament the decisive role in English political life.

Despite its emphasis on equality, Locke's theory did not mean that every citizen had equal political rights. Women and the majority of men had no right to vote, which was generally limited to those adult males who owned property and paid taxes on it. Everyone was nevertheless required to obey the laws that Parliament made (John Locke, *Second Treatise of Government*, ed. C. B. Macpherson [Indianapolis: Hackett Publishing Co., 1980] §§ 140, 157–8). Shortly after the Revolution of 1688, legislation stipulated that only those who derived a certain amount of income from their land were eligible to sit in Parliament.

When this background is considered, it becomes clear that Locke's theories supported the interests of the propertied class against the power of the king above and the envy of the wage-earning or unemployed masses below. On these matters see Locke, *Second Treatise of Government*, vii–xxi; Palmer, *History of the Modern World*, 173–7, 299–301.

[30] For Locke's argument see *Second Treatise of Government*; see also Taylor, *Sources of the Self*, 163–9; Clapp, "Locke, John," 498–500; Caponigri, *Renaissance to the Romantic Age*, 312–46.

Locke's theory of knowledge directly influences his philosophy of religion. Locke was a religious man who accepted God's existence, but he wished to explore the grounds on which a person might reasonably accept God's existence and revelation to humanity. In his effort to clarify these matters, Locke acknowledged that there are satisfactory proofs for God's existence and held that many aspects of revelation are also accessible to natural reason. Those points that fall beyond the reach of human knowledge can also be accepted as true provided one has been persuaded that God has revealed them. In sum, Locke understands faith as an assent to specific propositions and subordinates that assent to the canons of reason.[31]

On the basis of such convictions Locke held that religion is a matter between each individual and God. The Church is therefore an association of those who wish to worship God publicly and serve their own salvation at the same time. Locke considered personal conscience to be inviolable and taught that the Church was to be tolerant and never seek to constrain anyone's conscience.[32]

The need for rational thinking and the primacy of the individual governs Locke's moral theory. His ultimate principle is that things "are Good or Evil, only in reference to Pleasure or Pain" (*Essay*, II, 20:2). In practice, experiences of physical pain or mental uneasiness usually lead people to take action that is designed to diminish them. However, this need not be an automatic reaction, since people can stand back from feelings of uneasiness and consider rationally what is the greatest good that ought to be pursued here and now. Once that good is

---

[31] Locke is explicit on this point:

> *Faith* is nothing but a firm Assent of the Mind: which if it be regulated, as is our Duty, cannot be afforded to any thing, but upon good Reason; and so cannot be opposite to it. He that believes, without having any Reason for believing, may be in love with his own Fancies; but neither seeks Truth as he ought, nor pays the Obedience due to his Maker, who would have him use those discerning Faculties he has given him, to keep him out of Mistake and Errour. . . . He that makes use of the Light and Faculties GOD has given him, and seeks sincerely to discover Truth, by those Helps and Abilities he has, may have this satisfaction in doing his Duty as a rational Creature, that though he should miss Truth, he will not miss the Reward of it. For he governs his Assent right, and places it as he should, who in any Case or Matter whatsoever, believes or disbelieves, according as Reason directs him. He that does otherwise, transgresses against his own Light, and misuses those Faculties, which were given him to no other end, but to search and follow the clearer Evidence, and greater Probability (*Essay*, IV, 17:24).

[32] Nicholas Wolterstorff, "Locke's Philosophy of Religion," *Cambridge Companion to Locke*; Caponigri, *Renaissance to the Romantic Age,* 314–5; Clapp, "Locke, John," 501–2.

identified, its absence causes feelings of uneasiness that motivate the person to act so as to attain it. Locke declared that in determining the good a person should defer to the law God has decreed, for such a response shows due respect for God's will as well as God's rewards and punishments. The importance of God's will and the decisive role of pleasure and pain give a voluntaristic and hedonistic texture to Locke's moral theory.[33]

Principal Characteristics of Locke's Philosophy

John Locke's philosophy exemplifies an empirical form of rationalism. Its rationalistic quality is evident in the primacy assigned to questions of human knowledge; the assumption that human beings are innately capable of rational thought; and the normative function of reason in all areas, including faith, revelation, and morality. Although these qualities also characterize Cartesian thought, Locke's empiricism distinguishes him from his French predecessor. Empiricism presupposes that knowledge comes from one's experiences of the world and accumulates as a result of sensory data and careful reflection on the ideas they stimulate.[34]

Locke's philosophy reflects a strongly individualistic view of human beings. The gathering and processing of sense data are activities that each person is to perform independently. Knowledge thereby acquired is the basis of the free and independent judgments about truth that are the foundation of moral action. The same autonomous individual stands at the heart of Locke's political thought. He allows no room for paternalistic or authoritarian forms of government, the impositions of any ecclesiastical body, or the notion that people are inherently social in nature.

Lockean theory tends to fracture the unity of the human person. By suggesting that each individual needs to step back from experiences and rationally evaluate them in light of an ultimate good, Locke implies that the self can be distilled out from its experiences, identified

---

[33] Taylor, *Sources of the Self*, 168–71; Wolterstorff, "Locke's Philosophy of Religion," 180–2; J. B. Schneewind, "Locke's Moral Philosophy," *Cambridge Companion to Locke*, 199–225.

[34] When the term "rationalism" is applied to Lockean thought, it is used in a broad sense and aims only to highlight the decisive role he attributes to reason. In this case it does not mean that Locke employs an abstract, a priori epistemology similar to that of Descartes. This clarification is necessary because the word "rationalism" is often used to identify a specifically Cartesian approach that is the polar opposite of empiricism. See Williams, "Rationalism," 69; Clapp, "Locke, John," 489–91, 496.

with consciousness, and set in opposition to matter and sense experience. That sets the human person off from the body and constricts it to a radically private and intangible mode of existence. It also means that Locke's system involves a mind-matter dualism similar to that of Descartes.[35]

Another characteristic of Locke's approach is its orientation toward greater human control over the world, others, and oneself. To assert that experience is the fountain of knowledge is to suggest that it is possible to influence the learning and understanding of others by manipulating their experiences. Although that had many implications for social policies, it had direct application to the theory and practice of childhood education. In a similar way, Locke understands moral action as a means to obtain results that the agent will subjectively experience as good. Moral life is another arena in which people, endowed with reason and prompted by self-interest, exercise control over the world and themselves.[36]

The Influence of Descartes and Locke

Descartes and Locke have both exercised a strong influence over later thinkers. A number of philosophers followed the path of Cartesian rationalism with its abstract method and mathematical paradigm of knowledge. Those who considered Locke's experience-oriented empiricism to be more congenial worked to develop that approach.[37] Whichever approach they adopted, later philosophers inherited the divorce of mind and matter that Descartes and Locke had both endorsed. Many of them presupposed that physical matter, regarded as inherently meaningless, had nothing in common with the mind, which was identified with the person. That assumption complicated all efforts to formulate a satisfactory account of human knowledge, which has been a primary concern since the seventeenth century. It also made it ex-

---

[35] Aarsleff, "Locke's Influence," 262–5; Taylor, *Sources of the Self*, 171–3.

[36] Taylor, *Sources of the Self*, 169–76; Aarsleff, "Locke's Influence," 259–60; Crane Brinton, "Enlightenment," *EP* 1–2:520.

[37] Among those who took a Cartesian approach were Nicholas Malebranche (1638–1715), Benedict Spinoza (1632–77), Gottfried Willhelm Leibniz (1646–1716), and Christian Wolff (1679–1754). Prominent in the empiricist line were George Berkeley (1685–1753) and David Hume (1711–76).

The contrasting epistemologies of Descartes and Locke can be traced back to ancient thought. More proximately, they reflect the methods of early modern scientists, which included abstract geometrical and mathematical tools as well as careful observation of physical phenomena and the accumulation of experimental data.

tremely difficult to set forth an adequate and coherent account of the moral life.[38]

As they wrestled with these fundamental problems, powerful centrifugal forces pushed philosophers farther apart and increased the pluralism within Western thought. Those differences reflected the divergent approaches of Descartes and Locke and the effects of their mind-matter dualism. They can also be attributed to the world view that scientific work helped to inaugurate, which stresses human knowledge and control while depreciating the material universe as a source of meaning for those enterprises. Another factor is the fracturing of the Western Christian tradition. Once it divided over matters of faith, the West lost a respected source of consensus on the meaning and purpose of human life. The inability of a divided Christianity to perform this service left the field wide open to intellectual pluralism on foundational issues.[39] These considerations help to account for the proliferation of diverse and incompatible accounts of human life and the failure of modern thinkers to locate the common grounds on which a new consensus might be constructed.

THE ENLIGHTENMENT

The cumulative effects of social and political changes, early modern discoveries concerning the universe, and philosophical teachings

---

[38] See Collingwood, *Idea of Nature*, 103–5.

[39] The multiplicity of Christian bodies helped to discredit faith as a source of consensus about God, the universe, and the meaning of human life. In the absence of a generally shared religious faith, thinkers tended to search elsewhere for their premises and elaborated widely differing positions on basic philosophical issues. Divided Christianity thus constitutes an intellectual and cultural problem of foundational importance. Speaking of its impact on thoughtful persons today, one Lockean scholar has written:

> Thus with respect to epistemology in general and the epistemology of religious belief in particular, we are living in a new intellectual situation; none of us has any idea whatsoever as to what form this new situation will eventually take. The worry to which Locke addressed himself remains with us, however: when the tradition handed down to one is fractured and pluralized, so that one can no longer order one's life and belief by the wisdom of unified tradition, to what then does one turn? The answer that Locke articulated and defended with visionary power and philosophical subtlety was that one is to appeal to the deliverances of reason—or more broadly and fundamentally, to those points of direct insight into the facts of reality. That answer, in my view and the view of many others, is unacceptable. But once we have rejected Locke's answer we are back to his question: when tradition is fractured, to what does one turn for the ordering of life and belief? (Wolterstorff, "Locke's Philosophy of Religion," 197–8).

eventually transformed the outlook of the European people. Underway at least since the Renaissance of the fifteenth century, that shift of attitudes and thinking was essentially complete by the latter decades of the seventeenth century. That marks the beginning of the Enlightenment, the period of about a century in which the new habits of thinking achieved dominance in Europe.

Principal Tenets of the Enlightenment

The Enlightenment was a broad and heterogeneous phenomenon that differed from one area to another. Although it defies precise and accurate description, "in the widest terms, the Enlightenment may be designated as that movement in European culture which is characterized by a complete confidence in the power of 'reason' to dispel the obscuring clouds of ignorance and mystery which had weighed upon the human spirit; and precisely by doing so, to render men at once happier, and morally and spiritually better."[40]

Assumed to be essentially the same in all human beings, reason was conceived as the power to learn about the world, know what nature decrees for human life, and plan one's actions accordingly. Reason asserts that all persons are created equal, have equal dignity, and ought to have equal rights. It works against prejudice, bias, and fantasy; grants no recognition to the supernatural; and excludes divine revelation and anything else that does not conform to nature. With nature as the standard, it is possible to identify the errors, unnatural occurrences, and irrational customs that have accumulated over time. Relying on reason and nature to guide them, people can create a society of understanding, justice, and peace—a heaven on earth. A complex and powerful movement, the Enlightenment did not fail to have significant effects wherever it took hold.[41]

The Enlightenment did not occur spontaneously or by accident. Although the methods and findings of Harvey, Galileo, Newton, and their colleagues found a strong cultural resonance, they cannot by themselves account for the change in popular attitudes that took place. The same can be said concerning the writings of Descartes, Locke, and other philosophers. Scientific advances and philosophical thought

---

[40] Caponigri, *Renaissance to the Romantic Age*, 272.

[41] Oskar Köhler, "The Enlightenment," *History of the Church*, ed. Hubert Jedin and John Dolan (New York: Seabury, 1980) 6:342-4; Brinton, "Enlightenment," 519–24; see also Caponigri, *Renaissance to the Romantic Age*, 275–8; Roy Porter and Mikulas Teich, eds., *The Enlightenment in National Context* (Cambridge: Cambridge University Press, 1981), which discuss the Enlightenment's influence in various places.

were able to reshape society's outlook thanks to the work of certain people in France, the *philosophes*. Although they were neither scientists nor philosophers, the *philosophes* took a keen interest in the intellectual issues of their day and successfully popularized the new outlook through conversation, social organizations, and writing. The chief agents of this transition were Fontenelle, Voltaire, and the *Encyclopédie*.

Fontenelle

Bernard le Bovier de Fontenelle (1657–1757) began the process of popularization. Perhaps his most important contribution was his book *The Plurality of Worlds,* which appeared in 1686, the year before Newton published his *Principia.* In this volume Fontenelle related scientific achievements to the general public in a way that was understandable and appealing. His work applied the scientific outlook to ordinary human life and showed how it might transform attitudes and thinking. In so doing, Fontenelle also demonstrated the effectiveness of printed materials in spreading the new outlook among the public.

As secretary of the Académie des Sciences, Fontenelle had many opportunities to shape public opinion through the eulogies he delivered when a member died. He used those occasions to proclaim the superiority of science or modern thought for the benefit of the wider society. He typically portrayed the deceased as the son of middle-class parents who wanted him to study theology and join the clergy. This path was always rejected because of what Fontenelle described as poor teaching methods and theology's penchant for trading in mere words. Sooner or later the deceased encountered the brilliance of Descartes or the incontrovertible truth of geometry. Such moments of conversion delivered the person from ancient prejudices, useless pursuits, and obsolete institutions. They opened the way to the enlightened study of science and philosophy. Giving their lives to these disciplines was the ultimate virtue and glory of those whom Fontenelle eulogized. In delivering these addresses, Fontenelle spoke directly to the public at large, which was now generally literate and ready to assimilate a new way of thinking. His eulogies also carried an undertone of resentment toward the educational establishment and the Church, themes that would become more prominent with the passage of time.[42]

Voltaire

Voltaire was the pen name used by François Marie Arouet (1694–1778), probably the single most effective evangelist of Enlightenment

---

[42] Butterfield, *Origins of Modern Science,* 172–9.

ideas. Although not an original thinker, Voltaire used his sharp wit, clear mind, and skill as a writer to oppose abuses of power in his own country—especially arbitrary court judgments, cruel punishments, and religious persecutions—which he judged to be the inevitable result of authoritarian rule. In response to these offensive conditions, Voltaire carried out a lifelong campaign for human rights, the rule of law, and a humane system of criminal justice. He pursued these goals mainly through letters, philosophical novels, and articles written for the *Encyclopédie*.

Voltaire's program had a strongly intellectual dimension. Following his English mentors, he held that truth does not reside in theories created by the mind but comes from sensate experiences and a careful analysis of them. Nature is the source of truth, and reason the sole medium by which it is grasped. Inspired by Newtonian astronomy, Voltaire felt great awe at the sight of the heavens, and this deepened his conviction that the universe was created by a supreme being who deserves to be revered. He was indebted to Locke for his political theories, especially the affirmation of individual rights and freedom. Locke supplied the intellectual grounds beneath his call for civil rights and equality for all citizens, the toleration of religious diversity, and a state that is governed by laws and not the arbitrary will of its rulers. Voltaire was convinced that these imperatives were firmly grounded in nature and reason.

Voltaire's program made him a hero to the middle class and poor of France but an enemy to those in power. He resented the mindless opposition of reactionary clergy and academics to any proposal for change. He blamed the Church for persecuting religious minorities and for its complicity with an oppressive government. Voltaire's reliance on nature and reason left no room for God's grace, a sense of the transcendent, or supernatural revelation, and he ridiculed Church doctrines as empty and self-serving. He condemned the Church as a benighted, manipulative institution and priests as greedy, immoral, and parasitic. His bitter attacks against the Church incited hatred of it and stoked the fires of anticlericalism. He did much to convince people that faith is the hallmark of ignorance, eccentricity, and self-interest and is antithetical to the factual, scientific, and reasonable in human life.[43]

The Encyclopédie

The *Encyclopédie* was a major reference work whose original twenty-eight volumes were published between 1751 and 1772. It was pro-

[43]Norman L. Torrey, "Voltaire, François-Marie Arouet de," *EP,* 7–8:262-70; see also Brinton, "Enlightenment," 520–1; Cragg, *Church and the Age of Reason,* 237–42; Caponigri, *Renaissance to the Romantic Age,* 352–5.

duced by two remarkable editors, Jean le Rond d'Alembert (1717–83) and Denis Diderot (1713–84), who had drunk deeply from Enlightenment wellsprings. The significance of the *Encyclopédie* went well beyond its effort to open the sciences to a general audience. It sought to show that disparate areas of learning were linked by an underlying unity and set forth the essential principles and content of each. Ultimately it aimed "to change the general way of thinking."[44] In other words, its editors intended that the *Encyclopédie* should promote the Enlightenment's agenda. By bringing sound knowledge to the many, they wanted their work "to deliver mankind from the slavery of ignorance and superstition, to bring it to the promised land of rationality."[45] An examination of its articles discloses this perspective. The scientific approach is applicable to all of life's problems; humanity betters itself by using reason; supernatural faith is to be rejected; a humanistic approach to ethics is best; the state should be egalitarian and function under a limited monarchy. These positions, the underlying spirit of synthesis and systematization, and its overtly pedagogical purpose made the *Encyclopédie* "an effective instrument for the cultural education of France, especially of the middle classes."[46]

Other Predisposing Influences

Certain background factors also contributed to the *philosophes'* success. One was the proliferation of such scientific and mechanical devices as clocks, windmills, telescopes, microscopes, and pumps for air and water. Greater familiarity with such machinery made it easier for people to conceive of the universe as a mechanical object that could be studied and organized to serve human needs. A second factor was the impact of travel and reports about the life and culture of distant peoples. Once they became acquainted with other societies, Westerners found it more difficult to assume that their religion was privileged and their virtues superior. Many began to think that religious beliefs merely reflected historical or cultural influences while morality depended upon a common human nature.[47] A third phenomenon was the emergence of a middle class that was literate, growing more numerous, and increasingly sensitive to social, economic, and political

---

[44] From Diderot's article "Encyclopédie," as quoted in Arthur M. Wilson, "Encyclopédie," *EP*, 1–2:506.

[45] Caponigri, *Renaissance to the Romantic Age*, 359.

[46] Ibid., 358; see also 356–62 and Wilson, "Encyclopédie."

[47] Theologically, that was a momentous step because it implicitly denied that Christ is the incarnate Savior of all or that the economy of salvation enjoys divine sanction as the Catholic tradition has asserted. Köhler, "The Enlightenment," 345.

conditions. This was the constituency that Enlightenment proponents primarily addressed.[48]

The Christian tradition supplied many of the Enlightenment's principal themes and was another source of its cogency and power. The notion that reason illuminates a person finds a precedent in Augustine's view of knowledge. The claim that human reason can arrive at a knowledge of truth by examining nature reflects the Aristotelian tradition and the legacy of Thomas Aquinas. A suspicion of human authority, reverence for each person, and sensitivity to the interior life have been perennial in Christian thought and piety. The notion of a perfect society to be achieved at some point in the future drew from the Judeo-Christian concept of heaven. Bias and error replaced sin as the most destructive personal defect, while the agent of salvation was no longer a transcendent God but persons enlightened by reason.[49]

The Enlightenment's Impact on the Western Outlook

The Enlightenment exercised great influence because it was able to change the way Europeans understood themselves and their society, the world, and the universe. The significance of that shift of outlook can be appreciated by considering three of its most important features.

The first is the notion that the rational mind and physical matter are two radically different kinds of reality. That idea supplanted the traditional view that the person is a composite body-soul unity who occupies a fitting place within a meaningful universe. The split between mind and matter has brought forth the disembodied "self," which is identified with the intangible activity of knowing and willing and set in contrast to a universe of matter that is knowable, quantifiable, and controllable but devoid of human meaning.

Second, the Enlightenment restructured the relationship between the person and the community. No longer are persons understood primarily in terms of the community that nurtures and sustains them. The individual is emphasized so strongly that the community recedes into the distant background. What replaces it is a society conceived as the creature of autonomous individuals. There tends to be a sharp contrast if not an adversarial relationship between the private domain and

---

[48] Collingwood, *Idea of Nature*, 8–9; Cragg, *Church and the Age of Reason*, 46–7; Butterfield, *Origins of Modern Science*, 103–7, 179–82, 195–6; Köhler, "The Enlightenment," 345, 378–80.

[49] Köhler, "The Enlightenment," 342–7. It is a terrible irony that the better future promised by the Enlightenment has included two world wars, genocide, and other catastrophes.

rights of individuals on the one hand and the requirements of society on the other.[50]

A third effect is the denial or trivializing of the transcendent dimensions of human life. Reality and knowledge, human society and human agency, religion and morality are no longer commonly understood in light of a personal God and a supernatural horizon from which they draw their deepest meaning. Instead, these foundational realities are situated within a natural frame of reference in which human reason reigns supreme. The shift from a transcendent to an immanent world view prepared for the secularization of European culture and thought, encouraged a purely philosophical view of God, and promoted an expansive assessment of human capacities to know the material world and improve the condition of humanity.[51]

Some Consequences

One effect of this shift is the common assumption that learning depends upon a careful study of material reality that yields valid observations and reasonable conclusions. This view has stimulated important technological advances on a wide front and invigorated scholarship in many fields, including ecclesiastical studies. To cite only one example, influenced by the scientific method scholars have posed many new questions to the biblical text and inquired into the process of its composition. Their work has thrown the religious, historical, literary, and archaeological background of the text into high relief and contributed to a better understanding of the people and circumstances behind the text.

Closer study of the natural dimensions of religious faith involves certain risks, especially if knowledge is presumed to arise solely from an examination of physical reality. Such an assumption leaves little

---

[50] See, for example, Ian S. Markham, *Plurality and Christian Ethics* (Cambridge: Cambridge University Press, 1994) 14–5; Anthony Arblaster, *The Rise and Decline of Western Liberalism* (New York and London: Basil Blackwell, 1984) 21–3, 38–54.

[51] Caponigri, *Renaissance to the Romantic Age*, 278; Cragg, *Church and the Age of Reason*, 242–5; Crane Brinton, *A History of Western Morals* (New York: Harcourt, Brace & Co., 1959) 293–307. Many Enlightenment figures readily professed a religious devotion but focused it on the universe and its splendor. They understood God only as the Creator who made the universe and assures that it runs properly. God was not considered to be a personal divinity who cares about human beings or intervenes in human affairs to save and call people to eternal life. On this see also Ernest Campbell Mossner, "Deism," *EP*, 1–2:326-36; Brinton, "Enlightenment," 521–2; Michael J. Buckley, *At the Origins of Modern Atheism* (New Haven and London: Yale University Press, 1987) 37–41.

room for the supernatural or the Christian tradition.[52] It discredits faith as a valid source of knowledge about human life and an adequate basis for action in the public arena. That view tends to consign faith to the domain of individual preference, but it supports naturalistic forms of religion as well as agnosticism and atheism, which have all proven their appeal to educated people.[53]

In the political arena, the Enlightenment laid the foundation for government based upon the consent of the people. Its defense of the individual and its opposition to cruel punishments have enhanced human dignity. It promoted the legal protection of human rights, greater toleration in civil society, and many programs of social and human improvement. These advances are to its credit. At the same time, individualism and notions of state sovereignty caused a dramatic shift in the public position of the Church. In constitutional democracies where authority rests ultimately with the citizens, the Church tends to be set off from the state and regarded as a voluntary association of individuals. In countries with authoritarian rule, the Church has fallen under the often destructive power of civil magistrates. In either case, the Church confronts situations very different from those it knew in earlier centuries.[54]

The Enlightenment's influence is also visible in the counter movements that developed in its wake. Its sterile rationalism and disregard for the transcendent stimulated the Methodist movement of John Wesley. Its exaggerated claims concerning nature's inherent goodness fed the Jansenist reaction and encouraged its negative assessment of human nature. In seeking communion with God through the aban-

---

[52] Modern studies have sometimes caused problems for believers, notably when they suggested that Moses could not have written the entire Pentateuch, cast doubt on the Bible's reckoning of time, or contradicted the Genesis account of creation. These tensions have sometimes been difficult to resolve and have occasionally led to ill-considered rejections of faith in the name of science and valid scientific findings in the name of faith. See Alexa Suelzer and John Kselman, "Modern Old Testament Criticism," *NJBC*, 1113–29; K. Grobel, "Biblical Criticism," *IDB*, 1:407-13; S. J. DeVries, "Biblical Criticism, History of," *IDB*, 1:413-8; Yves Congar, *A History of Theology*, trans. Hunter Guthrie (Garden City, N.Y.: Doubleday, 1968) 187–9; Cragg, *Church and the Age of Reason*, 248–9.

[53] For further consideration of the phenomena of natural religion and atheism in the modern world, see Taylor, *Sources of the Self*, 234–84; Buckley, *Origins of Modern Atheism*.

[54] See Guido de Ruggiero, *The History of European Liberalism*, trans. R. G. Collingwood (Boston: Beacon Press, 1959) 50–73, 395–406; Heinrich A. Rommen, *The Natural Law: A Study in Legal and Social History and Philosophy*, trans. Thomas R. Hanley (St. Louis: Herder, 1947) 79; Cragg, *Church and the Age of Reason*, 209–33; Alec R. Vidler, *The Church in an Age of Revolution* (Baltimore: Penguin Books, 1974) 236; Markham, *Plurality and Christian Ethics*, 10–7.

donment of all personal effort and the fostering of complete inner tranquillity, Quietism presupposed that humans can do little to improve themselves. German pietism and Kant's ethic of duty constituted attempts to compensate for the rationalism and utilitarian tendencies of the Enlightenment. An immoderate fascination with the abstract and mechanical gave way to the Romantic period's celebration of humanity's historical and transcendent dimensions.[55]

Effects on Ethics and Moral Life

Although the modern Western outlook strongly emphasizes individual rights, it has had great difficulty in formulating a satisfactory account of the moral life. Once physical matter is seen as having extension but no qualitative aspects, the universe and human nature cannot be the basis of the good in any real or substantive sense. Nature and creation, at least as they had traditionally been understood, disappear from the moral discussion, and the same is often the case with the community. Since they presuppose an excellence in human nature that ought to be developed, character and virtue also drop out of the picture. The moral good then has to be founded upon the only fonts of meaning that are left: quantitative considerations, the mind, and the will. These sources establish the moral good and anchor its defense against the freedom of individuals. They have given rise to several different accounts of human moral life.

One seeks to identify the good with desirable consequences of human action, which can be reckoned in terms of the immediate result or assessed in net quantitative terms; for example, the greatest good for the greatest number. More specifically, the good can be seen as the useful—an action that accomplishes a beneficial outcome is deemed to be morally good. Beneficence, the ability to improve the situation of others, is often cited as constituting the good that is to be done. The good can also be linked to an emotional or sensible result, usually described as happiness or pleasure as opposed to pain or discomfort.

The rejection of physical nature and the human community as sources of the moral good has led to a reliance upon formal or procedural criteria, usually a prescribed manner of acting. Accordingly, an action will be judged morally good if it complies with such criteria as fairness, justice, equity, and respect for the autonomy or human

[55] On these topics see Cragg, *Church and the Age of Reason*, 25–31, 141–56; Brinton, *History of Western Morals*, 232–4; Caponigri, *Renaissance to the Romantic Age*, 443–80; Jordan Aumann, *Christian Spirituality in the Catholic Tradition* (San Francisco: Ignatius Press; London: Sheed & Ward, 1985) 228–40.

dignity of others. It is also common to find the criterion of universalization cited as a source of morality; that is, an act is deemed to be morally good only if it would be good in all comparable cases without exception. Although these approaches leave no room for a substantive theory of natural law, they emphasize personal and human rights and the requirement of equity among different individuals.[56]

Whatever approach is taken, the turn away from nature has encouraged strong tendencies to rationalize the moral enterprise or base it on the will. Moral life is rationalized when assertions about the moral good depend on having the right ideas or using the mind in the correct way. Rationalism sometimes embraces the facts of human experience, while at other times it ignores them as irrelevant. The notion that moral life is a function of the will characterizes other moral theories and includes all those that derive the good from the will of superior authority, whether or not it is reasonable. A voluntaristic current in ethics has reinforced the opinion that moral life is primarily a matter of duty or obligation rather than a way to live the virtue of faith or realize an excellence that is latent in one's being.[57]

These presuppositions and approaches help to account for a strong inclination to dismiss transcendence, emphasize the individual, and depreciate authority in deliberations about the good. They have given rise to a tendency to see morality as a private matter, which complicates efforts to conduct a satisfactory public discussion of moral issues or craft an account of moral life that can claim a consensus. This environment also affects the moral consciousness of Christian believers because it introduces a wide range of ethical presuppositions into the Church community, undermines communication on important issues, confuses discussions about authority and personal consent, and increases the chances that people will misunderstand one another's

---

[56] Although the term "natural law" has been an integral part of moral and legal thought for many centuries, it underwent a series of changes in the early modern period and has taken on various and sometimes incompatible denotations. A modern bias in favor of the individual against the community, the church, and the state has done much to push the concept of natural rights into prominence while giving it a specific tone and content. The complex historical, intellectual, and political background of the terms "natural law" and "natural rights" suggests that they should be understood and used with care. On these matters, see A. P. d'Entrèves, *Natural Law: An Introduction to Legal Philosophy* (London: Hutchinson University Library, 1970) 51–64, especially 59–62; John Finnis, *Natural Law and Natural Rights* (Oxford: Clarendon Press; New York: Oxford University Press, 1980) 198–230; Arblaster, *Rise and Decline of Western Liberalism*, 23–32; Rommen, *Natural Law*, 70–123.

[57] Taylor, *Sources of the Self*, 3, 75–90; Alasdair C. MacIntyre, *After Virtue: A Study in Moral Theory*, 2nd ed. (Notre Dame, Ind.: University of Notre Dame Press, 1984) 36–61.

views and intentions. The wide divergence between traditional and culturally prevailing views also hinders an effective conversation between the Church and society on important common issues.[58]

SUBSEQUENT DEVELOPMENTS

Events since the end of eighteenth century have demonstrated the influence of the Enlightenment on Western attitudes and thinking. The intervening period includes other developments that have shaped the modern world and the Catholic Church's position in it. Of particular interest are the French Revolution, the Industrial Revolution, the influence of European liberalism, the Church's experience in the United States of America, and the effects of historical consciousness.

The French Revolution

The French Revolution, customarily dated from the storming of the Bastille on July 14, 1789, drew its power from the grievances of the lower classes against the established order and long-standing class animosities within French society. Once the revolution began, it set in motion a complex and often violent series of events that could not be curbed until it had run its course. By the time it was over, the French Revolution had destroyed the old social and political order and irreversibly altered many aspects of French life. It assigned the Catholic Church a new position in French society, reshaped popular attitudes inside and outside the Church, and influenced the policies of the Holy See for well over a century.

The French Revolution was occasioned by a serious financial crisis. France owed a great deal of money, largely due to the expenses of waging war and maintaining an army and a navy. Since the state did not have enough income to settle these debts, King Louis XVI had to convoke the Estates General, which was the only entity that had authority to impose new taxes and revise the financial system. As the Estates General was preparing to meet, social and political conflicts led to a constitutional crisis. On June 17, 1789, that crisis assumed revolutionary dimensions when the Third Estate declared itself to be the National

---

[58] These matters are discussed in Brinton, *History of Western Morals*, 308–28; Taylor, *Sources of the Self*, especially 3–90. See also Alasdair C. MacIntyre, *Whose Justice? Which Rationality?* (Notre Dame, Ind.: University of Notre Dame Press, 1988) 1–11; idem, *After Virtue*, 6–22; Arblaster, *Rise and Decline of Western Liberalism*, 16–21, 28–37.

Assembly, claimed full legislative authority, and announced that it would write a new constitution for France.[59]

The National Assembly acted as it did in order to defend the professional and business interests of the middle class, or *bourgeoisie*, which was its main constituency. But its action also energized the peasants and the urban poor, who took to the streets to press their own claims for justice and equality. Under pressure from below, the National Assembly legislated an end to serfdom and tax privileges in France and decreed that all would be equal before the law. It set forth the governing principles of the new order in the Declaration of the Rights of Man and Citizen.[60] Soon afterward the National Assembly repealed laws that were offensive to the lower classes and undertook a thorough dismantling of the older order. In November of 1789, in order to settle the state's outstanding debts the Assembly confiscated the Church's property and put much of it up for sale.

That drastic step required the authorities to consider the Catholic Church's place in revolutionary France and make new arrangements for it. What resulted was a series of laws to provide for the financial support of the clergy and the institutions the Church had operated. More importantly, on July 12, 1790, the Assembly enacted the Civil Constitution of the Clergy, legislation that abolished monasticism, aligned the system of dioceses with civil jurisdictions, provided for the civil election of bishops without regard for papal prerogatives, and required state approval for the publication of papal acts. Pope Pius VI rejected this law and condemned the revolution that had produced it. The Assembly then required the clergy to swear their loyalty to the Civil Constitution of the Clergy. About half complied and the rest refused, a situation that also sowed division among the French laity.[61] In

---

[59] The Estates General was composed of three estates that together represented the entire French nation. The clergy constituted the First Estate, the aristocrats the second, and everyone else belonged to the third. The Estates General of the entire nation had not convened since 1614, when it sat as a tricameral body. This arrangement was rejected by the Third Estate in 1789 because it would have left too much power in the hands of the aristocrats, whom the middle class heartily resented. The Third Estate demanded that all three estates should sit as one body, which would have favored the Third Estate, since it was as numerous as the other two groups combined. When this proposal was rejected, the Third Estate unilaterally imposed its more radical solution. Palmer, *History of the Modern World*, 351–2, 354–9; John McManners, *The French Revolution and the Church* (London: SPCK, 1969) 19–23.

[60] This declaration was issued on August 26, 1789; for the text, see de Ruggiero, *History of European Liberalism*, 66–8. Its similarity to the Bill of Rights in the U.S. Constitution has often been noted.

[61] For the text of the Civil Constitution of the Clergy, see Ehler, *Church and State Through the Centuries*, 239–49. The requirement of the oath of loyalty, enacted on

the wake of this episode, hostility toward the Church intensified and anticlerical attitudes deepened. The campaign to dechristianize French life, which began in 1793, reflected the same antagonism and demonstrated how extreme some revolutionaries had become.[62]

In the early 1790s the revolution entered a more violent phase. The bourgeoisie and the lower classes continued to eye one another suspiciously, even though they both opposed the aristocracy and its reactionary aims. The revolution took on international dimensions when aristocrats and disillusioned revolutionaries began to seek the help of foreign armies in an attempt to restore the old order by force. That led to a series of wars, strengthened revolutionary fervor in France, and fostered a climate in which counter-revolutionary activity drew a very severe response. The Terror followed; this was the period of about a year in which some forty thousand people were put to death. After the summer of 1793 the violence abated, but France remained unstable for the remainder of the decade. The French Revolution came to an end on November 27, 1799, when Napoleon Bonaparte carried out a coup d'etat and took control of the country.[63]

The Impact of the French Revolution

The French Revolution inaugurated an era of political, social, and economic turmoil. Its destruction of the established order encouraged patriots in other lands to rebel against foreign rule or bring to birth

---

November 27, 1789, is considered by many to be the one act that was most responsible for engendering the deep hostility between the Revolution and the Church. Palmer, *History of the Modern World*, 364–6; Vidler, *Church in an Age of Revolution*, 15–8; McManners, *French Revolution and the Church*, 38–46.

[62] On the antireligious dimension of the French Revolution, see McManners, *French Revolution and the Church*, 86–105; Michel Vovelle, *The Revolution Against the Church: From Reason to the Supreme Being*, trans. Alan José (Columbus: Ohio State University Press, 1991); Jean Dumont, *La Révolution Française ou les prodiges du sacrilège* (Limoges: Criterion, 1984).

[63] Once in power, Napoleon decided to reach a settlement with the Church, which occurred with the Concordat of 1801. The Holy See gained unquestioned jurisdiction over all Catholic clergy but accepted the loss of Church property to the state. The Catholic faith could be practiced without hindrance, the clergy would be salaried by the state, and other faiths given freedom of expression. See Vidler, *Church in an Age of Revolution*, 18–21; McManners, *French Revolution and the Church*, 140–50. Extracts from the Concordat of 1801 can be found in Ehler, *Church and State Through the Centuries*, 252–4.

This discussion of the French Revolution has followed Palmer, *History of the Modern World*, 350–85; Vidler, *Church in an Age of Revolution*, 11–8; McManners, *French Revolution and the Church*.

their own national state. Its ideology of equality and individual rights found currency wherever people confronted authoritarian or oppressive systems. It demonstrated that the peasants, urban workers, and unemployed were able to rise up in order to secure their social, political, and economic goals. The French Revolution also showed that it is very difficult to control the energies that a revolution releases and that such a step can have unpredictable and destructive consequences. It warned that when a revolution goes too far, it loses popular support and increases the strength of conservative reactions. On all these points, the French experience was to be repeated time and again during the nineteenth century.

The French Revolution traumatized the Catholic Church. The violence and the injuries inflicted on the Church made its leaders more suspicious toward progressive social and political movements and more sympathetic to traditional political, social, and economic systems. They especially resented the demand that priests swear to abide by the Civil Constitution for the Clergy, since in addition to ignoring papal authority it opened deep fissures within French Catholicism and increased the alienation between the Catholic Church and important elements of French society and culture. Ironically, that episode made the papacy a touchstone of Catholicism in France in a way that had not been the case before. Furthermore, the increased respect for the Roman Pontiff strengthened ultramontanist currents in the Church and supported the process by which the Holy See took a great deal of Church authority into its own hands and asserted its prerogatives ever more vigorously on a wider range of issues.[64]

Along with many Catholics, the Holy See took the French experience as a paradigm for modern Western society and a lens through which its affairs were to be viewed and interpreted. The cumulative influence of the French Revolution and this official response to it has been great and has done much to shape the relationship between the Catholic Church and modern Western societies since that time. The Church has tended to oppose progressive movements, which has alienated people who were convinced that an established political or economic order needed to be changed or replaced. A generally adver-

---

[64] Ultramontanism represents both a theoretical position and a political strategy. In general, Ultramontanism attributes more authority to the pope than canon law and theology have traditionally recognized and seeks to settle problems through a papal decision that is imposed on the contending parties. Ultramontanists appeal to papal authority in order to resolve intrachurch questions or as a counterweight to secular authorities. See Frederick J. Cwiekowski, "Ultramontanism," *The New Dictionary of Theology*, ed. Joseph A. Komonchak and others (Collegeville: The Liturgical Press, 1991) 1064–5.

sarial relationship between the Church and society has made it more difficult for believers to take their place in the secular city and be fully accepted there. The Church's often negative attitude has not favored a constructive engagement with modern society and culture. A stronger and more assertive papacy helped to project these judgments and attitudes throughout the Catholic Church and to delay the day when they could be reconsidered.

The Industrial Revolution

The "Industrial Revolution" refers to the remarkable series of developments that occurred as machines replaced hand tools in the production of goods. That process began in England around the year 1780 and came to maturity in the early decades of the nineteenth century, when it also began to appear on the Continent and in the United States. Industrialization brought many advantages to the countries in which it occurred, made some people very wealthy, but also created a large underclass of workers and their families who lived in poverty. The overall effect of the Industrial Revolution on economic and social life was so dramatic that it provoked a wide range of responses, including the theories of Marx and Lenin and the social teachings of Pope Leo XIII.

The remote origins of the Industrial Revolution can be located in the Revolution of 1688, in which the English landowning class extracted a share of political power from the monarch and the aristocracy.[65] With their newfound influence the landowners obtained a series of laws that allowed them to fence off and privatize large tracts of land that had been used in common. Along with the introduction of better farming methods, privatization made agriculture much more efficient, which increased crop yields and forced farm workers into the general labor market. By providing abundant goods for overseas markets, the agricultural revolution stimulated international trade and increased England's wealth, helping it to gain control of the seas and acquire a colonial empire. At home it benefited from plentiful labor, sufficient capital to underwrite new commercial ventures, and the managerial expertise to oversee the entire enterprise.

But there was a serious problem: England could only sell what it could produce, and production was severely limited by the hand-based methods of the time. To cite one example, cotton fabric was in short supply because it required manual labor at every step, from the field to the finished bolt of cloth. The urgent need for a more efficient manufacturing process stimulated the invention of a remarkable series

[65] See note 29 in this chapter, above.

of machines that de-seeded the raw cotton, spun it into thread, and wove the cloth. As a result, England was able to meet the world's demand for cotton and profit handsomely as it did so. Another advance came with the invention and improvement of the steam engine, which ran the new machines, made mines more productive, and supplied power to ships and railroads.

The wholesale mechanization of industrial production had dramatic social consequences. Industrial efficiency demanded that factories should be situated close to the sources of fuel. That accounts for their construction near the coal fields of northern England and Scotland. Because they offered work, the factories attracted many people and stimulated the growth of nearby cities. But this large-scale migration involved many problems. Cities became overcrowded and living conditions deteriorated. Although factory jobs involved long hours, the wages were insufficient to support a family. To make up the difference, women and children also took factory jobs, which usually required no special skills. But for all that, there was still no security. When business turned bad, employees were laid off and lost their income. It is fair to say that many people lived and worked under very difficult conditions.[66]

The Industrial Revolution has done much to fashion the modern world as it exists today. It gave Western Europe the economic, political, and technological power that enabled it to establish hegemony over distant peoples during the nineteenth century.[67] It convinced many other nations that an industrial economy is the foundation of wealth, power, and a better standard of living. But it has also disrupted traditional ways of life and widened the gulf between socioeconomic classes in a given society and between industrialized and nonindustrialized nations. In such circumstances, poverty and inequity have caused social conflicts, political instability, and contestation over ideology and the proper organization of economic life.

The Industrial Revolution has raised some difficult questions for the Church and its members. Does the cycle of production and consumption constitute a sound basis for human life? Is it necessary or desirable to accept the economic and political inequities that have usually resulted? How should the Church assess the human and theoretical conflicts that occur and respond to the people who are adversely affected? What do people owe to their community and what claims do individuals have on the community and its resources? These questions require

[66] Palmer, *History of the Modern World*, 425–35; de Ruggiero, *History of European Liberalism*, 43–50.

[67] Palmer, *History of the Modern World*, 543–9; 608–47.

careful consideration of the prerequisites of human flourishing and the community's contribution to it and have important doctrinal, political, and pastoral dimensions.

Liberal Individualism

Although the Industrial Revolution reflected the wholesale mechanization of industrial production, it was propelled forward by the entrepreneurs who sought to expand their businesses and earn as large a profit as the circumstances permitted. This spirit of private enterprise reflected a deeper intellectual current that is usually known as "liberal individualism" or simply "liberalism."[68] Liberalism is important not only for its impact on the Industrial Revolution but also because it has deeply influenced contemporary Western thinking, attitudes, and institutions.

Because liberalism was a diffuse movement without a set form or content, it is difficult to describe exactly. At its core, however, liberalism seeks to secure for the individual the greatest possible measure of freedom. It promotes one's ability to think, believe, and act with minimal restraint on the part of church or state authorities. It opposes all political, religious, or intellectual orthodoxies that would bind the individual. Suspicious of any kind of official or group power, liberalism tries to protect individual freedom as much as possible from encroachment.[69]

Liberalism drew its content and power from many diverse sources. The Renaissance fascination with the individual and its celebration of human capacities provided one stimulus. The commercial expansion that began in the late fifteenth century encouraged private initiative and the practice of capitalist entrepreneurship. Religious sources were also decisive. By denying papal authority in religion, the Reformation rejected what was the oldest and arguably the most

---

[68] This discussion employs the term "liberalism" according to its historical meaning, which may be quite different from contemporary usage in some countries. It is a historical irony that people and groups who espouse key tenets of traditional liberal individualism often describe themselves as political and economic "conservatives," while those who defend the political and economic interests of poor and working-class people are frequently known as "liberals."

[69] See Arblaster, *Rise and Decline of Western Liberalism*, 10–4; Peter Steinfels, "The Failed Encounter: The Catholic Church and Liberalism in the Nineteenth Century," *Catholicism and Liberalism: Contributions to American Public Philosophy*, ed. R. Bruce Douglass and David Hollenbach (Cambridge: Cambridge University Press, 1994) 23–4; Harold J. Laski, *The Rise of European Liberalism: An Essay in Interpretation* (London: Unwin Books, 1962) 13–6.

important institutional authority in Europe. Its emphasis on the priesthood of all believers suggested that authority ultimately rests in private and not official hands. The Reformation's focus on the individual's inner experience and direct relationship with God has had a similar effect. The Catholic Church's own conflicts with civil monarchies and its respect for personal conscience also helped to weaken the claims of authoritative bodies and preserve a safe haven for individual persons.[70]

After a period of latency, liberal ideas came together and achieved dominance in the Enlightenment. Liberal thinking supported the American Revolution of 1776, the French Revolution of 1789, and many of the revolutions that convulsed Europe and Latin America during the nineteenth century. Although these events reflected many other influences as well, all sought to replace an established authoritarian order with one that would limit state power, protect individuals, expand their liberties, and promote their economic interests. Liberalism gave rise to free-enterprise theory and sustained the permissive legal and economic climate on which the Industrial Revolution depended.[71] It also supported the notion that individuals should be free to hold nonconforming opinions and pursue their own goals without interference from the state, provided only that the rights of others are not violated.

As it developed, liberalism helped to popularize the view that truth is to be established in an open market where all opinions are welcome and each person is free to judge, without interference by others, what is true or good. Liberalism's suspicion of established powers, its tendency to foment political revolution, the freedom it offered to the captains of industry, its embrace of acquisitiveness, and its distaste for

---

[70] See de Ruggiero, *History of European Liberalism*, 13–23; Arblaster, *Rise and Decline of Western Liberalism*, 15–37, 95–125.

[71] According to classic free-enterprise theory individuals act out of their own self-interest, and the only fixed laws are those that are intrinsic to economic life itself, for example, the law of supply and demand. Therefore, employers try to keep wages as low as possible and resist tariffs, government-imposed regulations, labor unions, and anything else that would hinder entrepreneurial freedom or drive up the costs of production. Any help given to the unemployed should be meager enough to motivate them to return to work at low wages. The government's task is to assure public security and guarantee the sanctity of contracts but leave most other matters in the private sector. Adam Smith, whose *Wealth of Nations* appeared in 1776, set the theoretical foundation for these ideas, which helped to guide the course of the Industrial Revolution and the circumstances of working people at that time. See Palmer, *History of the Modern World*, 433–5, 437; de Ruggiero, *History of European Liberalism*, 123–35.

objective criteria of truth profoundly influenced the affairs of Europe and the Americas during the nineteenth century. Its influence continues to be strong.[72] Liberalism has had a significant impact within the Catholic Church. Some of its members have accepted the view that individual rights, the rule of law, constitutional government, the open discussion of important issues, and a participatory approach to decision making are desirable in any society. Many have assumed that missionary or apologetical work in the larger society requires the Church to recognize these concerns, address them forthrightly, and to the extent possible, reflect them in its own procedures. The influence of the liberal ethos has affected the discussion of authority, conscience, the nature and binding quality of moral norms, and the status of "dissent" in the Church.

Although liberalism has found an echo in Catholic souls and can claim some support from the tradition, the popes have generally been hostile toward it. They have remembered the heavy price that the French Revolution exacted from the Church. That experience and the civil disorders of the nineteenth century have led them to defend the established social and political order and to intensify their resistance to the liberal ideology that seemed to foment violence and subversion. Catholic convictions about community, truth, and authority also stimulated opposition to liberalism.[73]

The Catholic Experience in the United States of America

The United States has offered a very different setting for the faith, service, prayer, and witness of a Catholic Church whose roots went deep into the soil of European history, politics, and thought. Among

---

[72] John Stuart Mill strongly defended the liberty of individuals against the encroachment of the group. His book *On Liberty*, published in 1859, offers a philosophical basis for liberal individualism. Mill is also known for his utilitarian approach to ethics. See Owen Chadwick, *Secularization of the European Mind in the Nineteenth Century* (Cambridge: Cambridge University Press, 1975) 28–33.

The foregoing discussion reflects Palmer, *History of the Modern World*, 433–5, 437, 455–69; Laski, *Rise of European Liberalism*; de Ruggiero, *History of European Liberalism*; John Langan, "Catholicism and Liberalism—200 Years of Contest and Consensus," *Liberalism and the Good*, ed. R. Bruce Douglass and others (New York and London: Routledge, 1990) 105–24; and the classic work, Max Weber, *The Protestant Ethic and the Spirit of Capitalism*, trans. Talcott Parsons (New York: Scribner's, 1958).

[73] The relationship between the Catholic Church and modern liberalism, although complex and ambivalent, has been a critical element in the Church's internal affairs. See, for example, Steinfels, "Failed Encounter"; Langan, "Catholicism and Liberalism." This topic will receive further attention in chapter 11, below.

the most significant causes of that uniqueness are the continuing influence of Protestant religious convictions and the particular effects of the Enlightenment on American customs, attitudes, and government. The religion of the Reformation was perhaps the most formative influence in the English colonies. Many had voyaged to America in order to escape persecution or find a place where they could freely practice their faith. Presupposing that a harmony should exist between faith and civil life, the early colonists founded a number of political-religious communities that reflected Anglican, Congregational, and other Reformation-based beliefs as well as their English political habits. Time and circumstance tempered the initially strict religious laws of some colonies, a process hastened by an ever-expanding spectrum of beliefs among the population. However, tolerance and accommodation did not annul the effects of religion on the consciousness and customs of the American people. These include respect for law; the need of personal initiative, upright morality, and education; a sense of divine favor and mission; and the idea that government depends upon social contract and general participation. Well into the era of independence, there remained a sense that the United States was a Protestant country. To this day many Americans consider that theirs is a Christian society.[74]

American attitudes and institution were also shaped by the Enlightenment as it had developed in England. Because the Revolution of 1688 had limited the power of the monarchy and secured the supremacy of Parliament, there was no further need of violence to overthrow a tyrannical regime or to defend individual rights and liberties. The Church of England had shown itself to be sympathetic to the claims of reason as Locke and others had set them forth, so there was little point in declaring war on the Church. In other words, by the middle of the eighteenth century the Enlightenment had already impressed itself on many of England's economic, political, and religious institutions. As a result England and its American colonies did not experience the revolutionary violence, class hatreds, hostility to religion, and impassioned secularism that convulsed the French. Although voices of opposition were never lacking, the Enlightenment extended its influence in those lands largely through custom and consent.[75]

[74] See Sydney E. Ahlstrom, *A Religious History of the American People* (Garden City, N.Y.: Doubleday Image Books, 1975), which offers the most thorough examination of the subject; also Henry Steele Commager, *The American Mind: An Interpretation of American Thought and Character Since the 1880's* (New Haven and London: Yale University, 1950) 162–95.

[75] Ahlstrom, *Religious History of the American People*, 418–36; Roy Porter, "The Enlightenment in England," *The Enlightenment in National Context*, 1–18. The classic

When they worked in tandem, religious convictions and Enlightenment ideology proved to be very effective in forming American attitudes and institutions. One result was a strong accent on individualism, which is evident in a tradition of free speech, encouragement of private enterprise in the pursuit of one's business and personal interests, the belief that reason and freedom are the keys to progress, and the multiplication of religions. Closely allied is the conviction that the government's powers come from the people and must be strictly limited, especially since individual rights are so precious. Another consequence is the constitutional bar against any law that would establish a religion in the United States or prohibit its free exercise. This provision was a practical necessity given the religious diversity of the American people, but it also reflected a strong desire to circumscribe state authority and leave religion to the conscience of each person. This constitutional arrangement had no precedent in European experience.[76]

The customs, attitudes, and culture of American society have presented the Catholic community with some unique problems and opportunities. The individualism that thrives in the United States often runs counter to the essentially communitarian basis of Catholic faith and praxis. It can lead people to think that religion is a purely private and interior matter that responds to no objective grounds or ecclesial authority, and that one's religion, or lack of it, is simply a matter of personal preference.[77] In politics and economics, individualism has given rise to the idea that one's activities in these areas have little to do with faith and should not be evaluated in light of the common good or the needs of the poor.

The Catholic Church has also drawn extraordinary benefits from American culture and society. Since it has never exercised civil power in the United States, there has been no legacy of anticlericalism to hinder its work. Because the Church was never identified with the economic or political establishment, it was free to embrace immigrants and working people and be accepted by them as a friend. Finally, the American tradition to exclude the government from religious affairs

---

study of the American Enlightenment is Henry F. May, *The Enlightenment in America* (New York: Oxford University Press, 1976).

[76] Commager, *American Mind*, 162–95; Bernard Bailyn, *The Ideological Origins of the American Revolution* (Cambridge: Belknap Press, 1967); Morton G. White, *The Philosophy of the American Revolution* (New York: Oxford University Press, 1978); Russel B. Nye, *This Almost Chosen People: Essays in the History of American Ideas* (n.p.: Michigan State University Press, 1966) 104–63 (esp. 104–16), 208–55.

[77] See the sociological data published by Robert N. Bellah and others, *Habits of the Heart: Individualism and Commitment in American Life* (New York: Harper & Row, 1986), especially 142–63, 219–49.

has removed all threat of state control or supervision of Catholic life. Constitutionally guaranteed freedoms of religion, assembly, speech, and the press have offered the Catholic Church a favorable environment in which to carry out its many activities. It has offered a new context in which to rethink Catholic teachings on freedom of conscience and the relationship between Church and state. The contribution of John Courtney Murray to this reconsideration has been especially important and is reflected in documents of the Second Vatican Council.[78]

Historical Consciousness

Throughout the early modern period scientists and philosophers assumed that the universe is composed of inert matter that tends to be at rest unless something intervenes to cause motion or activity. Although motion is caused by human agency or some natural process, it was ultimately attributed to God's creative act. The universe was seen as a giant clock and God the clock maker. Toward the end of the eighteenth century those metaphors and the mechanistic concept of nature that lay behind them came under increasing stress. One reason was the Enlightenment's view of human progress, which conflicted with the notion that things tend to remain unchanged. Another was a better knowledge of history and a new interpretation of history itself.

In the early modern era people tended to assume that the ancient Greeks and Romans had established the norm for good writing, the arts, and human living in general. They assessed their own activity in light of the standard their ancestors had set. This earlier view rested on the assumption either that historical change masks an underlying and much more important continuity or sameness in human affairs or that change is essentially cyclical, with alternating moments of success and decline. However, once people compared the defects in ancient works with the unparalleled accomplishments of modern science and literature, they began to think that human history was neither superficial nor cyclical but progressive in nature.

Scientific findings seemed to support this progressive view of history. Fossils and other evidence showed that plants and animals have become extinct or undergone major changes in a short time. These findings contradicted an older notion that all living things have a se-

---

[78] See E.E.Y. Hales, *The Catholic Church in the Modern World: A Survey from the French Revolution to the Present* (Garden City, N.Y.: Doubleday, 1960) 148–68; John Courtney Murray, *We Hold These Truths: Catholic Reflections on the American Proposition* (Garden City, N.Y.: Doubleday Image Books, 1964).

cure place within a stable universe.[79] Geological studies revealed that the earth is not inert but has changed dramatically. Research into the composition and behavior of molecules suggested that motion is intrinsic to them and is constitutive of physical reality. On the basis of these findings many people abandoned the notion that the human race, plants, animals, and the universe itself are fixed and immutable. They concluded that all these realities need to be understood temporally as well as spatially.

This shift of outlook has been of capital importance. The older idea that the universe is a machine that had been built and powered by an intelligent Creator gave way to a new view that sees all reality as essentially fluid. It tends to assume that activity gives rise to structure and not the other way around. There is an inclination to accept evolution as a fact of life and to associate knowledge with the apprehension of change, flux, or motion rather than with unchangeable realities whether tangible or intangible. In the political realm this new consciousness supported the idea that history entails an inexorable tendency to overcome class divisions and bring forth a just and equitable society.

More recently, historians have thrown the discontinuity and human character of past events into high relief and acknowledged that all accounts of history will be affected by the historian's own humanity and the particular concerns and biases it entails. This perspective emphasizes the contingency of historical events and the need to do justice to the unique, temporally situated, and culturally conditioned quality of persons and events. It excludes the notion that history unfolds by any sort of necessity, whether sacred or secular. If freedom and contingency prevail and if history is not preordained to follow any particular course, then the past does not control the present, and persons have greater influence over the future than many had assumed.

The term "historical consciousness" refers to the conviction that temporal events are marked by discontinuity, that human persons are historical beings, and that any adequate account of human life must duly acknowledge its historicity. To be sure, there are different interpretations of historical consciousness and its implications, some more moderate than others. However, there has developed a general agreement that historicity is essential to persons, reality, and knowledge. The emergence of historical consciousness constitutes a major intellectual and cultural landmark.[80]

---

[79] The landmark event was the publication in 1859 of Charles Darwin's *Origin of Species*, a study foreshadowed by work done in earlier decades.

[80] John W. O'Malley, "Reform, Historical Consciousness, and Vatican II's Aggiornamento," *TS* 32 (1971), especially 595–8. See also Collingwood, *Idea of Nature*, 9–27,

Within the Church, historical consciousness has reinforced the conviction that policies and practices need to be constantly updated in light of changing times and circumstances and has made resistance to such accommodation seem to be reactionary and contrary to pastoral needs. Awareness of historical change has helped theologians to understand why doctrines are sometimes formulated differently from one age to another and how the Church's understanding of them can develop. But the recognition of historical development has entailed certain problems. Once it is admitted that history affects the understanding and formulation of doctrine, it becomes more difficult to show how the substance of doctrine can remain immune from change. The effect of historical flux on moral life has been particularly controversial. Some have suggested that if reality, persons, and human knowledge are conditioned by change, then the requirements of upright morality might also change with time. In any case, considerations of temporality and contingency have increased the weight given to particular persons, times, and circumstances in deciding whether actions are good or evil and has called attention to the personal interests of moral agents and those who reflect upon or teach the moral requirements of human life.

Although the question of history is difficult and some proposals have been problematic, Christian believers have good reason to take the matter seriously and respond constructively. Christian faith is a historical faith that affirms that God has intervened in human affairs through mighty deeds on behalf of the chosen people and ultimately through the life, death, and resurrection of Jesus Christ. The Christian tradition confesses that God exercises a providential care of people in every age. Therefore each generation needs to interpret the signs of the times as best it can and shapes the course of history as it enacts its own response. Apologetical and evangelical considerations invite believers to account for human history in a way that not only does justice to faith but also responds to contemporary questions and experiences. If this task is done well, it can strengthen faith and make a positive contribution to discussions in the wider community. Finally, it is useful to consider the high cost of denying or minimizing historical change or underestimating the importance of the questions that it entails. If believers fail to offer a cogent account of history, they cede its interpretation to others and allow their theories to prevail by default. The

---

133–6, 142–57, 174–7; Butterfield, *Origins of Modern Science,* 222–46; Reinhold Niebuhr, *Faith and History: A Comparison of Christian and Modern Views of History* (New York: C. Scribner's Sons, 1949) 14–34.

influence of Marxist views of history shows that this course of action can have extremely unfavorable consequences.[81]

REFLECTIONS

In the period between the sixteenth and eighteenth centuries the European world view underwent a series of changes that reshaped its attitudes, culture, political life, religious perspectives, and view of the human person. In any attempt to appreciate these developments, it is well to remember that they grew out of the experience of the West and reflected important events in its history. Although it might well affect them, the modern outlook is foreign to non-Western peoples and to the tradition and praxis of the Catholic Church. This suggests that when Westerners and those of other cultural traditions encounter one another, both sides might benefit by paying attention to the diverse presuppositions, resources, and expectations they bring to a common enterprise or to assessments of one another. Similarly, it is useful for Westerners themselves to take stock of the contrasting outlooks that prevail in the Church and in the wider society. Such awareness can help to avoid confusion and misunderstanding, promote respect for others, and support a constructive response to a fundamental but unavoidable tension.

The conflict between the Western outlook and the Catholic Church helps to account for the suspicion and animosity that have often marked the Church's relationship with modern societies. To some degree this reflects the fact that these societies were often forged in opposition to supernatural faith, traditional authority, and the claims of corporate entities, especially the Catholic Church. That the Church's relationship with the modern world continues to be marked by suspicion and conflict suggests that historical antitheses are still charged

---

[81] See R. G. Collingwood, *The Idea of History,* rev. ed., ed. Jan van der Dussen (Oxford and New York: Oxford University Press, 1993); Herbert Butterfield, *Christianity and History* (New York: Charles Scribner's Sons, 1949), especially 113–29; Jean Daniélou, *The Lord of History: Reflections on the Inner Meaning of History,* trans. Nigel Abercrombie (London: Longmans; Chicago: Henry Regnery, 1958) 149–67; Alan Richardson, *History Sacred and Profane* (Philadelphia: Westminster Press, 1964) 212–41. Butterfield has noted how paradoxical it is that Christians, who continually address human failure, should have allowed Marxists to construct a theory of history around this reality and gain considerable influence among historians and others (Butterfield, *Christianity and History,* 42). See Alasdair MacIntyre, *Marxism and Christianity* (Notre Dame: University of Notre Dame Press, 1984).

The Catholic Church's struggle with the problematic of faith and history will receive further attention in chapter 11, below.

with energy. To the extent that it exists, that alienation taxes the respect, fairness, and patience of all parties. It invites the Catholic Church to consider its own responsibility for this troubled relationship and the impact of the resulting tension on its life, thought, and ministry.

To be sure, the relationship between Church and society is complex and will vary from place to place. Believers will usually be able to commend many aspects of contemporary culture, attitudes, and practices. Still, the modern Western outlook does not place a premium on supernatural faith or support those who try to follow Christ. There is no longer general agreement that the moral life requires people to acknowledge their social nature and the claim of truth about human life and the particular issues that must be decided each day. Authoritative acts, the arts, and the media of mass communication tend to be assessed in terms of personal or group interests rather than what is upright or good for the community. To the extent that this is the case, it will present the Church with several important challenges.

If the prevailing culture is hostile or indifferent to faith, believers will need to point out what they find deficient, account for their objections, and then give voice to Christian faith and defend it as reasonably as possible. In this connection, constructive conversations with representatives of the scientific, journalistic, entertainment, and academic communities seem especially urgent. There is also an evangelical imperative. In response to the dynamics of faith and charity, believers need to preach and give witness to the Gospel in a way that is faithful, accessible, and persuasive. The critical process of inculturation likewise demands careful attention.[82] Fidelity to faith and truth does not allow the Church to ignore the failures and exaggerations of a society or its culture. But if believers maintain too much distance from modern societies, address them with too negative a voice, or fail to approve what is noble and good, people will be unlikely to consider their critique or hear the gospel they preach. Successful inculturation allows the Church community to participate in the life of a nation, be accepted by it, and carry out its mission of witness, worship, and service more fruitfully. These considerations also warn against universalizing the Western experience or failing to consider non-Western societies in light of their own background and merits.

The cultural denial or trivialization of the transcendent dimension of human life constitutes a subtle but powerful attack on Christian faith.

---

[82] For an introduction, see Lucien Richard, "Inculturation," *The New Dictionary of Catholic Social Thought*, ed. Judith A. Dwyer (Collegeville: The Liturgical Press, 1994) 481–3.

Without a transcendent, personal, and saving God, Jesus Christ can be no more than a remarkable figure in ancient history. Ecclesial traditions lose their sacred aspects and retain merely archival significance. The eschatological dimensions of human life dissolve into fantasy. The Church becomes only another group within society, and Church authority a means for those in power to further their own interests. Faith will be little more than a symptom of ignorance or irrationality. These implications suggest that when a culture leaves little room for the transcendent, it also tends to validate unbelief, discourage Christian faith, and emarginate believers. Because cultural unbelief constitutes an intellectual statement and a way of life, it invites the Church community both to make a competent and sustained intellectual response and to give the kind of witness that can persuade fair-minded, spiritually hungry people that its way of life is worthy of their participation and commitment.

The contemporary Western outlook has had an equally strong impact on the moral life. It has depreciated supernatural faith, physical reality, and the community while promoting the individual to a decisive position in the moral enterprise. It tends to take personal rights, freedom, desires, and interests for granted. To the extent that this is the case, the moral life will be characterized by an adversarial relationship among individuals and the consequent need to reconcile their competing interests in a rational and equitable way. This approach contrasts sharply with the traditional Catholic conviction that moral life is to form a response to God's saving actions in human history, manifest grace and virtue, reflect human nature and the reality of things in general, and recognize the normative function of community. These points of tension or incompatibility have important practical consequences, for they affect the very integrity of a faith-inspired moral life, the objective grounds and general application of moral imperatives, and the entire range of social and political moral issues. These considerations suggest that current efforts to undertake a critical examination of modern Western views of the moral life need to continue. They urge pastors, theologians, and laypersons to pay close attention to the effects of outlook and presupposition on moral thinking and attitudes, especially among members of the Church.

Moral life embraces motivation and intention. By giving primacy to individuals and taking their desires and interests largely for granted, the modern outlook leaves itself little room to judge the moral quality of personal motivation. Although the criteria of equity and universalization can moderate behavior, they have less to say about the quality of desires. To the extent that personal motives go without moral evaluation, they will seem to be of little or no importance in the moral life.

The practical result is to license a wide array of human motives. The under-appreciation of motivation as an integral component of human action stands in sharp opposition to the traditional Christian concern for the quality of one's interior disposition, especially its insistence that Christians are to love God and neighbor wholeheartedly and to avoid cupidity in all its forms. Underlying this concern for interior rectitude is the basic Christian imperative to conversion, an all-encompassing dynamic that includes intention and motivation as well as external actions.

Many members of the Church will be subject to competing influences and will hear two often incompatible messages about faith and moral life. That conflict can be confusing, especially when its causes are not pointed out. It can lead unsuspecting believers to bring an unduly secular outlook to bear on issues that pertain to their Christian commitment. It can introduce serious distortions into discussions of Christian faith and morality and make it more likely that people will misunderstand Church teachings. It therefore seems urgent that the chief components of the modern Western world view should be identified and understood. It is also important to delineate the likely impact of that world view on faith and moral life. Greater clarity on these points can reduce confusion, help people to appreciate traditional presuppositions, and understand discussions of faith and morality in the appropriate context.

Although it is surely influential, modern Western thinking does not always constitute the best framework in which to consider intellectual and practical issues in the Church. Certain tensions—for example, the relationship between the intellect and the will, the unity or multiplicity of knowledge and reality, how interior consent is to be reconciled with objective truth, the issue of personal conscience and ecclesial authority, and the need to reconcile the hierarchical and communitarian dimensions of Church decision making—have been all but perennial in the Catholic tradition and would continue to claim attention even if the Enlightenment had never occurred. These considerations suggest that theologians and pastors need to place important issues in their larger historical, intellectual, and canonical contexts. Doing so can help to disclose the content and dimensions of a problem, contribute to a better assessment of it, and promote a more adequate response.

Taken together, modern European scientific, cultural, and intellectual developments have shaped the experience of many people and radically altered the context in which the Church lives and serves. That new world, very different from the Middle Ages, has confronted the Church with many challenges to its faith, moral life, institutional integrity, and ability to carry out its mission. However urgent, those challenges were not the only ones facing the Church in recent centuries. As the previous chapter has shown, it also had to address long-standing abuses, respond to the doctrinal assertions and practical manifestations of the Protestant Reformation, and promote Christian life among its own members. The following chapter will examine the Church's response to these challenges.

10

God's Grace, the Church, and Christian Life

The Catholic Church entered the modern age weakened by old conflicts, debilitating scandals, and grave pastoral problems. While the Church was still struggling with its domestic troubles, the Protestant Reformation precipitated a new emergency. It provoked religious warfare, brought new Christian communions into being, and demanded that the Catholic Church justify its traditional faith and praxis. At about the same time, the foundations of Europe's political, economic, intellectual, and cultural life began to shift. As that transformation proceeded, it profoundly changed the European outlook. People became more willing to deny the transcendent dimensions of life, diminish or control the churches' activity in the public arena, and assign faith to the private life of individuals.

Throughout this momentous and often difficult period, Church life and work continued. Worship and the tasks of pastoral care are required in bad times as well as good. In all seasons priests and people are called to hear God's word; respond in faith, hope, and charity; and help their neighbors see the face of God. Theologians need to continue their study of Scripture and tradition if they are to interpret the faith well to new generations. Bishops need to be good servants of the faith, unity, and mission of the Church.

These external challenges and internal imperatives strongly influenced Church life during the sixteenth through the eighteenth centuries. This chapter will consider official responses to contemporary challenges and note the activities of particular individuals and groups.

It will seek to identify their impact on the faith, thought, and moral life of later generations.

The first section will consider the work of the Council of Trent (1545–63). That council formulated an official response to the doctrinal assertions of the Protestant Reformation and promulgated canons to suppress abuses and protect the integrity of Catholic life. Its decrees on faith, worship, and reform have had a direct bearing on moral life and deeply affected how later generations of Catholic believers have understood and lived it.

While the Council of Trent was formulating its response to these problems, Ignatius of Loyola was making a pivotal contribution to the Church's spiritual and pastoral well being. Ignatius showed that even in troubled times it is possible to turn one's heart to Christ and act for the greater glory of God. The order he founded, the Society of Jesus, extended the blessings of education and pastoral care to peoples near and far and constituted a new paradigm for vowed religious life in the modern world.

The Council of Trent and the Society of Jesus were committed to sacramental penance, and both sought to give the Church competent and worthy confessors. The pursuit of that goal brought about important changes in the preparation of priests and prompted theologians to write new textbooks on penitential practice, which became the literature of moral theology. Because they formed many generations of priests and helped to shape the spiritual and moral outlook of post-Tridentine Catholicism, these manuals of moral theology also require attention.

The following section will account for the emergence of a theology that vigorously defended the respective roles of human nature and divine grace and eventually concluded that human beings have two ends, one natural and the other supernatural. This much sharper contrast between nature and grace had important long-term consequences. It encouraged a later generation of theologians to accept the divorce that had alienated the Church and the world and to differentiate faith and reason much more sharply. This theology of nature and grace affected intellectual developments, the catechesis provided to the Catholic people, and official policies toward the wider society.

THE COUNCIL OF TRENT

By the year 1530 it had become obvious that the Catholic Church faced an unprecedented crisis. Ecclesiastical abuses continued to cause widespread scandal. The Protestant Reformation, already sinking its roots deep into the soil of northern Europe, challenged the very legitimacy of traditional Catholicism and raised the specter of religious warfare. Many people believed that only a general council could solve these problems and bring a measure of peace to the Church, but curial resistance and the political situation militated against that course of action. Facing a rapidly deteriorating situation, Pope Paul III summoned general councils in 1534 and 1542, but war and political conflicts made it impossible to hold them. In 1545 circumstances became more favorable, and the long-awaited council finally opened in December of that year at Trent in northern Italy.[1]

This section will discuss those aspects of Trent's decrees that pertain to the moral life. Of particular interest are its decisions concerning original sin, justification, the sacrament of penance, Church reform, and seminaries.

The Council's Goals and Procedure

The Council of Trent's basic agenda was settled at an early stage. Pope Paul III's Bull of Convocation stipulated that the council would deal with "whatever things pertain to the purity and truth of the Christian religion, to the restoration of what is good and the correction of bad morals, to the peace, unity and harmony of Christians among themselves, of the princes as well as of the people."[2] Once the council was under way, however, a dispute arose between those who wanted it to concentrate on Church reform and those who believed that

---

[1] In the fifteenth and early sixteenth centuries, the Holy See did not wish to convoke a general council, fearing that to do so would reignite the conflict over the locus of supreme authority in the Church, strengthen the conciliarist party, and open the door to objectionable decrees, including those aimed at the Roman Curia.

The Fifth Lateran Council (1512–7) would appear to be an exception. However, it remained under the direct control of Popes Julius II and Leo X and included few but Italian prelates. Due to papal unwillingness to have meaningful reform, this council had little effect in the Church. For its decrees, see Tanner, 1:595-655.

For the prehistory of the Council of Trent, see Hubert Jedin, *A History of the Council of Trent*, trans. Ernest Graf (New York: Thomas Nelson & Sons, 1957) 1:5-581; Giuseppe Alberigo, "The Council of Trent," *Catholicism in Early Modern History: A Guide to Research*, ed. John W. O'Malley (St. Louis: Center for Reformation Research, 1988) 211–26; Jill Raitt, "From Augsburg to Trent," *Justification by Faith: Lutherans and Catholics in Dialogue VII*, ed. H. George Anderson and others (Minneapolis: Augsburg Publishing House, 1985) 200–17; Owen Chadwick, *The Reformation* (Middlesex and Baltimore: Penguin Books, 1972) 264–73; Hermann Tüchle, "Réponse et résistance: Les forces nouvelles et le concile de Trente," *Nouvelle Histoire de l'Église*, ed. L.-J. Rogier and others (Paris: Éditions du Seuil, 1963–75) 3:149-67.

[2] From H. J. Schroeder, trans., *Canons and Decrees of the Council of Trent: Original Text with English Translation* (St. Louis, Mo. and London: B. Herder, 1941) 9.

doctrinal issues were primary. The participants settled that problem by agreeing to deal with both matters simultaneously. They also decided that the council would not try to resolve theological controversies among Catholic theologians. In considering doctrinal issues its purpose would be to identify the principal positions of the Reformation and, to the extent that they were objectionable, declare the faith and praxis of the Catholic Church in opposition to them. Those decisions guided the work of the council and account for the content, tone, organization, and limitations of its decrees.[3]

The Decree on Original Sin

Enacted on June 17, 1546, the Decree on Original Sin was among the first of Trent's actions. Incorporating the teaching of the Councils of Carthage (418) and Orange (529)[4] on the nature and effects of original sin, it asserts that Adam's sin had spiritually destructive effects and was transmitted to all his descendants by physical generation. On account of original sin all human beings come into the world guilty in God's eyes and have no capacity to overcome their alienation from God. For that, the human race must depend completely upon Christ, who is its only source of forgiveness and reconciliation. In opposition to merely forensic notions of justification, the council emphasizes that baptism takes away the guilt of original sin so that the baptized become "innocent, stainless, pure, blameless and beloved children of

---

[3] The Roman Curia, religious orders, and residential bishops sometimes sharply differed about what should be reformed and how; this too affected the work of the council. On early decisions about Trent's agenda and approach, see Jedin, *Council of Trent,* 2:7-165.

Insofar as they respond to Reformation teachings, Trent's decrees were conditioned by several circumstances that did not promote accurate understanding, including the polemical nature of the debate, the very different backgrounds and concerns of the parties, intemperate statements, and the equivocal or novel use of theological terms. One of the goals of the Catholic-Lutheran dialogue today is to clear away historical misunderstandings and arrive at a fair and accurate grasp of what each Church believes. This attempt has already borne considerable fruit. On these issues see Alister E. McGrath, *Iustitia Dei: A History of the Christian Doctrine of Justification* (Cambridge and New York: Cambridge University Press, 1986) 2:72-4, 85; Stephen J. Duffy, *The Dynamics of Grace: Perspectives in Theological Anthropology* (Collegeville: The Liturgical Press, 1993) 232–3, 249–50; Anderson, *Justification by Faith.*

[4] These two sources are respectively discussed in chapters 4 and 5, above. For a review of the sources and history of Catholic teaching on original sin, see Piet Schoonenberg, *Man and Sin: A Theological View* (Notre Dame, Ind.: University of Notre Dame Press, 1965) 124–77.

God" (Can. 5)[5] and are qualified for admission into heaven. Nevertheless, baptism does not free a person from concupiscence, which, although it is not sinful in the proper sense of that word, is "a result of sin and inclines to sin" (Can. 5). The Decree on Original Sin established the basis for the council's later work on justification.[6]

Justification

Although Catholic theologians had often considered the process of justification, they never confronted so direct and powerful a challenge as Martin Luther presented in the early sixteenth century. Because justification is central to Christian faith and practice, the Catholic Church had no choice but to respond. But formulating that response was not an easy task, for Luther had raised new questions for which there were no ready answers. Moreover, Catholic theologians held incompatible views about justification and disagreed in their assessments of Luther's doctrine. These factors and the foundational importance of the subject required the Council of Trent to spend a great deal of time on it. What resulted is probably the council's most carefully considered decree.[7]

Two basic decisions governed its work on this topic. The first was a determination that the decree on justification would respond to Reformation teachings, especially those attributed to Martin Luther. Consequently, the council did not aim to write a comprehensive treatise but limited itself to Catholic doctrine on contested points. For that reason the Decree on Justification is no more than a partial statement of Catholic faith on the subject. The second decision controlled the organization of the Decree. Very early in the deliberations the council recognized three distinct situations in which persons either receive or live the grace of justification: the time of first conversion, when adult unbelievers receive God's word with faith; the extended period of Christian life, when one's living in grace ought to deepen and intensify; and

---

[5] The quoted text is from Tanner, 2:667.

[6] For the full text of the decree see Tanner, 2:665-7; or DS, 1510-6. Following the Council of Carthage and in opposition to Anabaptist teachings (see Chadwick, *Reformation*, 189–97; Pelikan, 4:277-9) the council included infants among those who are guilty on account of original sin and asserted their need for baptism (Can. 4). It excluded the Blessed Virgin Mary from its Decree on Original Sin (Can. 6). For more on the Decree on Original Sin, see Jedin, *Council of Trent*, 2:132-63; Duffy, *Dynamics of Grace*, 221–6; Henri Rondet, *Original Sin: The Patristic and Theological Background*, trans. Cajetan Finegan (Staten Island: Alba House, 1972) 169–75.

[7] Pelikan, 4:253, 279-89; Jedin, *Council of Trent*, 2:171; McGrath, *Iustitia Dei*, 2:63-8; J. Rivière, "Justification," *DTC* 8/2:2106-64.

the moment of reconversion, when a Christian who has fallen into grave sin is forgiven and reconciled once again to God and the Church. The decree gave specific consideration to each of these moments of grace and justification.[8]

The Decree on Justification

Building on its earlier Decree on Original Sin, the council first considered the initial justification of an adult unbeliever. Even though people retain a measure of free will, it is impossible for anyone to be freed of original sin either by natural powers or by their obedience to the Mosaic Law. God the Father has offered humanity forgiveness of original sin through the merits of Jesus Christ, who died for all. However, only those who receive the grace of Christ by means of baptism, or at least the desire for it, are forgiven or justified. Prior to the moment of justification there is a process of preparation in which the person, helped by divine grace, turns toward God. Neither justification nor anything that prepares for it reflects a person's merits; both depend entirely on God's free gift of grace. Justification brings personal sanctification as well as a forgiveness of sin, and it should be crowned by a firm resolution to keep God's commandments as befits a friend of God (ch. 10).[9]

---

[8] Chapters 1–9 considered the moment of first justification; chapters 10–3, human cooperation with God's grace in the course of Christian life; and chapters 14–6, the situation of the baptized who have fallen into grave sin.

In preparing the Decree on Justification the council abandoned the unitary format it had used in writing the Decree on Original Sin. Instead, it presented a positive exposition of Catholic doctrine in the sixteen chapters of the decree and then a statement of what Catholics were obliged to affirm or reject in the thirty-three canons that followed. The canons set forth precise, enforceable requirements, while the chapters supplied rich, authoritative material for preachers and teachers to use in their work among the Catholic people.

See McGrath, *Iustitia Dei*, 2:80-6; Jedin, *Council of Trent*, 2:307-10; Roger Haight, *The Experience and Language of Grace* (New York: Paulist Press, 1979) 105–9; and the text of the decree.

[9] See chapters 1–9 (Tanner, 2:671-4; DS, 1521–33).

In the course of its discussion the council described what it meant by the term "justification." It "consists not only in the forgiveness of sins but also in the sanctification and renewal of the inward being by a willing acceptance of the grace and gifts whereby someone from being unjust becomes just, from being an enemy becomes a friend, so that he is an heir *in hope of eternal life*" (ch. 7, Tanner, 2:673; the italicized words are in the original text and quote Titus 3:7).

The council asserted that barring a special revelation, "no one can know, by that assurance of faith which excludes all falsehood, that he has obtained the grace of God" (ch. 9; see also ch. 12; Tanner, 2:674, 676). Behind this position was the con-

The council then addressed the situation of the baptized. It affirmed that justified persons "grow and increase in that very justness they have received through the grace of Christ, by faith united to good works" (ch. 10).[10] That requires humility and the observance of the commandments as well as an ongoing effort to live "sober and upright lives" (ch. 11).[11] Faithful Christians commit daily or venial sins without ceasing to be just. But their performance of good works is not sinful at all, even when they are motivated by the wish to receive eternal life. The reward of salvation, which is God's gift to those who have faithfully persevered to the end of their lives, is to be sought in a spirit of dependence on God, "with fear and trembling, in labors, watchings, almsdeeds, prayers and offerings, in fastings and chastity" (ch. 13).[12]

Finally, the decree turned to the situation of those who by grave sin have lost the justifying grace they received in baptism. With the help of grace such a sinner can be justified anew by means of the sacrament of penance, which embraces repentance, confession, absolution, and works of satisfaction. Grace is lost not only by the sin of apostasy from faith but also by other mortal sins that leave faith intact. The council concluded its positive exposition with a summary that explains how persons can be said to have a justification or merit of their own without compromising the gratuity and necessity of God's grace (chs. 14–6).[13]

Justification and Christian Life

The council's vision of Christian life is intensely theocentric and deliberately anti-Pelagian. The initiative in offering a person grace and justification always belongs to God, and all aspects of a positive human response require a previous and ongoing gift of Christ's grace.

---

cern that the contrary view might encourage religious and moral laxity among the faithful as well as the awareness that with freedom they could reject God's gift of grace through grave sin. Duffy, *Dynamics of Grace*, 243.

[10] Tanner, 2:675; DS, 1535.

[11] Quoting Titus 2:12 (Tanner, 2:675; DS, 1536–7).

[12] Quoting Phil 2:12 and 2 Cor 6:5-6 (Tanner, 2:676; DS, 1541).

[13] Tanner, 2:676-8; DS, 1542–9. The decree concludes with a series of thirty-three canons on justification (Tanner, 2:679-81; DS, 1551–83).

The Decree on Justification was unanimously adopted during session 6 on January 13, 1547. For further discussion, see Haight, *Experience and Language of Grace*, 109–14; Carl J. Peter, "The Decree on Justification in the Council of Trent," *Justification by Faith*, 218–29; Duffy, *Dynamics of Grace*, 229–50; McGrath, *Iustitia Dei*, 2:68-80; Rivière, "Justification," *DTC*, 8/2:2164-92; Jedin, *Council of Trent*, 2:166-96, 239–310; Pelikan, 4:279-89.

Grace helps an adult person turn from sin and toward justification. This predisposition for justice involves "the faith that comes from hearing" (Decree on Justification, ch. 6).[14] Such faith gives rise to hope in God's favor and a true love of God who is all good. This process involves sincere repentance of one's sins and the commitment to live an upright Christian life in keeping with the commandments (ch. 6). Justification actually takes place when the "merits of the passion of our lord Jesus Christ are communicated" to a person. At that moment "the love of God is poured out by the agency of the holy Spirit in the hearts of those who are being justified, and abides in them." Divine love grafts people into Christ and infuses the virtues of faith, hope, and charity into them. These theological virtues make them living members of Christ's body and enable them to live a committed and fruitful Christian life. Accordingly, "the reborn are immediately ordered to preserve the justice freely granted to them through Jesus Christ in a pure and spotless state like a best robe, so that they may carry it before the tribunal of our lord Jesus Christ and possess eternal life" (ch. 7).[15]

The decrees on original sin and justification presuppose that human life is an essentially religious enterprise. People come into the world alienated from God through the sin of Adam but called to communion with God through the grace of Christ. Tension between sin and salvation characterizes the entirety of a person's journey through life. It is evident when one hears God's word and must decide how to respond. It is present when a faithful Christian experiences concupiscence, the inclination to sin. It is at issue when a gravely sinful Christian is offered the grace of conversion and either embraces or ignores it. Endowed with a real if wounded freedom, persons can and ought to cooperate with God's gracious offer of justification and salvation. But freedom also allows them to refuse. Throughout their lives persons freely resolve the conflicting attractions of grace and sin, and in so doing they decide the ultimate question of human life.[16]

The implications of this view for Christian moral life are great. Above all, Christian moral life is to be understood primarily in terms of alienation and reconciliation, sin and grace. The need to resolve the

---

[14] Tanner, 2:672, alluding to Rom 10:17.

[15] Tanner, 2:673-4.

[16] The council asserts that although original sin has weakened human freedom, it has not extinguished it. Concupiscence is a "tendency to sin," but it "cannot harm those who do not give consent but, by the grace of Christ, offer strong resistance." Decree on Original Sin, Can. 5 (DS, 1515; Tanner, 2:667). The Decree on Justification likewise assumes human freedom when it says that, helped by God's grace, persons can "turn towards their own justification by giving free assent to and co-operating with this same grace" (ch. 5; DS, 1525; Tanner, 2:672).

ongoing tension between the saving grace of Christ and the attraction of sin endows moral life with an inherently religious quality. This is evident in the council's discussion of the preached word, baptism, penance, and the works of charity that the just are urged to perform. Christian moral life is therefore not to be seen as simply the product of human will, wisdom, or goodness. It draws its strength and takes its direction from the divine gifts of faith, hope, and charity, which are the fruits of grace in the justified. Obedience to the commandments is surely required but is secondary to the grace-related prerequisites that the council identified. Maintaining the primacy of grace helps to preclude Pelagianism, legalism, and scrupulosity in Christian life and makes it possible for a believer to practice Christian faith with a sense of joy and gratitude to God.[17]

The Sacrament of Penance

The sacrament of penance presented a formidable problem to the Council of Trent. This ritual was used infrequently by the Catholic people and had been wounded by priestly vice and incompetence.[18] Protestant Reformers had attacked Catholic praxis as a human invention that had no biblical warrant and caused spiritual harm. As if these challenges were not enough, the doctrinal aspects of sin and penance are such that no single approach can be fully satisfactory. Penance constituted a complex problem whose tangled historical, disciplinary, pastoral, and theological dimensions defied easy analysis or solution.

Two early decisions governed the council's consideration of penance. The first was procedural. Following its earlier determination to differentiate doctrinal and disciplinary issues, the council decided to address the dogmatic dimensions of penance and leave its disciplinary and administrative aspects to be considered later. That decision pushed

---

[17] This discussion owes much to Philippe Delhaye, "Les leçons morales du décret tridentin sur la justification (session VI)," *StMor* 28 (1990) 177–93. Although the Council of Trent related justification to baptism and penance, it failed to mention the Eucharist. Both baptism and penance point to the Eucharist as an integral part of a committed Christian's life. Although theological reflection and the witness of traditional Church praxis can supply for this omission, it is regrettable that Trent left this void in its decree. Later decrees on the Eucharist (DS, 1635–61; Tanner, 2:693-8) and on the Holy Sacrifice of the Mass (DS, 1738–59; Tanner, 2:732-7) responded to concerns other than the place of the Eucharist in the life of the believing community.

[18] On popular attitudes toward penance and problems attributable to priests, see, for example, André Duval, "Le concile de Trente et la confession," *MD* 118 (1974) 133–45; Louis Vereecke, "La confession auriculaire au XVIe siècle: Crise et renouveau," *StMor* 21 (1983) 52–6.

the doctrinal dimensions of penance into the spotlight and led the council to determine that the basic issue was the sacramental quality of penance, that is, whether Catholic penitential practice reflected the will and mandate of Christ. Once the question was posed in those terms, it was not difficult for the council to judge that the traditional praxis was fully validated by divine authority and then to base its decree on that fundamental assertion.[19]

The second decision involved a dispute over how the council should frame its defense of sacramental penance. Some wanted to emphasize the primordial dynamic of *metanoia*, or the personal turning from sin to God. That approach would align penance with important scriptural texts and the Decree on Justification. Others proposed that since the Protestant Reformers had attacked the practice of the Christian people, it was necessary to defend the rite of penance as the Church actually celebrated it. The council acknowledged the virtues of the first proposal but adopted the other one. That decision accounts for the decree's heavy emphasis on such practical matters as ecclesiastical power, priestly authority, and the judicial dimensions of penance.[20]

The Chapters and Canons on Penance

The Council of Trent's document on penance opened with a preamble that recognizes the close relationship between justification and penance.[21] In the body of the document, composed of nine chapters and fifteen canons, the council sought to address twelve objectionable propositions that had been attributed to Protestant Reformers.[22] It asserted the necessity of penance for those who have fallen into grave sin after baptism, the sacramental quality of penance, and that it is distinct from baptism. Contrition is the most important of the penitent's acts. Prompted by God's grace, contrition prepares for and leads to forgiveness and reconciliation. Confession to a priest of all the mortal sins one remembers is required "by divine law" and includes specification by number, kind, and any circumstances that change their nature (ch. 5 and Cann. 6–7).[23] This also permits the priest to exercise his ministry

---

[19] On the power and authority of the Church, the priesthood, and the sacramental economy as key points of contention between Catholics and Protestants, see Duval, "Le concile de Trente et la confession," 149–53; Pelikan, 4:256-7, 262–74.

[20] See Duval, "Le concile de Trente et la confession," 145, 156–8.

[21] DS, 1667; Tanner, 2:703.

[22] A. Michel, "La Pénitence de la Réforme à nos Jours," *DTC*, 12/1:1069-86.

[23] DS, 1679, 1706–7; Tanner, 2:705, 712. Carl Peter has discussed the meaning of the phrase "by divine law" in this context; see "Auricular Confession and the Council of Trent," *CTSAP* 22 (1967) 185–200; idem, "Integral Confession and the Council of Trent," *Concilium* 61 (1971) 99–109.

with due responsibility and equity. Venial sins can be omitted without any fault because they do not cut a person off from God's grace and can be forgiven in other ways. The minister of the sacrament is a duly authorized priest whose absolution truly forgives the penitent's sins. Because binding and loosing "is like a judicial act," penance involves legal jurisdiction in the Church and requires that the priest be duly authorized if he is to absolve validly (ch. 6; also ch. 7 and Cann. 9–10).[24] The same considerations support the practice by which higher authority reserves to itself the absolution of more heinous sins. Finally, works of satisfaction are also essential to the penitential process. They help to deter future sins, correct the effects of past sins, overcome the hold of sin on a person, and promote conversion in the penitent (chs. 7–9 and Cann. 11–5).[25]

Penance and Catholic Life

The council's decision to emphasize the personal, ritual, and juridical requirements of sacramental penance influenced Catholic life for generations. By taking a praxis-oriented approach it reassured priests and people that the Church's ritual of forgiveness is not only legitimate but decisive for a sinner's standing with God. Just as a person becomes sinful through free and culpable evildoing, so a sinner is forgiven through free and praiseworthy acts of repentance, confession, and satisfaction in cooperation with the ministry of the Church. That reflected the traditional view that people enact their relationship with God in the course of their moral life and through the Church's sacraments. Finally, by adding a detailed explanation of Catholic penitential praxis, the council provided an authoritative charter for preaching and teaching. By framing its decree in personal, ecclesial, and practical terms, and by communicating it by word and worship, Trent's decree on penance gained great formative power.

---

[24] DS, 1684–8; 1709; Tanner, 2:707-8, 712.

[25] See DS, 1667–93, 1701–15; Tanner, 2:703-9, 711–3. The chapters and canons, which the council did not specifically call a "decree," are part of a larger document that also considers the sacrament of extreme unction, now known as anointing of the sick. It was enacted on November 25, 1551, during the fourteenth session of the council. In the background was the declaration of the Council of Florence, issued on November 22, 1439, concerning the sacraments. For its description of penance see DS, 1323; or Tanner, 1:548; see also A. Michel, "Pénitence," *DTC*, 12/1:1046-7.

For further discussion, see Michel, "Pénitence," *DTC*, 12/1:1086-113; Duval, "Le concile de Trente et la confession," 156–9; Bernhard Poschmann, *Penance and the Anointing of the Sick*, trans. Francis Courtney (New York: Herder & Herder, 1964) 196–202.

Trent's practical defense of penance was not without risks. By viewing sins as discreet acts, emphasizing the acts of the priest and the penitent, and insisting upon the juridical dimensions of the sacrament, Trent favored the impression that Christian life is primarily a matter of behavior. Its practical approach can suggest that what matters most in Christian life is the avoidance of sinful acts or at least the confession of those acts to a confessor in order to receive his absolution. That impression is problematic because it depreciates God's grace and the primordial requirement of conversion to God through Christ and assigns a de facto priority to human efforts. In fact, Trent taught the very opposite, namely, that God always has the initiative in Christian life, that the grace of Christ is primary, and that conversion to God is the most important moral imperative. But unless later generations studied the text on penance with care and interpreted it in light of the Decree on Justification, they were likely to overlook these basic assertions or fail to relate them sufficiently to penitential praxis and catechesis.[26]

Decrees on Church Reform

In all of its working sessions the Council of Trent enacted decrees that were designed to suppress abuses, reform canon law and Church administration, and assure that the clergy were competent, worthy, and dedicated to pastoral service. Some of its legislation targeted such vices as simony, greed, and clerical concubinage.[27] The council also tried to assure that the Catholic people received the pastoral care they

[26] Pope Pius IV's bull of confirmation, *Benedictus Deus* (January 26, 1564), increased the risk that Trent's decrees would be misunderstood. To protect the Church from erroneous or tendentious instruction, he prohibited anyone lacking papal permission from publishing "any commentaries, glosses, annotations, scholia on, or any kind of interpretation whatsoever of the decrees of this council. . . . For if difficulties and controversies relative to those decrees shall arise, their explanation and decision we reserve to ourselves, as the holy council itself has also decreed." Schroeder, *Canons and Decrees*, 271. For the Latin text, see 534–5; or DS, 1847–50.

In addition to taking their textual and theological background into account, it is well to remember that Trent's chapters and canons on penance were not meant to be a comprehensive treatment of sin and forgiveness but a focused response to specific problems in the mid-sixteenth century.

For more on the interpretation and assessment of Trent's document on penance, see Duval, "Le concile de Trente et la confession," 153–6, 158–9; Vereecke, "La confession auriculaire au XVIe siècle," 62; Alberigo, "Council of Trent," 219–23; Robert E. McNally, "The Counter-Reformation's Views of Sin and Penance," *Thought* 52 (1977) 152–4, 165–6.

[27] For example, session 21, Cann. 1, 9 (Tanner, 2:728, 731–2); session 25, chapter 14; and the Decree on Indulgences (Tanner, 2:792-3, 796–7).

had every right to expect. It renewed ancient requirements that bishops and pastors should reside among their people, preach God's word at least on Sundays and other major feasts, explain the sacraments, teach the way of salvation, and celebrate God's worship in a fitting way.[28] It established standards for clerical life and service; admission to the episcopate, presbyterate, and other clerical ranks; and appointment to offices of pastoral care.[29] Such legislation did more than try to remove conditions that had grievously injured the Church. It emphasized the spiritual and religious heart of Catholic life and gave it renewed vitality. Taken as a whole, the council's reform decrees laid the foundation for a rebirth of faith, piety, and pastoral care in the postconciliar era. Some historians believe that they were even more important for later centuries than Trent's decrees on doctrine and the sacraments.[30]

Legislation Concerning Seminaries

Among the council's decisions, the decree on seminaries was to have an especially deep impact on the life of the Catholic people. The council recognized that the decree on penance could only bear pastoral fruit if confessors were both virtuous and competent. It knew that the goal of better preaching and teaching likewise demanded a well-qualified clergy. For these reasons the council had to address the problem of priestly ignorance, incompetence, and immorality.[31] Because those difficulties reflected the failure of customary approaches to clerical education as much as any personal derelictions, they could only be abated if a new and more effective approach to clerical preparation was adopted. With that in mind the Council of Trent required

---

[28] For example, session 5, Cann. 9–12 (Tanner, 2:669-70); session 6, chapters 1–2 (Tanner, 2:681-3); session 14, Can. 2 (Tanner, 2:714-5); session 23, Can. 1 (Tanner, 2:744-6); session 24, Cann. 4, 7 (Tanner, 2:763-4).

[29] For example, session 22, Cann. 1–2 (Tanner, 2:737-8); session 23, the eighteen canons of the Decree on Reform (Tanner, 2:744-53); session 24, Cann. 1, 12, 18 (Tanner, 2:759-61, 766-7, 770-2); session 25, chapter 1 (Tanner, 2:784-5).

[30] See, for example, Pelikan, 4:290; also note 33, below.

[31] The council's diagnosis of this problem is evident in the following passages. Because of the irresponsible actions of some bishops, "it often happens that people are ordained, though unsuitable, untrained and ignorant, who have been rejected by their own bishop as incapable and unworthy" (sess.14, Can. 2 [Tanner, 2:715]). "It is public knowledge that many are admitted to holy orders with hardly any process of selection" (sess. 21, Can. 2 [Tanner, 2:728]). "Some illiterate and incompetent rectors of parish churches are unsuitable for sacred ministries, and others destroy rather than build up by the immorality of their lives" (sess. 21, Can. 6 [Tanner, 2:730]).

that seminaries were to be established in all parts of the Catholic world.

Trent's canon on seminaries embraced all major elements of clerical education. It presupposed that the process of religious preparation needed to begin early, "before habits of vice take firm hold on so many." The purpose of the seminary was "to provide for, to educate in religion and to train in ecclesiastical studies a set number of boys . . . whose character and disposition offers hope that they will serve in Church ministries throughout life." The canon stipulated the principal areas of study and preparation, which included "administering the sacraments, particularly all that seems appropriate to hearing confessions." It enacted detailed provisions that sought to guarantee that seminaries had adequate financial support and a staff of properly qualified teachers.[32]

The need for a reliable means of clerical education, the comprehensive nature of this canon, and the wisdom of its formulation all helped to make the seminary one of the strongest and, eventually, most influential of post-Tridentine institutions. Although its early development was slow and uneven, the seminary mediated Trent's doctrinal, canonical, personal, and pastoral requirements to succeeding generations of priests, who in turn brought them to the Catholic people. The symbiosis between decree and seminary accounts for much of Trent's impact on later centuries.

The seminary constituted a new and very different institution of higher learning that gradually took its place alongside the older universities. It aimed to serve the pastoral needs of the Church; its audience was clerical; and its agenda embraced the personal formation as well as the intellectual preparation of its students. The university dealt with a much wider range of professional and academic disciplines; its student body was far more diverse, and formational goals were not so sharply focused, if present at all. The seminary and the university provided very different environments in which to research, teach, and study theological subjects. Their respective relationships with hierarchical authority on the one hand and the broader society on the other were also dissimilar.

Although the Tridentine canon on seminaries was reasonable and necessary under the circumstances and its contribution great, it involved certain adverse consequences. Once seminary theology was institutionally segregated from the academic life of the university, it risked becoming disconnected from the other sacred and human sciences and losing vital contact with the major issues of the day and the

---

[32] Session 23, Can. 18; Tanner, 2:750-3.

people who discuss them. The pastoral purposes of the seminary are not well served in those cases. The more academic theology of the university can also suffer when it is free of pastoral concerns. Without a responsibility for the preparation of priests or a similar commitment, those who teach or study theology can find it more difficult to maintain its essential orientation to the Christian life.[33]

St. Ignatius of Loyola and the Society of Jesus

No adequate understanding of modern Catholic life is possible without recognizing the formative influence of St. Ignatius of Loyola. Being associated with Ignatius changed the lives of countless individuals, and the religious order he founded, the Society of Jesus, has made decisive contributions to the life and ministry of the Church. A phenomenon at once charismatic and institutional, the Society of Jesus is renowned for its spiritual outlook, missionary commitment, and educational accomplishments. It offered the Church a new paradigm for religious orders and stimulated the foundation of new communities of men and women religious. Jesuit theologians and educators created the first textbooks designed to support the preparation of worthy confessors, the so-called manuals of moral theology. With due respect for the other religious orders that also provided effective service and witness in the early modern era, this section will consider the contribution of St. Ignatius and the Society of Jesus to Catholic life.

St. Ignatius of Loyola

Born in Basque country in 1491, Iñigo López de Loyola[34] appears to have displayed little interest in religion while he was a youth. After an academically meager early education, he was taught the essentials of life and behavior at the royal court. His activities as a young man were

---

[33] Many consider that of all Trent's enactments, its provision for the seminary education of priests had the greatest impact on the Church in later centuries. Vereecke, "La confession auriculaire au XVIe siècle," 63; idem, "Le concile de Trente et l'enseignement de la théologie morale," *De Guillaume D'Ockham à Saint Alphonse de Ligouri: Etudes d'histoire de la théologie morale moderne 1300–1787* (Rome: Collegium S. Alfonsi de Urbe, 1986) 495–6; Chadwick, *Reformation,* 279. See also Rivière, "Justification," *DTC,* 8/1:2106-64; Paul F. Grendler, "Schools, Seminaries, and Catechetical Instruction," *Catholicism in Early Modern History,* 323–4.

[34] Iñigo was Ignatius' baptismal name and the one he used exclusively until he was in his early forties. At that time he began to use the name Ignacio, believing it to be an alternate form of Iñigo. Because tradition knows him as Ignatius, this discussion will use that name throughout. See John W. O'Malley, *The First Jesuits* (Cambridge and London: Harvard Univeristy Press, 1993) 29.

unexceptional and included episodes of brawling and illicit relationships with women. Ignatius became a soldier, and on May 20, 1521, while defending Pamplona against a French army, he suffered grave wounds to both of his legs. Those injuries ended his military service and began a lengthy period of convalescence at home. During that time he underwent a personal conversion that completely changed his life.

At the family home at Loyola, Ignatius had nothing to read save a book on the saints and Ludolph of Saxony's *Life of Christ*. After reading these books he began to wonder if he might do great things for Christ in the manner of a St. Francis or a St. Dominic. He also considered resuming his accustomed way of life. What proved decisive for Ignatius were the inner feelings associated with these alternatives. The thought that he might continue as a courtier or a soldier distressed him. Contemplating a radically Christian life brought him peace and consolation. He took those experiences as a sign of God's will and resolved to set his life on an entirely new course.

As soon as he was well enough to travel, Ignatius went to the Benedictine monastery of Montserrat. There he wished to give his conversion a more formal and public expression. After a night of prayer he ritually abandoned his weapons, took up the staff of a pilgrim, and put on the clothing of a beggar. Under the guidance of the novice master he spent three days reviewing his life and its sinfulness. He then made a sacramental confession in which he named his past sins, manifested his sincere repentance, and promised that he would henceforth live as a committed disciple of Christ. Having definitively repudiated his old way of life, Ignatius planned to make a pilgrimage to the Holy Land. Before he could realize that goal, however, a deep personal crisis overtook him.

After leaving Montserrat, Ignatius went to Manresa, where the plague and other circumstances detained him for about a year. During that time he discovered Thomas à Kempis' *Imitation of Christ,* a book that remained important to him throughout his life. He adopted a severely ascetical way of life. Tormented by doubts about his confessions, Ignatius lost his interior peace and even contemplated suicide. He sought help from various advisors but to no avail. Having decided to follow the lead of his interior experiences, Ignatius was able to resolve his crisis, moderate his penitential practices, and recover peace of soul. This phase of his life included some powerful experiences and visions that seemed to come directly from God. Ignatius kept track of all these events, especially whatever helped him to respond well. His experiences enabled him to help and console others, and with that purpose in mind, he began to commit them to writing. The notes Ignatius made at Manresa formed the core of the *Spiritual Exercises,* a book that he continued to edit for the next twenty years.

In the fall of 1523 Ignatius arrived in Jerusalem, where he hoped to spend the rest of his life helping souls. But political circumstances prevented him from remaining, and so with great reluctance he sailed back to Europe. Ignatius then returned to school, convinced that more education would make him better able to help souls. That began a long period in which Ignatius first studied the liberal arts at Spanish institutions and then philosophy and theology at the University of Paris. By the time he finished in 1535 he had become a master of arts.

Ignatius' years at Paris were decisive ones. He had acquired a fine education, an attachment to the theology of Thomas Aquinas, and an abiding respect for the university's pedagogical system. He had consolidated his commitment to poverty, simplicity of life, and the ministries of catechesis and spiritual guidance. Ignatius formed lasting friendships with six of his fellow students, largely due to his deep interest in the spiritual lives of others and his ability to help them make a radical commitment to Christ through the Spiritual Exercises.[35]

In the early months of 1534 the seven "friends in the Lord" resolved to embrace lives of poverty and seek ordination to the priesthood. Their aim was to go to Jerusalem, but if that was not possible they would accept whatever work the pope assigned them. They consecrated these decisions by means of vows, which they pronounced on August 15, 1534, at the chapel of St. Denis in Paris. Although most of them did not intend their vows to give rise to a new religious order, that was the fruit their common commitment would eventually bear.[36]

The Foundation of the Society of Jesus

In the years immediately following, the small group of friends lived in poverty as they preached, gave the Spiritual Exercises, and worked as volunteers in two Venice hospitals. In 1537, unable to go to the Holy Land, Ignatius and two of his companions decided to go to Rome in order to seek an assignment from Pope Paul III. En route he had his famous vision at La Storta, in which Jesus asked Ignatius to serve him

---

[35] For a sketch of these six men (Pierre Favre, Francis Xavier, Diego Laínez, Alfonso Salmerón, Nicolás de Bobadilla, and Simão Rodrigues) and their relationships with Ignatius, see ibid., 29–32.

[36] Pierre Favre had been ordained in July, 1534; most of the others became priests on June 24, 1537.

This review of the early life of St. Ignatius is indebted to William V. Bangert, *A History of the Society of Jesus* (St. Louis: Institute of Jesuit Sources, 1972) 3–17; and especially O'Malley, *First Jesuits,* 23–33.

and God the Father. The vision also placed Ignatius at the side of Jesus, who was carrying his cross. That experience convinced him that the name *Compagnia di Gesù*, "Society of Jesus," which the group had been using informally, was to be their official name.

By early 1539 the members of the *Compagnia* realized that they needed to reconsider their purposes and organization. In a series of meetings from March until June of that year they reviewed the traditional monastic rules but found that none was suitable for them. They composed a new document, the "Five Chapters," which they hoped would provide a strong foundation for their own life and work. Ignatius submitted that document, which is also known as the "Formula of the Institute," for papal approbation. By means of the bull *Regimini militantis ecclesiae* of September 27, 1540, which was a restatement of the "Five Chapters," Pope Paul III formally approved the Formula and established the Society of Jesus as a new religious order in the Church. Ten years later Pope Julius III issued another bull, *Exposcit debitum*, which solemnly reconfirmed the foundation and slightly modified the original Formula of the Society of Jesus.[37]

According to that latter bull the chief purposes of the new religious order were

> to strive especially for the defense and propagation of the faith and for the progress of souls in Christian life and doctrine, by means of public preaching, lectures, and any other ministration whatsoever of the word of God, and further by means of the Spiritual Exercises, the education of children and unlettered persons in Christianity, and the spiritual consolation of Christ's faithful through hearing confessions and administering the other sacraments. Moreover, this Society should show itself no less useful in reconciling the estranged, in holily assisting and serving those who are found in prisons or hospitals, and indeed in performing any other works of charity, according to what will seem expedient for the glory of God and the common good (*Const,* 66–7).

In another place Ignatius wrote that the "aim and end" of the Society was "by traveling through the various regions of the world at the order of the supreme vicar of Christ our Lord or of the superior of the Society itself, to preach, hear confessions, and use all the other means it can with the grace of God to help souls" (*Const,* 172, *Constitutions* [308]).[38]

---

[37] Both documents explicitly constitute the Formula as the rule that would govern the Society of Jesus. For an English translation of *Exposcit debitum,* which was dated July 21, 1550, see *Const,* 63–73. This account follows Bangert, *History of the Society of Jesus,* 16–22; O'Malley, *First Jesuits,* 32–6; see also *Const,* 36, 44–5.

[38] Even more succinct is this statement: "The end of this Society is to devote itself with God's grace not only to the salvation and perfection of the members' own

The First Jesuits and Their Ministries

These goals and objectives are clearly evident in the work of the first Jesuits. Even before formally approving the Society, Pope Paul III had sent some of Ignatius' companions on missions within Italy. Soon afterward two Jesuit theologians, Laínez and Salmerón, served at the Council of Trent. Others preached, taught, heard confessions, and gave the Spiritual Exercises in many parts of Europe. The Society established colleges to insure that young Jesuits received the education their ministries required. By means of these and the other schools they founded or staffed, Jesuits improved the quality of clerical formation, introduced better pedagogical methods, extended the benefits of a humanistic education, and helped to sustain the Catholic Reform.[39] Finally, their commitment to go wherever they were needed led many Jesuits to join the Dominicans, Franciscans, and Augustinians who were already serving in the missions overseas. During Ignatius' lifetime Jesuits had begun missions in Brazil and the Congo. The journeys of Francis Xavier and his companions to Goa, Japan, and the East Indies are well known. The dedication and work of the early Jesuits rekindled the sparks of faith and charity, conversion and understanding among the Catholic people, and helped to bring the gospel of Christ to distant lands.

Another measure of its effects on others can be found in the many young men who sought admission to the Society of Jesus. Although the new order had only about twenty members when it was established in

---

souls, but also with that same grace to labor strenuously in giving aid toward the salvation and perfection of the souls of their fellowmen." (*Const*, 77–8, *Constitutions* [3]).

[39] For more on Jesuit schools and educational methodology, see O'Malley, *First Jesuits*, 200–42; John W. Donohue, *Jesuit Education: An Essay on the Foundations of Its Idea* (New York: Fordham University Press, 1963); Allan P. Farrell, *The Jesuit Code of Liberal Education: Development and Scope of the Ratio Studiorum* (Milwaukee: Bruce, 1938). In addition to the formal education they offered in schools, colleges, and universities, the Jesuits also understood the importance of teaching Christian doctrine. Their catechetical efforts provided the people of the sixteenth century with a better grasp of faith and its moral implications and had a powerful influence on the development of catechetical practices. Peter Canisius and his catechisms are especially important in this regard. For the texts, see Fridericus Streicher, ed., *S. Petri Canisii Doctoris Ecclesiae Catechismi Latini et Germanici. Pars Prima: Catechismi Latini* (Rome: Pontifical Gregorian University; Munich: Officina Salesiana, 1933); for further discussion, see O'Malley, *First Jesuits*, 115–26; James Brodrick, *Saint Peter Canisius* (Chicago: Loyola University Press, 1962); Hermann Tüchle, "L'Église tridentine: Rénovation intérieure et action défensive (la Contre-Réforme)," *Nouvelle Histoire de l'Église*, 3:200-5; Grendler, "Schools," 315–30; X. Le Bachelet, "Canisius (Le B. Pierre)," *DTC*, 2/2:1507-37.

the summer of 1540, by the time Ignatius died in 1556 there were at least a thousand Jesuits, and by early 1565 that number had risen to about 3500. Although the remarkable growth of the Society of Jesus was not without risks and stresses, it validated Ignatius' new approach to religious life and certainly allowed the Society to sustain its numerous, varied, and far-flung ministries. Its apostolic successes and rapid expansion leave little doubt that the Jesuit "way of proceeding" was well adapted to the human, spiritual, and religious needs of sixteenth-century people.[40]

The Society of Jesus and Christian Life

Founded at a time when the Catholic Church was in disarray and Western Christianity was splitting apart, the Society stands as an eloquent reminder that in every age and season, amid scandal, ignorance, and all sorts of evil, people can receive God's word with open hearts and respond to it in a way that is prayerful, ecclesial, and rich in the fruits of charity. Ignatius' unreserved deference to the Church highlights its indispensable role in proclaiming the gospel, sustaining the hearer's response, and in guiding apostolic service. By insisting on this basic point and by focusing a piercing yet respectful light on the interior life of persons, Ignatius drew attention to the dynamic links among the word of God, faith, moral life, and the Church community.

With its vows, dedication to pastoral care, and commitment to prayer and the inner life, the Society of Jesus represents a traditional way of life that goes back through the friars and the monks to Augustine of Hippo, John Cassian, Benedict of Nursia, and the Desert Fathers and consecrated virgins of the ancient Church. That heritage was also shared by the Dominicans, Franciscans, Capuchins, Augustinians, Carmelites, and other communities of vowed men and women. But the Society of Jesus marks the appearance of a new kind of religious order. The Society was the first to commit so many of its members to the educational apostolate. The Jesuit superior general was given much greater authority than his counterparts in other religious orders. Jesuits do not wear a unique habit or chant the office in choir, and they are not bound to one diocese in the manner of secular priests or to one house as was the custom with monks and nuns. These novel provisions were intended to increase the Jesuits' ability to respond to pastoral needs whenever and wherever they arose.[41]

---

[40] Bangert, *History of the Society of Jesus*, 20–40. For an extensive discussion of the first Jesuits and their ministries up to 1565, see O'Malley, *First Jesuits*.

[41] See O'Malley, *First Jesuits*, 4–6, 14–20, 139–42; Bangert, *History of the Society of Jesus*, 42–4.

By its melding of the ancient with the unprecedented, the Society of Jesus gave the Church a new paradigm of religious life. That more modern approach was taken up by many new orders, notably the Oratorians, Lazarists, Ursulines, Daughters of Charity, and Visitandines, who also committed themselves to prayer and apostolic service in the name of Christ. Demonstrating the power of God's word in the lives of individuals and communities, these and other orders of men and women have performed many important ministries, including visiting the sick, teaching, caring for children, and in the case of priests, the perennial work of preaching and celebrating the sacraments. By their presence and activity they have given witness to God's presence in the modern world and strengthened the faith and moral life of countless persons.[42]

THE EMERGENCE OF MORAL THEOLOGY

Since the Fourth Lateran Council there had been a great deal of interest in all aspects of sacramental penance. With the passage of time, however, the discussion of penance flowed into two distinct channels. The theological issues were explored mainly by university professors who worked principally from the *Sentences* of Peter Lombard or, later, the *Summa theologiae* of Thomas Aquinas. Their treatises tended to be highly theoretical in nature. The practical and canonical aspects attracted the attention of bishops and priests who actually carried out the day-to-day work of pastoral care. They had written the *summas* of confessors to help priests respond well to the wide range of persons and cases they encountered. These books offered much practical advice but showed little interest in theory. By the sixteenth century the literature on penance generally fell into two very distinct genres, pastoral volumes that lacked a theological foundation and theoretical tomes that did not address pastoral concerns. Despite these works, many priests were incompetent.[43]

---

[42] Jean Delumeau, *Le Catholicisme entre Luther et Voltaire* (Paris: Presses Universitaires de France, 1971) 75–83; Hermann Tüchle, "Conséquences lointaines du schisme au siècle de l'absolutisme: Essor religieuse et confusion théologique, tentatives d'union," *Nouvelle Histoire de l'Église*, 3:274-88; Hubert Jedin, "Religious Forces and Intellectual Content of the Catholic Renewal," *History of the Church*, ed. Hubert Jedin and John Dolan (New York: Seabury, 1980) 5:567-74; for more on the spirituality underlying this religious reawakening and the major figures involved in it, see Jordan Aumann, *Christian Spirituality in the Catholic Tradition* (San Francisco: Ignatius Press; London: Sheed & Ward, 1985) 178–228. On the religious congregations of women, see Jo Ann Kay McNamara, *Sisters in Arms: Catholic Nuns through Two Millennia* (Cambridge, Mass., and London: Harvard University Press, 1996) 452–88.

[43] Vereecke, "Le concile de Trente et l'enseignement de la théologie morale," 497–500; Albert R. Jonsen and Stephen Toulmin, *The Abuse of Casuistry: A History of*

That was the context in which the Jesuits considered how they might prepare themselves to be good confessors, a ministry that they held in high esteem. Their deliberations were also shaped by the intellectual ethos of the Society: Ignatius and his companions had been well educated at the University of Paris and were convinced that intellectual competence was essential to ministerial success.[44] They therefore crafted a strategy that relied upon good scholarship and effective pedagogical methods to produce good confessors. That strategy helped to bring forth a new discipline, moral theology, and a new body of literature, the *Institutiones morales*, or "manuals of moral theology." The foundation of Jesuit colleges and the establishment of the seminaries called for by the Council of Trent provided a key institutional stimulus for these developments and guaranteed that they would have an attentive audience.

The manuals of moral theology formed many generations of confessors and exercised a primary influence on catechetics and on the religious and moral formation of the Catholic people up to the time of the Second Vatican Council. It is therefore necessary to examine this literature and note its understanding of the moral life. It will be important to identify the theological presuppositions behind this literature and take account of its strengths and weaknesses. That will offer a deeper insight into post-Tridentine Catholic life and today's pastoral and theological problems.

The Society's Preparation of Confessors

From its very beginnings the Society of Jesus determined the education and ministerial assignments of individual Jesuits in light of their

---

Moral Reasoning (Berkeley, Los Angeles, and London: University of California Press, 1988) 139–46. See also Servais Pinckaers, *The Sources of Christian Ethics*, trans. Mary Thomas Noble (Washington: The Catholic University of America Press, 1995) 257–8; Johann Theiner, *Die Entwicklung der Moraltheologie zur eigenständigen Disziplin* (Regensburg: Verlag Friedrich Pustet, 1970) 37–55; and the discussion on the *summas* of confessors in chapter 8, above.

[44] The Prologue to Part IV of the *Constitutions* [307] is significant:

The aim which the Society of Jesus directly seeks is to aid its own members and their fellowmen to attain the ultimate end for which they were created. To achieve this purpose, in addition to the example of one's life, learning and a method of expounding it are also necessary. Therefore, after the proper foundation of abnegation of themselves is seen to be present in those who were admitted and also the required progress in virtues, it will be necessary to provide for the edifice of their learning and the manner of employing it, that these may be aids toward better knowledge and service of God, our Creator and Lord.

See also O'Malley, *First Jesuits,* 101, 208–12, 232. For further discussion of the place of education in the Society, see Donohue, *Jesuit Education,* especially 3–62.

own capacities and the Church's needs. Some of its members received the university education that qualified them for professorships and similar positions, while others undertook a less demanding curriculum that was oriented to the pastoral ministries.[45] Because of its highly theoretical nature, however, a university education did not prepare a graduate to meet the more practical challenges involved in hearing sacramental confessions. The Society therefore needed to prepare all of its members to be good confessors. That office required some knowledge of theology and canon law, but it primarily demanded that the priest should be able to understand and evaluate a wide range of cases, know which canons and theological principles pertained to each, and make an appropriate response to each penitent. The Society's efforts to teach these pastoral competencies stimulated two important developments.

The first was pedagogical. In order to prepare its members to be good confessors the Society worked out a two-part educational strategy. First, it held weekly conferences on cases of conscience whose purpose was to improve the abilities of those who were either approaching ordination or already serving as confessors. Second, the Society inaugurated a two-year program of studies intended for Jesuits who were going to do pastoral work. Its principal subject matter was cases of conscience and involved a series of penitential case studies designed to teach future confessors the knowledge and skills they would need. This two-year pastoral program became known as the "short course," as opposed to the "long course" of university studies.[46]

The short course and the conferences on cases of conscience helped many non-Jesuits to become better confessors. Once the Council of Trent had stipulated that the bishop might require a priest to demonstrate his competence as a confessor,[47] many priests wanted to participate in these courses and conferences. The Society was happy to admit them to their own colleges. In addition, Jesuits sometimes taught in the diocesan seminaries that bishops were beginning to establish. These new institutions also needed a curriculum of studies that met the Council of Trent's requirements. The Jesuit short course was well suited to this purpose and was adopted by many post-Tridentine seminaries.[48]

[45] See *Constitutions* [351, 254–6, 394]; O'Malley, *First Jesuits*, 215.
[46] O'Malley, *First Jesuits*, 145–7; Vereecke, "Le concile de Trente et l'enseignement de la théologie morale," 501.
[47] Session 23, Can. 15 (Tanner, 2:749); see also Vereecke, "Le concile de Trente et l'enseignement de la théologie morale," 504–5.
[48] The desire of many priests to promote renewal in the Church enhanced the popularity of Jesuit presentations on cases of conscience. By the end of the

The second development concerned the material that was taught to future confessors. At first Jesuit theologians based their classes on the literature that was already available, mainly the *summas* for confessors and books on *casus conscientiae*, or "cases of conscience." However, those resources were not satisfactory because they ignored systematic considerations and failed to account for the solutions that were offered. Responding to these deficits, Jesuit educators began to organize their material systematically and to elaborate the theoretical grounds for their discussion of penitential cases. On both points they were strongly influenced by the *Summa theologiae* of Thomas Aquinas, whom Ignatius had firmly endorsed.[49] By the end of the sixteenth century the short course had well-formulated presuppositions and goals and a structure that organized penitential cases in light of the sacraments and the Ten Commandments.[50]

The Jesuit short course on cases of conscience, the strengthening of its content and structure, and the founding of colleges and seminaries dramatically improved the preparation of priests. But there was still something missing, namely, up-to-date books that supported the preparation of good confessors. Jesuit professors had written on cases of conscience during the sixteenth century, and it was only a matter of time before their books reflected the latest improvements in content, organization, and pedagogy.[51]

---

sixteenth century, diocesan bishops and other religious orders had noticed that such conferences brought many benefits and began to conduct them regularly for their own priests. Vereecke, "Le concile de Trente et l'enseignement de la théologie morale," 504–5; O'Malley, *First Jesuits,* 146. On the influence of the Society on Tridentine seminary legislation, see James A. O'Donohoe, "The Seminary Legislation of the Council of Trent," *Il Concilio di Trento e la riforma tridentina: Atti del convegno storico internazionale* (Rome: Herder, 1965) 164–6.

[49] O'Malley, *First Jesuits,* 145–7; Vereecke, "Le concile de Trente et l'enseignement de la théologie morale," 506–7; Jonsen, *Abuse of Casuistry,* 149–50.

[50] Also relevant to this development is the *Ratio studiorum,* an official document in which the Society set out a comprehensive plan of studies for all subjects and levels of education, including pedagogical considerations. It enshrined the distinction between the long course and the short course, included the latter's essential content and structure, and stipulated that the material should be organized around the sacraments and the Decalogue. Based upon two earlier versions, the definitive *Ratio studiorum* of 1599 governed Jesuit education until the Society was suppressed in 1773. See Bangert, *History of the Society of Jesus,* 105–6; Vereecke, "Le concile de Trente et l'enseignement de la théologie morale," 106–7; also Theiner, *Entwicklung der Moraltheologie,* 408–11.

[51] Of particular importance is the *Summa theologiae moralis* of Henrique Henriques (1536–1608), which appeared in 1591. This work is notable for its reliance upon the Ia-IIae of Thomas Aquinas' *Summa theologiae* and for being the first to use the term "moral theology" in its title. For more, see Theiner, *Entwicklung der Moraltheologie,*

The Emergence of Moral Theology

The first work to reflect these developments is Juan Azor's *Institutiones Morales,* which began to appear in 1600. Although this large three-volume work was based upon the contributions of sixteenth-century Jesuit theologians, it stands as a milestone in theological and pastoral life of the Church. It inaugurated a new literary genre, the "moral manuals," and a new discipline, moral theology, which is constituted by the typical presuppositions, concerns, and content of the manuals. For these reasons Azor's book warrants further attention.

Azor opens his work with a treatment of several preliminary topics, which generally reflect the sequence in the First Part of the Second Part of Thomas Aquinas' *Summa theologiae.* Azor examines "human acts," acts for which a person is responsible, and the distinction between good and evil acts. This is the context in which he broaches the subject of personal conscience. He reviews human emotions or passions, moral habits, the virtues, and sin, which he understands as a violation of law or rights. Finally he examines the divine, natural, and human laws that govern human acts. In time those theoretical considerations formed the content of "fundamental moral theology." Azor divides the rest of his work into four units, which deal with material he judges to be of great importance: the Ten Commandments, the seven sacraments, the three ecclesiastical censures,[52] and the states in life, including the human person's last ends. Within those

---

251–67; Vereecke, "Le concile de Trente et l'enseignement de la théologie morale," 506–7.

On the Society's preparation of confessors during the sixteenth century, see Jacques de Blic, "La Théologie morale dans la compagnie de Jésus," *DTC,* 8/1:1069-74; Theiner, *Entwicklung der Moraltheologie,* 57–249.

[52] The censures are spiritual penalties that canon law imposes upon members of the Church for specified serious offenses that are committed with grave moral imputability, willful stubbornness, and contempt for authority. Their purpose is medicinal, that is, to bring censured persons to reconsider their attitude, withdraw from contumacy, and comply with the demands of justice or Church order in a serious matter; once they have served this purpose, they must be lifted. According to present-day canon law, the three censures are (1) excommunication, which prohibits a baptized person from any ministerial involvement in the Eucharist or other cultic action, the celebration or reception of any sacrament, and the exercise of an ecclesiastical office or ministry, including acts of governance; (2) interdict, which is similar to excommunication except that it does not bar acts of governance or the exercise of an ecclesiastical office; and (3) suspension, which forbids a cleric from exercising some or all of the powers received with holy orders or a particular office. For the canon law of the Latin Church on ecclesiastical censures, see *CIC,* Cann. 1311–99, and the commentary in Thomas J. Green, "Book VI: Sanctions in the Church," *The Code of Canon Law: A Text and Commentary,* ed. James A. Coriden and others (New York and Mahwah, N.J.: Paulist Press, 1985) 893–941.

four units Azor considers the entire range of moral issues that might confront people in various times, occupations, and circumstances and also reviews the commandments, precepts, and canons that govern personal conduct. These practical issues became the domain of "special moral theology."[53]

Azor and the Moral Life

In what is arguably his most significant presupposition, Azor assumed that Christian moral life is governed by commandments, precepts, and canons. Although that might seem to be an unremarkable assumption, it profoundly influenced his view of moral life and its principal dynamics. Once Christian moral life is placed within an ultimately legal frame of reference, moral norms, freedom, and conscience must be reinterpreted accordingly. So fundamental a reorganization of moral life cannot fail to have dogmatic significance, which also needs to be considered in any assessment of this approach.

To assume that Christian moral life is governed by the provisions of higher authority is to imply that laws and precepts govern human conduct. If that is the case, it will be necessary to scrutinize the sources of law in order to know their precise degree of authority, and the laws themselves to see exactly what they prohibit or require. Especially in complex cases, that task requires the services of experts who know what the moral laws are and a way to publicize their rulings and settle disputed points. In addition, one will need to know which principles or norms speak to a given case and be able to apply them correctly. The challenge of correct application places a high premium on casuistry in moral decision making.[54]

To locate morality along the law-obligation axis is to change the meaning of personal freedom and the function of conscience. If law is the source of moral obligation, then in the absence of law there can be no moral necessity for a person to choose this option rather than that or even to choose at all. In other words, when no obligation binds them, people are free to do as they please. In such a situation, personal freedom has no norm and is simply a freedom of indifference.[55] In this

---

[53] Pinckaers, *Sources of Christian Ethics*, 260–2; Jonsen, *Abuse of Casuistry*, 153–5; Theiner, *Entwicklung der Moraltheologie*, 267–75.

[54] For further discussion of casuistry see Jonsen, *Abuse of Casuistry*, especially 101–51.

[55] Freedom of indifference is a corollary of voluntaristic, or will-based systems, and achieved great prominence in the wake of the fourteenth-century turn toward the will. It stands in contrast to freedom in a context where there is an objective norm for behavior that can be known by the intellect, as is the case with systems

system, therefore, personal freedom and obligation are antithetical, and all moral dilemmas can be reduced to the perennial conflict between them. Moral decision making occurs when persons decide whether they are bound by a moral norm or are free to act as they wish. That all-important judgment is the work of personal conscience.[56] To perform its task, conscience is to be informed by a knowledge of the relevant laws and the obligations they impose, and then is to apply them correctly to particular cases as they occur. In sum, moral life occurs as persons freely discern and accept the moral obligations that bind them and apply those obligations to particular issues, or determine that in a given situation they are free of obligation.

That view of human morality omits or depreciates certain foundational elements in Christian life. Azor did not do justice to grace, the ultimate end of the human person, or the human tendency to seek happiness, even though these points are essential to Thomas Aquinas' theology. Azor left these foundational topics aside because he considered them too speculative and extraneous to the ministerial work of future priests. Furthermore, once he had adopted a legal understanding of moral life, Azor was committed to a system that revolves around defined and thus limited obligations, with the minimalism and freedom of indifference that it entails. A minimalist approach to moral life is incompatible with one that bases Christian life on the grace and the gifts of the Holy Spirit, assumes that people freely act out of virtue and in pursuit of what will perfect them, and recognizes a dynamic toward human and spiritual excellence. When he treated these things at all, consistency required Azor to subordinate them to law or to view them as a means to help people know and fulfill their obligations. Of course,

---

such as that of Thomas Aquinas. See chapter 7, note 76, above. For a brief modern sketch of these two notions of freedom, see GS, 17. For a fuller discussion, see Pinckaers, Sources of Christian Ethics, 327–99.

[56] Azor understood and treated conscience differently than did Thomas Aquinas, who considered conscience to be an exercise of practical reason based upon the conviction that the good is to be done and promoted and evil avoided, aided by wisdom and the virtue of prudence. The diversity of their historical, intellectual, and institutional contexts helps to account for their contrasting views. On Aquinas' treatment of conscience and related topics, see, for example, STh, I, q. 79, aa. 11-3; Léon Elders, "La doctrine de la conscience de saint Thomas d'Aquin," RT 83 (1983) 533–57; Dennis J. Billy, "Aquinas on the Content of Synderesis," StMor 29 (1991) 61–83; Eric D'Arcy, Conscience and Its Right to Freedom (New York: Sheed & Ward, 1961) 33–47, 87–112; Jonsen, Abuse of Casuistry, 122–36; Louis Janssens, Freedom of Conscience and Religious Freedom, trans. Br. Lorenzo (New York: Alba House, 1965) 35–40; Ralph McInerny, Ethica Thomistica: The Moral Philosophy of Thomas Aquinas (Washington: The Catholic University of America Press, 1982) 105–16; Brian Davies, The Thought of Thomas Aquinas (Oxford: Clarendon Press, 1992) 232–9.

those generous souls who sought spiritual excellence remained free to pursue it and would be praiseworthy if they did so. But because perfection is not required as a matter of obligation, it was reckoned as a matter of counsel only, segregated from moral theology and consigned to the realms of mystical or spiritual theology.[57]

The Manual Tradition of Moral Theology

Because it offered a coherent and comprehensive discussion of penance-related issues, Azor's *Institutiones Morales* inspired others to publish similar works. Especially after Hermann Busenbaum published his acclaimed *Medulla theologiae moralis* in 1650, this new form of pastoral-theological literature achieved general acceptance.[58] Adhering to the path opened by Azor and Busenbaum, later theological writers produced a large body of literature, the manuals of moral theology, which dominated the field until the 1960s. Although the manual writers reflected the concerns and influences of succeeding periods and sometimes differed on matters of theory or practical judgment,[59] they shared similar presuppositions, methods, and goals. The discipline of moral theology derives its coherence and characteristic qualities from these common elements.

---

[57] F. Citterio, "Appunti per un capitolo di storia della teologia morale: Dal Tridentino al Secondo Concilio Vaticano," *ScCat* 115 (1987) 503–6; especially Pinckaers, *Sources of Christian Ethics*, 262–6; see also 266–73, 277–9.

[58] For more on Busenbaum (1600–68), see Theiner, *Entwicklung der Moraltheologie*, 312–5; John A. Gallagher, *Time Past, Time Future: An Historical Study of Catholic Moral Theology* (New York and Mahwah, N.J.: Paulist Press, 1990) 35.

[59] John Gallagher has identified three distinct but overlapping periods. The first (1540–1650) marks the early formation of the manual tradition. The second (1577–1879) is dominated by the Probabilism controversy, which concerned the correct resolution of a practical doubt about moral obligation. When the case was ambiguous and reputable theologians gave opposing judgments on it, was a person bound or free? Jesuit authors generally taught that if even a substantial minority of theologians held for freedom, then one was allowed to act on that view. Dominican authors usually required a majority of authorities to hold that there is no moral obligation. St. Alphonsus Liguori and many Redemptorist theologians adopted a mediating position. Rigorist and laxist proposals were also offered, but these were condemned by the popes. The third period (1879–1960s) was shaped by the neo-Thomistic era within modern Catholicism, which will receive attention in chapter 11, below. See Gallagher, *Time Past, Time Future*, 33–41; also Raphael Gallagher, "The Manual System of Moral Theology Since the Death of Alphonsus," *ITQ* 51 (1985) 1–16; Louis Vereecke, "La theologie morale du Concile de Trente à s. Alphonse de Ligouri," *StMor* 25 (1987) 7–24, especially 14; Jonsen, *Abuse of Casuistry*, 164–75; Pinckaers, *Sources of Christian Ethics*, 273–7; Delumeau, *Le Catholicisme entre Luther et Voltaire*.

That coherence was based upon the presupposition that moral life revolves around obligations that are imposed by law or divine authority, an assumption that inclined many manual authors to relate moral life ultimately to God's will rather than to God's wisdom. Their principal purpose was to provide the intellectual resources confessors need in order to resolve the cases of conscience that are presented in the sacrament of penance. The basic structure and content of the manuals usually involved three principal parts. The first was dedicated to topics of fundamental moral theology, including the human act, law, conscience, and sin. The second part considered a wide range of sins, usually treated as violations of the Ten Commandments, the precepts of the Church, and perhaps the virtues. The demands of justice and sins proper to particular states in life also fell within this part. The manuals concluded by discussing the requirements of canon law, especially as it pertained to the sacraments. In sum, the manuals aimed to define moral obligations and delineate the minimal requirements of Christian life in order to help priests teach and judge their people rightly.[60]

Historical and Theological Reflections

When the new discipline of moral theology is compared to the moral thought of Thomas Aquinas, it becomes clear that several significant

---

[60] Pinckaers, *Sources of Christian Ethics*, 266–73; Gallagher, *Time Past, Time Future*, 30–1, 44.

The exclusive concern with minimum requirements helped make moral theology a distinct discipline. The preface of one early twentieth-century manual presents the following disclaimer:

> We must ask the reader to bear in mind that manuals of moral theology are technical works intended to help the confessor and the parish priest in the discharge of their duties. They are as technical as the text-books of the lawyer and the doctor. They are not intended for edification, nor do they hold up a high ideal of Christian perfection for the imitation of the faithful. They deal with what is of obligation under pain of sin; they are books of moral pathology. They are necessary for the Catholic priest to enable him to administer the sacrament of Penance and to fulfil his other duties; they are intended to serve this purpose, and they should not be censured for not being what they were never intended to be. Ascetical and mystical literature which treats of the higher spiritual life is very abundant in the Catholic Church, and it should be consulted by those who desire to know the lofty ideals of life which the Catholic Church places before her children and encourages them to practise. Moral theology proposes to itself the humbler but still necessary task of defining what is right and what wrong in all the practical relations of the Christian life (Thomas Slater, *A Manual of Moral Theology for English-speaking Countries* [New York: Benziger Bros., 1908] 1:5-6).

shifts had taken place since his death in 1274. By the year 1600 theologians had largely abandoned the notion that moral imperatives arise from dynamics intrinsic to persons, their nature, and their ultimate end. Instead, they derived moral obligations from the commands of lawful authority. That basic shift suggests that the source of moral good had migrated from nature and its inclinations to law and its obligations, from the real to the commanded.[61] Theologians no longer located moral life within a larger theological whole but had begun to elaborate a "moral theology," understood as a discipline unto itself with its own goals, content, and method. Their focus had moved away from the primary dynamics of human and Christian life and settled instead on individual acts considered as such.

At first glance it is difficult to account for these fundamental shifts. Sixteenth-century Jesuit authors had taken Thomas Aquinas as their mentor and borrowed heavily from his *Summa theologiae*. Ignatius and the Society of Jesus certainly understood the primacy of grace, charity, and conversion in Christian life. They displayed apostolic generosity and a commitment to virtue. They recognized that sacramental penance has the power to inspire and express a sinner's turn away from sin to Christ. One must also assume that Azor and his colleagues were well aware that the Council of Trent had related the sacrament of penance to the process of justification.

As it happened, however, other influences carried the day and became the primary sources from which moral theology acquired its characteristic features. Since the end of the thirteenth century theology and pastoral care had flowed into different institutional and literary channels. The resulting dissociation of theoretical and practical concerns seriously compromised Azor's attempt to place pastoral care on a sound theological footing. Furthermore, in the wake of Stephen Tempier's condemnation of 1277 theologians were disinclined to attribute normative significance to nature and final causality. Impressed by God's power and freedom, they taught that God freely constitutes things as they are and establishes the norms that are to govern human acts. When God's will takes precedence over God's intellect, nature loses much of its normative quality, grace is more easily detached from moral life, and contingent singulars become much more important.[62]

---

[61] For further discussion of this important point see Thomas S. Hibbs, "A Rhetoric of Motives: Thomas on Obligation as Rational Persuasion," *Thomist* 54 (1990) 295–9; John Finnis, *Natural Law and Natural Rights* (Oxford: Clarendon Press; New York: Oxford University Press, 1980) 45–7; Jean Tonneau, *Absolu et obligation en morale* (Montreal: Inst. d'Études Médiévales; Paris: Vrin, 1965) especially 103–19.

[62] The Jesuit Francisco Suarez (1548–1617) is a key figure in this context. His voluntarist theory of law reflected the Western turn toward the will and strongly in-

Finally, Thomas' stable, comprehensive, and coherent world view must have seemed quite obsolete after the chaos of the intervening centuries and the dramatic changes that had overtaken European life during the sixteenth century, especially the sundering of Western Christianity. Those disturbing experiences also predisposed people to accept that authority and the fulfillment of specific obligations are essential to civil society and Christian life.[63]

NATURE AND GRACE

When the Council of Trent considered the respective contributions of divine grace and human freedom to personal justification, it framed its declarations in light of one overriding purpose: declaring Catholic faith in response to the errors it found in the Protestant Reformers' teachings. For this reason the council focused upon the two things that were required for justification, namely, God's free and unearned gift of grace and an adult person's free cooperation with that grace. Although these assertions drew the essential lines of Catholic doctrine, they did not detail how God's grace and human freedom interact in the drama of salvation. That was the primary issue that engaged theologians after the council.[64]

These post-Tridentine discussions had important doctrinal and pastoral consequences. They pushed the Church to sharpen its own understanding of nature and grace. They prompted theologians to emphasize the role of human freedom in justification and to orient grace primarily to acts rather than persons. The intellectual history of this era is also marked by certain exaggerations. Baian and Jansenist theories held that sin and grace are so powerful that they overwhelm human freedom. The need to rebut those views led theologians to develop the concept of "pure nature" and widen the distinction between nature and grace. Although these positions were also lacking in balance, they won general acceptance. Later generations of theologians

---

fluenced the later development of legal theory, ethics, and moral theology. For an introduction to his life and thought see John A. Mourant, "Suárez, Francisco," *EP,* 7–8: 30–3; Jorge J. E. Gracia, "Francisco Suárez: The Man in History," *ACPQ* 65 (1991) 259–66; Thomas E. Davitt, *The Nature of Law* (St. Louis: Herder, 1951) 86–108. For more on his voluntarism and how it compares with the thought of Aquinas, see Vernon J. Bourke, *Will in Western Thought: An Historico-Critical Survey* (New York: Sheed & Ward, 1964) 178; idem, *History of Ethics* (Garden City, N.Y.: Doubleday, 1968) 121–4; Finnis, *Natural Law,* 45–9, 337–42, 347–50.

[63] Citterio, "Appunti," 496–503; Bourke, *Will in Western Thought,* 171–8; see also the relevant discussions in chapters 8 and 9, above.

[64] Henri Rondet, *The Grace of Christ: A Brief History of the Theology of Grace,* trans. Tad W. Guzie (Westminster, Md.: Newman Press, 1967) 311–2.

took them for granted and assumed that they represented the traditional doctrine. The tacit canonization of this post-Tridentine theology of nature and grace had serious consequences. By encouraging believers to view the sacred and the profane in antithetical terms and by favoring a sharp contrast between Church and world, it helped to legitimate an official strategy of opposition to the post-Enlightenment world with its political, theological, disciplinary, and attitudinal byproducts. These results underline the importance of Post-Tridentine debates on nature and grace. The task of the present section will be to trace their development and point out their significance.

Baianism

Among the first to address the relationship between nature and grace was a Louvain theology professor, Michael du Bay (1513–89), who is usually known by his Latin name, Baius. Baius sought to oppose Reformation denials of human merit and to provide a true account of original sin and its effects on human salvation. He judged that the only way to do that was to bypass all Scholastic theological accretions and rely solely on St. Augustine of Hippo, whose writings he had carefully studied.

Baius presupposed that human nature includes all elements whose absence would inflict a significant loss on the human being. Human nature therefore requires the body's full subjection to the will and the person's full adherence to God. Full adherence involves the gift of the Holy Spirit, which God cannot withhold without inflicting an unjust deprivation on human nature. Baius taught that when innocent human beings persevere in obeying God's commandments, they are entitled to eternal life. Sin radically changes that situation. Once Adam disobeyed God's law, he and his descendants lost original innocence and became slaves to sin. Sinful human beings enjoy neither free will nor freedom of choice. All their acts are sins, and all their sins are mortal. Only God's gift of actual grace makes people do good and thus earn their reward. According to Baius, salvation or damnation does not reflect people's deliberation or use of freedom or whether they are in the state of grace or sin. Everything depends solely on actions; good acts merit salvation and evil ones damnation. But that in turn depends on whether God gives the grace necessary for sinners to perform good acts.

According to Baius, then, grace does not elevate nature but merely makes actions meritorious that would otherwise be sinful. Fallen humanity does not enjoy free will, and God is the sole arbiter of each person's eternal destiny. For Baianism, the giving of the Holy Spirit can be a natural necessity; eternal life is a reward due in justice rather than a gift given out of love; and both human nature and personal freedom can be compromised or suppressed. Its principal elements were condemned by Pope Pius V in 1568 and Pope Gregory XIII in 1580.[65]

Catholic Debates on Nature and Grace

When Catholic theologians tried to describe the relationships between nature and grace or between God's power and human freedom, they found themselves locked in controversy. Luis de Molina (1535–1600) and his Jesuit disciples were at pains to widen the scope of human freedom. In essence, they taught that God gives grace in light of divine foreknowledge of how human persons will use their freedom in any possible circumstance. That allowed Molinists to assert that good actions come forth from human freedom even though grace also empowers them. Domingo Bañez (1538–1604) and his Dominican colleagues rejected that approach. Strongly committed to God's role in salvation, they taught that good actions come from God's grace, which always accomplishes its intended effect without regard for anyone's foreseen merits.

This disagreement reflected political tensions, diverse pastoral concerns, and the fact that theological sources and Christian experience were both open to different interpretations. After giving them careful consideration, in 1607 the Holy See decided to tolerate both positions and, noting the heated nature of the dispute, warned the parties to stop arguing and refrain from accusing each other of heresy. Some time later, however, the Molinist approach underwent further development and eventually won the support of most theologians. The ultimate result of these discussions was to set the general contours of modern Catholic thought on human salvation and persuade most theologians that personal freedom plays a critical role in that process.[66]

Jansenism

Some years later another Louvain theologian, Cornelius Jansen (1585–1638), returned to the same issues. He was convinced that Baius

[65]Ibid., 313–21; Henri de Lubac, *Augustinianism and Modern Theology*, trans. Lancelot Sheppard (New York: Herder & Herder, 1968) 1–33; McGrath, *Iustitia Dei*, 2:90-3; see also DS, 1901–80.

[66]The debate between the Jesuit and Dominican schools of thought, often referred to as the controversy *de auxiliis*, is recounted in Rondet, *Grace of Christ*, 322–7; McGrath, *Iustitia Dei*, 2:93-5; Pelikan, 4:374-85. See also John M. McDermott, "The Neo-Scholastic Analysis of Freedom," *IPQ* 34 (1994) 149–65.

had been wrongly condemned and strongly felt that the Jesuit emphasis on human freedom was an affront to the power of God's grace. In a work entitled *Augustinus*,[67] published posthumously in 1640, Jansen taught that before his sin Adam had a natural claim on God's grace, which would support but not empower the good decisions of his free will. Fallen humanity, on the other hand, finds the attraction of sin so alluring that it cannot help but commit sin. Only the gift of God's grace enables a person to avoid sin and act worthily. But because God's grace is efficacious, it necessarily causes people to perform good acts. That does not mean that God gives grace to everyone. The ample evidence of sin in human life proves that grace is not given very frequently, which is another sign of its gratuity. The Catholic Church condemned key elements of Jansenist teachings in 1653 and again in 1713, especially because they overestimate innocent human nature and deny both God's universal salvific will and the free will of sinful people.[68]

The Response to Baius and Jansen

The response of Catholic theologians to Baianism and Jansenism focused on the basic errors they charged against these systems. Baius was indicted for having failed to uphold the gratuity of God's grace toward innocent human nature and denying free will in fallen human beings. His mistakes were attributed to a more basic confusion of the natural and supernatural orders. Against Baius, therefore, theologians tried to emphasize the difference between the natural and the supernatural, the gratuity of God's grace, and fallen humanity's ability to act freely in the face of sin and grace alike. Because these points had to be made and defended also in opposition to Jansenism, they took on great urgency and engaged theologians for long time. As a result, they stimulated Catholic theology to distinguish nature from grace ever more sharply and attach to the concept of "pure nature" an unprecedented content and meaning.

"Pure Nature"

The term "pure nature" refers to human nature as it would have been if God had never offered his grace and humans had not sinned. Because they knew that both these conditions are false, most patristic

---

[67] An ample summary of Jansen's *Augustinus* can be found in Nigel Abercrombie, *The Origins of Jansenism* (Oxford: Clarendon Press, 1936) 125–58, especially 126–53.

[68] For more on Jansenism see Rondet, *Grace of Christ*, 340–64; Abercrombie, *Origins of Jansenism*, 87–313; de Lubac, *Augustinianism and Modern Theology*, 34–117; also DS, 2001–7, 2010–2, 2301–32, 2400–2502.

and not a few medieval theologians had little use for this concept. They dealt with the actual condition of the human race and presupposed that humans had been created for union with God, had sinned, and need the grace God offers if they are to reach their goal. In other words, traditional theology accepted that human beings have a natural desire for an end they can attain only with God's help.[69] It was able to acknowledge this basic truth of human life without confusing or unduly separating the natural and the supernatural. Maintaining that older synthesis involved little difficulty so long as the traditional presuppositions went unchallenged.[70]

Once Baius asserted that innocent human nature requires the gift of the Holy Spirit and good behavior is entitled to a reward in justice, he moved the focus of the theological discussion from the actual condition of humanity to the hypothetical case of humanity before the Fall. Although that shift of horizons would have been enough to place the traditional synthesis under great stress, the logic of the Catholic response greatly increased the pressure on it. To deal with Baius' confusion, theologians emphasized the differences between nature and grace, which diminished the overall coherence of the inherited outlook. Against the subordination of grace to innocent human nature, they urged the gratuity of God's grace in all circumstances. That made it harder for them to claim that humanity has a natural desire for union with God. Against Jansenist assertions that fallen human nature is impotent, Catholic theologians insisted that it possesses free will and therefore has moral responsibility for its acts. That augmented the status of human nature in the presence of sin and grace alike.

The logic of their views led theologians to abandon the traditional synthesis and replace it with one that suited the campaign against Baianism and Jansenism. That process unfolded in several stages. First, sixteenth-century theologians reinterpreted their predecessors to make them say that persons only seek a merely natural fulfillment or try to know God simply as Creator. Second, in an effort to protect the gratuity of grace, they began to teach that God could, at least in theory, withhold grace from human beings. In that case, human nature would

[69] In the opening paragraph of his *Confessions* St. Augustine declared, "You stir man to take pleasure in praising you, because you have made us for yourself, and our heart is restless until it rests in you." Thomas Aquinas held that God is the last end of the rational creature, and "therefore God alone constitutes man's happiness" (*STh*, I-II, q. 2, a. 8; see also I, q. 2, Prologue).

[70] Rondet, *Grace of Christ*, 209–48; idem, "Le problème de la nature pure et la théologie du XVIe siècle," *RSR* 35 (1948) 483–5; Henri de Lubac, *The Mystery of the Supernatural*, trans. Rosemary Sheed (New York: Herder & Herder, 1967) 21–2, 25–47.

exist in a "pure" form and would pursue its purely natural ends without the help of grace. As that line of thinking became more mature, it pushed the concept of pure nature into greater prominence. Finally, although theologians originally invoked the notion of pure nature only hypothetically in order to highlight the gratuitous activity of God, it developed a life of its own and was eventually taken to describe an actual state of affairs. It then became possible to isolate human nature from grace and relate it to ends that were strictly natural. Of course, God remained free to add supernatural grace or withhold it in response to sin, but in neither case would God's action essentially change human nature or its activity. In the end, therefore, polemical needs, the tendentious interpretations of earlier theologians, and the impoverished condition of theology in that era led theologians to conclude that humanity actually exists in a state of pure nature, to which God can add supernatural ends and means that are entirely extrinsic to human nature. At the time few realized how novel this conclusion was or how influential it would prove to be.[71]

The Significance of These Developments

Although the debate between Molina and Bañez and the controversies set in motion by Baius and Jansen were conducted on the level of theological doctrine, these disputes had important moral implications. The Molinist emphasis on human freedom reflected the Jesuit awareness that efforts on behalf of spiritual conversion both presupposed and engaged personal freedom. The general acceptance of their approach emphasized the decisive role of human freedom in salvation and expanded moral responsibility in practice. Conversely, Jansenist teachings reflected a more severe judgment about human life and the conviction that God alone is responsible for personal salvation. In theory and in practice, Jansenists strongly opposed both the humanist strain in Western life and Jesuit efforts to defend human cooperation with salvation and to extend moral obligation no further than the minimum required by law. In rejecting Jansenist teachings, therefore, the Church vindicated human moral responsibility, reaffirmed that salvation requires free personal cooperation with God's grace, and kept moral obligations within human reach.

---

[71] The pivotal figures in the development of the notion of "pure nature" were Cajetan (1468–1534), Robert Bellarmine (1542–1621), and Francisco Suarez (1548–1617). This matter is extensively discussed in Rondet, *Grace of Christ*, 330–5; idem, "Le problème;" de Lubac, *Augustinianism and Modern Theology*, 118–310; see also idem, *Mystery of the Supernatural*.

The doctrine of pure nature involved a dualism that contributed to the further splintering of Western thought and culture. First and foremost, it legitimated efforts to understand the human person as a strictly natural, temporal, and secular being. In the wider society that way of thinking contributed to the rise of deism, naturalism, and atheistic accounts of human life and made it more likely that people would base their lives on a truncated if not false view of the human condition. When they saw people taking this approach, theologians, having validated the sharp distinction between nature and grace, could do little more than develop their own accounts of natural morality and try to show that nature itself proves that God exists and has spoken to humanity. Those enterprises served important apologetical purposes, but they fell outside the domain proper to theology. Theology focused on supernatural revelation, understood as God's communication of what was to be believed or done for salvation. That view helps to account for a highly intellectual or rational approach to revelation, faith, and theology.

The separation of nature and grace had equally significant effects on the theological understanding of Christian life. To affirm that human beings live and act independently of God's grace is also to imply that God's saving activity takes place independently of the created order. If that is the case, then the workings of grace and the response of faith do not intersect with ordinary human experience and will have to be relocated from a "natural" arena to one that is "supernatural." That has several important consequences. A sharper differentiation of nature and grace will tend to compromise the unity of Christian life and introduce deep fissures between spirituality and theology and between Christian moral life and faith. In addition, if natural moral considerations and the process of grace and justification belong to opposite sides of the nature-grace divide, then moral theology will tend to gravitate toward the domain of nature and away from the economy of salvation, or perhaps try to do justice to both but then be vulnerable to severe stresses against its internal unity. Phenomena that are not easily categorized either as natural or as supernatural will tend to drop out of the theological picture. As a result, theologians will depreciate people's sense of God's presence in their lives and their yearning for communion with God and underestimate the importance of such potentially decisive events as the preached word, sacramental worship, and people's daily encounter with questions of faith and sin, conversion and commitment to Christ.[72]

---

[72] Herman-Emiel Mertens, "Nature and Grace in Twentieth-Century Catholic Theology," *LS* 16 (1991) 242–50; Karl Rahner, "Nature and Grace," *Theological*

REFLECTIONS

This chapter has examined the work of a general council, followed a sinner as he turned to Christ and established a religious order that would help others to do the same, and seen the effect of theological reflections on intellectual and pastoral life. The events of this era suggest that ecclesial faith prompted a wide range of responses: corporate and juridical, theological and educational, charismatic and personal, pastoral and liturgical. Whether they reflected long-standing currents in Western life, responded to external challenges, or honored the perennial imperatives of Christian faith, the varied activities of the sixteenth and seventeenth centuries had a cumulative effect and helped to shape the religious and moral life of believers since that time.

In this period Catholics continued to believe that commitment to Christ engages a person in the Church's life of worship and service and requires respect for ecclesiastical authority. The Council of Trent explicitly reaffirmed the ecclesial dimensions of Catholic faith and enacted decrees that improved the Church's ability to mediate God's presence to people and help them respond in faith, hope, and charity. Theological activity, the preparation of the clergy, pastoral work, and the life of the religious orders took place within the Church and under the authority of its leaders. From one perspective none of this was exceptional, for it represented the ongoing practice of an ancient tradition of faith. However, in an age when the Protestant Reformation emphasized the direct relationship of each believer with God, these corporate dynamics marked Catholicism off more sharply from other expressions of Western Christianity. As European culture itself grew more individualistic, the Catholic Church was likely to find less sympathy and provoke more opposition within secular society. As the general environment became less congenial to ecclesial faith and authority, the Church was also more likely to become problematic for Catholics themselves.

Within the Church there was a great deal of concern over the practical organization and circumstances of Christian life. The Council of Trent addressed structural problems, ministerial nonfeasance or malfeasance, and personal vices in the Church. It promulgated many reform decrees and demonstrated special concern for preaching, sacramental worship, and the preparation of priests. Ignatius of Loyola and his associates carefully adapted the Society of Jesus to the needs and conditions of the age. The manuals of moral theology were acutely

---

Investigations (Baltimore: Helicon Press; London: Darton, Longman & Todd, 1966) 4:165-9; Rondet, *Grace of Christ*, 323, 327; de Lubac, *Mystery*, xi–xiv, 5; idem, *Augustinianism and Modern Theology*, 35–8, 261–2, 292–6.

conscious of the realities and problems of daily life. This concern with practicalities was prompted by a deep and abiding conviction that God uses the things and events of daily life to call people to faith, repentance, and service and that people enact their response in the same setting. That conviction made it urgent to remove scandalous conditions that hindered or prevented the Church from being an instrument of God's word and presence and to conform key elements of Church life to their sacred functions. The same awareness that daily life has transcendent significance guided the lives and work of pastors, saints, scholars, and ordinary members of the Church in this era.

A remarkable solicitude for a person's interior response accompanied this concern for tangible realities. Trent had underlined the freedom with which persons respond to God's grace and included the secret sins of one's heart among those that are to be brought to sacramental penance. St. Ignatius was convinced that interior experiences can disclose God's will and urged that careful attention be paid to them. He placed the spiritual consolation of the faithful among the chief purposes of the Society of Jesus. The council's wish to promote the spiritual formation of seminarians and theologians' recognition that sin requires free consent emphasize the importance of one's interior life. These considerations show once again that Catholic life embraces matters of the heart as well as hierarchical structures, sacramental rituals, traditional practices, and the community. Church leaders understood the decisive quality of people's interior experiences and responses. They recognized that the external observances of Christian life are to be informed by a free, generous, and sustained personal commitment to Christ and his Church. An adequate understanding of Catholicism is possible only if these interior and personal dynamics are duly considered along with its external and ecclesial dimensions.

When this fuller picture is taken into account, it becomes clear that the dynamics and imperatives of Catholic faith are also the dynamics and imperatives of the believer's moral life. The primary need for people to give free cooperation to the movements of God's grace has been noted. Trent's legislation to suppress scandalous conditions reflects its concern that moral and religious offenses easily turn people away from faith and encourage further evil. When it detailed the behavioral and interior requirements for sacramental penance, it emphasized the links between a persons' moral lives and their standing in the Church and before God. The attraction and contribution of the religious orders and the renewal of the pastoral ministries likewise reflected an awareness that religious factors shape a person's moral life and that moral decisions govern one's religious life. These considerations emphasize once again that the moral and religious aspects of human life are united in a close and reciprocal relationship. They suggest that specific moral issues are to be assessed in light of Christian faith and its religious dynamics, and vice versa. They urge caution when religious imperatives seem to overlook human freedom or when moral imperatives are inadequately grounded in the dynamics of Christian life.

The events reviewed in this chapter and the intellectual currents that waxed strong at the beginning of the modern age sometimes worked against the overall integrity and unity of Christian life. Trent's decision to uphold the practical dimensions of sacramental penance as it was celebrated at that time and the manuals' emphasis on behavioral requirements tended to overshadow the interior aspects of unity with God and the overriding necessity of conversion. The general view that moral life was governed by specific obligations and burdened by a multiplicity of sins made it more difficult to appreciate the personal generosity to which Christ calls each disciple. The rise to dominance of the concept of pure nature and its segregation from the supernatural domain generated considerable stress against the overall unity of Christian life. These developments helped to shape the experience of the Catholic people at that time and made it more likely that later generations would also labor under fractured or truncated views of Christian life. They call attention to the intellectual currents and the practical judgments that contributed to this problem. They suggest that, in the final analysis, Christian life requires that its various constituents should not only be expressed in an orthodox way but that they need to be understood and lived in a way that is essentially complete, duly integrated, and responsive to the proper priorities.

The pastors, theologians, religious, and ordinary believers of this earlier age left a complex legacy to their sons and daughters of the nineteenth and twentieth centuries. These later generations found themselves living in societies that had become more secular, less sympathetic to faith, and prone to challenge or dismiss the Church, especially when conflicts arose. It is now time to consider the life and activity of the Church in the modern world.

11

The Church in the Modern World

As the modern Western outlook established its hegemony over the intellectual, cultural, political, and economic life of Europe, the general environment grew more hostile to the Catholic Church. The Enlightenment's reliance on reason and nature excluded supernatural faith while its individualism depreciated the community, its traditions, and authority. Modern notion of progress made the Church seem to be a bastion of superstition and reaction, an obsolete institution at best, an intolerable obstacle at worst. Political theories either marginalized the public dimensions of faith or subjected them to state control. Throughout much of the nineteenth century these new habits of thought and the example of the French Revolution fanned deeply felt resentments and inspired a series of revolutions against the prevailing social, economic, and political order. These intellectual and practical developments often appeared to threaten the Church's religious and political interests and were viewed with alarm by its leaders.

The need to respond to these challenges dominated the Holy See's agenda throughout the nineteenth century and well into the twentieth. As soon as it was able to do so, it determined to resist the new order that had served up such bitter fruit. It deployed the Church's political, disciplinary, pastoral, and intellectual resources in a comprehensive strategy that involved tough defensive measures and other responses. Along with all that had provoked it, that strategy helped to establish the adversarial relationship between the Church and the world that was part of Catholic life and thought at least until the 1960s.

The Second Vatican Council (1962–5) reconsidered that entire approach. Drawing upon important theological developments in the preceding decades, it reoriented the Church to its sources, tradition, interior dynamics, and apostolic mission. Recognizing that important changes had taken place in the world and acutely sensitive to the Church's responsibilities there, the council adopted a more positive attitude toward the wider society. Its decisions on these fundamental matters have broad implications for the moral life of believers.

The task of this chapter is to review some of the principal moments in the Church's relationship with the modern world of the nineteenth and twentieth centuries, note certain developments in theology and domestic policies, and consider their effects on Catholic religious and moral life.

The first section will discuss the Church's response to the wide range of threats that liberal individualism spawned in the nineteenth century. Organized around a vigorous assertion of papal authority, that response brought important elements of Catholic life under the Holy See's immediate supervision and placed them in a decidedly defensive and adversarial posture. Besides shaping the Church's relationship with contemporary society, that process had a strong influence on Catholic intellectual life.

A second area of interest is the historical and intellectual background of the Second Vatican Council's reconsideration of Catholic faith and life. Despite strong incentives to intellectual conformity, Catholic scholars were able to conduct original research into important aspects of history, philosophy, the Scriptures, and Christian thought and practice. Their work called attention to the sources of the Church's faith and underlined the decisive influence of history on its faith, theology, and policies. Once these and parallel developments had matured, they undermined the older outlook and supplied the resources that were indispensable to the council's work.

The Second Vatican Council will be the subject of the third section. The council renewed the Church's contact with its scriptural, intellectual, and liturgical sources, clarified its mission, and mandated a more cooperative, friendlier attitude toward the modern world and separated Christians. Because they are so fundamental, these decisions have the potential to transform Catholic religious and moral life.

The Church Against the Modern World

Although the shift from a largely Christian and medieval outlook to one that is primarily secular and modern had been underway in Europe for many centuries, Catholic bishops and scholars were slow to appreciate what was happening or to mount an effective response to it. It took the trauma of the French Revolution and its aftermath to convince Church leaders that they could no longer afford to be passive or tolerant. Once they awoke to the religious, intellectual, and political realities of the modern world, they determined to respond vigorously in order to protect and strengthen the Church against all that might threaten it.

The Post-Revolutionary Challenge to the Church

By the beginning of the nineteenth century the Holy See had grasped the reality of the situation that confronted the Church. The French Revolution had confiscated the Church's schools and property, fomented a schism among its members, and tried to dechristianize French society. To many observers those were the practical consequences of the liberal individualism that had fueled the Revolution in the first place. Because that ideology locates the source of political power exclusively in the will of the people, it leaves no room for Church authority in the life of a nation, even a Catholic one. It breeds indifference to faith and can expel religion from public life. Liberal ideology also holds that individuals have a right to freedom of conscience, assembly, worship, and the press. Catholic leaders found such views to be unacceptable because they seemed to subordinate truth to individual opinion, undermine public morality, and depreciate supernatural faith.[1]

In the 1820s the Holy See was still reeling from the Revolution and was in no mood to indulge those who held that the Church should compromise or agree with modern approaches to faith or political life, especially when they were French Catholics. In that environment, Félicité de Lamennais (1782–1854) proposed that the common consent of society is the norm of truth and opens the way to a knowledge of God. Although these ideas were objectionable, the political views of Lamennais were even more alarming, especially since they had received wide publicity through his journal, *L'Avenir*. Distressed at the close relationship between the Holy See and the French monarchy, Lamennais and his associates declared that faith would be better served if the Catholic Church severed all official ties with the state, endorsed the liberal platform, and accepted it as a basis for its spiritual mission.

Although Lamennais recognized papal authority over that mission, Pope Gregory XVI rejected these proposals. Shaken by a liberal-inspired revolution in the Papal States in 1830, he issued two encyclical letters

---

[1] Edgar Hocedez, *Histoire de la Théologie au XIXe Siècle* (Paris: Desclée de Brouwer; Brussels: L'Édition Universelle, 1948–52) 2:159-60; Yves Congar, "L'Ecclésiologie de la Révolution Français au Concile du Vatican sous le signe de l'affirmation de l'autorité," *L'Ecclésiologie au XIXe siècle*, ed. Maurice Nédoncelle (Paris: Cerf, 1960) 89–90.

that rejected the philosophical and political views of Lamennais and condemned the book he wrote in response to papal criticisms. Gregory's interventions deterred others from defending liberalism on the basis of principle, but they did not preclude Catholics from proposing that governmental neutrality toward religion and individual freedoms might sometimes work to the Church's advantage.[2]

Nowhere did liberalism impact the Holy See more immediately than in Italy, especially when it threatened papal sovereignty over the Papal States and the city of Rome. As was the case elsewhere, Italian nationalism waxed strong during the nineteenth century. Under the banner of individual freedom and equality of rights, it sought to bring forth a single Italian state. But it was not possible to achieve this goal so long as the Austrians held part of northern Italy and the popes retained civil jurisdiction over Rome and the Papal States. That situation gave rise to a bitter struggle that had important religious as well as political consequences.

When he began his pontificate in 1846, Pius IX won the applause of liberals everywhere for having acceded to demands for representative government and for his other progressive steps. But he quickly fell from favor after he refused to help force the Austrians out of Italy. Italian nationalists had tried but failed to expel the Austrians by military action and blamed their defeat on the pope's refusal to send his army to fight alongside them. Angry Roman crowds became so unruly that on November 24, 1848, the pope had to flee south to the port city of Gaeta. Although the French restored him to Rome in 1850, Pius' political position remained insecure, especially since Italian nationalists and the Piedmontese government in Turin were still looking for a chance to take control of papal territories.

These events deeply affected Pius IX. The trauma of 1848, the spectacle of civil disorders in many other parts of Europe during that same year, the deliberately secular and anticlerical texture of many contemporary societies, and the continuing threats against papal jurisdiction persuaded Pius and his advisors never again to cast a sympathetic eye toward liberal ideology or countenance assaults against duly constituted authority. On the contrary, if liberalism and the modern world meant indifference

---

[2] Gerald A. McCool, *Catholic Theology in the Nineteenth Century: Quest for a Unitary Method* (New York: Seabury, 1977) 43–6; Alec R. Vidler, *The Church in an Age of Revolution* (Baltimore: Penguin Books, 1974) 68–72; E.E.Y. Hales, *The Catholic Church in the Modern World: A Survey from the French Revolution to the Present* (Garden City, N.Y.: Doubleday, 1960) 90–9; Hocedez, *Histoire de la Théologie*, 2:161-79. For the encyclicals against Lamennais, *Mirari vos* (August 15, 1832) and *Singulari nos* (June 25, 1834), see Claudia Carlen, ed., *The Papal Encyclicals 1740–1878* (Wilmington, N.C.: McGrath Publishing Co., 1981) 235–41, 249–51.

to faith, irreligious legislation, the exclusion of the Church from public life, the overthrow of legitimate governments, and hostility toward the Roman pontiff, then the papacy would stand against them with all the power and resources at its disposal. The loss of the Papal States in 1860 and the seizure of Rome by the Piedmontese in 1870 stiffened the Holy See's resolve and deepened its sense of grievance.[3]

Early Responses

As the nineteenth century opened, the Catholic Church was in no position to respond effectively to intellectual assaults or practical injuries. The impoverished state of Catholic philosophy and theology, the suppression of the Society of Jesus in 1773, and the loss or preemption of Catholic universities left the Church virtually mute in the face of modern ideologies. Revolutionary violence, state interference in the affairs of local churches, the imprisonment of two popes, and insufficient numbers of clergy likewise contributed to the Church's paralysis.

Once it began to recover from these dire circumstances, the Holy See gradually established the foundation for a stronger response. In 1814, Pope Pius VII revived the Society of Jesus, an action that restored a trusted and intellectually accomplished order to the Church's service. His successor, Leo XII, worked diligently to improve Catholic university education, and in 1824 he returned the Gregorian University to the Society. That action gave Jesuit scholars a strategic venue for their work and the papacy a much needed academic resource. Beginning in 1815 the Holy See concluded concordats with many European monarchies, thereby bringing a measure of stability to its political relationships. The rejection of Lamennais and his book, already noted, shows that by 1832 the Holy See had found its voice and was prepared to make it heard. By mid-century the papacy had grown strong enough to craft and execute a comprehensive response. As he surveyed the irreligious and hostile forces arrayed against him and the Church, a chastened Pius IX was more than ready to act.[4]

---

[3] Hales, *Catholic Church in the Modern World*, 100–6, 115–22; see also Hocedez, *Histoire de la Théologie*, 2:170-1; Peter Steinfels, "The Failed Encounter: The Catholic Church and Liberalism in the Nineteenth Century," *Catholicism and Liberalism: Contributions to American Public Philosophy*, ed. R. Bruce Douglass and David Hollenbach (Cambridge: Cambridge University Press, 1994) 19–44.

[4] Hales, *Catholic Church in the Modern World*, 59, 62, 72–89; Vidler, *Church in an Age of Revolution*, 21; Hocedez, *Histoire de la Théologie*, 1:13-26, 52; Yves Congar, *A History of Theology*, trans. Hunter Guthrie (Garden City, N.Y.: Doubleday, 1968) 177–82.

Papal Authority Confronts Liberalism

The heart of the Holy See's strategy was a forceful assertion of papal authority. That approach offered several advantages. First of all, it directly answered the claims of liberal thought. To uphold papal authority was to declare that the Church is a structured, hierarchical, and juridical society and deny that faith is a purely spiritual and interior phenomenon. It was to draw attention to divine revelation and to the public and objective grounds of Christian faith and contradict the notion that the Church is simply a voluntary association of individuals who are free to practice religion any way they see fit.[5] Second, although a more vigorous exercise of papal power abridged the prerogatives and reduced the diversity of local churches, it enabled the papacy to mount a coordinated defense against liberal thought and its practical consequences. Supported by strong Ultramontanist currents,[6] the Holy See encouraged the growth of Catholic organizations that might resist liberalism and strengthen the Church as a distinct counter-society.[7] It assured that the same policies were observed throughout the Church. These measures underlined the importance of faith for all dimensions of human life—including social, economic, and political affairs—against the attempts by some secular authorities to circumscribe or control the practice or influence of faith in the public arena.[8]

A more assertive papacy and its policy of defense and opposition led the popes to supervise and control Catholic intellectual life more closely than they had ever done before. Their campaign against objectionable theories and assertions helps to account for the more frequent appearance of encyclical letters, the greater recourse to the Index of

[5] The high point of the movement to promote papal authority and the strongest vindication of it was the First Vatican Council's solemn definition of papal primacy and infallibility in 1870; see DS, 3050–75. For Latin and English texts of the dogmatic constitution *Pastor aeternus*, see Tanner, 2:811-6.

[6] For a description of Ultramontanism, see chapter 9, note 64, above.

[7] The Vatican newspaper *Civiltà Cattolica* played a prominent role in the effort against liberalism. Pius IX had presided over its founding in 1850 and entrusted it to the Jesuits. Throughout the rest of the century it promoted a staunchly Ultramontanist perspective, broadcast the teachings of Roman theologians, and faithfully supported the political and theological interests of the Holy See. Its reputation as a semiofficial source gave it considerable influence among an ever larger readership in the Church. Hocedez, *Histoire de la Théologie*, 2:350-2.

For further discussion of Ultramontanism as it developed in various parts of Europe see Congar, "L'Ecclésiologie de la Révolution Français"; 95–106; Roger Aubert, "La Geographie ecclésiologique au XIXe siècle," *L'Ecclésiologie au XIXe siècle*, 11–55.

[8] Congar, "L'Ecclésiologie de la Révolution Français," 87–91; Joseph A. Komonchak, "The Ecclesial and Cultural Roles of Theology," *CTSAP* 40 (1985) 16–8.

Forbidden Books, and the publication in 1864 of the *Syllabus of Errors*.[9] The Holy See also intervened in order to specify what was to be taught or held by Catholic theologians and philosophers. That positive effort of control culminated in the 1879 encyclical letter of Pope Leo XIII, *Aeterni Patris*, which required Catholic scholars to adhere to the doctrine of Thomas Aquinas.[10] As the Holy See insisted on greater conformity and cooperation with its program of defense and opposition, Catholic intellectuals lost a good deal of their traditional liberty, within the limits of orthodox faith, to debate with one another and to propose different ways of addressing doctrinal or pastoral problems.

Hierarchical Authority as a Theological Source

As Church authority assumed an ever higher profile, Roman theologians did their part by emphasizing the prerogatives of the hierarchy in general and the Roman pontiff in particular. Jesuit theologians at the Gregorian University elaborated a theology that presupposes the necessity of divine revelation if people are to know what they must believe and do for their salvation. That purpose also requires that God's revelation, which includes the natural law, should be safely preserved over time and taught to the Church with clarity and certitude. As the duly appointed successors of Christ's apostles, the bishops carry out these necessary functions with the assistance of the Holy Spirit. The rest of the Church is to recognize the teaching authority, or magisterium, of the hierarchy and receive its teachings with obedience and

---

[9] John P. Boyle, "The 'Ordinary Magisterium': Towards a History of the Concept," *HJ* 20 (1979) 380–1.

The *Syllabus of Errors* was a summary of propositions that had already been condemned in encyclical letters and other papal interventions. The bald formulation of many of the objectionable statements and the absence of the original literary context allowed many to view the *Syllabus* as a crude and unreasonable document and Pius IX as an extreme reactionary who rejected democratic government in principle. For excerpts in English translation see Sidney Z. Ehler and John B. Marrall, eds., *Church and State Through the Centuries: A Collection of Historic Documents with Commentaries* (London: Burns & Oates; Westminster, Md.: Newman Press, 1954) 282–5; or Louis L. Snyder, *Fifty Major Documents of the Nineteenth Century* (Princeton: Van Nostrand, 1955) 116–20; for the Latin text and references to earlier sources, see DS, 2901–80. The encyclical letter *Quanta cura*, which accompanied the *Syllabus*, can be found in Carlen, *Papal Encyclicals 1740–1878*, 381–6. For the background to these texts see Hales, *Catholic Church in the Modern World*, 123–32; Hocedez, *Histoire de la Théologie*, 2:375-7.

[10] See Claudia Carlen, ed., *The Papal Encyclicals 1878–1903* (Wilmington, N.C.: McGrath Publishing Co., 1981) 17–27. For a discussion of this encyclical, see McCool, *Catholic Theology in the Nineteenth Century*, 226–40.

gratitude. In the words of the Gospel, whoever hears the authorized teachers hears Christ himself (see Luke 10:16). Later proponents of this theology located Church teaching authority primarily in the Roman pontiff.

This theology of hierarchical authority drew its strength from long-standing trends in Catholic thought as well as the Ultramontanism and controversial needs of the nineteenth century. Its impact on Catholic life and thought since that time has been great. By attributing great importance to the hierarchical functions of handing down and teaching matters of faith and morals, it endowed contemporary official teachings with unprecedented dignity and status and recognized them as a theological source to be respected by all believers, theologians included.[11] Quite apart from the content of those teachings, that theology tends to place the Scriptures, the Fathers, and the other monuments of faith in a shadow and diminish their influence over theological discussions and official teachings.[12] Although that basic tension and an analogous one in the domain of morals has produced serious strains, it has also stimulated valuable theological research into the relationships among the scriptural word, the Church, faith, and knowledge.[13]

Faith and Reason

Another contribution of Catholic scholars to the Church's strategy was their response to liberalism's assumption that human reason alone

---

[11] The classic statement of this position is found in Pope Pius XII's 1950 encyclical letter *Humani generis*, 18, 20; DS, 3884–5.

[12] See, for example, *Humani generis*, 21.

[13] For a review of this theology and those who principally developed it (e.g., Giovanni Perrone, Carlo Passaglia, Clemens Schrader, John Baptist Franzelin, Domenico Palmieri, and Louis Billot) see T. Howland Sanks, *Authority in the Church: A Study in Changing Paradigms* (Missoula, Mont.: American Academy of Religion and Scholars' Press, 1974) 21–128; for the historical and theological background of the present discussion, see 11–20; also see Avery Dulles, *A Church to Believe In: Discipleship and the Dynamics of Freedom* (New York: Crossroad, 1984) 103–32; Francis A. Sullivan, *Magisterium: Teaching Authority in the Catholic Church* (New York: Paulist Press, 1983), especially 24–51; John P. Boyle, "The Natural Law and the Magisterium," *Readings in Moral Theology No. 3: The Magisterium and Morality,* ed. Charles E. Curran and Richard A. McCormick (New York: Paulist Press, 1982) 430–60; idem, "Ordinary Magisterium"; idem, *Church Teaching Authority: Historical and Theological Studies* (Notre Dame: University of Notre Dame Press, 1995); Yves Congar, "A Semantic History of the Term 'Magisterium'"; idem, "A Brief History of the Forms of the Magisterium and Its Relations with Scholars," *Readings in Moral Theology No. 3,* 297–331.

provides sure knowledge of the truth necessary for human life. That view, which is a form of rationalism, leaves no place for supernatural revelation and tacitly denies that people have any need of it. Because rationalism constituted a powerful and appealing system of thought, it was urgent that Catholic thinkers disprove its claims and show that faith makes a valid contribution to human knowledge. That rebuttal was largely formulated by Joseph Kleutgen, S.J. (1811–83), who traced the problem to the defects of post-Cartesian thought. Reacting against liberal rationalism, Kantian idealism, and several Catholic responses that he judged to be faulty, Kleutgen drew upon the resources of an earlier Scholasticism to account for human knowledge and the validity and certitude of Christian faith. Presupposing a sharp distinction between nature and grace, he held that the resources of natural reason can establish that God, who cannot deceive, has spoken to humanity through Jesus Christ and that Jesus is God's accredited channel of revelation. Unaided reason does not prove the doctrines of faith but can show that the act of faith is entirely reasonable. Once posited through grace and freedom, the act of faith gives a person access to the necessary and certain truths of divine revelation.

Approaching the matter that way, Kleutgen was able to confront rationalism on its own ground and still uphold the supernatural and gratuitous quality of faith. Although he places great confidence in human reason, he assigns it a subordinate and largely apologetic role. Based squarely on faith, theology is to develop the implications latent in the eternal truths of divine revelation by means of a deductive approach that yields necessary and certain conclusions. Reference to other theological or historical sources has no purpose save to buttress or illuminate the truth that is already known by faith. That approach reflected the sharp contrast between reason and faith and between the Church and the world that marked Kleutgen's era. It dovetailed with the theology of Church teaching authority just noted. It grounded a sustained effort to attack liberalism with its own weapons and to present a reasoned defense of faith and morality to the larger society. Although his approach depreciated history, community, and the more spiritual, nonpropositional forms of knowledge, it commanded wide acceptance.[14] It

---

[14] These defects can be attributed in good measure to Kleutgen's sources and education. Rather than working directly from the texts of Thomas Aquinas and other representatives of high medieval Scholasticism, Kleutgen relied upon later commentators, notably Francisco Suarez (1548–1617). It also appears that his thinking reflected the Scholasticism of the German Enlightenment, largely dominated by Christian Wolff (1679–1754). The tendency of Kleutgen and his contemporaries to rely upon abstract, deductive, and juridical approaches and their interest in certitude and necessity seem to reflect the presuppositions, methods, and concerns of

is taken for granted in the First Vatican Council's statement on reason and faith, *Dei Filius;*[15] informs Pope Leo XIII's encyclical on Catholic intellectual life, *Aeterni Patris;*[16] and has continued to be influential until well after the Second World War.[17]

Capital and Labor

A prominent feature of nineteenth-century life was the plight of the working class and the economic and political turbulence that resulted from its grievances. Although the Church was slow to understand those developments or to appreciate their economic and political dimensions, during the second half of the century local leaders gained a much better grasp of the matter. Among them, Bishop Wilhelm von Ketteler of Mainz (1811–77) was especially important and exercised a primary influence on Pope Leo XIII (1878–1903). Drawing upon those resources and his own experience, Pope Leo took up the contentious problem of capital and labor in an 1891 encyclical, *Rerum novarum.*[18]

Since the beginning of the Industrial Revolution the economic condition of the workers had become quite difficult and had precipitated bitter arguments over how to respond. On the one hand, liberal economic principles declared that wages and working conditions were determined by whatever a worker agreed to accept. That contract was not to be questioned, even if it seemed to be unfair or reflected the poor bargaining position of most workers. The inequities that resulted from that approach provoked socialists to offer a very different remedy. They viewed workers as an oppressed class whose rights could be secured only if private property was abolished and goods held in common. Socialists promised that their approach would give everyone a

---

an age considerably later than that of Thomas Aquinas. See Giorgio Tonelli, "Wolff, Christian," *EP,* 7-8:340-4; Vernon J. Bourke, *History of Ethics* (Garden City, N.Y.: Doubleday, 1968) 163–4; A. Robert Caponigri, *Renaissance to the Romantic Age* (Chicago: Henry Regnery, 1963) 402–3, 429–33; Congar, *History of Theology,* 180, 185; McCool, *Catholic Theology in the Nineteenth Century,* 28–9, 186–7; see also chapter 10, note 62, above.

[15] Tanner, 2:804-11; DS, 3000–45; also the discussion in McCool, *Catholic Theology in the Nineteenth Century,* 216–26.

[16] Carlen, *Papal Encyclicals, 1878–1903,* 17–27; Congar, *History of Theology,* 184–7.

[17] This discussion has primarily followed McCool, *Catholic Theology in the Nineteenth Century;* see also Hocedez, *Histoire de la Théologie,* 1:131-51, 2:27-182, 289-366, 395-9; 3:45-52, 190-221; P. J. FitzPatrick, "Neoscholasticism," *CHLMP,* 838–52; Thomas Franklin O'Meara, *Church and Culture: German Catholic Theology, 1860–1914* (Notre Dame and London: University of Notre Dame Press, 1991), especially 25–50; Boyle, *Church Teaching Authority,* 30–42.

[18] For the text see Carlen, *Papal Encyclicals 1878–1903,* 241–61.

fair share of society's resources. Both of these positions had attracted the support of Catholics.

Against the socialists, Pope Leo defended private property and insisted that it was essential to the well being of workers and their families. Against the liberals, he condemned greed and abusive working conditions and denied that a contract can be merely the private affair of two individuals. Rather, the arrangement between owners and workers needs to be evaluated in light of its social and communitarian context and the requirements of human dignity. Wages must afford a decent living to an employee and his family. Working people have an inherent right to form unions to better their personal and economic situation, which states are to respect. The notion of class conflict and the suggestion that capital and labor are necessarily opposed are both erroneous. Community binds everyone together; owners and workers should act toward each other in a just, fair, and respectful way; and both should contribute to their society. The state is to guarantee that each person is equal under the law, "safeguard the community and all its members" (*Rerum novarum,* 35), and see to the proper fulfillment of distributive justice.

Rerum novarum marks a new turn in the Church's relationship with the modern world. In the context of nineteenth-century affairs, it represented a more positive engagement by the Church with contemporary society and its problems. Pope Leo based his proposals on a careful assessment of the facts and the various responses that had been put forward. Although he called for personal virtue, the pope recognized that social, economic, and political realities needed to be viewed structurally and judged on that basis. He highlighted the ideological substructure of both liberal and socialist proposals and countered with a very different program that was grounded in the Gospel as well as natural rights and obligations. In so doing, he reminded everyone that Christian faith needs to be translated into suitable action on behalf of justice and peace in society. Leo's encyclical on capital and labor made a deep impression in his own day and began an important new tradition of thought, literature, and action on social issues in the Catholic community.[19]

---

[19] William Murphy, "In the Beginning: Rerum Novarum (1891)," *Building the Free Society: Democracy, Capitalism, and Catholic Social Teaching,* ed. George Weigel and Robert Royal (Grand Rapids: Eerdmans, 1993) 1–30; David Hollenbach, "Modern Catholic Teachings Concerning Justice," *The Faith That Does Justice: Examining the Christian Sources for Social Change,* ed. John C. Haughey (New York: Paulist Press, 1977) 210–5; idem, *Claims in Conflict: Retrieving and Renewing the Catholic Human Rights Tradition* (New York: Paulist Press, 1979), especially 43–50; Hocedez, *Histoire de la Théologie,* 3:184-90. For a general introduction to Catholic social thought, see

The Modernist Crisis

The animosity between the Catholic Church and the world of the nineteenth century was in some respects the product of unresolved tensions over the relationship between faith and history. Does faith reflect nothing more than human needs and aspirations, or is it based on firm objective foundations that persons need to acknowledge? How can faith, which pertains to eternal truths known by divine revelation and transmitted by authorized witnesses, be reconciled with natural knowledge and sound reasoning, which recognize no formal authority and are historically conditioned? By the turn of the twentieth century research into Christian origins, the history of dogmas, and especially the interpretation of the biblical text had given these questions new urgency. Some Catholics saw the issue in terms of a dilemma: to adhere to Catholic faith was to lose the respect of educated people, while to embrace the findings of modern scholarship was to compromise one's standing in the Church. To resolve this painful conflict some proposed that faith should be understood as a purely historical phenomenon that reflects the aspirations and requirements of contemporary society. They asserted that this notion of faith would boost the Church's credibility and enable it to serve people more effectively.

Modernism is the outlook or disposition that produced that proposal. Although some of the laity and perhaps a bishop were Modernists, most of its proponents were priests, including such leaders as Alfred Loisy (1857–1940) and George Tyrrell (1861–1909). Modernists located the essence of Christianity in its spirit. They believed that faith and doctrine have no stable or objective basis but evolve with the cultural and historical circumstances. Although Modernism was more a movement than a clearly defined set of teachings, its basic premises can be allowed only at the cost of stripping Catholic faith of its grounds and integrity and denying the Church any adequate basis on which to challenge or evangelize contemporary societies.

Pope Pius X (1903–14) condemned Modernism in 1907. In his encyclical *Pascendi Dominici gregis*[20] the pope left no doubt that he con-

Charles E. Curran and Richard A. McCormick, eds., *Readings in Moral Theology No. 5: Official Catholic Social Teaching* (New York and Mahwah, N.J.: Paulist Press, 1986). For developments from the time of Leo XII until the 1960s, see Richard L. Camp, *The Papal Ideology of Social Reform: A Study in Historical Development 1878–1967* (Leiden: E. J. Brill, 1969); Jean-Yves Calvez and Jacques Perrin, *The Church and Social Justice: The Social Teaching of the Popes from Leo XIII to Pius XII (1878–1958)* (London: Burns & Oates; Chicago: Henry Regnery, 1961).

[20] Claudia Carlen, ed., *The Papal Encyclicals 1903–1939* (Wilmington, N.C.: McGrath Publishing Co., 1981) 71–97. For the Latin text, see *ASS* 40 (1907) 593–652; for the essentials, DS, 3475–500. Two months earlier, the Holy See had published

sidered Modernism to be an extremely dangerous heresy. He synthesized its disparate elements into a coherent whole, analyzed it in detail, and stated the Church's official response. Pius ordered local bishops to take a wide range of actions to uproot Modernism from the Church and prevent it from returning. These measures, which were to be applied with "diligence and severity" (*Pascendi*, 49), included dismissing Modernist sympathizers from seminary and university faculties, careful screening of candidates for ordination, censorship or prohibition of books, supervision of priests' gatherings and their literary work, and the establishment in each diocese of a "Council of Vigilance." These councils were to seek out "every trace and sign of modernism both in publications and in teaching, and, to preserve from it the clergy and the young, . . . take all prudent, prompt and efficacious measures" (55). In a later intervention Pius required professors to clear their textbooks and course contents with the bishop. He also promulgated an oath against Modernism, which was to be sworn by all priests prior to their ordination and whenever they assumed important offices or ministries.[21]

Pope Pius X defeated Modernism's threat to the Catholic Church at a heavy cost. Especially after 1910 the acute sensitivity of research into the historical dimensions of the scriptural text deterred Catholics from attempting to do significant work in that area. In the post-Modernist decades competent and faithful Catholic scholars fell under suspicion, and some of them were personally sanctioned or saw their works suppressed. As time passed there was a greater expectation that everyone would abide by what had been authoritatively established and resist the appeal of "novelty." There developed an atmosphere of suspicion, defensiveness, and vigilance that lasted until the time of the Second Vatican Council.[22]

---

the decree *Lamentabili*, which condemned sixty-five propositions associated with Modernism. See Bernard M. G. Reardon, ed., *Roman Catholic Modernism* (Stanford: Stanford University Press, 1970) 242–8; also DS, 3401–74; or *ASS* 40 (1907) 470–8.

[21] For the essentials, see Roy J. Deferrari, trans., *The Sources of Catholic Dogma* (St. Louis and London: Herder, 1957) 549–51; or DS, 3537–50; the full text of the document *Sacrorum antistitum*, issued as a *motu proprio*, can be found in *AAS* 2 (1910) 655–80.

[22] Michael V. Gannon has offered this portrayal of the situation in the U.S.A.: "The Church of the United States was overcome by a *grande peur*. As 1908 proceeded on its course a gradually enveloping dread of heresy settled over episcopal residences, chanceries, seminaries, and Catholic institutions of higher learning. Security, safety, conservatism became national imperatives. Free intellectual inquiry in ecclesiastical circles came to a virtual standstill. The nascent intellectual movement went underground or died. Contacts with Protestant and secular thinkers were broken off. It was as though someone had pulled a switch and the lights had failed all across

The Significance of These Developments

Any fair assessment of this period will acknowledge that liberal individualism and Modernism were incompatible with Christian faith and would dissolve the Church's integrity and mission. In response, Catholic leaders expanded papal authority, organized the Church against internal and external dangers, and developed an intellectual rebuttal to rationalist thinking. These steps involved important consequences for Catholic religious and moral life.

First of all, the Church's strategy of defense hindered its members from developing a more satisfactory response to principal questions of the day, especially the relationships between Christian faith and human history and between sacred authority and secular science. Against liberalism and Modernism the popes rightly insisted upon the objective quality of religious truth. But the Church also needed to acknowledge the historical dimensions of the Scriptures, Jesus Christ, and the Catholic intellectual tradition. Such an acknowledgment would have made it possible for scholars to craft a more adequate account of faith, address the basic issues raised by modernity, and help believers to make better sense of their participation in a contingent and historical world. At the time, however, official policies and the prevailing intellectual presuppositions obstructed that course of action. In the meanwhile people were given to understand that the world is a thoroughly secular place; modern thought is dangerous and perhaps heretical; faith and truth are unchanging; and therefore Catholics do well to adhere closely to the faith, discipline, and teachings of the Church.[23]

An extensive and forceful use of papal authority also characterizes this period. In addition to the actions that have already been noted, the popes issued a long series of encyclicals and allocutions in which they

---

the American Catholic landscape" ("Before and After Modernism: The Intellectual Isolation of the American Priest," *The Catholic Priest in the United States: Historical Investigations,* ed. John Tracy Ellis [Collegeville: St. John's University Press, 1971] 340–1).

On Modernism generally, see Roger Aubert, "La théologie catholique durant la première moitié du XXe siècle," *Bilan de la théologie du XX siècle,* ed. Robert Vander Gucht and Herbert Vorgrimler (Paris: Casterman, 1970) 1:423-8; idem, "Modernism," *SM,* 4:99-104; Hales, *Catholic Church in the Modern World,* 169–92; Raymond E. Brown and Thomas Aquinas Collins, "Church Pronouncements," *NJBC,* 1167–74; Reardon, *Roman Catholic Modernism;* Avery Dulles, *The Assurance of Things Hoped For: A Theology of Christian Faith* (New York and Oxford: Oxford University Press, 1994) 100–4; Marvin R. O'Connell, *Critics on Trial: An Introduction to the Catholic Modernist Crisis* (Washington: The Catholic University of America Press, 1995). For a review of official policies and actions concerning Scripture studies, see Brown, "Church Pronouncements," 1167, 1170–2.

[23] Aubert, "La théologie catholique," 427–8.

have addressed a wide range of political, disciplinary, doctrinal, and moral issues. Their teachings have provided clear and publicly accessible norms and reflections on many issues, but in so doing they have also made the problem of integration more acute. When there seems to be a conflict, how are papal teachings to be reconciled with other respected doctrinal sources? How does the papal office relate to other acknowledged authorities? Because these questions have ecclesial, pastoral, theological, and personal dimensions, they can be complex and difficult to address. They have pushed the issues of personal conscience and ecclesial authority into high relief, placed the spotlight on the relationship between authority and truth, and complicated the relationship between theologians and bishops. The currency of these issues and the pastoral turbulence they sometimes generate can be attributed at least in part to the Church's strategy of response to liberalism and Modernism.

WINDS OF CHANGE

The defensive, adversarial strategy of the nineteenth and twentieth centuries had an impact on practically all important areas of Catholic life. Although intellectual pursuits were especially sensitive and scholars fell under close supervision and control, they managed to carry out groundbreaking investigations into important historical, scriptural, philosophical, and theological questions. In fact, by working faithfully in an often unfavorable environment, scholars were able to establish the intellectual foundations on which the Second Vatican Council constructed its very different understanding of the Church's domestic life and its relationship with the world. Also decisive were the biblical and liturgical renewals and the simple fact that the world of the early 1960s was very different from that of 1860 or 1910. This section will review these developments and show how they provided the resources and experiences that enabled the council to reorient the Church to its own sources and give it a much more open posture toward the modern world, its people, history, and cultures.

The Intellectual Foundations of the Council

Pope Leo XIII's insistence that Catholic scholars adhere to the doctrine of Thomas Aquinas proved to be one of the most fertile sources of intellectual development in the early twentieth century. As they pursued a better understanding of St. Thomas, scholars deepened their knowledge of Scholastic texts and the substantive issues discussed in them. They saw more clearly that their medieval predecessors differed among themselves and that the historical context was indispensable to a sound understanding of the questions they treated and the positions they took. As their own competence increased, some scholars began to engage modern thought in a more positive if still critical way. That interchange provided a catalyst for the transcendental Thomism of such figures as Maurice Blondel (1865–1949) and Joseph Maréchal (1878–1944). Moving away from the late-nineteenth-century apologetic, Blondel related faith to the inner longing for God that people commonly experience. His approach offered a way to reunite experience, spirituality, and faith in a way that had not been done in centuries.[24] It also provided a basis on which Karl Rahner, S.J. (1904–84), Bernard Lonergan, S.J. (1904–84), and others constructed their systems of thought.[25]

Because the campaign against Modernism had made biblical research too sensitive, many scholars turned instead to the Fathers of the Church, medieval theology, and the background of Church doctrines. Their patient and steady efforts not only produced critical editions of important texts and clarified their meaning but highlighted the strong Augustinian currents in the tradition and the intensely spiritual concerns of ancient and medieval theologians. By the beginning of the Second World War they had published a large number of studies that made these sources more widely accessible. What was even more significant, their findings demonstrated that Christian sources were historically situated, diverse in nature, and highly attuned to the spiritual dynamics of Christian life. Their research undermined the notions that dogmas are invariable and that the Church in every age has stated and understood them in the same way. They showed that the rationalistic approach to faith, in vogue since the nineteenth century, did not represent a traditional consensus. Once they lost confidence in that prevailing view, theologians had to formulate a more satisfactory account of religious truth. If that effort succeeded, it might enable the Church to respond more positively to contemporary needs.[26]

[24] On Blondel, see Yves M.-J. Congar, *Tradition and Traditions: An Historical and a Theological Essay,* trans. Michael Naseby and Thomas Rainborough (New York: Macmillan; London: Burns & Oates, 1966) 215–7; Mark Schoof, *Breakthrough: Beginnings of the New Catholic Theology,* trans. N. D. Smith (Dublin: Gill & Macmillan, 1970) 49–53; Gerald A. McCool, *The Neo-Thomists* (Milwaukee: Marquette University Press, 1994) 45–50; Dulles, *Assurance of Things Hoped For,* 107–10.

[25] Aubert, "La théologie catholique," 424–9; FitzPatrick, "Neoscholasticism," 847–52; John A. Gallagher, *Time Past, Time Future: An Historical Study of Catholic Moral Theology* (New York and Mahwah, N.J.: Paulist Press, 1990) 151–8; McCool, *Catholic Theology in the Nineteenth Century,* especially 241–67; idem, *Neo-Thomists.* McCool highlights the pluralism that emerged as scholars tried to revive Thomistic philosophy.

[26] Aubert, "La théologie catholique," 429–32.

By the end of the Second World War the sweeping implications of earlier historical, philosophical, and theological research had begun to appear. In 1946 Henri de Lubac, S.J. (1896–1991) published *Surnaturel*, a detailed study of the relationship between nature and grace, including the origin and use of the term "supernatural" itself. De Lubac showed that the Fathers and Thomas Aquinas did not distinguish natural and supernatural ends and that this distinction became prominent only much later. He argued that the weight of the tradition supports the view that persons are created for union with God and have an inner desire for it. With divine grace this longing for God can give rise to personal faith. Although de Lubac produced strong evidence for those views, some theologians greeted them with dismay. Their problem was as alarming as it was simple: if de Lubac was correct, then the prevailing understandings of nature and grace and of philosophy and theology could no longer be sustained. Moreover, to suggest that the supernatural order is somehow embraced in the natural is to cast doubt on a key premise of the Church's rejection of Modernism and threaten to widen the path to historicism, immanentism, and pantheism. De Lubac's book stimulated much theological discussion, drew a response from Pope Pius XII,[27] and provoked personal restrictions against its author. Nevertheless, the power of de Lubac's evidence and argument eventually won the day, and the traditional synthesis he had recovered became another pillar of the Second Vatican Council.[28]

In the period following World War II these philosophical, historical, and theological studies supported a general *ressourcement*, or return to the sources. Perhaps the most important and best known representative of this movement is Yves Congar, O.P. (1904–95). From his youth Congar had been deeply interested in Christian unity. Prompted by

---

[27] *Humani generis*, 25–6; DS, 3890–1.

[28] Henri de Lubac's book *Surnaturel: Études historiques* (Paris: Aubier, 1946) and the foundational issue of nature and grace have generated a great deal of literature. See, for example, idem, *Augustinianism and Modern Theology*, trans. Lancelot Sheppard (New York: Herder & Herder, 1968); idem, *The Mystery of the Supernatural*, trans. Rosemary Sheed (New York: Herder & Herder, 1967); idem, *A Brief Catechesis on Nature and Grace*, trans. Richard Arnandez (San Francisco: Ignatius Press, 1984); see also Hans Urs von Balthasar, *The Theology of Henri de Lubac: An Overview*, trans. Joseph Fessio and others (San Francisco: Ignatius Press, 1991); Joseph A. Komonchak, "Theology and Culture at Mid-Century: The Example of Henri de Lubac," *TS* 51 (1990) 579–602; Karl Rahner, "Nature and Grace," *Theological Investigations*, trans. Kevin Smyth (Baltimore: Helicon Press; London: Darton, Longman & Todd, 1966) 4:165-88; Schoof, *Breakthrough*, 108–15; Stephen J. Duffy, *The Graced Horizon: Nature and Grace in Modern Catholic Thought* (Collegeville: The Liturgical Press, 1992) especially 50–84. In 1983 Pope John Paul II appointed Henri de Lubac to the College of Cardinals.

that and other contemporary concerns, he undertook detailed studies of the Church as the Catholic tradition has understood and lived it. Among his many writings Congar produced landmark studies on the laity, the ecclesial tradition, and the reform of the Church.[29] By emphasizing the scriptural, baptismal, sacramental, collegial, and spiritual dimensions of Church life, Congar offered believers a much richer and more fruitful insight into the Church and counterbalanced a theology that tended to be overly juridical and hierarchical. Although he too suffered from official sanctions, Congar became a primary influence at the Second Vatican Council and the intellectual force behind much of its work on revelation and tradition, the Church, the laity, and Christian unity.[30]

The Biblical Renewal

Although the Holy See had discouraged scholars from treating sensitive exegetical issues, Pope Pius XII inaugurated a more constructive policy in his 1943 encyclical *Divino afflante Spiritu*. In that letter Pius recognized that the biblical text is composed of different kinds of writing and explicitly endorsed the use of historical-critical methods in dealing with it. He encouraged Catholic scholars to address issues that they had previously bypassed and to interpret the sacred text in light of sound evidence as well as the Catholic tradition. Pius' encyclical opened a new era of scriptural studies in the Catholic Church. As scholars attended to technical questions they saw how important were the religious meaning of the sacred text and the historical dimensions of the economy of salvation. Their work amplified the power of the Scriptures to speak to people's hearts and call them to conversion. It prompted moral theologians to give greater priority to the properly Christian dynamics of moral life.[31] The biblical renewal's most impor-

---

[29] Yves Congar, *Vraie et fausse réforme dans l'Église* (Paris: Éditions du Cerf, 1950); idem, *Lay People in the Church: A Study for a Theology of Laity*, rev. ed., trans. Donald Attwater (Westminster, Md.: Newman Press, 1965), originally published in 1953; idem, *Tradition and Traditions*, originally published in 1960 and 1963.

[30] Schoof, *Breakthrough*, especially 93–108, 194–200, 210–4; Aubert, "La théologie catholique," 444–57, 461–5, 471–3; see also Avery Dulles, "Yves Congar: In Appreciation," *America* 173, n. 2 (July 15–22, 1995) 6–7. In 1994, shortly before his death, Yves Congar also became a member of the College of Cardinals.

[31] The influence of biblical studies can be seen, for example, in Fritz Tillmann, *Die Idee der Nachfolge Christi* (1934), which bases moral theology on the following of Christ; Gerard Gilleman, *The Primacy of Charity in Moral Theology* (first published in 1952); Bernard Häring, *The Law of Christ: Moral Theology for Priests and Laity*, whose original German text began to appear in 1954. Häring's insistence that the moral life expresses one's response to God's personal call has been especially influential.

tant contribution was simply to open God's life-giving word more fully to pastors, theologians, and ordinary members of the Church.[32]

The Liturgical Movement

After beginning in the 1830s as a Benedictine reform movement, the liturgical renewal spread to the Church at large both in Europe and beyond, including North America. This renewal was fueled by a study of liturgical texts and practices as well as by the popular participation that is inherent to the liturgy. As scholarship uncovered how the Church worshiped in the past, it drew attention to the differences between some contemporary customs and what earlier praxis had consecrated. Research had also emphasized the scriptural foundations, christocentric nature, symbolic power, and participatory texture of the liturgy. Baptism emerged as a sacrament of initiation into the Church, the Eucharist as the primary celebration of communion with God and neighbor in Christ, and penance as the way the Church reconciles grave sinners to God.

While scholars pursued their studies, the liturgical movement embraced an ever widening circle of laity and clergy. Besides helping to propagate scholarly findings, this grass-roots involvement brought personal and social concerns to the fore and highlighted the liturgy's tendency to bring faith and daily life together. Papal actions to promote music in the liturgy, encourage more frequent Communion, and revise certain aspects of Catholic worship called yet more attention to the liturgy. Pope Pius XII's 1947 encyclical *Mediator Dei* confirmed the legitimacy of the liturgical movement and began a period in which the Holy See allowed numerous changes in Catholic worship. By the early 1960s many people had concluded that a more radical reform of the Roman liturgy was needed and expected that the Second Vatican Council would mandate it.[33]

For the recent history of moral theology, see Josef-Georg Ziegler, "Théologie morale," *Bilan de la théologie du XXe siècle,* ed. Robert Vander Gucht and Herbert Vorgrimler (Tournai-Paris: Casterman, 1970) 2:520-4; Joseph Comblin, "La théologie catholique depuis la fin du pontificat de Pie XII," *Bilan de la théologie du XX siècle,* 1:490-1; Aubert, "La théologie catholique," 432–4; Gallagher, *Time Past, Time Future,* 140–83; Raphael Gallagher, "The Manual System of Moral Theology Since the Death of Alphonsus," *ITQ* 51 (1985) 6–14; Häring, *Law of Christ,* 1:22-33.

[32] Brown, "Church Pronouncements," 1167–8, 1170–1; Aubert, "La théologie catholique," 429–31; 449–53.

[33] Virgil C. Funk, "Liturgical Movement, The (1830–1969)," *The New Dictionary of Sacramental Worship,* ed. Peter E. Fink (Collegeville: The Liturgical Press, 1990) 695–715; Aubert, "La théologie catholique," 438–9; 455–7.

Changes in the World

Profound transformations in the world at large also contributed to the work of the Second Vatican Council. In many countries liberal democracies had replaced national monarchies even as others began to fall under the rule of fascist or communist dictators. In that new international order the Church discovered that it shared much in common with the Western democracies, especially an abiding opposition to Nazi and communist regimes. Contrary to earlier fears, experience demonstrated that the Church could do quite well in a liberal society. Reflecting on the Catholic experience in the United States, John Courtney Murray, S.J. (1904–67), developed a theology of religious tolerance that was based not on expediency but on the principle of respect for human dignity and the right of personal conscience to be free of coercion. The rise of secularism, common experiences in wartime, and positive encounters among members of different Christian communions promoted the ecumenical movement. Travel, technology, and more efficient means of communication had given people better knowledge about their world and easier access to one another. The cumulative effects of these and other changes were great and encouraged the Second Vatican Council to take a fresh look at the modern world and the Church's relationship with it.[34]

THE SECOND VATICAN COUNCIL

When the elderly Cardinal Angelo Roncalli succeeded to the See of Peter in 1958, no one expected that he would call an ecumenical or general council. When he made that surprising announcement on January 25, 1959, some people assumed that the upcoming council would ratify the Church's defensive stance, adopt the prevailing school theology, and solemnly condemn the errors of the modern world. But the Second Vatican Council did not take that approach. It decided to renew the Catholic Church through a more vital contact with its scriptural, liturgical, and dogmatic sources. It reconsidered the relationship between the Church and the contemporary world and called for a cooperative approach to common problems.

---

[34] John Langan, "Catholicism and Liberalism—200 Years of Contest and Consensus," *Liberalism and the Good,* ed. R. Bruce Douglass and others (New York and London: Routledge, 1990) 109–14; Robert W. McElroy, "Murray, John Courtney," *The New Dictionary of Catholic Social Thought,* ed. Judith A. Dwyer (Collegeville: The Liturgical Press, 1994) 650–3; Richard J. Regan, *Conflict and Consensus: Religious Freedom and the Second Vatican Council* (New York: Macmillan, 1967) 1–11.

Pope John's Charge to the Council

In his formal convocation of the Second Vatican Council, Pope John put forth a positive vision of the Church and its place in the world. In a word, Pope John portrayed the Church as the servant of human society. In the name of Jesus Christ, the Church is to promote whatever makes people's lives more human, remind them of their true dignity, and lead them to their eternal goal. That requires the Church to read "the signs of the times" (Matt 16:3) with keen interest and work cooperatively on society's problems. In response to Christ's will, the council should promote Christian unity through apt presentations of doctrine and fraternal charity.[35] Pope John's opening address to the council reiterated these themes and stressed the primarily pastoral nature of its task. It was not enough for the Church to preserve its doctrines with fidelity; it had a responsibility to reformulate them so that contemporary people might more readily understand and apply them to their lives. He suggested that the council should be merciful rather than severe and should prefer to explain Catholic teachings instead of condemning errors.[36]

An Overview of the Council's Work

In the opening sentence of the first document it promulgated, the council left no doubt that it fully shared Pope John's perspectives and concerns: "It is the goal of this most sacred Council to intensify the daily growth of Catholics in Christian living; to make more responsive to the requirements of our times those Church observances which are open to adaptation; to nurture whatever can contribute to the unity of all who believe in Christ; and to strengthen those aspects of the Church which can help summon all of mankind into her embrace" (*SC*, 1).[37] To achieve those goals the council undertook a series of reflections on the Church's origin, life, and mission; reassessed the world, its history, and the Church's relationship with them; and upheld the dignity of the human person. In the course of framing its views on these fundamental matters, the council developed several other topics that are integral

[35] For an English translation of Pope John's apostolic constitution *Humanae salutis* (December 25, 1961) see Walter M. Abbott, ed., *The Documents of Vatican II* (New York: America Press, 1966) 703–9. For the official Latin text, see *AAS* 54 (1962) 5–13.

[36] Abbott, *Documents of Vatican II,* 710–9. For the Latin text, see *AAS* 54 (1962) 786–95.

[37] English translations of the texts of Vatican II are taken from Abbott, *Documents of Vatican II.* The official Latin text of *SC* can be found in *AAS* 56 (1964) 97–134. *LG* is in *AAS* 57 (1965) 5–67, and most of the other documents are in *AAS* 58 (1966). See also Tanner, 2:820-1135.

to Christian life and service, notably God's word, faith and conversion, history, conscience, the dignity of the human person, and the liturgy. As it presented the basis, goals, and dynamics of Catholic faith, the council developed its personal, social, and pastoral implications and brought its moral dimensions into high relief.

The Church as Sign and Instrument of God's Plan

The council taught that God created the whole world in order to dignify human beings with a share in divine life. Sin disrupted this plan, but it did not stop God from acting on behalf of human salvation. From the earliest time God prepared for the Church, especially by intervening in the history of Israel and giving the Covenant. "Established in the present era of time, the Church was made manifest by the outpouring of the Spirit. At the end of time she will achieve her glorious fulfillment." Then, all the just who have ever lived "will be gathered together with the Father in the universal Church" (*LG*, 2).

Jesus Christ is the highest revelation of God his Father and the means by which God's plan of salvation is to be accomplished. Christ's obediential death brought humanity the forgiveness of sin and reconciliation with God that it needed. Jesus Christ established the kingdom of God on earth, and all are called to become adopted sons and daughters of God in Christ (*LG*, 3; see also *DV*, 5). After his death and resurrection the Holy Spirit was sent upon his disciples in order to make the Church holy and give it ready access to the Father. Bringing gifts of truth, unity, and perpetual renewal, "the Spirit dwells in the Church and in the hearts of the faithful as in a temple" (*LG*, 3–4). "A fellowship of life, charity, and truth" (*LG*, 9), the Church's mission is to bring everyone into full union with Christ and "to proclaim and to establish among all peoples the kingdom of Christ and of God" (*LG*, 5; see also 1, 3).

Christ's community is formed of those who hear his word with faith (*LG*, 5). Because it lives by the Holy Spirit, the Church is the body of Christ. Baptism unites new members with the death and resurrection of Christ and adds them to his Church. Although they come from all peoples, the faithful are united with God and one another and celebrate that communion in the Eucharist. Despite a diversity of gifts and functions in the Church, the faithful are to be one in love and, amid the trials of the present life, be "molded into Christ's image until He is formed in them" (*LG*, 7). At once hierarchical and mystical, visible and spiritual, earthly and blessed with heavenly gifts, the Church is called to disclaim earthly glory and carry out its mission in humility, self-sacrifice, and repentance until the end of time (*LG*, 8).

The Church as Friend of Humanity

Turning its attention specifically to the mission of the Church, the council declared that the Church is "truly and intimately linked with mankind and its history." Instead of maintaining a posture of suspicion and alienation toward the world, the council expressed compassion and claimed solidarity: "The joys and hopes, the griefs and the anxieties of the men of this age, especially those who are poor or in any way afflicted, these too are the joys and hopes, the griefs and anxieties of the followers of Christ. Indeed, nothing genuinely human fails to raise an echo in their hearts" (*GS*, 1).

These convictions and its respect and love for all humanity impelled the council to open a candid discussion of human experiences, striving, and history, including the meaning and goal of life. It promised to conduct its part of that dialogue with a humane and caring disposition and in the light of Christian faith: "The Council brings to mankind light kindled from the gospel, and puts at its disposal those saving resources which the Church herself, under the guidance of the Holy Spirit, receives from her Founder. For the human person deserves to be preserved; human society deserves to be renewed. Hence the pivotal point of our total presentation will be man himself, whole and entire, body and soul, heart and conscience, mind and will." In that presentation the Church will aim "to give witness to the truth, to rescue and not to sit in judgment, to serve and not to be served" (*GS*, 3; see also 40–2). That task requires the Church to scrutinize "the signs of the times" in light of faith, and find apt means to speak to contemporary people about the basic questions of human life (*GS*, 4).[38]

The Human Person

In order to establish an adequate basis for its response to urgent questions about society and human activity in the world, the council set forth its view of the human person. Drawing upon the resources of experience and faith, it declared that God created the human race with the ability to know and love its Creator and to use the rest of creation for worthy purposes. Created male and female, persons are inherently social by nature and need suitable relationships with others if they are

---

[38] Knowing that it must "recognize and understand the world in which we live, its expectations, its longings, and its often dramatic characteristics" (*GS*, 4), the council offers its assessment of them in *GS*, 4–10. That assessment is important also because human "happenings, needs, and desires" contain "authentic signs of God's presence and purpose," which the Church needs to understand (*GS*, 11).

to live and develop fully.[39] Although man and woman were created good, they abused their freedom by seeking fulfillment in opposition to God. That rebellion constitutes sin and has radically disrupted all human relationships. Sin accounts for the struggle between good and evil that constantly affects persons, groups, and institutions. Jesus Christ has come to free the human race from the bonds of sin and open the way to true and lasting fulfillment (*GS*, 12–3).

Although composed of body and soul, the person is one. The body is good and may not be despised even though it is wounded by sin and can be turned to evil purposes. Of even greater importance is human interiority, for by turning within, to the heart, persons can discover their spiritual nature and encounter God. Human intelligence has brought forth remarkable advances in many fields and is further evidence that persons are superior to the material universe. Such a great gift needs to be perfected by wisdom, which bids a person always to love what is good and true. Although sin has imposed hazards and limitations, intelligence makes it possible for persons to know reality with certitude (*GS*, 14–5).

Those observations on interiority and intelligence lead to a consideration of personal conscience. In their depths, each person finds the voice of conscience, which calls for the good to be loved and evil to be avoided, not only in general but also in particular circumstances. The person is to obey conscience as the voice of God and as a matter of personal integrity and dignity. Despite its highly personal and interior qualities, conscience mediates the objective requirements of human life. Conscience calls for cooperative efforts to learn truth and to find genuine solutions to human problems. It prompts persons to avoid arbitrary choices and to embrace objective moral norms. Conscience maintains its dignity when it errs in good faith but not when error occurs through culpable negligence or a habit of sin (*GS*, 16).[40]

Above all, the council insisted that the human person can be fully understood only in the light of Jesus Christ. By taking on human nature, Christ ennobled it with divine dignity and identified himself with all of his brothers and sisters. By his loving death and resurrection Christ brought humanity forgiveness of sins and reconciliation with God and one another. By being conformed to Christ through the gift of

---

[39] The council gave fuller attention to the social dimensions of humanity in *GS*, 23–32.

[40] The council also recognized the importance of conscience as a path to God: "Those also can attain to everlasting salvation who through no fault of their own do not know the Gospel of Christ or His Church, yet sincerely seek God and, moved by grace, strive by their deeds to do His will as it is known to them through the dictates of conscience" (*LG*, 16).

the Spirit, the Christian is renewed and enabled to fulfill the law of love. Although the Christian struggles against evil and experiences death, "linked with the paschal mystery and patterned on the dying Christ, he will hasten forward to the resurrection in the strength which comes from hope." Because everyone has the same ultimate end and Christ died for all, God offers every human being the possibility of salvation in Christ (*GS*, 22).

The Council's Moral Vision

The council's understanding of faith and human life is comprehensive and dynamic, and it overflows with significance for moral life. Its teachings are based upon the faith conviction that all things come forth from God and are meant to return to God. All realities and all persons therefore have a divine origin and end that are inherent to them. For the same reason, history involves God-given tendencies that are intrinsic to it. Although sin has seriously compromised the integrity of created things and generated strong countercurrents in history, God has intervened to free the human race from sin and bring his original plan to completion. These affirmations give rise to corresponding imperatives. God's creative intention, reflected in things and in history, is to be respected. God's saving word to persons is to be heard, and God's call is to be answered. These responses are required because they comply with God's will, respect the nature of things, and serve the true good of human beings.

These are the principal imperatives of Christian moral life as the Second Vatican Council presented it. However, because the council intended to promote a deeper understanding of Christian faith and faith's influence on believers' consciences, it did not want to leave its deliberations at the level of generalities. It therefore amplified certain important aspects of faith and underlined their moral implications. Its discussions of God's word, the grace of Christ, the Church, the world and its history, and the human person are especially important.

God's Word

The word of God enjoys a privileged position in Christian life. Along with sacred tradition, the Scriptures are "the supreme rule of faith." They are of paramount importance to the liturgy and must nourish and rule "all the preaching of the Church" (*DV*, 21, 24). Because the word is indispensable to its life, unity, and mission, the Church must never fail to preach it. "By the proclamation of the gospel, she prepares her hearers to receive and profess the faith, disposes them for baptism, snatches them from the slavery of error, and incorporates them into Christ so that through charity they may grow up into full maturity in Christ" (*LG*, 17; see also *LG*, 42; *DV*, 2, 7). Preaching is to nourish the People of God with the Scriptures "thereby enlightening their minds, strengthening their wills, and setting men's hearts on fire with the love of God" (*DV*, 23; see also *SC*, 24).[41]

The divine word is addressed directly to persons and claims them unreservedly. A wholehearted personal response, which the council identifies with faith, is the first requirement that the word of God presents to its recipient. "'The obedience of faith' (Rom. 16:26; cf. 1:5; 2 Cor. 10:5-6) must be given to God who reveals, an obedience by which man entrusts his whole self freely to God, offering 'the full submission of intellect and will to God who reveals,' and freely assenting to the truth revealed by Him" (*DV*, 5; see also *GS*, 24).[42] Understanding faith as a complete self-gift to God overcomes the minimalism and rationalism that often characterized the previous period and places the dynamics of response to God and communion with God at the very center of Christian life. In this light it becomes clear that faith includes both conversion from sin and evil and a dynamic toward Christian perfection (See *SC*, 9; *LG*, 7, 9, 10, 11, 40, 42). The freedom necessary to the response of faith underlines its moral significance at all points: when a person first turns toward God, when faith is explicitly confessed, and at every moment afterward (*DH*, 10; see also *GS*, 17).

The Gift of Grace

Integral to the council's teaching on God's word and the response of faith is the necessity of God's grace. "In order that we may be unceasingly renewed in him (cf. Eph. 4:23), He has shared with us His Spirit who, existing as one and the same being in the head and in the members, vivifies, unifies, and moves the whole body" (*LG*, 7; see also *LG*, 4, 8). When it speaks of faith, the council hastens to add: "If this faith is to be shown, the grace of God and the interior help of the Holy Spirit must precede and assist, moving the heart and turning it to God, opening the eyes of the mind, and giving 'joy and ease to everyone in as-

---

[41] The council declared that the Scriptures are to be easily accessible to the people (*DV*, 22) and that the laity have the right to "receive in abundance" from their pastors the assistance of the word of God (*LG*, 37). It reminded bishops that preaching is preeminent among their duties (*LG*, 25), adding that "the ministry of preaching is to be fulfilled with exactitude and fidelity" (*SC*, 35. See also *SC*, 52; *GS*, 43).

[42] The internal quotation is from a text of Vatican I (DS, 3008). For more on the response of faith, see Dulles, *Assurance of Things Hoped For*, 139–42.

senting to the truth and believing it'" (*DV*, 5).[43] In addition, God's grace must empower the efforts of unbelievers to do God's will as it is known in conscience as well as the faithful's own implementation of God's word and their participation in the liturgy (*LG*, 16, 42; *SC*, 11). The council's teaching on divine grace emphasizes the religious quality of Christian moral life and is to be borne in mind whenever the latter is considered.

The Life and Mission of the Church

The Church's life can be understood as a response to the word and grace of Christ. For that reason, faith, ongoing conversion, and the call to perfection are integral to Christian moral life. In addition, the will of Christ and the requirements of Church life include the commands to love one another and to protect and promote the unity of the Church. Closely related is a shared responsibility to the mission of the Church, which is to be carried out in humility and self sacrifice, and an obligation to manifest a special concern for the poor, the weak, and the sinful. Each member of the Church needs to "bear witness to Christ and give an answer to those who seek an account of that hope of eternal life which is in them (cf. 1 Pet. 3:15)" (*LG*, 10; see also *GS*, 24). All of the faithful are called to pray, participate in the sacraments, and contribute their own gifts in a generous and cooperative spirit (*LG*, 7–13).[44] These imperatives and the context in which they arise reflect the inherently ecclesial texture of Christian moral life.

The World and Human History

Among the most striking aspects of the council's doctrine are its positive reassessment of the world and its acknowledgment that the world and the Church can be adequately understood only if their historical dimensions are recognized. The dramatic changes recorded in the twentieth century alone are enough to demonstrate that history has a decisive impact on human life. God's creation of all things with the

---

[43] Internal quotations are from the Second Council of Orange (DS, 377) and the First Vatican Council (DS, 3010). Also pertinent is this statement: "Man, redeemed by Christ the Savior and through Christ Jesus called to be God's adopted son, cannot give his adherence to God revealing Himself unless the Father draw him to offer to God the reasonable and free submission of faith" (*DH*, 10).

[44] The council held the liturgy in such esteem that it dedicated a separate document to this aspect of Church life. The Constitution on the Sacred Liturgy should be consulted for further discussion of the liturgy's importance to Christian life and for the norms established for its reform and renewal.

intention to gather them up at the end of time communicates an even deeper significance to the universe, human beings, and their history. Furthermore, to confess that God has done great things in history, especially through Jesus Christ, is to declare that human history has a transcendent meaning that people need to understand and respect. The Church has the mandate to interpret that history and to bear witness to its claims so that all people can be reconciled, uplifted, and blessed through a living faith in Christ. These considerations have important implications for moral life.

First, because "all things are endowed with their own stability, truth, goodness, proper laws, and order," the world and the sciences have an autonomy that is to be respected (*GS*, 36; see also *GS*, 41). For that reason, there can be no excuse for shirking one's temporal responsibilities; on the contrary, Christians are to "discharge their earthly duties conscientiously and in response to the gospel spirit" (*GS*, 43).[45] This imperative has great significance for the life and work of the laity.

Second, the Church is to acknowledge its own solidarity with the human race and its history. This full acceptance of the human condition supports and promotes a cooperative relationship between the Church and the world and establishes a constructive framework for the apostolate (*GS*, 1–2; see also *LG*, 17).

Third, the transcendent horizon of human life precludes any attempt to absolutize the world or human history. The fact of sin and its many destructive effects require divine salvation and establish the context of the Church's worship, witness, and service. Because it finds no lasting home in this age, the Church is to consider itself a pilgrim in a foreign land and act as the humble servant of the Lord and all its neighbors (*LG*, 8, 16; and *GS*, 37).

Fourth, although the Church awaits no further public revelation, Jesus remains the Lord of history and continues to act in that forum on behalf of his people. Therefore believers need to scrutinize the signs of the times in light of the Gospel. This should allow them to draw out the implications of historical events for effective witness and service. The same historical flux requires the Church to reformulate its doctrines so that their saving truth is accessible to people of different times and places. The same is true of the Scriptures: "This accommodated

---

[45] In this connection the council bluntly criticizes an outlook that would locate religion "in acts of worship alone and in the discharge of certain moral obligations" and segregate it from the rest of temporal affairs. "This split between the faith which many profess and their daily lives deserves to be counted among the more serious errors of our age." Furthermore: "The Christian who neglects his temporal duties neglects his duties toward his neighbor and even God, and jeopardizes his eternal salvation" (*GS*, 43).

preaching of the revealed Word ought to remain the law of all evangelization" (*GS*, 44; see also 4, 41, 62; *LG*, 2, 9; *DV*, 3, 5, 19).

Finally, the council's reassessment of the world and human history led to a wholesale reconsideration of the responsibilities of Christian laity. The council's conclusions are explicit:

> A secular quality is proper and special to laymen. . . . The laity, by their very vocation, seek the kingdom of God by engaging in temporal affairs and by ordering them according to the plan of God. . . .
> They are called [to the ordinary circumstances of life] by God so that by exercising their proper function and being led by the spirit of the gospel they can work for the sanctification of the world from within, in the manner of leaven. In this way they can make Christ known to others, especially by the testimony of a life resplendent in faith, hope, and charity. The layman is closely involved in temporal affairs of every sort. It is therefore his special task to illumine and organize these affairs in such a way that they may always start out, develop, and persist according to Christ's mind, to the praise of the Creator and the Redeemer (*LG*, 31).[46]

The council's positive evaluation of the world and its people, its blessing of secular affairs, and its acknowledgment that history is of decisive importance rank among its most significant statements. By committing the Church to these positions and justifying them on factual, doctrinal, and mission-related grounds, the council oriented Christian moral life toward human society and the movement of history.[47]

The Human Person as Norm for Activity

When it called the faithful to a committed engagement in temporal affairs, the council recognized that it was not possible to specify the moral requirements of all conceivable cases (*GS*, 33, 43) but that an appropriate norm for moral action was still required. To answer this need, the council turned to the person and declared that activity in the world is to respect the requirements of human dignity and those of the community. Person and community do not confront one another as adversaries; rather, "the progress of the human person and the advance of society itself hinge on each other. For the beginning, the subject and the goal of all social institutions is and must be the human person, which for its part and by its very nature stands completely in need of social

---

[46] The council issued a separate Decree on the Apostolate of the Laity, which should be consulted.

[47] For more on these important points, see Marie-Dominique Chenu, "Une morale 'séculière,'" *StMor* 24 (1986) 251–6; Josef Fuchs, "The Christian Morality of Vatican II," *Human Values and Christian Morality*, trans. M. H. Heelan and others (Dublin: Gill & Macmillan, 1970) 70–4.

life" (*GS*, 25). This basic assertion gives rise to a general norm of human activity: "In accord with the divine plan and will, it should harmonize with the genuine good of the human race, and allow men as individuals and as members of society to pursue their total vocation and fulfill it" (*GS*, 35). The council elaborated more specific imperatives in light of the dignity of each person and the good of human society.

On the one hand, the dignity of the human person is the foundation of certain rights and responsibilities. "Therefore, there must be made available to all men everything necessary for leading a life truly human, such as food, clothing, and shelter; the right to choose a state of life freely and to found a family, the right to education, to employment, to a good reputation, to respect, to appropriate information, to activity in accord with the upright norm of one's own conscience, to protection of privacy and to rightful freedom in matters religious too" (*GS*, 26). The council continues:

> In our times a special obligation binds us to make ourselves the neighbor of absolutely every person, and of actively helping him when he comes across our path, whether he be an old person abandoned by all, a foreign laborer unjustly looked down upon, a refugee, a child born of an unlawful union and wrongly suffering for a sin he did not commit, or a hungry person who disturbs our conscience by recalling the voice of the Lord: "As long as you did it for one of these, the least of my brethren, you did it for me" (Mt. 25:40) (*GS*, 27).[48]

On the other hand, a "merely individualistic morality" is not enough. Rather, everyone is to "consider it his sacred obligation to count social necessities among the primary duties of modern man, and to pay heed to them." In that light, the council asked everyone to contribute to the common good according to their ability and the needs that exist. It rejected efforts to evade just moral and legal duties toward one's society, especially when doing so would compromise the well being of others. These observations highlight the close connection between Christian faith and work on behalf of social justice in the secular city (*GS*, 30).

The Significance of the Council for Moral Life

The council's most important contribution was to reorient the Church to its sources and mission and to renew the Church's relation-

---

[48] The text condemns certain activities because they are opposed to life itself. It calls for respect and love for "those who think or act differently than we do in social, political, and religious matters too" (*GS*, 28). It rejects discrimination on the basis of "sex, race, color, social condition, language, or religion," and calls for "excessive economic and social differences" among people and groups to be addressed so that the requirements of justice and human dignity may be met (*GS*, 29).

ship with the world, its people, and its history. Once the council took those foundational steps, it obtained a suitable context in which to consider Christian life and to identify its starting point and purposes, its norms and dynamics. On that basis the council unfolded imperatives that appeal directly to human freedom and are thus inherently moral in nature. Because those imperatives come from faith and shape one's response to God and neighbor, the council's elaboration of moral life was profoundly religious. By placing Christian moral life so squarely on ecclesial foundations and by drawing out its implications in such detail, the council turned a new page in the theological and pastoral history of the Church. The true dimensions of the council's work and its significance for moral life become even clearer when it is considered in the context of earlier thought and practices.

The council based the moral requirements of Christian life on the dynamics of faith and conversion, the facts of contemporary human experience, and the mission of the Church in the modern world. That approach allowed moral imperatives to emerge from human realities as they are known and interpreted by reasonable people in the light of faith. It presupposes that freedom is essential to the religious-moral response, asks nothing less than the gift of self to God and neighbor, and emphasizes that all are called to Christian holiness and to the perfection that befits the children of God. These teachings contrast with an earlier presupposition that moral life is governed by obligations that are imposed by lawful authority. In that framework specific commands or precepts call for due obedience; persons judge whether they are under obligation or are free to do as they wish and determine their actions accordingly. By binding its moral doctrine so closely to grace as well as to the faith and mission of the Church, the council gave moral life a much sturdier religious foundation, highlighted the intrinsic nature of its requirements, and protected it against legalism and minimalism.

The council reminded Catholics that they are to guide their moral and religious life in light of objective factors. These include the realities of the created universe, the events of history, and divine revelation as it is known in faith. The council upheld the responsibility and authority of the Church's pastors to illuminate the truth and guide the lives of the faithful and called upon believers to respond with *obsequium religiosum,* a submission born of religious commitment.[49]

---

[49] The term *obsequium religiosum* appears in the council's discussion of hierarchical authority (*LG,* 25). The Latin word *obsequium* is difficult to translate into English, all the more so since theological and pastoral considerations tend to affect one's translation. See Boyle, *Church Teaching Authority,* 63–78; Umberto Betti,

However, the council also manifested a profound reverence for the interior life because it is the seat of freedom and intelligence and a privileged forum in which persons encounter and respond to God. God is the ultimate authority or norm for personal conscience and takes precedence over all human authorities.[50]

When it manifested this respect for interiority and the sanctity of conscience, the council was not contradicting its statements on objectivity or introducing anything new to the Catholic tradition. However, when they are taken together, its teachings on these points constitute a more complete and more balanced account of the matter than would be the case when any of its components are absent or depreciated. In a principled and authoritative way, therefore, the council has contributed to a better understanding of human knowledge and the religious-moral response that follows. That more adequate account is important in its own right. It corrects an earlier tendency to emphasize objectivity and authority at the expense of interiority and the role of conscience, even while cautioning against the opposite extreme. Freedom is essential to moral life and the response of faith but is always to be exercised according to truth. Ecclesial authority is to illuminate truth and do so in a way that is respectful of persons and the sacred forum of conscience, in which God encounters and calls each one (*GS*, 16–7).

Integral to the council's comprehensive religious outlook is its mandate to the laity. By their baptism and a commitment born of grace and faith, laypersons have apostolic responsibilities that are to be discharged wherever they live and work. They are to engage their faith as well as their particular competencies, conscientiously determine what their practical contribution and witness are to be, and act accordingly. While they will often need the support and guidance of the clergy, the council observed that pastors cannot specify the moral requirements of every problem, nor do they have that responsibility (*GS*, 43). This vision of lay activity in the world stands in sharp contrast to earlier

---

"L'ossequio al magistero pontificio 'non ex cathedra' nel n. 25 della 'Lumen Gentium,'" *Antonianum* 62 (1987) 432–61; Joseph Komonchak, "Ordinary Papal Magisterium and Religious Assent," *Readings in Moral Theology No. 3*, 67–90; Basil C. Butler, "*Infallibile: Authenticum: Assensus: Obsequium*: Christian Teaching Authority and the Christian's Response," *DL* 31 (1981) 77–89; idem, "Authority and the Christian Conscience," *Readings in Moral Theology No. 3*, 171–87; Sullivan, *Magisterium*, 153–73; Francis A. Sullivan, *Creative Fidelity: Weighing and Interpreting Documents of the Magisterium* (New York and Mahwah, N.J.: Paulist Press, 1996) 23–4. The translation used here is based upon Sullivan's discussion of the issues.

[50] See Joseph Ratzinger, "The Dignity of the Human Person," *Commentary on the Documents of Vatican II*, ed. Herbert Vorgrimler, trans. W. J. O'Hara (Freiburg: Herder; Montreal: Palm Publishers, 1969) 5:127-36, especially 134.

attempts to base it on a specific mandate from the hierarchy or to subordinate Christian moral life to determined commands and prohibitions. It decisively abandons an approach that sifted pure nature from a supernatural order and deemed the world to be antithetical to the Church and dangerous to the faithful.

Closely related to this reconsideration of the world is the council's reevaluation of history. It acknowledged the importance of historical events because they are an important medium through which God acts. History presents dramatic challenges to peoples and individuals and is the arena in which the Church lives and carries out its mission. The council's turn toward history contrasts with an earlier campaign to oppose novelty and resist significant changes in Church thought and praxis. Moreover, to accept that the signs of the times are to be scrutinized in the light of faith, to acknowledge the inescapably prudential nature of many moral judgments, and to assert that doctrine, preaching, and liturgy all need to be accommodated to contemporary conditions is to imply that history is more decisive for Catholic life than had been admitted. It is also to make theologies that base moral life too exclusively on immutable principles seem to be incongruous.

To be sure, the council did not deny the importance of nature or repudiate a natural-law approach to moral decision making, but by attributing a pivotal significance to history, it did make the question of integration more acute. What is the relationship between nature and the "signs of the times," and what weight should each have in religious and moral reflection? How should contingent historical factors and eternal and unchanging realities be related? What is the place of moral principles, and what is the role of prudence in a person's moral life? These questions are not easy to answer and can be expected to occupy ordinary Christians, theologians, and pastors for some time to come.

Another way to grasp the significance of council's work is to consider the relationship between moral life and the sacramental celebrations of the Church. From a very early time the Church has relied upon sacramental penance to address the reality of sin within the Christian community, help sinners walk the path of conversion, and reconcile them to God. It has used the same forum to evangelize and catechize those who, although baptized, remain uncommitted. These pastoral goals and the range and magnitude of the problems have given the rituals of penance a pivotal place in Christian life, pastoral care, and theological reflection. At the same time, penitential concerns have sometimes favored an outlook that would exaggerate the threat or reality of sin, orient Christian life primarily to the avoidance of sinful acts, and see penance as the most important moment in a person's sacramental life.

In the light of this history, the council's declaration that the Eucharist is "the fount and apex of the whole Christian life" is striking (*LG*, 11; see also *SC*, 10). By upholding the centrality of the Eucharist, this statement underlines the work of God in Christ, the positive dynamics of faith, the normative quality of communion in Christian life, and the overriding claims of charity. Although it does not detract from the rightful place of penance or the other liturgical celebrations, it does mean that the moral life of the faithful should primarily draw its energy and direction from the Eucharist, including its cultic, neighbor-oriented, and self-sacrificial dimensions, and be expressed in them. The council's vindication of the Eucharist as the primary sacrament of Christian life is a significant contribution to moral life and to a more balanced, authentic, and fruitful sacramental praxis.

Finally, by renewing the Church's contact with its sources, dynamics, and mission, the council rendered much of the prevailing theology inadequate. It required theologians to update their respective disciplines so that they conformed to the fundamental requirements and imperatives of Catholic faith as the council had set them forth. Theology is to be "renewed by livelier contact with the mystery of Christ and the history of salvation." Moreover, "special attention needs to be given to the development of moral theology. Its scientific exposition should be more thoroughly nourished by scriptural teaching. It should show the nobility of the Christian vocation of the faithful, and their obligation to bring forth fruit in charity for the life of the world" (*OT*, 16). Although this mandate is brief and general in nature, it highlights pivotal areas in the council's work of renewal. It urges moral theologians to reconsider their responsibilities, sources, and methods and to make specific and far-reaching changes so that moral theology can help the faithful to worship, witness, and serve as they should. The council's injunction is further evidence that it meant to bring about a thorough renewal of Catholic religious and moral life.

REFLECTIONS

In the two centuries since the French Revolution the Catholic Church has been preoccupied with the world around it, especially European social, political, and cultural developments. For most of that period it found much in its environment to be hostile and therefore acted to protect its faith, institutional integrity, and members from external threats. The Second Vatican Council also took contemporary realities seriously, and its mandate for a new relationship with the world was similarly informed by the sources, life, and mission of the Church. Taken as a whole, therefore, this period throws the Church-world relationship into high relief, calls attention to the reciprocal influence between that relationship and the domestic life of the Church, and highlights the perennial need to discern and meet the requirements of faith.

Throughout this period the Catholic Church wrestled with the facts of history and its interpretation. At first some pointed to history as proof that Christian faith was groundless or at least stood in need of constant modification. Historical change and the needs of modern civilization were the pretext for sustained political and ideological attacks against the Church. In that environment it was perhaps to be expected that bishops and theologians would insist that truth is eternal, faith supernatural, and the Church unchanging. It is understandable that they should have viewed history as a problem that intruded from without, one that arose from false premises and erroneous thinking. However, once the Church was reminded that history is a principal medium of divine providence and the context in which popes and councils fashioned their decrees and theologians their writings, it became impossible to maintain that earlier statement of the problem. The weight of Christian sources and the economy of salvation persuaded the bishops to acknowledge the importance of history and frame theological and pastoral issues accordingly. Once the Second Vatican Council took those steps, it officially accepted the new terms of the question and recognized that history intersects with faith and all other important points in Christian life. It is now clear that faith and the moral response, pastoral care and apostolic service, can be adequately understood and fruitfully carried out only if their temporal dimensions are duly taken into account.

Besides addressing the issue of history, the council reoriented the Church to its faith, sources, and mission. It recalled the history of salvation, the centrality of Christ, and the primacy of the word for Christian life. It ordered a renewal of the liturgy and emphasized the need for all to participate actively and fruitfully. The Church is to preach, serve, and witness in the wider community; humanize the world; and help all people to live in keeping with their human dignity. Each member of the faithful is to take part in the Church's life, contribute to its unity, and promote its mission. These reminders and injunctions reflect Christian faith and the council's wish to renew the Church in its light. They trace the contours of Christian life and honor moral imperatives that flow from a Catholic faith commitment. They call attention to the religious sources, communitarian context, and apostolic purposes of faith; speak to people's hearts and minds; and respond to urgent needs in the Church and the world. The council's teachings therefore have the capacity to energize and redirect religious and moral life and constitute an ongoing challenge to everyone in the Church.

The council's reflection on the sources, life, and mission of the Church led it to change the focus and complete the picture in several areas of Church life. God was described as the fulfillment of human yearnings and faith as the free gift of self. The council related Christian moral life to the sources, dynamics, and goals of faith; accepted that the world and its history are integral to the entire discussion; and vindicated the call and mission of laypersons. It declared its reverence for the human dignity and conscience of each person. It upheld the word of God as the "the supreme rule of faith" and the Eucharist as "the fount and apex of the whole Christian life." Such statements were firmly rooted in the tradition, and none of them constituted a denial of any point that is essential to Catholic faith and life. However, when the council's actions are examined in the light of the theological situation that prevailed up to that time, it becomes clear that they corrected the balance, changed the axis, and moved the center of gravity among key elements of Christian life. Especially when they are taken together, these alterations constitute a restatement of Catholic faith as a foundation for human life. Such changes of gestalt and emphasis are likely to occasion considerable ferment, especially as some of their implications are teased out. But if the council's work is received and implemented in light of its sources, concerns, and goals, it is likely to stimulate constructive changes in theology, pastoral care, and Christian life.

Nevertheless, the record recommends both wisdom and patience. If history demonstrates the fact of change, it also shows that important changes take place gradually and often with difficulty. The medieval outlook did not easily yield to early modern discoveries about the universe. The alienation of important segments of European society from the Church took time, and so did the formulation and implementation of the Church's response. The contours and dynamics of Catholic life as they stood in the mid-twentieth century developed slowly and can be expected to perdure for some time. However, the council was a major event in the life of the Church. Its documents are readily accessible, and its teachings and decisions carry great authority. It has begun to change the thought, spirituality, and praxis of the Church and will continue to do so. These considerations suggest that the postconciliar period is likely to continue for an extended period and involve tensions between old and new that play out in many areas of Church life. As the years go by, unforeseen challenges and problems will also demand attention and leave their own imprint on Christian life. As it continues to carry out its daily responsibilities, the Church will abandon some habits of life and thought and learn others. This process can be expected to engage the faith and good judgment of everyone concerned, require them to remain attentive to God's word and the signs of the times, and place a high premium on the Eucharist and the commitment to charity that are the heart of Christian life.

Epilogue

This study has considered a wide range of persons, issues, and events and tried to show their place and importance in the bigger picture. Each has been presented with the hope that they would, when taken together, compose a portrait that highlights some of the sources and shaping of Catholic moral life. This Epilogue offers an opportunity to summarize and reflect on its scriptural, historical, intellectual, and liturgical aspects.

Principal Dimensions

That portrait gained its depth from the dynamic, temporal quality of its subject. Israel and the Church came into being on the basis of particular persons and events. These communities have a long history that includes traditions of faith, worship, learning, reflection, and a wide range of experiences. Moreover, there can be little doubt that the past continues to influence and set a standard for the life, faith, thought, and action in the Church community today. Persons also act in response to contemporary circumstances and in order to make things better for themselves, their children, and generations yet unborn. The faith-inspired hope that God will intervene with power to bring justice and peace to the human race strongly reinforces this future-oriented perspective.

Moral life obtains its breadth from the wide range of contemporary realities and challenges that confront persons and groups at any given moment. Sometimes the issues pertain to individuals, as when circumstances bear on one's integrity, relationship with God, or standing in the community; or when they require people to control their conduct and interior motivation. At other times they concern an entire community, as is the case with war or civil strife, structurally rooted injustices, matters of international trade, the cultural or legal life of the larger society, or the integrity and holiness of the Church. Moral life is always framed by present realities, claims, and conflicts and is enacted as people consider and then respond to them.

The third dimension of Christian moral life is arguably the most important: transcendence. Although the temporal and contemporary dimensions of human life are of the essence, acknowledging them does not adequately distinguish a community of faith from other human societies. Its uniqueness is closely bound to its characteristic affirmation that creation and human affairs mediate the providence and call of a God who is Lord of the universe, time, and the present moment. An acute sensitivity to the transcendent prompted the Israelites to take a keen interest in historical events and the Christian community to remember God's actions in Christ and defer to the apostolic tradition. But the present moment is equally important. The Scriptures display an intense concern for "today" and a conviction that "now" might be the time of salvation. If it is, the person or community being addressed is to seize the moment and respond decisively then and there. The witness of prophets, saints, and repentant sinners throughout Judeo-Christian history illustrates the urgency and life-changing power of these moments of grace.

The Sacred Scriptures

The moral life of the Christian community finds its earliest precedents in the experiences, faith, infidelity, and reflections of the Hebrew people; its focal point is the life, death, and resurrection of Jesus Christ, whose significance for the human race is set forth on the pages of the New Testament. Although these events ended some twenty centuries ago, they determine the principal lines and dominant tones of the overall portrait. They introduce the perennial question of faith; emphasize its historical, personal, and social qualities; and show what a fitting response involves. As the life of God's people unfolds in the scriptural texts, the importance of God's word and the community's fidelity, worship, witness, and ongoing reflection become more apparent, and its relationships with the world and the larger society likewise assume higher profile.

The Christian tradition has always revered the Sacred Scriptures as God's inspired word and an indispensable source for faith and life. The Second Vatican Council has reiterated the Church's deference to the biblical word, called for theology to be more completely nourished by it, reminded bishops and other clergy that preaching the word is a primary responsibility, and restored the Scriptures to their proper place in the liturgy. These actions emphasize the foundational importance of the Scriptures for the Church and all its members, whatever their rank, responsibility, or station. The Scriptures set forth the signs of God's actions on behalf of the human family, show how they engage moral life, and emphasize the decisive importance of a people's responses for their relationship with God and the People of God. The Scriptures draw out the impact of faith on worship, interior acts, and behavior; they emphasize the need for love of God and neighbor, and they call all the faithful to care for the peace and unity of the Church community.

In the Scriptures challenges to faith and moral responsibility often arise from the same circumstances and are resolved in tandem. Particular events such as the Exodus, the activity of Moses and other prophets, the Babylonian Exile, the ministry of Jesus and his apostles, call for faith in God and obedience to God's requirements. The power of evil and the suffering of innocent people are also fully acknowledged, especially since these realities can lead people to believe that God is unjust, capricious, or nonexistent and to live accordingly. Whether circumstances carry the stamp of the divine or the brutal, they have the potential to engage the heart and mind, the conscience and life, of those who are overtaken by them. The scriptural authors are acutely aware that such experiences can stimulate faith or disbelief and that moral life is inextricably involved in the process of personal deliberation and response to them.

There can be no doubt that, for the Scriptures, repentance is integral to the response of faith. To have the all-holy God approach is to have one's creatureliness, failures, and sinfulness thrown into very high relief. And if God's purpose is reconciliation and friendship with human beings, then repentance and forgiveness are essential to that end. Repentance is not limited to the first moments of faith but is to characterize the believer's life forever after. By the same token, to renege on one's commitment to repentance and faith by means of grave sin is also to repudiate one's friendship and unity with God. The inextricable unity of faith and repentance needs to receive due recognition in personal life, theological reflections, worship, and pastoral care.

The Scriptures are equally clear in laying out the principal contours of Christian moral life. God's word is to be heard and done, especially as it comes forth from the Lord Jesus. The sick, the poor, the sinful, and the lost are to receive special attention and hopefully be gathered in and lifted up. The intentions of the heart are as important as words and deeds. It is necessary to watch for the time of salvation, seize the moment when it arrives, and place one's entire life under God's rule. Generosity, carrying one's cross, and positive accomplishments are required; the good left undone can be as decisive as the evil inflicted. The peace and unity of the Church community are fundamental to God's plan and are to be respected and promoted by all Christians. The community's worship and moral life are closely bound; both are to be upright and marked by charity.

These and other biblical requirements are well known, but they do not always receive the emphasis they require, nor have their implications been sufficiently drawn out and brought to bear on Christian moral life. Giving full value to the scriptural word will honor the Second Vatican Council's exhortation. It will help theologians, pastors, and ordinary members to appreciate the Christian faith as a foundational virtue and commitment, acknowledge the transcendent and ecclesial qualities of moral life, and respond to the proper priorities as they carry out their responsibilities.

History

The story of Israel and the Church speaks of persons and events that are signs of God's intervention in human affairs. It shows communities as they wrestle with the challenges of faith in a God who has changed their history and claims their lives. The record embraces a wide range of human experiences and actions; it includes instances when people suffer injustice or are rescued from evil and times when God seems to be absent as well as moments charged with divine energy. Especially when they occur repeatedly, human experiences can exert great power in people's lives, shape their moral acts, and influence their response to God. The Scriptures ponder all such moments in light of faith and with a keen awareness of the mysteries of the human heart. The persons and details may be particular, but the story is perennial; it speaks to the conscience and freedom of all persons as they work out their own response to the claim of faith in the midst of life. Whether the arena is personal, pastoral, or theological, there is every reason to take human affairs seriously and to appreciate their importance for faith and moral life.

People deliberate and respond to their experiences in light of prevailing interpretations of human affairs. This has prompted believers to assess these interpretations and, in many cases, to craft accounts that more adequately respond to contemporary experiences and employ new intellectual resources as well as the light of faith. Job's anguished response to misfortune and injustice, other scriptural writers' convictions about God's kingdom or the arrival of the end times, St. Augustine's *City of God*, and Thomas Aquinas' *Summa theologiae* show how faith can interpret human experiences, answer people's need for understanding, illuminate their consciences, and guide their lives. These few examples highlight faith's inherent tendency to understand

and interpret God's actions in history and human actions in an economy of grace. They should encourage qualified members of the Church to develop accounts of human affairs that are faithful, true to life, and appealing to persons of competence and experience.

A closely related question is the relationship of a community of faith to the larger society, its people, culture, thought, and political system. Over the centuries there have been many changes on both sides of this equation: the mutual embrace of the early Christian Church and the Graeco-Roman Empire transformed both Church and society; the same dynamic can be observed as Catholicism moved into a very close relationship with the nations of Western Europe and as that relationship dissolved in recent centuries. The alienation of many Western societies from the Church and its acceptance by non-European peoples have created a new if also more complex situation with its own challenges and opportunities. There is a pressing need to understand better what the Church community can or in fact does adopt from the peoples among whom it lives and what it should say to them and ask of them. A sound grasp of the Church-world dynamic is required if the life, worship, and mission of the Church are to be assessed adequately and carried out well.

Knowledge and Reason

Faith entails thought. This is already evident in the early pages of Scripture, where the universe is presented as God's good work and the Exodus as sufficient grounds for faith. Careful reflection is presupposed in those passages that stipulate the legal, moral, and cultic requirements of Hebrew faith or depict sinful actions. The same holds true for the New Testament, in which preaching and teaching often involve considered arguments and doctrine is assessed for its conformity to truth. As a rule, scriptural books cannot be adequately understood until their theological subtexts are brought to light.

In the early Christian centuries the apologists engaged the religion, mythology, literature, and morals of Graeco-Roman society. Bishops catechized, preached, and guarded the unity of their churches; they conserved the apostolic tradition and rebutted erroneous doctrines. There is little question that to be successful these activities needed to be properly focused, truthful, accessible to the audience, and persuasive. The intellectual dimensions of faith are also evident as some of the Fathers drew upon Stoic resources and Augustine brought Neoplatonic thinking to bear on the doctrinal, spiritual, and pastoral issues of his day. Among the most important legacies of this period is the incorporation of ancient philosophical resources into the Christian tradition.

Later centuries bear their own witness to the intellectual aspects of faith. In the Middle Ages the monks demonstrated the power and effects of the Augustinian approach to scholarship. Analytical logic and Aristotle's corpus of writings stimulated the development of new ways to understand, organize, and express Christian faith and its implications for living. By the sixteenth century many schools of thought had developed, each with its own way of conceiving and accounting for the Christian life and describing the place of moral life within it. The conflict between Protestant and Catholic Christians in the West revolved around doctrinal issues. In the modern period the legacies of the Council of Trent and the Enlightenment have focused attention sharply on issues of truth, knowledge, certitude, and teaching. Such issues have attracted attention and concern in large measure because they bear so heavily on faith and moral life. Today's interfaith discussions and public conversations on cultural, legal, moral, and other matters of common concern require technical competence, insight, and an ability to engage informed people in a constructive way.

There can be no doubt that Christian faith will continue to tax the intellectual capacities of believers today. They will wish to consider the many points of intersection between faith and intellectual life and to become familiar with key issues as they have developed in the past, including their religious and moral implications. Some problems have been perennial and can be expected to reappear, at least between the lines, in contemporary discussions. These include the relationships between the abstract and the concrete, the general and the particular, the one and the many, the eternal and the historical, authority and reason, truth and conscience, and nature and creation. Other questions concern the nature of reality and knowledge and the extent to which mind, heart, and will ought to govern one's response to God. The authority of bishops to judge the orthodoxy of statements about faith and their participation in theological discussions have ancient precedents but remain contemporary issues. The same is true of divine grace and theological anthropology. These last topics deserve special attention.

The Church's teachings on grace and justification arise on scriptural foundations. The Fathers were acutely sensitive to the reality of grace, particularly when they spoke about the Church, worked out baptismal and penitential praxis, or confronted those who cast doubt on the necessity of the grace of Christ for salvation. Augustine of Hippo, Thomas Aquinas, and the Councils of Carthage, Orange, and Trent each made a major contribution to the ecclesial tradition on grace. This now well-developed body of doctrine describes the relationship between God and human beings and outlines its implications for salvation, sin, freedom, and the Christian life in general. The necessity and primacy of divine grace are recognized in the Church's canonical tradition and embodied in its liturgical life. Grace is altogether foundational for the life of the Church and all of its members. Despite these facts, the record demonstrates that earlier moral theologians generally ignored this doctrinal tradition and did not sufficiently integrate Church teachings on grace, faith, and justification into their accounts of moral life.

It is necessary to address these deficits. The moral implications of the doctrinal tradition on grace and justification need to be explored more fully, and accounts of Christian moral life need to draw more generously from that tradition. By the same token, moral theologians do well to base their reflections on the Scriptures, the liturgy, and other properly Christian sources as well as those that are common to all human beings. Such a revision of method and approach promises to do better justice to the properly theological foundations of Christian moral life and to enhance the coherence of the theological enterprise. It can also be expected to support more balanced portrayals of moral life and to reduce the likelihood that they tacitly disassociate morality from faith and salvation or relate them only superficially. If settled doctrine on grace and justification gains more influence on accounts of Christian morality, there will be less risk of giving the erroneous impression that salvation depends upon morally upright acts that can be performed by anyone solely on the strength of natural freedom, knowledge, and effort.

Liturgical Worship

Liturgical worship has been integral to the faith and moral life of the believing community since its beginnings. Worship marked the Sinai Covenant, and the Temple stood at the center of Hebrew life. Jesus respected the liturgical traditions of his people, and his disciples set the foundations of public worship in the Christian Church. The Bible testifies that liturgy requires an upright moral life and emphasizes its theological dimensions.

In the early Christian era baptismal catechesis and rituals manifested an acute awareness that catechumens need to be taught the history of salvation and helped to advance in repentance and faith. Baptism seals the new Christian with the Holy Spirit, confers forgiveness of sins, and formalizes one's commitment to Christian life. The life of the Church follows from baptism; it is based upon the priority of God's initiative, the gift and necessity of grace, the scriptural word, and the ongoing, comprehensive requirement of faith and repentance. It entails an upright moral life, adherence to the apostolic tradition, care for the *communio* of the Church, and service in charity to those in need. In the Eucharist the assembly celebrates these gifts, thanks God for them, and seeks divine help for its life of repentance, faith, and charity. Those members of the Church who renege on their baptismal commitment through grave sin lose their place in the eucharistic assembly. They need to do sincere penance and require the Church's judgment, help, and prayer if they are to be reconciled anew. In later centuries the tradition of ecclesiastical penance developed and became ever more complex.

By the end of the fourth century the catechumenate and ecclesiastical penance were already undergoing significant change. Some aspects of this evolution can be praised as insightful or responsive to pressing needs; others can be criticized as unwise or unhelpful. Taken as a whole, however, these developments reflect the Church's conviction that Christian life emerges from God's word and from the waters of baptism, is based on faith and repentance, and is to be lived in an informed, committed, morally upright, and mission-oriented manner. If anything, the complex histories of Christian catechesis and ecclesiastical penance show how seriously earlier generations took these requirements and their responsibility to mediate them to new generations and circumstances.

The liturgy remains an integral part of Christian life. In its breadth, depth, and content, liturgical worship reflects human life and proclaims that it is to be lived in the economy of divine grace. As the community gathers for prayer, it brings all of its experiences, concerns, failures and successes, hopes and fears, to a celebration of God's actions, word, and ongoing presence. Each participant is reminded that he or she has been reconciled and gathered in the name of the Lord. The community offers praise and thanks for divine gifts, confesses its sins, and prays for the needs of all. The preaching ought to interpret contemporary concerns in light of the word and encourage the congregation to carry its worship into daily life through service and charity. The liturgy calls attention to the decisive importance of the present moment and looks forward to a new Day of the Lord, encouraging sinner and saint alike and consoling those who are heavily burdened. Its symbolic elements evoke the heavenly and the earthly and can mediate God's love and stir the human heart in a way unequaled by spoken words.

Along with the witness of holy men and women, liturgy can help moral theologians to situate their reflections within the proper context, sort out important methodological and substantive issues, and develop accounts of moral life that more closely reflect the faith, circumstances, and mission of the ecclesial community. Liturgy manifests the context of Christian life for ordinary members of the Church, engages their moral life, and underlines its religious significance. Centered around the Eucharist as "the fount and apex of the whole Christian life" (*LG*, 11), worship illuminates, guides, and empowers them as they continue their daily activites. It likewise affords an unparalleled perspective from which they can reflect more deeply on the intersection of faith and moral life in the Church.

Abbreviations

AAS	*Acta apostolicae sedis*
ACPQ	*American Catholic Philosophical Quarterly*
AdvHaer	Irenaeus of Lyons. *Adversus haereses* (Against Heresies)
ASS	*Acta sanctae sedis*
ColCis	*Collectanea Cisterciensia*
CC	*Cross Currents*
CDH	Anselm of Canterbury. *Cur Deus homo* (Why God Became Man)
CFaustMan	Augustine of Hippo. *Contra Faustum Manichœum* (Reply to Faustus the Manichean)
CHLMP	Norman Kretzmann, ed. *The Cambridge History of Later Medieval Philosophy: From the Rediscovery of Aristotle to the Disintegration of Scholasticism, 1100–1600.* Cambridge and New York: Cambridge University Press, 1982.
CIC	*Codex iuris canonici* (Code of Canon Law, 1983)
Conf	Augustine of Hippo. *Confessiones* (Confessions)
Const	Ignatius of Loyola. *The Constitutions of the Society of Jesus.* Trans. George E. Ganss. St. Louis: Institute of Jesuit Sources, 1970.
CTSAP	*Catholic Theological Society of America Proceedings*
DBap	Augustine of Hippo. *De baptismo* (On Baptism)
DBT	Xavier Léon-Dufour, ed. *Dictionary of Biblical Theology.* Rev. ed. Trans. P. Joseph Cahill and others. New York: Seabury, 1973.
DCatRud	Augustine of Hippo. *De catechizandis rudibus* (The First Catechetical Instruction)

DCivDei	Augustine of Hippo. *De civitate Dei* (The City of God)
DCorGrat	Augustine of Hippo. *De correptione et gratia* (On Rebuke and Grace)
DDoctChr	Augustine of Hippo. *De doctrina Christiana* (On Christian Instruction)
DDuaAn	Augustine of Hippo. *De duabus animabus, contra Manichaeos* (On Two Souls, Against the Manichaeans)
DGestPel	Augustine of Hippo. *De gestis Pelagii* (On the Proceedings of Pelagius)
DGratChr	Augustine of Hippo. *De gratia Christi* (On the Grace of Christ)
DGratLibArb	Augustine of Hippo. *De gratia et libero arbitrio* (On Grace and Free Will)
DH	Vatican II. *Dignitatis humanae* (Declaration on Religious Freedom)
DivInst	Lactantius. *Divinae institutiones* (The Divine Institutes)
DL	*Doctrine and Life*
DMorMan	Augustine of Hippo. *De moribus Manichaeorum* (On the Morals of the Manichaeans)
DNatBon	Augustine of Hippo. *De natura boni* (On the Nature of Good)
DNupCon	Augustine of Hippo. *De nuptiis et concupiscentia* (On Marriage and Concupiscence)
DOfMin	Ambrose of Milan. *De officiis ministrorum* (On the Duties of the Clergy)
DPaenA	Ambrose of Milan. *De paenitentia* (On Penance)
DPaen	Tertullian. *De paenitentia* (On Penance)
DPecMerRem	Augustine of Hippo. *De peccatorum meritis et remissione* (On the Merits and Forgiveness of Sins)
DPud	Tertullian. *De pudicitia* (On Purity)
DS	Henricus Denzinger and Adolfus Schönmetzer, eds. *Enchiridion symbolorum: Definitionum et declarationum de rebus fidei et morum.* Ed. xxxv emendata. Barcelona: Herder, 1973.
DSpirLit	Augustine of Hippo. *De spiritu et littera* (On the Spirit and the Letter)

DTC	*Dictionnaire de Théologie Catholique.* Paris: Letouzey et Ané, 1923–50.
DV	Vatican II. *Dei verbum* (Dogmatic Constitution on Divine Revelation)
EBT	Johannes B. Bauer, ed. *Encyclopedia of Biblical Theology: The Complete* Sacramentum Verbi. New York: Crossroad, 1981.
EglTh	*Eglise et théologie*
EP	Paul Edwards, ed. *The Encyclopedia of Philosophy.* New York: Macmillan Publishing Co. and The Free Press; London: Collier Macmillan Publishers, 1967.
EpCor	Clement of Rome. *Epistle to the Corinthians*
Essay	John Locke. *An Essay Concerning Human Understanding.* Ed. P. H. Nidditch. Oxford: Clarendon Press, 1975.
ETL	*Ephemerides theologicae lovanienses*
Exhort	Clement of Alexandria. *Exhortation to the Heathen*
FS	*Franciscan Studies*
FZPT	*Freiburger Zeitschrift für Philosophie und Theologie*
GS	Vatican II. *Gaudium et spes* (Pastoral Constitution on the Church in the Modern World)
HC	Hubert Jedin and John Dolan, eds. *History of the Church.* New York: Crossroad, 1965–81 (some volumes identified as *Handbook of Church History*).
Hefele	Charles Joseph Hefele. *A History of the Councils of the Church from the Original Documents.* Trans. William R. Clark and others. Edinburgh: T&T Clark, 1883–96.
HJ	*Heythrop Journal*
HTR	*Harvard Theological Review*
IDB	George A. Buttrick and others, eds. *Interpreter's Dictionary of the Bible.* New York: Abingdon Press, 1962.
Int	*Interpretation*
IPQ	*International Philosophical Quarterly*
ITQ	*Irish Theological Quarterly*
JEH	*Journal of Ecclesiastical History*
JRE	*Journal of Religious Ethics*

LG	Vatican II. *Lumen gentium* (Dogmatic Constitution on the Church)
LS	*Louvain Studies*
Luscombe	D. E. Luscombe. *Peter Abelard's Ethics.* Oxford: Clarendon Press, 1971.
MD	*Maison-Dieu*
Med	René Descartes. *Meditations on First Philosophy: With Selections from the Objections and Replies.* Trans. John Cottingham. Cambridge: Cambridge University Press, 1986.
Mon	Anselm of Canterbury. *Monologion* (Soliloquy)
MS	*Monastic Studies*
NJBC	Raymond E. Brown and others, eds. *The New Jerome Biblical Commentary.* Englewood Cliffs, N.J.: Prentice-Hall, 1990.
NRT	*Nouvelle revue théologique*
NTS	*New Testament Studies*
NV	*Nova et vetera*
OT	Vatican II. *Optatam totius* (Decree on Priestly Formation)
Paed	Clement of Alexandria. *Paedagogus* (The Instructor)
Pelikan	Jaroslav Pelikan. *The Christian Tradition.* Chicago and London: University of Chicago Press, 1971–89.
Pros	Anselm of Canterbury. *Proslogion* (Address)
RB	*Revue Biblique*
RHE	*Revue d'histoire ecclesiastique*
RHPR	*Revue d'histoire et de philosophie religieuses*
RSPT	*Revue des sciences philosophiques et théologiques*
RSR	*Recherches de science religieuse*
RST	*Religious Studies and Theology*
RT	*Revue Thomiste*
RTAM	*Recherches de théologie ancienne et médiévale*
SC	Vatican II. *Sacrosanctum concilium* (The Constitution on the Sacred Liturgy)
ScCat	*La Scuola Cattolica*

SJT	*Scottish Journal of Theology*
SM	Adolf Darlap, ed. *Sacramentum Mundi: An Encyclopedia of Theology.* London: Burns & Oates; New York: Herder & Herder, 1968–70.
SP	*Studia patristica*
STh	Thomas Aquinas. *Summa theologiae*
StMor	*Studia moralia*
Tanner	Norman P. Tanner, ed. *Decrees of the Ecumenical Councils.* Washington, D.C.: Georgetown University Press, 1990.
TDNT	Gerhard Kittel, ed. *Theological Dictionary of the NT.* Grand Rapids, Mich.: Eerdmans, 1964.
TRHS	*Transactions of the Royal Historical Society*
TS	*Theological Studies*

Index of Principal Names and Subjects

(Italicized pages give a definition or description.)